P9-DNN-627

DISCARDED

STEP INTO A WORLD

Other books by Kevin Powell

In the Tradition: An Anthology of Young Black Writers (1993)
Co-edited with Ras Baraka

recognize, poetry (1995)

Keepin' It Real—Post-MTV Reflections on Race, Sex, and Politics (1997)

STEP INTO A WORLD

A Global Anthology of the New Black Literature

Edited by Kevin Powell

SOUTH HUNTINGTON
PUBLIC LIBRARY
2 MELVILLE ROAD
HUNTINGTON STATION, N.Y. 11746

John Wiley & Sons, Inc.

New York • Chichester • Weinheim • Brisbane • Singapore • Toronto

809.8989
Ste

Permissions credits appear on pages 459–65 and constitute an extension of this copyright page.

This book is printed on acid-free paper. ♾

Copyright © 2000 by Kevin Powell. All rights reserved

Published by John Wiley & Sons, Inc.
Published simultaneously in Canada

Design and production by Navta Associates, Inc.

No part of this publication may be reproduced, stored in a retrieval system, or transmitted in any form or by any means, electronic, mechanical, photocopying, recording, scanning, or otherwise, except as permitted under Section 107 or 108 of the 1976 United States Copyright Act, without either the prior written permission of the Publisher, or authorization through payment of the appropriate per-copy fee to the Copyright Clearance Center, 222 Rosewood Drive, Danvers, MA 01923, (978) 750-8400, fax (978) 750-4744. Requests to the Publisher for permission should be addressed to the Permissions Department, John Wiley & Sons, Inc., 605 Third Avenue, New York, NY 10158-0012, (212) 850-6011, fax (212) 850-6008, e-mail: PERMREQ@WILEY.COM.

This publication is designed to provide accurate and authoritative information in regard to the subject matter covered. It is sold with the understanding that the publisher is not engaged in rendering professional services. If professional advice or other expert assistance is required, the services of a competent professional person should be sought.

Library of Congress Cataloging-in-Publication Data:

Step into a world : a global anthology of the new Black literature / edited by Kevin Powell.
    p.   cm.
  Includes bibliographical references and index.
  ISBN 0-471-38060-1 (cloth : alk. paper)
    I. Powell, Kevin.

                                                                    00-043300

Printed in the United States of America

10 9 8 7 6 5 4 3 2 1

Dedicated to all the writers, all the artists, and all the people who struggle to make their voices heard and their heartbeats felt

and for Joe Wood, a brilliant young writer—
wherever you are, your spirit is missed by many. . . .

"This volume aims to document the New Negro culturally and socially,—to register the transformations of the inner and outer life of the Negro. . . ."

—ALAIN LOCKE, THE NEW NEGRO (1925)

"You say one for the treble two for the time come on—Speech is my hammer bang the world into shape/Now let it fall—Huuh!/My restlessness is my nemesis/It's hard to really chill and sit still/Committed to page/I write a rhyme, sometimes won't finish for days/Scrutinize my literature from the large to the miniature. . . ."

—MOS DEF, "HIP HOP" (1999)

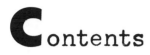ontents

PART FIVE

Poetry

Acknowledgments

SO MANY TO THANK, SO LITTLE SPACE. First off, mad props to the gods, the goddesses, and the ancestors for life—and this world we call home, for now.

I want to thank Wiley publisher Gerry Helferich and Wiley editor in chief Carole Hall for greenlighting this anthology and making it a reality. 'Nuf respect to both of you.

I especially want to thank Chris Jackson, my editor, for the clear vision, for the no-nonsense directions and proddings, and for the uncanny ability to sift through my numerous late-night e-mails, faxes, and phone calls as we molded this thing into shape. Man, if the literary world had more editors like you, not only would more of us get published, but there would be much better literature to read. Thank you, thank you, thank you.

I also want to give a shout out to Jabari Asim, a most selfless writer and editor. When I look at the cats who compose this anthology, I realize a number of them were initially suggested by you. In an age where so many of us writers desire to be stars, quickly running down résumés, appearance schedules, and advance sums and booksale figures, it is good to know that someone from the new school is, well, old school—and mad real. Thank you for the two-way dialogue all these years, son!

There are, of course, a number of folks who contributed to the evolution and completion of this anthology in one manner or another. If I leave out names, please know it is not intentional and that your help has been measured by my heart and soul, like forever, yo: Andrew Wylie, Jeff Posternak, and Lisa Halliday of the Wylie Agency; Kalamu ya Salaam, E. Ethelbert Miller, Quincy Troupe, Dr. Jerry Ward, Kadija George, Bridgett Warren, Ruth Forman, Rohan Preston, Teresa Washington, Kwame Dawes, Colin Channer, Tisa Bryant, Tijan Sallah, Elisabeth Dyssegaard, Tanure Ojaide, Anson Gonzalez, Vanessa Richards, Allison Joseph, Sabrina Miller, Charles Larson, Maria McCloy, Kenya Dilday, Bridgett Davis, K Sanneh, Lauren Summers, American Program Bureau, Maureen Carter, Itumeleng oa Mahabane, Gail Smith, Kupenda Auset, Darius James, Michael Datcher, Cheo Tyehimba, Dimitry Leger, Jennifer Howard, Tracy Sherrod, Nicole Aragi and the Watkins/Loomis Agency, Alan Light, Kenneth Carroll, Lenard D. Moore, Valerie Boyd, Tony Medina, Wayde Compton, Bernardine Evaristo, Jeffrey Shotts, Eisa Ulen, John Keene, Michele Kort, Charlie Braxton, Nalo Hopkinson, and Michelle Whelan, among many others. I thank you all, and all the writers who submitted work.

STEP INTO A WORLD

The Word Movement

all you golden-black children of the sun,
lift up! and read the sky
written in the tongue of your ancestors.

—HENRY DUMAS, "BLACK STAR LINE"

Between the concrete cracks and digital domination of this new millennium, we have the Word Movement. No big surprise here: black people can talk—and they can write, too. Been proven before, with Wheatley and Dunbar, with the Harlem Renaissance (thank you Zora, Langston, et al.), the Negritude writers (thank you Leopold, Aime, et al.), the Black Arts Movement (thank you Sonia, Amiri, et al.), and those hype-ass Nuyorican cats (thank you Miguel *and* Miguel, et al.). So what makes this period different, this essay necessary, here—and now? Might be that a lot of heads who participate in this thing rubber-stamped "the scene" done forgot "the scene" did not just erupt when *you* decided to spit a poem at an open mic set last week. "The scene" is as old as Trey Ellis's famous essay, "The New Black Aesthetic," which dates back to the late 1980s. There Trey broke down what was happening with post-Soul colored culture, including Vernon Reid and the Black Rock Coalition, Lisa and Kellie Jones, Fishbone, and Russell Simmons, among other hot girls/boys on the block. Throw in how big hip-hop already was (and how black nationalistic it was about to become), and how much our ghetto villages would eventually define the new black artistic energies from—to paraphrase Public Enemy—the boulevard to the bourgeois, and it is clear, yo, that we were manifesting a movement right up under the nostrils of that ridiculously vapid decade.

Uh-huh, the 1980s, that period when Ronald Reagan then George Bush (the daddy, not the "W") made things unsafe, spiritually, physically, psychologically, for the Negro everywhere. For example, when I began my journalism career as a twenty-year-old in December 1986, my first assignment was covering the murder of Michael Griffith by white thugs in Howard Beach, Queens. While we cruise-controlled through mind-numbing Reaganomics, black America was gradually losing itself to the triple threat of crack, gun violence, and AIDS. Except some of us were too blunted on the times to know what was hitting us until we'd been slapped silly. But there was optimism. On our political front Jesse Jackson told us to keep hope alive (back when Jesse was as hip as the hip-hoppers) and Louis Farrakhan let da man know, with *his* words, if you mess with Jesse then you messin' with him.

But it was the burgeoning literary environment that provided the most intense wet dreams for the future: besides Ellis's "The New Black Aesthetic," one could not ignore his well-received first novel, 1988's *Platitudes,* nor his place as one of only a few young writers in Terry McMillan's otherwise old school 1990 anthology *Breaking Ice.* Meanwhile *The Village Voice* in New York City was fast becoming an incubator for new jack black wordsmiths such as Carol Cooper, Greg Tate, Lisa Jones, Lisa Kennedy, Nelson George, Barry Michael Cooper, and Harry Allen. Back then I eagerly awaited every Wednesday for the next issue, wondering what these writers had to say about Brooklyn—then as now a haven for black artists, thinkers, and movers and shakers, and, really, the new Harlem—about black gangs, about black music as different as Teddy Riley's and Cecil Taylor's, about the new black film craze. Little did these writers know they were inspiring the next wave of cultural critics like Colson Whitehead, Joan Morgan, Joe Wood, Danyel Smith, Scott Poulson-Bryant, Touré, dream hampton, Christopher John Farley, Veronica Chambers, and this writer, among many others. And little did these cats know they were actually the pioneers of the Word Movement.

What's more, certain words stuck to the mental vocab during the 1980s: like apartheid, like consciousness, like activism, like poetry. I understood and appreciated verse because I had gotten drunk on Shakespeare, Keats, Dickinson, and all them other dead white people back in high school. But it was a whole other thing to *hear* poetics by folks named the Last Poets, Mutabaruka, Linton Kwesi Johnson, and Gil-Scott Heron; or to hear the musical manifestos of Bob Marley, Fela, and Steel Pulse, and to be enticed by the agitprop telepathy of Boogie Down Productions, De La Soul, and N.W.A. Moreover, I learned words could spark controversy. Did not fully understand—then—all the fuss over Alice Walker's *The Color Purple*—book and film—but sure knew it was bugged how words caused so many blacks to be upset. Although I was on the wrong side of the issue at the time (I was mad at Alice because most men were mad at Alice and I figured I'd go along for the ride) I dug the fact that sister-girl had the guts to put down on paper—words—what she felt was truth.

What Alice Walker felt is what some in this generation were beginning to feel: that words, if used effectively, could mean something, could become something, could mean a taste of power. Not just any words, mind you, but the right words. Words like those scribbled by Jean-Michel Basquiat on his art. Words like the provocative theater pieces of George Wolfe, the butt-naked lyrics of Prince, the parodies in Robert Townsend's *Hollywood Shuffle* and Keenan Ivory Wayans' *In Living Color.* Words as revelatory as a John Edgar Wideman meditation, words as familial as a Rita Dove poem, words as elastic as an August Wilson play, words as love-soaked as an Audre Lorde discourse, words as pointed as a bell hooks proclamation, words as plaintive as a Toni Morrison novel. Words like *She's Gotta Have It.* Saw that film and was shocked by the brashness of Spike Lee. How he used words, starting with that title, to shed some light—his black male light—on the dynamics of sisters (uh, aiight, a sister) and brothers. Then dug the way Spike upped the ante, two films later, with *Do the Right Thing.* Words: a phrase we been sayin' around the way for years suddenly had new meaning, an impact, a political significance. Yeah, do the right thing. Do the right thing and make black films like Spike did, for yourself and on your own terms. Do the right thing, speak your mind, and *not* care what white folks think about what you sayin', ya know? Do the right thing and be bold, dun: If they raped Tawana Brawley then we gotta do the right thing. If they killed Yusef Hawkins in Bensonhurst, Brooklyn, then we gotta do the right thing. If they won't let Nelson Mandela go free, then we gotta do the right thing. Them words, words like Public Enemy, bold prophets of rage, spinning hip-hop, like a bottle, from the cold-gettin'-dumb era to:

Elvis was a hero to most
But he never meant _____ to me you see
Straight up racist that sucker was
Simple and plain
Mother_____ him and John Wayne
— "Fight the Power"

So, yeah, some of us young writers knew we were on to something big, something magical. Shucks, glad to be, really. Post–Civil Rights America hadn't been too kind to colored people—parents nor the children. Some of our parents had been movement workers, or Black Panthers, or Communists, or nationalists, or assimilationists. Some, like my moms, felt the only reason King got killed was because he talked too much, and too loudly. Some loved white folks, some hated white folks. Some of our parents loved white folks and hated themselves, while some hated white folks and thought that meant they loved themselves. Meanwhile, some of us children are blacker than my Kenneth Cole joints, and some of us are high yella and, as Malcolm Gladwell puts it, "white enough to pass, but black enough to know better." And some of us do pass, culturally, racially, or both. Some of us are biracial and our parents—the black one and the white one—had to creep like TLC so as not to disturb all the sleeping bigots on the planet. Some of us come from famous families: a father who is a superstar writer, an aunt who is a world-renowned activist. Some of our families are from more humble origins and simply cannot understand why we waste our time writing. Some of us were raised Christian, or Muslim, or Jewish, or some combination thereof; and some of us come from homes where our parents would not allow god—spelled in all lower-case letters—to even think about stepping through the door. Some of our families embrace Afrocentricity and sent us to Afrocentric schools, celebrated Kwanzaa instead of Christmas, and gave us nice African-sounding names. Some of our families, like my immediate family, don't think they are African at all and that is all that needs to be said. Some of us are the first generation in our families to attend college, or an integrated college, and some of our families have long been associated with higher education. Some of us have been directly or indirectly victims of the prison-industrial complex, and some of us have written quite passionately about the criminalization of blackness. Some of us know what it is to have a mother and father stay together forever, and some of us have become writers because our parents ain't together, ain't been together, and, as poet Natasha Trethewey says in her biography, we are "interested in absences, in memory and forgetting, our common language of loss."

Loss, yes Lawd, like the minds and souls lost in Vietnam. Loss, yes Lawd, like the minds and souls lost to those other wars waged where parents, children, communities, regions, nations, have been cracked open, scattered, destroyed. With drugs. With alcohol. With self-hatred. With gang violence. With domestic violence. With neocolonial violence. With police violence. With spiritual violence. With this identity and that identity, with kente cloth and yarmulke, or headwrap and skullcap. With middle-class bliss and working-class nightmare—and vice versa. With gender politics and politicized gender. With sexual orientation and orientation toward sex—or not. With multicultural heaven, and integrated horror show. With the pain born of oppression and ignorance and deception and self-deception, and promises made and stuffed, quickly, into the hypocrite's jewelry box. And we came/come out of all this madness to be, say, Imani Tolliver, to compose verse that reveals the scar tissues:

> when I was little my father stole my pussy
> small, purple and pink
> it was mine
>
> —"GIN AND JUICE"

Yup, raw-dog like that, like hip-hop, sound track for a fragmented generation: somewhere between those nasty, smelly jheri curls and Michael Jackson's moonwalk outta himself, hip-hop started to matter, too. I would argue that there would be no major movement among young scribes had there been no hip-hop, which is basically spoken words over a boom-bap ba-boom-bap boom-bap-bap ba-boom-bap. Truth is black folks been talkin' junk for years—see Louis Jordan, Moms Mabley, Malcolm X, Fannie Lou Hamer, Muhammad Ali—but the opportunity for hip-hop to catch wreck had much to do with what Nelson George called, in book form, *The Death of Rhythm and Blues*. By the late 1980s, with the exception of innovators like Prince, much of R&B was recycled garbage, whereas the spoken "songs" of hip-hop were remarkably fresh, eclectic, exciting. Be it Run-DMC or Salt N Pepa, The Geto Boys or Too Short, Big Daddy Kane or MC Lyte, hip-hop catalyzed young black verbal expression as had not been done since the 1960s, at least here in America. Hip-hop also represented the first black music where its originators could care less what white people thought of them. In other words, gone, for the most part, were the coded language and immaculately groomed attire *and* behavior of the Motown days. Hip-hop started at the bottom, and we bottom-dwellers know words—be it the words of a graffiti writer or an MC—are the one sure way to identify ourselves, to become visible, to matter.

Furthermore, in many ways there is a direct link between, say, the Harlem Renaissance's Langston Hughes, the Black Arts Movement's Amiri Baraka, and hip-hop in that the "words" were (and are) literally taken from the mouths of the people. For there is a musicality to our daily language, and the best of our writers have always understood that. No coincidence, then, that some of the most talented "spoken word" poets around today—Tony Medina, Ruth Forman, Willie Perdomo, and Sarah Jones are some of the few who actually have skills—turn out to be those who are best able to showcase the language and lives of the common folk. And brilliant young fiction writers like Victor LaValle and Ricardo Cortez Cruz have heavily "sampled" the vernacular and attitudes of hip-hop in their work. For they are hip-hop and hip-hop is them and hip-hop is, at its root, about wordplay. Or, better still, the Harlem Renaissance had the blues, the Black Arts Movement had jazz and the sounds of Motown, and the Word Movement has hip-hop.

Paul Beatty's highly publicized triumph at the Nuyorican Poets Café's inaugural grand slam contest, in the spring of 1990, was a watershed moment for the Word Movement. It was, in a sense, the bridge from the 80s into this new thing. Part of Paul's prize: publication of his poetic tome, *Big Bank Take Little Bank.* A lengthy profile in *The Village Voice* only reenforced Beatty's importance to this new scene. Los Angeles born and bred, Beatty's work captured the spirit of our postindustrial, media-saturated, computerized age. Like a hip-hop artist (although Beatty is not, and was not, a "hip-hop poet"), Beatty stitched together social commentary, pop cultural samples and sound-bytes, and autobiographical mini-tales to create poetry that spoke to our microwave times:

> sssssssoundcheck
>   onetwo   onetwo
>   my boy   elroy
> suicidal drumtech in full effect
> son of jane
> and george jetson
>
>   miscegeny creation of hanna barbaric
>   claymation science
>
> —"DOGGIN THE ROCKMAN"

Beatty's work and that *Voice* article prompted me to find and call him, not just to offer congratulations, but also to ask Beatty to contribute to an anthology Ras Baraka and I were compiling at the time. Eventually entitled *In the Tradition: An Anthology of Young Black Writers,* and published in the winter of 1993, this book, which contained fifty-one mainly twentysomething poets and fiction writers, would be the first of a series of anthologies attempting to announce my generation's arrival as writers. That, however, was not the original intention of *In The Tradition.* The initial idea for the collection, born in the fall of 1988, was to feature poets from Howard and Rutgers, where Ras and I attended college, respectively. But, within a few months I suggested to Ras that we broaden the anthology to include young and emerging black writers whether they had attended college or not. (I was thinking of Ras's father, and *Black Fire,* the landmark collection the elder Baraka edited with Larry Neal. Indeed, our anthology title would come from a 1984 poem by Amiri Baraka.) By the winter of 1989 we had reached out to Marie Brown, one of the best-known black literary agents in America, and with Ms. Brown's support, the process officially began. Little did we know it would take four years to find a publisher willing to put out *In the Tradition.*

No matter, because those early days of the Word Movement were heady ones. Besides Beatty, Elizabeth Alexander published *The Venus Hottentot* to much critical acclaim; a whole crew of Spelman student-writers, like Kupenda Auset, were inspired by visiting professor Sonia Sanchez and local heroine Pearl Cleage; California-based poet and essayist Michael Datcher edited the important anthology *My Brother's Keeper,* while another Cali inkslinger, Ruth Forman, picked up the 1992 Barnard New Women Poets Prize for *We Are the Young Magicians.* In St. Louis, Jabari Asim, Ira Jones, and

Andrea Wren, mentored by Eugene Redmond, created a new voices reading series, launched *Eyeball,* a periodical designed to showcase the best writers of the Word Movement, and published several chapbooks, including *Young Tongues.* In Philadelphia, Major Jackson and Wadud Ahmad combined on performance pieces while Jackson curated programs uniting established and emerging writers. In Boston, a motley crew of poets and fiction writers including John Keene, Tisa Bryant, Sharan Strange, Kevin Young, and Patrick Sylvain christened themselves the Darkroom Collective, harking back to the days of the Harlem Renaissance and those parlor trysts. Many of us have gotten to know each other via readings, letters, phone calls, in apartments, in lofts, on subways, on street corners while perusing bookstands, and as we've read and performed our work at the Brooklyn Moon Cafe in New York, at Vertigo Books in Washington, at the Painted Bride in Philadelphia, at Ebony Square in New Orleans, at the World Stage in Los Angeles, at the National Black Arts Festival in Atlanta, and at the Cave Canem black writer retreat, which changes venues year to year. And publications such as *Callaloo, Drumvoices Revue, Crab Orchard Review, African Voices,* and *Obsidian II* and *III* have all published the work of this new generation, much in the same way that *Crisis* and *Opportunity* did during the Renaissance.

As we were getting our literary macks on, established writers got their batteries recharged big-time, dun. For example, it was extraordinary to witness three black women—Toni Morrison, Terry McMillan, and Alice Walker—on *The New York Times* best-seller list simultaneously. That feat said that thoughtful black literature could be taken seriously and could sell a bundle of books. And of course we cannot forget that Walter Mosley, E. Lynn Harris, and Nathan McCall shut down the notion that black male writers were not getting their propers. Each of these writers became best-sellers in the 1990s, while maintaining wildy different styles of writing. I took particular notice of McMillan and Harris because they represented a new approach to black literature: combining highly confessional "fiction" with grassroots marketing savvy. While McMillan had already published a few books prior to *Waiting to Exhale,* her breakthrough, she had carefully nurtured a core audience of loyal readers who would ultimately generate colossal sales. Harris self-published his first novel, then transformed the massive response into a cottage industry around his later, big house-produced works. Besides opening up literature to black women of all stripes and the black gay male community as it had never been done before, McMillan and Harris were influencing the young writers of the Word Movement. We now had a blueprint for self-publishing and, eventually, for distributing our work via new outlets like the Internet. The goal was not just to write, but to aggressively inform the public of our efforts.

It was this quest, though, for public attention and accolades that would taint the Word Movement. I feel this began around the same time I appeared on the first season of MTV's "The Real World," the New York City edition, in 1992. The producers knew I was a poet and asked if they could film me reading my work. I took them straight to the Nuyorican. Much to my chagrin, only a few months later MTV was recruiting poets for poetry "commercials" and a poetry unplugged special. While I cringed at the sight of some of these spots, the fact is television and, eventually, films such as *Love Jones* and *Slam* were inspiring thousands—and perhaps millions—of people to get down with the Word Movement. What's more, the spoken-word scene was one of the key elements and agitators for the Word Movement's overall growth and development. In other words, would so many people, today, give a damn about literature if it had not been for this poetic eruption?

The flip side, however, is the fact that the MTV-ization of the Word Movement has placed an overemphasis on the poetry, which is commonly referred to as "spoken word," while ignoring other important genres of writing, like fiction, criticism, and drama. Additionally, poets who are more concerned with how their work stands (up) on the page as opposed to how well they can, à la a rapper, titillate an audience, are either deemed mediocre poets or forgotten entirely, save the small circle of us who actually appreciate literature beyond the oral hedonism of the now. And far too many of the poets who have self-published their work, or have sent out poetic missives via the Internet, by and large do not want *critical* feedback on their material.

I have had a number of younger writers around the country ask me for literary advice, then either disrespectfully cut me off or not respond to my suggestions on authors to read—be it Lucille Clifton, Pablo Neruda, or Seamus Heaney. The same it's-all-about-the-benjamins mentality that has gripped hip-hop also has a chokehold on the Word Movement. In my many travels—some forty states and virtually every major American city, big and not so big—it has become painful to sit through open mics as one poet after another reads a poem concerning their sexual fantasies, how much they hate white people, black men being "gods" and black women "queens," or if the poet wants to get particularly deep, some combination of the aforementioned. Ain't tryin' to be a hater, but as this scene has evolved into a verbal free-for-all, I suspect that a lot of cats are not reading, and could care less about how their work stands the test of time. In fact, many a young writer has stated to me, emphatically, "I don't read anything because I don't want to be influenced by other people," or, incredibly, "I don't have time to read." Oh, okay. Or, as Willie Perdomo frames it, the Word Movement has become something akin to a hustle:

> I spot the spoken word racketeers
> who get close enough to put bugs
> in my ears
> buy me a few beers
> and extend open invitations to the studio
> to lay down a track or two
> for a couple of points
> so they can dig into my pockets
> when I fall asleep.

> —"Spotlight at the Nuyorican Poets Café"

On the fiction side, poor imitations of McMillan and Harris have popped up everywhere. As was the case with the music industry where every major label had to have a "gangsta" act, suddenly every big publishing house has to have a "fiction" writer who jacks the dialogue of a beauty salon or barbershop and passes it off as good literature. Toss in a catchy, black vernacular-driven title, a colorful cover, and a blurb or two from a nonliterary "star," and, *Bling! Bling!* Gold is on the way. It seems to matter little how well any of these writers can actually write. As contributor Debra Dickerson declares in her stinging piece,

> It is ironic that the same mainstream recognition of the black literary imagination that is fueling the boom in black books is also responsible for the dumbing down of that imagination.

—"SHE'S GOTTA HAVE IT"

This "dumbing down" has been so profound it even permeates newer genres of writing, such as hip-hop journalism. When I worked at *Vibe* as a staff writer, along with Joan Morgan and Scott Poulson-Bryant, our vision was to make the publication a "black" *New Yorker* or *Vanity Fair. Vibe,* like *The Source* before it (and its important early 90s writers James Bernard, Reginald Dennis, and Kierna Mayo), did, I feel, do some meaningful work, at least in the beginning. But somehow and somewhere we got lost in the haze of advertisement dollars, sensationalized headlines, and we writers and editors clamoring to be as famous as the music artists we were profiling. Thus, inevitably, that dream, too, derailed. I cannot go anywhere, be it a college campus or an obscure bar in a 'hood somewhere, anywhere, without a younger cat telling me he wants to be—no, he says, he *is*—a hip-hop journalist, in spite of the fact that he has had mininal or no training (be it formally or not) as a reporter, as a researcher, or as a cultural critic. When I ask these newer new jacks about their knowledge of black music, if it ain't DMX, Dr. Dre, or whoever is hot at the moment, they ain't feelin' it— or *you* for asking. Sadly, too many young music critics know *nada* about music beyond what is on the local urban station. And names like Amiri Baraka and Greg Tate are foreign to many. Indeed, with the proliferation of hip-hop magazines the past few years, and the explosion of the hip-hop dot-coms, now virtually anyone can proclaim him or herself a music journalist, grab a phat salary and title, with perks, and have a cover story without knowing how to construct a paragraph, let alone an article. So what we have, fam, in a nutshell, is the Word Movement, like hip-hop, in a crazy holding pattern trying to figure out which route to fly next.

I started thinking of editing another anthology of my generation of black writers a few years back. As the Word Movement veered into something unrecognizable, I quietly xeroxed poems, articles, essays, and reviews, and clipped newspaper and magazine pieces, and purchased the books and CDs of basically every young black writer I came across. If I was going to do this book, it had to include good writers, and not just the writers I knew, or who lived in New York City, or in America. Also, it did not matter if they were famous or not, whether they were signed to a major house and had big-time agents, or if they had only sold a handful of books or chapbooks at their local café. I simply refused to believe that there was not more than a handful who could throw down with a pen and a pad.

I also combed through the numerous anthologies published since *In the Tradition:* the ones that featured writers born after a particular year, as well as the ones that, myopically, contained only "award-winning" or "noted" young writers; the ones on black men, on black women, on fatherhood, on motherhood; the ones on black gay men, on black lesbians; the ones on black love, on black eroticism, on spoken-word artists, on Mumia Abu-Jamal; and the ones that featured only poetry, or only speculative fiction . . . and so on. I knew I did not want to do a niche or specialized anthology. That, rather, I wanted this anthology to be regarded as a definitive text of this era, as the mouthpiece for the Word Movement, much in the same way that *The New Negro* and *Black Fire* represented their times. Which also meant I could not put together a collection that only contained my (literary) friends, or writers and kinds of literature I favored. If I was going to do this, I thought, I would have to cast a wide net in search of some of the best and brightest writers of the Word Movement.

The call went out, officially, in August 1999, and seven months later I dwindled approximately 250 submissions—from as near as the next block in Brooklyn to as far away as Fiji—to the 106 writers—52 women and 54 men—gathered here. My criteria for inclusion was simple: I wanted writing that was great or exceptionally good, where writers showed an obvious understanding and mastery of craft, and did not rely on what I call "sob stories" or "gimmicks" to propel a piece, like a death in the family, an addiction, or some other tragedy. Anyone, I feel, can write a tearjerker, but few are able to write a tearjerker that, because of technical competency, has me remembering that piece days, weeks, months, years from now. It is for that reason that many of the pieces in this anthology are previously published material, with a few notable exceptions, like Daniel Wideman's wonderful essay "Your Friendly Neighborhood Jungle."

It goes without saying that this anthology features writers who have been and will continue to produce incredible bodies of work: Edwidge Danticat, Junot Díaz, John Keene, Allison Joseph, Ben Okri, Daphne Brooks, and Lynell George, to name but a few. And while I have involved newer, lesser-known heads, rest assured these writers, such as Taigi Smith, Wayde Compton, Eisa Davis, Howard Rambsy II, and Samwiri Mukuru, are cats I believe we will be hearing from for years to come. I also wanted to include writers who have been doing solid work, in relative obscurity, and with the most incredible amount of humility. Writers such as Lisa Teasley, who writes poetry, fiction, essays, and criticism, and is a prominent painter yet cannot convince a big house to take a chance on her completed novels. And I wanted timeless, classic pieces, like Donnell Alexander's "Are Black People Cooler than White People?" and Scott Poulson-Bryant's very prophetic "This Is Not a Puff Piece," about rap icon Puff Daddy, because they declare, conclusively, that we do have something to say, and we are doing so in new and amazing ways.

I decided to call this collection *Step into a World—A Global Anthology of the New Black Literature* because you, the reader, will literally be taken on a journey around the planet. Borrowed from a KRS-One rap song, the main title also reflects my desire not to participate in these artificial boundaries of geography. We *are* African people, as Teresa Washington infers many times in her epistolary epic "An Atlantic Away: A Letter from Africa." No doubt. While most of the writers are based here in the United States, it is not lost on me how many were either born or have roots in the Caribbean, or in Africa. The fact that so many of the fine young West Indian and African writers live either in England or the States says much about our postcolonial tribulations, and much about the need to be in spaces where we can tell our stories straight up, no chaser.

While far too many nations to list are directly or indirectly accounted for in *Step into a World,* contributors are actually based in nine countries and on three continents. As the subtitle suggests, this global assemblage of new black voices was exciting to orchestrate. Using a telephone, a fax machine, snail mail, and especially the Internet, I was able to communicate with writers in ways that were impossible during the making of *In the Tradition.* Indeed, I am clear that *Step into a World* would not exist this quickly, if at all, without the aid of the digital revolution. Fewer than 5 percent of the writers who submitted work, as well as of those in the book, do not have an e-mail address. I cannot begin to describe my joy as poems, letters, e-mails, short stories, author biographies, and other items made their way to me by way of my e-mail address. It is quite astonishing to connect with places I long to visit, such as South Africa, Amsterdam, Trinidad and Tobago, and Vancouver, Canada.

You, the reader, can approach *Step into a World* in many ways. First, the book can be approached by its six sections: Essays, Hip-Hop Journalism, Criticism, Fiction, Poetry, and Dialogue. All of the sections are alphabetized. And while it is common to see Essays, Criticism, Fiction, and Poetry in anthologies, I wanted to include newer forms of writing. While I remain somewhat critical of the type of hip-hop journalism taking place today, I cannot ignore the fact that a number of young writers desire to dive in because of some of the pieces presented in this section. Moreover, this marks the first time hip-hop journalism is given its own space in book form. Among the genre's A-list mind squad represented here is Harry Allen, widely regarded as the first writer dedicated completely to hip-hop journalism.

In terms of the Dialogue section, I felt it important to highlight the various ways our generation communicates, among each other, and with the world. So we have an address, a manifesto, letters, and an e-mail. It is my thinking that some or all of these forms will grow in popularity in the coming years as more traditional modes of writing become too time-consuming for our cellular sensibilities.

The second way the anthology can be accessed is by cross-referencing the various pieces. For example, there are resonances between the fiction of Danzy Senna's "Caucasia" and the nonfiction of Lonnae O'Neal Parker's "White Girl." Both explore biracialism, albeit in different ways. As a matter of fact, practically every theme one can think of is touched upon in *Step into a World,* be it racial identity, gender oppression, sexual politics (for both the straight and gay and lesbian communities), AIDS, crack, social apathy, capitalism, birth, death, and spirituality. And hip-hop, the sound track for a good portion of this generation of writers, cuts and scratches its way through this anthology. No, not everyone collected here is a hip-hop head, but to ignore the music would be to ignore what is happening with global youth culture.

Finally, what is fascinating to me are the contributors' biographies. When you read the background information—and dig between the lines—a striking mosaic develops of these 106 writers, who range in age from twenty-three to forty-three, and were born between 1957 and 1977. These bios offer a closer glimpse at writers whose lives cover the Civil Rights Movement, as well as independence movements in the Caribbean and Africa. What you will notice, too, is much relocation and displacement, across cities, states, seas, oceans, continents. There is an undeniable searching at hand. Some of the writers provide explanations for that searching when you turn from their bios to their respective pieces. Some do not. What is understood is that we are one people, but then again we are not.

I feel it must be stated that the absence of any serious political motion paralleling the Word Movement speaks to some of the confusion manifested in even our finest work. Let us not forget that while the Harlem Renaissance was happening there was the Garvey Movement. Or that many of the Negritude writers in the Caribbean and Africa supported or participated in the battles against the European colonial powers. Or that the Black Arts Movement came on the heels of the Civil Rights and the Black Power Movements. The Word Movement is, in some ways, both political and apolitical. Political in the sense that any time a black person decides to put down on paper what he or she feels, that in itself is a political act. Apolitical in the sense that far too many young writers, including some in *Step into a World,* are only concerned with their individual lives—and careers—and have not given much thought to the fact that our very ability to be writers and artists stems from previous and ongoing struggles.

Be that as it may, I was not interested in forcing any sort of unity with *Step into a World.* Our diversity is our beauty, our strength, our work-in-progress. And I respect the right of every writer to do what she or he pleases. Indeed, it is thrilling to bring together such eclectic voices, be they straight, gay, lesbian, or bisexual; b-boy, bohemian, or bourgeois; progressive or conservative; male or female; college professor or grassroots activist; slam champion or Cave Canem participant; experimental fiction writer or best-selling author; Northerner or Southerner; American or West Indian; Latino or Canadian; European or African.

With all these layers and complexities, it is hard to say where black literature—or black people—are headed next. Kevin Baldeosingh's "Do Books Matter?" raises an interesting question in this day of short attention spans and, it seems, sadly, increasingly shorter attention spans for literature that requires some level of mental stamina. Perhaps the answer does lie in the work of those writers who are best able to take current events, current language, and massage and manipulate them, then give them back to the people. And perhaps the Internet is a place "serious" writers need to explore if they aim not to become obsolete and forgotten as the dot-coms continue the push toward global rule. We writers now know the multimedia assault—cable TV, desktop publishing, the Internet—is a real and present danger to our livelihoods and our future. Not only have these technologies democratized the space for all would-be writers, but it has made it doubly difficult for those of us who are trying to be craftspeople—and not simply famous writers for the moment—to maneuver.

Yet it is remotely possible all this will change if the so-called economic prosperity looming over America comes to a sudden and screeching halt. It is remotely possible that as AIDS and other social maladies persist in beating our communities down, our writings will cough up a stark social realism unseen since the Depression-ridden 1930s. Or it is remotely possible that this will be one of the last generational anthologies to appear in this form as the information age makes books and any object larger than a Palm Pilot or cellphone absolutely obsolete. And downloading "e-books" may very well become the new thing for the majority of readers.

This is the world we have inherited, this is, as James Baldwin once said, our birthright. The Word Movement shall go on, we shall go on, the globe will continue to roll in both merriment and utter confusion. While *Step into a World* certainly does not recommend hard and ready solutions to our plethora of concerns, it does, because of the brilliance of so many of these writers, offer interpretations, joys, sorrows, songs, sermons, and, at the end of the day, possibilities that there is something beneath our words—and beyond these pages.

Kevin Powell
Brooklyn, New York
The Year 2000

PART ONE

Essays

"I wrote these words for everyone/Who struggles in their youth/Who won't accept deception/Instead of what is truth."

—Lauryn Hill, "Everything Is Everything" (1998)

Donnell Alexander

Are Black People Cooler than White People?

I'M COOL LIKE THIS:

I read fashion magazines like they're warning labels telling me what not to do.

When I was a kid, Arthur Fonzarelli seemed a garden-variety dork.

I got my own speed limit.

I come when I want to.

I maintain like an ice cube in the remote part of the freezer.

Cooler than a polar bear's toenails.

Cooler than the other side of the pillow.

Cool like me.

Know this while understanding that I am in essence a humble guy.

I'm the kinda nigga who's so cool that my neighbor bursts into hysterical tears whenever I ring her doorbell after dark. She is a new immigrant who has chosen to live with her two roomates in our majority-black Los Angeles neighborhood so that, I'm told, she can "learn about all American cultures." But her real experience of us is limited to the space between her Honda and her front gate; thus, much of what she has to go on is the vibe of the surroundings and the images emanating from the television set that gives her living room a minty cathode glow. As such, I'm a cop-show menace and a shoe commercial demi-god—one of the rough boys from our 'hood and the living, breathing embodiment of hip hop flava. And if I can't fulfill the prevailing stereotype, the kids en route to the nearby high school can. The woman is scared in a cool world. She smiles as I pass her way in the light of day, unloading my groceries or shlepping my infant son up the stairs. But at night, when my face is visible through the window of her door lit only by the bulb that brightens the vestibule, I, at once familiar and threatening, am just too much.

Thus being cool has its drawbacks. With cool come assumptions and fears, expectations and intrigue. My neighbor wants to live near cool, but she's not sure about cool walking past her door after dark. During the day, she sees a black man; at night what she sees in the shadow gliding across her patio is a nigga.

Once upon a time, little need existed for making the distinction between a nigga and a black—at least not in this country, the place where niggas were invented. We were just about all slaves, so we were all niggas. Then we became free on paper yet oppressed still. Today, with as many as a third of us a generation of two removed from living poor (depending on who's counting), niggadom isn't innate to every black child born. But with the poverty rate still hovering at around 30 percent, black people still got niggas in the family, even when they themselves aren't niggas. Folks who don't know niggas can watch them on TV, existing in worlds almost always removed from blacks. Grant Hill is black, Allen Iverson is a nigga. Oprah interviewing the celebrity du jour is a black woman; the woman being handcuffed on that reality TV show is a nigga.

The question of whether black people are cooler than white people is a dumb one, and one that I imagine a lot of people will find offensive. But we know what we're talking about, right? We're talking about style and spirit and the innovations that those things spawn. It's on TV; it's in the movies, sports and clothes and language and gestures and music.

See, black cool is cool as we know it. I could name names—Michael Jordan and Chris Rock and Me'shell Ndegeocello and Will Smith and bell hooks and Li'l Kim—but cool goes way back, much further than today's superstars. Their antecedents go back past blaxploitation cinema, past Ike Turner to Muddy Waters, beyond even the old jazz players and blues singers whose names you'll never know. Cool has a history and cool has a meaning. We all know cool when we see it, and now more than at any other time in this country's history, when mainstream America looks for cool we look to black culture. Countless new developments can be called great, nifty, even keen. But, cool? That's a black thang, baby.

And I should know. My being cool is not a matter of subjectivity or season. Having lived as a nigga has made me cool. Let me explain. Cool was born when the first plantation nigga figured out how to make animal innards—massa's garbage, hog maws and chitlins—taste good enough to eat. That inclination to make something out of nothing and then to make that something special articulated itself first in the work chants that slaves sang in the field and then in the hymns that rose out of their churches. It would late reveal itself in the music made from cast-off Civil War marching-band instruments (jazz); physical exercise turned to public spectacle (sports); and street life styling, from pimps' silky handshakes to the corner crack dealer's baggy pants.

Cool is all about trying to make a dollar out of 15 cents. It's about living on the cusp, on the periphery, diving for scraps. Essential to cool is being outside looking in. Others—Indians, immigrants, women, gays—have been "othered," but until the past 15 percent of America's history, niggas in real terms have been treated by the country's majority as, at best, subhuman and, at worst, an abomination. So in the days when they were still literally on the plantation they devised a coping strategy called cool, an elusive mellowing strategy designed to master time and space. Cool, the basic reason blacks remain in the American cultural mix, is an industry of style that everyone in the world can use. It's finding the essential soul while being essentially lost. It's the nigga metaphor. And the nigga metaphor is the genius of America.

Gradually over the course of this century, as there came to be a growing chasm of privilege between black people and niggas, the nature of cool began to shift. The romantic and now-popular image of the pasty Caucasian who hung out in a jazz club was one small subplot. Cool became a promise—the reward to any soul hardy enough to pierce the inner sanctum of black life and not only live to tell about it but also live to live for it. Slowly, watered-down versions of this very specific strain of cool became the primary means of defining American cool. But it wasn't until Elvis that cool was brought down from Olympus (or Memphis) to majority-white culture. Mass media did the rest. Next stop: high fives, chest bumps, and "Go girl!"; Air Jordans, Tupac, and low-riding pants.

White folks began to try to make the primary point of cool—recognition of the need to go with the flow—a part of their lives. But cool was only an avocational interest for them. It could never be the necessity it was for their colored co-occupants. Some worked harder at it than others. And as they came to understand coolness as being of almost elemental importance, they began obsessing on it, asking themselves, in a variety of clumsy, indirect ways: Are black people cooler than white people and, if so, why?

The answer is, of course, yes. And if you, the reader, had to ask some stupid shit like that, you're probably white. It's hard to imagine a black person even asking the question, and a nigga might not even know what you mean. Any nigga who'd ask that question certainly isn't much of one; niggas invented the shit.

Humans put cool on a pedestal because life at large is a challenge, and in that challenge we're trying to cram in as much as we can—as much fine loving, fat eating, dope sleeping, mellow walking, and substantive working as possible. We need spiritual assistance in the matter. That's where cool comes in. At its core, cool is useful. Cool gave bass to 20th-century American culture, but I think that if the culture had needed more on the high end, cool would have given that, because cool closely resembles the human spirit. It's about completing the task of living with enough spontaneity to splurge some of it on bystanders, to share with others working through their own travails a little of your bonus life. Cool is about turning desire into deed with a surplus of ease.

Some white people are cool in their own varied ways. I married a white girl who was cooler than she ever knew. And you can't tell me Jim Jarmusch and Ron Athey and Delbert McClinton ain't smooth.

There's a gang of cool white folks, all of whom exist that way because they've found their essential selves amid the abundant and ultimately numbing media replications of the coolness vibe and the richness of real life. And there's a whole slew more of them ready to sign up if you tell 'em where. But your average wigger in the rap section of Sam Goody ain't gone nowhere; she or he hasn't necessarily learned shit about the depth and breadth of cool about making a dollar out of 15 cents. The problem with mainstream American culture, the reason why iron's been elevated to raison d'être status and neurosis increasingly gets fetishized, is its twisted approach to cool. Most think cool is something you can put on and take off at will (like a strap-on goatee). They think it's some shit you go shopping for. And that taints cool, giving the mutant thing it becomes a deservedly bad name. Such strains aren't even cool anymore, but an evil ersatz-cool, one that fights real cool at every turn. Advertising agencies, record company artist-development departments, and over-art-directed bars are where erstatz-cool dwells. What passes for cool to the white-guy passerby might be—is probably—just rote duplication without an ounce of inspiration.

The acceptance of clone cool by so many is what makes hip hop necessary. It's what negates the hopelessness of the postmodern sensibility at its most cynical. The hard road of getting by on metaphorical chitlins kept the sons and daughters of Africa in touch with life's essential physicality, more in touch with the world and what it takes to get over in it: People are moved, not convinced; things get done, they don't just happen. Real life doesn't allow for much fronting, as it were. And neither does hip hop. Hip hop allows for little deviation between who one is and what one can ultimately represent.

Rap—the most familiar, and therefore the most emblematic, example of hip hop expression—is about the power of conveying through speech the world beyond words.

Language is placed on a par with sound and, ultimately, vibes. Huston Smith, a dope white guy, wrote: "Speech is alive—literally alive because speaking is the speaker. It's not the whole of the speaker, but it is the speaker in one of his or her living modes. This shows speech to be alive by definition . . . It possesses in principle life's qualities, for its very nature is to change, adapt, and invent. Indissolubly contextual, speaking adapts itself to speaker, listener, and situation alike. This gives it an immediacy, range, and versatility that is, well, miraculous."

Which is why hip hop has become the most insidiously influential music of our time. Like rock, hip hop in its later years will have a legacy of renegade youth to look back upon fondly. But hip hop will insist that its early marginalization be recognized as an integral part of what it comes to be. When the day comes that grandmothers are rapping and beatboxing as they might aerobicize now, and samplers and turntables are as much an accepted part of leisure time as channel surfing, niggas will be glad. Their expression will have proven ascendant.

But that day's not here yet. If white people were really cool with black cool, they'd put their stuff with our stuff more often to work shit out. I don't mean shooting hoops together in the schoolyard as much as white cultural institutions like college radio, indie film, and must-see TV. Black cool is banished to music videos, sports channels, and UPN so whites can visit us whenever they want without having us live right next door in the media mix. Most of the time, white folks really don't want to be part of black cool. They just like to see the boys do a jig every once in a while.

At the same time, everyday life in black America is not all Duke Ellington and Rakim Allah. Only a few black folks are responsible for cool. The rest copy and recycle. At the historical core of black lives in this country is a clear understanding that deviation from society's assigned limitations results in punitive sanctions: lynching, hunger, homelessness. The fear of departing from the familiar is where the inclination to make chitlins becomes a downside. It's where the shoeshine-boy reflex to grin and bear it was born. Black rebellion in America from slave days onward was never based on abstract, existentialist grounds. A bird in the hand, no matter how small, was damn near everything.

Today, when deviation from normalcy not only goes unpunished but is also damn near demanded to guarantee visibility in our fast-moving world, blacks remain woefully wedded to the bowed head and blinders. Instead of bowing to massa, they slavishly bow to trend and marketplace. And this creates a hemming-in of cool, an inability to control the cool one makes. By virtue of their status as undereducated bottom feeders, man niggas will never overcome this way of being. But, paradoxically, black people—who exist at a greater distance from cool than niggas—can and will. That's the perplexity of the cool impulse. As long as some black people have to live like niggas, cool, as contemporarily defined, will live on. As long as white people know what niggas are up to, cool will continue to exist, with all of its baggage passed on like, uh, luggage. The question "Are black people cooler than white people?" is not the important one. "How do I gain proximity to cool, and do I want it?" is much better. The real secret weapon of cool is that it's about synthesis. Just about every important black cultural invention of this century has been about synthesizing elements previously considered antithetical. MLK merged Eastern thought and cottonfield religious faith into the civil rights movement. Chuck Berry merged blues and country music into rock 'n' roll. Michael Jordan incorporated the old school ball of Jerry West into his black game. Talk about making a dollar out of 15 cents.

Out in the netherworld of advertising, they tell us we're all Tiger Woods. He plays the emblematic white man's game as good as anyone. Well, only one nigga on this planet gets to be that motherfucker, but we all swing the same cool, to whatever distant ends. The coolness construct might tell us otherwise, but we're all handed the same basic tools at birth; it's up to us as individuals to work on our game. Some of us have sweet strokes, and some of us press too hard, but everybody who drops outta their mama has the same capacity to take a shot.

G WTW

SO WHAT CAN I TELL YOU ABOUT A BUNCH OF UNFORTUNATE NIGGERS stupid enough to get caught and hanged in America, or am I supposed to say lynched? I'm assuming this aggressive tone to establish a little distance from these images of the despised and dead, the better to determine the usefulness of this project, which escapes me, but doesn't preclude my writing about it. Too often we refuse information, refuse to look or even think about something, simply because it's unpleasant or poses a problem, or raises "issues"—emotional and intellectual friction that rubs our heavily therapeuticized selves the wrong way. I didn't like looking at these pictures, but once I looked, the events documented in them occurred in my mind over and over again, as did the realization that these pictures are documents of America's obsession with niggers, both black and white. I looked at these pictures, and what I saw in them, in addition to the obvious, was the way in which I'm regarded, by any number of people: as a nigger. And it is as one that I felt my neck snap and my heart break, while looking at these pictures.

In any case, America's interest in niggers—and people more than willing to treat other people as niggers—is of passing interest since America's propensity to define race and the underclass through hateful language, and hateful acts is well-known, and discussed. What isn't talked about that the largely white editors (who constitute what we call Publishing), have in hiring a colored person to describe a nigger's life. For them, a black writer is someone who can simplify what is endemic to him or her as a human being—race—and blow it up, to cartoon proportions, thereby making the coon situation "clear" to a white audience. To be fair, no such offensive non-ideas were put to me when this present collaboration was suggested, but would my inclusion in this book, as the nearly ahistorical, "lyrical" voice have been suggested if I were not a Negro? Or am I "lyrical" and ahistorical because I am a Negro? I am not going to adopt a mea culpa tone here, since I agreed to supply what I have always thought of as a soundtrack to these pictures, which, viewed together, make up America's first disaster movie.

But before I can talk about these pictures, such as the picture of the beautiful black guy with the incredibly relaxed shoulders who has been whipped—front and back—and who does not reveal anything to us (certainly not with his eyes) except his obvious pain: his flesh-eating scars, and the many pictures of people with their necks snapped, bowels loosened, feet no longer arched—before I can talk about any of the "feelings" they engender in me, I want to get back to the first question I posed: What is the relationship of the white people in these pictures to the white people who ask me and sometimes pay me to be Negro, on the page?

Of course, one big difference between the people documented in these pictures and me is that I am not dead, have not been lynched or scalded or burned or whipped or stoned. But I have been looked at, watched, and it's the experience of being watched, and seeing the harm in people's eyes—that is the prelude to becoming a dead nigger like those seen here, that has made me understand, finally, what the word "nigger" means, and why people have used it, and the way I use it here, now: as a metaphorical lynching before the real one. "Nigger" is a slow death. And that's the slow death I feel all the time now, as a colored man.

And according to these pictures, I shouldn't be talking to you right now: I'm a little on the nigger side, meant to be seen and not heard, my tongue hanged and with it, my mind. But before that happens, let me tell you what I see in these photographs: I see a lot of crazy looking white people, as crazy and empty-looking in the face as the white people who stare at me. Who wants to look at these pictures? Who are they all? When they look at these pictures, who do they identify with? The maimed, the tortured, the dead or the white people who maybe told some dumb nigger before they hanged him, You are all wrong, niggerish, outrageous, violent, disruptive, uncooperative, lazy, stinking, loud, difficult, obnoxious, stupid, angry. Prejudiced, unreasonable, shiftless, no good, a liar, fucked up—the very words and criticism a colored writer is apt to come up against if he doesn't do that woe-is-me Negro crap and has the temerity to ask not only why collect these pictures, but why does a colored point of view authenticate them, no matter what that colored person has to say?

In writing this, I have become a cliché, another colored person writing about a nigger's life. So doing, I'm feeding, somewhat, into what the essayist George W. S. Trow has called "white euphoria," which is defined by white people exercising their largesse in my face as they say, Tell me how you've suffered. Isn't that what you people do? Suffer nobly, poetically sometimes even? Doesn't suffering define you? I hate seeing this, and yet it is what I am meant to write, since I accepted the assignment, am "of the good," and want to know why these pictures, let along events, have caused me pain. I don't know many people who wouldn't feel like a nigger looking at these pictures, all fucked up and hurt, killed by eyes and hands that can't stand yours. I want to bow out of this nigger feeling. I resent these pictures for making me feel anything at all. For a long time, I avoided being the black guy, that is, being black-identified. Back then, I felt that adopting black nationalism limited my world, my world view. Now I know from experience that the world has been limited for me by people who see me as a nigger, very much in the way the dead eyes and flashbulb smiles in these photographs say: See what we do to the niggers! They are the fear and hatred in ourselves, murdered! Killed! All of this is painful and American. Language makes it trite, somehow. I will never write from this niggerish point of view again. This is my farewell. I mean to be courtly and grand. No gold watch is necessary, as I bow out of the nigger business.

In my life as a city dweller, I have crossed dark nighttime streets so as not to make the white woman walking in front of me feel fear. I have not deliberately come up behind a neighbor opening the door to our apartment building, so as not to make him feel what colored people make him feel: robbed, violated, somehow, I have been arrested on my way to school, accused of truancy. Once, when I was coming out of a restaurant with a friend, four or five cops pinned me to a wall, pointing guns at my head, I looked just like someone else. This is not to be confused with the time I sat with the same friend in his car, chatting, me in the back seat leaning over my friend's shoulder, and suddenly the car was flooded with white lights, police lights, and the lights on the hoods of their cars were turned on, and five or six cops, guns out of their holsters and pointed at me, were ordering me to get out of the car. We thought you were a car-jacker, they said, as I stood in that white light which always reminds me of movie premiere lights, you know, where people look like all dressed-up shadows as those lights hit them, getting out of their cars?

This is what makes me feel nigger-ish, I'm afraid: being watched. I go to parties with white people. Invariably, one of them will make a comment about my size. They say, We'd know you anywhere, you're so big! I mean, you're so distinctive!, when they mean something else altogether, perhaps this: we have been watching you become what our collective imagination says you are: big and black—niggerish—and so therefore what? Whatever. As long as it can be lynched, eventually.

Once or twice I thought I might actually get killed in my New York of cops and very little safety—a nigger casualty, not unlike the brilliant Negro short story writer and poet Henry Dumas, who was shot and killed in a subway station in Harlem, another case of "mistaken identity" in a colored village? He was thirty-three years old when he was killed in 1968 and had written at least one short story that I consider a master-piece, "Ark of Bones," a story made distinct by the number of lynchings that fill the air without being explicitly referred to. All those colored tragedies, even before you've had a chance to grow up, Dumas seems to say in this tale of two boys who are ignorant of their history, and then not. That is their rite of colored male passage: having to drag all those lynchings around with them, around their necks: those are their ancestors. Too bad when violent deaths define who you are. Here's a little of the narrator, Fish, and his voice, which is all he has: "Headeye, he was followin' me," Fish begins. "I knowed he was followin' me. But I just kept goin', like I wasn't payin' him no mind." What Head-eye and Fish eventually see, walking through a wood where maybe a cousin was lynched, maybe not, is an ark floating on a river. The ark is filled with the bones of their black ancestors. The ark carrying those bruised bones is "consecrated" ground, but it is divine ground that can never settle, since its home is a stream. Those bones keep moving, like the dead niggers on these pages. Every time you turn a page, they move.

But back to the idea of being watched by (primarily) white editors and being lynched by eyes. What I mean is that so much care, so much care is taken not to scare white people simply with my existence, and it's as if they don't want to deal with the care, too: it makes their seeing me as a nigger even more complicated. I know many, many colored people who exercise a similar sensitivity where white people are concerned, anything to avoid being lynched by their tongues or eyes. Certain colored people want to lynch you, too. They are competitive, usually, and stupid people who believe that if they work hard and sell out they can be just like most white people and hate niggers even more than they do since they "know" them. Those colored people are, in some ways, worse than white people, since they imagine that they are the some-times-lynched class, as opposed to the always-lynched. Fact is, if you are even half-way colored and male in America, the dead heads hanging from the trees in these pictures, and the dead eyes or grins surrounding them, it's not too hard to imagine how this is your life too, as it were. You can feel it every time you cross the street to avoid worrying a white woman to death or false accusations of rape, or every time your car breaks down anywhere in America, and you see signs about Jesus, and white people everywhere and your heart begins to race and your skin becomes clammy, and the perspiration sticks to your flesh, just like Brock Peters in the film version of "To Kill a Mockingbird," where he's on trial for maybe "interfering" with a white woman: it's her word against his but her word has weight, like the dead weight of a dead lynched body.

Once you're strung up, as they say in "The Ox-Bow Incident," or maybe the Maureen O'Hara version of "The Hunchback of Notre Dame," or maybe in "In Cold Blood," or once they've fixed a pain in the neck for you, as they say in "His Girl Friday" (all these movies have lynchings in them, or make reference to lynchings), once that's happened, what happens to your body? Did the families in these pictures stand at the periphery and wait for all to be over, when someone, maybe the youngest among them, could climb the tree and cut Cousin or Mother or Father down? It's hard to see if any of the lynched have anything but rope and eyes staring at them in these pictures. When they were lynched their humanity was taken from them so why not their families? They have no names in these pictures—maybe addresses, I don't know, since I couldn't look past the pictures, really. What difference would it have made to get the facts of any of these lives, white or colored, right? Don't we want this story to go away?

I'm ashamed that I couldn't get into the history of these people. I saw these pictures through a strong light that my mind put up, to obscure what I saw when I looked at all these dead niggers, their bodies reshaped by tragedy. I think the white light I saw was the white light those cops put on me. If you look at any number of old newsreel pictures taken at the big Hollywood premieres held at the Pantages, or Grauman's Chinese, in the nineteen thirties, forties, or fifties, some of the guests walking past the movie lights—klieg lights—look like shadowy half people trying to fill their suits or dresses. People as penumbrae. That's the light I saw when I looked at these pictures: it made the people in the pictures look less real. When I thought of that white light, I thought of my introduction to the South, where many of these niggers were killed: it was sitting in a darkened movie theatre with my mother and little brother, watching a revival of "Gone With the Wind," which some people called "GWTW." We ignored the pitiful colored people in the film because we wanted to enjoy ourselves, and in Margaret Mitchell's revisionist tale of the South, Vivien Leigh was so pretty. We couldn't think of those dumb niggers hanging from the trees in some field or another in Atlanta or outside of it, even though we knew about that by then. I'm sure we did though I don't think I'd heard Billie Holiday sing "Strange Fruit," about all those black bodies swinging in the Southern trees. At any rate, I didn't like Billie Holiday for a long time: her voice didn't make sense to me, nor did those black bodies, nothing so terrible was ever going to happen to me in Brooklyn, where I was considered cute and knew I would live forever. The world was going to love me forever. Whites and blacks.

I could make them love me, just as Vivien Leigh made so many men fall in love with her before the fall of Atlanta, in a movie that came out around the time Billie Holiday was singing "Strange Fruit," and perhaps that's an interesting thing to try now, watching GWTW to the sound of Billie Holiday singing "Strange Fruit." See her black bodies and weariness smeared all over Vivien Leigh's beautiful face, and Hattie McDaniel's ridiculous one.

Sitting in the movie theatre, watching GWTW for the first time, I was in love with Vivien Leigh and not all those niggers, the most hateful among them being a brown-faced, oily-skinned carpetbagger who looks at our Vivien Leigh with some kind of lust and disgust. I hated him then because he intruded on the beautiful pink world. Leigh's girlishness could have smothered me; I would have made her forget that I was colored and that she could lynch me if she wanted to because I knew I could make her love me. But how do you get people to ignore their history? I never thought of those things when I had love on my mind.

In the middle of the movie, Vivien Leigh as Scarlett suffers, and says she will never suffer again, and I loved her so much I didn't want her to suffer. As I grew up, I retained that feeling toward women who looked like my first movie star love: I didn't want them to suffer, even though they, like Vivien Leigh as Scarlett, could lynch a nigger to pay for all their hardship: God didn't make people of her class and wealth and race to suffer. For sure, Scarlett, in real life, might have lynched a nigger in order to make that person pay for all the inexplicable pain she had gone through and eventually come out the other side of, a much better person.

After that, her world might have looked completely different.

Race Natters—The Chattering Classes Convene on Martha's Vineyard

Angela Ards

"ONE-TWO-THREE! FARRAKHAN, FARRAKHAN," CORNEL WEST CHANTED TO check the mikes. It was a curious moment during "A Conversation on Race," the panel discussion featuring 10 of the country's more prominent black scholars held Labor Day weekend on Martha's Vineyard. Sponsored by the W. E. B. Du Bois Institute, self-described as the nation's oldest research center on African and African American studies, the dialogue was ostensibly called in response to the national conversation on race President Clinton launched two months ago.

Toward the end of the three-hour seminar, a middle-aged white man in the 400-plus audience asserted that the one black leader able to articulate a national plan of action around race was Minister Louis Farrakhan, and would the esteemed professors behind the dais comment on that? West, after adjusting the mikes, sought to temper the questioner's perception by downplaying Farrakhan's support. "His national organization is roughly only the size of the two biggest Baptist churches in Brooklyn," said the Harvard professor of Afro American studies and religion, who has no mass constituency. Farrakhan's rise, West argued, is merely the result of the crisis of black leadership, which is itself a reflection of the crisis of American leadership—spineless—refusing to tell the truth, refusing to be honorable. . . . Look at the black leadership! Who is not already subsumed by the establishment, while Farrakhan says plainly, "You're catching hell and you know it"?

Of course, these constituencyless panelists posing as African American spokespersons are thoroughly "subsumed by the establishment," with few plainspeakers among them. Not only was Farrakhan absent, so were traditional but fading race leaders Jesse Jackson and the NAACP's Kweisi Mfume. Rather, the Edgartown conversation, held in the sterile clapboard walls of the Old Whaling Church, was mild, modulated, borderline weary. "I for one am sick and tired of discussing the race problem," declared Du Bois Institute director Henry Louis Gates Jr., who moderated the discussion. Would the institute be doomed to sponsor such an event same time next century? he wondered glumly.

But his own introductory comments departed little from the same old same old. Gates trotted out the oft-quoted Du Bois remark—"The problem of the 20th century will be the problem of the color line"—that was probing and poignant in 1903 but feels parochial today amid the browning of America. In fact, before the event, Gates said that "the president's initiative must consider how the forces of economics and gender will fundamentally influence the matter of race even more in the 21st century." Yet the issues confronting African Americans were framed only in terms of black men. Gates cited horrific statistics indicating that in 1990, 2,280,000 black men were ensnared in the in the criminal justice system, while only 23,000 received college degrees. That's a ratio of 99 to 1; the ratio for white men is 6 to 1. But black women's issues didn't even get the perfunctory footnote treatment customary at race events sponsored by supposedly less progressive groups such as the Nation of Islam or the NAACP. And if, as Gates waxed prosaic on the Du Boisian prophecy, "ethnic difference [amid] economic differentials and economic scarcity" is the problem of the new millennium, the all-black panelists performing before a predominantly white, affluent Vineyard crowd did little to expand the black-versus-white paradigm that now frames race relations.

In fact, minstrelsy came to mind, with the performative tone set early on by Anna Deavere Smith. She presented three characters from *Twilight,* her play about the 1992 civil unrest that engulfed Los Angeles: a white former president of the police commission who refers to the black gang members attempting a truce as "these curious people," a Korean liquor store owner who sympathized with the plight of African Americans until her business was looted and destroyed, and a black gang member who—in a truncated piece, with the least political insight—mused abstractly on the meaning of his tag.

I often get the feeling Smith worries that a mostly white audience might think she's privileging the African American perspective, so she goes out of her way to shortchange it. But a purpose is served. The president's proposed conversation, as well as the event at Edgartown, helps white people learn the vocabulary of race, which they have not had to speak until now, as the melting pot gets murky. At one point, Anita Hill described—without translation—her hometown of Norman, Oklahoma, as a "sundown town" to explain why there is no sizable minority presence there today. Many whites in the audience were visibly lost, and those without a black friend handy to translate had to deduce meaning from context.

If the conversation is ever to be clear, Americans must discard the vague terms *race* and *racism,* said former Black Panther Kathleen Cleaver, and start discussing white supremacy. Otherwise, "how can you have a conversation about race that does not succumb to the dictates of the subtext of white supremacy," asked this now visiting professor at Cardozo Law School, "especially now, when we have Republican goon squads working like hell to restore not only the symbols but the substance of white supremacy?" Such as chain gangs, church burnings, and the revocation of affirmative action.

There was a lot of talk about how there had been enough talk already, but few concrete ideas were offered on how to improve race relations. Christopher Edley, former special counsel to the White House's committee on affirmative action and current consultant to the president's recently appointed seven-member race advisory board, naturally supported Clinton's race initiative, arguing that "conversation sets the stage for an engagement that can be transforming." Harvard law professor Randall Kennedy suggested that blacks be treated as individuals under the law, and his colleague Charles Ogletree offered a broad 25-year plan for social transformation.

Mainly, however, there were observations. Sociologist Orlando Patterson said that despite the deluge of literature decrying black middle class success as "volunteer slavery"—a clear shot at Vineyarder and author Jill Nelson's memoir—more than 70 percent of African Americans are "pretty content" with their lot, according to some obscure Gallup Poll only he seemed to have seen.

Patricia Williams was the only panelist to register unease about participating on an all-black, all-academic panel. "The structure," she said, "is one that repeats some island—and I don't mean Martha's Vineyard—an islanding of the conversation." Hill echoed that sentiment when she noted that the Vineyard conversation was very different from one that would occur in her hometown, a place, she says, "where the civil rights movement happened—almost." Indeed, it was only very late in the evening that the discussion reached beyond panelists' statistics and anecdotes to the outside world, as West mentioned the march against police brutality that occurred in New York the morning of the seminar.

Savvily timed to coincide with the president's Vineyard vacation for maximum media coverage, "A Conversation on Race," at $50 per ticket, was a lucrative fundraiser for a worthy cause, the Du Bois Institute. Gate's Harvard Dream Team of black scholars is bringing to the field of African American studies—inside and outside—a level of legitimacy and outside of academia—a level of legitimacy and respect that it has never before enjoyed. Yet just what recommendations the president and his advisory council could glean from this event is dubious, since none of them was present.

Still, Gates was clearly satisfied. "Just getting people this smart together, and an audience this smart, that was my goal. This was like a seminar at a university. Someone says, 'Why are we here?' Someone says, 'I'm glad we're here.' Someone says, 'I disagree with you.' Someone says, 'You're full of shit.' And that's great! We took three hours tonight, and these people would have sat for two more."

Panelists were mobbed by fawning audience members seeking autographs after the event, and then ushered into vans waiting to spirit them to a posh party hosted by Diane Sawyer and Mike Nichols, where Carly Simon and Jessye Norman performed spontaneous duets. Also on hand was software magnate and budding patron of black cultural causes Peter Norton, who underwrote the 1995 "Black Male Show" at the Whitney Museum, and recently purchased a rambling oceanside house on the Vineyard that is to serve as a retreat for Harvard professors.

It's a long way from hardscrabble Piedmont, West Virginia, to the exclusive enclaves of Martha's Vineyard, and Gates couldn't seem more pleased to have arrived. "I happen to love this island," he enthused. "This is the most thoroughly integrated place in the United States in August—by race, ethnicity, religion, and gender, no doubt." And what of the "economic differences" he'd urged Clinton to consider as integral to improved race relations? Is the island integrated by class? "No," Gates acknowledged, without apology. This is a very middle-class place." No doubt.

<hr>

Valerie Boyd

In Search of Alice Walker

ON A WARM, WET OCTOBER EVENING, PEOPLE ARE GATHERING AT THE Crowne Plaza Hotel in Macon, Georgia. Local movers and shakers, and working-class black folks—Macon's backbone—have come to have dinner with Alice Walker, to hug her neck, as we say here in the South, and to watch her receive the 1997 Shelia Award from the Tubman African American Museum, the town's vanguard cultural institution.

The event promises to be a homecoming of sorts. Many of Alice Walker's relatives live in Macon. And as they make their way to the tables reserved for them, they are all aglow. Alice's older sister Ruth Walker-Hood is here with her 14-year-old grandson. One of Alice's big brothers has driven from Eatonton—their hometown.

I, along with several other members of the Alice Walker Literary Society, have come from Atlanta. An international organization, the society was founded at Spelman College and Emory University last May.

But I was baptized in Walker's words more than 15 years ago by the late great novelist Leon Forrest, in an African American literature class where he encouraged students to revel in Walker's work. Since then I've consumed each of her books with a kind of hunger. And like more of the people gathered at this banquet, I am watching the door, looking for Alice.

This is not the first time that I've been in a small Georgia town looking for Alice Walker. Just a few weeks earlier, on a radiant spring day, I'd driven to Eatonton, about 75 miles east of Atlanta.

I'm not sure what I was looking for there, but I do know that as I've become more and more of a writer, I've felt a growing sense of connection to Alice Walker. Like her, I was born and raised in Georgia, though Eatonton is a far cry from Atlanta, my hometown. And like her, I count Zora Neale Hurston, another black southern-born writer, as my literary foremother. Recently it occurred to me that if Zora is my spiritual and artistic grandmother, then Alice—who put a marker on Hurston's weed-choked grave in 1973—is my mother. So I suppose I drove to Eatonton, to borrow Alice's phrase, in search of my mother's garden.

Heading into town I am greeted by a flurry of signs: one huge billboard with Confederate flags adorning each side urges passersby to "Join the sons of Confederate Veterans." "You're not in Atlanta anymore," I tell myself. "You're in Georgia."

Other signs follow, including the one I've been looking for: "Welcome to Historic Eatonton, home of Joel Chandler Harris, Alice Walker." Her name is in smaller type below his. On the sign Eatonton brags that it is "Close to Everything . . . Next to Perfect."

In short order there are more signs inviting me to visit the Uncle Remus Museum and reminding me that Eatonton is the birthplace of Uncle Remus' literary master, Joel Chandler Harris. I don't see any more signs about Alice Walker.

When I walk into the little yellow house that is home to the Tourist Information Center, I am greeted by a woman with platinum blond hair and wide blue eyes. As her eyes do a quick sweep, checking out my purple batik pants and down-the-back dreadlocks, I tell her that I would like to explore the local attractions. Handing me a stack of brochures, she recommends the Uncle Remus Museum, the Tour of Homes, and two nearby recreation areas.

"What about Alice Walker?" I ask.

"Of course," she perkily responds and gives me a lilac-colored brochure. On the front there's an old photograph of Alice Walker, taken when she was still wearing a 'fro, that appeared on early editions of *In Search of Our Mothers' Gardens*. The literary chronology in the brochure hasn't been updated since the publication of *Possessing the Secret of Joy* in 1992. Still I'm heartened by the fact that the brochure even exists and that it promises an Alice Walker Driving Tour. Somewhat apologetically the woman warns me not to "get out and walk around on the property because Alice Walker still has family who live in the area."

"Really," I ask, "what family?"

"Sisters and cousins, I believe," the woman replies. Actually, the brochure says that Alice's brother Fred lives at the Grant Plantation, their mother's birthplace. It doesn't mention that two more brothers—Jimmy and Bobby—are also among the town's 4,737 residents.

"Has the chamber of commerce asked Alice Walker about doing more to mark her origins in Eatonton?" I ask.

Bright-eyed as ever, the woman replies: "Yes, we have. Since she's alive and all, she just doesn't want us to do a lot. And I can't blame her. I'd probably be the same way if I was her. I mean, the Uncle Remus stuff is dead. But she's still alive, and she's still got family here. So we try real hard to protect her privacy."

Privacy is important to Alice, her sister Ruth acknowledges. But according to Ruth, any efforts Eatonton wants to make now to honor Alice Walker may be too little, too late. "Alice has reached the very top of her field. And she's done it without the support of her hometown, and I'm quite sure she doesn't need it now." But Ruth believes that others need it: "It's important to give these kids someone to look up to."

The first place I find on the "Driving Tour" is the Wards Chapel A.M.E. Church. Despite the warning, I get out of my car. A warm breeze rustles through the congregation of trees on the side of the tiny white church, and I notice that the yard seems to attract more than its share of butterflies. There's a small purple sign—maroon really—on a wooden stake in the churchyard. The metal sign has an icon of a woman sitting in a rocking chair, recognizable as Celie from Walker's Pulitzer prizewinning novel, *The Color Purple*. The sign says that this church is where "Alice Malsenior Walker was baptized and faithfully attended services."

Later Ruth Walker-Hood tells me that because the old church's members "are scattered to the four corners," these days it is only used for an occasional funeral.

The church is, as Alice Walker has written, "simple, serene, sweet." And despite the too-high grass around the steps, the broken window panes, and crushed Budweiser cans strewn in the backyard, there is something about it that remains alive. Perhaps it's the butterflies and the birds, which seem to guard the church from malevolent spirits. I wonder if the cardinals and robins ever fly through the broken glass and into the sanctuary during the eulogies or while the choir is sending some soul home with "Amazing Grace."

Across the street is the cemetery where Alice's parents, Willie Lee Walker and Minnie Tallulah Grant Walker, are buried along with other family members. A purple sign marks the spot. Surely Alice Walker had something to do with the stone on her mother's grave. It says simply: "Loving South, Great Spirit."

Farther up the road another sign indicates the site of the home where Alice Walker grew up. But the small wooden cabin sitting on the huge expanse of farmland looks too new. Less than two miles away is the house where Walker was born. Just outside the rather foreboding fence that protects the property is a purple sign; behind it stands a stubby tree. A funeral flower is laid lovingly at the foot of the tree next to a white cross with a name that at first glance appears to be "Janie" stenciled across it. I think of Janie from Zora Neale Hurston's novel *Their Eyes Were Watching God,* about which Walker has said, "There is no book more important to me than this one." On closer inspection I see that the name of the person being remembered here is Jamie. As I wonder who this Jamie was, the intoxicating smell of pine trees wafts through the air.

I drive on, looking for the fifth and final stop on the tour—the Grant Plantation, Walker's mother's birthplace. Despite several attempts I never find it. The only sign I see is for Uncle Remus Realty, which features a nattily attired, dancing white rabbit—Br'er Rabbit, I suppose.

At the Uncle Remus Museum, situated in the center of town, the rabbit hailing passersby is a dirty gray, but still nattily dressed. The museum is catty-corner to the Putnam Middle School. The kids have a good view of the former slave cabin that became the museum in 1963—the same year another famous Georgian, Martin Luther King Jr., gave his "I Have a Dream" speech.

Joel Chandler Harris is heralded—in this town, damn near worshiped—as the creator of Uncle Remus. But even Harris admitted his creativity was questionable. In a interview he described Uncle Remus as "not an invention of my own, but a human syndicate, I might say, of three or four old darkies whom I knew. I just walloped them together into one person and called him 'Uncle Remus.' "

Alice Walker wrote about the effect Harris' fiction had on her life in her essay "The Dummy in the Window: Joel Chandler Harris and the Invention of Uncle Remus," which she included in *Living by the Word:* "Joel Chandler Harris is billed as the creator of Uncle Remus. Uncle Remus told the stories of Br'er Rabbit and Br'er Fox, all the classic folk tales that came from Africa and that, even now in Africa, are still being told. We too, my brothers and sisters and I, listed to them. But after we saw *Song of the South* [the 1945 film that features Uncle Remus telling his tales to a group of little white children], we no longer listened to them. They were killed for us. In fact, I do not remember any of my relatives ever telling any of those tales after they saw what had been done to them."

Discussing her hometown's exaltation of Harris' Uncle Remus, she wrote: "There was also, until a few years ago, an Uncle Remus restaurant. There used to be a dummy of a black man, an elderly, kindly, cotton-haired darky, seated in a rocking chair in the restaurant window. In fantasy, I frequently liberated him, using Army tanks and guns. Blacks, of course, were not allowed in this restaurant."

Almost to my surprise, I am allowed into the Uncle Remus Museum. Kathryn Walden, a gracious southern belle, greets me warmly and invites me to sign the guest book. She proudly announces that I am the thirty-fifth adult visitor of the day, that about a thousand visitors arrive every month, and that people have come from all 50 states and 38 foreign countries.

I had heard that there was a folder of information on Alice Walker here at Uncle Remus headquarters. (Perhaps to put both of the town's famous African Americans under one roof.) But Mrs. Walden says, "No, we don't have anything on her here," emphasizing the last word. "I hope they're going to do something for her, like start a museum, but we don't have anything about her here."

As I cautiously make my way around the museum, I am captivated by newspaper clippings describing the Harris Centennial Celebration on December 9, 1948, the day that would have marked his one hundredth birthday. Alice Walker had been born just a few years before the big event, on February 9, 1944. Reading the news stories I wonder if Alice and her siblings were among the children in the parade that one reporter described: "And the descendants of Uncle Remus' darky friends took part too, with Negro school children marching along."

Next to a basket filled with bolls of cotton, an old tin poster advertises Uncle Remus brand syrup. It features a picture of a smiling, bearded black man—the typical portrait of Uncle Remus—and the words "Dis sho am good."

"Joel Chandler Harris and I lived in the same town, although nearly one hundred years apart," Alice Walker has said. "As far as I'm concerned, he stole a good part of my heritage. How did he steal it? By making me feel ashamed of it."

The Eatonton-Putnam County Library carries most of Alice Walker's books, and in the library's computer her name appears 40 times. (There are 40 references to Br'er Rabbit, and 42 to Joel Chandler Harris.) I ask one of the librarians if there is a special Alice Walker collection. She seems to want to educate me about Walker's versatility as a writer. "No, we don't have a special collection separate from everything else because she writes all kinds of books. Some are fiction, some are poetry, some are essays."

"I'm familiar with her work," I interrupt.

"Now, I do have a vertical file of clippings I've kept over the years in my office," she offers.

"Are the materials in the vertical file accessible to the public?"

"Yes, well, I can bring the materials out to you." Somewhat reluctantly, the woman steps through a glass door. She returns with a thin manila folder. "Here it is," she announces.

Trying to suspend my disbelief, I phrase my question delicately: "This is everything you have, right?"

"Uh-huh. You can sit right there and go through it," she says, pointing to a table within her eyeshot, so she can make sure I don't try to sneak off with this treasure chest of information.

The most recent clipping in the folder is from 1994, and it's not even about Alice but her daughter, feminist writer and activist Rebecca Leventha Walker. The most recent clippings about Alice herself are undated stories from the Eatonton *Messenger* concerning her 1992 visit to the town with television newswoman Diane Sawyer for *Prime Time Live*. Among the other gems there is a review of her first published book of poetry, *Once*; a copy of an essay she wrote in 1975 for *Ms.* magazine on Flannery O'Connor; a *New York Times Magazine* cover story from 1984; and the local paper's extensive coverage of the premiere of the film version of *The Color Purple* at the now closed Pex theater in Eatonton.

Alice's sister Ruth, who organized that premiere, is surprised when I tell her that the library has copies of most of Alice's books. "Once upon a time," she says, "the library had two *Color Purples* and that was it."

Still, you cannot buy a book by Alice Walker in Eatonton—but Joel Chandler Harris' books are for sale at the museum.

Alice Walker strides into the hotel ballroom looking smart in a black tuxedo-style pantsuit. Before heading for the dais, she stops at a table near the door where many of her relatives are sitting. She embraces everyone at the table and introduces them to her traveling companion, a tall Hawaiian woman. Shortly after Alice and her guest are seated, an elderly black man walks up to the dais. Alice stands up to greet him. He envelops her hands in his and says, "To all these people you're Alice Walker, but to me, you'll always be Baby Alice."

It will be this way all night—warm hugs, warm smiles, warm words. A letter from Georgia's first lady, Shirley Miller, the wife of Governor Zell Miller, is read. She writes that Alice Walker has been "a jewel in the state of Georgia's crown for many years."

After receiving the Shelia Award, which is given to black women of high achievement, Walker hugs the crowd with soft loving eyes. "I haven't been in Macon in a long time," Walker begins." I used to come as a little girl to see my family. . . . "

Earlier in the day, Walker says, she had gone to Eatonton to visit her parents' graves. She draped a lei—made by her friend's mother—around her mother's tombstone. She then went to visit her first-grade teacher, who still lives there.

After the program, Alice Walker is attentive to each well-wisher, careful to spell the names correctly as she signs her books for about two hours. Later, at the home of the museum director, Walker converses easily on a range of subjects with a small group of guests. The talk ranges from the political situation in Cuba to her recent appearance on *Sesame Street,* and her upcoming novel, *By the Light of My Father's Smile*. When the conversation moves to female genital mutilation and starts to get depressing, she smoothly changes the subject. "It's important for good people to be happy," she says firmly. "Are you happy?" she asks one guest. He says he is. She says she is too. It's easy to believe her. She is kind, relaxed, magnanimous, comfortable in her body, in her skin, in her life. She is at home.

This celebration in Macon may be as close to a hometown embrace as Alice Walker is going to get, despite the claim Eatonton makes on its Web site that it is "A town known for proudly honoring its heroes."

On the same Web site a three-page article on the history of the town predictably includes several lengthy paragraphs on Joel Chandler Harris, along with a photo of Br'er Rabbit and a link to the Uncle Remus Museum Web page. A short paragraph on Alice Walker follows in which greater emphasis is given to Whoopi Goldberg and Oprah Winfrey and their contributing to Eatonton when they starred in *The Color Purple,* than to the town's most famous daughter.

How is it that in her hometown a woman whom the *Washington Post* has called "one of the best American writers of today" is made subservient to Joel Chandler Harris (surely a less accomplished writer and, arguably, a plagiarizer, if you count the black folk tales as stolen texts)?

I put this question to Jim Marshall, the president of the Eatonton-Putnam Historical Society. He tells me that the society and the chamber of commerce "have been trying for several years to raise money for an Alice Walker marker" to go in a small garden in the side yard of the chamber's office. The garden is full of purple flowers, he says, and they "want to call it the Color Purple Garden or the Alice Walker Garden." He doesn't remember which.

I don't remember seeing the garden when I was in Eatonton, nor did anyone mention it or the fund-raising efforts for a marker, but I listen on. "Right after the premiere of the movie," he says, they started trying to raise about $6,000 for a large granite or marble monument. (That was more than ten years ago.) "That kind of money is hard to raise in a small community," he explains.

Marshall recommends that I talk with Jimmy Davis, one of the local black officials. But Davis, a county commissioner and a member of the chamber of commerce, says he knows nothing about any fund-raising effort. "I would be glad to give a donation, and I know of several organizations that would be happy to give too."

Later Marshall takes a slightly different tack, claiming in a what-more-do-you-people-want tone that "people in the community have supported the Color Purple Foundation." Started by Ruth Walker-Hood 11 years ago, the foundation provides college scholarships for needy rural youngsters, regardless of race. Ruth "deserves a great deal of credit" for pushing the foundation, Marshall says, adding, "I really admire her spunk."

No sooner do I agree with his assessment of Ruth than he says, "If Alice made more of an effort like that toward the community, people might respond more positively toward her."

"An effort like that." The words ring in my ears as I thank him for his comments and hang up the phone. Alice Walker, Ruth says, has been the foundation's biggest financial supporter. I suppose that's not the kind of effort Marshall is talking about. Perhaps he means if Alice were chattier with the locals—the local white folks, that is—they might give her the recognition she deserves. Being an internationally acclaimed Pulitzer prizewinning author just isn't enough.

Before our conversation ended, Marshall told me that Ruth Walker-Hood is a good friend of his. I wonder if he'd be surprised at her blunt assessment of the situation. "If Alice were white, her books would be all over Eatonton, just like that Uncle Remus crap they've forced down our throats all our lives."

The Uncle Remus Museum may be the best a town Eatonton can do.

A certain kind of mythic black figure looming large and languid in the ancestral memories of many white Southerners, Uncle Remus is a fiction, sprung from the fantasies of a white writer who lifted his stories from black folk culture. He is a servile, gentle happy cartoon character of a black man with no sense of history, no awareness of injustice, no anger—and no weapons.

Unlike Uncle Remus, Alice Walker is real. She is outspoken, sexual, political, intrepid, inspired, and occasionally angry. And her mind and her pen are her weapons.

In short, for a town like Eatonton, Alice Walker is dangerous. For this reason, at least for now, a woman like Alice Walker can't be truly honored in Eatonton. Uncle Remus will have to represent us all.

Mama's Girl Veronica Chambers

IN TWO WEEKS, MY BROTHER MALCOLM WILL BE TWENTY-ONE. RIGHT NOW he is sitting in jail. I am sitting in my cubicle at *The New York Times,* where I am an editor. If there is a worse place to receive this information, I can't think of it. When my twelve-year-old half brother calls me with the news, I must curl over my desk and whisper into the headset. All around me are white faces, no one that I can turn to and say, "You know, my brother's been arrested—I've go to go." Lucky, then, that it is almost five and I can just pack up my stuff and leave.

At home, I call my mother, who calls my father. I stopped speaking to my father three years earlier when I decided I had had enough of all the drama. My father still lives near Philadelphia, where my brother has been arrested. The week that my brother is in jail, we play this weird game of telephone—my brother talks to my father, who talks to my mother, who talks to me. At first my mother and I are extremely calm, we discuss the details with a clinical detachment. This is not the first time my brother has been arrested. It's about the millionth time that we've pow-wowed over Malcolm and wondered, What should we do, what should we do?

But the evening news sets me on edge—I see my brother in every young black man. Just as prejudiced as some white people, I find myself thinking, *They all look alike!* It amazes me that however many hundreds of years after Diaspora and a splitting apart of a people, the family ties between black men and women are so visually evident. But that's too easy. The deeper issue is that the resemblance between my brother and all these other young black men bothers me because I'm wondering, *How will* they *know this is my brother? How will* they *know not to hurt him?* I think of another black man, Alexandre Dumas, and his tales of the Three Musketeers. Set within the context of the inner city, Dumas's motto, "All for one and one for all," has scary connotations for young black men. You go, I go. And every other street corner has a story about how Peter took the bullet for Paul. I spent the better part of the night crying, as I always do, hot and heavy, angry tears.

Just the week before, I'd spoken to Malcolm. He was living with his girlfriend, a twenty-year-old woman with two kids, neither of whom were his. "How are you eating?" I asked him. He told me that his girlfriend got food stamps. His answer implied that he wasn't dealing drugs anymore. I didn't like the idea of my brother living on welfare, but since he had a complete aversion to working for minimum wage, I decided not to push it.

Once I'd gotten out of college, I'd joined my mother in the crusade to save my brother. I grew up with the understanding that the world is a harder place for black men than it is for black women. That it is easier for a black woman to get a job than it is for a black man. I knew there was a way that the world made black men angry and that as a black woman, you worked around it, you kept your cool, you kept things together.

After five years of frustration, though, my mother and I had recently made a pact to restrict our efforts to words of support and guidance and not to give my brother any more cash because it never seemed to do any good and it might even have done some harm. If he wanted to live off a girlfriend's welfare, that was his business. But it turned out that was just another lie and now he was in jail. My mother and I guessed it was a drug offense and we were right: possession with intent to distribute. It was a charge that sounded familiar, like something I'd seen on a rerun of *Miami Vice.*

My cousin Guille, streetwise and familiar with the territory my brother had made his home, warned me to stop worrying about him. "He's out there doing what he wants to do," she said. "Malcolm doesn't care about anyone but himself. He'd take your last dollar, your rent money, your food money, and he wouldn't think twice about it. Look out for yourself."

But the success I had found in journalism made it hard not to wish my brother would find similar satisfaction in his life. Once again I was the super sister, thinking of what I could do to help him, and then I thought of the red winter coat and my heart hardened a little bit.

A year before I joined *The New York Times* I was living and working in Los Angeles. I hadn't heard from my brother for almost six months. He was hard to track down. He shuttled between Atlantic City and New York, living with different friends and different girlfriends. He wasn't good about letting me or my mother know his current phone number and address. The last phone number I had for him was a beeper number that didn't work.

In early December, my brother calls me. He is in Atlantic City again. It's already begun to snow back East. My brother says he does not have a winter coat and is walking around in a denim jacket. He wants to know could I send him money for a coat? I remember our pact and tell him that I will send him an actual coat instead.

It's odd to go winter-coat shopping in southern California. Not that it doesn't get cold at night, but it's never so cold that you have to bundle up in layers. As I walk through the mall, feeling coats for bulk, checking the labels to see if they are water-resistant, considering colors, I think about winters when I was small. My mother would get up first, shower, and get dressed. She would turn on the oven and leave the door open to warm up the tiny kitchen. Our apartments were always freezing and we couldn't afford space heaters. My mother would wrap my brother and me up in a blanket, walking us through the cold apartment into the bathroom. We'd take quick showers, then my mother would walk us back to the kitchen where she'd have our clothes laid out in front of the oven. I loved how warm the clothes felt against my skin, the turtleneck and jeans toasty from the oven's heat. It wasn't something I thought about, this ritual of warmth. I thought everyone got dressed in front of the oven in the winter and I assumed it was something I would do for the rest of my life.

It wasn't until college, my junior year, when I lived in an on-campus house that I had the opportunity to adjust the heat in my room for the very first time. I kept the thermostat at 80°. My roommate was a white girl from the Midwest who loved the fresh air so much that she insisted on keeping the windows open, even during the brutal Massachusetts winter.

"You can always put on more clothes," she said, padding around in her Birkenstocks and socks.

"I *can't* get warm enough," I told her. I wanted it so hot that I was sweating. I wanted it so hot that I could sleep with only a sheet even in the middle of December. I wanted to explain to this girl about the cold apartments I grew up in, to tell her about getting dressed in front of the oven and the way my mother would boil tea for us at night so that we were warm enough to sleep. I wanted to explain what heat meant to me, how I had to have it, how I had to control it, but I never did. I didn't want her pity more than I wanted the heat.

I think of this girl and the oven and my mom when I am shopping for a coat for my brother. I buy him the biggest, most expensive red coat I can find.

I tell my mother about the coat, about the Christmas package I'd put together for Malcolm of CDs, a book, and the coat. My mother has just moved to Miami with my stepfather. She is still looking for a job and doesn't have much money. She asks if she can split the cost of the coat with me and make it a joint Christmas present. I agree and sign a card with both our names, though the truth is, I will never ask for her half of the money.

I leave my office early and take the package to the post office the next afternoon. I circle the block until I find a parking spot close to the front door. I lug the box out of the hatchback. A young guy dressed in a suit and tie holds the door for me. He looks like one of the budding studio execs that work in the mailroom at Columbia Pictures, just across the street. I push the package near the windows, then stand patiently in line. It is two or three weeks before Christmas, but I know that Christmas mail can be slow and I don't want my brother to be presentless on Christmas Day.

I am called to window #1. The thirtyish guy behind the counter is from South Central. He has a Gheri curl and a Snoop Doggy Dogg drawl. I like him because he keeps pictures of his beautiful baby daughters by his window and he calls me ma'am. He laughs when he sees the pitiful job I have done trying to seal the box with masking tape. "What did I tell you about this cheap tape?" he says, taking out the industrial-strength good stuff from beneath his desk. "You're lucky you got me and I'm gonna help you out. But do me a favor. Treat yourself to some good quality tape for Christmas, okay?" I laugh and agree.

"Malcolm X. Chambers," he says, reading the label. "That's a helluva name. Is this a present for a man out East?"

I shake my head. "Nah, it's for my little brother." I smile at him. There is something about this guy that just makes my day.

"Have a good one, ma'am," he says. I wish him the same and speed back to my office.

I remember it all so clearly even though it was just one of many gifts I was able to give that season, one of the many trips I took to the post office, one of a million errands to run before I took off for Christmas. It is so clear in my memory because it was one of those rare days when you just feel infused with love. I still believed that loving my brother would help see him through the mess he'd made of his life.

I spend Christmas in Miami with my mother. Not a word from my brother. Neither my mother nor I know how to get in touch with him. New Year's also goes by without a peep. Then sometime in early January, he calls me. "What's up, V?" he says, in that slow guttural delivery that so many guys like him have—an urban panther's growl.

"Malcolm!!!" I screech in what my brother calls my black Valley Girl speak. "Where have you been? What's going on? Why haven't you called?"

He pauses. "Yo, I've been busy. It's rough out here, V."

I don't want to ask because I don't want him to feel that I'm being obnoxious, but I can't help it. "Did you get the coat?"

He pauses again. "Yeah, the coat. Yeah, it was phat. But yo, it was too small so I gave it to my friend 'cause you know, he's smaller than me."

"You did what?" I hiss, barely audible.

"It was too small so I gave it to my friend." The tone in his voice warns me not to push the point any further.

I'm trying to think how not to turn this into a fight. I'm trying to think how to keep my cool. It's been almost a month since my brother's last call and if I piss him off, it could be months before he calls again. "Malcolm," I say as calmly as I can manage, "Malcolm, that coat was an extra-large. How could it not fit?"

My brother sucks his teeth. He knows this conversation is going to drag on and he's not pleased. "Yo, it fits in the shoulders and stuff, right?" he says, lapsing into a sweeter, more explanatory tone. "But the sleeves were too short. And V, I ain't got no gloves."

Whenever we were kids and we tried to outsmart my mom, she always used to turn to us and say, "I was small, too, you know. I wasn't born big. I was your same size and I had your same sneaky thoughts." Sitting on the phone with my brother, I'm thinking the same thing. He must take me for a real fool. Not only do my mother and I buy him this really nice coat that he says he needs badly, he doesn't call to wish us a Merry Christmas or a Happy New Year, let along thank us. He gives the coat away. No gloves. Please. He lied. He wanted money and instead he got a coat he didn't need or want.

Now my brother is in jail and I am home in my apartment. I can't sleep. I'm having nightmares. I think about my brother all day, can't shut him off and do my work. I want to ask for a leave of absence at work, but I know that I can't. I am one of only two black editors. There is a constant and incredible pressure for me to succeed. A leave of absence opens the door for talk of incompetence. I can't explain to the people I work with where I've come from, what I'm dealing with. I don't think they would understand. Honestly, I don't think they want to know.

My brother's girlfriend calls to inform me of the prison's visiting hours. I tell her I'll try to make it, but I don't know how. This is one of those times I wish I worked at a factory or that I pushed papers at some nameless, faceless place where nobody cares where you came from or what you're about. But I don't. I have a career. So I am relieved at the end of the week when my brother is released from jail.

A month later, I go to visit my mother for the Fourth of July weekend. We are on the beach and we are wearing matching swimsuits. The day before, we were running around the mall like teenagers, trying to stay one step ahead of my stepfather and my boyfriend. We raced over to the swimsuits on sale. I had taken one over to my mother—cream with mesh netting that I thought would look good against my brown skin. "What do you think of this?" I'd asked her. She turned, laughing. She was holding the same suit. We'd each offered to choose another—dressing alike seems a little too Mommy Dearest—but we loved the design and after my mother pointed out that we live in separate states, we agreed to dress like twins, just for the day.

The waves are crashing hard. It is hurricane season and the ocean is temperamental. My mother still has not learned how to swim. Neither have I. The four of us—two men, two women—stand just a few feet in, jumping the waves when they come, splashing each other in between, until the rain forces us indoors.

In the house, my mother and I sit at the table and talk. The conversation turns inevitably to my brother. Despite all the things we have worked out, how we relate to my brother is the one thing that always makes me feel like I can't stand her. There is a saying that black women mother their sons and raise their daughters; when it comes to my mother, the saying is too true. My mother raised me—there were a lot of hard times, times when we both were hurt and angry, nevertheless I am the woman I am today because of her. But my mother let my brother walk all over her ever since he was a child. Her way of looking after Malcolm was something I'd emulated, not only out of concern for my brother, but to please my mother. Eventually, though, I became so fed up that I got tougher on him. I felt sympathy and wanted to support Malcolm and all the young brothers in his situation. But unlike my mother and the black women of my childhood, I wasn't going to support a black man at the expense of myself. This realization changed everything about how I viewed Malcolm, how I viewed my mother, and how I viewed my father. It was like we were all playing this black woman–black man game and then I moved my piece right off the board.

"If I could do things differently," she says, her voice small and helpless, "I would've been more strict with you children."

I cannot hide my frustration. My fists are clenched, my whole body is stiff. The same rain that we were dashing through a few moments before is giving me a migraine. Although he is twenty-one, she still considers him the measuring stick by which she will be judged as a mother. If he straightens up and does well, she will consider herself a good mother. If he never gets his act together, she will be a failure. So many times I've tried to explain to my mother that there is a difference between circumstance and choice. My brother and I grew up under the same circumstances, but we made a million different choices along the way. The circumstances we could not control, but the choices were ours to make.

"You do your best," my mother is saying. She doesn't listen to what I tell her, and I hate it when she ignores me like this. But the truth is, the same advice I give her, I still find hard to follow. This is one of the things that makes us so much alike. I tell her she's not a failure because of what my brother does or does not do. Yet I feel like I won't ever be able to enjoy my life fully, to enjoy my successes without guilt as long as my brother is out there dealing drugs and getting arrested and beginning to think of jail as a second home.

Once when I was in college, I went swimming alone. It was early spring, March, barely warm enough to go in the water, late in the day, sunset. I went swimming alone though I can barely swim, not knowing even how deep the sublime campus river was. I waded into the cool water, deeper and deeper until I got a cramp in my leg and felt myself being pulled under. I was pulled under a footbridge as the dusk of late afternoon turned into the pitch black of night. I could not stay up. My wet palms slid along the mud wall of the riverbank. I felt myself falling and then resigned myself to falling, tired from the struggle. Then I decided to shout. I felt I had to try and shout. So I pushed up and screamed. I screamed again, though my head was full of water and it sounded like a whisper. I was screaming and whispering at the same time. Then I saw someone, then I couldn't see and only felt someone. Then I was lying on the side of the river. Wet and cold, but alive.

I know my brother is out there swimming. I know that he can barely swim. I know that the day is darkening on him. I know that he is sometimes tugged under because he can disappear for weeks on end. I know that he is resigned to falling in. I know that he thinks he will survive as a ghetto merman but he is falling in. I know that in water oxygen is finite. I know that he may come up this time or next, but there may come a time when he does not come up at all.

I know what it's like to nearly drown. When your arms are tired and your legs are dead weight. When your body betrays you and there is nothing and no one to hand on to. Even now I can still summon the fear. And what I fear more than anything is that if my brother spires to the surface, if in a moment of clarity he shouts and it only comes out as a whisper, will anyone hear him? Will anyone help him? Will I be able to hear or help? Or will he, resigned and tired, sink back to the bottomless bottom?

My brother at three was practically mute; he refused to speak until he was almost four years old. He spoke only through me, some strange gibberish that I cannot now recall. Now that my brother is a big strong black man, with big strapping black man problems, I long for our secret language. I imagine that I could whisper those words into his ears and I would become more powerful than his homeboys, that the call of our secret language would be more powerful than the call of the streets. But he is no longer three and I am no longer six, and the words we made up are lost forever.

The Visible Man

Trey Ellis

WHEN I ARRIVED IN FLORENCE IN 1981, I WAS SURE A BLACK FACE IN ITALY would be no novelty. Yet during the six months of my sophomore year abroad from Stanford, about the only time I saw another black American was when I looked in the mirror. My perceptions and loyalties shifted; I became closer to white American students than I had been in the States. Every Stanford girl was called *Biondina* (Blondie) even if her hair was dark brown. A Santa Barbara surfer and I were now both minorities.

Yet as I slowly learned to express myself in Italian with fewer appeals of *"Come si dice?"* ("How does one say?"), my allegiance began to tilt from the Californians to the Italians. Other students also itched to experience behind-the-scenes Tuscany, but somehow, it seemed easier for me. In my case, being a minority was nothing new: I grew up in Irish and Italian-American middle and working-class suburbs outside Ann Arbor and New Haven. Hearing an Italian child shout *"Guarda, mamma, un nero"* ("Look, ma, a black man") before the mother slapped the child's pointing finger was cute compared with watching old ladies in Connecticut cross the street to avoid sharing the sidewalk.

In fact, I soon metamorphosed from an ugly American into one of those insufferable school-year-abroad students who pretend to have been born Continental. I started to dress better and gesticulate with my hands. I almost wanted to take up smoking. In the mornings I'd peer over my bowl of *caffè latte* at the other students' soggy presweetened cereal as if I'd never dumped out whole boxes of the stuff just to get at the plastic snap-together spaceships. Back in my New Haven neighborhood I'd bridled aggressively against my own Yankee assimilation. But in Florence, speaking Italian, I was soon over-aspirating my c's, trying to mimic the Tuscan accent. I'd say *"Hoha-Hola hon la hannuccia horta"* ("Coca-Cola with a short straw") in a more flagrantly Florentine way than any descendant of Dante.

Physically, of course, I could never pass for an Italian. On the streets I was usually mistaken for an African drought refugee. Old women would stop and squeeze my arm. *"Sei uno dei nostri Eritrei?"* ("Are you one of our Eritreans?") one once asked, soothed by seeing her weekly church contribution made flesh. Others, after discovering I was an *Americano nero,* assumed I was some kind of civil-rights celebrity. *"Ce l'ho un sogno!"* somebody once said to me—"I have a dream!"

Yet Italians accepted me more readily than any people I've ever know. They shared with me their Easter dinners, their beach houses, their grandparents. Every weekend a pack of us would hike 500-year-old cobblestone streets to visit little-known hillside monasteries or hunt the Chianti region for obscure grape festivals. I was an absolutely equal member of a wonderful group of Italian friends who—except for me—had known each other since high school.

Then at year's end I had to leave. On the plane home I thought about why Italy had embraced me so effortlessly. Sicily is just 90 miles from North Africa and, thanks to Moorish incursions as far north as Naples, I was fooled daily in the streets, waving to Sicilians I mistook for high-yellow Alabamans. Northern Europeans see themselves as pure, while all Mediterraneans to them are hot-blooded Afro-Europeans. They're right. As for this Afro-American, finding myself among people who liked to sit outside with friends and lyrically argue and seduce and brag, I felt as comfortable in a piazza as on my grandparents' front stoop.

Back at school, I didn't realize how uncomfortable I sometimes felt in the States until I remembered how at home I'd felt in Italy. So after graduation and months of rejection as a TV comedy writer in New York, I knew it was time to get back on the plane.

When you arrive in a new country and know that you're only staying a few months, you can afford to fiddle with your identity. But returned to Florence this time and not knowing when or if I'd ever go home, I began to act less Italian. Despite my Italian friends' jokes, I resumed eating eggs in the mornings and drinking cappuccino at night. No longer insecure about the language, my ridiculous Tuscan mellowed to standard Italian. I realized that as a foreigner, my entire mystique was my black Americanness.

I brought two duffel bags, 20 pages of my unfinished novel and savings for two months. The savings stretched to 3½ months until finally Italian stereotypes about blacks landed me a job. I walked into a store called Sarallo Sport to buy a windbreaker, and the owner asked me if I'd ever seen a black skier. He'd just seen one of us in a documentary about Aspen and was fascinated. Black skiers *are* indeed rare, but I told him I happened to be one of them. He offered me a part-time job selling ski equipment. I knew he just wanted a walking marketing gimmick, but my stomach decided *va bene*.

That inspired me to see what other stereotypes I could exploit. After constantly being asked loony questions about black tanning and hair care, I figured I deserved at least one perk. So after work one evening I stopped by the Silhouette Club, Florence's toniest gym. I sort of hinted to the manager that I was a world-famous athlete and personal trainer. "*Come* Carl Lewis," I told him. He let me go to the gym for free until a spot opened up for a weight trainer. I knew he felt that having a black American work out in his Italian gym was a gold star of approval—like Chinese people eating in a Chinese restaurant.

Soon my days found a routine: until noon I'd fill page after page of the same three-ring notebook I'd been using for schoolwork since the eighth grade. My novel, *Platitudes,* was inching forward at 12 pages a week.

Lunch was pasta or risotto and frozen fish sticks, then I'd floor my Ciao moped to the other side of town and my jobs. I'd tell people to lift harder at the Silhouette Club (*"Più forte! Ancora, pigro!"* "Harder! One more, lazy!") until four, then cross the street and sell skis at Sarallo Sport ("*I bastoncini non devono arrivare fino all' ascella,*" "Your ski poles don't have to reach your underarms") until seven. That left me an hour to inhale dinner and speed through crazy Italian rush-hour traffic to the Scuola Leonardo Da Vinci. There, two other Americans and I taught English to Italians. My work day would end about 10:30.

At Easter, my friends Vanni, Francesca, Rainer, Vanna, Laura and I rented a former Winter Olympics bunkhouse just outside Cortina d'Ampezzo for a week. As I carved an intermediate trail on packed powder, the Italians were as shocked at seeing a black skier as my boss had been back in Florence. They yelled down at me from the chair lift, *"Nero! Nero!"* I tried to escape celebrity, skiing the back side of Cortina where the German-speaking Alto-Adigiani live. Springing through a beautiful field of moguls, I heard screams from overhead, *"Schwartz! Schwartz!"*

Enough. I stopped and took in the crown of white mountains that surrounded me without end, aggressive in their beauty. My head ballooned with one thought: I was the only person with skin this brown, hair this curly, for as far as the eye could see. There, in the most wide-open place I'd ever been, claustrophobia overcame me.

On the way back to Florence an old song came on the radio, and my friends sang along, floating back on their sweet memories of high school. I prided myself in knowing contemporary Italian pop better than all my friends, yet no matter how long I stayed, I'd never share their childhood recollections. And they'd never dream of *Lost in Space.*

I knew then I would visit Italy for the rest of my life, but that I'd never emigrate. I couldn't imagine myself in 10 years, a stranger in every land. I needed to move on, but I wasn't ready to go home.

A visiting childhood friend lugged the 353 pages of my novel's rough draft back to the States in a waterproof cocoon of trash bags and tape. The reward to myself for finally completing it would be a great trek. But after Florence I wasn't about to hostel-hop through Europe like every other American post-grad traveler. No, my Grand Tour would be of Africa. I'd try to hitchhike through Greece to Egypt, down to Kenya, across Uganda and Zaire to Nigeria, then north through the Sahara to Tunisia and, finally, back to Florence. In Africa I hoped to find high adventure and to discover just how far I hadn't come from my family's first home.

I landed in Cairo, where an Egyptian my age put his forearm next to mine and said "Look my brother, we are the exact same color." He then ushered me to a slimy hotel costing 15 times my allotted budget. After that night, however, Africans treated me as a heroic civil-rights freedom fighter. They wouldn't let me spend my money. I couldn't eat all the food they offered. I couldn't carry all the gifts they gave.

Floating down the Zaire (formerly the Congo) one night, in the middle of a continent three times larger than the United States, I looked out at the wide black expanse of river, the low and dark silhouette of zillions of trees and the white fireworks of far-away tropical lightning, and I thought, for the first time in my life, for as far as I could see, I was a majority.

It was only then that I knew I was ready to come back home to America. For a while.

——————————————————————————————————— **Ekow Eshun**

Return to the Planet of the Apes

IN THE FUTURE, BLACK PEOPLE WILL BE EITHER INVISIBLE OR EXTINCT. I know this because I have watched men journey to the great planet Jupiter in *2001: A Space Odyssey,* I have glimpsed a time when machines rule the world in *The Terminator* and when Morlocks menace the last remnants of society in *The Time Machine,* and I have seen no one who looks like me. There is a particularly pointed illustration of this in *Planet of the Apes* when Charlton Heston—who plays Taylor, an astronaut from our present, crash-landed on a future Earth where apes have enslaved a dumb, submissive humanity—comes face to face with all that is left of his black co-pilot from the same disastrous space mission. Last seen being dragged off by some burly gorillas, Taylor's colleague has been lobotomized, stuffed, and turned into a glass-eyed museum exhibit for the citizens of Ape City to stare at. When I first saw that scene it freaked me out. Still does sometimes. But maybe that's my own fault for taking fiction as fact. After all, everyone can tell the difference between fantasy and reality, right? So what does it mean when you take the visions of tomorrow created by science fiction movies seriously and start to wonder what they say about your own place in the world today?

When SF films peer into the future, often their aim is to highlight the absurdities of the present day. No more is this so than with *Planet of the Apes* and the four sequels that followed it. *Planet* was made in 1968, the year I was born. And the film's startling imagery—gorillas on horseback herding humans like cattle, Taylor discovering the ruins of the Statue of Liberty—has lived with me since I first saw it on TV as a child. Look at it my way. It is 1979. You are 11, trying to negotiate the delicate racial politics of the school playground. All the kids are listening to Two Tone and ska and find themselves simultaneously seduced by the multi-racial ethic of the rude boy and the racist rhetoric of the National Front, whose spray-painted slogans can be found in any school yard across the country at the time. Their invective is mouthed by shorn-headed children too young to care about the good or bad sense involved in arguing that Pakis and Yids and wogs are taking over the country. You turn on the TV and *Love Thy Neighbour,* a comedy about a white bigot and his wife, who wake up on morning to find a West Indian couple have moved in next door, is screening to gales of canned laughter. Change the channel and The Black And White Minstrel Show—white people crooning songs from the American South in black-face make-up—is peak-time family viewing. Somehow, no one apart from you seems to notice how strange a society is in which kids parrot racist slogans like they would nursery rhymes and the caricaturing of different races passes as popular entertainment. It feels as though you occupy a place outside of object time and space in a parallel world of subjective pain: your own personal science fiction movie—*The Brother from Another Planet.*

Under the circumstances, *Planet of the Apes* feels virtually real. In the film, Taylor is intelligent and articulate, but his voice is denied him and his appearance prompts suspicion and loathing. Through the course of the movie, he is forced to ask fundamental questions about who he is and where he fits into a world which doesn't seem to want him. He experiences a sense of alienation and a consuming anger at the unfairness of his treatment. In other words, he discovers what it's like to be black in a white world. There are other movies which have tried to tackle racial transference head-on, such as Melvin Van Peebles' *Watermelon Man* and the eighties teen flick *Soul Man,* both of which have white characters who become black. Yet the route they chose, satire, never rings as true as the far more fantastic premise of *Planet of the Apes.*

It's received wisdom that after the first movie, the Apes series went into decline, reaching rock-bottom with the spin-off TV show of the seventies. Certainly, the films do progressively lose their way, the quintet's complicated chronology eventually forming into a ball of confusion. In the sequel, *Beneath the Planet of the Apes,* Earth is destroyed by bomb-worshipping mutants. But with the movies still popular, the producers wrung three prequels from the concept—*Escape from the Planet of the Apes, Conquest of the Planet of the Apes* and *Battle for the Planet of the Apes.* Yet however cynically they were made, each follow up still carries an allegorical weight. In *Conquest,* for instance, the apes are a subjugated slave class, who plot their eventual liberation from humanity in secrecy. Here the racial metaphor is explicit, although it is apes who have become the heroes and humans the racist oppressors. *Planet of the Apes* is often described as nightmarish. And in a way this is an appropriate description in that the reason nightmares frighten is because within them is a truth too difficult to deal with during waking hours. Others might offer their own interpretations of the Apes movies but when you grow up suffering jokes about monkeys and bananas at school and kids think it's funny to call you Urko—after the chief gorilla in the TV spin-off series—the nightmare doesn't lie in an Earth ruled by apes but in the far crueler world of humans. Like they say in Ape City, "Beware the Beast Man."

The Sports Taboo: Why blacks are like boys and whites are like girls

THE EDUCATION OF ANY ATHLETE BEGINS, IN PART, WITH AN EDUCATION IN the racial taxonomy of his chosen sport—in the subtle, unwritten rules about what whites are supposed to be good at and what blacks are supposed to be good at. In football, whites play quarterback and blacks play running back; in baseball, whites pitch and blacks play the outfield. I grew up in Canada, where my brother Geoffrey and I ran high-school track, and in Canada the rule of running was that anything under the quarter-mile belonged to the West Indians. This didn't mean that white people didn't run the sprints. But the expectation was that they would never win and, sure enough, they rarely did. There was just a handful of West Indian immigrants in Ontario at that point—clustered in and around Toronto—but they owned Canadian sprinting, setting up under the stands at every major championship, cranking up the reggae on their boom boxes, and then humiliating everyone else on the track. My brother and I weren't from Toronto, so we weren't part of that scene. But our West Indian heritage meant that we got to share in the swagger. Geoffrey was a magnificent runner, with powerful legs and a barrel chest, and when he was warming up he used to do that exaggerated, slow-motion jog that the white guys would try to do and never quite pull off. I was a miler, which was a little outside the West Indian range. But, the way I figured it, the rules meant that no one should ever outkick me over the final two hundred metres of any race. And in the golden summer of my fourteenth year, when my running career prematurely peaked, no one ever did.

When I started running, there was a quarter-miler just a few years older than I was by the name of Arnold Stotz. He was a bulldog of a runner, hugely talented, and each year that he moved through the sprinting ranks he invariably broke the existing four-hundred-metre record in his age class. Stotz was white, though, and every time I saw the results of a big track meet I'd keep an eye out for his name, because I was convinced that he could not keep winning. It was as if I saw his whiteness as a degenerative disease, which would eventually claim and cripple him. I never asked him whether he felt the same anxiety, but I can't imagine that he didn't. There was only so long that anyone could defy the rules. One day, at the provincial championships, I looked up at the results board and Stotz was gone.

Talking openly about the racial dimension of sports in this way, of course, is considered unseemly. It's all right to say that blacks dominate sports because they lack opportunities elsewhere. That's the "Hoop Dreams" line, which says whites are allowed to acknowledge black athletic success as long as they feel guilty about it. What you're not supposed to say is what we were saying in my track days—that we were better because we were black, because of something intrinsic to being black. Nobody said anything like that publicly last month when Tiger Woods won the Masters or when, a week later, African men claimed thirteen out of the top twenty places in the Boston

Marathon. Nor is it likely to come up this month, when African-Americans will make up eighty per cent of the players on the floor for the N.B.A. playoffs. When the popular television sports commentator Jimmy (the Greek) Snyder did break this taboo, in 1988—infamously ruminating on the size and significance of black thighs—one prominent N.A.A.C.P. official said that his remarks "could set race relations back a hundred years." The assumption is that the whole project of trying to get us to treat each other the same will be undermined if we don't all agree that under the skin we actually are the same.

The point of this, presumably, is to put our discussion of sports on a par with legal notions of racial equality, which would be a fine idea except that civil-rights law governs matters like housing and employment and the sports taboo covers matters like what can be said about someone's jump shot. In his much heralded new book "Darwin's Athletes," the University of Texas scholar John Hoberman tries to argue that these two things are the same, that it's impossible to speak of black physical superiority without implying intellectual inferiority. But it isn't long before the argument starts to get ridiculous. "The spectacle of black athleticism," he writes, inevitably turns into "a highly public image of black retardation." Oh, really? What, exactly, about Tiger Woods's victory in the Masters resembled "a highly public image of black retardation"? Today's black athletes are multimillion-dollar corporate pitchmen, with talk shows and sneaker deals and publicity machines and almost daily media opportunities to share their thoughts with the world, and it's very hard to see how all this contrives to make them look stupid. Hoberman spends a lot of time trying to inflate the significance of sports, arguing that how we talk about events on the baseball diamond or the track has grave consequences for how we talk about race in general. Here he is, for example, on Jackie Robinson:

> The sheer volume of sentimental and intellectual energy that has been invested in the mythic saga of Jackie Robinson has discouraged further thinking about what his career did and did not accomplish. . . . Black America has paid a high and largely unacknowledged price for the extraordinary prominence given the black athlete rather than other black men of action (such as military pilots and astronauts), who represent modern aptitudes in ways that athletes cannot.

Please. Black America has paid a high and largely unacknowledged price for a long list of things, and having great athletes is far from the top of the list. Sometimes a baseball player is just a baseball player, and sometimes an observation about racial difference is just an observation about racial difference. Few object when medical scientists talk about the significant epidemiological differences between blacks and whites—the fact that blacks have a higher incidence of hypertension than whites and twice as many black males die of diabetes and prostate cancer as white males, that breast tumors appear to grow faster in black women than in white women, that black girls show signs of puberty sooner than white girls. So why aren't we allowed to say that there might be athletically significant differences between blacks and whites?

According to the medical evidence, African-Americans seem to have, on the average, greater bone mass than do white Americans—a difference that suggests greater muscle mass. Black men have slightly higher circulating levels of testosterone and human-growth hormone than their white counterparts, and blacks over all tend to have proportionally slimmer hips, wider shoulders, and longer legs. In one study, the Swedish physiologist Bengt Saltin compared a group of Kenyan distance runners with a group of Swedish distance runners and found interesting differences in muscle composition: Saltin reported that the Africans appeared to have more blood-carrying capillaries and more mitochondria (the body's cellular power plant) in the fibres of their quadriceps. Another study found that while black South African distance runners ran at the same speed as white South African runners, they were able to use more oxygen—eighty-nine per cent versus eight-one per cent—over extended periods: somehow, they were able to exert themselves more. Such evidence suggested that there were physical differences in black athletes which have a bearing on activities like running and jumping, which should hardly come as a surprise to anyone who follows competitive sports.

To use track as an example—since track is probably the purest measure of athletic ability—Africans recorded fifteen out of the twenty fastest times last year in the men's ten-thousand-metre event. In the five thousand metres, eighteen out of the twenty fastest times were recorded by Africans. In the fifteen hundred metres, thirteen out of the twenty fastest times were African, and in the sprints, in the men's hundred metres, you have to go all the way down to the twenty-third place in the world rankings—to Geir Moen, of Norway—before you find a white face. There is a point at which it becomes foolish to banish speculation on the topic. Clearly, something is going on. The question is what.

2.

If we are to decide what to make of the differences between blacks and whites, we first have to decide what to make of the word "difference," which can mean any number of things. A useful case study is to compare the ability of men and women in math. If you give a large, representative sample of male and female students a standardized math test, their mean scores will come out pretty much the same. But if you look at the margins, at the very best and the very worst students, sharp differences emerge. In the math portion of an achievement test conducted by Project Talent—a nationwide survey of fifteen-year-olds—there were 1.3 boys for every girl in the top ten per cent, 1.5 boys for every girl in the top five per cent, and seven boys for every girl in the top one per cent. In the fifty-six-year history of the Putnam Mathematical Competition, which has been described as the Olympics of college math, all but one of the winners have been male. Conversely, if you look at people with the very lowest math ability, you'll find more boys than girls there, too. In other words, although the average math ability of boys and girls is the same, the distribution isn't: there are more males than females at the bottom of the pile, more males than females at the top of the pile, and fewer males than females in the middle. Statisticians refer to this as a difference of variability.

This pattern, as it turns out, is repeated in almost every conceivable area of gender difference. Boys are more variable than girls on the College Board entrance exam and in routine elementary-school spelling tests. Male mortality patterns are more variable than female patters; that is, many more men die in early and middle age than women, who tend to dic in more of a concentrated clump toward the end of life. The problem is that variability differences are regularly confused with average differences. If men had higher average math scores than women, you could say they were better at the subject. But because they are only more variable the word "better" seems inappropriate.

The same holds true for differences between the races. A racist stereotype is the assertion of average difference—it's the claim that the typical white is superior to the typical black. It allows a white man to assume that the black man he passes on the street is stupider than he is. By contrast, if what racists believed was that black intelligence was simply more variable than white intelligence, then it would be impossible for them to construct a stereotype about black intelligence at all. They wouldn't be able to generalize. If they wanted to believe that there were a lot of blacks dumber than whites, they would also have to believe that there were a lot of blacks smarter than they were. This distinction is critical to understanding the relation between race and athletic performance. What are we seeing when we remark on black domination of élite sporting events—an average difference between the races of merely a difference in variability?

This question has been explored by geneticists and physical anthropologists, and some of the most notable work has been conducted over the past few years by Kenneth Kidd, at Yale. Kidd and his colleagues have been taking DNA samples from two African Pygmy tribes in Zaire and the Central African Republic and comparing them with DNA samples taken from populations all over the world. What they have been looking for is variants—subtle differences between the DNA of one person and another—and what they have found is fascinating. "I would say, without a doubt, that in almost any single African population—a tribe or however you want to define it—there is more genetic variation than in all the rest of the world put together," Kidd told me. In a sample of fifty Pygmies, for example, you might find nine variants in one stretch of DNA. In a sample of hundreds of people from around the rest of the world, you might find only a total of six variants in that same stretch of DNA—and probably every one of those six variants would also be found in the Pygmies. If everyone in the world was wiped out except Africans, in other words, almost all the human genetic diversity would be preserved.

The likelihood is that these results reflect Africa's status as the homeland of Homo sapiens: since every human population outside Africa is essentially a subset of the original African population, it makes sense that everyone in such a population would be a genetic subset of Africans, too. So you can expect groups of Africans to be more variable in respect to almost anything that has a genetic component. If, for example, your genes control how you react to aspirin, you'd expect to see more Africans than whites for whom one aspirin stops a bad headache, more for whom no amount of aspirin works, more who are allergic to aspirin, and more who need to take, say, four aspirin at a time to get any benefit—but far fewer Africans for whom the standard two-aspirin dose would work well. And to the extent that running is influenced by genetic factors you would expect to see more really fast blacks—and more really slow blacks—than whites but far fewer Africans of merely average speed. Blacks are like boys. Whites are like girls.

There is nothing particularly scary about this fact, and certainly nothing to warrant the kind of gag order on talk of racial differences which is now in place. What it means is that comparing élite athletes of different races tells you very little about the races themselves. A few years ago, for example, a prominent scientist argued for black athletic supremacy by pointing out that there had never been a white Michael Jordan. True. But, as the Yale anthropologist Jonathan Marks has noted, until recently there was no black Michael Jordan, either. Michael Jordan, like Tiger Woods or Wayne Gretzky or Cal Ripken, is one of the best players in his sport not because he's like the other members of his own ethnic group but precisely because he's not like them—or like anyone else, for that matter. Élite athletes are élite athletes because, in some sense, they are on the fringes of genetic variability. As it happens. African populations seem to create more of these genetic outliers than white populations do, and this is what underpins the claim that blacks are better athletes than whites. But that's all the claim amounts to. It doesn't say anything at all about the rest of us, of all races, muddling around in the genetic middle.

3.

There is a second consideration to keep in mind when we compare blacks and whites. Take the men's hundred-metre final at the Atlanta Olympics. Every runner in that race was of either Western African or Southern African descent, as you would expect if Africans had some genetic affinity for sprint. But suppose we forget about skin color and look just at country of origin. The eight-man final was made up of two African-Americans, two Africans (one from Namibia and one from Nigeria), a Trinidadian, a Canadian of Jamaican descent, an Englishman of Jamaican descent, and a Jamaican. The race was won by the Jamaican-Canadian, in world-record time, with the Namibian coming in second and the Trinidadian third. The sprint relay—the 4 ×100—was won by a team from Canada, consisting of the Jamaican-Canadian from the final, a Haitian-Canadian, a Trinidadian-Canadian, and another Jamaican-Canadian. Now it appears that African heritage is important as an initial determinant of sprinting ability, but also that the most important advantage of all is some kind of cultural or environmental factor associated with the Caribbean.

Or consider, in a completely different realm, the problem of hypertension. Black Americans have a higher incidence of hypertension than white Americans, even after you control for every conceivable variable, including income, diet, and weight, so it's tempting to conclude that there is something about being of African descent that makes blacks prone to hypertension. But it turns out that although some Caribbean countries have a problem with hypertension, others—Jamaica, St. Kitts, and the Bahamas—don't. It also turns out that people in Liberia and Nigeria—two countries where many New World slaves came from—have similar and perhaps even lower blood-pressure rates than white North Americans, while studies of Zulus, Indians, and whites in Durban, South Africa, showed that urban white males had the highest hypertension rates and urban white females had the lowest. So it's likely that the disease has nothing at all to do with Africanness.

The same is true for the distinctive muscle characteristic observed when Kenyans were compared with Swedes. Saltin, the Swedish physiologist, subsequently found many of the same characteristics in Nordic skiers who train at high altitudes and Nordic runners who train in very hilly regions—conditions, in other words, that resemble the mountainous regions of Kenya's Rift Valley, where so many of the country's distance runners come from. The key factor seems to be Kenya, not genes.

Lots of things that seem to be genetic in origin, then, actually aren't. Similarly, lots of things that we wouldn't normally think might affect athletic ability actually do. Once again, the social-science literature on male and female math achievement is instructive. Psychologists argue that when it comes to subjects like math, boys tend to engage in what's known as ability attribution. A boy who is doing well will attribute his success to the fact that he's good at math, and if he's doing badly he'll blame his teacher or his own lack of motivation—anything but his ability. That makes it easy for him to bounce back from failure or disappointment, and gives him a lot of confidence in the face of a tough new challenge. After all, if you think you do well in math because you're good at math, what's stopping you from being good at, say, algebra, or advanced calculus? On the other hand, if you ask a girl why she is doing well in math she will say, more often than not, that she succeeds because she works hard. If she's doing poorly, she'll say she isn't smart enough. This, as should be obvious, is a self-defeating attitude. Psychologists call it "learned helplessness"—the state in which failure is perceived as insurmountable. Girls who engage in effort attribution learn helplessness because in the face of a more difficult task like algebra or advanced calculus they can conceive of no solution. They're convinced that they can't work harder, because they think they're working as hard as they can, and that they can't rely on their intelligence, because they never thought they were that smart to begin with. In fact, one of the fascinating findings of attribution research is that the smarter girls are, the more likely they are to fall into this trap. High achievers are sometimes the most helpless. Here, surely, is part of the explanation for greater math variability among males. The female math whizzes, the ones who should be competing in the top one and two per cent with their male counterparts, are the ones most often paralyzed by a lack of confidence in their own aptitude. They think they belong only in the intellectual middle.

The striking thing about these descriptions of male and female stereotyping in math, though, is how similar they are to black and white stereotyping in athletics—to the unwritten rules holding that blacks achieve through natural ability and whites through effort. Here's how Sports Illustrated described, in a recent article, the white basketball player Steve Kerr, who plays alongside Michael Jordan for the Chicago Bulls. According to the magazine, Kerr is a "hard-working overachiever," distinguished by his "work ethic and heady play" and by a shooting style "born of a million practice shots." Bear in mind that Kerr is one of the best shooters in basketball today, and a key player on what is arguably one of the finest basketball teams in history. Bear in mind, too, that there is no evidence that Kerr works any harder than his teammates, least of all Jordan himself, whose work habits are legendary. But you'd never guess that from the article. It concludes, "All over America, whenever quicker, stronger gym rats see Kerr in action, they must wonder, How can that guy be out there instead of me?"

There are real consequences to this stereotyping. As the psychologists Carol Dweck and Barbara Licht write of high-achieving schoolgirls, "[They] may view themselves as so motivated and well disciplined that they cannot entertain the possibility that they did poorly on an academic task because of insufficient effort. Since blaming the teacher would also be out of character, blaming their abilities when they confront difficulty may seem like the most reasonable option." If you substitute the words "white athletes" for "girls" and "coach" for "teacher," I think you have part of the reason that so many white athletes are underrepresented at the highest levels of professional sports. Whites have been saddled with the athletic equivalent of learned helplessness—the idea that it is all but fruitless to try and compete at the highest levels, because they have only effort on their side. The causes of athletic and gender discrimination may be diverse, but its effects are not. Once again, blacks are like boys, and whites are like girls.

4.

When I was in college, I once met an old acquaintance from my high-school running days. Both of us had long since quit track, and we talked about a recurrent fantasy we found we'd both had for getting back into shape. It was that we would go away somewhere remote for a year and do nothing but train, so that when the year was up we might finally know how good we were. Neither of us had any intention of doing this, though, which is why it was a fantasy. In adolescence, athletic excess has a certain appeal—during high school, I happily spent Sunday afternoons running up and down snow-covered sandhills—but with most of us that obsessiveness soon begins to fade. Athletic success depends on having the right genes and on a self-reinforcing belief in one's own ability. But it also depends on a rare form of tunnel vision. To be a great athlete, you have to care, and what was obvious to us both was that neither of us cared anymore. This is the last piece of the puzzle about what we mean when we say one group is better at something than another: sometimes different groups care about different things. Of the seven hundred men who play major-league baseball, for example, eight-six come from either the Dominican Republic or Puerto Rico, even though those two islands have a combined population of only eleven million. But then baseball is something that Dominicans and Puerto Ricans care about—and you can say the same thing about African-Americans and basketball, West Indians and sprinting, Canadians and hockey, and Russians and chess. Desire is the great intangible in performance, and unlike genes or psychological affect we can't measure it and trace its implications. This is the problem, in the end, with the question of whether blacks are better at sports than whites. It's not that it's offensive, or that it leads to discrimination. It's that, in some sense, it's not a terribly interesting question; "better" promises a tidier explanation than can ever be provided.

I quit competitive running when I was sixteen—just after the summer I had qualified for the Ontario track team in my age class. Late that August, we had travelled to St. John's, Newfoundland, for the Canadian championships. In those days, I was whippet-thin, as milers often are, five feet six and not much more than a hundred pounds, and I could skim along the ground so lightly that I barely needed to catch my breath. I had two white friends on that team, both distance runners, too, and both, improbably, even smaller and lighter than I was. Every morning, the three of us would run through the streets of St. John's, charging up the hills and flying down the other side. One of these friends went on to have a distinguished college running career, the other became a world-class miler; that summer, I myself was the Canadian record holder in the fifteen hundred metres for my age class. We were almost terrifyingly competitive, without a shred of doubt in our ability, and as we raced along we never stopped talking and joking, just to prove how absurdly easy we found running to be. I thought of us all as equals. Then, on the last day of our stay in St. John's, we ran to the bottom of

Signal Hill, which is the town's principal geographical landmark—an abrupt outcrop as steep as anything in San Francisco. We stopped at the base, and the two of them turned to me and announced that we were all going to run straight up Signal Hill backward. I don't know whether I had more running ability than those two or whether my Africanness gave me any genetic advantage over their whiteness. What I do know is that such questions were irrelevant, because, as I realized, they were willing to go to far greater lengths to develop their talent. They ran up the hill backward. I ran home.

Lisa Jones

Are We Tiger Woods Yet?

FORGET ABOUT BILL CLINTON'S BRIDGE TO THE 21ST CENTURY. LET'S hitch a ride on Tiger Woods, our Cablinasian golden child. One-man totem of the new "race-blind" America. This "General Powell in a Nike Hat," who, as he was described in the promotional video that aired before the Masters, "transcends ethnic groups and age groups." (Let the multiracials cast in the Nike ads say, "I am Tiger Woods.") Or as Tiger's Asian mama says: He who is the "Universal Child." The One who, according to his black ("flavored" with Chinese and Cherokee) daddy, Big Poppa Earl Woods, the former Green Beret, is "qualified through his ethnicity to accomplish miracles." And boy do we need one.

Regardless of his ups and down on the greens, Tiger Woods has been a winner in Image America since the day he turned pro. And his future is assured because, as Woods told us in the news conference announcing his recent union with American Express, he's got his master "brand plan" all figured out. First the historic Nike deal, then the ads, the book deal, the apparel with its own logo (burgundy and black, says Nike, representing his multiracial background). Now it's the credit card and the watch. And next year, as Tiger Inc. scales contract after contract, the beverage and the car. We're sure to see Tiger's smith mug for decades to come.

It didn't take long for Woods to mortgage himself to the multinationals. Of all the deals closed this year, his coupling with American Express is symbolic perfection. The card is such an emblem of instant gratification—not just of the plastic-loot kind, but of the American dream (which, as we've been told, is the story of Tiger Woods). Just charge it. Perhaps you'll never have to pay for it. "It" being social change, of course. Social change achieved magically, without remedies, except a little consumer recognition and a lot of bootstrap pulling. A recent letter to the *Times* gushed that Woods's real achievement as an athlete was that he had done everything without "preferences" or "set-asides," as if the solution to America's race problem is just a matter of colored folks being more like Tiger and Mike.

Whites have always celebrated black champions as evidence of their own lack of bias. In the continuum, Tiger fills an important function circa 1997. He's living proof of a camera-ready racial harmony, achieved without America having to lift a finger. He's Dr. King in the green jacket, convincing us that despite the O.J.'s, the Rodney Kings, the Mark Fuhrmans, the Texacos, the resegregation of American schools and communities, we have reached the mountaintop.

More and more it is this "image equity," this *illusion* of change—offered by Image America when it crowns deities like Tiger—that stands for substantive change. And not only does image equity stand for change, it stands stubbornly in the face of fact. Minority numbers down at state law schools in Texas and California because of the dismantling of affirmative action? Don't worry, guys like Tiger are on TV. Nike's hired Tiger as a pitchman and is rallying against racist golf courses? Just ignore the company's exploitative employment practices in Asia.

Tiger's racial politics, even fuzzier than Fuzzy Zoeller, make him a particularly ripe token of his age. In the Tiger era, the waters of race are murky as ever. Racism transmogrifies at every turn, disguised as poverty, as educational inequities, as unemployment. While institutional racism digs its heels in deeper, race mutates into further abstractions: Cablinasian superstars; black female officers of the Ku Klux Klan. Clarence Thomas, the ultimate affirmative action poster boy, arguing that segregation is not inherently immoral; pierced "wiggers" blasting nigga-kill-nigga hip-hop from retro boom boxes.

Tiger's mix of impulses around race is a muddy stew of his mere 21 years on the planet and an almost *Star Trek*-ian brand of humanism. Woods thanks black golf pioneers after his Masters win, yet expresses anger at being called African American. Woods brags in interviews that he reads all his racist hate mail, yet says he has no interest in being the "great black hope." Woods, at Nike's urging, becomes a marketing-friendly racial provocateur, but says if he could split himself down the middle, he'd choose his Thai side. Woods takes time to make peace with Fuzzy, yet passes on Clinton's invite to the Jackie Robinson anniversary at Shea Stadium. Woods tells *Fortune* magazine that he doesn't think he has "transcended the issue of race," then doubles back and says he might have—"It's just kind of hard to see from my side sometimes."

Woods has not shied away from the mantle of role model, so he has to expect that his choices around identity are up for public critique. Certainly he has a right to claim whatever racial moniker he prefers. But his Cablinasianism reads more like a privilege ploy than a healthy empowerment strategy for mixed-race identity. Indeed, Cablinasianism constructs multiracialism as a teacher's note excusing Tiger and others like him from the race debate. And it definitely doesn't challenge race and class hierarchies. (Note which ethnic prefix leads Tiger's nom de plume: Caucasian.)

Lurking behind Woods's coronation in Image America, and the wrangling over his identity, is the nagging truth that black America, circa 1997, is not Tiger Woods. Every day we see federal and state governments chipping away at what Tiger's life really represents: access for those long denied.

A most appropriate companion story to the rise of Woods is the resurrection of Proposition 209. Less than a week before the Masters victory, the referendum, which pulls the plug on affirmative action in California, was upheld, reversing a lower court's decision. In Berkeley, students (around Tiger's age) who protested this turnaround were beat up by cops and arrested. (Where was the national coverage of this story?)

The doors of opportunity that Tiger himself once walked through are shutting, while the nation gloats over him. Media coverage made much of his Masters victory corresponding with the 50th anniversary of Robinson integrating baseball and kick-starting the modern civil rights movement. But in the words of *Boston Globe*'s Derrick Jackson, "the denial of racism is such that [these] comparisons were done with straight faces, instead of a sickened shame that we've gone 50 years and we're still cheering token successes."

The real symbol, the wake-up call of young black America is not the multiracial millionaire Tiger Woods. It's Malcolm X's 12-year-old grandson, Malcolm Shabazz. Shabazz, as we know, set the fire that, a month after Tiger's Masters victory, killed his own grandmother, Betty Shabazz. Young Shabazz's act eerily recalls the firebombing of his grandparents' house more than 30 years ago. It's an old story: our immediate enemy used to the Man. But now, some argue, it's what the Man has planted within.

A documentary about the death of a young rapper that screened recently on PBS focused on the fact that the leading cause of death of African American men ages 18 to 24 is murder, followed by AIDS. This is a familiar enough statistic; repeated so often without remedy we've become immune to it. But the documentary took this verity beyond nameless, faceless figures.

It urged that, the next time we watch a group of these young men, in a school yard or on a basketball court, we commit their faces to memory and be reminded that one in five will be killed at the hands of another black man. A second will end up spending more years of his life in an "overfunded prison," to quote Derrick Jackson again, than in an "underfunded school." Some of these black men might be Tiger Woods's poor Cablinasian relations from Compton, regardless of the ethnic moniker they choose.

We can salivate over Tiger's endorsement contracts and records off the tee, but who and what forces are out here working to reverse gruesome statistics such as these? No answer on the horizon. Only Marvin Gaye still singing in the background, mercy, mercy me.

On the Disappearance of Joe Wood Jr.

Robin D. G. Kelley

ON JULY 16, THE *NEW YORK TIMES* RAN A BRIEF ARTICLE ABOUT THE disappearance of Joe Wood. The thirty-four-year-old book editor was attending the Unity '99 conference of minority journalists in Seattle, Washington, when he decided to do a little bird-watching in the Longmire area of Mt. Rainier.

The evidence suggests that he was traveling alone and unequipped for hiking, and at least one eye-witness reportedly saw Joe Wood on July 8, the day he set out on his excursion. The witness remembers warning him of a particularly unstable snow bridge. Days later, his abandoned car was discovered in a parking lot at Longmire. Whatever the circumstances, by the time the article ran Joe Wood had been missing for eight days.

Later that night, John F. Kennedy Jr., Carolyn Bessette Kennedy, and Lauren Bessette perished in a tragic plan crash, their young lives cut short in the icy waters of the Atlantic Ocean. Their disappearance, the search, and the awful realization that there would be no survivors spurred the entire nation into a state of mourning. Then Joe Wood really disappeared.

Like many others, I felt deeply saddened by the deaths of these three young and talented people, and moved by the rich and detailed portraits of John, Carolyn, and Lauren painted in vivid technicolor by the television and print media. But I wanted to know what happened to Joe Wood, my friend. I spent the weekend channel surfing, web surfing, thumbing through the latest editions of local newspapers for anything about Joe, but there was no other news beyond the Kennedy tragedy. For many of us who know and love Joe, it turned out to be a particularly frustrating weekend. Where were the search parties for Joe? What did the Civil Air Patrol plan to do? Had they found any witnesses? Then late Tuesday night, five days after learning of Wood's disappearance, I ran across a short article from the *Seattle Post-Intelligencer* (July 19, 1999) posted on the web. It confirmed what I had heard by word-of-mouth from Wood's vast network of friends and acquaintances: he had not been found and the National Park Service decided to call off the search. Outraged, many of us called and faxed the National Park Service's office at Mt. Rainier asking that the search continue.

Maybe Joe Wood was no John F. Kennedy Jr., but does that mean he deserved to be jettisoned from the media, lost and forgotten? Is the life of this young and incredibly talented black man really so insignificant compared to Mr. Kennedy's? Like Kennedy, Wood was full of promise. Besides being one of the most dynamic editors at the New Press and a former senior editor at the *Village Voice,* Wood is regarded as one of the most talented writers of our generation. His essays are generally autobiographical, exploring issues such as race, color consciousness, sex, masculinity, and the problems of coming of age in a post–Civil Rights generation. His prose is pure poetry, metaphors rising from the page, a thousand pictures of meaning packed into short staccato phrases. His book reviews, like his brilliant meditation on critic Albert Murray's most recent works published in the *Village Voice* a couple years back, are always incisive and thoughtful. And his edited book *Malcolm X: In Our Own Image* (1992) has few peers in the burgeoning field of Malcolm studies. If there was a single theme in all of Joe's writings it is that black people are extremely complicated and diverse, and while our burdens are often collective and shared, what goes on in our families and communities is beautiful, four-dimensional, multicolored chaos.

Like "John John," Joe also touched many lives as a writer, editor, and friend. Somewhat soft-spoken with an infectious smile and an affinity for baseball caps, Joe had a way of bringing laughter to a room in a quiet way. Every time I ran into him or engaged him on the phone, we would end up exchanging hilarious stories that ultimately revolve around the absurdity of being black in a world that cannot see you unless you conform to certain stereotypes. Joe was neither a Buppy (Black Urban Professional) nor a gangsta nor an au naturel vegetarian dredlock-wearing guy. He is just . . . Joe—cosmopolitan, extremely well-read, kinda cool, and like me, about 5 percent nerd. And he possesses one of the most brilliant minds I have ever encountered. After graduating with honors from Yale University, he moved almost immediately into New York's hippest literary circles, writing for the *Village Voice* when it was cutting edge and exciting. Indeed, Joe once told me that the controversial critic Stanley Crouch helped him land a job there. As my editor on at least two different projects, Joe was a dream to work with: he listens patiently, reads with the care of a highly paid surgeon, makes every effort to understand your intentions, and he takes charge.

So why did Joe disappear? Why did someone with so much talent and promise and popularity completely evaporate from the media? Why was his tragedy—a tragedy that has rocked many people in the world of writing—not worthy of even one-tenth the coverage given to the Kennedys? I'm not naive enough to expect equal time, but the abrupt manner in which Joe completely dropped out of the news compels us once again to ask: What is a black man's life worth? Given how few of us occupy the literary world, and how few truly brilliant minds there are in the world generally, the prospect of losing a Joe Wood is devastating. And the possibility of losing his legacy, his history and contribution, his very presence is equally devastating. Sadly, perhaps Joe's own words explain why the nation doesn't mourn the loss of Joe Wood, or why the nation doesn't know enough to mourn his loss. In what now seems like an eerie passage from his essay "Malcolm X and the New Blackness," he discusses his dual life as a black kid in the Bronx and a student at the elite Riverdale High School located just inside the Bronx County line. Joe wrote, "My family and neighbors were not Kennedys—we worked and we were too black." And as any celebrity photographer will tell you, when you're too black, you are more susceptible to being lost in the shadows.

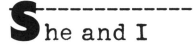

Bruce Morrow

She and I

I DO NOT NOW WHY I LOVE HER, BUT I DO SO MUCH. WE ARE NOT CLOSE, we are not good friends, we do not talk for hours on the phone or get together on holidays and "catch up." In fact, I rarely see her and seldom talk to her. A call once a year would be enough for me. I wonder if it's the same for her.

She likes to decorate things; I like only functional items. She has light peach silk wallpaper in her living room, brass tables with smoked glass tops, a cocoa-colored couch and loveseat positioned in front of a window concealed from the world by copper-colored vertical blinds. I, on the other hand, bought curtains a couple of years ago because my boyfriend, of six years at the time, was tired of waking up at sunrise, which is always my wont. I usually find my furniture in the garbage, in the basement of my building, in piles on street corners every Tuesday and Thursday night. A coffee table with red tile mosaic top. A silver plated floor lamp without glass shade. A variety of old wooden school chairs with petrified gum stuck underneath.

She has visited my home in the last ten years as often as I've visited hers. I cleaned my apartment for two weeks for her first stay. I scrubbed the floors, cleaned the windows, bought curtains (my other reason for getting window treatments), bought new sheets and washed them before putting them on the bed. I bought tickets to a Broadway show because I knew that she would expect that on a visit to the Big Apple.

People from Cleveland know what to expect when they come to New York City: tickets to a play; a visit to at least one museum; treacherous rides on the too hot or too cold or too crowded subway; and lots and lots of walking. She knew to bring comfortable sneakers because taking cabs everywhere could get really expensive and the subway doesn't always go directly where you want it: to the well-lighted marquee of the theater ten minutes before curtain call or, after the theater, the front door of Orso, which serves the best fancy pizza appetizers in town, with thin crust, pesto, and goat cheese. New York City tourists love to eat pizza at dives named Famous Ray's or Original Ray's or Ray's Famous Pizza even though John's on Bleecker Street and V&T's across the street from the Cathedral of St. John the Divine are the places I would most recommend.

She thinks I eat out all the time. But, truth be told, I don't even think about eating; it's better for my figure, which I try to work out at least five times a week at the fancy-ass expensive gym down the street from my office.

On her first visit to my apartment, the only time we ate at home was in the morning. She volunteered to make pancakes, my favorite food of all time (with chunky slices of cheddar cheese on the side instead of bacon), but I insisted on keeping things simple. Scrambled eggs and toast. Cold cereal with fresh fruit. One morning when I was feeling energetic, I made oatmeal with bananas and cinnamon.

It was on that first day of her first visit to my apartment in New York, when, after finishing a breakfast of eggs and toast, she asked: "Do you want me to clean the coffee maker for you?" I was already nervous enough about eating with my mother and my boyfriend in our little eat-in kitchen in our one bedroom apartment that I'd scrubbed from top to bottom; but this observation sent me over the top. From some far off place deep inside my head, perhaps close to the hippocampus, the brain's memory center, a panic started. And it was true: the only thing I'd forgotten to clean after cleaning for two whole weeks before my mother's first visit was the coffee maker, which is one of the only kitchen appliances that I use on a regular basis because most of the time my lover and I leave our apartment at 8 A.M. and don't return until 10 P.M. My gym fatigued body just won't allow me to eat high caloric complex carbohydrates while watching the 11 o'clock news.

We didn't really get to spend a lot of time alone together on her first visit to my apartment in New York, which was on the occasion of my graduation from the Columbia Writing Program because a relative in Brooklyn died suddenly and we ended up spending the last four days of her seven day visit riding for almost two hours out to Flatbush to be with family, to go to the wake and, on the third day, to go to the funeral. At the burial ceremony, we both cried, just a little.

On her first visit to my apartment in New York City, my friends kept saying that we looked exactly alike, put a red wig on me, add a few freckles, and we could be sisters.

When she was young, she was always skinny. When I was young, I had to wear husky size pants. I look in the mirror today and I still see a fatso.

She likes to shop—loves to shop!—and at the age of twelve, thirteen, I would go with her to Kmart or Zaires, Halle's or Higbee's or May Company, or, later on during my high school years, Saks Fifth Avenue at Beechwood Place, the most expensive mall in the Cleveland area. I would follow her through aisles lines with silk dresses and wool suits, gold jewelry and leather gloves, clutch purses and felt hats—all in pursuit of the perfect Easter Sunday outfit. While my brother would refuse to join us because he wanted to play ball down the street, I would follow her for hours, approving and disapproving her selections. The grey jersey over the red hot chiffon. The Anne Klein over the Liz Claiborne. Black pumps instead of gold-toned loafers.

She seemed to never form an opinion; I always had one. However, she could become very opinionated if the price was too high. If an item was deemed a must-have but wasn't on sale, she would not even try it on, but say instead, "Now that's sharp; now I could wear something like that," as she pressed the Yves Saint Laurent strapless number to her body, swaying from side to side, not quite ready to put it back on the rack.

We were so close, real close, almost like sisters.

I don't remember ever wanting to try on dresses with her, but I do remember wanting to see her in the dresses. I wanted to give my opinion and have her value it. Above all else, I wanted to be with her. All alone with her on some journey, just she and I shopping in the designer women's department of Saks on a late Saturday afternoon.

After she'd exhausted herself and made a few small purchases, we'd head down to the young men's department. To accommodate my big butt and thick thighs without leaving too much room in the waist, she would suggest I try on dress pants with large double pleats in the front. At the age of thirteen I was too old for huskies. She'd make me turn around and check the construction of the waistband to see if she could easily make the necessary alterations. Let it out a half inch in the back. Add one inch cuffs. I never complained because double pleats were very much in style in the mid to late 1970s.

When I was growing up she always let me do what I wanted. If I wanted to take piano lessons, she found a teacher, borrowed a piano from a distant relative, and made room in the dining room for the antique white upright piano (Lesters, Philadelphia) and the small piano bench (not matching; this was before she redecorated and sent the piano back to the distant relative from which it came). I took drawing lessons at the Cleveland Museum of Art, swimming lessons at the neighborhood pool, went ice skating on Fridays with my brother and cousins. When I applied to a private college in Rochester, she protested that we just couldn't afford it. But when I got accepted she only said that it would be tough, I'd have to get a job and keep my expenses down.

For a while we both sang in the same choir, the Youth and Young Adult Choir of St. Matthew's United Methodist Church. She was a soprano, I a tenor. Until I left for college, we always went to choir practice together on Wednesdays and sang together on Sundays.

College was like a dream for me. I could just be free, gay and free, freely gay. I didn't have to worry about my large extended family of aunts and uncles and cousins and second cousins and great aunt and uncles, who all lived in walking distance from me and were the center of my social life. I've always been gay; as far back as I can remember, I've always had to keep secrets about myself, hide my attraction to the boy next door, not get caught playing with dolls or jumping rope or holding my hand just so.

But I'm sure my mother always knew her firstborn was a big sissy.

I remember loving to play with her hair. As if she were my living doll, I'd sit on the couch and she on the floor, and I would scratch her scalp before she went to bed. I'd put her hair up in the different styles I admired on models in magazines, *Ebony*,

Essence, Vogue, and *Cosmopolitan.* Rita Hayworth and Diahann Carroll were my ideals: with a little help from Clairol, her hair color matched Rita's; and because of her high forehead, Diahann's hairstyles worked well with the shape of her face. She'd compliment me for being so creative and, when she got dressed up to go out for the evening or church on Sunday morning, she would try to recreate my sculptured hair creations.

Did I stop playing with her hair after I went away to college or was it before that? Did I grow out of it or was it something we both thought was too telling an act? I do not know.

We've never been that close since.

"So are you dating anyone?" one of my aunts asked on my first visit back home from college.

"So who's your girlfriend up there at college?" my grandmother asked and giggled like a teenager.

She, on the other hand, never asked about my love life. Privacy was—and is—very important to us both.

We both love secrets, love to keep secrets, love to pretend that the secrets don't exist.

We both procrastinate. My bills are never paid on time. I'm always late for appointments. It's gotten so bad that I now get several extensions each year before filing my income taxes even though I know I'm getting a refund.

Some people might say I work on CP time (colored people time, that is), but don't let the tables turn. I cannot stand waiting on others. I'm not a patient person. Even though I don't pace back and forth in the subway station while waiting for the train, in my mind, I've worn a deep groove.

It wasn't until I was filling out my college applications that I asked my mother what my father's name was. Because my mother was divorced at the time from her husband and my stepfather of fourteen years, I did not want to put his name down even though he was the only father that I knew. Maybe that's why I waited until the deadline to fill out the applications. Procrastination is all about avoiding. And she and I are both good at avoiding. She could have told me sooner about my father. She could have told me more about him. Where did she meet him? Why didn't he act more responsibly? Just because my mother married a man that wasn't my father when I was still very young, three or four, I still should have been told more about this man, my father, who I cannot even imagine. His eyes. His smile. His ears that stick out just like mine. I might have seen a photograph of him in a plastic bag in the bottom of the china cabinet but as soon as I would look away from it I would forget what I had seen. Somewhere in my mind, deep in the hippocampus, there's a little film clip of my Aunt Justine suggesting to my mother that she should tell me about my father; I'm on the floor playing cards or watching TV; and my mother, as non-confrontational as ever, is avoiding the subject. Does she say, *Later, I'm going to wait until he's older.* Does she tell my aunt that it's none of her damn business, *why don't you have children of your own and then you can raise them as you see fit?* Does she say, *Yes, you're right, it's time. Bruce I want you to know who your father is. Go down stairs and get that bag of photographs in the bottom of the china cabinet and bring it up here. There's something I want to show you.* I can't remember. I cannot remember. There are so many different endings to this little film that my mind starts overheating and the film suddenly freezes, then bubbles and melts into a flashing white light of truth just as I'm seeing his face, morphing into my own face, for the very first time.

I do not for the life of me remember the name she told me to write on those stupid college applications.

Is that when we started growing apart?

I fell in love with a beautiful half Chinese, half Jamaican girl my first year at college. I fell in love with a beautiful boy with skin the color of charcoal my sophomore year. I joined gay organizations on campus, had all gay friends, read gay books and magazines, went to gay clubs and gay films and gay picnics. Except for Christmas, I didn't go home for vacations. When I did go home, I reverted back to my old self: shy, antisocial, secretive. The husky momma's boy.

After college I moved to New York and became the biggest homo around. I joined gay organizations, had all gay friends, read all gay books, subscribed to all gay magazines, danced at gay clubs, watched all gay films, and marched down Fifth Avenue every last Sunday in June in the Annual Gay Pride Parade.

It wasn't until I broke up with my first New York City boyfriend that I called my mother and told her I was gay. I didn't think it was necessary until then. She was quiet for a while then said she would have rather not known. She said she was now worried about me living in New York, I had to be careful, what with AIDS and all that. I assured her I was having very safe sex and she got really quiet again. Was that too much information, too many secrets revealed? During that moment of silence I could faintly hear another phone conversation leaking in, two women laughing and speaking in Spanish. Were they telling each other secrets too? Were they afraid that one day they wouldn't know each other at all, wouldn't recognize those awful gold loafers they shouldn't have bought ten years ago anyway? While the silence between my mother and myself grew, I strained to hear what the two women were saying but all I could understand were the often repeated words *mira, mira* (look, look . . .) and *pero, pero* (but, but . . .). Living in New York City, I should learn more Spanish and maybe date some cute Latino.

I took a Spanish course once, but I never learned the language. When I traveled to Puerto Rico, and the Dominican Republic, and Mexico I had to rely on my boyfriend to decipher the menu.

"When are we going to visit your family?" he asked over and over again. "I want to see where you grew up. Let's go visit your mom."

I had no interest in visiting the Buckeye State.

When we had time we usually headed to the beach, Cape Cod, Florida, or, on special occasions, the Caribbean.

After not visiting Cleveland for a couple of years, my mother started asking when I was coming home. I am home, I would say. Who wants to go to Cleveland? Why don't we meet somewhere else, Cuba for Christmas maybe or Bali for New Year's.

Perhaps I was waiting for her to extend the invitation to my boyfriend too and she soon did.

"When are you and Roger going to visit?" she asked finally. But I still didn't want to go. I was too worried, too uptight, too ready to second guess her objections to me and my boyfriend sleeping in the same bed in her house.

She was coming to the realization that her oldest son wasn't going to show up unexpectedly at her door one day without bringing his boyfriend, significant other, or whatever you want to call him. Roger, that's his name. A three bedroom house is a big lonely place for one person.

I shrugged off any good will she extended.

I was afraid. I was scared of being gay around my family and scared of some random display of homophobia. I was scared that everything would be the same, that I was the same even though I was the adventurous son living the high life in New York City. I didn't want to go back there. Back there I was a sissy, a punk, an unpopular nerd, a fatso in husky size pants. A precocious boy that liked shopping in the Ladies' department. Even though I've tried to come out to each and every relative that I've talked to, somebody might ask when I'm getting married and, if not, if I have a steady girlfriend even though Roger would be standing right beside me.

She and I are not close because I won't let us be close.

There's probably some developmental theory about the distance that's grown between her and myself but I'm not a psychologist.

Twelve years after my coming out call to my mother and nine years with my present boyfriend, I finally found myself back in Ohio. We were going to a wedding in Michigan and Roger, my boyfriend, got his chance. I couldn't get out of it. She, too, seemed eager for us to visit. As Roger and I drove into the city of Cleveland, I kept feeling like I was lost but knew the way home. I-70. I-95. Downtown. The new baseball stadium, Jacobs Field. The new basketball arena, Gund Arena. Carnegie Avenue (pronounced car-NAY-gie in CLEVE-land) lined with ugly billboards and dumpy looking brick faced buildings until we get to the sprawling multileveled campus of Cleveland Clinic, then University Circle, home to Case Western Reserve University, Severence Hall, and the Cleveland Museum where I learned to use ebony pencils, charcoal, pastels, and large pads of newsprint on Saturday mornings. All while I'm fidgeting in my seat, pointing things out to Roger, I'm peaceful on the inside. I know this place; this place knows me. The Rapid Transit Authority. The shifting lanes of Cedar Road swaying up to Cleveland Heights. Coventry. Oh, bohemian Coventry Road, famous for its 60s happenings, the place for gays and alternatives to coexist. Coventry where poets still own the sidewalks. Coventry where a guy openly winked at me when I was fifteen and where I first went on a date with a man almost twice my age.

The houses get bigger then smaller. There's the Cedar-Lee Theater and my old high school with the Mickey Mouse clock on top. The McDonald's has been replaced with a mammoth Thai restaurant. Some of my favorite trees are missing, here, there, killed by some blight, destroying the tunnel of trees effect that made the neighborhood look a hundred years old, which it is. There's our house with gold aluminum siding, black shutters, white columned porch, and green artificial turf covering the front stairs. Yuck. How silly. How decorated. How something. What's up with outdoor carpeting anyway? I used to help her plant geraniums in pots on the front porch, cut the dead blossoms off the rose bush so new ones could grow. We'd sit on the front porch, she and I, my mother and I, watering the grass and surveying the suburban paradise around us. She'd tell my stories and sometimes she'd forget and call me girl. *Girl,* she'd scream, *you wouldn't believe it if you saw it.* I'd scratch her scalp and fix her hair and she'd braid my hair so I'd have a big fluffy afro in the morning. We were so close.

She and I were as close as the w and e in we.

Standing in the driveway holding our bags, Roger's beaming and I'm shaking. Upset that I've lose my keys—I don't have keys to these locks—I knock too loud, too many times. No sound. We didn't call to let her know exactly when we were arriving because we wanted it to be a surprise. I ring the bell and knock again. That's her. I can hear her walking down the stairs, fumbling with the locks, opening the door. Her hair's up in a french twist like the one I tried to replicate from a picture of Catherine Deneuve in *Cosmopolitan*. Her face has filled out and I can see a slight sag around her jaw but there's no way anyone would guess she's over forty-five. She stares at me and I at her. For a brief moment I forget where I am: not looking in a mirror. She kisses me and hugs me and I can smell her skin, her hair. It would be so nice, I think, to go back and be her best friend, to sing together, to go shopping together. I want pancakes with cheddar cheese for breakfast, lunch, and dinner. She hugs Roger next and calls us inside. The screen door screeches shut like it has for the last thirty years. And before you know it I'm home.

White Girl?

Lonnae O'Neal Parker

I HAVE A 20-YEAR-OLD WHITE GIRL LIVING IN MY BASEMENT. SHE HAPPENS TO be my first cousin. I happen to be black. Genes are a funny thing. So are the politics of racial declaration.

My 5-year-old daughter, Sydney, calls her Cousin Kim. Kim's daddy calls my mother his baby sister. Kim's father is black. Her mother is white. And Kim calls herself white. At least that's what she checks off on all those forms with neat little boxes for such things.

She grew up in southern Illinois, Sandoval, population about 1,500. There were 33 people in her high school graduating class. Counting Cousin Kim, there was half a black. I used to think Kim lived in a trailer park. But one day she corrected me. We live in a trailer home, she said—"my mother owns the land."

The black side of Kim's family is professional. Lawyers, doctors, Fortune 500 company execs. We have an uncle who got a Ph.D. in math at 21. The white side of Kim's family is blue collar. Less formally educated. Some recipients of government entitlement programs. Not to draw too fine a distinction, but color is not the only thing that separates us.

I brought Kim to Maryland to live with me after my second child, Savannah, was born. She is something of an au pair, if au pairs can hail from Sandoval.

Back home, Kim had run into some trouble. Bad grades, good beer. She came to D.C. to sort it all out. To find a way to get her life back on track. And she came to get in touch with the black side of her family—and possibly herself. She may have gotten more than she bargained for.

This is a story about how a close family can split right down a color line without ever saying a word about it. The details belong to Cousin Kim and me, but the outline is familiar to anyone for whom race is a secret or a passion or an issue or a decision. The story is scary in places. Because to tell it, both Kim and I have to go there. Race Place, U.S.A. It is a primal stretch of land. It shares a psychic border with the place where we compete for the last video, parking space at the mall or kindergarten slot in that elite magnet school. Where we fight over soccer calls, and elbow each other to secure Tickle Me Elmos for our kids. It is the place where we grew up hearing black people smell like copper and white people smell like wet chickens. Where everybody knows that whites are pedophiles and gun nuts. And blacks smoke crack. Where interracial couples still bother us.

You've gotta pass through Race Place in order to make it to Can We All Get Along, but most everybody is looking for a shortcut.

For Kim and me, there are no shortcuts. We meet in the middle, from opposite sides of a racial divide. It is the DMZ and our shields are down. We may lose friends, black and white, for telling this truth so plainly. Still, alone together, we begin.

Do you remember the first time somebody called you "nigger"?

I do. I was on vacation in Centralia, Ill., where both of my parents were born and raised. Five minutes from where Cousin Kim grew up. It was the early 1970s, and I was maybe 5 years old.

Two white girls walked up to me in a park. They were big. Impossibly big. Eleven at least. They smiled at me, "Are you a nigger?" one of the girls asked.

On the segregated South Side of Chicago where I lived, it was possible for a black child to go a very long time and never hear the word "nigger" directed at her. But I wasn't on the South Side, and after five years, my time was up.

I stood very still. And my stomach grew icy. My spider senses were tingling. Where had I heard that word before? "I, I don't know," I told her, shrugging my shoulders high to my ears.

The first girl sighed, exasperated. Then the other repeated, more forcefully this time, "Are you a nigger? You know, a black person?" she asked.

I wanted to answer her. To say something. But fear made me confused. I had no words. I just stood there. And tried not to wet my panties.

Then I ran. I turned quickly to look over my shoulder just in time to hear a rock whiz past my ear and plop into a nearby creek.

"You better git, you little Ne-gro!" somebody else, a white boy, yelled at me from a few feet away. I kept running, and this time, I didn't look back.

For the rest of the day, I harbored a secret. I harbored the shame for longer. I knew I was black. I had found out the year before. I remember because I had confronted my father, demanding to know when my blond hair and blue eyes would kick in. Like the Miss Breck shampoo girl on television. Like the superheroes on "Superfriends."

Only white people have blond hair and blue eyes, my dad said. "And we're black."

The wicked witch, the headless horseman, the evil stepmother and all the bad guys on "The New Adventures of Scooby Doo" wore black. Black eye, black heart, Black Death, black ass. Mine was a negative, visceral reaction to the word.

Five years old was old enough to know I was black. It was old enough for somebody to call me a nigger.

And it was certainly old enough to feel like one.

That would be the first time.

It is early June, and Cousin Kim and I are about to watch "Roots," the landmark 1970s television miniseries about a slave family. Kim says she's heard of the movie but has never seen it. So I go to queue the video in the cassette player, but first I make a cup of tea. And straighten the pillows on my couch. Then I check my voice mail.

I am puttering. Procrastinating. Loath to begin. Because I don't know if our blood ties are strong enough to withstand slavery. And I am scared to watch "Roots" with a white girl. Scared of my anger. Scared of my pain. Scared that she won't get it. Scared of how much I want her to. Scared of the way race can make strangers out of family.

It has been nearly a year since Kim first came to live with me. She was a cousin I barely knew. She had visited my husband and me in the summer of 1994, when our daughter Sydney was a baby. The first time she had ever seen so many black people in her life, she would later say.

Before that, there were brief visits with my mom and quick kisses at my college graduation. Over the years, I heard much more than I ever saw of Cousin Kim. Kim's father had a black family. His kids were adults when Kim was born. Later, his wife died. And though they are now a public couple, my uncle and Kim's mom never married.

My girls adore Kim. And when she goes to get Sydney from school, the little black prekindergartners rush her at the door, greeting her with wide smiles and hugs and shouts of "Hi, Cousin Kim!"

This past year, we've laughed over sitcoms and shared private jokes. We've talked about old boyfriends, gone shopping and giggled over family gossip. Still, up to now, we've never been down that black-and-white brick road.

I was shocked to hear that Cousin Kim considered herself white. I found out only because she had to fill out some forms to get into community college. Because I asked her if they had a box for race. Then I asked her what she checked. I was ready to tease her pointedly for checking off "other." In between. Not quite either.

I was prepared to lobby her—to drop science about the "one-drop rule." In slave days, that meant that if you had a drop of black blood, you were singing spirituals and working for somebody for free. Trying not to get beaten, and trying to keep your babies from being sold—even if the massa was their daddy. Color gradations were a legacy of the plantation system. And although light was favored, one drop gave us a common destiny.

Shackled all of us darkies together.

Later, one drop meant that blacks were able to form a common cultural identity. To agitate for the common good. Because light mulattoes lynched as easily as dark Africans. But one drop also meant there have always been those who could pass. Who required writ, or testimony, or a declaration of intent to make them black. For whom race has always been a choice.

Cousin Kim would be one of these. Her eyes are bright blue-gray and her skin has only a suggestion of color. Generations of careful breeding have worked out all her kinks. To white folks, she looks white. And mostly, that is how they treat her. Like one of their own.

Still, I was ready to cast her lot with the sisters. You know half-black is black, I was ready to say. I was ready for "other." I wasn't ready for "white." Or that familiar sting of rejection.

I have The Sight. Like my mother before me. Like most black people I know. It is a gift. A special kind of extrasensory perception. We may not be clairvoyant enough to determine the location of the rebel base. Or have the telekinesis it takes to shatter a glass ceiling.

But we can spot some Negro on you from three generations away.

It reveals itself in a flash of expression. A momentary disposition of features in repose. The curl of a top lip that seems to say "Nobody knows the trouble I've seen."

We have The Sight because we are used to looking at black people. Used to loving them. We know the range of colors black comes in. Because there's always somebody at our family reunions who could go either way. And because we are worldly people, and we know how these things go.

The Sight is a nod to solidarity. It is a reaction against dilution and division. It is the recognition that when people face overwhelming odds, you need to know who can be compelled to ante up and kick in.

We use it to put a black face on public triumphs that look lily white. And to "out" folks who might act against our interests without sharing in the consequences.

No matter how many times she thanked "the black community" for embracing her music, we knew Mariah Carey was part black. And long before he opened his mouth, we saw something in Rock Newman's eyes, even though they are blue.

When people wanted to call actresses Jennifer Beals or Troy Beyer beautiful, we were eager to point out their black roots. Eager to claim New York Yankee Derek Jeter and Channel 4 newscaster Barbara Harrison. Old folks swear Yul Brynner was black and that was why he kept his head shaved. And speculation persists, despite the fact that Georgia representative Bob Barr has affirmed his whiteness. Understand. It's not that we don't respect Tiger Woods, himself a Cablinasian. We just don't think it will help him get a cab in D.C.

My cousin calls herself white and I see a side of me just passing away. Swallowed up by the larger, more powerful fish in the mainstream. And I wonder if that will be the future for my family., some who look like Kim—others who look like me but have married white, or no doubt will. And I wonder, ultimately, if that will be the future for black people. Passing themselves right out of existence. Swearing it was an accident. Each generation trading up a shade and a grade until there is nothing left but old folks in fold-up lawn chairs on backyard decks who gather family members close around to tell nostalgic tales that begin "Once upon a time when we were colored . . ."

And I think to myself, I wish there were some things that we just wouldn't do for straight hair. And I think of the struggle and the history and the creativity lost. And I trust that the universe will register my lament.

When my cousin calls herself white, I see red. And I hear echoes. "Well, I don't really consider myself black . . . "

Or maybe it is laughter.

Cousin Kim is having a hard time with "Roots." Not her own, the movie. I'm not having an easy time myself.

She isn't ready for the stuff they left out of her history books. I am unable to restrain my commentary. Or my imagination. Sometimes my tears.

Ever heard of Calvert County, I ask Kim bitterly when a teenage African girl is sold at an Annapolis auction as a bed wench to Robert Calvert. Kim didn't know that Maryland had ever been a slave state.

There is a scene where kidnapped African Kunte Kinte won't settle down in his chains. "Want me to give him a stripe or two, boss?" the old slave, Fiddler, asks his Master Reynolds.

"Do as I say, Fiddler," Reynolds answers. "That's all I expect from any of my niggers."

"Oh, I love you, Massa Reynolds," Fiddler tells him. And instantly, my mind draws political parallels. Ward Connerly, I think to myself. Armstrong Williams. Shelby Steele. Hyperbole, some might say. I say dead-on.

"Clarence Thomas," I say to Cousin Kim. And she just stares at me. She may be a little tender yet for racial metaphors. I see them everywhere.

Kim is 20 in the way of small-town 20-year-olds all over the country. Her best-best friends are Jenny and Nikki and Theresa. They send letters, e-mail one another and run up my phone bill. She takes classes, takes care of my children and passes time painting her nails and watching "The Real World," on MTV. I tease her about being Wal-Mart-obsessed.

Cousin Kim walked out of the movie "Glory" when she was in 11th grade. When Denzel Washington got lashed with a whip and cried silently. Couldn't handle it, she said. "I just didn't want to see it. I couldn't stand the idea of seeing someone literally beat." Avoidance and denial are twins in my family. In others as well.

When Kim was growing up in Sandoval, they didn't celebrate Black History Month, she says. "Not even Black History Week. We just had Martin Luther King Day."

The town was not integrated. Her father was the only black person she saw regularly. "And I don't consider him black," Kim says. My uncle is not one to disabuse her of that notion.

Kim's dad ran his own sanitation business. He was a hard-working, astute, sometimes charming businessman. A moneymaker. And my mother says people used to say if he had been white, he would have been mayor of Centralia. Of course, Kim has never heard this. In fact, "we've never had a conversation about race in my house," Kim says casually. And for a moment, I am staggered. But I am not surprised.

My mama's people have always been color-struck. Daddy's, too, for that matter. Black folks know the term. It is part of an informal caste system that has always existed in the black community.

It is a form of mental colonialism. A shackle for the mind. A value system that assigns worth and power to those traits that most closely resemble the massa.

If you're light, you're all right. If you're brown, stick around. If you're black, get back, people used to say.

I am light; my husband is dark. When my daughter Sydney was born, everybody wanted to know who she looked like. They weren't asking about her eyes. They wanted to know what black folks always want to know when a baby who can go either way on the light-dark thing is born. Whose color is she? What kind of hair does she have?

The hair can be a tricky thing. Nothing for that but to wait a few months until the "grade" comes in good. But for color, we've got it down. We're a race of mad scientists, fervently checking the nail beds and ear tips of newborns to precisely determine where they'll fall over the rainbow.

My paternal grandmother was a very light woman with straight hair and black features. She had an inspection ritual she performed on all new babies in the family. A careful once-over to check for color and clarity before she pronounced judgment. I didn't know this until I introduced her to Sydney when she was about 6 months old.

She sat my baby on her lap. After a few minutes, she announced her findings. "Well, her color is good. And her hair ain't half bad considering how black that nigger is you married."

Hmmmm. You know these days we try to stay away from divisive pronouncements on color, I wanted to tell her. We don't want to handicap our daughter with crippling hair issues.

But please. My grandmother might have hit me if I had tried to spout some nonsense like that. More to the point, particularly among the elders, there is a certain unassailable quality to the color caste logic. A tie-in with life chances. And my grandmother was nearly 80. So I took the only option available under the circumstances. I smiled sweetly and said thank you. Because, after all, this was high praise.

"Watch out for your children!" had been a favorite admonition passed down from my maternal grandmother. The one I shared with Cousin Kim. She wasn't talking about bad influences or oncoming traffic. She was talking about a kind of Breeders' Cup standard for black love. At least the kind that ended in marriage. Light skin, good-hair (a compound word), light eyes. that was the Triple Crown.

Early on, I learned there is a premium placed on my particular brand of mongrel. I am Red, as in Red Bone. Or Yellow, for High Yellow. Or light, bright and damn near white.

I used to be able to break into a full genealogy incantation in an instant, with attention paid to the whites and Native Americans in my family tree. Because that white girl was still running around my head asking me if I was black. Because black and ugly always came in the same breath.

But I credit white folks with my slow evolution toward racial consciousness. We moved to a suburb of Chicago when I was 9. And we arrived squarely in a middle-class dream.

I had always been shy. A good student. With long hair. Teachers loved me. And always, a few black girls hated me. "White dog," they called me—no, wait, that's what they called my sister. I was a "half-white bitch." Theirs was a reaction. A rage. A demonstration of the only power they had, the only power perhaps they thought they would ever have. The power to bully. But back then, I didn't know that. I had "A Foot in Each World" but couldn't get my head into either.

I don't remember my moment of political and aesthetic epiphany. It was more of a slow dawn, I think. An incremental understanding of the forces that were working around me. Certainly, watching white folks pack up and leave the neighborhood in herds made an imprint. And when a white boy spat on me at a park, I took that very personally. But it was the trickle of small slights that accumulated over the years that combined to make one point very clear.

High Yellow was just a lighter shade of black.

To be in Chicago in 1983 when Harold Washington, a big, dark, deep-black intellectual, was elected mayor was to see the face of racism. To watch the way that hate contorts the features and purples the skin. White folks were rabid. Foaming at the mouth. A few white newscasters could barely read their copy. A flier circulated through my high school featuring a big-lipped black caricature chowing down on watermelon. The city would have to be renamed Chicongo, it said. And I understood.

Ultimately, race is political. And I am a partisan.

Sometimes I still hear that white girl ask me if I am black. And now I have an answer. Pitch. Cold. Blacker than three midnights. As black as the ace of spaces. I'm so black that when I get in my car, the oil light comes on.

I've decided that it is unhealthy for us to surrender to white sensibilities, including the ones that mock us from inside our own heads. We have all been guilty of dumbing down our humanity—like white folks can't process nappy hair—and it's time to help them raise the bar.

Kim has a friend whose daddy was in the Ku Klux Klan. A poster-sized picture of a finger-pointing Klansman adorned her living room wall. "I felt like Clarice Starling in 'The Silence of the Lambs' whenever I went over there," Kim says. "Like the first time she went to the jail and saw Hannibal Lecter."

The father didn't ask if Kim was part black. Kim didn't tell. She just sat on the edge of the couch with her hands and legs folded. "I kept praying, oh God, he's going to see something on me and know that I am mixed." So she stared straight ahead. And she sucked her lips in a reverse pucker the whole time she was there. Trying not to make herself too obvious, she says. Trying not to look black.

When she was in fifth grade, Kim's dad took her to a basketball game. And the bleachers went silent. Then they got whispery. Some folks already knew her dad was black. After that, everybody did.

"They used to tease me," Kim says with a shrug. She is reluctant to talk. So I press her, "Let's see, it went something like this, "Nigger-lips, nigger-lips, nigger-lips." Kim won't look at me.

The grandparents of one of Kim's friends didn't like black people. They didn't know about Kim's daddy. When the girls visited these folks, they weren't allowed to watch "The Cosby Show" because the grandfather didn't want a black man in his living room.

"I hate the N-word," Kim says. It is late. We've finished another installment of "Roots," and Kim is unsettled. Ready to talk. Tripping over her pent-up thoughts. "Whenever somebody said 'nigger' in class, everyone would turn around and look at me. I hate that word. I hate that the first thing they associate with that word is me."

When she was a freshman at Sandoval High, Kim wore a T-shirt with Martin Luther King Jr. on the front and Malcolm X on the back. "They all looked at me as if to say 'Oh, my God, she really isn't white.'" She grins when she says this.

Around 1993, Kim says she started getting into the "movement." Started watching "Yo! MTV Raps" and "The Cosby Show." Started being hungry for black culture.

She gave a civil rights speech to her sophomore English class. Her teacher thought it was a little angry. That summer, when my daughter Sydney was a baby, Kim came to D.C. We toured the White House and saw the first lady. But it was the Father's Day tribute at a friend's house where a group of us read proclamations and praised all the things we loved best about black men that got her. That let her know there was a different world than where she came from.

Her mother said she seemed different when she returned. Kim says she's always been different. In a town where everybody knows everybody and the social hierarchy is simple and uncolored, Kim is an anomaly.

"I've never technically fit in Sandoval," Kim says. "I've never had the small-town mentality. Then, after I moved out here, I thought maybe I do. Maybe I'm just a little bit country."

"I'm really trying to figure out who I am."

Some of that goes with 20-year-old territory. It's a no woman's land. Biologically grown, legally not quite, emotionally uneven. But Cousin Kim's 20 is more complex than most. She's never tried to deny the fact that her dad was black. But she has never had the resources or the tools to embrace that side of herself. She is provincial. Unexposed. Underdressed as a black girl. Searching.

On the phone or when she goes home to visit, Kim is still white. But in my house, she is a real root sister. Neither are affectations. It's just the way her cards fall. Kim is, I suppose, the ultimate insider. Privy to our private jokes. The ways we laugh at white people. And at each other. A black spy in her world. A white fly on the wall in mine. A study in duality.

We have also had some growing pains in my house. And I am quick to assign blame. Quick to play the race card.

Cousin Kim smokes. I am hard pressed to name anybody else who smokes. Especially anybody young and black. I want her to stop, and I make the questionable lead. "You need to leave that nasty white girl [expletive] alone," I tell her. Initially when I said it, Kim just looked at me meekly. Now, she gives me the finger.

Ours is a jocularity. Aided by silent code. Reinforced by a power imbalance.

Reverse racism, I suppose some would call it. I don't think so. I believe white folks would know if blacks were ever to really reverse racism. We call them countermeasures. Cousin Kim, I ask her, if you hate me because I am black and I hate you because you killed my babies, is that the same?

It is a rhetorical question. Because in my house, we do not hate. We merely understand that there are those who do. So we strive for balance. We try not to resort to negative campaigning. Sometimes we succeed. Occasionally we fail. But we always make the effort. Because fear leads to anger, anger leads to hate and hate leads to suffering. We do not need Yoda to tell us this. It is something people on the dark side have always known.

A couple of months ago, Katie Couric made me mad. I had to vent with Cousin Kim. For a week, the "Today" show devoted a segment to tracing family histories. And Couric's roots go back to Alabama. When cotton was king and the Courics were part of the ruling family.

You could buy fertile land cheap, the segment said. And the Courics did. The family prospered and included a Civil War governor and a member of Congress.

Couric toured the family cemetery and recounted the stories behind the headstones. Then she said, "Slaves lie in unmarked but well-tended graves nearby."

That was it. No acknowledgment that these "slaves" were people her family bought and sold. That some of them might be her kin. That no matter how smart or talented or hard-working she is, her privilege was codified, her head start generations long. That it came at the expense of somebody else's freedom. No mention of any attempt to trace those other lives to see how they fared. Maybe that would have been too much to hope for. But how about an expression of regret. A mea culpa. An "I'm sorry—wish you were here."

Genealogy is about "our simple stories, not forgotten," Couric said. Interesting choice of words. Black families have stories, too. Ones we don't forget. That get passed down to our kids.

My great-grandmother shot a white man who tried to rape her in Mississippi, and the family had to scatter. My grandmother's family, who hadn't been able to get in on that fertile-land-for-cheap deal, was dirt poor and although she was the only one of her people to finish high school, there was no money for college. At 17, my mother sat outside a Birmingham train station crying because they told her she was too colored for the white side and too white for the colored side. On a family vacation, we were turned away from an empty motel lot because the manager said there were no vacancies. In college, when I told a white journalism professor I wanted to work at The Washington Post, he said, "Doing what? Sweeping floors?"

Cousin Kim, I say. Which is better? The kindly massa or the sadistic overseer? And Kim doesn't answer. Neither, I tell her. They are the same. Two parts of a whole. Today, folks won't just walk up to you and call you "nigger lips." Well, they might, but mostly it is the benign racists who are killing me softly. They don't recognize themselves in the mirror. They didn't mean anything by it. They harbor no ill will. They just don't care enough to step outside their comfort zone.

I understand that proclivity. Often I share it. Most of us are too self-involved to dig up in the psychic pain of others. But when your family has owned slaves, indifference is a self-indulgence you forfeit.

More than 300 years of chattel slavery. 129 years of terrorism and de jure Jim Crow. Thirty-four years—one generation—of full legal enfranchisement. I don't know, seems a little corrupt for white folks to cry colorblind now. We go to the Race Place because these days, I find privileged indifference as culpable as malice aforethought. When you step on my toes, I may not retaliate in kind, but you must know that I will say ouch. Loudly. Such that it disturbs your peace. Then you say, "I'm sorry." Then help me heal. After that, we can all get along nicely.

Cousin Kim nods her head yes. I believe she really gets it this time. But perhaps that's just wishful thinking.

Cousin Kim and I have watched all six parts of Alex Haley's "Roots." And three parts of "Queen." Then we did an hour of WHMM's "Black Women on the Light Dark Thing." We have talked and we have shared. And still she is white. And I am as black as ever.

"We're lucky," the biracial woman Alice said in "Queen." We can choose. Who'd choose to be black? Black is hard. White is so much easier."

Still. I want my cousin to be black for me. For the little girl who ran from a rock thrown at her head. For all the niggers I have been. I want her to be black because I'm still afraid of casual monsters in white-girl clothes. Not because they might hurt me, but they might hurt my children. Not because they hate. But because they teach 5-year-old black girls to hate themselves. And black people of all ages to suck in their lips.

Cousin Kim still chooses white not only because she looks white, she says, but "because I was raised white," and because most white folks don't know the difference. Probably it is easier. Maybe to some people she is selling out—but I also know that is an option a lot of black folks would like to have.

If I'm honest myself, maybe I'm one of them. At least sometimes, if I think about my husband or brother getting stopped by the police for speeding. Or maybe at Tysons Corner, when tears burn my eyes as I watch a sales clerk wait on everybody but me. My anger is hot and righteous. But I'd give it up for a simple "May I help you?" any day.

Every day the world lets me know I'm black. And I wonder what it would feel like not to carry that, just for a while. Probably guilty. Probably relieved. Probably a lot like Cousin Kim.

There are no easy choices, but I think I understand my cousin's. Maybe I did all along. I just had to tell our story to realize it. But understanding and acceptance are not the same. Cousin Kim is white but conflicted, and I still sting with rejection. So alone together, we linger.

Race. The final frontier.

The Race Place isn't crossed in a day. You can't pass through it in the time it takes to watch a miniseries. We traverse the Race Place in fits and starts, inch by inch, over the course of a lifetime. Or maybe two. Sometimes our progress is steady. And sometimes we are dragged for miles back to the beginning, chained behind a pickup truck, and have to start all over.

The overarching reality is that realities overarch. And jockey for head space.

The extremes are easy to condemn, but the vast middle is where most of us live. Where we raise our families. And where we hope that life's lessons land a little softer on the behinds of our children than they did on our own.

A few days ago, Cousin Kim said she got into an argument with her ex-boyfriend over "The Wonderful World of Disney." The characters in the old cartoons are racists, Kim said. Look at the crows in "Dumbo." "I won the argument," she says. "He told me 'Kim, you think too much.'"

Cousin Kim smiled. And I smiled. Because this is what I want for her. To think. To challenge. To recognize. To get it. If she does that, then maybe she doesn't have to be black.

Still, I can't help giving her a silent "right on, little sister." You just take your time. We're family. And I'll be here to hip-you-up if you ever change your mind.

Taigi Smith

What Happens When Your 'Hood Is the Last Stop on the White Flight Express?

IT IS ALMOST THANKSGIVING IN NEW YORK CITY AND BETWEEN TRIPS ON THE D train and fifteen-hour workdays, I barely feel the autumn leaves crunch beneath my feet. My body shivers from the November chill, while my nose, red from windburn, runs uncontrollably. I find myself wishing for the comforts of home and smile because in a few days I will be in San Francisco, sitting at my mother's table, full of Thanksgiving sweet potatoes, pasta, and if I'm lucky, turkey. I laugh out loud because at forty-something, my mother is still unconventional and has yet to cook a traditional Thanksgiving dinner. She instead faithfully replaces the turkey with a simpler bird: cornish hen.

I cannot wait to see Harold, my wannabe stepfather, and tell him that for the first time in my life I was almost fired. I wonder if he will understand when I describe being verbally reprimanded last week by my boss, a white man, who blackballed me simply because I asked that he address me as an adult and not as a "kid." What will Harold's face say when I tell him that I was called "insubordinate" and "out of line" for expressing my views, and in the end, offered a demotion instead of dismissal? I am sure that he will bless me with his southern-spun, New Orleans-bred, project wisdom, imparting that type of insight that will make me laugh, cry, and get mad all at the same time just because his words will be so real, yet so emotionally disruptive. In the end, his words will cut deep and he will tell me that in their eyes I will never be a white girl, but always a nigger girl who must never, ever forget her place.

Will my mother, who, like me, spent several years in New York, recognize that at twenty-four years old, I have found myself bordering insanity and unsure of where the next year, let along my entire life, will lead me? Will she be able to see that working at a TV network has made me aggressive, competitive, and edgy, or will she be deceived by the nice clothes, make-believe smile, and pleasant demeanor? I am heading home, to the streets of the Mission, in search of my comfort zone, Shotwell Street, the place where the memories are good and the streets familiar. While I am home, I will visit Mi Rancho, the yellow *marqueta* on the corner of Twentieth and Shotwell owned by a local businessman named Jorge. In our neighborhood, Jorge was *el rico,* owning not only *una marqueta,* but a *taqueria* and, even better, a gold two-door Mercedes. Mi Rancho was the community hub, a place we shopped for last-minute needs like *leche, frijoles,* and Calistoga water. Jorge's prices were notoriously high and his vegetables rotten, but his breads and pastries were legendary in my neighborhood. They were sweet, flaky, and hands down the best in the Mission. It was in Mi Rancho that I was caught stealing for the first time. The shame of having to face Jorge every day after being caught with the pilfered chocolate bar may have saved me from a life of kleptomania. As expected, Jorge told my mother about my thieving ways and she in turn slapped the hell out of me in front of everyone in the store. That is a day I'll never forget.

I hope that Angel, the old man with the dark sunglasses, will be around to say hello. He always greets me like our meeting is a chance encounter, a gift from heaven. I remember when Angel and I first met. I was five and he'd left a cake for me in a big, pink box near my door. He was a skinny man who always wore a fresh-pressed, beige windbreaker and gave me a buck or two every now and then in exchange for my childish stories of adventure. He lived upstairs in an immaculate two-room studio all by himself and though he rarely spoke of family or received visitors, something very mystical was happening with Angel. He had a way of seeing things you thought he didn't see and knowing things you didn't tell him. He always remembered my birthday, fed Coco, the dirty, stray dog, and gave me knowing glances every time he caught me doing something I wasn't supposed to do. When he wasn't cleaning our building, he was looking out of his second-floor window, observing, and perhaps seeing those things we thought he didn't see. I'm sure I'm not the only person he caught doing wrong. Angel took twilight walks at 4:00 A.M., cruising the San Francisco red light district for young men. It was not until many years later that my mother told me of Angel's homosexuality and his walks on the wild side. My mother, a housekeeper, worked for doctors, and she told me Angel was gay after she referred him to a well-known urologist when a backed-up urethra damn near killed him. But at this moment, I only want to see Angel use his wrinkled hands to tell me I've grown and hug me like he always does. His whispery voice will scream "Ta—shi!!!" as he welcomes me, his long-lost daughter, home.

Perhaps it is the anticipation of going home that causes me to lose myself and flash back to better times, simpler times.

It was the summer of 1980 and I was a tall, skinny, eight-year-old girl with big feet and wild braids. We had gathered at out usual spot on 20th and Shotwell to shoot the breeze and amuse ourselves. Like so many other city kids, there was little for us to do on the long days of summer. We were the children of bus drivers, housekeepers, migrant workers, the unemployed and mentally ill. We lived together on this block of land in apartment buildings, surrounded by automotive shops, and single-family homes in the heart of the Mission, America's Latino pit stop for high hopes and big dreams. Some families had come seeking refuge from the bloody wars that ravaged El Salvador and Nicaragua during the 1980s, while others had immigrated toward *el Norte* to escape the desperation of Mexico's barrios. My mother, a twenty-four-year old single parent, found the Mission through a friend, and although she'd never admit it, Moms was a hippie seeking solace from the craziness of Haight-Ashbury, the legendary stomping ground of Wavy Gravy, the Grateful Dead, and reefer-toking flower children. Somehow, Moms had convinced Max, the Irish owner of the building, to rent her a small one-bedroom apartment in the Mexican neighborhood for less than $200 a month. My mother and I were one of a handful of black families in the neighborhood, so it was almost impossible not to notice us. As a four-year old, I only remember Max's frizzy gray hair, dingy overalls, hammer, and workmen's boots. He was an old man who lived in the basement of the limestone, three-story building, with a friendly face and pleasant demeanor. I only know that Max disappeared one day and my four-year-old memory doesn't remember saying good-bye. Soon after, a lesbian woman named Ramsey became our new landlord and I never saw Max again.

My building was shouting distance from the San Francisco Fire Department, and for years I listened to the sounds of the big red trucks speeding quickly down the streets of the barrio, racing to save homes, personal possessions, and, most importantly, life. From my window, I watched the firefighters go through their daily drills each morning at 6:00 A.M. They ran laps, did jumping jacks, and put out mock fires in an imaginary burning building. Every spring, rookie firefighters would clean up our block and plant saplings in barren patches of land. Today, those saplings are the full-grown trees that line Shotwell Street.

The Mission of the 1980s was a cultural mecca filled with music and dance. On the far corner of Twentieth and Shotwell was an old garage that had been transformed into a dance studio. For months on end, you could hear the sounds of Brazilian drums resonating from the walls of the once vacant garage. At night, women and men would emerge from the building salty with sweat, glistening, and exhausted. You could hear them chattering incessantly, in Spanish and English, about Carnaval, the Mission's answer to the legendary Rio de Janeiro event. Dancers would pack the dance studios that laced the Mission to practice the twenty-four-hour festival of samba, salsa, and steel drumming. It was during Carnaval that my neighborhood's women adorned themselves in fifty-foot high feathered headpieces and barely-there thong bikinis to parade up Mission Street twisting, gyrating, shimmying, and singing. It was during Carnaval that a woman could take off her bikini top and flaunt her breasts without embarrassment or inhibition during this wry celebration of femininity and woman-hood. It was not until I, at twelve, put on my own bikini and feathers and danced with the Brazilian troupe Batucajé that I realized the electricity generated when women of color come together as one to celebrate themselves as beautiful, cultural, and creative beings. It was here that we could dance, and sing, and sweat, and flaunt ourselves and our bodies like no other time during the year. This was *our* Carnaval.

I remember the rallies on Twenty-fourth and Mission and the sounds of political activists demanding freedom with the words "No More, No More, U.S. Out of El Sal-vador." These were the same activists who denounced the American-inflicted blood-shed in Nicaragua, and again, their banners of resistance waved when the American government found it necessary to invade Grenada. The activists were white, Latino, young, and old—most of all, they were loud and unrelenting. Their demands would be heard for miles around, and although it took years for the bloodshed to end, the activists never gave up. Instead, they found refuge on this little stretch of California land, and chose to fight the bloodshed in Central America instead of ignoring it. It was here, on Twenty-fourth Street, across from McDonald's and near the BART station, that political literature was handed out, like clockwork, every weekend. It was on this street that the rallies raged, every Saturday, until the violence died down. Who would have thought that again, almost twenty years later, these same people would still be fighting for freedom?

> *Why do I keep thinking about Duane, the Vietnam veteran who told me
> what it was like returning to the United States after the war? This country
> was a cold, foreign place. It was no longer home. Things had changed during
> his absence and Duane was now a pariah in his own country.*

I finally made it home and Thanksgiving was just a few days away. And while the warmth and familiarity of my mother's apartment endured, something strange had happened to the neighborhood. I'd only been away for about two years, but the Mis-sion I knew had somehow transformed itself into a place I found hard to navigate, let alone recognize. The number of brown faces in my neighborhood had diminished and I was trapped in an unfamiliar place filled with caucasoids and trendy bars. The most noticeable change was the "For Sale" sign on the Mi Rancho property that boldly announced that Jorge was closing his doors. The smells of *pasteles* had disappeared and sadly, Angel was nowhere to be found. I asked my mother about him, and she said he'd packed up in the dead of night, returning to Mexico and leaving nothing behind except the silence of his absence. Angel knew his departure would be painful, so he spared us the agony of having to say good-bye and instead vanished. But today I wonder if Angel was able to see the changes taking place in the neighborhood before any of us even sus-pected it. Did he see the white developers surveying our block and chose to pack up instead of being put out?

> *Gentrification: The displacement of poor people and people of color. The
> raising of rents and eradification of poor people from neighborhoods once*

considered unsavory. A money-driven process in which landowners and developers push people out of their homes without thinking about where they will go. Gentrification is a premeditated process in which an imaginary bleach is poured on a community and the only remaining color left in that community is white. Only the strong coloreds survive.

The word on the street was that the neighborhood was being taken over by white people and there was nothing that the people of color could do about it. People were being packed up and pushed out in record numbers to make way for yuppies and New Media professionals who would pay exorbitant rents to reside in what the *Utne Reader* called "One of the Trendiest Places to Live in America." The streets of the Mission were now lined with Land-Rovers and BMWs. Seedy neighborhood bars now had bouncers and were serving $10 raspberry martinis. Abandoned warehouses had not been converted into affordable housing, but instead into fancy lofts costing between $300,000 and $500,000 and not so ironically, the Army Street Projects had been demolished, leaving hundreds of people displaced and possibly homeless. Today, a barren piece of land surrounded by a fence sits where the projects used to be. The message was clear. It was time for the blacks and browns to get out. The whites were moving in and that was it.

For black, Latino, and poor people, "gentrification" is just another word this country uses to exploit its colored and disenfranchised. Ask the blacks being pushed out of Harlem about the meaning of "gentrification." Ask the Puerto Ricans of the Lower East Side where they will go when Alphabet City no longer contains the letters P and R. And where are young, African American artists and writers supposed to live now that the bohemian hot spot Fort Greene, Brooklyn, has become a haven for white professionals with rents starting at $900 per month for cramped, ramshackle studios? Whether you call it "gentrification" or "revitalization" the translation is simple: Whites Only. In the end, we're only asking to be left alone in the communities we've worked so hard to create. Is it really too much to ask for a place called "home"?

Although my building in San Francisco had been spared from the claws of wealthy land bandits, it had mutated into a cultural war zone, spurred on by economic and racial disparities. In fact, the entire community had became a war zone where guerrilla tactics were the weapons of choice. Someone was posting up signs all over the neighborhood urging people to deface the live/work lofts, scrape up the fancy, high-priced vehicles that filled their streets, and flatten yuppie tires. This vigilante had become a sort of folk hero in the neighborhood and his signs were part of an underground movement called "The Urban Yuppie Eradication Project." His posters urged his fellow Missionites to burn down the million-dollar lofts and make life hell for the new pioneers. In defense, the yuppies held their own rally, interestingly enough, on the corner of Twenty-fourth and Mission, the home of the infamous political protests of the 80s. Although the local media came out for the event, only a few yuppies were brave enough to show up. My mother had formed a sort of guerrilla coalition within her own building. Evidently, the new whites living there were trying to take over and eventually wanted to fill the place with filmmakers, writers, and other artist types. They were communicating via e-mail with the building manager to secure new vacancies for their people, and while the plan almost worked, they failed to fully homogenize the building.

It was these same people who viewed me with suspicion when I returned to Shotwell Street. Their icy glares easily translated into "What are *you* doing here?" I'd been gone for almost two years and none of these people knew me, and so they naturally became suspicious of the black girl "loitering" around the building. It really didn't matter that I'd spent almost twenty years of my life there. To them, I was another brown face that they were working to get rid of.

Perhaps it is the sense of loss I feel that causes me to lose myself and flash back to better times, simpler times.

I was sulking in a corner and pouring my heart out to Marcy, my next-door neighbor, because for the third day in a row Jimmy and J.J. were calling me Medusa, and pulling the long, scraggly braids that my mother forced me to wear until I was thirteen years old. They'd spent the days tormenting me about my outdated clothes and the blue Holly Hobbie lunch box my mother made me carry to school every day. The truth is, we spent almost everyday "cappin'" on each other—this meant that we found new and ingenious ways to make fun of each other's mommas, sneakers, hair, bikes, torn-up apartments, and anything else that could be dissected and put under the microscope of ridicule. Like so many other days, me, J.J., Jubie, Jimmy, Nateena, Marcy, Maria, Robert Jr., Joe, Jerry, Greg, Damon, Darryl, and Sharon were hanging on the steps of 567 Shotwell listening to N.W.A. and Eazy-E on a broke-down piece of radio. For a while, we became a breakdancing crew. The guys would do the breakin' and the girls would stand on the sidelines doing the uprock. And then we became a bike-racing clique, racing our BMX's up and down Capp, Folsom, South Van Ness, and Harrison like madmen. I was a tomboy and got my Huffy at Toys 'R Us for my birthday, and in typical Shotwell fashion, my new bike became the butt of jokes for weeks. None of the other kids on the block could get past the fact that my dirt bike had a long, black, banana seat. And when the ridicule was over, neither could I. For months, my mother yelled at me because I never rode the bike that she'd worked so hard to buy, but I chose her screams over the torment of my peers. And then we became a skateboarding crew and would skate up and down Shotwell, oftentimes injuring ourselves and breaking an arm or two in the process. My skateboard was destroyed when I jumped off while racing down a hill. The board went crashing into the street and was crushed in half by a car. Defeated, I walked home with half of a skateboard in each hand. Again, my Shotwell buddies were there to receive me as I walked toward the 567 building with tears streaming down my face. Fortunately, it was my "cheap" skateboard that was the target of ridicule this time and not me.

Jerry was a big, chunky boy with a mop of black hair. He, like all the other boys, made it a point to terrorize me whenever possible. I'll never forget the day he threw a match at me and burned a hole in my purple Danskin bodysuit. My mother would have told his mother, except we all knew that there was something different about Jerry's mother. His mom never said much. She simply spent her days looking out of the window, and would occasionally yell from her fourth-floor apartment to no one in particular. She came outside once in the twenty years I lived on Shotwell, spending most of her time watching life pass by from the peach-colored apartment structure across the street from my house. She'd watch from that window for days on end, looking sickly, demented, and old. Her hair, like Jerry's, was black and wild, but it contained streaks of gray. She was mysterious and scary—witchlike, to say the least. It was not until some years later, after she died a mysterious death, that I learned that Jerry's mother was mentally ill. She suffered from some type of dementia caused by the strange mix of alcohol and depression. Perhaps it was the pain of watching her husband walk up and down Shotwell Street in a drunken haze day after day that finally did her in.

Reality brings me back to the present and forces me to look at the situation at hand. I am old enough to realize that things can no longer be taken at face value.

I needed so badly to say "This is my neighborhood, I grew up here," but my anger silenced me. The stares had as much to do with the Ford Explorer I was driving, the clothes I was wearing, and the Mills College degree I carried as they did with the color of my skin. I'd been in New York long enough to realize that there really wasn't a thriving black community in San Francisco. Back East, my closest friends drove Benzes and Suburbans. We lived well, but worked hard. We vacationed in Martha's Vineyard, Miami, Negril, and Belize and were on the cusp of becoming the next generation of leaders. Erica was the creative director for John Singleton and Tony headed up a multi-million-dollar clothing company. Fred was a successful Avid editor who made close to $150,000 a year and Courtney was in charge of video promotions for Sony Music. I had managed to become a freelance writer and a producer for a major television network. Many of us had started our own businesses. We'd become lawyers and music-industry moguls who were making power moves and big money. It was the ignorance of these new age yuppies that annoyed me more than anything else. There was no way that they'd ever respect me as a black woman because they were not used to dealing with black people in positions of power, let alone a little black girl hanging around the Mission driving a Ford Explorer. In their eyes, I was an impostor, some strange breed of black person they just didn't understand. What they didn't know was that not only had I come from the Mission, but I was smart enough to realize that there was something fundamentally wrong with the way they were using money and power to take away land that never belonged to them in the first place. Historically, California was the home of the Indians, the Aztecs and Mayas. This was Latino land and they were taking over Latino soil—again.

It is the evil that prowls behind the martini bars, lofts, and hipster sushi spots that scares me. More than the air of wealth that permeates the neighborhood, it is the air of superiority that angers me. It is the look of hate I receive when I go home that aggravates me. It is the look that says "We are willing to take over this neighborhood at all costs" that leaves me wondering about the future of my friends and neighbors. It is the realization that people of color have never—and will never—have a place to truly call our own. I have thought about returning home to organize my fellow Missionites, but doing so would mean giving up the life I've worked so hard to create in New York and I am not willing to make that sacrifice. At times I become resentful because, secretly, I wish my mother and her neighbors would more aggressively organize themselves to save the neighborhood. I am angry because from a distance I am watching my neighborhood slip from their grasps in a way that is quick and painful, and there is nothing that I can really do about it from so far away. What disturbs me most of all is that this whitening of the Mission has taken place under the thumb of a fellow African American, slick mayor Willie Brown. If you cannot trust a black mayor to have the best interests of people of color at hand, who can you trust?

As my mother's only child, it is my responsibility to make sure that she will continually have a place to live, whether that place be in San Francisco or elsewhere. But what is to become of all the other mothers and grandmothers in the Mission whose children have neither the income nor sensibility to realize that their parents' well-being is in their hands? I've often wondered where they expect us, black and brown people, to go when the entire nation falls to the mighty reign of gentrification. It is as if the developers and people in power are trying to push us off the ends of the earth. If the earth were flat, instead of round, would black and brown people find themselves pushed over the edge in a literal way? I imagine a world in which we are lined up, with our belongings, household items and such, and told that in America, there is no longer room for people like us—poor and working-class people. In these nightmares I have, my mother is searching not only for a new apartment, but for a new planet called home. This is the bleaching of America, the nationwide phenomenon where people who look like me are pushed to the outer boroughs, the unsavory places where no one, black or white, wants to live. It is a modern theory embraced only by those who are fortunate enough to afford the sky-high rents, luxury apartments, and loftlike living.

It is here that it becomes difficult to write this essay. I am facing my own hypocrisy and I am torn.

It is 1999 and I pay well over $1000 a month to live in a Brooklyn community where the amenities include a twenty-four-hour liquor store, a marijuana delivery service, illegal all-night gambling, and numerous buildings for Section 8 families and people on welfare. I live in one of several buildings earmarked for upwardly mobile professionals—and white people. Throughout the neighborhood, signs of "revitalization" are cropping up. There are the white kids walking smugly down the street, sometimes riding rickety bikes or skateboards. Internet businesses are opening up alongside dance studios and I, for one, have a fully renovated apartment with brand-new appliances and superfast, T-1 Internet access. I am on the cusp of this revitalization, and while I have an amazing apartment in the midst of the 'hood, I am more than conscious of the fact that those around me may not be here for long, I am sure they look at me and all the other professionals moving in and wonder "What are *they* doing here?" Do my low-income neighbors realize that the new buildings being put up like wildfire are not for people like them, but for people like me, who can afford to pay inflated rents for renovated apartments in the 'hood? The people who live in my area probably don't see the change that is forthcoming, and, in the end, it will be they who will suffer from the effects of gentrification this time and not I. It is when I come home at night and see the brothas hustling across the street and listening to music all night long that I realize that I may have switched sides in this fight over land. It is when I call the police because I'm not trying to hear Biggie or Puffy at 3 A.M. in the morning that I realize that "they" really don't want "us" here and they'll do everything to keep "us" out. I cringe when I hear people yelling outside of windows and when I see young women fighting with their "baby daddies." But that's life in this 'hood, and 'hoods everywhere, so at this point it is me who must adapt and not them. If you accused me of being a hypocrite, I'd painfully agree with you, because at this juncture, I am clearly on the other side. At this moment, I am the bad guy.

> *Picture this. I am drinking Chai Lattes at Starbucks on Washington Ave. I don't look at the people who view me with suspicion. I ignore them and instead continue talking on my cell phone. I say to myself "What are these people doing here?" and breathe a sigh of relief as I watch the bulldozers tear down what used to be the brick Section 8 building on Prospect Place. Will this be me in five years?*

I am fighting with myself at this moment because I don't want them to take over my San Francisco neighborhood, but three thousand miles away, in another state, and another community, I am "on the front lines of gentrification," as a neighbor so politely put it just a few days ago. I am struggling to deal with my own class issues and realize that while my mother still cleans houses, I am a thriving member of the middle class. I feel proud and guilty at the same time and not really sure where my future will take me, both as an individual and as a human being. I have worked hard for every-thing that I have and feel no need to save anyone who has not been as fortunate as I but, at the same time, I realize that while I have managed to achieve a level of profes-sional success, others have not been as fortunate as I.

> *It is too hard to talk about my own hypocrisy. I constantly remind myself that this is a story about where I've been. It frightens me to think about where I might be going.*

In the Mission, these days called The Mission Deluxe, I lived neck and neck with Mexicans, El Salvadorans, Cubans, Filipinos, whites, gays, artists, blacks, heroin addicts, prostitutes, cholos, street vendors, dancers, and migrant workers. It is here that I rode roller skates with metal wheels, learned to speak Spanish, and fell in love with Curtis, my forbidden soulmate. It is in that building on Shotwell Street that Curtis secretly left letters stashed near the fire extinguisher that professed his undying love for me. Was Angel, the old man upstairs, watching? I remember when most white people were either too scared or too good to venture into the Mission unless they were look-ing for cheap drugs or cheap sex. There was a time when silent gangsters roamed the streets clad in Ben Davis jeans, Dickies, and Sir Jackets. They claimed gangs like HHG (the Twentieth Street Happy Home Boys), XIII (Trece), and LTM (Little Time Mission Gangsters) and drove souped-up Impalas and Caddys that bounced up and down to a hydraulic beat. The sounds of "oldies" could be heard for blocks around as these men cruised up and down Mission Street wearing red bandanas, dark sunglasses, and sex appeal like a second skin. Perhaps it was the threat of these silent gangsters that kept the yuppies away, for everyone knew that the men of the Mission protected their own and killed if necessary. That's just the way it was. Whatever the cause of their absence, I find myself wishing for the days of old. For us, the inhabitants of the Mission, this place was more than somewhere to buy expensive coffee and million-dollar lofts. It was where we laid our roots, memories, and bloodlines. For some, it would be a final resting place, but that is all gone now. I fear that it is only a matter of time before the building I grew up in is sold and converted into condominiums, or loft spaces.

Once again I find myself flashing back. This time the memory is not so pleasant—I find myself in direct confrontation with myself.

It is 1984 and I am on my way to school on a misty, cool San Francisco morning. I walk alone because all of my friends attend another school—I am in a program for gifted students at Everett. It is almost 8:00 A.M. and I am carrying both my army green backpack and the blue Holly Hobbie lunchbox I hate so much. And I pass them like I do most mornings. They are the drunk men who are sprawled outside of that bar on Nineteenth and South Van Ness. These are not derelicts, but fixtures in my community, men who cherish the smooth, hard tastes of Night Train and Thunderbird wine. At twelve, I am too young to judge and instead stare at them and imagine what dreams must hop through their heads. Sometimes one of them will awake and sing a Mexican ballad, shaking the others from their alcohol-induced stupor. But today the men are silent; they are draped over one another and snoring. The other migrant workers have left for the orchards, but these men are too tired and too hung over to search for work; and so they sleep on that corner, as they do most days after a good night of drinking. The bar, a second home to them, is discreet with heavy black doors and tinted windows. Because I am too young to know the value of a good drink, I continue on to school—perhaps I will learn something new today. When I return home, the bar will be shut tight, and like most days, the sleepy old men with names like Miguel, and Rafael, and Jaime will be gone.

For years, the sounds of laughter, Latin guitars, and the wailing voices of *mariachis* could be heard drifting through the cracks of that neighborhood dive. An occasional knife fight or barroom brawl was to be expected behind the doors of this nameless place. Tequila, *Negro Modelo,* and Night Train were the drinks of choice and it was here that one could slam a shot for a buck twenty-five. Fast forward. It is 1998. I am sipping chocolate martinis in what was once an immigrants' watering hole. A jukebox replaces the *mariachis* and top shelf liquor takes the place of Night Train. On this evening, Ron and I are talking and he's trying to convince me to marry him. I'm thinking that I haven't seen this guy in years and he's obviously a bit tipsy, but I thank him for his compliments, order another chocolate martini, and think for a second about my boyfriend back home. And then I see him. He is a short man, only a few inches above five feet and wearing dirty gray pants and a button-down shirt. His eyes are red and glazed over and he's barely able to stand. He sings a song and I recognize the accent—it is from Juarez or Tijuana. He jibbers something profane in Spanish and appears to be confused by the sea of white faces (and me!). The jukebox is playing a song by the latest alternative rock group and I'm waiting impatiently to get my twenty-five cents' worth of old school Dr. Dre. And as Juan, or José, or Ramon, or Jorge searches the room for his *compadres,* it becomes evident that this place he'd once known so well is now as foreign as this country. He blinks his eyes a few times and tries to shake himself from this drunken haze, but soon realizes that what he's seeing is no illusion, but reality. He stares silently at the blond woman with the multiple tattoos and pierced lip and wonders where his friends might be. He has never seen white people in this bar and it's obvious that he's lost—confused, to say the very least. As he looks at her, I stare at him and relate, if only for a second, to his longing for days gone by. And then he turns from her and looks at me as if to say "What are you, *una negrita,* doing here with *todos los gringoes?*" In that space we lock eyes and I allow him to see my shame while I share his sadness. My *ojos* tell him that I too am disconnected, lost in a place I knew so well. Like the old man looking for a drink, I am saddened, disillusioned, and disgusted by the change in scenery, and, like him, I also feel powerless. He glances around a bit more, struggles to his feet, curses a few words in *Espanol,* throws down his tequila, closes his eyes as if to say *Adiós por un tiempo último,* and stumbles out of the door.

Texaco

Natasha Tarpley

The skin of children, hugging tightly rib cages and collar bones, rounding to elbows and knees, secures them in their notions of speed, of agelessness, of flight. We will always run this way, hitting and breaking the wind with our fists. And we will always be smooth, our faces do not crumble, our spines will never bend us toward the ground. Someday we will grow wings from our arms and shoulders, someday when we are angels.

Summer dusk passed to dark. Our upturned faces watched the sun, a faded pink Red Hot someone sucked all the sticky crimson heat off of, descend on us like a blessing. Those nights, Mom and Daddy let us stay out even after the sky had called in all of its colors; had turned itself the deep purple of windows like the closed eyes of a sleeping house.

We preyed on a different light: the yellowish green or white sparks of lightning bugs. Waited breathless for the first sudden twinkle that signified the beginning of the chase. With one hand clasping an empty pickle jar, the other fishing the air, we ran after the lightning bugs' sporadic flickering. Those nights nothing seemed beyond our reach. Life was just another thing to hold in our sweaty palms, to collect in empty jars and containers with lids screwed on so tightly, not even air could escape.

In the afternoon after school, two or three times a week, my sister and brother and I made the trek from our house up to the Texaco station to replenish our candy supply. For some reason, the Texaco station was the only place our parents would let us walk without them, although it was just as far away—three or four long blocks—as anyplace else we might have imagined walking, and we had to cross a busy street to get there. We didn't argue the point.

At the Texaco, we made our selections from rows of clear plastic and glass containers full of penny and five cent candies—PAL penny gum, Now and Laters, pronounced Nowlaters or Nowalaters, Lemonheads and wine candy, also known as Jolly Ranchers—lining the shelves behind a thick sheet of foggy bulletproof glass, which ran the length of the counter.

There was no glass when we first started coming here. We could rest our hands on the counter and watch the man count out our purchases, even reach into one of the containers ourselves if we got bold. There was a "mini-mart," one of the first combo gas station/convenience stores in our area, that you could walk around in. Mom or Daddy sometimes sent us there to buy something they needed for that night's dinner, or an item they had forgotten to get in the "real" store. You could squeeze the loaves of bread and choose the softest; hold cans of pop from the cooler against your cheek to find the coldest.

That was in the late seventies, soon after my youngest sister was born and my parents sold our house on 91st and Michigan to buy the two-flat building on 68th and Chappel. By 1981, the entire area behind the counter had been sealed off by an impenetrable wall of glass. We crowded into the narrow rectangular area between the counter and the entrance, joining the single-file line, snaking all the way to the rear wall and then doubling back on itself, of people waiting to place gas and cigarette orders at the window up front.

The door leading to the mini-mart had been soldered shut, although the market was still open. The cashier would yell out whatever it was you wanted and someone else behind the counter would run into the mini-mart area to get it. If what you bought was too big to fit through the revolving window at the register, someone would bring it around for you. You could no longer touch the thing you wanted until you paid for it, and even then, you had to take whatever they gave you.

To get to the Texaco station, we took the back way, through the alley, pushing into the territory of the big boys. Boys who were rumored to belong to the much feared (and revered) Disciples gang, stories of whose escapades permeated our insulated neighborhood of middle class black families. Boys who slithered into our yard, past our fence, past my parents' hopes that private schools, a relatively stable family and money would be enough to keep them out.

They came to steal the sour green apples that grew on the tree in our backyard, and once, all of our bikes from our basement. Big boys you couldn't help but love for their badness, the rudeness of their walk. Big boys, bad boys, invincible, infinite, despite our best weapons against them. One time, we concocted a poison in our garage, made from paint, mud, glue, water and worms, and injected it into apples strategically placed in the crux of the tree's thick limbs, and on the window sill of the garage facing the alley. None of the big boys ever took the bait.

When the poisoned apples didn't work, our next line of defense was our parents. Once Mom actually spanked one of the boys who had come into the yard and called her a bitch when she asked him to leave. This was a time before bullets would be fired quicker than words; a time when adults didn't fear children as enemies. After the spanking, Mom invited the boy, who was around eleven or twelve, to come over and play in the yard some time. He seemed to consider the invitation for a moment, standing there, scrawny, snot-nosed and puffy-eyed, at the edge of our yard. But his eyes rapidly glazed over, his lips curling into a defiant scowl, as he mumbled something about coming back to kick all of our asses, before turning and stepping back into the alley. I saw a big boy cry that day; the way he didn't run away when Mom released him, how his gaze lingered. I remember his face when I see the faces of other big boys flashing across the screen on the evening news, flickering past me on the street. And I wonder if maybe their eyes aren't really the stones everyone says they are, but really are more like eggshells, a yolk of uncried tears swimming around inside.

Those Texaco afternoons, walking through the alley gave us some of the big boys' badness—before we discovered our own. It was the place where we tested speed and boundaries, leaning against the one thing certain in our lives: We were always close to home.

One afternoon, after we had made the trek, and were sitting on the sun-warmed sidewalk in front of our house, counting and separating our candy into small mounds on our laps, our friend Darryl—whom we called Egghead Darryl, because of the extreme oval shape of his head—walked up to the fringes of our circle to give us some news. Darryl lived across the alley with his grandfather in the three-flat building behind our house. He had come to report that there had been three murders in the apartment above his last night.

"Y'all seen the news today?" he asked us, arms crossed, chest puffed out slightly with the importance of his story. We shook our heads, no. A whole family had been "wiped out," he said matter-of-factly, stabbed to death while they slept. We knew them. We saw the mother, a black woman, and the father, a white minister, all the time cleaning behind their building, unpacking groceries from their car, calling for their kids. We had played with the children, a girl named Rhonda, who was around my age, nine or ten, and her brother, Steven, who couldn't have been more than five. They weren't part of the group of kids we hung out with from the neighborhood. They almost never played piggy or running bases with us in our driveway. They never rode their bikes up and down the block. But we knew them.

As Darryl told it, the father's son from a previous marriage, who was white and crazy, hated his father for marrying a black woman. So he broke into their apartment and stabbed everybody inside. Rhonda, who was away at camp, was the only one who survived. Imagine going away for a week and coming home to find your entire family gone, never coming back. Imagine being the only one left.

After that day, we didn't walk up to the Texaco nearly as often. And when death boldly stepped out of the alley and entered our house, taking our father two summers later, we stopped going altogether. We went inside, most days before the sun had set all the way. Nobody waited for dark. We watched the lightning bugs sometimes, as they shimmered up to our windows. But too soon, even that light dimmed and faded away. We turned instead to the steady blue stream emanating from the television, the light that could survive encased in glass, the faces we knew would still be there smiling and alive the next morning.

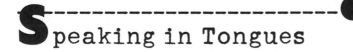

Speaking in Tongues

Touré

MAGNIFIQUE! SUMMER À PARIS AVEC UN APPARTEMENT ALL TO MYSELF IN THE 10th arrondissement. No host family, no youth hostel. I would magically learn francais via the world-famous méthode immersion! I would venture beyond the touristy parts and see the real City of Light! I would have the time of my life! Before setting off into my first Parisian night alone, the friend who had lent me her place told me, in richly accented English: "Chéri, in Paris there's not guns, but there's a war of attitude. If you are too nice, they run you over." I laughed. I'm from Crooklyn. Who gon' mess wit me?

On the métro a woman with Janet Jackson braids and three friends in tow asked me, "Avez-vous une cigarette?" and moments later she and I were sitting down at a café on the Place de la Bastille for a drink. Her friends, a girl and two young men, sat at the closest possible neighboring table. Janet pointed to them. "Tu les invites?" Can they join us? Sure. Two rounds later the bill arrived: 450 francs, about $75. Everyone looked at me. I learned the hard way that "inviter" also meant to pay for.

After a moonlight walk through le Quartier Latin, everyone—Janet and her sister, her sister's too-quiet boyfriend and his cousin, a tall, lanky wannabe rapper sporting a Kangol cap—ended up at my place. The only English they knew were Snoop Doggy Dogg lyrics, so I had to struggle along in French, exhausting myself to complete basic sentences. They taught me some new words—doudoune (bubble jacket), défoncer (to get high)—and street slang, which inverted syllables of words so that appartement became tementappart and garetteci meant cigarette. French conversation flowed past me, but each sentence I comprehended and each one I painstakingly constructed was empowering. I felt like an infant wobbling free of Mom, gaining confidence from the smallest footsteps.

Around 2 A.M. I felt a yawn coming on. I asked my new friends if I could see them tomorrow. But they didn't want to leave. It's too late to be on the street, they insisted. Besides, they said, Janet's only 16. If she were caught out after midnight they'd all be detained by the police. Why can't we stay here? they asked. I wanted to be nice—what could be the harm?—but Janet had initially said she was 20. Had she lied before, or was she lying now? And once I was asleep among four strangers in a house I was responsible for, anything could happen. I demanded they leave. So they lay down— two on my couch, two in my bed.

It was as though I wasn't there. I began walking around yelling: "C'est chez qui?! C'est chez qui?!" To which they'd say, "Chez vous," and then lie back down. First 3 o'clock, then 4 o'clock came and went while they dozed or spoke to one another in a rapid stream, sometimes clearly about me, gesturing at me as I stood a few feet away, refusing to slow down for me. At one point Janet's sister started screaming at me. I grabbed bits of her tirade—"Tu m'énerves!"—and somehow knew she was saying, "You're annoying me!" Incroyable.

French words whirled around the room like Hitchcockian birds. I felt erased from the world—and, with no ability to express myself, I was. Whom could I turn to for help? Most likely, my neighbors spoke no English. And if I called the police and they too spoke no English, I would be paralyzed. Language is symbolic action and I could do nothing. The man I was in Brooklyn, as quick and agile with words as an athlete is with his body, was gone, replaced by a tongue-tied oaf. Language, I felt then, is a place, a geographical region, and if you don't know the terrain your access is restricted. Masters of French, Janet and her friends walked freely in a mental country where I could only toddle on the border. I felt as though I wasn't in the room with them, and, in a sense, I wasn't.

I had to make myself matter. I had to outfox them. I grabbed the phone and dialed in a blur. I roared into the receiver what was happening to me. English spitting out so fast the words tripped over one another—*these kids won't even pay attention to me!* After a minute I hung up.

Janet and her gang regarded me with new eyes. Now that English counted for something, I did too. "Tu as telephoné qui?!" she asked. I wouldn't tell her whom I had called. They became nervous. And I became visible. I was part of the world again. The sun began peeking through the window and the smell of fresh-baked croissants from the boulangerie below wafted into the apartment, and the four gathered their things and made their way out. They never guessed I'd spoken to no one.

Your Friendly Neighborhood Jungle

Daniel J. Wideman

THE FIRST STORY I REMEMBER WRITING COINCIDES WITH MY EARLIEST memory of Africa. It was a collaborative project, "The Adventures of Obi," which my father, my brother, and myself worked on for a few weeks in the cave-like basement of the house on Harney Street. The basement was where my father's study was in those days—I remember it being dark, from the cherrywood paneling and the lack of light underground; and I also remember it being strictly off limits at all other times—the kids had to stay out of Dad's hair so he could work.

Dad did the illustrations. Pencil sketches of village scenes, imagined African rivers, voluminous stores of weaponry of all kinds (universal young boys' obsession demanding these images, I'm sure). I was so impressed by his drawing ability, none of which I managed to inherit. I can't recall precisely our "artistic process"; but if I had to guess I would say that he'd sketch a scene, then Jake and I would describe what we saw in it, Dad patiently transcribing our fanciful narratives. It's interesting to me that I think back on this project as play, though of course my father intended some sort of edification to be part of it. He is the one who introduced the name Obi—Igbo for chief—for our chief protagonist. Through memory's haze I can't say for sure but I certainly don't recall him stressing the "African men are all kings and princes" motif; nevertheless the concept of our nobility was planted. Embedded in the language we would one day excavate and understand, he must have imagined this. My father knew the journey to self-esteem begins and ends with language, with the words you carry in your head. Identity is always more about what you tell yourself than what you profess to others.

So as we sketched and scribbled in the basement, Obi was just a boy in a loincloth, and neither African boyhood nor the loincloth were yet loaded symbols to us. A boy traipsing around our imaginations in the fictionalized/fantasized African landscape we invented for him. Obi was a game we played, like tag, existing only on the precious few days we were permitted entry into Dad's inner sanctum. Transforming and transcending his space; not knowing, as I do now, that a writer's study can be prison and dungeon, desolate cave as well as comforting cradle and creative incubator. Regardless of where it is, a study is always subterranean. Always dark territory, where the only religion practiced is the science of maieutics. Space where the subconscious and the conscious struggle to meet, where they grapple and what emerges is sometimes intact; often scarred beyond recognition though in most stories scarring is a good and exciting, even a necessary outcome.

Remembering studies and stories today; sitting here in my new study in North Carolina—is it a coincidence I picked the highest point in the house? The room is perched atop our home and has a big, bright west-facing window that lets in lots of southern sunshine and a gorgeous view of the stand of loblolly pines across the street. Trees tall, erect, and slender as pens; in the dark their silhouettes are so many feathered quills, the ground a vast inkwell, the stars above just so many luminous dots on the i's in the story the tree-pens would write across the blank slate of the nightsky; the story they would write if a Hand strong enough to pluck them up, quiet enough to listen to their whispers, brave enough to set them down might dare to do so.

I remember the sense of mystery, connection and exhilaration swirling through the room as we put our "Obi" book together. A feeling of emboldened giddiness that looking back now I am able to identify as the seeds of empowerment only because I've watched the same look pass across the faces of the teenagers in my black history classes. The awakening evidenced in a physical straightening, a literal rejuvenation of carriage.

This retelling of those times is a masala of memory, conjecture, fanciful hopes and revised and revisited sensibilities. A story. A path to the past I follow unswervingly until one of any number of encumbrances announces itself. I have a choice then. Stop at this particular layer of excavation, shelve the shovels and engrid the evidence; or push on. I can either allow the narrative to flare and vanish, to bravely peter out like a match swallowing itself to prolong the light; or I can keep talking, re-remember, leave the path in search of new fuel to fan the flame.

I remember the emotions triggered by the act of invention much more clearly than I can recall specific words or the shape of a plot. I remember the electric ambience in the room, though I've forgotten the particular contours of the African epic we dreamed up together. I vividly remember an experience I can only describe as detached propinquity; the moment many writers describe as the point the story "took on a life of its own." The characters you had to labor so diligently to prop up suddenly arise on their own and miraculously take a few tentative steps by themselves. The narrative a balloon you've struggled to inflate; a balloon frustratingly tethered and inert; each day an exercise in the increasingly implausible; hoping your hot breath can become helium; one day gaping as the balloon does a dance, magically shuffles off its moorings and floats away. Leaves you anchored to terra firma, but carries your last whisper aloft, the final wish you desperately exhaled now the lifeblood of the story. You become a spectator, delighted and surprised by each shift in the story's course; while at the same time you are as close as the wind; have in fact *become* the gentle, imperceptible yet insistent breeze beneath its wings.

Obi was many people at once. He quickly became hero and alter-ego to my brother and me. Trapped in the desiccated plains, buried in the barren, frigid netherzones of Wyoming winters we appropriated the geography of Obi's Igbo village. Seen through his/our new eyes, a new universe burgeoned in our backyard. Rocky Mountain cottonwoods sprouted thick tropical vines which concealed all manner of menacing African fauna. Like children everywhere, we invented and colonized a new world in one or two languid afternoons. Obi was guide and imaginary playmate, comrade-in-arms and braver, stronger self.

For my father, the story was a bridge to the Africa he knew we would not learn about in school. A carefully constructed counter-image he used as a foundation to lead us into a deeper awareness of our history. Achebe was *his* guide, he'd recently been beguiled by *Things Fall Apart* and in fact would pass that magical novel on to me and make sure it was one of the first "grown-up" books I ever read. Our father was a rising black artist and intellectual teaching at an overwhelmingly white university; raising a multiracial family in a tiny, arch-conservative, ranching outpost in a state with more cattle than people. Although we were young and oblivious to the social turbulence, the professional struggles and private conflicts bedeviling our father, signs of his distress and frustration would erupt in occasional frightening flashes that jostled and dislodged our sense of order. I remember, in particular, his ranting tirades against two TV programs my brother and I couldn't get enough of.

We were, like almost all American kids who had a TV in the 1970s, Tarzan fanatics. The reruns of the Johnny Weismuller originals as well as the plethora of updates and spinoffs— *Tarzan and Jane, Cheetah, Tarzan's Tales*—I can't even recall all the titles, they were myriad and omnipresent. Most weekdays after school, if you flipped the channels with enough patience and aplomb you could catch at least one show featuring if not Tarzan himself than an equivalent king-of-the-jungle-themed episode. And Saturdays were an all day buzz for the Tarzan addict. Right alongside the Looney Toons in the morning, one click over from *Wide World of Sports* and movie "classics" all afternoon. Johnny and his bone-pierced buddies, his savage sycophants, swung from vine to vine, hour after hour.

We loved nothing more than echoing the signature guttural roar which commenced each episode: that trademark quasi-feline, not-quite-human, pied-piper-of-the-Nile, Southern (as in south of the Equator) Rebel Yell.

My father would hear our pitiful, prepubescent jungle squalls and come running. "Turn that shit off." But it was always more joke than command. Most often he'd join us in front of the set and we'd grin and beat our chests and jump around the room looking for all the world much more like Cheetah the chimp's cousins than our brave archhero. Meanwhile my father would ridicule and degrade the "skinny, pale cracker" on the screen, set up a steady stream of invective, a paean of disgust. Jutting his jaw and lumbering around exaggerating Tarzan's pseudo-Native jungle mumble: "Me Tarzan. Me dumb. Me shit in woods. Me got African spear up me white ass."

We would answer by scolding him "Da-ad!," pronouncing his name in two syllables, in the singsong way kids employ to convey the horrible embarrassment inflicted by a goofy parent.

"Tarzan doesn't talk like *that*."

At the same time, unable to watch his shenanigans and simultaneously keep the hints of smiles from colonizing the carefully tightened corners of our mock frowns, we understood at some level that Tarzan did, in fact, speak *just* that way. That Dad sounded ridiculous and funny and ignorant when he talked like that precisely because he sounded just like Tarzan. His mimicry and the tacit commentary embedded within it meant we quickly came to associate the monkey babble, the grunts and oonga-boonga talk with the silly white man in the loincloth. Though the Africans in these shows were depicted as Sambo savages, and spoke the same nonsense language, somehow they never sounded quite as cartoonish as Tarzan to our ears. Dad never lampooned the natives, or rather, when he did it was never with the same intensity, the same pointed focus.

His consistent presence while we watched the Tarzan shows, along with the nonstop satire and subtextual narrations, the endless interruptions, ensured we never took the King-of-the-Jungle too seriously. We never allied or affiliated ourselves too closely with him for fear of falling within the compass of Dad's barbs and verbal assaults. We forged a form of silent compromise—Dad would tolerate our obsession, allow us to watch our favorite program, as long as we tolerated his incessant repostes and critiques. We could watch Hollywood's fantasized Africa to our hearts' content, but only if we never forgot that it was fantasy. Sinister, stupid, vacuous fantasy; as silly and as far beyond African reality as that teen-wolf, hormonal, voice-cracking banshee bellow we bounced delightedly off the family room walls.

Mr. Rogers' Neighborhood was the other program that never failed to magically summon my father from wherever he was—the study, the bathroom, the yard, an MLA conference in San Francisco and cause him to instantaneously materialize in the room beside us. The "ding-ding" of the trolley on its way to "visit the land of make-believe" a Pavlovian bell, my father bounding into the room jaws agape, mouth foaming, ravenous and impatient to rip a large chunk out of poor Fred Rogers' tight white behind.

"Won't you please, won't you please, please won't you be . . . my neighbor."
It is twenty-plus years later and I can still hear it—his favorite phrase, the tease, the needle that never failed to get our gander up.

"Mr. Rogers is a faggot."

"No he's not, Dad, HE IS NOT!"

The routine so honed he eventually abbreviated it, walking in front of the TV, pinching his nose to mimic Mr. Rogers' overly nasal stereotypical white-suburban diction and barking out a staccato *"Faggit!,"* then running out of the room.

I remember being furious, shouting after him, "Is Not! IS NOT!" Like all profoundly successful teases, it got to the point he didn't even have to say the word, didn't even have to be in the room to "get" me, all he needed was a hint, an intimation:

"Won't you please, won't you please . . ." from the screen.

A disembodied nasal scat from the kitchen, *"Na-Nat!"* enough to get me going, cook my little goose, ruin the next five minutes of the program.

"He isn't a faggot. You're the faggot!"

"Ba-bap!"

"Shut <u>up</u>!"

"Shut up," nostrils squeezed shut.

"Don't talk like that!"

"Faggot!"

"IS NOT!"

It was years before I discovered, or before I allowed myself to register at a conscious level, the fact that *Mr. Rogers' Neighborhood* was filmed and produced in Pittsburgh. Looking back I realized the endearing familiarity of Mr. Rogers' voice was intimately connected to his Pittsburgh accent. This was why I found him so strangely soothing and reassuring (and thus was thrown into seemingly disproportionate degrees of consternation when I hear him ruthlessly mocked and demeaned). Fred Rogers was, indeed, my father's neighbor. Another native Pittsburgher. The city skyline one could occasionally glimpse in the background was my father's hometown, the trolley to Rogers' utopian make-believe kingdom would have to have run past the steel mills, on iron ties laid down by African American workers in the early part of this century.

Suddenly I had a context. A prism through which it became possible to fathom my father's seemingly irrational cruelty toward this innocent denizen of public broadcasting. The vitriol and disgust which would cause him to introduce such an ugly and inappropriate epithet in front of young, impressionable kids. His own boys. His antipathy so far surpassed the standard adult, knee-jerk distaste for lovable, cuddly kiddy shows (witness the "Blow up Barney" Society) it had baffled me for many years. A grown man now myself, watching the credits roll one afternoon with my little cousins, seeing the studio's address and the puzzle pieces finally fell into place.

Here was a black man born and raised in the Pittsburgh ghetto of Homewood watching his two sons grow up galaxies away in rural Wyoming, fawning and gushing over Mr. Rogers and his land of "pretend." Our dominant, living, daily connection to his hometown, to our grandmother's city, this obnoxious, giddy, Ward Cleaver clone leering at us through the TV screen, inviting us every afternoon to come play in his neighborhood. My dad watching helplessly as we, in our innocence, were naturally enthralled and entranced by this Disneyburgh, but the father-figure tour guide so distant, so different, so opposite to him that their loose accidental kinship could only be gleaned from the way they both pronounced the local football team's name, the franchise named for the proud legacy of the steel industry: "Stillers." Even hearing Fred allude to them an intolerable appropriation of territory Dad considered his own—he couldn't bear the thought of his sons growing up rooting for Mr. Rogers' "Stillers" instead of Homewood's.

My father grew up terrified of venturing into the part of the city where Fred Rogers lived. Mr. Rogers' neighborhood was an alien planet, a place populated by people living lives a black boy could get in trouble for daring to imagine, let alone trying to emulate. A neighborhood where they wouldn't let black kids into the city pools so my father never learned to swim. Fred Rogers' Pittsburgh was the reason an athlete gifted enough to win a basketball scholarship to the University of Pennsylvania, talented enough to garner international acclaim as a writer, rich enough to build a summer house on a lake in Maine, to this day cannot volunteer to chaperone his children, his granddaughter, for an afternoon swim, lest they stray deeper than the six-foot level he can safely negotiate.

Mr. Rogers' neighborhood was the place where black teenagers had to wear homespun turbans, genuflect, and pretend to pass as East Indians to get into the "whites only" theaters, the only place in town to see a first-run movie. The owner knew damn well what brand of nigger lay beneath the elaborate rags and towels piled up haphazardly on top of dark heads. He knew, but also couldn't ignore the grubby coins clinking in a herd of black pockets lined up to fill his till. So the turban ritual evolved as a solution, self-negation, humiliation just part of the price of the ticket, popcorn not included.

My father is not a rabid homophobe. Or if he is, it is not part of this story. But as a young man, a new father, a writer paid to smithy words for a living, he found the anvil bare. Found himself speechless; devoid of the vocabulary that could speak to spell out this particular pain. Watching his sons, his young men, become smitten by everyone's favorite neighbor, patriarch of America's favorite neighborhood. Half ashamed, half guilty to admit a stupid kids' show could light this kind of fire in him. Still, the flames impossible to smother. No insult, no epithet strong enough to carry the complex weight of the anger this engendered, and even if he crafted one that could, he wouldn't dare unleash it in all its ferocity upon tender ears, upon our young hearts.

So he settled for "faggot," foregrounding the properties of weakness, the notions of diminished manhood and inadequacy that might help him imagine, and one day help me to see, this man's smug smile erased, his eyes cast down and the incriminating color of his hands hidden, buried deep in his pockets, his pale face framed by the humiliating folds of faux-Indian cloth as he shuffles his way into unwelcome territory, into a hostile, darkened theater balcony deep inside somebody else's friendly neighborhood.

PART TWO

Hip-Hop Journalism

"I'm goin' to my media
assassin/Harry Allen,
I gotta ask him/Yo Harry,
you're a writer, are we
that type?/Don't believe
the hype"

—Public Enemy,
"Don't Believe
the Hype" (1988)

Harry Allen

Hip-Hop Hi-Tech

The race which first learns to balance equally the intellectual and the emo-tional—to use the machines and couple them with a life of true intuition and feeling such as the Easterns know—will produce supermen.

SINGER/SCHOLAR/ACTIVIST PAUL ROBESON MADE THIS STATEMENT IN London's *Daily Herald* back in 1935, so he obviously wasn't talking about hip-hop or modern electronics. But he could have been.

Hip-hop is a modern music, in the sense that its arrival speaks to a particularly modern comfort with, and access to, electronic technology. It is an intrinsically electronic African-American music, the first which, from its inception, performance or creation was impossible without electronics. How fitting that one of the form's first innovators, Joseph Saddler (a/k/a Grandmaster Flash), did not go to the School of Music & Art to ply his trade but to Samuel Gompers Vocational School to become an electronics technician.

Hip-hop was the first African-American music that one could get on cassette, albeit bootleg form, from the beginning (way before you could get it on wax). The first box I ever saw advertised was the Panasonic "Dyn-O-Mite" 8-track tape model, which was out around '75 or '76. Remember this? It came in three colors: red, white, or blue. It featured both a plunger on top that you pushed down to change the tape channel and *Good Times'* J.J. as its print ad spokesman. In addition to presaging the explosion of portable prerecorded music, now re-exploding in Jeeps and Maximas everywhere, I'd like to think that hip-hop also helped along at least three demises: that of 8-track, an unrecordable format, that of Jimmie Walker, Panasonic's inner-city loudmouth, and that of TV producer Norman Lear's master-slave stranglehold on situation ghetto comedies.

Hip-hop humanizes technology and makes it tactile. In hip-hop, you make the technology do stuff that it isn't supposed to do, get music out of something that's not supposed to give you music quite that way. You squeeze it, rip at it, and do other things with the equipment that mess viciously with your warranty. "I don't believe this!" yelled the white girl who was engineering at our high school radio station the first time I played "The Adventures of Grandmaster Flash on the Wheels of Steel." "I mean, what is this? Wreck-the-*Record?*" This wasn't just culture shocked. This was culture rocked, soon to become culture jocked.

If African-American music holds the voice as a musical and tonal ideal, what more efficient way to reach that musical ideal than to just play the vocal you idolize? In hip-hop, no higher praise can be given a vocalist than to cut 'n' scratch their voice. Call it a form of ancestor worship. The scratch is incantatory.

"Hip-hop lives in the world of sound— not the world of music—and that's why it's so revolutionary," says ultrapercussionist Max Roach in a strangely aborted *Spin* interview. "What we as Black people have always done is show that the world of sound is bigger than white people think." Hip-hop is so boastful, so bodacious, so full of its bad self that it dares to claim what is, basically a mistake (the scratch) as its musical point of departure, and techno-crap like turntables, mixers, and samplers as instruments in their own right. "They smiled when I told them I played turntables. They laughed when I sat down to play." In hip-hop, the DJ gets the last laugh.

Going Way Back

D.J. Marley Marl reportedly has one of the most advanced home studios in hip-hop, where he produced cuts on the *Colors* sound track and his just-released *In Control, Volume 1*. In-house, he also does digital recording, mixing, and audio sweetening for film and video.

Back in Queensbridge, he didn't always have it this good. "First there was like, some column speakers, some PA speakers," he says of his beginnings, "two turntables— **Gerrard**, **BSR**, other people had **1100A**s. They stopped makin' 'em. I still got a pair, though. They're like, the first, old, *def,* **Technics**, he laughs. "The first mixer I ever used was actually a receiver. I used to go back and forth on the balance knob [laughs], before I even really seen a mixer, and I had another amp for the cue so I could hear. What was that? '78, '77, '76 . . . It was way back."

"I don't know, electronically, who he was around, in what environment," says D.J. Red Alert upon hearing Marley's reminiscence. "He was probably around more of the disco era, Disco Twins, Fantasia . . . you know. Now for us, we was low-budget, we was comin' up, everbody was into [Technics] **210**s and a **Clubman** mixer. That was the first mixer everybody knew how to jump to before they got to a **Gemini**, and also **Numark**. But everybody felt like they was important when they got ahold of a **GLI**. And then another thing that everybody knew, that if you ever had this amp, in the Bronx, you had respect. It was called the Big Mac—**Macintosh**, one of the most powerful amps around. After a while, people started building up their systems."

The Basics

In some ways, today hip-hop electronics comes down to a mike, two turntables, a mixer, a drum machine, a sampler, an amp, and two bass-heavy speakers. In some ways, it don't come down to any of that. Know how you can read music magazines, and you'll see some guitarist say, "I like the Phaser G-75. It gives me more coloration in my low-end tones. But I don't know —the Parsec N70 is brighter at the high end," and they'll go on in specific detail about the particular effects they get from equipment? Why don't hip-hop artists talk like that? A lack of education, right?

Cool brother/Public-enemy-et-al. Producer Hank Shocklee tells why: "They don't care. None of that stuff matters, because all they know is what hits them. They don't care about, 'Oh, my vocals are up 2dB and that's too much here.' Most rappers are just gonna pick up a mike in the studio, blow into it, say a few things, and then determine if they like the way that voice sounds. If they don't like that way their voice sounds, they want *another* mike. And they'll keep finding a mike until they get one that they like! They don't know in terms of *technology* why they like it because, no, they don't have time for that. Hip-hop demands more of you than knowing what instruments, or knowing the technology. Hip-hop is more of an innovative situation. You have to spend more time in being innovative than in knowing the technology.

"I mean, nobody *cares* that Mantronik is one of the most technological whizzes there is. Nobody cares that he knows all the technology there is to know in hip-hop. Everybody knows that Mantronik makes a bullshit record."

Technics of the Trade

"My techniques are invincible, so why even try 'em?"

Sir Ibu of Divine Force says the pun from his single, "Holy War (Live)," was unintentional. Acknowledged. That doesn't take anything away from the fact that in hip-hop, Technics is synonymous with "turntables," having a grip on the market that is, at least numerically, unassailable. At present, the model 1200 is the DJ's weapon of choice. However, Divine Force made "Holy War," their hiccupy, hyperrhythmic testimony to the fact of Djing, with D.J. Enerjizer slicing on another model.

"I think they was SB-1s, SB-L1's, sum'n like that. The direct drives. We had Jizer cut it while I rhymed. Then once we did that, we laid in 'Funky Penguin,' with the turntables. Then we layed in "Amen Black Brother," with the turntable too. So only the beginning, from Eddie Murphy, was sampled. That's why it sounds so rough, that's why it sounds so raw and live: it was done *live* in the studio. Like how it started, back in the parks. 'Cause we didn't have the technology at that time. We just knew about two turntables and a mixer and a MC."

"Phonograph records are in a sense a contradiction of the meaning of the music," writes jazz historian Martin Williams in his book, *The Jazz Tradition.* "That is, they tend to make permanent and absolute music that is created for the moment, to express the meaning of the moment."

"Yeah, *right,* says the DJ as he loads another permanent and absolute copy of "Catch a Groove" on the turntable, so he can de-ermanent-ize and de-absolute-ize it. He knows better: that every record can be scratched, and that every record with scratching can be scratched. Like the particle physicists who break open atoms, hoping to later dig out their most elementary particles, dope DJs break open breaks, searching for the answer to hip-hop's most basic, yet unanswered question: how small is a piece of fund?

DJ Grandmaster Flash, lead man with the notorious, recently re-disbanded Furious 5, is still trying to find out. I asked the inventor of the **Flash Former**, a device for simplifying the Transformer scratch (marketed by mixer maker Gemini), what does a DJ look for in turntables? "Well . . . ," Flash pauses, "I can't say, 'cause I've got a turntable series coming out, for DJs! But let me just tell you this. Motor torque is one thing. Once a record is placed on the table, how much weight can you put on it before it'll come to a complete halt while in the ON position? On what angle does the arm sit? The suspension, how it's suspended up in the air, the tracking of the arm, and also the skating of the arm—how well will that arm lock in the groove, regardless of how thin the record was recorded? How well will it stay in the groove once you start scratching it? There's like four other factors—which I can't speak on—that weren't covered in a [Technics] turntable that's pretty important."

You're saying Technics is ideal only because the people who use them probably don't know how to do better? "I think the ultimate turntable they've *ever* made was the 1100As. When that 1100A came out, the platter sat extremely high off the base. The motor torque, it was the best I've ever felt. *Extremely* strong. You could damn near lean on it, and it would almost try to pull you along. What's important with that is that when you're spinning back, if that turntable is at least three-quarters up to speed, it's just up to the human being to be able to just push it. So that last quarter will be compensated for in the push. You go to the turntable on the left—BAM! Then you go to the turntable on the right—BAM! It won't be, *beeeeeeyaaaaamm*! Where a lot of turntables do that due to motor torque and, under pressure, that motor can't stand it. It can't get up to speed."

Why do you think the 1200s dominated the scene so long? "It was the trendy turntable to use and it was the best thing happening with the modern, technologized turntable. You have some turntables that cost three and four and five times more than this, but they service other applications. Like, there's a turntable called the Thorens. When it comes to disco blending, to lock-to-speed, it's the best thing happening right now, because that's their forte. But a Thorens is a really dainty turntable."

Well, what problems would a DJ face with two Thorens turntables? Flash doesn't take a breath. "Scratching. As soon as he rubbed it back, the platter would stop. And also, their weights are suspended on wire, which would cause the arm to waver as soon as you try to bring it back and forth. See, that arm is made for, once you set it down, it's sat down and you don't touch it, otherwise you're gonna have problems."

Finally, how many turntables, besides the classic 1100As, have you owned in your career? "About five sets. I've been through SL-23s which is Technics, I had Sl-20s, I had SL-220s, I had Duals, BSRs, and I got the Technics once again, which is the 1200s." Suddenly, Flash's voice gets very soft, as though he were kicking quiet bass to a fly girl. "A turntable can really last with me 'cause I've got a light touch. I'm not extremely hard on a turntable, but it's just gotta be able to do what I ask."

Sampling: Issue or Non-Issue?

They say that I sample/But they should sample this/My pit bull—

"CAUGHT, CAN WE GET A WITNESS," PUBLIC ENEMY

Tell the truth—James Brown was old/Til Eric and Ra came out with 'I Got Soul'/Rap brings back old R&B/And if we would not/People could of forgot—

"TALKIN' ALL THAT JAZZ," STETSASONIC

Like the cover for their first album, *On Fire,* the cover for Stet's latest single is graphically hip-hop defiant. Along with the band are, front and back, photos of hands in the blatant act of preparing samples. You can almost see fingerprints.

A sampler is basically a sonic copy machine, though a much better, more flexible copy machine than any model you've every seen. There are a few of them on the market, but the standard is the $2500 **Akai S900**, which boasts "11.75—63.3 seconds sampling time." Record the sound of these pages turning as your TV plays the "One Life to Live" theme in the background. Or record your boss yelling. Or a piece of Kool & the Gang, whatever, for up to 63 seconds. Loop it, so it plays end-on-end forever, or hook the S900 up to a keyboard and play whatever you recorded in a scale.

Then, there are the sampling drum machines such as the **Emu SP1200**. Tape the sound of a James Brown snare, a scratch, or a cough. The SP1200 don't care. Load it into the machine, hit one of its drum pads, and the sound plays back percussively. The privilege costs $3000.

Even with the arrival of these samplers, sampling is nothing new. Turntables have always been used in hip-hop as a form of sampler, and one cannot look at popular American music—of which America is the casing, Europe the fuse, and Afraka the gun powder—without realizing that it all "samples" from other sources. I mean, Elvis launched a career and sold a billion records by spit-shining r&b jams and "sampling" African-American song and dance styles. Gospel lyrics consist almost entirely of "sampled" writ, reworked bits and pieces of Bible text. The difference is that the King James Version is in the public domain, as are, unfortunately, African-American song and dance styles. James Brown's "Funky Drummer," Bob James's "Take Me to the Mardi Gras," Sly Johnson's "Different Strokes," and now Elvis's cover of "Tutti Frutti" are all registered with the US Copyright Office.

Ear magazine, October '87 issue: Saxophonist Henry Threadgill on hip-hop: "Well, the biggest change about rap music and hip-hop, to me, is that the rhythm is monolithic, which has nothing to do with anything associated with the evolution of Black music or any other music. You have regression, total regression in terms of rhythm in this music.

"What's most important, though, is that you've got a lot of people who are not musicians doing this stuff."

I asked Hank Shocklee what he thought of this last point, "OK," he said. "So? Who said that musicians are the only ones that can make music?

"Hip-hop is, 'You better make something *dope*.' If you can use a BSR turntable," he laughs, "if you can use a Mr. D.J. Microphone and two Close 'n Plays, they don't care. It just better be dope! Like I said, it doesn't have anything to do with the machines. You just better stay up on the times."

Homophobia: Hip-Hop's Black Eye

Farai Chideya

IT WAS THE DAY, MAYBE THE ONE DAY, THAT THE UNTHINKABLE HAPPENED: Troubled trash tabloid the *New York Post* developed a social conscience. On October 24 of last year, its front page was graced with a smiling snapshot of teenage dancehall reggae artist Buju Banton—above huge black letters spelling HATE MUSIC. The snapshot was from "Boom Bye Bye," the single on which Banton proclaimed: "Two men necking/Lying in a bed . . . Get an automatic or an Uzi instead/Shoot them now."

A couple of months later, on the British TV show *The Word*, dancehall star Shabba Ranks supported Bantona and added, "If you forfeit the laws of God Almighty, you deserve crucifixion." The resulting attention back in the States from Ranks's statements led the *Tonight Show* to cancel a pending March booking. What landed Banton on the front page and yanked Ranks from Leno's show was an aggressive media campaign by a New York–based gay-rights groups called the Gay & Lesbian Alliance Against Defamation (GLAAD), an organization whose recent successes in voicing its agenda has heated up longstanding tensions between gays and the hip-hop community. GLAAD has been somewhat successful at exacting retribution from hate-speech perpetrators; Banton, Ranks, and Marky Mark (who, also on *The Word,* supported Ranks's right to state his opinion) have all reluctantly signed to do anti-gay-bashing public service announcements on radio and TV, while even the radio stations that aired "Boom Bye Bye" offered unctuous public apologies. And each new twist in the saga has been accompanied by articles in the New York papers, as well as reports in the national media ranging from *Newsweek* to *Us.*

In the past, many rappers never thought twice about letting their hatred loose on the mike. Chubb Rock says, "You know I'll slap a faggot." "The Big Daddy law," says Big Daddy Kane, "is anti-faggot." Public Enemy's Flavor Flav has gone on record with antigay remarks, and Ice Cube rhymes "true niggas ain't gay." The "true niggas" Cube raps about are gangstas, the AK-47 toting, 40-swilling embodiments of urban manhood whose image sells millions of albums to black and white listeners Gangstas—real ones, or the kind created out of thin air by a rapper's lyrical finesse—have become the street preachers of urban reality. And according to hard-core rappers, there's no room in that reality for being gay.

Homophobia is as American as apple pie—as witnessed by the "moral" outrage that stymied President Clinton's push to end the ban on gays in the military. And rap, of course, is not alone in its antigay lyrics. Heavy metal is, like rap, music that defines maleness for its adolescent fans, a kind of maleness that makes gays outsiders. Axl Rose, on the cusp of superstardom, sang, "Immigrants and faggots/They make no sense to me" in Guns N' Roses' "One in a Million." But there's one crucial difference between the two musical genres: Metal doesn't—and doesn't have to—shoulder the same moral and cultural weight that rap does. How may times have you seen ol' Axl interviewed about the mood of the white community? The leaders of the hip-hop nation, however, are regularly called on to represent an entire race. "Some people call R.E.M. the most important band in American," says Jonathan Van Meter, editor of the hip-hop magazine *Vibe.* "But when are they on CNN or on the cover of *Time?*" Public Enemy called rap "black America's CNN," and rappers such as the Oakland-based Paris believe the messages behind rap lyrics are not just listened to but heard. "I know they are," Paris says. "They are the reason why people listen."

"With the forced exile, incarceration, and execution of black leaders, rappers have become the spokesmen for the black community," says Michael Franti, leader of Disposable Heroes of Hiphoprisy, whose "Language of Violence" is perhaps the only anti-gay-bashing rap. But a lot of these spokesmen are barely through adolescence. "When you're 16, you want to drive a car, get drunk, have sex," says Franti, who appeared on that very same British TV show one week after Shabba Ranks with the words FUCK HOMOPHOBIA written on his chest. "Those are the symbolic rites of manhood, and the most important one is heterosexual virility. And the way to say you're the most virile is to say you're the least homosexual or 'soft.'"

GLAAD public affairs director Donald Suggs—an African American—has taken heat for targeting primarily black artists, yet makes no apologies for his media crusade. Currently on the agenda: a postering campaign against Brand Nubian, whose "Punks Jump Up to Get Beat Down" includes the lines: "Fuck up a faggot / Don't understand their ways / And I'm not down with gays." The posters, a play on the parental warning stickers, read "Societal Advisory, Homophobic Lyrics." (Brand Nubian declined to comment for this article.) "Everybody wants to talk about artistic freedom," says Suggs, "but nobody wants to talk about artistic responsibility."

Suggs is battling not just individual rappers, but a whole system of belief. In the black community, as in America as a whole, many beliefs about gays have their roots in religion. Shabba Ranks stated that his comments on *The Word* were "premised upon . . . my childhood religious training." Rappers such as Buju Banton and Chubb Rock look to Christianity, too, while Cube and Brand Nubian look to Islam. Saying "the devil made me do it" is nice, but saying "God made me do it" is even better.

But Suggs won't accept the homophobia, or the reasoning behind it. "There are so many things in hip hop and dancehall that are against religion: killing, adultery. If people really followed religion, half these songs wouldn't be out there." The moral authority of religion, now and throughout history, has allowed artists such as Cube and Ranks to remain mired in wrongheaded dogma without having to consider progressive change.

Religious beliefs aren't the only factor shaping the conventions of the hip-hop nation: Many otherwise well-informed texts from the new doctrines of Afrocentrism play the same role. In the seminal book *Afrocentrism*, Molefi Asante calls homosexuality a trait learned from the white bourgeoisie that "makes the [gay] person evaluate his own physical needs above the teachings of national consciousness." And popular books such as *The Isis Papers* offer much the same argument: that white society emasculates black men and makes them gay.

"I think effeminate traits in black men are glorified by the white media," says Paris, who formed his own label after Time Warner–owned Tommy Boy Records rejected his presidential assassination-fantasy "Bush Killa." "Prince and Michael Jackson—who are these she-women supposed to be? They cross over [to white audiences] because they're androgynous." The former Nation of Islam member adds, "I can't be the rapper in hip hop that stands up for the gay cause. It's not something I agree with, if you get down to it." But he takes pains to add, "As far as beating people down, I'm not into that. To each his or her own."

To Paris, the whole debate over hip hop and homophobia seems tangential. "We're getting killed, our women are being raped. Considering that we are on a collision course for destruction, the issue of homophobia is trivial." Many in the black community see gays, whom they view as socio-economically well-off, as pretenders to the uncomfortable throne of disadvantage. Being black is an instant visual distinction, but as long as gays keep their mouths shut, those who question the gay-rights agenda argue, they can live their lives free of harassment. In a May 17 *New Yorker* article, Harvard professor Henry Louis Gates, Jr., chided the black community for its lack of compassion for gay rights: "For those blacks and whites who viewed last month's march on Washington with skepticism, to be gay is merely an inconvenience; to be black is to inherit a legacy of hardship and inequity." But that standard of discrimination is flawed, Gates went on. For example, mainstream leaders, especially religious ones, can still talk about hating gays in ways that they can no longer talk about hating blacks. "In short," Gates says, "measured by their position in society, gays on the average seem privileged relative to blacks; measured by the acceptance of hostile attitudes toward them, gays are worse off than blacks."

The constant positioning of one group against the other is, of course, absurd, and denies the fact that many "true niggas" can be and are gay and lesbian. The fact that one of those brothers waving their hands in the air might be gay, or one of the front-row cuties in full Kente dress might snuggle up at night with the girl right next to her, is never acknowledged.

Even with the ubiquitous misogyny of rap, sexism is a little less openly nihilistic than homophobia. Women, after all, are always valued by the guys for some reason, even if they're the wrong ones (receptacle, breeder, "easy on the eye" sexual wallpaper). But the hip-hop nation, as defined by some of its most prominent citizens, has absolutely no use for gay men and women.

Many in the hip-hop community argue that stories such as the *Post's* are driven more by antiblack sentiment than any honest regard for the good of gay America, acting as yet another excuse for the hostile mainstream media to spew antirap rhetoric. James Bernard, an editor at the *Source* and the author of an upcoming book on Ice Cube and South Central L.A., feels that the outcry over hip hop's homophobia is just good old-fashioned rap-bashing. "I'm not trying to defend particular lyrics, but I think these guys have taken more heat than they deserve," he says. "The rap industry has so many seminars on these issues." Bill Adler, a rap publicist who also produced a booklet criticizing Ice Cube for anti-Semitism, disagrees. "If you cover this topic at all," he says, "you can't help but do it justice."

Monica Lynch, head of Tommy Boy Records, recognizes that the media card can be played two ways. "Rap in general draws a disproportionate amount of media sensationalism," she says. "I think that there's a tremendous fear of black males. A lot of what you hear in rap today, the bitch-ho-lyrics, is man trying to be man. And sometimes you hear the phrase 'The oppressed becomes the oppressor.' But I'm not a young black male; I try not to judge that. I would just say there's a real insecurity about their own masculinity, and they [take it out on] gays, women, or anyone else that they see as being weaker."

But while women have stepped up tot he mike to challenge the gansta stereotype (or to join in on their own terms), gay rappers are not allowed or not interested in entering what Lynch calls "the jousting ring" of rap. "Women, gays, Jews, Koreans; whatever [rapped about group] it may be, there may be lyrics deemed hate mongering. It's the rapper's right to be there and their right to be full of shit. But there is always an open invitation for the next person to get on the mike and do battle and counter these things. A lot of people get bloody noses, but you've got to fight back," she says, adding she believes there could be openly gay rappers under the right circumstances.

But what are those circumstances? For gays and lesbians, the present lyrical atmosphere, and the lack of hardcore authenticity that gayness represents, may be too much to overcome. Could there ever be, say, a gay gangsta rapper? "I don't think so," says Paris. "No way."

LA rapper Yo Yo agrees. Street credibility, she says, "would be a problem, 'cause people wouldn't be able to deal with it." Yo Yo, who favors Clinton's moves to end the gay ban in the military, supports GLAAD'S antihomophobia campaigns. "If I felt like my life was in danger, I'd stand up," she says.

"I did this thing on my new album with [dancehall artist] Idle Joe," Yo Yo continues. "He said this word 'batty boy.' And I was singing it, singing the male part, and my friend told me what it means [the West Indian equivalent of 'faggot']. I went through this thing trying to get it off this album. I tried to have them bleep that out—I don't want anything like that on the album. But it was too late, and I feel bad about it. Society has made it so easy for people to discriminate. It's hard for you to stop it—it makes you look stupid if you say anything."

Gay members of the hip-hop industry are in a precarious position. Those who are openly gay often condemn homophobia, but say the lyrics don't bother them personally. Van Meter has taken his licks for being a gay white man in what is traditionally a straight black man's world. Russell Simmons, who was originally involved in the launching of *Vibe,* the Quincy Jones–Time Warner hip-hop publication, pulled out because *Vibe* "didn't hire one straight black man," he claimed in an interview with the *Washington Post.* Says Van Meter, "I guess I didn't anticipate the criticism I'd come under. But I feel that my sexuality is irrelevant, that I've adequately defended myself.

"The idea that hip hop is homophobic is exaggerated," he says. "If [Naughty By Nature's] Treach refers to his father who left him as a fag, he's not really calling him a fag. I love that song. I'm willing to accommodate what appears to be homophobia because I love the music so much." But songs such as [this, he] admits, "walk that line."

RuPaul, the skyscraper-tall black drag queen whose "Supermodel" hit No. 1 on the dance charts, has much the same attitude. "I'm not bothered by it and I thank God they have the freedom to say it," RuPaul says. "It doesn't make me lose sleep at night. Let them go on and do their own thing. They'll burn themselves out." Although RuPaul claims to have been "discriminated against by every community there is: black, white, straight, gay, lesbian," the singer doesn't place any particular emphasis on hip hop.

So who does hip hop's homophobia hurt? Suggs believes it contributes to rejection of and sometimes violence against gays of color. He argues that the antagonism between straight and gay blacks masks the common enemy of racism, saying: "[Straight blacks] don't realize that gay blacks are discriminated against in the white *and* gay communities." Matt Foreman, the executive director of the New York Gay and Lesbian Anti-Violence Project, which provides counseling and aid to victims of bias crimes, believes hip hop's lyrics have a deep effect on young listeners. He likens it to studies that show a correlation between depictions of violence on television and actual violent crimes. "What we know empirically is that young people, those under 18, are disproportionately the perpetrators of antigay violence," Foreman says. "Of the 662 antigay bias crimes reported to us last year, 31 percent were committed by people under 18, 52 percent by people aged 18 to 29. The popular media has a direct impact on the way young people act. It's absurd to think that a [music] group that can influence fashion across the country in profound ways doesn't have an effect on behavior. Kids will dress like them, go out and buy the clothes, but they're not listening to the lyrics?"

But Foreman isn't a fan of GLAAD's tactics: He thinks they're too weak. "I think we take a much more hard-line approach to this stuff than GLAAD does," he says, adding that he's never seen GLAAD's anti–Brand Nubian posters on New York's streets. "We thought they let Marky Mark off the hook too easily. My perspective is that [hip–hop] lyrics, which are homophobic both in that they're degenerating and that they're encouraging violence, are unique [in pop music] in terms of how many there are and the lack of outrage over them. We don't have any problem condemning these lyrics, urging people to boycott the record producers, but GLAAD has a problem saying that. I don't know if it's because we're right there with the people who bear the brunt of this stuff, but we just have a much more," he pauses, "*violent* attitude to these people.'"

For some targets, the perception of gayness is enough. P.M. Dawn's Prince Be was shoved off the stage of the Sound Factory in January 1992 by KRS-One (Kris Parker) of Boogie Down Productions. The attack may have had something to do with rumors about Prince Be's sexuality—as well as the fact that Be has refused to term his groups melody-suffused music rap. "A lot of hard-core hip hop isn't down with P.M. Dawn," Prince Be says with supreme understatement. "It would be real dangerous for someone [in the hard-core community] to talk about gayness. What would have to change at the same time would be the consciousness of the whole hip hop hard-core crowd, and of the whole world.

"A lot of people thought I was gay and I just wouldn't acknowledge it," he says. The question came up when he appeared on the U.K. television show *The Word,* the same show Ranks later went on. "They asked me if I was gay, and I said it doesn't matter. But then it leaked out to some people in the States, and I had to straighten it out," he recalls. "Do I like men? No. Am I gay? I don't think so. "But," he laughs, "I seen *The Crying Game,* and that girl's fly!'"

Few rappers are willing to laugh at the tension that exists around gay issues today, but some are making strides to bridge the gap between the gay and hip-hop communities. Victoria Starr, a radio programmer who is a lesbian and has a woman's music show on WBAI, shared a panel with Ice-T at the New Music Seminar two years ago. "I didn't even have to push him," she says of his public change of heart of homosexuality. "He talked about how he used to say things in concert like, 'If you have AIDS, don't clap.' Then people told him that wasn't cool. He said, 'Look, we're all victims of society, and we grow up learning these things.' "

"I'm working on a book on k.d. lang," says Starr. "Could she have come out five years ago? She was working in country music, which was probably as bad as rap. Hip hop is so rapidly homophobic that maybe it would kill someone's career to come out. Ninety percent of gay people could come out, but for someone in hip hop maybe that's not possible."

Rap music, for all its flaws, is still the CNN of black America. The problem isn't too much free speech, but not enough. The hip-hop nation, with a painful few exceptions, is unwilling to stand up and call gay-bashing rhymes wack. So now gays and lesbians are trying to break the lyrical silence. For example, GLAAD, in conjunction with the New York group Out Youth, is bringing together young gay and lesbian rappers in a competition for a cash prize. Says Suggs, "We wanted to show Brand Nubian who was out there." What's needed is an editorial from *inside* the hip-hop community that comes out strong against those who love to hate. Finding a "true nigga" who can rock the mike—and who's gay—may be the only way.

The Death of Rock n' Roll

Cheo Hodari Coker

THE HISTORY OF POPULAR MUSIC IN AMERICA GOES SOMETHING LIKE THIS: Niggas invent it. White boys steal it. Niggas invent something else. White boys steal that. Niggas take it all the way out—pushing the edge of cacophony, rage, sound, and fury (read: Funkadelic). White boys ignore it, protest it, downright reject it, ban it, and bury it, only to come back to it a few years later and take the whole thing outright (read: Primus, the Red Hot Chili Peppers, and Jane's Addiction). Who would have thought that in the '90s it would be the hip-hop elite wearing Versace, Hugo Boss, and outfits from the L.L. Bean catalog and the white kids bringing back shell-toe Adidas, Kangols, and calling themselves "nigga" with, dare I say it, niggerific affection?

Strange country this is. Strange, twisted, contradicted, confused, brilliant, and insane—warped and dashed out to the rest of the world on fiber-optic cables at 56-bytes-per-second.

Bebop fueled the musical revolution that Charlie Parker and Dizzy Gillespie were attempting against swing in the mid '40s. It was music the critics called vulgar; the degenerate musical ravings of drug addicts. Now bebop is heard in jazz clubs around the world that most black people can't even afford admission to—and that's when it's being appreciated. Most of the time it's being played as dinner music to a crowd who wouldn't know Kenny Kirkland from Kenny G. And rap music—widely heralded as the generation's bebop—is following the same sad path.

Now it's kids from the Valley and Scarsdale breakdancing and lindy hopping in Gap ads, nary a black or Puerto Rican in sight. Now it's Run of Run-DMC—who boasted in "Rock Box": "Calvin Klein ain't no friend of mine, don't want nobody's name on my behind"—rapping the virtues of the Gap while bopping down a runway. Rappers who would have been lucky swigging St. Ides in a commercial are now selling Sprite. And speaking of St. Ides' former posterboy Ice Cube, the Los Angeles rapper and N.W.A. co-founder who wanted nothing but "bitches and money" back in 1989—is featured today on American Express billboards alongside such luminaries as David Geffen, Martin Scorcese, Spike Lee, and Magic Johnson. Like the others, he isn't identified by name—you're supposed to know who he is.

What does this have to do with the music? Everything. Rap no longer just reflects urban America's angst—it represents that of all Americans. All of the country's rage: its contradiction, its obsession with materialism, sex death, and the operatic bliss of love and rejection. Because rock and roll just can't cut it anymore.

There are the obvious signs—that rap outsells every other genre of music, including country; that Lauryn Hill won Album of the Year; and that Def Jam's sales (with a roster that includes Jay-Z, DMX, LL Cool J and Foxy Brown) are up 200%, while Interscope's (with Marilyn Manson, No Doubt, Nine Inch Nails) have dropped 28%. But there are also subtler ways rap has infiltrated this country's culture—when *GQ* used the word "disses" on their cover, or when the 50-year-old white lady in line at the bank tells someone they look "jiggy." Or the fact that the only new rock bands that sell massive units—like The Offspring, Limp Biskit, Korn, Sugar Ray, and Beck—have all adopted elements of the rap aesthetic, musical or otherwise.

But you'd still be missing the point. The point is, even the rock kids don't want to rock anymore. Billy Corgan used just as many break-beats as he did guitar-riffs on the latest Smashing Pumpkins album. Alanis Morrisette, same story. And if there isn't a clearer sign of rock and roll's demise, it's the rise of an artist like Eminem.

It's not that Eminem's been trumpeted as yet another great white hope in rap. (He's no Rakim.) And it's not that he embodies what Sam Phillips, the Sun Records owner who championed Elvis Presley, referred to when he said "find me a white man who sounds like a black man and I'll make a million dollars."

The important thing is that the 24-year-old rapper (né Michael Mathers) has chosen rap—not rock and roll—to be his outlet to speak to his people. Not even five years ago, this self-described crack smoking, coke sniffing, mushroom toking, gun clapping maniac would have had a guitar, a heroin habit, and dreams of being the next Kurt Cobain.

Instead he's made one of the first authentic white hip hop records for the simple fact that he's been able to make the music fit his specific life experience, and he's completely honest about it. It's not harkening to the rhymes and styles of the by-gone old school like the Beastie Boys, or white apology à la 3rd Bass, or out-gangstering other white boys with attitude like House of Pain. Eminem is no gangster or thug. He's just one of a whole generation that has fallen through the cracks—neglected by parents who do more drugs than he does, not fitting in with the black and Latino kids he grew up with who will never really accept him as one of their own—even if he has adapted their culture.

Eminem's made a record so irreverent and shocking that it could have been made by Ice Cube circa 1990. But this white kid did it and made it fit into his world. His lyrics about slipping date rape drugs in the drinks of 15-year-old girls for sexual purposes ("Guilty Conscience"), singing your daughter a lullaby while dumping the bodies of her mother, stepfather and stepbrother off a pier ("97 Bonnie & Clyde"), or turning your drug-addled rage and alienation into music that functions as well in Nebraska as it does on Hollywood Boulevard ("I Just Don't Give a Fuck").

It's about hip hop being as identifying a mark on one's disaffected psyche today as Mick Jagger was over 30 years ago when he thumbed his nose at the establishment by saying the plastic salesman on TV "can't be a man, 'cause he doesn't smoke the same cigarettes as me."

It's about the death of rock n' roll.

Run-DMC sounded the first death knell back in the early and mid-'80s. The guitar, coupled with the hard beat, has always been at the center of their sound—whether it was "Rock Box," "King of Rock," or even the stripped-down classic, "Sucker MC's." It had no guitar, but it felt like a rock record—not the rap records everyone was used to.

The Sugarhill Records era of rap, from 1979 through 1983, just as it established the music in the mainstream, misdirected it at the same time. With the noted exception of "The Message," most records of that were glorified disco records—a snappy phrase here, a chorus there, and something simple that could make you pat your feet. The aggressive sound that was hip hop, in the parks and in the clubs, wasn't represented in the recording studio.

Back in the days, the pioneer DJs like Kool Herc and Afrika Bambaataa made it a point to flip rock records on their ear—to take a snippet of something here, and a little bit of something there, and make a track hard yet danceable. Billy Squires' "The Big Beat," Led Zeppelin's "When the Levee Breaks," and Deep Purple's "Smoke on the Water" were some of a number of records that might end up in the mix. The DJ would isolate the hardest part of the drum and extend it between two copies—making for an endless break, two seconds that could become five minutes.

With "Here We Go," Run-DMC had something that made them different than everyone else. They stripped away all of the bullshit—no sequins, no Indian headdresses, nothing extra. They just rocked some Adidas, striped Lee's, a leather jacket and a whole lot of attitude. It was hard, in your face, grab your balls. It was rock and roll—even if they weren't calling it that.

By the time they recorded "Walk This Way" in 1986, Run-DMC were rock and roll. The Aerosmith classic was a favorite breakbeat—even though the first three seconds were the only part of the album any B-Boy cared about. In fact, until the recording session, no one in the group even knew who Aerosmith was. Anytime D or Run asked Jam Master J for the beat, they would say "throw on *Toys in the Attic*," which they thought was the name of the group, not just the name of the LP.

But by the time they re-recorded it, everything changed. The first thing was that they revitalized Aerosmith's career (those guys should Run-DMC a dollar for every record they sell). But more importantly they broke the stigmatization of the categorization of rap and rock and roll.

In the video, after Steven Tyler busts through the wall separating the two bands (and genres), Run gives the rocker a look of such utter contempt, and coolness, that anybody looking could see what he was saying. Head cocked to the side, in the coolest B-Boy stance, his face said: This is my world. Your day is over. All that spandex shit is dead. We can take your shit, word for word, flip it over, and still do it better than you do. The dismissive hand gesture, as he turned his back, sealed it—rock was on the way out.

But back then, even though a lot of kids gravitated to Run-DMC, and the Beastie Boys, rock still ruled. There was Bon Jovi, Mötley Crüe, and Van Halen. There were the alternative guys that were creeping on a comeup—REM, U2, and Depeche Mode. And, if we're talking pure pop, Madonna and Prince still had the capacity to shock.

But then came Guns N' Roses, with fire in their sound and desperation in their eyes. The pure white boy was making a comeback. Axl sashaying on stage, Slash leaning back real cool, his black top hat covering his eyes, his face hidden by a mess of curls. A classic rock sound that was melodically based, with hooks and choruses that people could follow, rebellious lyrics that lashed out at hypocrisy and urged living for the moment, and angry, back-the-fuck-off-me *Beggar's Banquet* style.

The Sunset Strip was alive again, and MTV began to reflect the paradigm shift away from prissy groups like Rick Ocasek and the Cars, Huey Lewis and The News, and Peter Gabriel. Along came lots of beer, the rumblings of a heroin epidemic making a comeback, and white girls with long legs in cutoffs, high heels, and silicone titties. Guns N' Roses pushed the latter '80s envelope back to '70s levels of excess—wild parties, misogynistic aggression, danger, and reckless abandon.

Yeah, it was cool. It was bold. But there were too many Roses. Where were the guns?

Ganster rap had those guns. Once N.W.A. and the Geto Boys took Schooly D and BDP's stance to another level, rap gained a heavy metal edge.

The rule since the '50s and the days of the sock hop, had been this: pick the music that pisses your parents off the most and that becomes your generational sounding board. The parents of the '50s were into Sinatra and Perry Como. They didn't want their kids to have anything to do with crazy niggas like Little Richard and Chuck Berry, with their tales of fast cars and sexual innuendo filtering out between the words.

And those baby boomer kids grew up, smoked some dope in the '60s, grew long hair, had some free love—and maybe if they stayed in the game long enough, did like KC and the Sunshine Band and, you know, "do a little dance, make a little love, get down tonight." But that was it. By the mid '80s, they had settled into their 40s, and into their fortunes. Hair was cut, suits were bought, flower power was dead, and it was all about money and society. The night belonged to *Dallas, Dynasty,* and *Falcon Crest.* The vote belonged to Ronald Reagan.

So fine, little Johnny has a G'N'R poster, long hair, girls. I understands that. Hell, I listened to Zeppelin back in the day myself.

But now little Johnny's cut off all his hair, he's wearing black, and wants to be down with a group called Niggers With Attitudes? Playing that noise that I heard when I was coming home from work the other day—even after I rolled up my windows. I hate that. What is that? That's not music. I work with black guys every day, hell, I even have a drink sometimes with Bill Johnson, he's a black guy, cook, hard worker, Lakers fan like me. But even he would agree that there's a difference between black guys and niggers. What kind of role model is a nigger?

The most aggressive kind. Rap became the soundtrack for the alienation age. Here was something that finally, parents couldn't understand—a window into a world of sex and death that seemed so much more urgent (read: real) than any of that devil worshiping shit. And the more you listened, the greater the window opened.

When creative, sampling groups like A Tribe Called Quest and De La Soul came into the mix, they not only gave you the aggressive, hard stuff, but pushed the sound in directions that had never been heard before. Rakim, Big Daddy Kane, Kool G Rap, Chuck D of Public Enemy, and KRS-One, took elocution to a whole new level—and were actually talking about more than love or their dick.

The music was going in so many different directions at once that suddenly everything was brand new. It was histories, cultures, opinions that had been suppressed for years, suddenly springing forth in so many different ways, coming back stronger and harder the more the mainstream tried to compartmentalize it.

MTV ran *Yo! MTV Raps* as an experiment, and were embarrassed and shocked when it became the highest rated show on the entire network. You could keep Public Enemy and N.W.A. off the radio charts and the airwaves, but it didn't matter. Kids from all walks of life were coming to the shows and buying the records, even if they didn't always understand the music. It served its purpose, it was about the eradication of white society in general. Rap kept creeping—and damn it, even the record companies couldn't stop it—it kept showing up its rock and roll peers.

By the time SoundScan was introduced, N.W.A. had outsold their mainstream competitors three-to-one with no airplay, and had the numbers to prove it. Ice Cube could come out with a record years later telling the editor of *Billboard* to muthafuck himself—and every one of his records in the Soundscan age, with the exception of *War and Peace,* have debuted as No. 1 on that magazine's chart.

Rock n' roll was dead—even if it was in denial.

Now we're heading toward a universal art from where hip-hop techniques set the musical paradigm for all genres. Everything, from television commercials to *Sesame Street,* uses breakbeats. Most rock singers have given up trying to sing all together—mostly what they do is sing talk in a style that's all but rap in name. DMX, Jay-Z and almost every other rapper you can think of rules *Total Request Live.* The only reason MTZ hasn't morphed into BET is because the powers that be at Viacom just don't want to acknowledge that 85 percent of MTV's viewers, if given a choice, wouldn't give a shit if they stopped playing rock and roll altogether—those that care watch it on VH1.

And Puff Daddy's doing Led Zeppelin covers—and we're in a time where half the people in the studio, not to mention buying the record, have the audacity to ask the question "Who the fuck is Jimmy Page?"

Confessions of a Hip-Hop Critic

dream hampton

"I SEE THAT BITCH DREAM, I'M STABBING HER," METHOD MAN, ONE OF RAP'S fastest rising stars, let it be known. He was looking for me. He was furious after reading an album review I wrote in *The Source,* a rap magazine. The article fleetingly compared him to Busta Rhymes of Leaders of the New School, whose sophomore album was actually the subject of my article. Apparently I'd struck a nerve in that sensitive place called the male ego. In his mind, I'd accused him of hip-hop's equivalent to treason—jacking someone's style. Almost six months later, at the Los Angeles airport LAX, I spotted Method Man's group Wu-tang Clan outside of my terminal. Apparently we had the same flight home to New York. I barely remembered Method's beef; I waved at the member of the group that I knew and rushed inside to make last-minute changes on my ticket. Method had never seen me before. When he walked up to me, all beautiful and smiling, he was expecting to walk away with my phone number. He held both my hands in his—he was warm and earthy. I knew as awkward as it'd be, I'd have to fess up.

"dream hampton." I added my last name so he'd know exactly who he was talking to. He dropped my hands immediately. Stepped back a little.

"Look I know you're looking for me but in my heart of hearts I felt that way and I didn't mean for you to take it like a dis but I gotta do my thing as a writer and I never meant for you and Busta . . ." We went back and forth like that for a while—artist and critic (and fan), brother and sister, I knew what was at stake. I had to be honest, confident, intelligent, and unafraid or there was a good chance Method would have used those large hands to slap me in the mouth—and that was real. He'd felt disrespected, and his neighborhood and our youth culture have taught him, and all black boys to react to disrespect with violence. Although I knew male critics who'd been approached by angry artists the same way, my being a woman made me particularly vulnerable.

In the back of my mind was Dee Barnes, the video show hostess who'd been assaulted at a crowded nightclub by Dr. Dre because he believed she had disrespected him by airing an interview with Ice Cube. At the time Cube and Dre were enemies and Cube dissed Dre. Dre was silently supported by a community in awe of his talent. Dee's pleas for allies went largely unheard.

By the time we were ready to board our flight, I'd earned Method Man's respect and provided him with some clarity about my intentions. "I'm really glad I met you," he told me before he walked away.

Before I moved to New York, before I ever met a rapper, I was a hip-hop fan. In the beginning I didn't really consider what it meant to be a girl and a hip-hop junkie. I just was. It was the soundtrack to my high school years, the music I roller-skated to in junior high, and the music all my little boyfriends, and some of my girlfriends, practiced making. There have been few things in my life that have inspired me like KRS-One's *By All Means Necessary* or Public Enemy's *It Takes a Nation of Millions.* I shook my butt to Rakim and Doug E. Fresh. And I recognized my neighborhood, Detroit's east side, in the sex-and-violence tales from Too Short and N.W.A.

I started writing by accident. As a nineteen-year-old intern from NYU's film school hired to organize *The Source's* photo collection, I was always offering unsolicited opinions. As the only woman in the office I was forced to respond to the sexism and misogyny not only in the music, but within the magazine's pages. The guys thought it would be cute if I reviewed the Hoes Wit Attitude, a group whose debut album was presented by Eazy E of N.W.A. (Niggaz Wit Attitude). My assignment package included glossy photos of the Hoes in leather thongs with rifles standing between their legs and a poorly produced tape with lyrics about sexing Mandela. In my review, I included everything I'd learned from my contemporary womanist heroes Alice Walker and Pearl Cleage—I even spelled my name in small letters like bell hooks. I blasted H.W.A. for being antithetical to the women's movement in hip-hop, one spearheaded by progressives like Queen Latifah. I was offered that they'd confirmed boys' most twisted notions of womanhood—that "bitches ain't shit but hoes and tricks."

I'm not puritanical. I'm a firm believer that women should be able to exercise control of their sexuality. But for obvious reasons I'm suspicious about how much control the Hoes actually exercise. I'm also clear that the black woman's body being marketed, as it was once auctioned, has a direct relationship with our oppression, both black and female.

Three years later, I am unable to even respond to H.W.A.'s second release. This time the photos the music editor gives me have them in fur bikinis under expensive fur coats. I am spent. Exhausted. Cynical and jaded.

At twenty-two, after what feels like a lifetime of hearing brothers call sisters "bitches" and "hoes," I can no longer feign shock when I see women personifying these definitions. At last year's annual black music conference in Atlanta, "Jac the Rapper," it was clear that the weekend had turned into an event. Thousands of black folk my age showed up. Brothers stood around trying to look hard. Sisters, who'd also received their cues from their favorite music videos, did their best to be sexy for the brothers. Usually in daisy duke shorts and halter tops. They wanted the men, particularly the rap stars, to believe that they are as virile and in control as they imagine they are in their songs. There were several incidents of violence that weekend. Most of it was men assaulting women. But it was the totally believable rumor that a sister had been murdered, thrown from a thirty-second-floor balcony into the hotel's atrium, that made me realize how dangerous this game we play really is.

I'm frustrated that other brothers don't take up my cause, that they aren't mortally offended by their own misogyny.

I'm angry for feeling abandoned by my older sisters and brothers who dismiss hip-hop and my generation altogether. I'm offended that black leadership and black radio alike hold televised conferences where young folk are described in the abstract, as if we'd landed (rather than been raised) in our communities.

Consequently, I find myself in the uncomfortable and precarious position of defending great poets like Tupac, Snoop Doggy Dogg, and Kool G Rap when outsiders want to reduce them to monster misogynists and murderers. Because I love rap music, its cadences, intonations, and mood swings, I've recognized and struggled to reconcile the genius and passion of my brothers—even when it meant betraying my most fundamental politics. I'm in the same position I imagine I would have assumed had my peers been the eloquently sexist Ishmael Reed or genius/woman-beater Miles Davis. Hip-hop may be guilty of pimping and parading the worst of black America, but rap music cannot be made responsible for this government's institutional racism and sexism and our family's subsequent decimation.

I was glad I met Method Man too. I wasn't, however, convinced that I'd changed him in some way. The standard myth that there are good women worthy of men's respect and the others are—you guess it—bitches and hoes was one introduced to me by my grandfather. And I'm sure when Method and other brothers are confronted by a woman fiercely devoted to this culture we call hip-hop and this nation we call Black, one who can name break beats from hip-hop classics and is willing to challenge them to their face about their antirevolutionary sexism, they automatically label her an exception.

I'm not convinced "exceptional" is a totally safe space. Dee, for instance, was all of these things. But when Dre had a choice between confronting Ice Cube, who made the offensive remarks on the air in the first place, or the easier target Dee, he opted for the latter. He was silently supported by a community that needs its Black male heroes and finds its heroes dispensable, even annoying.

Sometimes I joke that if I could trade my generation of brothers in for a new set, I would. I can't. These are my peers, the brothers I have most in common with. The challenge for me and sisters like myself is to confront my brothers and our music with consistency, love, intelligence, and self-respect.

hip-hop feminist | Joan Morgan

MUCH HAD CHANGED IN MY LIFE BY THE TIME A MILLION BLACK MEN MARCHED in Washington. I no longer live in Harlem. The decision had less to do with gun-shot lullabies, dead bodies 'round the corner, or the pre-adolescents safe-sexing it in my stairwells—running consensual trains on a twelve-year-old girl whose titties and ass grew faster than her self-esteem—and more to do with my growing desensitization to it all. As evidenced by the zombie-like stare in my neighbors' eyes, the ghetto's dues for emotional immunity is high. And I knew better than to test its capacity for contagion.

So I broke out. Did a Bronx girl's unthinkable and moved to Brooklyn—where people had kids and dogs and gardens and shit. And a park called Prospect contained ol' West Indian men who reminded me of yet another home and everything good about my father.

It is the Bronx that haunts me, though. There a self, long deaded, roams the Concourse, dressed in big bamboo earrings and flare-legged Lees, guarding whatever is left of her memories. I murdered her. Slowly. By sipping miasmic cocktails of non-ghetto dreams laced with raw ambition. I had to. She would have clung so tightly to recollections of monkey bars, sour pickles, and BBQ Bontons, slow dances to "Always and Forever," and tongue kisses *coquito* sweet—love that existed despite the insanities and rising body counts—that escape would have been impossible.

It is the Bronx, not Harlem that calls me back. Sometimes she is the singsong cadences of my family's West Indian voices. Or the childhood memories of girls I once called friends. Sistas who refused the cocktail and had too many babies way too young. Sistas who saw welfare, bloodshed, dust, then crack steal away any traces of youth from their smiles.

Theirs are the spirits I see darting between the traffic and the La Marqueta vibes of Fordham Road. Their visitations dog my equanimity, demanding I explain why this "feminism thing" is relevant to any of their lives. There are days I cannot. I'm too busy wondering what relevance it has in my own.

> . . . And then came October 16, the day Louis Farrakhan declared that black men would finally stand up and seize their rightful place as leaders of their communities. . . . It wasn't banishment from the march that was so offensive—after all, black women have certainly convened at our share of closed-door assemblies. It was being told to stay home and prepare food for our warrior kings. What infuriated progressive black women was that the rhetoric of protection and atonement was just a seductive mask for good old-fashioned sexism. . . .
>
> Kristal Brent-Zooks, "A Manifesto of Sorts for a New Black Feminist Movement," *New York Times Magazine*

The "feminist" reaction to the Million Man March floored me. Like a lot of folks, I stayed home to watch the event. My phone rang off the hook—sista friends as close as round the corner and as far away as Jamaica moved by the awesome sight of so many black men of different hues, classes, and sexual orientations gathered together *peacefully* for the sole purpose of bettering themselves. The significance of the one group in this country most likely to murder each other—literally take each other out over things as trifling as colors or stepping on somebody's sneakers—was not lost on us. In fact, it left us all in tears.

Still, as a feminist, I could hardly ignore that my reaction differed drastically from many of my feminist counterparts. I was not mad. Not mad at all. Perhaps it was because growing up sandwiched between two brothers blessed me with an intrinsic understanding of the sanctity of male and female space. (Maintaining any semblance of harmony in our too-small apartment meant figuring out the times my brothers and I could share space—and the times we could not—with a quickness.)

Perhaps it was because I've learned that loving brothers is a little like parenting—sometimes you gotta get all up in that ass. Sometimes you gotta let them figure it out *on their own terms*—even if it means they screw up a little. So while the utter idiocy inherent in a nineties black leader suggesting women stay home and make sandwiches for their men didn't escape me, it did not nullify the march's positivity either. It's called being able to see the forest *and* the trees.

Besides, I was desperately trying to picture us trying to gather a million or so sistas to march for the development of a new black feminist movement. Highly, highly unlikely. Not that there aren't black women out there actively seeking agendas of empowerment—be it personal or otherwise—but let's face it, sistas ain't exactly checkin' for the f-word.

When I told older heads that I was writing a book which explored, among other things, my generation of black women's precarious relationship with feminism, they looked at me like I was trying to re-invent the wheel. I got lectured ad nauseam about "the racism of the White Feminist Movement," "the sixties and the seventies," and "feminism's historic irrelevance to black folks." I was reminded of how feminism's ivory tower elitism excludes the masses. And I was told that black women simply "didn't have time for all that shit."

While there is undeniable truth in all of the above except the latter—the *shit* black women don't have time for is dying and suffering from exorbitant rates of solo parenting, domestic violence, drug abuse, incarceration, AIDS, and cancer—none of them really explain why we have no black feminist *movement*. Lack of college education explains why 'round-the-way girls aren't reading bell hooks. It does not explain why even the gainfully degreed (self included) would rather trick away our last twenty-five dollars on that new nineties black girl fiction (trife as some of it may be) than some of those good, but let's face it, laboriously academic black feminist texts.

White women's racism and the Feminist Movement may explain the justifiable bad taste the f-word leaves in the mouths of women who are over thirty-five, but for my generation they are abstractions drawn from someone else's history. And without the power of memories, these phrases mean little to nothing.

Despite our differences about the March, Brent-Zooks's article offered some interesting insights.

> . . . Still, for all our double jeopardy about being black and female, progressive black women have yet to galvanize a mass following or to spark a concrete movement for social change. . . . Instead of picking up where Ida B. Wells left off, black women too often allow our efforts to be reduced to the anti-lynching campaigns of the Tupac Shakurs, the Mike Tysons, the O. J. Simpsons and the Clarence Thomases of the world. Instead of struggling with, and against, those who sanction injustice, too often we stoop beneath them, our backs becoming their bridges. . . .

Why do we remain stuck in the past? The answer has something to do with not just white racism but also our own fear of the possible, our own inability to imagine the divinity within ourselves. . . .

I agree. At the heart of our generation's ambivalence about the f-word is black women's historic tendency to blindly defend any black man who seems to be under attack from white folks (men, women, media, criminal justice system, etc.). The fact that the brothers may very well be in the wrong and, in some cases, deserve to be buried *under* the jail is irrelevant—even if the victim is one of us. Centuries of being rendered helpless while racism, crime, drugs, poverty, depression, and violence robbed us of our men has left us misguidedly over-protective, hopelessly male-identified, and all too often self-sacrificing.

And yes, fear is part of the equation too, but I don't think it's a fear of the possible. Rather, it is the justifiable fear of what lies ahead for any black woman boldly proclaiming her commitment to empowerment—her sistas' or her own. Acknowledging the rampant sexism in our community, for example, means relinquishing the comforting illusion that black men and women are a unified front. Accepting that black men do not always reciprocate our need to love and protect is a terrifying thing, because it means that we are truly out there, *assed out* in a world rife with sexism and racism. And who the hell wants to deal with that?

Marc Christian was right. *Cojónes* became a necessary part of my feminist armature—but not for the reasons I would have suspected back then. I used to fear the constant accusations—career opportunism, race treason, collusion with "The Man," lesbianism—a lifetime of explaining what I am not. I dreaded the long, tedious conversations spent exorcising others of the stereotypes that tend to haunt the collective consciousness when we think of black women and the f-word—male basher, radical literary/academic black women in their forties and fifties who are pathetically separated from real life, burly dreadlocked/crew cut dykes, sexually adventurous lipstick-wearing bisexuals, victims. Even more frightening were the frequent solo conversations I spent exorcising them from my own head.

In time, however, all of that would roll off my back like water.

Cojónes became necessary once I discovered that mine was not a feminism that existed comfortably in the black and white of things. The precarious nature of my career's origins was the first indication. I got my start as a writer because I captured the sexual attention of a man who could make me one. It was not the first time my externals would bestow me with such favors. It certainly would not be the last.

My growing fatigue with talking about "the men" was the second. Just once, I didn't want to have to talk about "the brothers," "male domination," or "the patriarchy." I wanted a feminism that would allow me to explore who we are as women—not victims. One that claimed the powerful richness and delicious complexities inherent in being black girls now—sistas of the post–Civil Rights, post-feminist, post -soul, hip-hop generation.

I was also looking for permission to ask some decidedly un-P.C. but very real questions:

> Can you be a good feminist and admit out loud that there are things you kinda dig about patriarchy?

Would I be forced to turn in my "feminist membership card" if I confessed that suddenly waking up in a world free of gender inequities or expectations just might bug me out a little?

Suppose you don't want to pay for your own dinner, hold the door open fix things, move furniture, or get intimate with whatever's under the hood of a car?

Is it foul to say that imagining a world where you could paint your big brown lips in the most decadent of shades, pile your phat ass into your fave micromini, slip your freshly manicured toes into four-inch fuck-me sandals and have not one single solitary man objectify—I mean roam his eyes longingly over all the intended places—is, like, a total drag for you?

Am I no longer down for the cause if I admit that while total gender equality is an interesting intellectual concept, it doesn't do a damn thing for me erotically? That, truth be told, men with too many "feminist" sensibilities have never made my panties wet, at least not like that reformed thug nigga who can make even the most chauvinistic of "wassup, baby" feel like a sweet, wet tongue darting in and out of your ear.

And how come no one ever admits that part of the reason women love hip-hop—as sexist as it is—is 'cuz all that in-yo-face testosterone makes our nipples hard?

Are we no longer good feminists, not to mention nineties supersistas, if the A.M.'s wee hours sometimes leave us tearful and frightened that achieving all our mothers wanted us to—great educations, careers, financial and emotional independence—has made us wholly undesirable to the men who are supposed to be our counterparts? Men whose fascination with chickenheads leave us convinced they have no interest in dating, let alone marrying, their equals?

And when one accuses you of being completely indecipherable there's really nothing to say 'cuz even you're not sure how you can be a feminist and insist he "respect you as a woman, treat you like a lady, and make you feel safe—like a li'l girl."

In short, I needed a feminism brave enough to fuck with the grays. And this was not my foremothers' feminism.

Ironically, reaping the benefits of our foremothers' struggle is precisely what makes their brand of feminism so hard to embrace. The "victim" (read women) "oppressor" (read men) model that seems to dominate so much of contemporary discourse (both black and white) denies the very essence of who we are.

We are the daughters of feminist privilege. The gains of the Feminist Movement (the efforts of black, white, Latin, Asian, and Native American women) had a tremendous impact on our lives—so much we often take it for granted. We walk through the world with a sense of entitlement that women of our mothers' generation could not begin to fathom. Most of us can't imagine our lives without access to birth control, legalized abortions, the right to vote, or many of the same educational and job opportunities available to men. Sexism may be a very real part of my life but so is the unwavering belief that there is no dream I can't pursue *and achieve* simply because "I'm a woman."

Rejecting the wildly popular notion that embracing the f-word entails nothing more than articulating victimization, for me, is a matter of personal and spiritual survival. Surviving the combined impact of racism and sexism on the daily means never allowing my writing to suggest that black women aren't more than a bunch of bad memories. We are more than the rapes survived by the slave masters, the illicit familial touches accompanied by whiskey-soured breath, or the acts of violence endured by the fists, knives, and guns of strangers. We are more than the black eyes and heart bruises from those we believed were friends.

Black women can no more be defined by the cumulative sum of our pain than blackness can be defined solely by the transgenerational atrocities delivered at the hands of American racism. Because black folks are more than the stench of the slave ship, the bite of the dogs, or the smoldering of freshly lynched flesh. In both cases, defining ourselves solely by our oppression denies us the very magic of who we are. My feminism simply refuses to give sexism or racism that much power.

Holding on to that protective mantle of victimization requires a hypocrisy and self-censorship I'm no longer willing to give. Calling rappers out for their sexism without mentioning the complicity of the 100 or so video-hos that turned up—G-string in hand—for the shoot; or defending women's reproductive rights without examining the very complicated issue of *male choice*—specifically the inherent unfairness in denying men the right to choose whether or not *they want* to parent; or discussing the physical and emotional damage of sexism without examining the utterly foul and unloving ways black women treat each other ultimately means fronting like the shit brothers have with them is any less complex, difficult, or painful than the shit we have with ourselves. I am down, however, for a feminism that demands we assume responsibility for our lives.

In my quest to find a functional feminism for myself and my sistas—one that seeks empowerment on spiritual, material, physical, and emotional levels—I draw heavily on the cultural movement that defines my generation. As post–Civil Rights, post-feminist, post-soul children of hip-hop we have a dire need for the truth.

We have little faith in inherited illusions and idealism. We are the first generation to grow up with all the benefits of Civil Rights (i.e., Affirmative Action, government-subsidized educational and social programs) and the first to lose them. The first to have the devastation of AIDS, crack, and black-on-black violence makes it feel like a blessing to reach twenty-five. Love no longer presents itself wrapped in the romance of basement blue lights, lifetime commitments, or the sweet harmonies of The Stylistics and The Chi-Lites. Love for us is raw like sushi, served up on sex platters from R. Kelly and Jodeci. Even our existences can't be defined in the past's simple terms: house nigga vs. field nigga, ghetto vs. bourgie, BAP vs. boho because our lives are usually some complicated combination of all of the above.

More than any other generation before us, we need a feminism committed to "keeping it real." We need a voice like our music—one that samples and layers many voices, injects its sensibilities into the old and flips it into something new, provocative, and powerful. And one whose occasional hypocrisy, contradictions, and trifeness guarantee us at least a few trips to the terror-dome, forcing us to finally confront what we'd all rather hide from.

We need a feminism that possesses the same fundamental understanding held by any true student of hip-hop. Truth can't be found in the voice of any one rapper but in the juxtaposition of many. The keys that unlock the riches of contemporary black female identity lie not in choosing Latifah over Lil' Kim, or even Foxy Brown over Salt-N-Pepa. They lie at the magical intersection where those contrary voices meet—the juncture where "truth" is no longer black and white but subtle, intriguing shades of gray.

This Is Not a Puff Piece

Scott Poulson-Bryant

There are people in fashionable society who, throughout their lives, carry with them the burden of their scandals, as ineradicable from their personalities as a tattoo on their forearm.

—DOMINICK DUNNE

PROLOGUE: BEFORE ANDRE HARRELL FIRED PUFF DADDY, THERE WAS ANOTHER story. Before he walked into Puffy's office on that nasty hot evening on July 8 and told his protégé that there was room for only *one* king at the castle called Uptown Entertainment; before Andre Harrell told Puffy that he would have to take his new record label, Bad Boy Entertainment, elsewhere; before Puffy packed up his office; before the telephone lines burned with theories (*Andre's threatened by Puffy's success. Andre was pressured from higher-ups at MCA. Andre's bosses never liked Puffy anyway; they never understood him, never tried to, Puffy's just a troublemaker*); before Andre was saying that Puffy "had particular ways he wanted to do things that weren't in the direction I wanted Uptown to go. . . . "Before all that, before Andre decided that Puff Daddy was "unnecessarily rebellious," there was another story to be told about Puff Daddy. A story that started like this . . .

As hip hop makes its mad dash toward the finishing line of high capitalism, it will need a hero. And there he is, shirtless, the waistband of his Calvin Klein boxer briefs peeking perilously over the edge of his black shorts, the skull tattoo on his left breast gleaming red, mingling with the other guests at Uptown Entertainment president Andre Harrell's party in a posh suburb in northern New Jersey. It is summer 1992 and it's the weekend that Whitney married Bobby and the cream of black entertainment society has invaded this coast for the show. The FOAs (Friends of Andre) swim in the pool, jam to Kid Capri on the 1 and 2's, and play shirts-on-skins b-ball on the court out front, waiting for the catered food to arrive from the Shark Bar, Manhattan's West Side eatery of choice for black entertainment types. Russell Simmons is there, and Veronica Webb and Keenan Ivory Wayans and Babyface. But Puff Daddy is the only one with a briefcase, one of those shiny, bomb-protectant joints, opening it and closing it periodically to show folks the information inside; initial artwork for the logo of Bad Boy

Entertainment. And his first words to me, as I make my way onto the back porch, are not hello or even hi how are you, but, instead, "Yo, nigga, why you frontin'?" Frontin', as in not calling him when I said I would.

We'd actually met a few weeks earlier at a fashion show, and after introductions and small talk, he'd said to me then, "You should write a piece about me." Not only, I thought, is he an A&R man, party promoter, stylist, video director, record producer, and remixer, but he's also his own publicist. It's that kind of boldness, that confident sense of purpose, that drives Sean "Puff Daddy" Combs along the path to success he has chosen. Indeed, he is a boy wonder, and, at 22 years old, possibly the second-youngest record-company president—just two months behind Dallas Austin—when Bad Boy launches this year. Codirecting and costarring in the videos of Mary J. Blige and Jodeci—the jewels in his young crown of achievement—he inspires the same kind of awe and jealousy usually reserved for a front-and-center star. There is so much to do, in fact, that he employs two live-in assistants to manage his growing schedule of meetings and growing roster of acts.

And Puffy cherishes his status, thrives on the exuberance of his youth and its possibilities. He likes the hanging-out nature of his work—the club-going and party-hopping, keeping on the very edge of what's young and black and hip. But Puffy brings something else to his behind-the-scenes machinations—he's his own best logo. The postcards announcing the debut of Bad Boy feature Puffy in all his cultivated B-boy glory, shirtless and seated underneath a lonely streetlamp in one, poised behind jail-like bars, his arms raised dramatically, in another. He has the aura of a performer; quite possibly he is the only A&R executive in the business with as many groupies as his artists. He's the shadowed love man in Mary J. Blige's "Reminisce" video and the placard-carrying strutter in Heavy D's "Don't Curse" clip. "Puffy," says Andre Harrell, "is the perfect icon. He embodies that kind of charisma and star power." In the fickle world of hip hop, Puffy created heroes and makes a hero of himself in the process.

But heroes, because they are heroes, usually bear the cross of their constituents' sins; heroes often take falls. And just after Christmas 1991, as he attempted to present a gift to his community in the form of a fund-raising celebrity basketball game, Puff Daddy's ascendancy almost came to its first abrupt and complete—some say inevitable—stop. What began as "an opportunity to get dressed up in your newest gear, a colorful event 'cause black folks always want something to go to to be colorful," as Andre Harrell put it, ended up as a tragedy that would reverberate around the globe. At the Nat Holman Gym at City College in Harlem, nine people were killed, victims of a stampede of bumrushing, overeager fans. Puffy was the promoter and organizer, and in the aftermath of the event, he found himself at the center of the serve-and-volley toss-up of laying blame and anointing responsibility. His name, once synonymous with all that was fierce, irreverent, and youthful about hip hop, was now the very definition of all that was fragile, violent, and immature.

"Puffy was a ham," says his mother. Before rolling off a litany of examples like a proud stage mother. He modeled with Stephanie Mills in a *Wiz* layout for *Essence*. He was a Baskin-Robbins ice-cream boy in another spread. But he'd always loved music. "I didn't know what he would do, but he was blasting me out of the house with this mixing kit I bought him when he was 13, making that noise, scratching those records."

The house was an apartment in Esplanade Gardens, a middle-class complex in Harlem. Then, when his mother's work for United Cerebral Palsy forced her to relocate to Westchester County, home became Mount Vernon, a mixed-race suburb just north of the Bronx. His father, who owned a limousine company, died when Puffy was three, and his grandmother raised him with his mother. "My mother was the man of the house," Puffy says now. "She was running shit."

But Sean—who became Puffy when he was about 12, in a game of the dozens—was looking to the future anyway, to Howard University, where he would find out what being the man was really about. "I knew they had mad girls down there, and parties, but I really wanted to get a black education." He found out in his first two weeks on campus that there was a world to conquer. "I was looking at things as a businessman by then," Puffy says, remembering his introduction to black college life. "Experiencing black people from all different lifestyles, different parts of the country. I had to learn from this."

He had to learn, basically, that it wasn't who you were but who you knew. He brought his Harlem flavor to bear by throwing parties that became the place to be Friday and Saturday nights on Howard's campus. "I started gaining friends from that. I could get anything I wanted on campus," he says. "If I needed to get my car fixed, I knew where to go. If I needed the English paper, I knew who to go to. If I needed an exam or some weed, I knew how to get it."

So: schoolwork could be bought; life was easy; Puffy had it made. But he admits now that his methods were suspect. "I had a lot of immature ways about me. I don't agree with all that stuff now. I had a lot of growing up to do."

Back in the late '80s, when Puffy was in high school and grooving into the wee hours to the beat of house music and hip hop, artists would come to clubs to film their videos. Puffy found himself dancing for Diana Ross, Fine Young Cannibals, and Baby-face. Seventeen years old and hungry for a life in entertainment, he was still confused: Should be he a shaker, doing the Running Man for admiring audiences? Or should he be a mover, actually running things as The Man? When he saw the "Uptown Kickin' It" video and the young brother named Andre Harrell at the front of the boardroom table, he decided he "wanted to be the guy sitting at the head of the table, pushing contracts aside after signing them." Heavy D, a fellow Mount Vernonite and a premier artist at Uptown, hooked him up with an interview that landed him an internship working Thursdays and Fridays. Up at five a.m. each Thursday to get to New York by 10, Puffy would make it back to Howard by midnight each Friday for his parties. Even sneaking onto the Amtrak, hiding in the bathroom to avoid paying the conductors, he was happy. "I didn't give a fuck," he says. "I was at Uptown."

"My vision for the company," says Andre Harrell, "was to create a label that was cool, that had that Harlem kind of cool hustler cachet to it." Puffy impressed Andre, "in his shirt and tie, doing everything right, real polite and respectful." But what he noticed underneath the polite attire was something else: "Puffy was a hustler." So when Kurt Woodley, the A&R director at Uptown, left the company, Harrell wasn't surprised that Puffy took him to lunch and asked to have the job. He was 18 years old.

His first project was Father MC's debut album, which netted a gold single and respectable sales, carrying on the too-smooth style that became Uptown's specialty with

Heavy D and Guy. But gathering dust were two other projects: Jodeci, a four-man singing group from North Carolina whose first record had passed without notice, and the future Queen of Hip Hop Soul, a Bronx girl name Mary J. Blige.

"Utilizing stereos at high volumes should be limited to VPs and Directors," reads a memo on the walls of some offices at Uptown Records. Puffy takes this seriously. His office actually vibrates with the force of the beat. As I walk in, Puffy's on the phone and before he cuts the call short I hear him say, "Nah, G, you think I'm gonna give the merchandising away? I come up with the flavor for my artists." The flavor for Jodeci and Mary J. Blige, Puffy's two biggest acts during his tenure as A&R man, came to him as a dream—soulful R&B singers in hip hop gear, a kind of mix-and-match approach that, in retrospect, seems absurdly obvious. A new genre was born. Hip hop soul, as Harrell calls it. Sound meeting sensibility at a typically contradictory African American crossroads. "And now, says Puffy, "everybody's trying to look like the groups that I put out, with the images I created."

Detractors point out that the style Puffy "created" is actually just an extension of his own Harlem homeboy style—that Jodeci, for instance, are just four Puffys on stage, playing out his own narcissism. "I wouldn't say they're exactly like me, but it's a combination of me and young black America," Puffy says. He stops, ponders for a second, and then continues. "But if I was a honey, I would probably be just like Mary J. Blige. A bitch. Not in the negative connotations of the word but like, 'That's a *bad* bitch.'"

It was in this spare, busy office that the groundwork of the Puffy business occurred. The wall unit holds a small collection of books skewed mostly toward music and black studies, various Uptown artists' 12-inch singles, and a large color television usually tuned to one video channel or another. A life-size cutout of Mary J. Blige stands at attention near the door, as if to greet visitors with the realization of Puffy's dreams. A cactus plan, prickly as Puffy often seems, rests on the windowsill. His beeper, on vibrate mode, scurries around his desk like an impatient child; Puffy answers pages constantly. That is, when he isn't working on the weekly column he writes for *Jack the Rapper,* an industry journal recounting radio activity of current records. Or when he isn't meeting with prospective artists, who wait in the anteroom and grin at each other in anticipation of playing their demos for the man who seems to represent the increasing visibility and force of urban black boys in contemporary music. ("I saw him in that Karl Kani ad," one of them said earlier, outside the office. "Who that nigga think he is?" "Puffy," responded another, "that's who.")

He is remarkably soft-spoken, communicating mostly through body language: He might break into a sliding dance move when describing his night out at Mecca or some other club-of-the-moment. Or stand stock-still with a hard-headed stare, daring you to convince him. When a young designer comes to show a video of his clothing collection, Puffy leaves the room after a glimpse at the screen, refers the video to Sybil, his assistant, then returns to the room and describes, to a T, what he saw only two seconds of.

One day in the summer of '92, Jodeci needed clothes for a *Regis and Kathie Lee* appearance. Puffy cabbed from store to store in downtown Manhattan, collecting baggy jeans and woolly skull caps, eating Chinese takeout, chatting into his cellular phone all the while. Late in the day, as I reached for my beeper, he said, "Damn, I never met a nigga get more beeps than *I* do." Pause: "I bet you one of those suburban kids, got good grades in school, went to college. You wanna win a Pulitzer prize, don't you?" This is Puffy: arrogant, boyish competition mixed with the seductive, coy recognition of ambition in others. I ask him later if he is conscious of the seduction. If, in fact, it gets him what he wants. "Anything I've wanted, I can say I've gotten it," he says, straightforwardly. "I just saw it and did it, you know? I observe. I always look at the situation before I speak and before I decide what I want. I don't just jump my ass buck naked into the firepit, I look at that motherfucker and see if there's any space."

After a long day of listening to demos, scheduling studio time, and preparing for the imminent debut of his own company, Puffy is headed home to the tony suburb north of Manhattan, in his white BMW, for a much-needed rest. In a contemplative mood, he takes a circuitous route through Harlem, crisscrossing the city streets as if on a memory mission, passing prostitutes on some side streets and lost-looking children on others. Here on the road, caught for a moment between the rarefied world of Uptown (the record company) and the rapidly deteriorating world of Uptown (his teenage stomping grounds), he talks about his dark side.

"A lot of my music is about pain. That's why the masses relate to it. It's attainable, people understand it. When Mary J. Blige sings about looking for a real love, it's fucked up, searching, you know? It's realistic shit."

As he drives up to a stoplight, he says, quietly, "I don't normally be smiling, real happy, youknowhumsayin'? Ain't nothing to be happy about. Things are fucked up. You got little kids starving, getting beat up, parents on crack, ain't got nobody to talk to.

"The only time I'm really happy is when I'm at a club or the rink and they play one of my records. The motherfuckers be screaming to it. They play one of my remixes and I see the look on their faces. Or I go to the concert and see all the kids dressing and looking like my artists.

"I could have got off on the highway, but I just have to drive through Harlem to remind me about all the fucked-up shit. How fortunate I am."

There's a story about Puffy that both his detractors and admirers like to tell. When he was a little boy in Mount Vernon, he wanted a pool, refused to swim in the public pool in the park. According to one version, Puffy begged and begged for the pool and was only happy when his mother took on a second job to pay for it. When Puffy tells the story, he describes the white kids across the street and how they teased him. "They would never invite me over. I used to cry. My Moms made sure she got me a pool that was two times bigger than theirs. It took her like a year to save for it and it was the only Christmas gift, nothing else, no socks, nothing. "I ask if he thought he was spoiled. "My mother tried to get me everything I wanted. She always sacrificed and didn't do for herself. Maybe by some other standards I was spoiled, but I don't think so. I never did no flipping-out brat shit on my mother."

When we get to his house, he tells me he bought it because of the pool. It's a beautiful split-level, small by the town's standards, but comfortable. Puffy shares it with his assistants Mark and Lonnie, who each have their own room off the main hall. Puffy's bedroom is dominated by the closets and roomy, boxy shelf space filled with sneakers and shoes. Downstairs, a pool table takes up most of the space in the rec room, off of which there's a bar and weight room and mixing room for late night scratching sessions.

Mark and Lonnie come in, carrying records and Puffy's suit, fresh from Agnès B. Shirts need to be ironed, so Puffy challenges Mark to a game of pool. The loser will iron. "I'ma make you my bitch tonight," Puffy tells Mark as they square up.

As Puffy wins game after game, the front door opens and his mother comes in, carrying paintings for the house. Everyone calls Mrs. Combs—a short, stylish woman with close-cropped hair—Mom. She eventually takes a seat at the bar and watches the game, telling me about her son's hustling nature. She tells me about Puffy's father, about how he was quite the player, the pool shark, how he would shoot pool and dice up around Lenox Avenue and 126th Street, and how Puffy probably gets his spirit, his competitiveness, naturally. Then her Mom-speak breaks in: *You should eat if you gonna go out. What are you wearing tonight? You want me to fix y'all some sandwiches?* And she does, heaping mounds of Steak-Umms with tomatoes and cheese.

Mark irons, Puffy dresses, Lonnie scratches on the turntables. Boys at home, before they become men in the street.

> *You can take Hollywood for granted like I did, or you can dismiss it with the contempt we reserve for what we don't understand. It can be understood too, but only dimly and in flashes. Not half a dozen men have ever been able to keep the whole equation of pictures in their heads.*
>
> —F. Scott Fitzgerald, *The Last Tycoon*

Hip hop has always been—and will always be—about fabulousness and myth. It's about building new stages to perform newer songs while wearing the newest clothes. But from its fitful birth on the cracked pavement that lined the blocks of upper New York City up until the mid '80s, when Run-D.M.C. rushed up the pop charts with the other American Realness acts (Springsteen, John Cougar Mellencamp), "hip hop" was "rap," ethnic and subcultural, taken for granted by the kids from around-the-way, dismissed by the High Pop tastemakers with the contempt they reserved for that which they didn't understand. But there were a few who could keep the equation in their heads. Russell Simmons and Fab 5 Freddy, for instance, saw the "in," saw the never-quenchable thirst of major labels and downtown art galleries as creating the next, and logical, pit stops for this new, evolving thing. Some called it selling out.

But there was another generation behind them, who could also keep the equation in their heads, as they danced up the residue of black power that seeped through the grooves of Public Enemy and KRS-One records. They were also watching the decade-defining shenanigans on *Dynasty* and buying into the record-breaking event called *Thriller* and imbibing the language of bigness, or largeness, as it would be called in hip hop parlance, where words come and go at a feverishly junk-bondish turnover rate.

Puffy is from that generation. They know that blackness means fierceness in the face of adversity. They know that you can yell "Fuck white people" or call yourself a "nigga" and make millions. Their first hip hop shows were often stadium-size or live freestyling on, of all places, MTV. They are conscious of their era, and they know they exist because they spend money on entertainment that tells them they exist. And closer to home, they saw that the people with the fresh cars and nice clothes were not parents of kids their age, but actually *kids* their age, kids with lethally legal and illegal businesses. Gettin' paid. Livin' large. Whether on the money-makin', boogie-down tip of the entertainment world or the hardcore of the street, black people could *own*. And what better to own and market, to turn into a mock grass-roots cottage industry, than the culture itself? Says one industry insider, "All these young boys wanna be in the music business to get large, when they would be out in the street selling drugs. The music industry is perfect for them, 'cause it's just a legal form of drug dealing."

Listen to Puffy talk about drive, about the reason he gets up in the morning: "The young kids—all the real motherfuckers across the world that's young and black—they need that real shit. Motherfuckers *need* that shit, youknowhumsaying'? They got to hear it. Like, if records stopped being made, motherfuckers would be jumping out of windows or something. That shit is almost like a drug."

That's also the reason he started throwing parties.

Hip hop parties had, for the most part, been banned in New York, due to an increasing amount of violence and recurrent, racist complaints about noise. But Puffy needed a nightlife. Why not just create one? "I found myself being this senior executive of A&R," he says now, "and I was like, yo, I wanted to use my power and my money and rent some of these clubs, so we could have a place to go." Kicking off his reputation with a Christmas party in 1989, when he was starting out at Uptown, he threw a fete for the industry, he says, "to kind of announce myself. It was real dope."

He teamed up with Jessica Rosenblum, a downtown club fixture, who once womaned the door at Nell's. She'd established a niche for herself by organizing social functions for the music industry and came with a reputation as a white woman on the hip hop make, one of the many white faces popping up more and more frequently on the scene. She and Puffy became partners with the opening of Daddy's House at the Red Zone, a home for hardcore hip hop where you could roll with the flavor to the latest beats, complete with live shows and plenty of attitude. "We were equal partners," Puffy says, "but I was more on the creative end, I knew more of the people. "Daddy's House received the imprimatur of the hip hop tastemakers and Puff Daddy became synonymous with the hippest underground jams in New York City. Rosenblum describes Daddy's House this way: "You know a party is a success when it turns up in a rap song. Daddy's House did."

But its success was short-lived. Fights began to break out. Jessica wanted to expand her own operation. Puffy had a regular job, with increasing responsibility. "It just started to become too much pressure for me," he says now. "And I was making money from work. I didn't want party promotions to be the main thing in my life."

But in December of 1991, one particular party would become the *only* thing in his life.

It all started when Magic Johnson announced he was HIV-positive. Puffy was upset and wanted to host a celebrity basketball game to raise both money and community awareness. Well-practiced by now in the art of promotion, on the day of the game Puffy had everything running smoothly. Heavy D had gotten involved in the plans, and by late afternoon a posse of usually reticent artists—Boyz II Men, Mary J. Blige,

Jodeci, Michael Bivins, EPMD—and hundreds of fans had shown up at the Nat Holman Gym.

"As it started getting dark, we had to shut the doors 'cause the line had got disorganized out front," Puffy says. "The police came in through the back door and we were like, 'Yo, there's too many people out there.' We told them we really needed their help. This white sergeant said okay and they all left the building out through the back and then like about an hour later, the people in the pay line started pushing on the doors. Inside the gym, it was only 40 percent capacity filled. But we weren't gonna let nobody else in. Anybody who got caught outside with tickets, we were gonna refund their money. We just didn't wanna take chances by opening the doors back up.

"But people started pushing from the outside and the doors just snapped off the hinges and people just started pouring in. People started jumping down the staircase. People started piling on top of each other and glass started breaking in the doors and people were getting scared and running.

"Pushing and pushing. It was more pressure. Then all of a sudden, I'm on the other side of the door, pulling people through so we could open some of the other doors, but even as we started pulling people in, more people were pushing through. We started screaming to people to get back, to back up. And like a few minutes later, we saw people passing out 'cause of the heat."

He pauses, drawing in a breath. "And we started seeing some scary shit. People's eyes were going back in their heads and I'm thinking, people could die out here. A big kid had gotten stuck in the door and we couldn't pull him through or anybody else. The cops were being called, but nobody was coming.

"And I could just feel it. I was thinking some of the people were dying or dead. People had started to regurgitate. Nobody was trying to give mouth to mouth resuscitation, so I started and other people started. One guy that I knew, we were trying to revive him for like 45 minutes. He was throwing up in my mouth but I didn't care. We were like, Yo, man, you gotta live. We were pumping his chest and breathing into him. And I'm seeing my girlfriend buggin' out because her best friend is there, not breathing, and I'm trying to give her mouth to mouth. And I start to feel this feeling, in the breath I'm getting back, that people were dead. I could feel the death going into me.

"Later," he continues, his voice quieter now, "I went home, and I kept saying to myself that it was all a bad dream, that I was gonna wake up. But I never woke up. And the next day we contacted the police and the mayor's office. But people just looked at the flyer and saw my name and Heavy D's name and started blaming everybody, people saying whoever threw the event must have fucked up. And the press started drawing conclusions before the actual investigation."

Accusations flew from all corners. The director of the student center at City College blamed the president of the Evening Student Government, claiming in *The New York Times* that she had misled him about "her skill in organizing such events, the size of the expected crowd and to whom the proceeds were to be donated." It turned out, also, that the AIDS education Outreach Program, the charity to which a portion of the proceeds were to have gone, was questionable. It had not been registered as a charity in Albany, according to the *Times*, and "was not known among anti-AIDS groups."

In televised press conferences, Puffy looked shrunken and young, hesitant in speech and demeanor. He went underground to avoid the ensuing melee of judgment. Even Rosenblum, whom Puffy had hired to work the door (not to co-promote, as was rumored), admits that the situation took its toll on him. "It made him learn to think things through," says Rosenblum now. "Puffy's used to telling people what he wants and having them execute it. Unfortunately, this time, the people working for him didn't fully execute the plan. It wasn't Puffy's *fault,* but it was his responsibility."

Says Puffy, "I started to lose it. I felt like I didn't want to even live no more. I was so fucking sad. The legal counsel was not to go anywhere, not to talk to anybody. But I wanted to go to the wakes and the funerals and try to provide some comfort, even though I knew my presence probably wouldn't have given comfort. But what I was going through, with the blame and stuff, was nothing compared to what the families were going through.

"I couldn't eat," he recalls now, sitting forward in his seat. "I was just sleeping, like a mummy. I didn't talk to nobody. And every time I turned on the news there was something about the event or the money or something.

"I was scared throughout the whole event. There's no big hero story to all this. I'd never had that much up against me. I had to be a man or die. And I was deserted. There was, like, fake, nosy support. But a lot of people I thought were my friends just fell by the wayside. I had my mother and my girl and Andre, and a few other friends.

"But I have to live with the fact that people meet me or see me and no matter how many platinum records I have or whatever, they'll think, 'Oh, that's the guy who murdered nine people at City College.' 'Cause they didn't check out the mayor's report that cleared me of all the blame. [The City Hall report actually found that Combs had delegated responsibilities to inexperienced associates and should have arranged better security to handle the expected large crowds.] But I imagine the pain the families go through and I understand that what I went through and will go through is nowhere near their pain. And that's the thing that kept me going, knowing if they had the strength to go on, I had the strength to go on and handle people looking at me and thinking whatever they're gonna think."

"The City College event grew him up quick," Heavy D says. "He was on a path where he could have destroyed himself. He was on a high, you know, he was 'Puffy!' doing all this stuff at his age. But every disaster has a delight. There's a lesson in disguise."

Always a "panicky young man," as Heavy D describes him, Puffy no longer moved with the same reckless, abandon, rushing headlong toward whatever goal he set. And even though outsiders looked to place blame on easy official targets like City College or the police, Puffy found the answer in the community that bred his style, his music, himself. "It wasn't that the tickets were oversold like people said. It wasn't the fire department's fault or the cops'. And it wasn't simply that 'niggas are crazy,' as people say," he says. "It's just that overall in the black community there's a lack of self-love. The majority of the kids weren't necessarily gonna put themselves in the position to get hurt, but when it came time to love their neighbors and move back, they couldn't love their neighbors because they didn't love themselves."

And that's probably the hardest thing for Puffy to accept: that, in essence, The City itself was responsible for the nine deaths forever linked to his name—The City and its dark side, which feeds on the constant restlessness of the shut-out and put-down, which takes away the places of recreation that might be a respite from the infrequent, hyped "events" kids are attracted to, the places where their heroes can shine bright and strong.

But Puffy's job was to create those heroes, and he had to go back to work soon after the tragedy. Jodeci and Mary J. Blige were blowing up around the country and bringing a whole new image of young blackness to the masses. Mary J. Blige's blasé, Uptown Girl attitude mixed with hip hop beats, and a talent-show vocal aggressiveness redefined the concept of the soul-shouting diva. Puffy was also at work on *Blue Funk,* Heavy D's darkest album, full of the pain of love lost and maturity gained. Jodeci became the standard-bearer of urban black-boy stoicism, but with a supple, gospel sound that made R&B edgy again.

And edginess is what Puffy likes. In the works was Bad Boy Entertainment, Puffy's own management and record company. During the aftermath of City College, says his mother, "A lot of people showed Sean their asses to kiss. I was there for him, and we became a lot closer, we started communicating better." She realized just how determined her son was about having his own company. "I didn't want him going down the drain," Mrs. Combs says now. "I told him not to worry, that we'd have our own thing. I had planned to help him all along, but this seemed like a good time. I invested in something for him."

"Puffy is a warrior, he'll go for his," says Andre Harrell. Sean wants Bad Boy to embody his own personal energy and philosophies. Bad Boy wants to be edgier, harder. They would sign a gangster rapper. I think Puffy wants to deal with more rebellious issues."

I ask Andre about Puffy's rebellion thing. He laughs and outlines his theory of Black Folks: There are "ghetto negroes, then colored negroes who are upper lower class or lower middle class who want to go to college and feel the need to be dressed up everywhere they go, you know, working with the system so the system will work for them. Then there's just Negroes, sayin', I've had a credit card for ten years, my father went to college. Puffy is somewhere between ghetto and colored. He is very much like Russell [Simmons]. Puffy was raised colored, went to private school. And that's why he wants to be rebellious. He didn't grow up where rebellious was just normal. Colored folks want to be down with the ghetto."

Late one Sunday night, Puffy and I sit in his white BMW, on East 21st Street in Manhattan, and I ask him about the ghetto thing and its influence on his music. He tells me that even though he didn't grow up in the projects, he was "always attracted to motherfuckers who were real, niggas who really didn't have a lot. Like, a person could live in the suburbs, but they may not have no friends there. You don't really have nothing if you don't have no friends and your mother is a single parent and she may never be around and you ain't really got shit."

"Are you talking about yourself?"

"Yeah, in a sense. But the majority of kids in the suburbs was *made,* you know? Their parents made them a certain way. These kids from the ghetto had no choice. They didn't have shit, but they were *real.*"

Finally he boils it down to its essence: "I don't like no goody-two-shoe shit. I like the sense of being in trouble. It's almost like a girl, yoknowhumsayin'? Girls don't like no good niggas. Girls like bad boys."

Heavy D believes that Puffy—the persistent kid from around the way, who found that all his dreams and nightmares could merge in a single moment—is "slowly yet surely realizing that what he has is a gift. In my opinion, Puffy was responsible for Father MC, Mary J. Blige, and Jodeci. Especially Jodeci. You gotta remember that they had a record out before, and they only blew up when Puffy got in the loop. But Puffy has to realize that that gift ain't for him. It's for other people."

With the debut of the Bad Boy artists, Puffy's ultimate test awaits him. The four acts on the roster are acts handpicked by Puff Daddy himself, not acts passed down for his overseeing. Although the first release, Notorious Big's "Party and Bullshit," featured on the *Who's the Man?* soundtrack, has an irresistible street flavor that seems to have caught the attention of the party people, it remains to be seen whether Puffy has the ears to go with his eye, whether he can see a project from its inception to its fruition with the same level of success. Faith, it seems, will show him the way.

Sitting in the car on 21st Street, Puffy is preparing to go into Soundtrack studios to remix Mary J. Blige's next single. Perhaps that, and recounting the City College nightmare, explains the sudden darkness in his manner. He leans back in the leather seat and sighs. "I just like talking to God, realizing that my shit ain't nothing, my problems are so minute. I pray every night, every day, I talk to God a lot. I carry a Bible with me all the time."

He pulls a tiny, tattered, dog-eared Bible from his back pocket and turns to Psalms. He reads: "The Lord is my light and my salvation; whom shall I fear? The Lord is the strength of my life; of whom shall I be afraid? When the wicked, even my enemies and my foes, came upon me to eat at my flesh, they stumbled and fell."

This is the text of Puffy's next tattoo.

EPILOGUE: Whatever the reason for Puffy's dismissal from Uptown—and we may never know the real reason, or, for that matter, the true nature of the relationship between Puff Daddy and Andre Harrell—both men continue to speak well of each other. Harrell's Uptown will continue to oversee the development of Bad Boy's first three artists—at Puffy's request. Puffy will retain the Bad Boy concept and has the freedom to develop his dream elsewhere.

Just three days after being fired, Puffy remained his cool and contained self. "My only regret," he says, quietly, patiently, "is that if I had any flaws, I could have been nurtured or corrected, instead of people giving up on me. Somebody older may think I have nothing to be angry about 'cause I did what they did in half the time. But I'm not ungrateful for what I've received." He sighs. "But this is just another chapter. This ain't no sad ending."

And he is right. It won't be long before there is yet another Puffy story to tell.

Live from Death Row

Kevin Powell

But some man will say, How are the dead raised up?
And with what body do they come?

—1 Corinthians 15:35

No one can just drop in on Death Row Records CEO Marion "Suge" Knight Jr. without feeling the magnitude of his reputation. No one.

On a cool Southern California evening, I arrive to see him at the Can-Am Building in Tarzana, a thirty-minute drive north of Los Angeles. I'm greeted by a tall, stone-faced, caramel-colored man with a walkie-talkie and a black windbreaker inscribed SECURITY. Rather than letting me into the tiny lobby area, he tells me to wait outside while he alerts someone within the single-story edifice that Suge has a visitor.

The budding legend surrounding 30-year old Suge Knight is such that damn near everyone—from fellow journalists to former and current Death Row employees all the way to a shoeshine man in West L.A.—warned me that Suge was "the wrong nigga to fuck with." The mere mention of his name was enough to cause some of the most powerful people in the music business to whisper, change the subject, or beg to be quoted off the record.

This is an especially hectic time for Knight and Death Row, whose "keepin' it real" mentality has the industry all shook up. Tha Dogg Pound's controversial debut album, *Dogg Food*—the breaking point in the relationship between Time Warner and Interscope Records, Death Row's distributor—was finally released last Halloween and shot to number one on the pop charts. As Snoop Doggy Dogg faced a murder charge in L.A., Knight secured a $1.4 million bond to bail Tupac Shakur out of prison in October and signed him up (both to Death Row Records and Knight's management arm). Shakur has been working feverishly on his Death Row debut—a double CD all written since Shakur's release, titled *All Eyez on Me* (twenty-eight cuts, including a duet with Snoop called "Two of America's Most Wanted")—partly because a return to prison still looms, pending appeals.

Meanwhile, work continues with singers Danny Boy and Nate Dogg, and rappers the Lady of Rage, Jewell, Sam Sneed, and others yet unheard of—to say nothing of the artists for whom Knight now "consults," including Mary J. Blige, Jodeci, and DJ Quick. Death Row is also backing record labels headed by Snoop (Doggystyle Records) and Tha Dogg Pound (Gotta Get Somewhere Records). Plus there's Knight's new Club 662 in Las Vegas and the vision of Dr. Dre directing movies for Death Row Films.

All these things are on my mind as I'm being frisked in the lobby of the Can-Am Building, now the permanent studio for Death Row, where talents as diverse as Bobby Brown, Harry Belafonte, and Barry Manilow once recorded. Around-the-clock protection is provided by a group of off-duty black police officers who work in Los Angeles. While Death Row isn't the group's only client, it's the biggest. According to the guard at the reception desk, "We're better security because we're all licensed to carry guns—anywhere."

Another tall, muscular black man escorts me back to Suge's office—the building also contains two state-of-the-art studios, a gym, and a space where Suge often sleeps. The man opens the door, and I'm struck by two things: a big, light-brown German shepherd rolling on the floor, and the fact that virtually everything in the room—the carpet, the cabinets, the sofa and matching chairs—is a striking blood red. I look at my escort; he reads my facial expression and says nonchalantly, "That's Damu. He won't bother you. He'd only trained to kill on command." On that note, I step gingerly into Suge Knight's office.

Knight's imprint is all over: from the sleek stereo system to the air conditioner (set way too cold) to the large-screen TV that doubles as an all-seeing security monitor. Right in front of his big wooden desk, outlined in white on the red carpet, is the Death Row Records logo: a man strapped to an electric chair with a sack over his head. I was told by another journalist that no one steps on the logo. No one.

Sporting a close-cropped haircut and a neatly trimmed beard, Knight strikes a towering pose. When he sits down to face me, with Damu (Swahilli for "blood") now lying by his feet, you can't help but notice the huge biceps itching to bust through his red-and-black-striped shirt. Muscle, say both his admirers and detractors, is the name of Knight's game. Speaking with a syrupy drawl, Suge (as in "Sugar") details the original mission of Death Row Records.

"First thing to do was to establish an organization, not just no record company," he says, his eyes looking straight into mine. "I knew the difference between having a record company and having a production company and a logo. First goal was to own our masters. Without your master tapes you ain't got shit, period."

As Knight speaks of Dr. Dre's *The Chronic,* which laid the foundation for Death Row in 1992, and Snoop's solo debut, *Doggystyle,* which proved that Death Row was more than just a vanity label, I can't help but notice how utterly simple and ghetto—in the sense that the underclass has always done what it takes to survive—his logic is. Ain't no complicated equations or middle-class maneuvers here, just, according to Knight, people getting what they deserve. And never forgetting where they come from.

"We called it Death Row 'cause most everybody had been involved with the law," Knight explains. "A majority of our people was parolees or incarcerated—it's no joke. We got people really was on death row and still is."

Indeed, there is no way to truly comprehend the incredible success of Death Row Records—its estimated worth now tops $100 million—without first understanding the conditions that created the rap game in the first place: few legal economic paths in America's inner cities, stunted educational opportunities, a pervasive sense of alienation among young black males, black folks' age-old need to create music, and a typically American hunger for money and power.

The Hip Hop Nation is no different than any other segment of this society in its desire to live the American dream. Hip hop, for better or for worse, has been this generation's most prominent means for making good on the long-lost promises of the civil rights movement. However, the big question is, Where does this pull-yourself-up-by-your-bootstraps economic nationalism end and the high drama that hovers over Death Row Records begin?

The music industry thrives on rumors, and Death Row is always grist for the gossip mill. Stories run the gamut from Knight and his boys using metal pipes in persuading the late Eazy-E to release Dr. Dre from Ruthless Records, to former Uptown

CEO Andre Harrell being strong-armed into restructuring Mary J. Blige's and Jodeci's contracts, to an alleged beef between Knight and Bad Boy contracts, to an alleged beef between Knight and Bad Boy Entertainment CEO Sean "Puffy" Combs, which some trace to the shooting death of one of Knight's close friends last October.

That incident, some say, has fueled a growing East Coast versus West Coast battle, and—so go the rumors—has led to reported threats on Combs's life. "I heard there was a contract out on my life," says Combs. "Why do they have so much hatred for me? I ask myself that question every day. I'm ready for them to leave me alone, man."

In an interview in last April's VIBE, Shakur suggested that Combs, the Notorious B.I.G., Shakur suggested that Combs, the Notorious B.I.G., Shakur's longtime friend Randy "Stretch" Walker, and others behaved suspiciously immediately following Shakur's shooting in New York on November 30, 1994. Exactly one year to the day after Shakur's shooting, Walker was murdered execution-style in Queens. (When contacted by phone after the murder, Shakur offered no comment.)

The drama had already intensified when Knight bailed out Shakur last October and brought him to Death Row. Shakur's "relentless new double album for Death Row includes a track featuring Faith Evans—one of Combs's artists and Biggie Small's wife—titled "Wonder Why They Call You Bitch." According to one source "Tupac and Faith are now very, very close." ("Me and Faith don't have no problems," says Shakur. When asked about the relationship beyond the studio, he replies, "I ain't gonna answer that shit, man. You know I don't kiss and tell.") While Knight has said repeatedly that he wants Death Row to be "the Motown of the '90s," the label's history is unfolding more like an in-your-face Martin Scorsese film than Berry Gordy's charm school approach.

I ask Knight about all the rumors. He shifts his weight in his chair and bristles. "When you become the best, it's more rumors, it's more people want to stop you, 'cause everybody want to be number one."

"Can we talk about any of these alleged incidents?"

"Say what you want to say."

I then recount my understanding of the Andre Harrell story as Knight stares at me. Before long, he's flipped the script, asking me what I would do if I wasn't receiving a fair deal.

"You should get the best deal you can get in this business," I respond.

Knight edges forward in his chair, proud he got me to agree. "See, people got this business mixed up," he says. "They want to go and talk about a person who fixin' to come and help you. They don't say nothin' about the motherfucker who beatin' people out they money. When you stand up for right, people should tip they hat to you and keep movin', and mind they own business."

Not totally satisfied with Knight's response, I wonder why rappers D.O.C. and RBX are no longer with Death Row Records, and why both have gone on record, literally, complaining of not being paid. But Knight's already defensive, and I don't want to get tossed out before I get to bring up other, more important questions.

"What about the methods you used to get Harrell to renegotiate those contracts?" I ask.

"It's like this. Was you there?"

"Nah."

"Then there's nothin' to talk about."

What Knight will talk about is how important it is for him and Death Row to stay rooted in the streets. The youngest of three children and a proud native of working-class Compton (where he still keeps a house), Knight was a star defensive lineman in high school and at the University of Nevada at Las Vegas before entering the music business in the late 1980s. It's not clear how he got into the game—some say he was the D.O.C.'s bodyguard during the N.W.A. days, while Knight maintains he started a music publishing business that earned a small fortune off Vanilla Ice's smash 1990 debut. Whatever the case, few individuals have as much drive as Knight: "Ghetto politics teaches you how to win and really be hungry. I never been the one who wanted to work with nobody. 'Cause I think if a motherfucker get you a paycheck—listen to how it sound, paycheck, like the paying you to stay in check. Can't nobody keep me in check."

Time Warner couldn't. It bowed to political pressure and announced it was selling its 50 percent interest in Death Row's profitable distributor, Interscope Records. Self-appointed gagsta rap watchdog C. DeLores Tucker couldn't. She may have helped get Interscope dropped, but she had no effect on Death Row's progress. In fact, at one point she met with Knight to get a piece of the action. He turned her down.

Despite all the community outreach Suge Knight does—the lavish Mother's Day dinners for single mothers, the turkey giveaways at Thanksgiving, the Christmas toy giveaways for Compton children—he has to know he puts fear in some hearts, that his I-don't-give-a-fuck persona unfurls itself long before people ever meet him in the flesh. Hip hop has always been about being straight-up, about being skeptical of the motives of the generation ahead of us, about creating shields (or myths) to protect our world from outsiders—Bob Dole, William Bennett, C. DeLores Tucker—who seek to come in and dominate us. With four-year-old Death Row Records as his sword and an aura Al Pacino's Scarface would be proud of, Suge Knight epitomizes that mind-set—but at what cost?

Listen to Knight summarize his modus operandi: "Black executives, they get invited to the golf tournaments. I don't give a fuck about all that. I'm not gonna play golf with you. When you playin' golf, I'ma be in the studio. While you trying to eat dinner with the other executives in the business, I'ma be havin' dinner with my family, which is the artists on the label." He pauses to emphasize his point. "Without your talent, you ain't shit."

Talent is something 30-year-old Grammy winner Dr. Dre, né Andre Young, has in abundance. On a different day in the Can-Am Building's studio A, hip hop's most sought-after producer is waiting for Tupac to show up and continue work on his new album. The Compton-born cofounder (with Knight) and president of Death Row, Dr. Dre has sold fifteen million records in the past decade. Six foot one, 200-plus pounds, Dre wears a beige Fila outfit, brown Timberlands, and a gold Rolex saturated with diamonds. If that isn't enough, a chunk of diamond and gold glitters on one of his fingers. Those adornments aside, I'm surprised how soft-spoken and shy the baby-faced Dr. Dre is in person, his eyes avoiding mine for much of the interview. To break the ice, I ask about the World Class Wreckin' Cru, his first group back in the early 1980s.

"Wreckin' Cru was a DJ crew. They used to call it that because it was the guys that came in after the party was over and broke down the equipment," Dre says, leaning closer to my tape recorder as he warms to the topic.

"We eventually made a record, and we had the costumes on and what have you. Back then, everybody had their little getups, you know, like SoulSonic Force, UTFO." Dre laughs at the memory. "That shit haunted me, but you know, I ain't ashamed of my past."

Dre grew disillusioned with the Wreckin' Cru's style and teamed up with a teenage rapper named Ice Cube. They performed live at clubs and skating rinks. "We used to take people's songs, you know, and change them and make them dirty. Like 'My Adidas' was—" Dre laughs hard from the gut up. "Cube had this thing called 'My Penis.' We rocked it, and people would go crazy. So we just took that and started making records with it. And with me being a DJ, I used to sit in the club during the week and make up beats just to play in the club. I would take somebody else's song and re-create it and make it an instrumental. So that's how I basically got into producing."

Eventually Dre decided to form a group, but he needed a financial backer. In 1986 he met Eric "Eazy-E" Wright, a former drug dealer and fellow Compton resident looking to pump his money into something legal. Dre produced an Eazy single called "Boyz-N-the Hood," and it was on. "We hustled the record every day for eight months," says Dre, "riding around in a jeep, selling it from record store to record store ourselves."

DJ Yella, an old Wreckin' Cru partner, joined Dre, Eazy, Cube, MC Ren, and short-term member Arabian Prince to form arguably the most influential rap act ever. N.W.A.'s 1989 landmark, *Straight Outta Compton,* introduced an entire nation to urban blight, West Coast style. The album, produced largely by Dr. Dre and released on the underground label Ruthless Records, went double platinum with virtually no radio play. Dre says he and Eazy started Ruthless, although it was Eazy and Jerry Heller—a middle-aged white man who'd previously worked with Elton John and Pink Floyd—who gained credit for building America's first multimillion-dollar hardcore rap label.

Despite his meteoric success, Dre grows bitter when describing the disintegration of Ruthless Records and his relationship with Eazy-E. "The split came when Jerry Heller got involved," he recalls. "He played the divide-and-conquer game. He picked one nigga to take care of, instead of taking care of everybody, and that was Eazy. And Eazy was just, like, 'Well, shit, I'm taken care of so fuck it.'"

When I reach Heller later by telephone, he reluctantly admits that Dre "was probably right. You know, Dre was a producer and a member of the group," he says. "Eazy was interested I in being Berry Gordy, so more of my time was spent with Eazy."

During the production of N.W.A.'s *Efil4zaggin* album, Dre decided he wanted out of his contract. He almost spits out the recollection: "I was gettin' like two points for my production on albums. I still have the contracts framed." Dre adjusts his Rolex. "I'm not no egotistical person. I just want what I'm supposed to get. Not a penny more, not a penny less."

That's where Knight came in. "Suge brought it to my attention that I was being cheated," he says. "I wanted to do my own thing anyway. I was going to do it with Ruthless, but there was some sheisty shit, so I had to get ghost." Exactly how Knight helped Dre "get ghost" depends on whom you ask. When I mention to Jerry Heller that Knight maintains he's never threatened or beaten up anyone to make a gain in the music business, Heller cracks an eerie laugh reminiscent of Vincent Price's on Michael Jackson's *Thriller*, then says, "I would say he's taking poetic license."

Dre gives Knight credit for coming up with the plan for Death Row in 1991. He assures me he and Knight are "fifty-fifty-partners. You know, me and Suge, we like brothers and shit. "These two buddies figured Dr. Dre's name was bankable enough to start a record label and get a distribution deal, but unbelievable, there were no takers at first. Finally Interscope took a chance and Death Row (the label was going to be called Future Shock, after an old Curtis Mayfield single, until Dre and Knight purchased the more dramatic handle from one of Dre's homeboys) has become the most profitable independently owned African-American hip hop label of the 1990s.

Death Row's first release, *The Chronic,* dissed Eazy-E and Jerry Heller numerous times. But when conversation turns to Eazy's death from AIDS last March, Dre grows solemn. "I didn't believe it till I went to the hospital." He sighs, rubs his chin, and collects his thoughts. "He looked normal. That's what makes the shit so fuckin' scary, man. But he was unconscious, so he didn't even know I was there." Obviously, adds Dre, the ensuing battle over ownership of Ruthless Records will affect Eazy's seven children. "That's who's really going to suffer from this. We were talking about doing an N.W.A. album and giving Eazy's share to his kids."

Dre's words stop suddenly. He's looking off somewhere, palming the back of his neck, perhaps reliving all the years of his life, personal and public: the Wreckin' Cru, N.W.A., his run-ins with the law, Death Row, all the awards and accolades, the offers to produce superstars such as Madonna, his and Ice Cube's long-awaited *Helter Skelter* album, Snoop's trial . . .

I pull Dre back into conversation by asking, "Would Death Row exist without you?" His expression becomes blank, then he begins to speak but stops himself and thinks for a moment. "Wherever I am, whatever I do is going to be the bomb shit. And people are going to benefit from it. I dunno, there might be another Dr. Dre out there somewhere." He laughs uneasily.

I ask him about his greatest fear. "I'm not afraid of anything at the moment," he replies. "Actually, I'm afraid of two things: God and the IRS." He laughs again. "That's it. You know, I get butterflies every time a record comes out. I'm, like, I hope people like it. I hope people buy it. But it's never no serious fear."

What matters most to Dr. Dre is the digestion and creation of music: "A lot of times when I'm at home kickin' it, I don't even listen to hip hop," he says. "I listen to all types of music." (He promises Death Row ventures into rock, reggae, and jazz.) Pushing forward in his chair, Dre, who's recently taken up the trumpet, taps his fingers on his left knee excitedly. "My personal opinion is, the '70s is when the best music was made. Some motherfuckers had orchestras! Had string sections and they'd have to sit there and orchestrate a song. And put some vocals to it. So they really got into it. Curtis Mayfield, that motherfucker was bad as shit. Isaac Hayes, Barry White, y'knowhumsayin'? them brothers was in there doing it."

Out in the crisp air of El Mirage Desert Dry Lake Bed (a grueling 100-mile trek north from Los Angeles) stands the $600,000 video set of "California Love," Tupac's phat first single (co-rapped and produced by Dr. Dre) from *All Eyez on Me.* The video, directed by Hype Williams, is loosely based on the flick *Mad Max:* Helicopters fly over-head, dirt bikes kick up sand, and everyone in the shoot—including Tupac, Dre, comedian/actor Chris Tucker, and a plethora of male and female extras—is wearing black leather shirts, vests, gloves, hats, and pants with metal spikes. Desert dust coats their faces, hands, and arms.

I haven't seen Tupac Shakur since our Rikers Island interview last January. I make my way to his trailer and knock. The door swings open, releasing a powerful gust of chronic smoke. There he is, the big eyes shining brightly, the smile still childlike and broad as an ocean, his exposed muscles—probably due to his 11-month bid—bigger than ever.

As Shakur is whisked away to a TV interview, I ask, "What do you think about this whole East Coast versus West Coast thing?" Tupac smiles that wicked smile and says, "It's gonna get deep."

What is even deeper is the way the word *family* has been mentioned by everyone associated with death Row, including newcomers like teenage R&B singer Danny Boy and rapper/producer Sam Sneed. In this often cruel and unjust world, it can't be argued enough how important it is to have people who've got your back. To have, as we say, "fam with ya." Shakur's journey—from Harlem and the Bronx to Baltimore to the Bay Area to Los Angeles to Atlanta and back to New York and now back to Los Angeles—has always been about that need for family.

A few weeks later I speak with Shakur via telephone. "The family part, to me—I'm not gonna be corny and be, like, 'Everybody on Death Row love each other,'" he says. "It's not like that. Nobody has beef internally. And if we do, we handle it internally.

"More than a family, Death Row to me is like a machine. The biggest, strongest superpower in the hip hop world. In order to do the things that I gotta do, we gotta have that superpower. Now we gotta expand and show exactly what a superpower is.

"At Death Row I don't have to worry about embarrassing nobody or standing out or doing something they don't want me to do. I'm still Tupac. At Death Row, I got my own shit. I'm independent. But this is the machine that I roll with.

"As for me and Suge, right now—as of today—we're the perfect couple. I can see this is what I've been looking for, managementwise. He rides like I ride. With Suge as my manger, I gotta do less. 'Cause before, niggas wasn't scared of me. So I brought fear to them. Now I don't have to do all that to get respect. 'Cause motherfuckers is scared shitless of Suge. I don't know why, cause Suge's cool. A lot of cowards are trying to make it like Suge's the scourge of the industry. All Suge's doing is riding. Making it so rappers can get what they due."

Back at the video shoot, as another TV crew tapes him, a hyper Tupac spreads out a stack of $100 bills just handed him by Knight, who stands in the background talking on a cellular phone. "This is why I signed to Death Row," says Pac to the cameras, "right here."

Shakur's antics hit me as poignant because—perhaps unwittingly—he's playing right into the hands of people who view rappers as foul-mouthed, money-sex-and-violence-crazed lowlifes who are poisoning America's youth. Of course, one of the beauties of the hip hop generation is that we really don't give a fuck what "outsiders" think about us. But in not giving a fuck, in having no agenda but our own selfish needs are we ultimately fucking all the people (family, real friends, ardent supporters) who see us as representative of dreams so often deferred?

I'm still pondering this a week later at the Los Angeles County Criminal Court Building. The washed-out, gray, nineteen-story structure looks as intimidating as any other courthouse, but this one is notable for its famous defendants: O.J. Simpson, Heidi Fleiss, Michael Jackson. I'm here to witness the *People vs. Calvin Broadu* (a.k.a. Snoop Doggy Dog) murder trial.

On the ninth floor, in department 110, room no. 9-302, Judge Paul G. Flynn is presiding over jury selection. Some 500 prospective jurors have been interviewed, and 11 have tentatively been agreed upon by the prosecution and defense. While the search for No. 12 continues, my eyes are on Snoop and his codefendant McKinley Lee—the accused triggerman—a dark-skinned young man with a shiny bald head and a thin goatee. In the interviews, Rodney King and O.J. Simpson come up often, as does the issue of race. While Lee pays close attention, especially to questions about potential jurors' views on rap music, Snoop, his permed hair pulled back into a bun, hunches over a legal pad, scribbling, looking up only when his lawyer David Kenner whispers into his ear.

During the lunch break, Snoop leaves the building with his bodyguard and friends (he's free to walk the streets because Knight bailed him out). Meanwhile, Kenner, a short, cock-diesel man with jet black hair, offers that Lee and Snoop acted in self-defense in the fatal shooting of Philip Woldemariam in August 1993. If convicted, both men face life imprisonment.

Kenner, who represents Death Row on both entertainment and criminal matters, insists that "Snoop Doggy Dogg is not on trial here; Calvin Broadus is. When you reach to a performer's interviews or their songs," Kenner says, "and try to extrapolate from that perceptions that you want to draw about the real person, to me it would be no different than saying Arnold Schwarzenegger is a cold-blooded murderer because of his last movie."

That point aside, Kenner expects the prosecution to bring Snoop's lyrics, videos, and interviews into evidence. Several people who have had contact with Snoop over the past three years, including this writer, have been subpoenaed as material witnesses. Just a few days earlier, charges against a third codefendant, Sean Abrams, were dropped. Kenner also asserts that serious questions of missing evidence have yet to be answered.

Returning just before proceedings resume, Snoop, as rawboned as ever in a dark green double-breasted suit, pauses to speak with me. "I'm straight, you know," he says, picking at the strands of hair cupping his chin. "Everybody's praying for me, and I want them to continue to pray for me."

I ask Snoop if he feels rap music is on trial. His eyes meet mine and narrow. "Yeah, it is. I can't really speak about it, but listen to me, it is."

What about critics who say this trial shows what rap music is all about—violence?

"It's God, giving us obstacles," he replies. "He puts everybody that's successful through obstacles to see if they'll maintain and become successful years down the line. So I'm ready for whatever."

"What do you say to people who look up to you as a hero?"

"Keep God first. Visualize a goal and try to reach it, and if you can't reach it, find something else other than the negative. Because that negative is a long stretch behind the wall—trust me."

There's no ignoring the violence pervading hip hop culture. Particularly when it seems to be reaching up to executive levels. In my interview with Suge Knight, I ask him about the murder in Atlanta of his close friend, Jake Robles. Does he really believe Puffy Combs, the biggest hitmaker on the East Coast, actually had something to do with it? Unnerved by the question, Knight changes the subject, and it isn't brought up again. However, when it's clear the interview is over, he says he has some things he wants to discuss with me.

For the first time that evening, Damu the dog raises up off the red carpet and turns in my direction. "I didn't like them questions you was asking me about the dead," Knight says, anger curling the corners of his mouth. "You mean the questions about Eazy-E?" I ask cautiously.

"Nah, that was my homeboy that was killed down there in Atlanta. I felt you was being disrespectful, and I don't forget things like that," Knight says matter-of-factly, his eyes boring into mine.

As Knight lectures me, the possible seeds of this supposed feud between Knight and Combs come to mind: Tupac Shakur wondering in VIBE last year whether Combs and Biggie Smalls may have known something about his being shot; rumors (strongly denied) that Shakur was raped in jail; Knight publicly dissing Combs—"You don't need no executive producer who's all over your record and in the videos"—at last year's televised *Source* Awards in New York; and finally, the murder of Knight's buddy in Atlanta.

The Atlanta story, according to eyewitnesses, goes a little something like this: SoSoDefRecords CEO Jermaine Dupri had a birthday party, which Knight and Combs attended. Later, both showed up at an after-party at the Platinum House. According to Combs, Knight turned to him after the shooting and said, "You had to have something to do with this." Given the high profiles of both Knight and Combs, it's ironic that there was barely any mention of the incident in the media.

Interestingly enough, both Knight and Combs are on record denying there's a beef. Knight: "For what? I'm a man. How does that look for me to go and have a beef with a person who's not a threat to me?" Combs: "I'm not a gangsta, and I don't have no rivalry with no person in the industry whatsoever. The whole shit is stupid—tryin' to make an East Coast/West Coast war. East Coast, West Coast, Death Row, Def Jam, or Uptown, I feel nothing but proud for anybody young and black and making money. [Some people] want us to be at each other, at war with each other. Acting like a bunch of ignorant niggas."

But there's no denying that tension's in the air. Some folks say it's the start of a hip hop civil war. I remember Dr. Dre saying, If it keeps going this way, pretty soon niggas from the East Coat ain't gonna be able to come out here and be safe. And vice versa."

Back in the office, when Knight feels he's gotten his point across, he and Damu turn and head over to his desk. I rise slowly, then exit.

Out in the night air, I sigh hard. This has not been an easy article to deal with. Too many people have warned me about what to say and what not to say, and that, to me, is not what hip hop is about. But then again, it's 1996 and shit is thick for black folks. When a people feel like social, political, or economic outcasts, it gets easier to consider taking one another out—even over the pettiest beefs—in the name of survival. Not even journalists are immune to this logic.

The tragedy here is that two of the most successful young black entrepreneurs ever could possibly end up hurt or dead over God only knows what. As VIBE went to press, there was talk of involving people such as Minister Louis Farrakhan or Ben Chavis in an effort to get both sides to make peace. The future of hip hop may ultimately depend on such a meeting.

How long Death Row Records will live remains to be seen. But like a true player setting his rules for the game, Knight predicts, perhaps not recognizing the double meaning of his words, "Death Row's going to be here forever."

Danyel Smith

Hit 'Em Up: On the Life and Death of Tupac Shakur

TUPAC SHAKUR: A FIERY FEROCIOUS MC, AN AUSPICIOUS ACTOR, A MAN SO beautiful he made you wanna touch the screen, the photograph, him. He made you wanna see those vanilla teeth, the wet sweet wild eyes, the fleshy lips, the lashes like fans like feathers on his fudgy skin. He made you want to kill him, defend him, make him your baby. He dared you to find the lies, to prove he's crazy. Tupac keeps you searching, even now, for the line between him and the him he put out there for you to see, for the line between being and acting, between how one rolls through life and how one rocks the microphone. Crazy motherfucker. Coward. Sucker. Sexist. Sex symbol. Superman. Provocateur. Hero.

He's another hero we don't need, and 'Pac's built, in death even, to last. From the start, his life was made-for-mythologizing, shrouded as it was in the tragedy of the Black Panther party. Because of his mother's affiliation with the group, Tupac's early existence was mingled with the plain logic of breakfast for everyone, in the ballsy resolve of guns in California's state capital, in the glamour and fraternity of leather peacoats and tams for any brother wanting to stand up and fight—or look ferocious and fab. And Tupac's adult biography has everything—money, music, movies, malfeasance—that makes us love and hate someone. No matter what wrong shit he was ever caught up in, he always had his other raised-by-Panthers/fuck-tha-police self to fall back on.

Tupac's five albums are equal parts striking and adequate. His dramatic (on-screen) performances were promising here and cartoony there. He never quite lived up to the brilliance of his Bishop in Ernest Dickerson's 1992 *Juice*. Onstage, his performances were spotty. Tupac, like many MCs, rode his own dick, seeming to care more about how he was coming off to his boys backstage than he did about the average Negro who paid to stand up in a hot club and catch 'Pac's fever for a moment.

Tupac's different lives were very much in league, though; none would have been vibrant without the others. He managed them, like he managed his blackness—with a fantastic, desperate dexterity. Like most American heroes, Tupac Shakur had glide in his stride, big guns, and leather holsters. But his life was about juggling plums while bullets nipped at his ankles. It was about defiance, women, paranoia, ego, and anger—and going out in a blaze of what he imagined to be glory.

In the late 1980s and early 1990s, Tupac Shakur was chiseling out an existence in Marin City, California's craggy slums. Oakland was known as Coke-Land back then, and though it was a bridge or two away from Marin, Tupac got over to the East Bay a lot, first hanging with his half brother Mocedes and a crew known as Strictly Dope, then with this white girl, Leila Steinberg, from Sonoma County, who was managing him, and then with the droll brothers who made up Digital Underground.

To what degree it is true will probably go forever untold, but the rise of the Bay Area dope game and Bay Area hip hop were massively intertwined. (Actual gangsters, their stacks of cash, and the music business have been linked since kids in the 1940s gave music a real economy.) It's no coincidence that as the crack cocaine market exploded, people like DU, Too Short, and MC Hammer blew up—as well as lesser-known talents like MC Ant, Ant Banks, K-Cloud & the Crew, Premo, and Capitol Tax. The Oakland Police Department Drug Task Force was using battering rams to bust down the doors of dope houses back then. Kids were getting a gross kind of paid while Highland Hospital yanked bullets from bodies. There seemed a ceaseless stream of mothers, groggy with grief, wailing on the news about a good child who was dead. MCs and songwriters responded to the havoc crack was wreaking on the East Bay.

Hammer's contribution was the innocuous "Pray," but Tony Toni Toné went to the soul of the matter with 1988's "Little Walter," an ode to a dope dealer who gets shot upon opening his front door. Club Nouveau's 1986 "Situation #9" (a Top 10 R&B hit) was another admonition: "The life that you're living / Is gonna catch up to you / And boy, I think you need some help." The immense vocals balanced the paranoid lyrics, and that chemistry may have inspired Tupac to ask Roniece Livias to sing in the background (along with David Hollister, who would go on to sing lead in the first incarnation of Teddy Riley's BLACKstreet) of his debut single, 1991's "Brenda's Got a Baby."

Tupac's "Brenda" deserts her newborn, sells dope, then sex, and ends up (in the video for the song) the silent star of a crime scene. He came to kick it with the DU crew one night on a plush Sausalito houseboat Jimi "Chopmaster J" Dright had rented while recording an album under the name Force One Network for Qwest Records. The bay rocked us softly while we listened to "Brenda's Got a Baby" three or four times. Tupac held on to a frayed piece of ruled paper with the lyrics.

"No, she ain't somebody I know," he answered somebody's question. Tupac curled himself forward and laughed. "Y'all some simple muthafuckas," he said. "She's one a them girls we all know." He was 20, I think. The verse he rapped on DU's 1991 "Same Song" had been like a single french fry for a growing boy: Now I clown around / When I hand around / With the Underground." Tupac felt he had more to say. His then-manager, Atron Gregory, was unable to convince Tommy Boy's Monica Lynch of Tupac's potential, but Interscope saw dollar signs in Tupac's worldview, and put up the dough so Tupac could have his say.

It all came out of him in *2Pacalypse Now* (1991), the words of a boy weary of doing the "Humpty Dance," and tired of standing on the corner in Marin City, selling weed. All the best sons on that album—"Young Black Male," "Rebel of the Underground," and the unwavering "Trapped," with Shock in the back murmuring "Nah / You can't keep the black man down"—are rank with the funk of a young man cooped up too long in somebody else's concept. *2Pacalypse* didn't sound like a DU spin-off because while the Underground Railroad production squad stuck with the liquid bassiness that had succeeded for Digital, they also went for a sound more incensed, impassioned, broken, and hateful. They added some Tupac.

Tupac's MC skills were just coming together back then. His words, especially in "Brenda," are over-enunciated and urgent. His writing, though, was clear and picturesque. Brenda was "in love with a molester / Who's sexing her crazy." And when Tupac says "Prostitute found slain / And Brenda's her name / She's got a baby," with Hollister and Roniece battling out in the background, moaning and repeating the name of Brenda over and over, the song is bold and melancholy—a crystalline morality tale. The line "She didn't know what to throw away / And what to keep," especially in the way Tupac hurls it out, consonants sharp and hard, says more about a young woman's angry bewilderment with life than some of the most adored female MCs ever have.

It was right before the release of *2Pacalypse Now* that Tupac, while in New York with Digital Underground, went to an audition with Ronald "Money-B" Brooks. Mun read before Ernest Dickerson, but didn't get called back. Tupac, who said he went along "just to trip," ended up being cast opposite costar Omar Epps's tormented Q as Bishop in *Juice*. While the training Tupac received during his high-school years at Baltimore's School for the Arts no doubt emerged at the unscheduled audition, the way he hustled himself into the reading demonstrated a kind of alertness to opportunity that can't be taught in the classroom.

In the film, Tupac and Epps battle it out for most lovely—both of them black as truth with brown eyes, matching each other stare for stare. Q wants "juice," but the kind Bishop gets drunk on is too corrosive. Bishop has killed Raheem, one of his best friends, and at the funeral, his easy duplicity is marrow-freezing. And later, when Q, trying to get his life back together, slams his locker shut only to find Bishop standing there, it's a vision of one hellborn. The movie house gasps were loud and in unison. "It's over," says Bishop. "Ain't nothin' nobody can do about it now." And like so many of the words that came out of Tupac's mouth which seemed to predict his end, they provide a peek into his state of mind. "You know what?" he says. "I am crazy."

Tupac played Bishop-as-bogeyman ingeniously. Dickerson placed him throughout *Juice* as a cloaked figure—at one point Bishop's red hood is pulled over his head, his face turned away from the camera, a fiend more likely to battle the X-Men than three of his buddies in Harlem. Tupac depicts Bishop's coldness as a hopelessness he finally submits to, even if it means embracing depravity. "You gotta get the ground beneath your feet, get the wind behind your back," says Bishop, after watching James Cagney get shot in *Public Enemy*. "And go out in a blaze of glory if you got to. Otherwise you might as well be dead your damn self." At the end of the film, to the strains of Cypress Hill's "How I Could Just Kill a Man," Q can't hold on to Bishop any longer. Bishop is hanging off the side of a building, Q holding on while he can. "Hold on, Bishop!" Q manages to say, then Bishop is gone—with us calling after him.

In 1991, Public Enemy was still the best band hip hop ever birthed. Touring with Anthrax, they came to the Calvin Simmons Auditorium in Oakland on October 20, the day that the Oakland Hills were burning down to the dirt. Smoke hung over the whole city, ashes fell to the ground like tiny gray snowflakes. Authorities were asking citizens to stay off the roads. Would the PE concert go on? Would Digital Underground roll to the show even though the condominium complex that housed three of the group's members was now among the ashes falling from the sky?

The mood backstage was bleak. This was only a few weeks before *Juice* came out, and somebody'd told me earlier in the day that Tupac had gotten in trouble with the police the day before, had gotten his ass beat in the middle of Oakland's tiny downtown. I saw him backstage, from across a long room, and he looked great. He was talking to someone; I could see his profile, and I knew that the story must have been exaggerated. I walked over to tell him what I'd heard and that he looked fine, and when I got up on him and his whole face was in my face I saw that the other side was puffed and scabby, his eye was swollen, there were scratches and small dents on his forehead—but just on the one side.

He laughed when he saw the expression on my face and gave me back his profile. "You like that better?" he said, with his usual toothy smile. "Nope!" he said, showing me his whole face again. "You gotta look! Look! Those motherfuckers had me on the ground and they bashed my head into the sidewalk over and over. On some bullshit! Hear me? Mad 'cause I had a check for seven grand in my wallet. I'ma sue 'em though. Watch me." And he just kept on like that, talking to everybody, real regular, no bandages. One side of him flawless, the other ruined as the hills in flames behind us.

"Holler If Ya Hear Me," produced by Randy "Stretch" Walker of Live Squad, is the best track (and it was never a single) Tupac Shakur ever recorded. It's the first number on 1993's *Strictly 4 My N.I.G.G.A.Z.,* and it barrels at you, churning and fired up. "'Cause I'm black born / I'm supposed to say 'peace' / Sing songs / And get capped on?" The lines are juicy with testosterone, every one rolling right into the next. "Pump! Pump! if you're pissed / At the sellouts living it up / One way or another / They'll be giving it up." He's going fast with the lyrics, the song revved up on the intoxicating, pretend energy that comes from saying what you want when you know it's only about itself, not about what really happens, or about what you're really going to do. But still, it feels divine.

"Oh, no / I won't turn the other cheek." And it's like, yes. Can we not turn the other fucking cheek? Can we revel at the blood heating up our hearts when we hear a black person espousing that? "I love it when they fear me," says 'Pac, and how lovely is that feeling when you have always been in fear? Tupac emits fat zaps of musical electricity—they first rouse, then dull, then burn.

Tupac, with "Holler," dispensed a buccaneer spirit—bandanna'd men, fancy women, romance, mutiny. It's what gangsta rap was about at its N.W.A. beginnings: no more Mr. Nice Guy. Let's be defiant in our songs and we'll feel, if not actually be, free. We'll feel a part of the patriarchal club—every line of a good gansta rap song being a warm hand on a soft dick, after all. And as usual, too—passive girls get the (sensual) benefit and pay the (political and spiritual) cost. Surrounded by rock nostalgia, hip hop fans believe that music "changed the world" before, so it can change the world again. Every time someone new arrives—Chuck D, Ice-T, Arrested Development's Speech, anyone from the Wu Tang Clan—and dares to state what he (and it's always a he) thinks about the world, blacks get hopeful, whites get excited, and then when things stay the same, everyone feels betrayed.

It was around this time he was arrested for shooting two off-duty cops on October 31, 1993, in Atlanta. Shooting cops? And living to tell the story? And beating the rap? He was beyond real. He rhymed about shooting people, and getting shot, and he lived it in real life, and he played it on film. He filled the hero spot in a way someone like Eazy-E never could, because Eazy wasn't easy to look at and Eazy never talked about his mama or any other female like he loved her.

"Keep Ya Head Up" was the gold single that carried *Strictly* to platinum status. The song contains a riff from the Five Stairsteps' "O-o-h Child," and vocals from the same Dave Hollister (credited this time as the "Black Angel") who contributed so mightily to "Brenda's Got a Baby." On each of Tupac's albums, he included at least one song that illuminated the side of himself that believed in good. "I wanna give a holler to my sisters on welfare," he says in "Head Up." "Tupac cares if don't nobody else care." Uplifting, pro-choice, and anti-abuse, "Keep Ya Head Up," "Dear Mama," and "Brenda" are the "good" songs, the ones that make Tupac unassailable in the eyes of his fans. "Head Up," especially, is used like shield and sword to defend him.

Tupac tells women he knows they're "Dying inside / But outside you're looking fierce." It's a little saccharine at points, yes, but as "Head Up"'s chart success proved, by this time, Tupac Shakur could say "Keep hope alive"over a decent loop and sell mega units. Tupac was smart enough to risk feeling and appearing "positive." (The song gave someone like Nas, for instance, nerve enough to do a song like "If I Ruled the World [Imagine That]" in 1996.) As author Reverend Michael Eric Dyson might put it, Tupac Shakur knew to give us a little God with our gangsta rap.

Tupac was at his best on *Strictly 4 My N.I.G.G.A.Z.,* still touched by Digital Underground's mischievous aura but standing on his own two feet, not yet doing time on Death Row. On "Representin' 93," Tupac names the brothers he loves—and in 1993, he was still referring to DU as his "real niggaz." "I Get Around" was pretty much a Digital Underground song with Tupac on lead. Listen and you can almost hear Shock-G in the studio telling 'Pac to lighten up a little bit—take a swim, have some sex, go platinum, live a little. Tupac was on his way to being deified or dead or both, is what everyone said. We watch him in his black Versace, knowing exactly which was correct.

In 1993's Poetic Justice Tupac is bald, extra slew-footed, and wears a huge nose ring. He looks pretty, but it doesn't matter because Regina King steals the movie from him, Janet Jackson, and Joe Torry. Much was made of Tupac playing a Regular Guy, not someone like Bishop, who was closer to what people believed to be Tupac's "real" personality, and therefore easy to play. He succeeded to a large degree, considering John Singleton's banal story line. What hurt the film most was the coldness between Shakur and Jackson. She'd requested he take an HIV test before she would even kiss him, and the sizzle, if there had been any, was imperceptible on the screen. In truth, Tupac wasn't easy around girls in his films or in his videos. There was bravado and awkwardness, but little smoothness.

Because of creative differences and attitude contradictions, Tupac got booted from Allen and Albert Hughes's *Menace II Society* and then Singleton's *Higher Learning.* Burning bridges all over Hollywood's colored section, Tupac ended up in *Above the*

Rim (1994), playing a murderous gangsta basketball scout. In the film, Tupac's bandannas coordinate with his every outfit, neatly folded and painstakingly pressed. He's like Doris Day at the beginning of 1959's *Pillow Talk,* perfectly dressed and bonneted and ready to rumble.

Tupac's character, Birdie, was flimsily written, but Tupac fully dramatized the deadness of soul certain killers must have. As in *Juice,* there are moments in *Rim* when Tupac captures the calm of bitter people who've been kicked when they were defenseless, the confidence that comes with constantly intimidating people. He does casual evil as deftly as John Malkovich, tells you all about Hades with his fringed eyes.

Above the Rim has its happy ending (Duane Martin's character goes to Georgetown on a basketball scholarship) but there's also Birdie's violent comeuppance. Marlon Wayan's character, Bugaloo, at the end of the film, raises a pistol to shoot Birdie. Tupac's mouth turns down in a sneer as the bullet hits him. He's pushed back, and his arms fly up over his head. In slow motion, Birdie looks like a spirit has entered him, or like he's pouring himself, in spurts, into some lover.

The spring Tupac was incarcerated—acquitted of sodomy and weapons charges, guilty of sexual abuse—his third album, *Me Against the World* (1995), was released, and debuted at number one on *Billboard*'s pop and R&B album charts. "Dear Mama," about Tupac's troubled but loving relationship with his mother, proved a perfect antidote to the charges. Particularly in a moment when some were beginning to wonder, If he didn't rape that girl in the hotel, why didn't he help her? Did he really nap through a gangbang? Why didn't he denounce his buddies like the guy who wonders, in "Keep Ya Head Up," "Why we take from our women / Why we rape our women / Why we hate our women"?

"Dear Mama," along with Tupac's appearance in court, bandaged and weak from the five bullets he took in the lobby of a New York City recording studio, smoothed his rough edges and filled in his story. And he didn't spend much time in jail, either. Tupac Shakur was rescued, like a true innocent, from New York's Clinton Correctional Facility.

Death Row Records CEO Suge Knight secured a bond for $1.4 million so Tupac could jet to southern California and begin recording what became the twenty-seven-song album *All Eyez on Me.* Tupac was entrenched in the Death Row camp by 1994, his production strictly L.A.-style. Tupac told me he couldn't deal with Atron Gregory "apologizing for him," and by 1995, Tupac was being managed by Suge himself, and had gone from being signed to Jimmy Iovine's Interscope to being signed to its subsidiary, Knight's Death Row Records.

Hip hop's first double album, *All Eyez on Me* went on to sell seven million units. Death Row cofounder and house producer Dr. Dre and Suge Knight were starting to fall out by the time Tupac began recording, and Dre produced only two tracks for *All Eyez,* one of them being the huge hit "California Love." Dre and Tupac trade verses, and Zapp's Roger Troutman, with his jheri curl and electronic voicebox still intact, makes the chorus unforgettable.

The rest of the album is mostly, to use one of Tupac's favorite words, simple. On "All about U," 'Pac, Snoop Doggy Dogg, Nate Dogg, and Dru Down chime in over a tinny sample of Cameo's "Candy." All of them, Tupac included, spit out labels for women—

shitty-ass ho', hoochie—and one of them (doesn't matter who) says, "Is you sick from the dick / Or is it the flu?" Great sexist songs like Raekwon's "Ice Cream," DJ Quik's "Sweet Black Pussy," and even Too Short's grotesque "Freaky Tales" have either silliness or genuineness or art at their core. They seduce with inspired beats and intriguing chauvinisms. Many of the ditties on *All Eyez* are repulsive not only because the production is tired, but because the misogynist themes are weak, and break under the pressure of two or three listens. You can't even respect them for their intensity, let alone be offended or scared.

And it's not like everything has to be about peer marriages or keeping your head up. Tupac is at his most alluring on *All Eyez*'s "How Do U Want It?" Words like "Tell me / Is it cool to fuck?" rumble from his mouth like dice. "Holla at Me" packs none of the same punch as "Holler If Ya Hear Me," but the last two songs on *All Eyez on Me* reflect 'Pac's fight-and-fuck, love-and-hate, boast-and-beg dichotomies. "Ain't Hard 2 Find" is 'Pac, E-40, B-Legit, C-Bo, and Richie Rich acting like he-men. If you wanna fight, I'm right here, is what these California soul brothers are saying. "Heaven Ain't Hard 2 Find," on the other hand, is Tupac at his macho sweetest, creating a scene complete with Alizé and "moonlight mist."

"We'll be best friends," he almost sings to his intended, "I'll be the thug in your life." Tupac sympathizes with his lover's hesitancy (if she wasn't hesitant, she'd be a hoochie in another song). Then he says "Love me for my thug nature," sounding foolish at first, but then desolate, and in the end, profoundly sad.

In *Bullet*, it's Mickey Rourke, as a bandanna'd white *cholo*, who's constantly getting in touch with his thug nature. The film opens with Rourke riding away from prison in a blue convertible with Barry White playing in the background. Tupac sports an eye patch, and rides around in the back of a limo slicing a mango with a switchblade, looking like somebody snatched him off the set of one of his own video shoots. Watching *Bullet* is like getting teeth pulled without Novocain while listening to the post–Lionel Richie Commodores. Tupac and Rourke look loaded most of the time (even when there's no need for them to) and reek of a desperation totally detached from their characters.

Bullet never made it to the cineplexes, and is easily forgotten in the face of *Gridlock'd,* a flat, goofy, good film Tupac starred in with Tim Roth, which was released six months after Tupac's death. When Tupac, as the heroin-addicted Spoon, says "Somehow I don't think this was my mother's dream for me," squinting as the drug dances through his blood, "Dear Mama" suddenly sounds less like an image Band-Aid. Spoon is a bass player/poet on the spoken word scene, and at the end, when he's kicked, and he raps a corny rhyme about life being like a traffic jam, he carries it off, but you can't imagine Tupac ever recording anything like that in real life, ever. The songs he recorded right before he was shot dead in Las Vegas bear no resemblance to anything in *Gridlock'd.*

The Don Killuminati: The 7 Day Theory (1996) is dreary because Tupac was no longer here when it came out, and powerful only in the quickest and most tragic ways. Tupac—rather, "Makaveli" as an ominous voice states—says in "Bomb First" that he's got "Thug Life running through my veins on strong." Then he chants, and it's pitiful, "West Coast ridah / Comin' up behind ya / Shoulda neva fucked wit' me." No? Well, they did, and now you're dead.

But dead or not, the mighty "Hail Mary" is one of Tupac's better songs (though in an attempt to sound ominous, Tupac sounds much like Shaquille O'Neal on the mike). "Come wit' me / (Hail Mary, nigga) / Run quick see . . . Do you wanna ride or die?" "White Man'z World" is 'Pac's usual shout-out to the sisters. In "Against All Odds," Tupac disrespects Mobb Deep, Nas, and Sean "Puffy" Combs, like he did so fervently in "Hit 'Em Up," a base diatribe/revenge fantasy Death Row released in June 1996. "I knew you niggas from way back," he says in "Odds" when he's not spitting out more spiteful disses about their personal skills ("Nas / Your shit is bitten"). In the song, Tupac is consumed with other people wanting and stealing his style, his life, his way of being.

Tupac, especially on his first two albums, considered himself blameless, made it clear, especially before he got down with Death Row and the whole L.A. ridah scene, that his life was not his fault. In *Strictly 4 My N.I.G.G.A.Z.'s* "Strugglin'" he says "Some call me crazy / But this is what you gave me." In that same album's "Pac's Theme (Interlude)," Tupac answers a pseudo-reporter's question, "I was raised in this society / So there's no way you can expect me to be a perfect person / I'ma do what I'ma do." He always did believe, or at least believed strongly when I knew him, that to be crazy in this world was to be normal, that to get along well in a place so inherently unfair was to have eaten yourself alive and then be living on the shit that you pushed out afterward.

Tupac made people uncomfortable. At his best, he called blacks and whites alike out of their complicity in a despicable system. He made thuggery-as-resistance appealing, urged us to be loud and wild and reckless. He was not trying to "rise above" the way things are. He was not trying to "be better." No one ever said what would happen if folks got tired of aspiring to dignity; Tupac showed one way it already is. "I love it when they fear me," he said. But more truly, he loved not fearing them. He was free when he didn't give a fuck about anything, including continuing his own life, when he felt like the world—for a change—was his.

Wasn't Tupac great when he wasn't getting shot up? Or accused of rape? Wasn't he just the best when he wasn't falling for Suge Knight's lame-ass lines and dying broke? Couldn't Tupac just have been your everything? He got you fired up, excited and hopeful about something you couldn't even name, then had you crying in the end for a smooth-skinned young man in a coffin, like always. But you wish him back for one more song, one more standoff with the cops, more jail time, more anything. You wish back the bright spectacle that was Tupac Amaru Shakur's noisy sad life. Short life. Thug life. Triple life. Afterlife.

The last sound on *The Don Killuminati* is that of bullets popping off. Helicopter blades beat the air into a small, inside-out tornado. Tupac is dead in the street. Blood everywhere. Police clearing the scene. Thug niggas stand on the periphery, girls cry. Commentators report the shooting of "Tupack Shaker." He's dead, they say, dancing from star to star at night, diving into Hell's seething sewers at dawn. Tupac bathes on Sundays in the tears we cry for him, wades like a slave through that troubled water.

PART THREE

Criticism

"I just want to innovate and stimulate minds/Travel the world and penetrate the times."

—Common, "The 6th Sense" (2000)

Angles of Vision

EVERY SIGNIFICANT ERA IN MODERN BLACK AMERICAN LITERATURE HAS been distinguished by a declaration, usually expressed by a leading artist, that best characterizes the direction, scope, and stylistic approaches that shape the work of the period. Every era, that is, until now.

A Little Background

Harlem Happenings (1925–1940)

"Each generation will have its creed," Alain Locke observed in 1925. In his introduction to *The New Negro,* the critic, educator, and philosopher lauded in his contemporaries a spiritual emancipation that would, he argued, lead to significant social and political gains. Echoing W. E. B. Dubois and James Weldon Johnson, Locke triumphantly proclaimed, "The mind of the Negro seems suddenly to have slipped from under the tyranny or social intimidation and to be shaking off the psychology of imitation and implied inferiority."

This remarkable transition, Locke predicted, would be propelled by a vanguard of men and women committed to the uplift of the race via a variety of disciplines, not the least among them art. A year later, Langston Hughes's essay "The Negro Artist and the Racial Mountain" confirmed Locke's vision of a generation of fearless, motivated artists committed to using their skills for the benefit of their people.

Hughes's condemnation of an "urge within the race toward whiteness, the desire to pour racial individuality into the mold of American standardization, and to be as little Negro and as much American as possible" was a direct response to an essay by George S. Schuyler, New York's resident black contrarian. In "The Negro-Art Hokum," Schuyler had denounced questing after racial identity as a futile waste of time and energy. "The Aframerican," he declared, "is merely a lampblacked Anglo-Saxon."

Furthermore, "the literature, painting and sculpture of Aframericans—such as there is . . . is identical in kind with the literature, painting, and sculpture of white Americans." His heavy-handed vitriol notwithstanding, Schuyler wasn't entirely wrong: Europe's influence on Harlem's cultural warriors was substantial and often easily detected. A passage from Countee Cullen, for example, could possibly have more in common with a Spenserian stanza than a blues-based Hughes riff. Hughes's response to Schuyler seems to be motivated less by genuine intellectual disagreement than by fundamental philosophical differences. Fighting fire with fire, Hughes lashed out at members of the "Nordicized Negro intelligentsia" who dismissed those forms of expression (in dance, everyday speech, and popular music, for instance) usually regarded as essentially "black" in favor of any cultural strands that could be construed as "white." Hughes advocated firsthand fellowship with "the low-down folks, the so-called common element." Without such familiarity, an artist was doomed to failure.

"It is the duty of the Negro artist," Hughes asserted, "if he accepts any duties at all from outsiders, to change through the force of his art that old whispering "I want to be white," hidden in the aspirations of his people, to "Why should I want to be white?

143

I am a Negro—and beautiful"? Hughes's exuberant equalization of blackness and beauty precedes the popularization of such by four decades—but we're getting ahead of ourselves.

The Wright Stuff (1940–1960)

The Wall Street crash of 1929 effectively dissolved the confluence of industrial prosperity, postwar optimism, and national interest in African American culture that made the Harlem Renaissance possible. By 1940, that unprecedented flourishing of black artistic excellence was merely a memory. The new decade began as the Great Migration finally ebbed, ending twenty-five years of large-scale exodus to the cities and factories of the North. The transformative population shift reflected itself in the literature as urban realism became a dominant motif. Thus, Jean Toomer's blood-soaked Georgia clay gave way to Richard Wright's rat-infested Windy City tenements; Zora Neale Hurston's leafy Florida hamlet was replaced by Gwendolyn Brooks's crowded Chicago kitchenette.

A significant change in the vernacular accompanied the pilgrimage from plantations to paved avenues. "Hip talk" or slang, often used to show one's common sense or "street smarts," contributed substantially to the new urban sensibility. The fresh, musical lingo caught the ears and interest of whites, who often appropriated it for their own use.

White fascination with black language and, by extension, black literature, should be regarded with suspicion, according to Wright. In fact, black literature should never be created with white audiences in mind. "The Negro writer who seeks to function within his race as a purposeful agent has a serious responsibility," he wrote in 1937. His "Blueprint for Negro Writing" spelled out the various aspects of that responsibility.

Rigid and relentless, Wright attacked his Renaissance predecessors as pen-packing petty bourgeoisie with misguided ambitions. At the same time, he acknowledged the value of the very trove of folklore long championed by Hughes, Hurston, and Sterling Brown: "Blues, spirituals, and folk tales recounted from mouth to mouth; the whispered words of a black mother to her black daughter on the ways of men; the confidential wisdom of a black father to his black son; the swapping of sex experiences on street corners from boy to boy in the deepest vernacular; work songs sung under blazing suns—all these formed the channels through which the racial wisdom flowed."

In Wright's view, black writers could no longer afford to perform parlor tricks for the amusement of wealthy white thrill-seekers, or to stifle their energies by asserting their humanity to the skeptical keepers of "high" culture.

No longer should a black artist strive to prove to whites that he is worthy to walk the earth as their equal; the responsible, revolutionary black scribe must engage his gifts in the epic battle of good (Marxism) versus evil (capitalism). "He is being called upon to do no less than create values by which his race is to struggle, live, and die," Wright declared.

For Wright, embracing Marxism as gospel did not involve replacing genuine creative processes with simple propagandizing. This could be avoided through the proper application of perspective, which he defined as "that part of a poem, novel, or play which a writer never puts directly upon paper. It is that fixed point in intellectual space where a writer stands to view the struggles, hopes, and sufferings of his people."

Both the spirit and the letter of his Blueprint illustrate Wright's struggle to reconcile his heartfelt activist leanings with his desire to create lasting art that transcends the level of protest. At times it appears that he's trying to convince himself, not his peers, of the efficacy of his formula. Ultimately, Wright acknowledged that the successful execution of a work of art matters more than the political position it advances: "Every first rate novel, poem, or play lifts the level of consciousness higher."

Many of Wright's fellows, including Ralph Ellison and Chester Himes, explored Marxism and found it lacking. Ditto for Wright himself, whose long, contentious break with the Party took public form in a 1944 essay entitled "I Tried to Be a Communist." Still, whether deliberately or unconsciously, most black writers took Wright's call for consciousness-raising to heart, supplementing the Harlem Renaissance's initial bold efforts with such exemplary works as Ann Petry's *The Street*, Gwendolyn Brooks's *Annie Allen*, and Ellison's modernist masterpiece, *Invisible Man*. (James Baldwin, Wright's onetime protégé, unwittingly confirmed his mentor's observations when he condemned him in "Everybody's Protest Novel," an overwrought essay that failed to have much of an impact beyond the white readers for whom Baldwin wrote it. Although it remains of interest as a historical document, its effect on Baldwin's fellow black writers remains difficult to measure.)

Perhaps most important, by insisting that artists become astute observers and committed participants in the political struggles of their times, Wright paved the way for the openly militant attitudes adopted by the architects of the movement that would follow. In turn, the Black Arts school celebrated Wright as an important philosophical ancestor whose best work—*Native Son* and *Black Boy*—enabled the articulation of a new and vital Black Aesthetic.

The Black Aesthetic/Black Arts Movement (1960–1970)

In 1960, when four black college students peacefully occupied the segregated Woolworth's lunch counter in Greensboro, N.C., their nonviolent approach typified the naive optimism of civil rights activists of that time. Woolworth's soon acceded to the students' demands, and the moral suasion techniques advocated by Martin Luther King Jr. and others seemed reasonable enough. But those techniques appeared to be hopelessly, painfully outmoded in just a few short years. By 1968, disheartened by the assassinations of King and Malcolm X, and frustrated with the government's reluctance to enforce the civil rights acts passed by Congress, masses of black people had begun to take to the streets. This time, though, they weren't singing "We Shall Overcome."

It was an amazing development: Little more than a century before, blacks who sought to become literate—let alone free—were often put to death. Now descendants of that same oppressed group were once again risking death while insisting upon a new vernacular, a lingo that whites, for the first time, were reluctant to appropriate: "Black Power!" "Freedom Now!" and a phrase that must have made Langston Hughes smile, "Black Is Beautiful!"

For artists, passivity had become completely passé. Instead of reaching down from a Talented Tenth perch to help their downtrodden brethren, black writers found themselves scrambling to keep up with the energized masses. In northern cities such as Detroit and New York, police interrupted rallies with bloodthirsty fervor; in Birmingham, Ala., and other southern backwaters, Bull Connor and his cohorts used firehoses and ferocious dogs while clubbing women and children with Third Reichian relish. Clearly, Petrarchan sonnets and Pindaric odes would not suffice.

But what *would* suffice? An art "that speaks directly to the needs and aspirations of Black America," Larry Neal suggested. In his groundbreaking 1968 essay "The Black Arts Movement," Neal chronicled the development of what came to be known as the Black Aesthetic. Citing the work of Amiri Baraka, Etheridge Knight, Ron Milner, and others, Neal called for poems, plays, novels, and essays that embodied the perfect marriage of form and function, literature that linked itself explicitly to the rebel spirit then blossoming in black communities across America.

"Black Art is the aesthetic and spiritual sister of the Black Power concept," Neal wrote. Etheridge Knight, a major poet of the Black Arts school, explained how this essential kinship was to be achieved: "The Black artist must create new forms and new values, sing new songs (or purify old ones); and along with other Black authorities, he must create a new history, new symbols, myths, and legends (and purify old ones by fire)."

For Neal, the purification process to which Knight referred would make abstractions obsolete, resulting in literature that could land in readers' minds like lightning bolts and shock solar plexuses like a solid uppercut. Reinforced by Hoyt Fuller, Addison Gayle Jr., Stephen Henderson and other perceptive critics, the Black Aesthetic was skillfully executed by artists who proudly adhered to its requirements. Among the latter, Haki Madhubuti (then called Don L. Lee) insisted on work that was fearlessly confrontational. "There is *no* neutral blackart; either it *is* or it *isn't,* period," he wrote in the preface to his 1969 collection, *Don't Cry, Scream.*

The Black Arts Movement's most accomplished proponent was Amiri Baraka, who wrote the most resonant poetry of the era and successfully popularized the concept in his poem "Black Art": "We want 'poems that kill.' / Assassin poems, Poems that shoot guns," he demanded.

Alfred Kazin once described early nineteenth-century America as "a time when people still looked to literary men for guidance." Ralph Waldo Emerson, the *éminence grise* of that time, wrote in 1839, "Ours is the revolutionary age, bringing man back to consciousness." Similarly, Larry Neal and others called for black literary men and women to inspire their brothers and sisters to a new form of consciousness—a new way of looking at and being in the world.

At its worst, art associated with this movement took on the flaws of the very system it sought to dismantle, including chauvinism, anti-Semitism, and homophobia. At its best, it dramatically reduced the distance between writer and reader, encouraging a mutually informative and enriching relationship whereby artists could interact frequently and freely with the people they aimed to serve. "The Black Arts Movement is radically opposed to any concept of the artist that alienates him from his community," Neal wrote.

In their landmark *Black Fire* anthology, Baraka and Neal refused to dismiss outright the assertions and experiments of their black predecessors; they saw their new movement as part of an enduring tradition of struggle, one that incorporates Hughes's "Negro Equals Beautiful" while rising to meet the challenges of an aggressively racist society. A Lance Jeffers contribution to *Black Fire* aptly illustrates this idea:

> and my own dark rage a rusty knife with teeth to gnaw my
> bowels,
> my agony ripped loose by anguished shouts in Sunday's
> humble church,

my agony rainbowed to ecstasy when my feet oversoared
    Montgomery's lime,
ah, this hurt, this hate, this ecstasy before I die,
and all my love a strong cathedral!
My blackness is the beauty of this land!

Women Ascending (1970–1990)

Marita Bonner's 1925 essay, "On Being Young—a Woman—and Colored" prefigured many of the themes that would be forcefully addressed during the 1970s. Her description of the black female condition shows a prescient understanding of the struggle to come:

> *"Still; quiet; with a smile, ever so slight, at the eyes so that Life will flow into and not by you. And you can gather, as it passes, the essences, the overtones, the tints, the shadows; draw understanding to yourself.*
> *And then you can, when Time is ripe, swoop to your feet—at your full height—at a single gesture."*

For white women seeking full enfranchisement, the time was ripe in 1963, when Betty Friedan's *The Feminist Mystique* launched the modern feminist movement. Black feminist concerns, on the other hand, were often submerged beneath the masculine (read macho) strains of the largely nationalist Black Arts Movement. By the dawn of the new decade, black women had grown tired of the twofold oppression they often endured. Up to this point, they had been willing to subdue their own intraracial concerns—black male chauvinism, few creative options, and limited opportunity for leadership, among others—in the struggle against the common enemy embodied by white racism and its Jim Crow restrictions.

Changing mores and civil-rights legislation, accompanied by the sexual revolution and a growing cohesion among mainstream feminists, encouraged black female artists and intellectuals to point their efforts in new and stimulating directions. At last black women would tell their own stories—and on their own terms. Maya Angelou, Toni Morrison, and Alice Walker were among the vanguard; each published her first major prose work in 1970. At the same time, Mari Evans, June Jordan, and other female poets joined Sonia Sanchez in adapting the aims of the Black Arts school to women's desire for full rights and recognition. Echoing Marita Bonner, Sanchez's noteworthy *A Blues Book for Blue Black Magical Women* lamented, "there is no place for a soft/black/woman."

For our purposes here, the most significant watershed was Toni Cade Bambara's *The Black Woman,* a collection of poems, stories, and essays that confronted the patriarchal aura of the cultural nationalist movement.

In her preface, Bambara also challenged the efficacy of the feminist movement, citing the works of Friedan and other icons such as Anaïs Nin and Simone de Beauvoir. "How relevant are the truths, the experiences, the findings of white women to black women? Are women after all simply women? I don't know that our priorities are the same, that our concerns and methods are the same, or even similar enough so that we can afford to depend on this new field of experts (white, female)."

"The first job," Bambara argued, "is to find out what liberation for ourselves means, what work it entails, what benefits it will yield."

Alice Walker, who contributed greatly to the foundation of what is now known as womanism, suggested combining critique of white feminist thought with celebrations of black female traditions, communities, and selves. While condemning the paucity of outlets available to black women artists, Walker celebrated the resourcefulness of her sisters. In "In Search of Our Mother's Gardens," her famous 1972 essay, she asks, "How was the creativity of the black woman kept alive, year after year and century after century, when for most of the years black people have been in America, it was a punishable crime for a black person to read or write?"

For Walker, her forebears' insistence on making "a way out of no way" is cause for eloquent defiance. "To be an artist and a black woman, even today, lowers our status in many respects, rather than raises it: and yet, artists we will be," she declared.

In "Toward a Black Feminist Criticism" (1977), Barbara Smith called for a decidedly feminist perspective to create new channels for black women's creativity: "A viable, autonomous black feminist movement in this country would open up the space needed for the exploration of black women's lives and the creation of consciously black women-identified art."

Smith, who would go on to edit *Home Girls: A Black Feminist Theology* in 1983, further observed that "the use of black women's language and cultural experience in books *by* black women *about* black women results in a miraculously rich coalescing of form and content and also takes their writing far beyond the confines of white/male literary structures."

This insistence on creating a space (and an audience) for woman-centered writing made possible the worldwide popularity of "serious" writers such as Angelou and Morrison while enabling the unforeseen rise of popular novelists such as Terry McMillan and Connie Briscoe. The flexible boundaries of black women's fiction became evident to the reading public at large in 1992, when McMillan, Walker, and Morris briefly shared choice spots on the *New York Times* best-seller list. Realizing Marita Bonner's long-ago dream, black women writers had risen to their full, glorious height. It was as if America's readers had taken to heart Mari Evans's proud pronouncement:

> I
> am a black woman
> tall as a cypress
> strong
> beyond all definition still
> defying place
> and time
> and circumstance
>   assailed
>   impervious
>   indestructible
>
> Look
>   on me and be
> renewed

Angles of Vision (1990–Present)

Like the other anthologies that began to appear during the nineties, *In the Tradition* (1992, Harlem River Press) arrived after a relative drought. Kevin Powell and Ras Baraka's compilation differed from the others in its emphasis on the poetry and fiction of a new generation, one whose members were the first to come to maturity after the epochal shifts of the '50s and '60s. In view of the fact that its contributors include several of the most skilled writers of the new generation (indeed, the future Hugheses, Hurstons and Ellisons), *In the Tradition* must be regarded as the seminal publication of the new era.

In a brief introduction linking themselves and their peers to the continuum of African American literature, Powell and Baraka confidently declared, "We are the movement, a new Black Consciousness Movement of poetry and fiction and art and music. . . ." This was perhaps overly enthusiastic, since no prevailing political ideology accompanied this generational shift, and no prevailing political ideology can be found in the work included. The kind of intellectual and philosophical cohesion that propelled some previous collections (e.g., *The Black Woman, Black Fire*) was notably absent in *In the Tradition*. This lack is almost certainly related to the fact that its contributors' maturity coincided with the rise of Reaganism and a national agenda almost completely devoid of civil-rights concerns. Hence the most sober component of Powell and Baraka's introduction: "We are children of the post-integration nightmare." While some of their fellow artists would likely take issue with that morbid phrase, few would disagree that the post-integration landscape has been strewn with both land mines and new opportunities. Prominent among the latter was a chance to investigate one's art more freely than ever before, with little regard for the possibility of censure from one's peers. Greg Tate has described such investigations as resulting from a post-liberated aesthetic. Trey Ellis, perhaps the best-known contributor when *In the Tradition* appeared, had already developed this idea further in a 1989 essay, "The New Black Aesthetic."

Whereas Langston Hughes had singled out the black middle class as the primary source of the self-hatred that, in his view, threatened to paralyze black artistic efforts, Ellis pointed to the middle class as the source of an artistic approach that, like Hughes's, is ultimately "black." But in Hughes's view, an upbringing in a middle-class household almost guaranteed artistic failure: "One sees immediately how difficult it would be for an artist born in such a home to interest himself in interpreting the beauty of his own people."

Ellis identified "Ishmael Reed, Clarence Major, Toni Morrison, John Edgar Wideman, George Clinton, David Hammons, and Richard Pryor" as "coming of age just as the Black Arts Movement was beginning to fade." According to Ellis, they are icons of the post-liberation generation. "My friends and I . . . have inherited an open-ended New Black Aesthetic from a few Seventies pioneers that shamelessly borrows and reassembles across both race and class lines," he wrote.

Examples of such line-crossing go back way beyond the '70s. Hughes and Hurston, for instance, were both masterful reassemblers. Despite their sarcastic treatment of "the niggerati" (their fellow black writers and artists), both writers used their college-trained powers of observation to hone their celebrated flair for everyday speech. Richard Wright, too, practiced cross-cultural transference; his later work in particular reflected both his interests in existentialism and the philosophical issues he picked up in Parisian salons. Despite occasional assertions to the contrary, black artists' borrowing have frequently crossed the lines to which Ellis referred.

But Ellis correctly showed that the environment surrounding the artists had changed. One of the consequences of that change has been a viewpoint that echoes Hughes's 1925 declaration. "We no longer need to deny or suppress any part of our complicated and sometimes contradictory cultural baggage to please either white people or black," Ellis observed.

Elise's observations, however compelling, are limited to the pursuits of a small band of middle-class artists. Little attention is given to poor and working-class artists of his generation whose work shows evidence of the same transformations. Like Power and Baraka, he is also overly optimistic in referring to a "movement" when there is little evidence of one forming along the lines he described. And although he pays appropriate homage to the Black Arts Movement pioneers, he avoids echoing their insistence that black art be judged according to its ability to "function" in the struggle. (It should be pointed out that many B.A.M. theorists, especially Neal, had softened their stances long since. In a 1976 essay, Neal acknowledged, "Literature can indeed make excellent propaganda, but through propaganda alone the black writer can never perform the highest function of his art: that of revealing to man his most enduring human possibilities and limitations.")

The absence of a prevailing sense of urgency should not lead one to deem the new generation as apolitical or apathetic. As Kalamu ya Salaam has observed, "Black writers have always had to face the issue of whether their work was primarily political or aesthetic." The new writers continue to engage this age-old conundrum, but do so in an environment that allows greater room for, among other things, preoccupations with style. Most of them would agree that the pressures of the wide world continue to remain strong and hostile. Those pressures, exacerbated by damaging judicial retrenchment and increasingly aggressive campaigns against affirmative action, are at least implicitly acknowledged in much of the writing being produced.

Nonetheless the post-manifesto generation's most accomplished writers tend to avoid overly simplistic portrayals of American and global society, and they also eschew assumptions of a monolithic black population. In fact, little is assumed and nothing escapes questioning, including the notion of a singular black community, and the existence/implications of "blackness" itself. Elizabeth Alexander, author of two acclaimed poetry collections, has articulated a philosophical strand that weaves its way through much of the new writing:

> I didn't want to write a poem that said "blackness
> is," because we know better than anyone
> that we are not one or ten or ten thousand things
> (From *Today's News*)

Of his own work, Hughes once said, "Most of my own poems are racial in theme and treatment, derived from the life I know." Hughes's life and knowledge are brilliantly distilled in such classic poems as "Daybreak in Alabama":

When I get to be a composer
I'm gonna write me some music about
Daybreak in Alabama
And I'm gonna put the purtiest songs in it
Rising out of the ground like a swamp mist

But what if, as in the case of post-manifesto poet Carl Phillips, the life you know is *not* overwhelmingly racial in theme and treatment? Phillips surely experiences as much difficulty flagging a New York taxi as any other black man, but the poetic world he inhabits appears closer to an international bazaar—one lined with tables piled high with delectable metaphors and choice allusions, all free for the taking—than a crowded Harlem street corner.

Phillips brazenly addresses this difference between his approach and that of a Famous Black Poet in his poem "Passing":

and I want to tell the poet that the blues
is *not* my name, that Alabama
is something I cannot use
in my business.

Kevin Powell's first solo collection, *recognize* (Harlem River Press, 1995), contains a poem paying explicit homage to Hughes. "Genius child" cleverly alludes to Hughes's oeuvre before concluding:

you, too, fragment
a dark vein
it sings
it sags
like a blues bag
weighing dreams
on lenox avenue

The fact that Phillips and Powell can take such disparate approaches, and each succeed at writing poems that "work" say much to the post-manifesto aura in which new black writers are creating.

To be sure, some black writers in each previous era wrote and flourished outside the prevailing cultural aesthetics of their age. Even as Langston Hughes was developing his Negrocentric ethos, Claude McKay was transforming sonnets into militant songs of defiance, and Countee Cullen felt perfectly comfortable composing poems such as "To John Keats, Poet at Spring Time." Robert Hayden, whom some Black Arts poets heartily denounced as shamefully apolitical and hopelessly out of touch, continued to write wonderful work even as some of his harshest critics attempted to pass off sloganeering as poetry; Ralph Ellison, who shared a mutual disgust with some of the architects of the Black Arts Movement, pursued his own fiercely independent investigations throughout the '60s and '70s.

Still, the sociopolitical conditions of the present age, the ever-expanding middle class, years of integrated schooling, and the sheer variety of black existence in this country all contribute to an atmosphere in which newer published writers are comfortable to follow their own inclinations, according to their instincts and idiosyncracies instead of ideologies. The independent writer, as it were, has become the norm rather than the exception.

The Soul of Black Talk

Erin Aubry

We have no models. The Black American has no antecedent. We, in this country, on this continent, in the most despairing terms, created an identity which had never been seen before in the history of the world. We created that music. Nobody else did, and the world lives from it, though it doesn't pay us for it. We are the only people in the world—in the world!—who know anything about this country. Nobody else does. Nobody . . . We are the only hope this country has.

—JAMES BALDWIN,
SPEAKING AT A 1980 SYMPOSIUM
ON BLACK ENGLISH

WE ARE NOT ALLOWED. FOR THE LAST 10 YEARS OR SO, I'VE HAD THIS UNEASY but oddly liberating daydream: Somebody white and usually well-meaning drops all sense of political correctness and demands, almost angrily, that I describe the black American experience in a single word. I refuse, at first—haven't I stood firm against racial monolithism all these years?—and then with a certain relief I fling aside my well-placed caution and reply: *otherness.*

This is what I don't say, can't say publicly, but what I increasingly feel, I am growing as accustomed to otherness as breathing, and as thoughtless of its existence. I've decided: In every possible way, from every conceivable angle, at each historical rest stop, from our bloody beginnings in America to now, black people have remained strangers in their native land. Unknown social quantities in our own skin and thus too wary of one another to coalesce around any single purpose for too long, black people have instead bound themselves together with culture and tradition that, ironically enough, boast the sharply defined life and robust purpose that have so frequently eluded us. It is a rarefied life that courses well above the racist American fray: jazz, tap dance, church on Sunday, blues, soul-food breakfasts, Mardi Gras, second-lining, hamboning on street corners.

And language—especially language. It didn't merely survive in the barren cold of otherness; it thrived in it. Growing up in South L.A. in a predominantly black neighborhood, I absorbed many ways of talking: strictly standard English at home, turbocharged New Orleans patois at family gatherings, the '70s-flavored rap of my peers that seemed to cut through any and all bullshit with a casual insolence. This was the epitome of cool to me, the patter of "ain't"s and "don't mean nothing"s and pointed disregard of verb tenses that seemed no less precise, and much more visceral, than the shiny language of the library books I routinely buried myself in. I was a product of both, could wield both to my advantage, could get over in ways in college profs never imagined. In the presumed sociolinguistic divide between haves and havenots, there is in fact vast connective turf that blacks claim as their own and white people know nothing of. This was where I first forged dreams of writing, of soaring; language, in all its transcendent glory and flat-out validation of otherness, was my getting place.

But that might change. As the recent furor over ebonics portends, language may prove to be something we can no longer be allowed to keep, even in our hearts. Again uncertain of ourselves, we are forced to publicly denounce blackspeak as bad, to laugh at it, to put it away with childish things. Language may no longer be our cultural property, but another one of our social impediments, like drugs and gangs. Dragged into the unflattering light of public opinion, ebonics has been roundly condemned, like affirmative action before it, as a bastard child with no place in our middle-class aspirations, and even less of a place in the hardy, albeit largely unrealized, American ideal of social equality. Such condemnations have all but drowned out the much larger issues upon which ebonics precariously rests: the ongoing miseducation—or non-education—of black children, the growing entrenchment of the black poor, and perhaps most insidious of all, the wholesale rejection of the very logical idea that black American culture is directly descended from African culture, at least in part.

I'm not entirely convinced that ebonics is a full-fledged language, but that is hardly the point; my realization that *we are not allowed* to contemplate the possibility is. James Baldwin said that the language forged by black people in this country "got us from one place to another. *We* described the auction block. *We* described what it meant to be there." But he added that it is knowledge we are forbidden to embrace; we have been consigned to letting others describe to us who we are.

I am no exception; like so many black people who consider themselves progressive, I initially dismissed ebonics as embarrassingly unprogressive. I decided later that I recoiled from it because I couldn't get beyond a word that was so brazenly black, and therefore, in my subconscious, devoid of value. I was thoroughly in hock with the well-turned dismissal of ebonics by *The New Yorker* (which chastised the Oakland school board for "dressing up in the rhetoric of defiance what looked for all the world like an admission of defeat") and publications loftier than that. I had to electroshock myself back to my belief that this country never takes any black issue seriously, except when it suits this political agenda or that, and even then "seriously" is far too strong a word. However forcefully we erupt on op-ed pages and radio talk shows over the controversy of the day, we like to forget that until that moment we have existed merely in the shadows. And as linguist Ernie Smith says, as long as "blacks are uncomfortable with their blackness—*apologize* for it," the shadows are where we'll remain.

> *I've been 'buked.*
> *And I've been scorned . . .*
> *I been talked about, sure's you're born.*
>
> —NEGRO SPIRITUAL

The fact that black inner-city kids have been stuck there for decades has disturbed few people, certainly not those who decry ebonics the loudest, who merely pretend to be disturbed now. What I hate is the facile, insufferably *serious* way in which the press has characterized black speech, picking it apart while at the same time accusing black people of being the cultural separatists. Despite assurances from coast to coast that we all belong—speaking the same language apparently qualifies as unity—the pundits busily put black people under glass like lab samples, or exotic flora. The suburban-driven *L.A. Times,* in its story about the Language Development Program at 95th Street Elementary School in South-Central, conveniently provided readers with a boxed "Ebonics at a Glance." In 100 words or less were snappy summaries of terminology, history, extent of use ("it is the predominant language pattern among many urban blacks and is used at least some of the time by most blacks"), teaching methods and so forth. For non-black America, black folks are always reducible.

Los Angeles Unified School District board member Barbara Boudreaux, who argued strenuously for an ebonics resolution similar to Oakland's, grumbles about reporters and critics making *her* out to be L.A.'s "ebonics lady." "The achievement of black kids is *not* on the mind of the populace, okay?" says Boudreaux, whose much-amended resolution was quietly shelved, pending further study. "The fact is, anything with the word 'black' in it throws people into a tizzy. I'm upset that people *aren't* upset about the right thing." For all the misconceptions it touched off, she was heartened by the Oakland board's action, because "it's black people taking a stand for black people. I hope this puts education on the front burner permanently."

Problem is, the ground-level nature of education is worlds away from the ethereal one of pop culture. Whites might find it difficult to reconcile the marginalization of black folks with the incalculable influence of rap music and jazz, and blues and gospel before it. Black literature from Paul Laurence Dunbar to Zora Neale Hurston to Baldwin, right on up to Toni Morrison, has defied marginalization by its very existence. Novelist and essayist Albert Murray argues in his most recent book. *The Blue Devils of Nada,* that the American aesthetic of self-invention, from Elvis to L.A.'s own Chicken Boy architecture, springs from the blues riff and its endless improvisational possibilities. And if blues, and a whole canon of classic black literature, ain't nothing but poetically wrought ebonics, how ironic—and hypocritical—that black English has become such a pejorative in the "real" world.

It's a false and intentionally misleading division, says Yvonne Divans Hutchinson, a longtime honors English teacher at Markham Middle School in Watts. "Our jargon, our idioms, our metaphors have pervaded American culture so much that you can't separate out black language from American language, or culture, even if you tried," she says. "Our language may have African speech patterns, but it's an *American* form of speech. It is certainly not as uneducated or as ungrammatical or ignorant or as dismal as people would have us believe." Linguist Geneva Smitherman, a veteran of past ebonics wars, puts it another way. "If black English is so god-awful bad," she sighs, "why is everybody still speaking it?"

Black people are mired in a thousand sinkholes, in the shadows, yet aspects of black culture—starting with language—are more public and profitable than ever. As rapidly as black youth are sliding into oblivion, rappers are acquiring millions, McDonald's airs gospel-style commercials, Coke debuts its "new phat bottle" billboard campaign featuring a faceless boy clad in gangsta-style baggy pants, and our own *Buzz* magazine lists "mad skillz" and other black-spawned phrases in its glossary of high-fashion runway speak.

As Smitherman once said, black language has crossed over nicely, thank you—black people haven't. We *do* sing America, as Baldwin and Murray and Langston Hughes concluded, though now we tend to dilute the music by singing it on cue for an expectant publisher or record exec. And when that happens, "black people are not allowing themselves humanity," complains Richard Yarborough, an associate professor of English and pro tem director of the Center for Afro-American Studies at UCLA. He cites the rash of contemporary black writers who are getting published not because they have anything terribly profound to say, but because they fashion their work to fit the hot publishing trends: lurid inner-city narratives, hollow musings on middle-class angst, all told in an unmistakable "black" voice. Blackspeak thus becomes less an expression of culture than a marketing concept.

Yarborough says it is the mature writer who doesn't resort to tricks, who knows to lead with story. "You could argue that Jervey Tervalon's book *Understand This*"—a novel set in pre-riot South-Central Los Angeles told from several different perspectives—"was written in ebonics, but it was a well-written book. It couldn't have had the same power and resonance that it did *without* the language." But Tervalon himself says the expectations of publishers subtly force even good black writers into such tricks, and resisting the pressure could stunt a career. Despite the success of his first novel, his current one, which features a black middle-class protagonist living in tony Santa Barbara, has failed to garner interest. "They were looking for *Understand This, Part 2*," he says of publishers. "They have defined ideas of what the black voice is, particularly for men—it's the up-from-the-ghetto story, the Nathan McCall memoir, the Monster Cody confessional. There's this idea that we are actually not whole *unless* we come from the ghetto. Unfortunately, writers will cannibalize themselves to get product out there. What makes things worse is that literary fiction is a hard sell."

Tervalon grew up in the Crenshaw district and graduated from Dorsey High. He says he was always, at best, a mediocre student of standard English; grammar and mechanics are still something of a struggle for him. In conversation he will sometimes say "mouf" instead of "mouth"—an ebonics speech pattern that is now common Internet knowledge (and the object of vicious ridicule in anonymous cyberspace). But Tervalon says what set him apart from a lot of black youth was his refusal to believe that he was speaking something substandard; that he focused on expression and ideas rather than mechanics. Fortunately for him, he intuited the difference between descriptive and proscriptive; that, he says, is rare. "If a black kid is repeatedly told he sounds ignorant, is ignorant, he or she will simply stop talking—they'll go inside," he says. "They lock themselves up. And we know what happens from there."

Don't you get it? Where I come from, it don't pay to talk white.
—GENE ANTHONY RAY
TO HIS ENGLISH TEACHER IN THE MOVIE *FAME*

I couldn't say "ain't" in my house. I couldn't say "dang," or "what you mean," or "I'm going over Sharon's house"—I was always going *to* Sharon's house. If I spoke that way, it had to be done furtively, like sneaking a smoke in the girls' bathroom. But outside, hanging out with friends in my neighborhood, I had to be equally careful about using speech too properly: It would mark me as a square, as being saditty and above-it-all—

an image already built into my light complexion and straight hair. I grew fearful of saying too much, of sounding both too precise and not precise enough; I grew fearful of *not belonging*, of being stranded alone in my otherness. Speech took on an almost metaphysical power; it could change my color before my eyes, like a chameleon's skin. So, like Tervalon, I turned to the written word. I created a space where I could talk at will, at inordinate lengths. But still I wondered: Who was I writing for?

Over the years, the question devolved into a taunt. As an adult, I found myself flinching inwardly at the sound of a boyfriend's speech, to the point of cold embarrassment for him and then complete severence from him. My proletarian raging against the black middle class was neatly blown away by a righteousness that erupted, against my deepest wishes, at *his* "ain't"s and "don't mean"s and "everybody like that"s. In public—and sometimes even in private—it wasn't poetry at all, but social malfeasance that branded him as incompetent, unfit. I assumed the power of the oppressor; words lost their shape-shifting powers and became fixed, ugly points that had to be covered up, like stains on a carpet. I hated myself and wondered again: Whose ear was I trying to win?

> *Black English is a systematic, rule-governed language system, with linguistic antecedents in Africa and America, forged in the crucible of struggle that is the Black American Experience.*
>
> —Geneva Smitherman in *Talkin and Testifyin*

The Authentic Negro Voice question crested during the black-literature movement of the '60s. Intentionally or not, writers claimed the raw, uncut language of the streets as real-deal blackspeak; it was re-born as a primary language, aesthetically if not politically. Assimilation was out; an unapologetic sense of otherness conveyed by this language was in. Imamu Amiri Baraka (né LeRoi Jones) set the tone with work that elegantly wed protest to poetry, epiphanies to the profane. Perhaps nothing describes the seething, survivalist nature of black English better than this climactic line from Baraka's play *Dutchman,* delivered by the black protagonist to a white woman harassing him on the subway: "Old bald-headed four-eyed ofays popping their fingers . . . They say, 'I love Bessie Smith.' And don't even understand that Bessie Smith is saying, 'Kiss my ass, kiss my black unruly ass.' Before love, suffering, desire, anything you can explain, she's saying, and very plainly, 'Kiss my black ass.'"

Baraka was a major influence for the poet Ojenke, an original member of the Watts Writers Workshop and a legend in his own right. "He was like a bolt of lightning for a lot of people, what he was saying and how he was saying it," says Ojenke, a bearded sage of a man who's always preferred "writing on the hearts of the people" to publishing anything. "He was more of an oral-tradition kind of guy," tapping into a pride of African heritage that swelled with the Black Power movement. But Ojenke says his own impassioned style, and those of many of his contemporaries, is most deeply rooted in the venerated tradition of the church: His father was a minister, and as a writer he absorbed the fiery hallmarks of a preacher—call-and-response singsonging, pointed repetition—alongside touchstone works by everyone from Homer to Dunbar. Another major influence was the avant-garde jazz of John Coltrane, who set non-mainstream language—black English—to music. And rap, Ojenke maintains, is simply another point on a cultural continuum, "a response by African people to their current conditions. Ebonics itself is a moot point, a fait accompli. It's already part of the American lexicon—you can't extricate it from that. Forms of expression will keep emerging, as long as we're here."

But if the '60s set black artists free, they also sowed fresh seeds of language-based class divisions that have flourished, to profoundly ill effects, a generation later. Black speech patterns had been studied since the 19th century, and the '60s rekindled an interest in the subject, particularly the question of whether its origins were primarily African or American. Geneva Smitherman, the first black scholar to author a book on the subject, *Talkin and Testifyin: The Language of Black America* (1977), described the conflict this way: The two major forces of the decade, social-change movements and Great Society programs stressing success through assimilation, "have not acted in concert. While blacks were shouting 'I'm black and I'm proud,' Anglos were admonishing them to 'be like us' and enter the mainstream. While you had black orators, creative artists, and yes, even scholars rappin in the Black Thang, educators (some of them black, to be sure) were preaching the Gospel that Black English speakers must learn to talk like White English speakers in order to 'make it.'" Inherent in black English was what she called "linguistic push-pull"—the push toward Americanization countered by the pull of Africanized patterns, a conflict that perfectly embodies what W.E.B. Du Bois called the "twoness" of the black psyche, the irresolution of place and identity. Now, 130 years out of slavery, resolution is hardly in sight. "The problem that no one wants to deal with," says Yarborough, "is that we are essentially a native population with immigrant problems."

But to merely attribute black language to the black disenfranchised—to pathologize it, in a sense—is to largely miss the point of the language itself, its richness and complexity and the inimitable way it forges words to style—delivery, emphasis and expression. What linguists clinically term "code-switching"—consciously switching from black English to standard, or melding the two—is what most black people I know have done their whole lives. Some may rail against ebonics publicly because they want to shore up image, but in the real world they will walk past a total stranger who is black, catch his eye, nod quickly and mutter the salutatory "Wha's up?" No further conversation required.

A friend of mine in the medical profession says the bonds assumed by such exchanges are a source of comfort and power, as well as a reminder that black people are perhaps not as estranged from each other as they've come to believe. "I'll walk past a group of black doctors I don't know, and we'll talk like we know each other," he says. "One time, a white doctor looked at me kind of perplexed and said, 'Oh, do you know them?' I didn't, not in the typical sense, but I *did* know them. That's why we use the language, too, to avoid detection by whites. And deep down, I don't think any black person wants to assimilate completely."

Nor should they, says Ernie Smith, an L.A.-based linguist and longtime proponent of the theory that ebonics is an African-based language that has merely been "relexified" to English. Smith believes that the notion of black talk as bad English—even using the term "black English"—simply reinforces our subconscious belief that nothing African is good or legitimate, that invoking the African half of African-American is tantamount to some kind of treason. "What people in effect are saying is that we have no ancestry, no history," huffs Smith, who was one of several black language experts and psychologists who attended the 1973 St. Louis conference on the language development of black children where the term "ebonics" was coined. "People take the white-supremacist stance, which assumes we came to this country with nothing, that our variety of English is on a deviant trajectory. I reject that."

Yet everything black seems on that trajectory, says Mansur Ali, an English and music teacher at Washington Prep High in South L.A. who has researched the African-American language connection. "We don't take our stuff seriously," he says. Language is simply the tip of the iceberg. "For example: We joke about 'colored people's time,' about being late and lazy, when it's likely a reflection of the African holistic concept of time—it's directly opposed to the Western, linear approach. We've mocked our traditions, or any possibility of them, ever since slavery. We still have not accepted certain things about ourselves. Ebonics provides us with a sense of identity, but we don't accept that either."

Indeed, in recent months people have been confessing a great, sudden unease with the way they talk, with how their friends talk. One friend of mine, a single mother of about 30, worries about the quality of company her daughter keeps; her classmates are passable, she says, "but girl, you *know*"—she rolls her eyes—"they talk pure ebonics!" Another woman, a longtime South L.A. resident born in East Texas, apologizes for her struggle to put together a certain phrase. "I guess I don't talk right—ebonics, you know," she sighs. "I need to go back to school, learn something."

We *can* profitably hew to a middle ground, argues Marcyliena Morgan, a UCLA assistant professor of anthropology who specializes in African linguistics. Morgan is not in the African-language camp, though she agrees that black people maintain a very rich, unique language tradition that should be given its propers. But she says that ultimately, the African argument is more emotional than logical. "We can be of African origin without speaking African," she says. "If I occasionally don't have subject-verb agreement, that's not an African argument, that's an argument based on typology. You have too many other linguistic influences to argue the Niger-Congo link."

Perhaps. But moderation on the part of black folks has not played well in this country. One of the many things we have grown to deny ourselves is subtlety, and the unpleasant truth may be that we must be extreme to be heard. That's a pity, because our ongoing struggles with fitting in, or not wanting to fit in, require as much finesse as we can muster. And it is only in the shadows that we can nurse the still-raw wounds of assimilation, examine the pain that still attends our efforts at honest self-perception, and save our kids from that pain in the meantime.

I am now only beginning to believe that *I am allowed.* I believe it in fits and spurts, in those Peter Pan moments when language lets me fly high enough to lose sight of the ground. It takes time and a slow, incremental buildup of faith that can be scattered to the wind without warning. I remember, as a graduate student of theater 10 years ago, sitting in the office of a professor who was convinced I had plagiarized a term paper because, he said, it didn't accurately reflect the way I spoke. "You speak . . . " He searched for the right words. "Off the cuff. Not very well." Not at all like the Voice in the Paper.

I laughed nervously then, condemned the man as a racist and eventually got the grade I deserved. But that old fear that the voice *wasn't* mine, that it was too proper and too colored and consigned me to the frozen outer reaches of otherness, overtook me. I retreated, again, to a kind of silence for years. I am breaking silence now.

Do Books Matter?

Kevin Baldeosingh

I AM NOT A BETTING MAN, BUT I'LL LAY TEN TO ONE ODDS THAT NOBODY has ever posed the above question in any form or fashion in any issue of the *Trinidad and Tobago Review.*

In the technical sense, of course, it is a silly query. Books obviously matter as repositories of information. But even the technical question may become relevant in a hundred years, if not sooner, when computers and diskettes are more widespread. Right now, though, I am using the word "matter" in the ideological sense and, therefore, the books I refer to are novels and didactic non-fiction.

It is usual among academics and other intellectual people to assume that books influence the world. This is mostly because, being bookish persons themselves, they think it impossible that lesser mortals could fail to be swayed by what they consider so important in their own lives. Dennis Craig, Vice-Chancellor of the University of Guyana, expressed the typical view in his opening remarks at the 1994 presentation of the Guyana Prize for Literature: "The creators of . . . good literature are those among us who . . . have the habit of holding up the mirror to nature and by so doing they show us who, what and how we are." Funso Aiyejina in the 1996 Xmas issue of the *T&T Review* opined, "In a complex multi-cultural society like the Caribbean, wholesome morally responsible stories and willed choices are mandatory in order for the society to engage itself in any meaningful self-interrogation." And one of the United States' foremost literary critics, Harold Bloom, feels entirely comfortable writing, "The Canon is the true art of memory, the authentic foundation for cultural thinking. Without the Canon, we cease to think."

This kind of egg-headedness is almost charming. The question of how the ideas contained in books are supposed to show people who do not read "who what and how" they are, let alone make them interrogate themselves, never occurs to academics. It is almost as though books are supposed to influence the masses of human beings by some sort of literary osmosis. What these intellectuals have failed to realize is that their assumption about the ideo-political importance of books is based on social systems which have been largely superseded in this century.

In the first place, people—both intellectual and otherwise—assume that books have extraordinary power mainly for religious reasons, in both the historical and psychological senses of the term. Historically, religion has been a major influence in shaping political structures and those religions which have had the most influence are those which have had books to confer authority—the Bhagavadgita, the Torah, the Bible, and the Qu'ran. People, being basically idolatrous, came to venerate these books as holy objects in themselves. In the Western world, as Greek logic permeated Jewish theology, religion became extended to non-spiritual areas such as philosophy and politics, as well as to the books containing their ideas. Communism and capitalism thus became religions, psychologically speaking, in their own rights. Nowadays, science has begun to suffer a similar fate, though fortunately its own rigor has so far kept it a few steps ahead of its zealots.

In the second place, even after Gutenberg invented the printing press and books became more widespread, the social structures which gave prestige to books did not start to wither until four centuries later. Thus, the assumption that books did indeed matter was in fact quite true until this century, although essayists and even poets were probably always more influential than novelists. This is because, before mass education and the Industrial Revolution resulted in widespread literacy, the people who could read and write were an elite in all senses of the term. Not only were they a small educated minority, but they also had economic and political power. There was thus a much shorter distance between ideas in books and the institutions of the world. (One should note that, historically, this has had as many bad as good effects.) But, as democracy and education became more widespread, the bridging structures which made the transformation from ideas to sociopolitical reality possible began to change and collapse.

Now, on the brink of the new millennium, we have a situation which our intellectual forebears of even the last 100 years would never have imagined in their wildest dreams: a mostly literate culture where most of the people who can read do not read. Not books, at any rate, and often not anything they don't have to.

Now in order for literature or any other sort of art to have practical consequences, it must affect persons with political or social clout. If books only help to shape a person's attitudes, this may have psychological effects on the particular individual. Indeed, I am sure that nearly every avid reader would be able to cite a book or books which have had a major impact on their life. But books can only have social consequences if they influence either a few powerful individuals, or so great a number of average persons that the ideas expressed become generally accepted. And that, in turn, can happen only if people read the books in the first place. As Mark Twain once said, "The man who does not read good books has no advantage over the man who can't read them."

There may still be societies where books actually exert sociopolitical influence. France and Britain perhaps; maybe the United States; and definitely in Iran, Egypt and Nigeria, where novels can get their authors murdered. But not the Anglophone Caribbean. The only Caribbean nation where novelists seem to receive sociopolitical recognition is Guyana and, if that is so, the state of that country does not reflect well on its writers' ideas. In Trinidad, I doubt very much that Prime Minister Basdeo Panday or the clico conglomerate president Lawrence Duprey or Archbishop Anthony Patin read West Indian novels or that, if they do, it affects their conduct in any significant way.

Insofar as authors have sociopolitical influence, it is not directly because of their books. Especially not in the Caribbean. Here, the influence of literary work is often separate from the work itself. What really matters is the intellectual reputation conferred upon writers by their books. The political and literary value of books are thus connected but separate, like the rails of a track. While this phenomenon is not unique to post-colonial cultures, it is certainly more the case for us. But since nearly all West

Indian writers live and work out of the Caribbean, the literary-cum-political train is naturally derailed.

Besides, the intellectual authority a person might get from writing a few novels may not be justified by the books themselves. Just because someone can write a socially perceptive novel does not necessarily make their political ideas practical, as with the reparation-for-enslaved-Africans theme in Earl Lovelace's *Salt*. Psychologically speaking, too, a high level of creative intelligence usually means a low level of analytical intelligence and vice-versa (hence the reason literary critics are often execrable fiction writers).

What exacerbates the situation is the elitism which underlies all Caribbean literature and, indeed, all Caribbean institutions. All societies have such elitist divisions and only a minority of nations—mainly European and a few Asian ones—have solved most of the problems which arise from non-meritocratic hierarchies. (The interesting exception is the United States, where the top one percent of the population owns more than the last 90 percent. That the US is also the world's only industrialized country with such high crime statistics and such low educational scores is probably not coincidental.)

You might say that our situation in the Caribbean is a little worse because of colonialism and our historical youthfulness. But we are not unique in this problem of class/elite/caste divisiveness, though all our pseudo-intellectuals like to blame history for our woes and not ourselves. And this institutional elitism, and the psychological insecurity of the individuals who represent the institutions, lead to parallel divisions in art and literature.

Perhaps because of such intellectual inferiority complexes, there has been little attempt to create a tradition of popular literature in the region. Instead, authors have always gone for the critical kudos. Admittedly, our socioeconomic situation makes it difficult for a writer to do otherwise—critical kudos get you university jobs—but difficult is not impossible. With perhaps the sole exceptions of *Miguel Street*, *The Lonely Londoners* and *The Duppy*, no Caribbean novels straddle that wide canyon between entertainment and erudition. This is a serious failure of both creativity and willpower, especially if one takes the position that literary fiction is crucial to our development as a people. Although I am myself a novelist, I don't take that position, but I do think that fiction which truly entertains inevitably educates, whereas educational fiction that fails to entertain educates poorly. Not incidentally, our writers' output of highly literary novels has also ensured that only a tiny intellectual elite reads Caribbean novels, even in Trinidad where popular novels like Mills&Boon romances and John Grisham thrillers have thriving sales.

The French novelist, essayist, playwright and philosopher Jean-Paul Sartre held that a writer should be measured by the direct action of his work upon the public. This view seems to me to have more validity than the alternatives. To assume anything else leads to the conclusion that art has some value independent of human beings, which is a problematical position.

If we adopt Sartre's view, then the most important writer in Trinidad now is not novelist V.S. Naipaul or Earl Lovelace, but newspaper columnist Keith Smith. After all, the Trinidadian public, which is the most literate one in the West Indies, reads newspapers rather than novels. And, even by other standards, there is little doubt that Smith is a writer of very high calibre. He may not be able to write novels, but his is no reflection on his ability to tell a story or convey ideas effectively. The difference between novelists and other writers is not usually creativity or intelligence, but plain stick-to-itiveness—i.e. the discipline to stay with the work till you have written about 60,000 words.

But you won't hear Caribbean critics acknowledging Smith as the equal of Lovelace in literary terms, let alone postulating that he is a more important Trinidadian writer than Naipaul. But Naipaul himself has suggested more than once that the novel is dead and that real writing is taking place elsewhere. I wouldn't go so far as Naipaul, because the sales figures don't support his contention and because he considers the only real novels to be literary ones. But certainly if one takes 'real' writing to be writing that effectively reaches people, which is part of what Naipaul meant, one would have to look at film scripts and magazine and newspapers for such work.

It is a hard task for literary people in the Caribbean to admit any such thing, though. Doing so would interfere with their elite self-image. For all their talk about 'transforming' our societies through literature, our intellectual elite rejects any sort of work which might actually have an effect. Sartre again becomes relevant: "Our critics are Cathars: they don't want to have anything to do with the real world except eat and drink in it . . . They get excited only about classified matters, closed quarrels, stories whose ends are known."

The small controversy in July over the use of obscene language in the play *Jean and Dinah* by Errol Hall illustrated this perfectly. Junior Telfer, director of the Little Carib Theatre where the play was staged, said, "My duty as a member of the board is to preserve everything that the Little Carib and Beryl McBurnie stand for. The Little Carib has never been associated with any controversial play." In other words, the Little Carib has never hosted a relevant play in its entire existence; and this, which should be a source of shame for Telfer, is apparently a source of pride. It is thus no cause for wonder that drama is pretty much ignored in our society.

Let's turn to Sartre again: "Art, of its essence, is opposed to that which exists . . . its value is one of terrorism; it is a weapon against traditional value and morality." But when local dramatists and other writers insist they are revealing us to ourselves, they are usually confusing metaphysics for analytical philosophy. This is also true of many Caribbean novelists, in particular Wilson Harris. And, since literary critics and other intellectuals usually buy into this confusion, Harris is naturally praised as though he has some deeper mystic insight into reality, whereas what he mostly has is a really obscure prose style.

This, I think, is the sticking point: books in the modern world can matter only if they are written in a readable fashion. Except for the early Naipaul, Selvon, Michael Anthony, Anthony Winkler and CLR James, all our writers have failed to do this. "One is not a writer for having chosen to say certain things, but for having chosen to say them in a certain way," wrote Sartre. "And, to be sure, the style makes the value of the prose. But it should pass unnoticed . . . In prose, the aesthetic pleasure is pure only if it is thrown into the bargain."

CLR in particular reveals the truth of this. James's ideas are all the more convincing because of the clarity of his prose—a clarity which adds to, rather than detracts from, his eloquence. But even CLR's ideas could only influence the society if many people read his books, or if the political and economic elites were persuaded by him. That didn't happen and still isn't happening.

As far as novels go, their value usually lies in the humanistic attitudes they express. But, again, such attitudes can become social reality only if sufficient numbers of people read the novels and are influenced by them. And that can only happen if Caribbean writers start writing good popular fiction and if academics get the confidence to mash up their own ivory towers. Until then, though, the assertion that books do matter will remain a fond illusion.

Daphne A. Brooks

The Other Side of Paradise: Feminist Pedagogy, Toni Morrison Iconography, and Oprah's Book Club Phenomenon

THIS PIECE WAS FIRST PRESENTED AT THE MODERN LANGUAGE ASSOCIation National Conference held in San Francisco, California, December 27-30, 1998:

I'd like to begin with several acknowledgments, as well as a disclaimer, and a confession: First, I'd like to thank Rachel Lee and Farah Griffin for their insightful suggestions and I'd like to give a special shout out to HARPO Productions for informing me that my paper had "no educational value or purpose," the requirements for receiving video footage from *The Oprah Winfrey Show*. The disclaimer is due to HARPO's resistance to providing me with an Oprah videotape for today. I've been forced to read from the actual transcript of Winfrey's program and I take no responsibility for what may come out of that. . . . My confession is that I've come to the realization that Oprah Winfrey is a terribly difficult subject on which to write . . . she's, in one sense, too easy to slag and too culturally relevant to not engage with. . . . Therefore, what I hope do this evening is to try to walk the line in between critically examining her book club work and trying to perhaps open the door for acknowledging its profound influence on classroom politics and textual discussion. Also while I won't be discussing *Beloved* the film, I want to leave open the possibility for discussion and/or comments. . . .

By the time that novelist Toni Morrison sat down with talk show host Oprah Winfrey and four other star-crossed viewers for a late-afternoon lunch of crabcakes and baked bruschetta, the world of letters had already begun an odd and unexpected dance with popular talk show culture in the fall of 1996. Earlier that year, Winfrey had launched what turned out to be her most successful venture as a talk show host—that of the segment known as "Oprah's Book Club." Designed with the goal in mind to, as the diva host proclaimed, "reintroduce reading to people who've forgotten it exists," Oprah's Book Club has ushered in a new era of "reading" as a popular and leisurely act in American culture. Perhaps even more surprisingly, the program has transformed Nobel laureate Morrison from her heralded position as black feminist icon of literary and academic discourses into a household name—quite literally. Headlines in popular and publishing trade journals that marveled over "Oprah's cultural revolution" and the "literary phenomenon of her book club" spoke of the sheer impact that Winfrey's program had on Morrison's book sales. Once the host had selected Morrison's third novel, *Song of Solomon,* as her second book club selection on October 18, 1996, within two months, twice as many copies of the novel were sold than in the previous nine years of its publication added together. Morrison, it seemed, had finally arrived in the homes of "middle America" and in the hands of what market analysts described as "virgin readers," Oprah's fifteen million viewers of "mostly women with spare time on their hands, and a taste for stories of personal drama."

This paper takes as its point of departure that initial moment when Morrison and her literary oeuvre took a seat at the table of popular media culture—an act that has inadvertently yoked consumer desire with racial, gender, class, as well as canon politics in the contemporary literary marketplace and one that has arguably effected or opened a space for effecting the nature of feminist pedagogy in its sheer popularity among a broad cross section of readers who may in face one day be our pupils in the classroom. What I will attempt to do is to examine the potential transformation of Toni Morrison and her work in the context of Oprah's Book Club, and particularly how, if at all, the incorporation of her novels in this context effects textual analysis and discussion. I examine the impact that the circulation of Morrison's work in the mainstream media has had on mass market literary culture and likewise, how Morrison's work and her popular iconography have been irrevocably altered by the relationship with the book club. In the year and a half since that initial program, Morrison released her seventh and perhaps most controversial text, *Paradise,* which was quickly snapped up as an Oprah's Book Club selection earlier this year as well. Oddly, however, the stakes have seemingly changed for both Winfrey and Morrison. This time around, Winfrey, in an effort to storm the gates of literary "high culture," took her club out of the kitchen of sumptuous snacks and tearful testimonials and into the ivied halls of Princeton University, where the author led a rare "study group" discussion on the text. Morrison, meanwhile, surfaced in mass periodicals ranging from *Time* and *Essence* magazine to the paparazzi section of *People Weekly,* which spotted her alongside film stars Tom Cruise and Nicole Kidman.

This provocative and compelling cultural chiasmus between Winfrey and Morrison clearly spawns perhaps more questions than answers. What, for instance, are the gains and potential losses—if any—of such a cultural shift? How might feminist theorists of color respond to charges that Winfrey has, in turn, "domesticated" the author and her work? Likewise, what does it mean to contend that Morrison has "politicized" and "intellectualized" the popular talk show? Is it possible to conceive of the book club phenomenon as an opening toward reconceptualizing coalition politics between "academic" and "nonacademic" women readers? (And by this I mean that, in a sense, you have diverse groups of readers represented, but their reactions to the text and their diverging processes of reading that they discuss perhaps yield more fissures than connections). Beyond simply "getting the country reading again," how does the sheer diversity of who reads, what is read, and how it is discussed in Oprah's Book Club complicate and challenge—if at all—the formation of conventional reader communities? Does Oprah's pronouncement that she envisions her program and the club as attempting to "make people's lives better" suggest an effort to reintroduce alternative forms of "pleasure" in women's lives (as Janice Radway contends in her landmark study of romance novels and the women who read them), or does the book club simply transmute and re-enact the vacuous terms of the talk show "spectacle of feeling"? Clearly, the club offers the potential to diminish the "dichotomy between elite and popular (mass) literature" that Radway, Cathy Davidson, and other feminist scholars of reader-reception theory have observed, but how do we address this lessening of the divide and simultaneously acknowledge the complexities of pedagogy and readership? In the great words of the queen of all media herself: for responses to these questions, stay tuned.

Getting in the Classroom with Oprah

On the same day on which Toni Morrison's third novel, *Song of Solomon,* was chosen as the second Oprah's Book Club selection, Friday, October 18, 1996, Barnes & Noble booksellers announced that its chain had sold a remarkable 16,070 copies of the novel on that day alone. Jacquelyn Mitchard, the first author selected for book club distinction, has likened the experience to "being struck by lightning" *(New York Times)* and Morrison herself has since marveled over the sheer numbers in book sales since becoming a feature of Winfrey's literary revival. Although the origin of the book club predates Winfrey's more recent and high-profile redemptive movement entitled "Change Your Life TV" by two years—and this is a phenomenon I'll be returning to later in the paper—the structure of participation as well as the overriding themes of the book club set a precedence for the show's cultural and ethical transformation—or at least the popular perception of that transformation. As one publishing trade magazine put it, "a mere 6 months ago, Oprah Winfrey was the visible face of a TV genre that was being held responsible for everything from moral turpitude to murder. Suddenly she is being hailed as nothing less than the savior of the printed word." Despite the troubling observation here that Winfrey was somehow more "visible" (read: spectacular in terms of race, gender, and, at times, girth) than her TV counterparts, the suggestion remains that Winfrey's program made a successful generic shift out of the increasingly "prurient" realm of talk show spectacle to more "high-minded" programming—thus leaving Jerry Springer to assume the role of whipping boy for the moral pundits.

Clearly, however, the fundamental structure of the book club draws heavily from the traditional structure and thematic vision of the daytime talk genre that Winfrey, herself, pioneered in the early '80s. In keeping with the confessional and sentimental format of the Oprah show, the book club guidelines request that viewers-turned-readers connect with the text on a deeply personal level and then make that connection public for consumption. Viewers are selected for inclusion in a videotaped discussion of the featured novel by way of an epistolary process wherein they are asked to read the current selection and write to the Oprah show, telling the program's staff "how the novel affected you . . . what did the characters mean to you? How did the story make you reflect on your own life?" Readers are essentially asked to testify discursively in regard to their relationship with the text in a bid to achieve a domestic intimacy with the show's host and the author of the selected novel, who attends the discussion taping as well.

Hence, rather than marking a major departure from *The Oprah Winfrey Show*'s broadly influential format, which largely centralized testimonials of domestic strife and reconciliation, the book club has essentially invoked that process from a literary standpoint. And, as arts journalist Christopher John Farley notes, each selection "reveal[s] itself to be a literary manifestation of Winfrey's own desires, fears and ghosts. Certain themes and topics are explored again and again, in book after book. Secrets. Child abuse. Physical abnormalities . . .on page 1 of the book club pick, *Ellen Foster,* by Kaye Gibbons, the narrator says, 'When I was little, I would think of ways to kill my daddy.' (*Time* magazine, 83)—a line which both anticipates and diverges from the instantly incendiary opening line of last January's club selection, Morrison's *Paradise,* which reads simply 'They shoot the white girl first.'" All of this begs the question, then, where does Toni Morrison—Nobel laureate, Pulitzer Prize winner, National Book Award recipient—fit into this literary constellation of dysfunctional pathos?

By far the most celebrated and arguably the most textually challenging book club author to date, Morrison and her two novels chosen for discussion—*Song of Solomon* and *Paradise*—seem to resist the easy soundbite/tabloid summary assigned to other authors and their works. As scholar Linda J. Krumholz attests in the recent anthology on pedagogical approaches to Morrison's work, *Song of Solomon* alone challenges the instructor as well as the pupil with its "density, it's multiple stories and perspectives, its poetic richness, and its allusive threads." (106) And although Winfrey has argued that "reading about similar experiences" to her own has provided her with nurture and enlightenment, this sort of a goal takes on a peculiar challenge when focusing on Morrison's work since the author, herself, confessed on the program that she relished the magic realist impulse as a writer—of "mak[ing] something familiar strange in a book" and vice versa. In this regard, her tests potentially resist the initial visceral safety and comfort that Winfrey and her followers so crave and seek in the book club spotlight novels. Seemingly, Winfrey's solution to this problem the first time around was to attempt to make Morrison and her literature more "familiar" to her audience. [I wish to turn to this initial program to examine what's at stake in terms of including Morrison in the book club discussion before tracing the trajectory to her more recent appearance this past winter.]

Like Water for Chocolate: Oprah's Book Club as Literary Discussion Group

Two programs were set aside for Morrison and *Song of Solomon* on *The Oprah Winfrey Show* in the fall of 1996. The first of these programs aired on November 18 and diverged somewhat in format from past and future book club sessions in that it featured Morrison in the studio and combined a short interview with the author in between "highlights" of the taped book club dinner, which had taken place several weeks before airtime at Winfrey's penthouse apartment in Chicago. This is our first introduction to the selected book club "cast," if you will (since even Morrison refers to the taped dinner as "a good movie," a comment we may wish to come back to in terms of the mildly histrionic visual narrative at hand), and the group consists of four selected viewers: Aileen, Cynthia, Celeste, and Melinda. Background information on each of the readers is limited to the soundbite labels prescribed to them in voice-overs by Winfrey, which segue into brief excerpts of the participants reading from their "winning" letters. For instance, Winfrey's description of "Cynthia Neal" as "a single mom" who "works as a service representative for New Jersey Bell" gives way to Neal's proclamation in her letter that "I read *Song of Solomon* many, many years ago, and loved the challenge of spooning the words to my brain." Melinda Foster Foyes, "a stay at home Mom from Raleigh, NC" explains that "*Song of Solomon* was awesome. I'd love to meet Toni and discuss this book." If memory serves me correct, all of the participants are African American, with the glaring exception of Celeste Messer, who, Winfrey confesses, "we fondly called . . . 'the rich white woman from Dallas'" and who becomes the memorable centerpiece of the program for reasons we will explore.

Several key themes are prefaced and established for discussion in this twenty-minute segment, which will give way to what I'm defining as the "mother of all book club dinner discussions." For instance, the process and experience of reading as a topic of discussion surfaces repeatedly with participants exchanging the method of approaching the text (e.g., Aileen: "I had to keep going back and read every word . . ." and Cynthia affirms that she could in no way "skim" *Song of Solomon*). Winfrey and her guests acknowledge the complexity of Morrison's texts—a subject that will recur as a topic of contention in future discussions. Cynthia commends Winfrey for her "bravery" in choosing *Song of Solomon* because of its "difficulty," which leads to a peculiar exchange rife with baptismal and seduction imagery. Winfrey claims in regard to encouraging her viewers to read Morrison's work that "I had to get you to wade in with me, okay?" to which Melinda replies "Right. I mean, it was—you lured me in. I appreciate it." Celeste, however, establishes her resistance to this seduction early on, proclaiming that: "I mean, it was like you were just poking me like bruises, and it was just, 'Read it again. You didn't get what I was saying there.' And it was like, 'I don't want to' or I just was uncomfortable." Symbolically badgered by the two black female icons in her presence, Celeste positions herself as the reluctant reader of the group. Not surprisingly, this comment sets into play the central drive of the book club session to come, that of comforting and converting the upper-class white female subject. Moreover, the overarching book club tenets that stress the instructive quality of a text as well as the politics of readerly confession and transformation come to a head more memorably in the figure of Celeste, "the rich white lady from Dallas."

Indeed, this spectacle of conversion becomes the crux of the *Song of Solomon* discussion programs, superseding and at times displacing textual analysis altogether. Breathlessly, Winfrey describes how "it was—something really incredible happened among us all. . . . Because Celeste, Little Miss White Lady Celeste here, and I say that because that's what she said to me in the letter that she wrote to me, she said, 'Oprah, I am so ticked at you. I don't understand why you would choose this book. . . . I am female and I'm white and I make a certain amount of money—a lot of money—and I've never been poor and I've never been abused and I don't know what you're thinking that I would have anything to do with this book.' By the end of the evening, it was Celeste who was crying louder than all of us at the table, as we all were doing at the table. You had a transformation, did you not?" To which Celeste replies in the affirmative. Here the anticipation of emotive spectacle is marketed for consumption and perhaps more troubling still is the structuring of the program around the white female viewer's literary and emotional awakening (and by this I mean that each commercial break during the mother-of-all-dinner-parties program is preceded by Oprah's juicy tag line, which urges viewers to stick around because "you're going to see laughter and tears and a breakdown that turned into a breakthrough").

The stage is thus set for the full one-hour program featuring the dinner party; its title alone—"Behind the Scenes of Oprah's Dinner Party"—suggests a kind of exposure and surreptitious voyeurism to which the program insistently panders. What's more and perhaps what's most legendary to those of us who tuned in for the initial airing of this program is the way in which the actual discussion of Morrison's text is relegated to the final twenty minutes of the show, and to be sure, the discussion takes on a rather unique life of its own. Seemingly here, the structure of the program operates as a self-conscious response to the earlier eruptions of fear and anxiety among novice Morrison readers such as Celeste. To read Toni Morrison in the context of Oprah's Book Club, Winfrey clearly attempts to calibrate the tenor at which her work will be received by viewers; though she can do nothing to alter the density of her text, Winfrey's strategy seems to be here to resituate the novel in the throes of domestic ritual and excess—an environment that her masses of female viewers will surely relish.

Thus, she repeatedly claims at the show's opening that "the dinner transformed lives" and assures that "even if you haven't read the book, it could help change yours. . . . .Even if you haven't heard of Toni Morrison, there's still so much wisdom that you can get out of this dinner, as I did. I think I know a lot in the world, but when I was in her presence, I felt like I was eleven. But if you're more into party planning than life lessons, you can get some great tips on planning a dinner party, too. This one was really—I must say—even though it was at my house—it was very beautiful." Winfrey's intro leads into a lengthy opening segment on the preparation for the gathering, ranging from tips on making homemade breadsticks, the painstaking care taken to flying in the best possible crab cakes (reportedly Morrison's favorite meal) from Maryland, and the meticulous energy that Winfrey's white male chef Paul has expended in the full-day preparation of pistachio pear tarts for dessert. In addition to her chef, Morrison's hairdresser Andre, a character familiar to fans of the Oprah makeover programs, makes a special appearance to instruct viewers on the proper etiquette and organization of place settings and fine china for the occasion.

While seemingly the invocation of the domestic here parallels the nineteenth-century cult of domesticity that Anglo writers such as Catherine Beecher espoused, Harriet Beecher Stowe invoked as a means to political reform, and African American activists such as Frances Harper and Pauline Hopkins transformed to suit their own purposeful, black Reconstruction agendas, Winfrey's positioning of domestic ritual and ceremony (I'm sad to say) aims much more locally in its pursuit of offering her viewers a fantasy of leisure and comfort. (I will say in defense of this moment that Winfrey seems to be establishing and promoting a legitimate, mainstream fan culture around black female lit figures such as Morrison and Maya Angelou and that this emphasis on material grandeur, while lacking the kind of broad political purpose I would hope for in the cultivation of domestic space, is, however, geared toward and perhaps ultimately admirable in its elevation of and revaluation of writers as cultural treasurers and pop phenoms to be properly feted.) The goal here, it seems, anticipating the theme of "Change Your Life TV," is to offer viewers a literal as well as a figurative window to a "better self," and thus book club reform (like the catch slogan used since the beginning of this season's Oprah) takes place ultimately and initially on the individual level.

This appears to be an underlying problem of the overall new format and evolving ideology of *The Oprah Winfrey Show*, by the way. I do not wish to suggest that Winfrey's program is not, for instance, responsible for incredibly active and charitable volunteer activities such as the Angel Network; indeed, Winfrey has become, along with her talk-show colleague Rosie O'Donnell, a kind of cultural icon in the spearheading of communal reform activities. Winfrey's new formal builds on this iconography; the "Change Your Life TV" programming format relics, for example, on different advice specialists in the fields of motivation, financial freedom, relationships, and a department known simply as "make peace with your parents." Ultimately, the format and the ethos promote a rhetoric of "responsibility"—a term that comes up repeatedly in Oprah's definition of the new programming edge. I am, however, concerned by Winfrey's professed perspective on these changes. In response to a critique that the show has become "evangelical," Winfrey replied in a recent on-line chat interview by saying that "It's a shame that we've evolved into the kind of society where evangelical is considered negative. . . . I call it good, spirit, making the right choices, taking responsibility for your life."

Mildly awash with the conservative language of welfare reform, Winfrey's comments embody the decontextualizing, largely apolitical direction of the book club programs as well. Although the "personal is indeed political," in the context of Winfrey's show, the self-actualizations and conversions which come as a result of the act of reading are kept at arm's length from any discussion of the social, political, and economic structures of power that potentially entrap many of Oprah's viewers. Change and transformation are limited to the self on *The Oprah Winfrey Show* and although reading theorist Elizabeth Hardwick has argued that, in the 1980s, the popular mainstream literary public did not "read for a validation of their own experience" (she cites the escapism of the supermarket romance novel as an example of this), I would argue that the book club, and particularly the famous *Song of Solomon* book club dinner, affirms and—to a certain extent—promotes the "average" reader's search for self-realization.

In what is most certainly a throwback to the nineteenth-century women's literary movement of edification, social conduct, instruction, and spiritual redemption, which novels such as *The Coquette* and *Charlotte Temple* typified and which as well influenced the production of African American conduct books in the latter half of the century, Oprah's Book Club frames the worth of the *Song of Solomon* sessions wholly in terms of individual transformation. Like the upper-middle-class women of late Victorian America who, Barbara Sicherman finds, found "freedom and possibility" and "a way of ordering, and understanding their lives" through the world of books, the Oprah show invokes literacy as an avenue for personal change and appeals to the same group of readers who, Radway contends, the long-standing Book of the Month Club has targeted: those readers "seeking a model for contemporary living and even practical advice about appropriate behavior in a changing world." (276)

At the center of Winfrey's movement to ignite the rhetoric of individual reform, Celeste, "the white lady from Dallas," arrives at the book club dinner with her literary discomfort and dislocation heavily in tow. Unlike Cynthia, the African American woman from New Jersey who confesses an early love for Morrison and who acknowledges that "I read these stories and I know these people," Celeste finds little in common with the *Song of Solomon* community. This confession Winfrey attests to "loving" while reading Celeste's attestation of alienation aloud for the group. Celeste adds that "I found it [the novel] kept sucking me down to a level I've never been before, and—and that was uncomfortable for me." Winfrey characterizes this reaction as a fear of

going "into Toni territory" and it is this fear, this ball of confusion and social dislocation that sparks the spectacle of sentimentality at the moment when Morrison finally
reads a passage from the novel, some forty minutes into the program. Against Morrison's hushed reading of the funeral scene in which the heroine Pilate mourns for her
granddaughter's death, Winfrey instructs viewers to listen and "you'll hear Celeste in the
background sobbing. In just a moment we'll explain why that scene hit her so hard."

Following the reading, textual discussion is displaced in favor of foregrounding
Celeste's emotional collapse before the cameras. Racked with pain, she engages in a
lengthy narrative, describing the birth of her stillborn son some sixteen years before
and her subsequent repression of trauma and grief—that is—until now. Not surprisingly, Morrison's rich, eloquent, and (dare I say) near-epic text is reduced here to a vehicle for the emotional awakening of the white female subject. Celeste's reaction remains
a poor and simplified cousin to that of the "empathic" antislavery epistles of white abo-
litionists that Saidiya Hartman has problematized and powerfully unpacked in her
study of nineteenth-century literature. Unlike this sort of figure who "must supplant
the black captive in order to give expression to black suffering," thus, in turn, effacing
the black figure altogether, Celete's "awakening" holds no space for even a cursory or
transitory response to the black female grief expressed in the passage; instead her feeling is limited to her self from beginning to end. The moment is an all-too-familiar one,
perhaps even mundane at this point for those of us in the academy who have witnessed
the repeated scene of what Ann duCille has cogently characterized as "the lure of
black women's fiction . . . its capacity to teach others how to endure and prevail, how
to understand and rise above not necessarily the pain of black women but their own."
(101) DuCille's concern, that "the texts of black women must be readable as maps,
indexes to someone else's experience, subject to a seemingly endless process of translation
and transference," is, of course, here all too real in the context of Winfrey's program.

Even Morrison herself is transformed into a "map" of sorts that will lead Winfrey's
viewers out of their putative misery. As Winfrey's tag line for an additional segment of
the program proclaims, "Here's a message for every person on the planet. . . . Take a listen, will you, to Toni Morrison, as she tells us her journey to becoming the writer and
the woman that she now is." As it turns out, Morrison is allowed her own autobiographical and confessional moment in the program as well and she offers a crafted narrative of her experiences as a writer, a publisher, and a single mother, and her journey
to self-fulfillment that comes to fruition, as she tells it, at the point when she decides
to "write down not just what I wanted to do . . . but what I thought if I didn't do, I'd
die." These two things turn out to be to mother her children and to write books. Shaping these comments into the format of the program, Winfrey quickly reminds her
viewers, "So the message is this: If you're feeling overwhelmed, take out a sheet of
paper, as Toni Morrison did, and write down the things you have to do or you believe
you will die if you don't. That is sure to put your life in perspective."

Here Winfrey continues her effort to mediate the space between converting
Morrison into a palatable and approachable domestic icon for her viewers—someone
who has more rather than less in common with them—and perhaps attempting to utilize the author's presence in this world of fine china and mood lighting as a kind of dis-
ruption to this domestic order and space. If, as Janice Radway contends, "romance
reading" operates "as a complex intervention in the ongoing social life of actual social

subjects, women who saw themselves first as wives and mothers," then too the book club seemingly follows this gesture by attempting to provide viewers with instructional alternatives for living. But clearly here these "lessons" come less as a result of the actual act of reading more from the intimate contact and safe, comforting space that the *idea* of reading conjures.

How much has changed for Oprah's Book Club in the two years since its inception? According to the Oprah website, the popularity of the club and viewer participation are at an all-time high. For the most part, the format of the club discussions has become even more extravagant, with its emphasis on preparing text-related meals and traveling to the geographical site of the selected narrative. Yet the one programming exception to these format revisions was when Morrison returned early this year to discuss her new novel *Paradise* on March 6, 1998. This particular program, a far cry from the *Song of Solomon* dinner, featured "twenty-two lucky participants" who accompanied Winfrey to Princeton University, where Morrison was to "lead a class discussion" on the text. And I've decided because of time to show you first the overview of the program to give you an idea of this session.

CLIP I: Start right before she goes back to January clip. The overview.

Oprah gets the final word there. More than any other selection of the book club, *Paradise* sparked viewer protestations of textual difficulty and incomprehension. Winfrey emphasizes here that the trip to Princeton, a place of "higher learning," will some-how hopefully aid the readers in their quest to release the "secrets" of the text. Morrison is again awarded a deified status here but the assumption and the desire is for her to play the role of textual authority for hungry pupils in her classroom rather than nur-turing matriarch of a dinner party.

Yet the problem of reader resistance to the novel is a significant one, slightly resem-bling that of Celeste's frustration with *Song of Solomon*. Winfrey, however, takes a dif-ferent approach to dealing with white female readers' obstacles in the *Paradise* program, attempting instead to quell and address certain reactions to the text at the opening of the show.

CLIP II: The black reader/white reader exchange (to laughter).

While the first audience member confesses her frustration with the nonlinear structure of the narrative, the second viewer expresses a more general difficulty with the text, that she "really wanted to read it" and "learn life lessons." Her question regarding whether there lies any "value in a book that is hard to understand" sets the tone, though, for perhaps the most remarkable and compelling aspect of this book club program in that the bulk of the show is focused on questions of "how to read," how to (as Oprah puts it) "open yourself" to texts that don't come with instruction manuals. Rather than shaping the text to meet the visceral needs of the readers, participants are asked to stretch themselves and reflect on strategies for accessing the textual complexity of *Par-adise*. In other words, the discussion aims to articulate and explore both the "event of reading" as well as the multiple meanings of the text (something sorely missing in the previous book club discussion).

Now, in closing, I have to confess that I feel slightly self-conscious championing this more recent Oprah's Book Club over the previous program. I would, of course, have to articulate my own biases in privileging a book club discussion that is so much more engaged with the literature that, as Oprah describes it, participants were forced to "wait to have dinner" until after the discussion (crab cakes and pecan droppings). Given my own position as a scholar invested in teaching literature by women of color and presenting this paper at the Modern Language Association Conference, it seems almost all too easy and too safe to end with a reaffirmation of more conventional strategies for textual analysis. What about, for instance, those other viewers and readers who have no interest in trips to Princeton or, for that matter, suggestions for flower arrangements when having a Nobel laureate over for tea? I want so much to resist the observation made by Frank Kermode nearly two decades ago where he insists that "To be realistic we have little to do with the oppressed, with the hapless victims of television and advertising, insofar as they constitute an inaccessible man. We have to do with the new Common Reader, who has to be our creation, who will want to join us, as people who speak with the past and know something of reading as an art to be mastered." (10)

Clearly, too many strides have been made since the time of Kermode's statement to include voices such as Morrison's—voices previously in the margins and now in many ways at the center (or at least some centers) of academic thought. And it seems that it is precisely because of these significant strides to elasticize and eclecticize (!) the walls of the canon that we, as feminist scholars of color, should continue to be engaged with the diverse and "hapless victims" of the media, particularly those women who look to Oprah's afternoon comfort zone, or for that matter Terry McMillan's pop tales of domestic strife and reinvention, or who groove to the sounds of Mary J. Blige and Lil' Kim and TLC. I'd like to believe that there's a space for these kinds of readers in the classroom or, maybe even more importantly, that there is room outside of the familiar walls of the classroom to discuss and enjoy and explore rather than eliding and eclipsing Morrison's wildly imaginative, elliptical prose. For as Barbara Christian reminds, "it was 'ordinary' black women, women in the churches, private reading groups, women like my hairdresser and her clients, secondary school teachers, typists, my women friends, many of whom were single mothers, who discussed *The Bluest Eye* or *In Live and Trouble* with an intensity unheard of in the academic world." To these women, Christian observes, "this literature was not so much an object of study but was . . . lifesaving." (64) Perhaps then the challenge for both Oprah Winfrey and for those of teaching literature by women of color is to discover and revel in that space that mediates the critical challenge of reading with the pleasure and inspirational value of intimacy with the text. That space, however, as my colleague Farah Griffin has pointed out to me, may for now only exist outside the spectacle of TV cameras.

She's Gotta Have It

Debra Dickerson

THERE WILL NEVER BE A RAINY AFTERNOON MONOTONOUS ENOUGH, A plane ride long enough, or a convalescence debilitating enough to justify reading Benilde Little's *The Itch* (Simon & Schuster, 286 pp., $23). There's no book here, only a collection of blackface paper dolls striking self-conscious poses.

According to the book jacket (perhaps the best writing in the book), *The Itch* is "the stirring story of a crisis-torn woman who discovers a depth of character and a sense of self she never knew she possessed." Tapping into the bottomless well that is black folks' justified hunger to see themselves reflected in the cultural zeitgeist, Benilde Little is only the latest hustler with a laptop and rap-album liner notes to crib slang from to cash in on her people's low literary expectations.

Her first book, *Good Hair,* was a bestseller and it, too, sucked in exactly the same way that *The Itch* does, and for a very simple reason: it's the same book. I read *Good Hair* hoping to find some ray of light, some way out of my duty to my intellect, my craft, my people, and my common sense. Big mistake. Huge. Just a hodgepodge of tired black stereotypes mouthing tired black grudges in such a literary monotone, the reader is tempted to side with the tired white cardboard cutouts propped up for ritual abuse in both books.

Again, the book jacket synopsis for *The Itch* is all you need to know: "Abra Lewis Dixon is the envy of the fashionable, professional women of her well-heeled social circle. She leads a charmed life—she has attended all the right schools, married very well, and enjoys every material comfort granted by her bourgeois existence. . . . It is only when her impeccable marriage turns suddenly shaky that Abra's insular utopia is left in pieces." In *Good Hair,* Alice-who-also-went-to-all-the-right-schools's impeccable engagement turns suddenly shaky and for the same clichéd, anemically developed reason. Alice has a coupla ham-fisted incest paragraphs scotch-taped to her "character"; Abra's "insular utopia" is clunkily overshadowed by her having grown up fatherless. These things affected the two greatly. We know this because we are told so (repeatedly) by Little, not because we are shown the effects of either trauma through the writing.

At least in *The Itch* it's page 4 before the distracting (and gauche) litany of designer names begins, the point of which is to establish the characters' bourgeoisity; Armani debuts in the second paragraph of *Good Hair.* Alice-Abra doesn't pack a bag; she packs a "Coach duffel" every time the character takes a trip (which she does a lot to show how upscale she is). In the movie *Good Fellas,* a wiseguy asks his gaudy wife how much money she needs for her latest shopping spree. She doesn't reply at all, just grins like the greedy bitch she is and spreads her thumb and index finger two inches apart. That's writing. That's character development. Alice-Abra would have said, "$3500, dahling. There's a Givenchy handkerchief I simply must have. You don't think that's decadent, do you? Do you?"

It is ironic that the same mainstream recognition of the black literary imagination that is fueling the boom in black books is also responsible for the dumbing down of that imagination. There is simply too much money to be made off tossing crumbs of this type before the starving black masses for any of the players—publishers, editors, agents, writers, Hollywood—to control themselves. If this keeps up, one day readers will open the latest black bestseller and all the pages will read simply: "Ditto, girlfriend."

My problem with *The Itch* (and its ilk) is not that it isn't highbrow lit-tricher destined for *Masterpiece Theatre.* There should be black beach reading, mysteries, westerns, and sci-fi, just as there are the white versions of all those genres. But just as we should say no to the drug dealers who would anesthetize us into accepting a poor substitute for happiness, we should just say no to the carpetbaggers who would peddle us such poor excuses for art. Those of us who cut our teeth on Ralph Ellison, James Baldwin,

Zora Neale Hurston, and Octavia Butler learned that good writing is always difficult to produce and often difficult to process. The next generation of black writers and readers deserves no less.

No Entry

Lynell George

I'VE ALWAYS HOPED MARDOU FOX WOULD FIND HER VOICE. INSTEAD, Mardou, the icy object of obsession Jack Kerouac so exhaustively lays bare in his solemn confessional *The Subterraneans,* remains an abstract, a black bohemian indistinct beyond her beauty, lost in the dusk of that first August afternoon on Montgomery Street. What was her version of the "bookmovie"? Listening for an opening, waiting for the hot air to clear, just how did this orphan/waif find herself center of this orbit, debating Kant, Reich and the verse of Baudelaire? One will never know. In the shower of Kerouac bios and photo memory books, counterculture lit anthologies and mountaintop conferences, Mardou, the woman who inspired a three-day Benzedrine bender and an astonishingly honest "tearbook," is for eternity referred to only by a jarringly unpoetic pseudonym—"Irene May." She "prefers her anonymity," beat biographers have for decades rhapsodized: I prefer to think that it is something much more grand: she sits guard over her remaining secrets.

Mardou's slight shadow pulled me in. Her less-than-half-told story jump-started my own rough ride with the beats. I had, a few years back, turned up my nose at *On the Road,* not able to comprehend what all those scruffy high-school boys at the back of the classroom whispered overtures about. I drifted, found it tedious, as one high time blended into the next. But, too, there was the poetry, the unstructured, alternative lifestyle (read: bohemia). And the promise of perpetual motion was thrilling—no rules, no ties, as one "leaned forward toward the next crazy venture beneath the skies." I began reading beat novels/bios/free verse the way others devour romance, mysteries or novels of grand historic proportion.

My '80s were Kerouac's '50s: the materialistic Reagan years chillingly mirrored the era of the Company Man, all staid and monochromatic. Campuses were silent; these were indolent days. Kerouac's books, like Robert Frank's or William Claxton's sifted-fight photographs or John Cassavetes's gritty, jittery film-of-the-times *Shadows,* all worked like Mr. Peabody's Way-Back Machine expressly tailored for an anachronism like me. Kerouac was a mad and careful chronicler of the moods, pace and colors of jazz, from bop to post-bop to West Coast cool—so I could, through the magic of "spontaneous bop prosody," watch my long-dead heroes swing.

Amid his journey novels and poignant sketchbooks—*Lonesome Traveler, Satori in Paris, Big Sur* and tales from the legend of Duluoz—Mardou introduced a unique element. She wasn't a kitten picked up off the soft shoulder of the road. Her desire to be an "independent chick with money and cuttin' around" was more than endearing, puffed-up hipspeak. I found exhilarating the notion of cutting one's own trail—though I recognized the unnoted limitations, the eclipsed freedoms afforded a black woman even within this "progressive" bohemian orbit.

Kerouac the sentimentalist (in the guise of protagonist Leo Percepied) could never move beyond precious invention. Submerged in his reveries, in his quixotic search for the "essence," an unencumbered self blinded him to prosaic reality (" . . . as I pass Mexicans I feel the great hepness I'd been having all summer on the street with Mardou, my old dream of wanting to be . . . Negro or an Indian or a Denver Jap or a New York Puerto Rican come true, with her by my side so young, sexy, slender, strange, hip . . ."). The subtleties lay beyond even his own sensitive grasp:

> I wanted to go into a bar for a wine, she was afraid of all the behatted men ranged at the bar, now I saw her Negro fear of American society she was always talking about but palpably in the streets which never gave me any concern—tried to console her, show her she could do anything with me, "In fact baby I'll be a famous man and you'll be the dignified wife of a famous man so don't worry" but she said "You don't understand" but her little girl-like fear so cute, so edible, I let it go.

Never mind her own aspirations, or that riding his coattails was not her dream of success. Her "fear" wasn't of American society—more precisely, her unease made her circumspect. She knew the ugly/violent manifestations of ignorance, of bigotry, hints of which Kerouac harbored himself.

Within Kerouac's prose and verse there was maybe an arm's-length understanding of the "Negro" culture, but he tended instead of deify or pay obsequious homage. The same went for women—those "bangtail" girls that Kerouac so demoralized in the now infamous *Visions of Cody* passage:

> As far as young women are concerned I can't look at them unless I tear off their clothes . . . I figure her cunt is sweet. This is almost all I can say about almost all girls and only further refinement is their cunts and will do . . .

Unwittingly or not, Kerouac etched the rules in stone. Somewhere in the middle of madness he gave the media something to chew on, an alluring hook. Then he sat back to watch the action: the Beat Generation, he quipped, was "a swinging group of new American men intent on joy."

That is the loaded quote that begins Barry Alfonso's overview of the beats, setting the tone for a recently release Rhino boxed set, *The Beat Generation.* The three-CD compilation doesn't upset those perimeters; rather it serves to reinforce them. Inside there are, as promised, a lot of men (mostly white) and a lot of joy (a.k.a. "Kicks"), with nods to black culture—bop, black hipster slang—from which the beats so liberally drew. A dizzying mix of kitsch meets sublime, the set is impressive in its scope and effective in its mood-setting powers, with Nelson Riddle's fluid and atmospheric "Route 66 Theme" and a plum slice of verisimilitude provided by investigative radio docs—Howard K. Smith's *The Cool Rebellion* and Charles Kuralt's *The Greenwich Village Poets.* Tying together various components from beat antecedents (Lord Buckley and Langston Hughes), bridges (Kenneth Patchen), inspirations (Dizzy Gillespie, Slim Gaillard, Charlie Parker) and new musings from the baby beats (Tom Waits), the collection also celebrates the holy beat trimvirate: Kerouac, William S. Burroughs (from

Naked Lunch), and Allen Ginsberg's "America," a reading resonant in its dispassion.

Young poets were miming the frenetic, out-in-front style of their favorite bopmen. Poetry was improvisation illuminated by rhythm and intonation. The voice evolved into a well-honed instrument.

But though bop and its progenitors are more than adequately recognized in *The Beat Generation,* you won't find Amiri Baraka (né LeRoi Jones) reading or artist/poet Ted Joans sermonizing. And even though black/Jewish poet Bob Kaufman is cited in the booklet—his photo and verse ("His Horn") given reverent space—these voices aren't part of this otherwise comprehensive keepsake.

During a one-on-one on Disc 3, Ben Hecht does do his feeble best to fish out the role of the "Negro" from a taciturn and marginally belligerent Kerouac: "He is the original beat," prompts Hecht. Kerouac enthusiastically agrees, then adds, "Negroes have a lot of fun . . ." To Alfonso's credit, he doesn't let this one slide: "It might've been news to many of the 'happy, true-hearted ecstatic Negroes of America' (Kerousac's description) that their lives were so untroubled."

Such careless and obtuse utterances are only a few of the things about Kerouac that have made me shudder, along with his writing disconcertingly in the voice of a 10-year-old Southern black boy in Pie. Then I wrestle with my notions of writerly love for the poet/visionary within him. Kerouac, our dear *Ti Jean,* is embarrassing like a much-adored great-aunt: so grand, but so aged, that she speaks her mind, uncensored and always out of turn.

Norman Podhoretz was high and outside in his projection that "bohemia was for the Negro a means of entry into a white world." In truth, it was a chance for white men to walk on the "wild side"—to excavate black culture, in the same way they scratched the surface of eastern philosophy or the romance of dusky Mexico. Their interest was only fleeting. Poet/artist Ted Joans may be remembered more for his "Rent-A-Beatnik" schemes than for his jazz-inspired recitations: Bob Kaufman's frenetic, evocative writing style and trailblazing efforts are never even duly noted. The rebel-spirited Kaufman, co-founder of the avant-garde (and still surviving) literary journal *Beatitude,* served as a model for resistance in free-speech battles between the city of San Francisco and its bohemians.

Baraka, the most recognized though seldom lionized beat of color, was feeling generous when he wrote, "Burroughs' addicts, Kerouac's mobile young voyeurs, my own Negroes, are literally not included in the mainstream of American life. These characters are people whom Spengler called *Fellaheen,* people living on the ruins of civilization. They are Americans no character in a John Updike novel would be happy to meet, but they are nonetheless Americans, formed out of the conspicuously tragic evolution of modern American life."

Baraka, however, must have known then what he knows most acutely now—that *our* outside is very different. It is an outside that a haircut, a shave or a change of dress will never alter. The young, white male bohemian "outsider" was really more insider than he cared to admit. Maybe this is why Baraka and others sought to create an "inside" of their own.

Joyce Johnson aptly titled her evocative memoir of the times *Minor Characters.* On the cover, eyes downcast, she is just out of focus; the lens is poised sharp on Kerouac, who sports a defiant half-scowl. Carolyn Cassady called her daybook-cum-autobio *Off the Road,* and most recently LeRoi Jones' ex, Hettie Cohen, filed her report: *How I Became Hettie Jones.*

These women were all outsiders cursed with a yen for constant motion. Their hopes and yearnings mirrored those of the men with whom—for better or worse—they found themselves feverishly enmeshed. "I started leaving home when I was six," writes Hettie Jones. "At night, in my narrow maple bed, under the starched, white, ruffled, pink-ribbon-threaded spread . . . I'd made up stories with myself as the hero of great seafaring adventures."

But after marriage, a baby or donning "straight" threads to hold down a 9-to-5, Jones and other women came to understand they could find no place for their thoughts turned prose: "With all her grand ambition," Jones realizes with a chill, "all she'd ever 'become' was Hettie Jones." And so it was. Joyce Glassman became Johnson, Cohen became Jones—these women assuming anonymous names, anonymous employ, only brushing elbows with the literati who paused to visit the suite of spartan rooms they called home.

Probably no one was as forgotten in the shadows as Mardou—a conundrum who, to "the subterraneans," was as shimmeringly exotic as she was mad. To herself, she was not as mad as she was lost. As Leo/Jack observed, she "sat in the corner by the window . . . being 'separated' or 'aloof' or 'prepared to cut out from this group' for her own reasons . . ."

She intended to sing on her own line, as Billie Holiday used to do.

Nose perpetually in book, I understood. Because I, too, am a "brown woman disposed to wearing dark clothes," who "was able to walk as fast as [the men] were." And I fell—hard—for this: "Nights that begin so glitter clear with hope, let's go see our friends, things, phones ring, people come and go, coats, hats, statements, bright reports, metropolitan excitements . . . the talk gets more beautiful, more excited, flushed happy faces are now wild and soon there's the swaying . . ."

To have Mardou's veteran eyes; to have sage advice from someone who knew what it was like to step through the ruins of civilization, finding beauty in those *Fellaheen* streets.

What About Black Romance?

Esther Iverem

This is for the lover in you . . .

—SUNG BY HOWARD HEWITT AND SHALIMAR

SITTING IN THE SUNNY RESTAURANT AT THE PARK HYATT HOTEL, Theodore Witcher is asked to name a Hollywood black romance. Pausing a moment, he leaps back decades and offers dusty "Mahogany," the inauspicious 1975 directorial debut of Motown music mogul Berry Gordy. It featured a painfully thin Diana Ross with a broad smile and bouncy hair playing opposite heartthrob-of-the-decade Billy Dee Williams.

"I can't say that I recall," Witcher says. "In the last generation of films, you pretty much arrive back at Diana Ross and Billy Dee."

Witcher is the 27-year-old director of "Love Jones"—which has made a name for itself as a new black romance. Opening last week was director Rusty Cundieff's "Sprung," which is quirky but offers more of a traditional, head-over-heels love story. What makes both films remarkable, first and foremost, is that they are actually black romances. The fact that Witcher, culturally savvy like the poetry café regulars in his film, cannot name a few recent black love stories, says a lot about Hollywood's avoidance of black love and sexuality on the screen. In the thousands of films and television shows that Hollywood has released, only a handful have depicted any substantial relationship between a black man and a black woman. As recently as the 1980s, "The Cosby Show" was unique on television in that it was often the only place to see a black man kiss a black woman.

"I guess that exclusion is something I've known about all my life," says veteran actress Ruby Dee. She appeared in her first film in 1949 and has played in her own real-life love story with her husband of nearly 50 years, Ossie Davis. But she has never starred opposite a black man in a love story. "It's one of the things stuck into your subconscious and it eats at you in little ways. You've received a certain type of propaganda about yourselves, about your relationships, about white people. Something creeps in of the enemy's propaganda."

Two years ago, Ebony magazine published the results of a survey of film historians, filmmakers and actors, who were asked to name the most romantic black movies. A 40-year-old musical, "Carmen Jones," topped the list. Rounding out the top 10 were: "Nothing but a Man" (1964); "For Love of Ivy" (1968); "Sounder" (1972); "Claudine" (1974); "Coming to American" (1988); "Jason's Lyric" (1994); "Lady Sings the Blues" (1972); "Mahogany" (1975); "Paris Blues" (1961); and "A Warm December" (1973).

Only two movies from the last two decades made the list. And a strong argument can be made that some of the movies aren't romances so much as dramas and comedies containing a thread of romance.

There is no comparison between these films and real love stories from Hollywood. Consider just the hits of the past film season. In "Jerry Maguire," Tom Cruise finally realizes the wispy blonde he married is his true love. In "The English Patient," dashing, wealthy Brits—smug benefactors of a colonized world—live risk-taking, interesting and passionate lives.

Though an aesthetic of white faces, aquiline features and flowing hair, we have been given a vision of what love and, as an extension, humanity, is. We've seen them all: average, well-meaning white people ("Sleepless in Seattle"); mob love ("Bugsy"); funky musicians ("A Star Is Born"); hooker as Cinderella ("Pretty Woman"); communists ("Reds"); military love ("An Officer and a Gentleman"); dying white people ("Love Story"); white people speaking in foreign languages (a favorite: "Wings of Desire"); elderly white people ("On Golden Pond"); even unattractive people ("Inventing the Abbotts").

There's something about the simplicity of a love story," says actress Theresa Randle, who has played the girlfriend/wife opposite Wesley Snipes and Michael Jordan, and is the star of Spike Lee's "Girl 6." That's why I love Lauren Bacall and all those people because they were in *real movies.* You sit there and you cry and you wait for who comes in the door."

For a substantive black film romance, go back to 1968 to "Nothing but a Man" with Ivan Dixon and Abbey Lincoln. Go to a foreign film, "Black Orpheus." In literature, turn to James Baldwin's "If Beale Street Could Talk," Zora Neale Hurston's "Their Eyes Were Watching God" or last year's novel "Tumbling," by Diane McKinney-Whetstone. (But even romance in literature may not make the transition to the screen. The hot affair between Easy Rawlins and Daphne in Walter Mosley's "Devil in a Blue Dress" was reduced on the screen to a single steamy scene.)

Or turn to the imagination. No doubt there was an African willingly captured by slavers just to follow an abducted loved one; recently emancipated blacks who walked the length of the country to find a lost spouse. There were fashionable lovers of the Harlem Renaissance; militant lovers of the 1960s.

"I miss seeing those images," says rapper and actress Queen Latifah of the scarcity of black lovers on-screen. "I would like to see every aspect of black human life in the world on the screen. But that is only going to happen if people write it and market it.

"I think that 'Waiting to Exhale' did a lot in that it sold," she adds.

A Question of Economics

Talk to directors, actors and film executives about the reasons for this love drought and, as always, when the subject of black film comes up, you will be presented with Catch-22s. The spiel starts something like this: Yes, Queen Latifah and everybody else, scripts with black romance *are* being written. But few if any blacks in Hollywood are in a position to green-light a film, and Hollywood will only invest in black films that white executives believe are sure moneymakers.

In recent years, the biggest black films have either been urban (ghetto) dramas or urban (ghetto) comedies. Director John Singleton's first film, "Boyz N the Hood," grossed $57.8 million domestically and was nominated for an Academy Award. His next effort, "Poetic Justice," was—though thematically scattered—sort of a love story, starring Janet Jackson and Tupac Shakur. But it grossed $27.5 million and was picked at by critics.

"The question becomes, 'Am I going to risk something on an unproven quantity?'" says Doug McHenry, director of the love story "Jason's Lyric" and producer of such films as "New Jack City" and "A Thin Line." "These are the type of calculations that filmmakers go through because we are being pressured."

"Because we are not entrenched in decision-making positions at the corporate level, we have to work even harder and be rejected even more," says actor Roger Guenveur Smith, who had his first and only film love interest in Spike Lee's "Get on the Bus."

"And a lot of that has to do with the cyclical nature of the business," Smith adds. "A western or a silly comedy will do well, and then every studio has to do a western or a silly comedy. For a while, there were five or six Black Panther projects floating around, but because 'Panther' did not do well all of those projects were squashed."

But the issue of black romance in film gets even more complex. If anyone is going to take a risk on a film, they are less likely to take such risks on black films, which are considered appealing to a niche market. McHenry estimates that there is perhaps a core audience of 6 to 7 million people—primarily age 14 to 25—for such films. In contrast, there is an estimated audience of between 40 to 50 million for each "general audience" film. While African Americans support general audience films—comprising up to

25 percent of moviegoers—white people generally do not support black films in the theater.

Smith thinks that expanding the currently limited marketing strategies for black films could improve the changes of success for black romances. He points to the success of independent films of the past season such as "Fargo," which earned a respectable box office draw and was allowed to slowly build a following. The movie that ushered in the new wave of black film, Spike Lee's independently produced "She's Gotta Have It," utilized an alternative release strategy with some success. The film, which followed a young black woman, Nola Darling, and her love affairs with three men, was arguably the first American film to treat lovemaking between black actors and the naked black body in an artistic fashion.

"She's Gotta Have It" didn't necessarily depend on the big opening weekend," Smith says. "And as it stands now, if films don't do big business on the first weekend, then they disappear."

On-Screen Sexuality

Yet the lack of black romances cannot be dismissed as merely an understandable corporate prerogative. To accept that reasoning would require ignoring Hollywood's extreme avoidance of black sexuality and its continual promotion of European standards of beauty as the romantic film ideal.

Half of the equation for a film romance, for example, requires a beautiful heroine. In the Hollywood version, the role is filled by white women—Meg Ryan, or Julia Roberts. They offer accepted models of sincerity and vulnerability. When Ryan gets that wide-eyed, glassy look in her eyes, she's the all-American daughter or sister wrestling with emotions and mating.

But no such sympathies or romantic sensibilities are developed for most black women on the screen. Up into the 1960s, the most common role for a black woman was that of a maid devoted to the care of whites. In the 1950s, the first television show to star a black woman, "Beulah," featured a large, bandanna-wearing actress, Louise Beavers. She declared herself in one episode to be so busy as a domestic that she wasn't "in the marketplace for a husband." The film image of the asexual black woman has carried down to the present day in the person of Hollywood's highest paid black actress—Whoopi Goldberg—who has played mammy roles ("Clara's Heart," "Corinna Corinna," "The Long Walk Home") or played *one of the guys*. The one semi-romance Goldberg is most easily remembered for, "Made in America," was opposite a white man, Ted Danson. Similarly, when Primestar, the satellite television service, polled Americans last year, singer Whitney Houston—who appeared opposite white actor Kevin Costner in the blockbuster hit "The Bodyguard"—was the only black actress cited as a favorite romantic heroine.

During the last three decades of film, the most consistent image of black sexuality shown on television and film has been that of a black prostitute. In '70s blaxploitation flicks such as "The Mack" or in seemingly innocuous television shows like "Starsky and Hutch," the black hooker was marked by, along with her hot pants, high heels and rabbit-fur jacket, all of America's sick mythology about the loose sexuality—and availability to white men—of black women. Today's hooker images are sometimes more subtle. Even in the love relationship between actors Will Smith and Viveca Fox in

"Independence Day," the black woman worked as a stripper.

"Black women and white women have totally different sexualized histories in America—two totally different paths," says Bridgett M. Davis, director of an independently produced film, "Naked Acts," that focuses on a young black woman's quest to love her body. "What is the effect on black women whose sense of their bodies has been based on them being placed on an auction block, stripped down to their waist, being raped, and then being told that they asked for it? That's a heavy history, and how do you climb out of that?"

Singer Toni Braxton, who is creating a stir with her nearly nude pose on the cover of Vibe magazine, told the publication there is a double standard for exposure and idealization of black vs. white bodies. "If an artist like Madonna is wearing her booty hanging out, she's considered a genius. But if a black person does it, we're considered skank whores or sluts," she said.

On the male side, the historical racial stereotype of the black buck seems to translate easily. Black actors like Wesley Stripes and Laurence Fishburne have been able to slip into lead roles in action dramas such as the current "Murder at 1600 Pennsylvania" (starring Snipes). White 20 years ago Hollywood wasn't ready to accept Billy Dee Williams as sort of a black Cary Grant, Fishburne has played very sexual roles opposite Ellen Barkin in "Bad Company" and opposite Irene Jacob in "Othello." In contrast, the sex in "The Bodyguard" between Houston and Costner was only hinted at with the hokey symbolism of his erect sword cutting her sheer scarf. When Vanessa Williams played opposite Arnold Schwarzenegger in "Eraser," no hint of any sexual attraction was allowed between them.

Even the best of the vintage black romances, "Nothing but a Man," "A Warm December" and "Claudine," avoid sex scenes, as if the lovers might burn a hole in the celluloid. The notable exception to this, of course, is "Jason's Lyric," starring Jada Pinkett and Allen Payne. In fact, the film was considered so hot that the movie ratings system initially threatened to slap it with a NC-17 rating. Director McHenry protested, saying that the ratings board was unaccustomed to seeing black lovers on the screen, and that it considered "pornographic" acts that were no more risqué than what had appeared in other films because the bodies involved were black. He eventually shaved some footage to get an R rating, yet some critics still described the film's sex scenes as "raw" and "graphic."

"If you have two black people making love, somehow that's steamier than other people," McHenry said at the time. Motion Picture Association of America President Jack Valenti denied his group was racist and accused McHenry of milking the press to promote his film. McHenry countered that the MPAA was picking on his film as a way of proving that it was doing its job.

Plastic America

Movies such as "Jason's Lyric" are often the efforts of emerging black directors. For many of these filmmakers, it has been a mission to portray on film the romantic and intimate relationships they have witnessed or experienced in real life.

"Love Jones" was something that, if we pulled it off, would be something we hadn't seen before," says Witcher of the film's depiction of romance among young, urban creative blacks. In Condieff's "Sprung," there is a startling moment that offers a self-reflexive comment on both the rarity of this type of film and the state of Hollywood's black films in general. Two lovers are in the park. He tells her his dream, to one day make a movie with friends and lovers who sit around and talk.

"Is it a black film?" she asks.

"It's black."

"No gangsters? No drugs? Nobody getting shot?"

"None of that."

"Humph. You ain't gonna make no money."

He differs.

"It's a love story," he says. "And everyone loves a love story."

The new wave of black directors has not always been successful in its attempts to depict romance. Independent film critic Jacquie Jones, for example, has been critical of how black women have been portrayed in the new crop of films. Despite its marketing strategy, "Love Jones" is less a love story than a story about the difficulties of connecting in the '90s. "Sprung" sets up a disquieting comparison between the more genuine love of its light-skinned stars (Tisha Campbell and Cundieff) and the tawdry attraction between its dark-skinned supporting actors (Joe Torry and Paula Jai Parker).

A major roadblock for black romances is that such films typically must be star driven. Of the two leading star contenders, Denzel Washington has expressed no interest in sexual scenes, and Whitney Houston—who comes off as stiff and artificial as a black Barbie on screen—has not yet developed the acting muscle to be a romantic heroine who elicits our sympathies. The two of them, starring in "The Preacher's Wife," were supposed to produce a romantic blockbuster. Instead, the chemistry between them was flat.

But in the hands of new directors and producers, Hollywood may creep closer to depicting actual black love on the screen. Think of all the baby steps. For example, in "Waiting to Exhale," a full-figured black woman walked away with the happiest ending of all. Though just a subplot in "Jerry Maguire," Cuba Gooding Jr. and Regina King gave one of the more realistic portrayals of a young black couple in recent film history. And in "Sprung," Campbell actually gets to play a pretty ingenue with normal drives for life, love and sex.

"It was a mandate and agenda to include tenderness between black men and women in my film because it's so rarely seen," says "Naked Acts" director Davis. "I think that it speaks to the whole of my creative effort, which is to reveal black folks' humanity in whatever guise."

Directors who have such an agenda believe that these images have a powerful impact.

"We swim in a sea of culture," says McHenry. "And that sea alters our expectations and how we treat each other."

"In all of this, we have not yet gotten to the point where we can celebrate our sexuality and beauty," says Davis. "I don't think that most white women know that even to be [angry] about objectification is itself a certain luxury. It suggests a certain history. I feel like, 'Objectify me. Make me the objective standard of beauty.'

"We all want to see our lives reflected on the screen," she adds. "The heart of our lives really is our sexuality. It cuts to the core of who we are as human beings."

Mark Anthony Neal

"It be's that way sometimes 'cause I can't control the rhyme."
Notes from the Post-Soul Intelligentsia

*'cuz ain't nothing better than the shit I got/making niggas jump off the roof,
it's roof top/I put the Hip in Hop/and the don't in stop/ and the clip on
glock/then I rock box your block/My hypothesis on this/is you niggas better
come to terms with my vocabulary quick or get dissed/My brain bleeds mental complex feed/Bring it on kid, I got exactly what you need . . .*

—KEITH MURRAY, *THE RHYME*

ONE OF MY EARLIEST MUSICAL RECOLLECTIONS IS RIDING IN MY UNCLE'S
car with my pops, driving down 168th Street in the Bronx listening to what I would
later learn was Junior Walker's "What Does It Take (to Win Your Love)?" The late
Walker's tenor sax continues to resonate among a spate of childhood memories that are
all cradled by the sounds of Soul that dominated the era. In truth I can barely imagine
a world without Diana Ross's seven-minute epic "Ain't No Mountain High Enough" or
The Spinners' "Mighty Love," though in fact this was the world that I faced as the Soul
tradition gave way to the unbridled nihilism of disco and the ragged emotion of funk.
Don't get me wrong, I got my original "groove on" listening to Funkadelic's "One
Nation Under a Groove," but somehow these were the sounds of a world slipping away
into an uncertain and unfamiliar future. Given these dynamics it seemed logical to
ignore the rudimentary sounds of a musical genre I would, a decade later, embrace as
my own and my generation's. If hip-hop was my music . . . was my future, it was noise
that I wasn't willing to hear as the '70s waned and Reagan's Roarin' '80s dawned.

The house parties and park jams that figured so prominently in hip-hop's early
development and that represent perhaps the last hospital social spaces afforded black
youth in the burgeoning post-industrial city, were often outside my concerns. Somehow hip-hop's appeal for me rested beyond its use as an aurally constructed notion of
space and physical site(s) for the invisible, though ever-present urban-determined
youth that the genre has been so readily associated with. Having giving up the Soul and
given up on funk a few years earlier, my impending maturity found refuge and its muse
in the pressing political and social issues of the mid- to late '80s. Fortunately, I was a
part of an ever-maturing generation that was thankfully spared cosmic interpretations
of our contemporary history via network miniseries, cinematic epics, and multicultural
school textbooks. Our history—the history of the modern Civil Rights movement and
its brash and angry offspring, the Black Power and Feminist movements—was shared
with us via its dominant icons: the common, God-fearing, everyday black folks whose
revolutionary charge was to simply transcend absurd and bizarre circumstances immediately and often. Yes, we would relive these moments in the living rooms, back
porches and church pews of our increasingly dispersed and mythical black nation, but

these were not our moments . . . these were not our stories. Those stories were neatly packed away with the memories of Diana's shrill voice urging us to "touch somebody's hand" and brother James saying it loud and proud.

Yet, we remained uniquely poised—this first post–Civil Rights, post-nationalist, post–Black Power, post–Gary, Indiana, post-integration . . .post-Soul generation—to interpret the political and cultural terrain of our own conflicted moment. Lacking many of the nostalgic ties that both defined and bound earlier generations of Civil Rights leaders and followers, we witnessed Jesse Jackson's two historic presidential campaigns, the rebirth and rise of the Nation of Islam, the first black Miss America, the child murders in Atlanta, Spike Lee's *Do the Right Thing*, the liberation of Nelson Mandela, and the publication of Alice Walker's *The Color Purple* as subjective strangers equally disdained by an old Negroid guard and a young generation of whites remorseful perhaps that they were the first generation who could not legally deny our freedom—or so we thought. But we were also a generation that would ultimately be politicized by the successful rise of the conservative Right, its predominant icon Ronald Reagan, and the failure of our leadership—elected and anointed—to adequately respond to the realities of black urban life in the 1980s and hazards posed by right-wing ideologues posing as legislators, presidential candidates, objective political pundits, and members of the Hollywood elite.

Hip-hop, whose early rhythms and cadences foreshadowed its oppositional potential a decade later, served as the ideal conduit for the inner rage of displaced, disadvantaged, and miseducated urban masses as well as the embryonic political musings of an urban-defined, college-aged, burgeoning post-Soul intelligentsia. In short, the "post-Soul" generation comes to maturity during and is thus marked by the incidents of black middle-class flight, a substantial deterioration in the quality of black public life, the unequivocal re-emergence of the conservative Right, and the failure of post–Civil Rights strategies to adequately respond to any of these life-affecting threats.

Writer/critic Nelson George first used the term "post-Soul" to delineate the cultural production of African Americans since the Blaxploitation era of the 1970s.[1] While I am appropriating the spirit of George's idea, I have a very specific context in which to apply the "post-Soul" theme. I believe the post-Soul intellectual to be a unique and transitional figure in the area of African American arts and letters. It is the critical musings of this generation of thinkers that will construct transitional social and political strategies for the twenty-first century, creating the necessary connections between our most recent political struggles and the struggles that will visit the generations that will immediately follow us. Unique in that we are, perhaps, our people's best intellectual hope to bridge the widening gap between yesterday's Civil Rights marcher and today's crack baby. Skeptical as we may be of the previous generation's watershed movement, they have endowed us with a spirit of purpose and the capacity to hope, though I believe in our darkest hours our sentiments remain allied with the pessimisms of the marginalized African American Diaspora of our urban centers. To be sure, though, the dissertations of the brothers and sisters of crack babies, if not former crack babies themselves, have yet to be written, though we may be uniquely positioned to facilitate their emergence.

Like the brash, young thinkers of the early twentieth century, whose New Negroness continues to inform the traditions of African American arts and letters, we are charged with navigating a new world defined by radical shifts in labor demographics, a bottom-to-top redistribution of wealth, and the development of computerized networks of communication that have redefined the very notions of communication, commerce, and public discourse. In our best moments we hope to eschew the "HNIC"[2] elitism that perhaps defined and limited some members of the generation of New Negro thinkers, by critically interrogating our positioning to the black urban masses that we aspire to empower and the tradition of black intellectual thought that informs us. Where this earlier generation of thinkers often failed to equally relate to the Phi Beta Kappa and the Harlem Dandy, we have little choice but to engage the B-Boy, the Buppie, and the many diverse manifestations of black identity that continue to proliferate. At the crux of this reality is to position ourselves beyond mere gatekeeper status of some truncated, sanitized, and historically determined version of blackness, but to broaden the context of what are concurrently individualized, communal, and socially determined constructs.

Our status, as intellectuals and academics, demands some allegiance to the staid plaster of the ivory tower and the middle-class lifestyle it affords, while the essence of our being—are some of us not the first and second generation of the most profound migration movement of the twentieth century?—lies in the "ghettohoods" that we called home. Brother Gil Scott-Heron was right, "home" is often where the "hatred" is, but his home, as Esther Phillips attested in her version of Scott-Heron's "Home Is Where the Hatred Is," has also been a place of love and sustenance, if not a living metaphor for human survival. Such realities can no longer be simply accepted as the dilemma that excuses our inability to adequately impact upon the social and political policies that most adversely affect our communities. This movement of "post-Soul" intellectuals is poised to redefine the nature and purpose of traditional arts and letters, on the one hand blurring often oppositional discourses of popular and academic expression, and on the other positing, as did earlier generations of black scholars, the academy as a site to influence public policy and to critically confront the specter of race in American society. Our mission differs from earlier generations of black scholars in that the white academy of desegregated America has emerged as the primary site of our scholarly endeavors, providing the context to access valuable resources but also to confront our growing marginalization (as intellectuals) from the concentrated mass of young black minds that continue to emerge from historically black institutions. Our abilities to counter these contradictions will be witnessed in our commitment to critically engage public discourse, popular culture, political activism, and the belief that our theoretical groundings serve as viable models of mass social praxis.

The intellectual sensibilities of the "post-Soul" intelligentsia are the dual product of America's segregated past and its failed attempts at an integrated present. Not simply "affirmative action babies"—the realities of post–Civil Rights race relations are simply more expansive than debates about set aside programs and quota systems—our access to predominately white institutions within academe, perhaps, represents the most compelling example of the success of the Civil Rights movement. But in many regards, our political groundings were most notable influenced, not by the traditional leadership of the Civil Rights movement, but by the largely urban intelligentsia that was locked out of the mainstream academy during the 1940s, 1950s, and early 1960s because of segregation in higher education, and who perceived the Negro academy as an increasingly limiting and inadequate paradigm to address the issues of the black urban North. This cadre of thinkers, though not expressly defined by the rigors of traditional academic life, were nevertheless devoted to examining the philosophical issues surrounding black identity in a highly industrialized moment. More compellingly, their work highlighted an alarming paradox within the African American Diaspora. As the masses of blacks became increasingly urbanized as a corollary to mass migration, the Negro intelligentsia remained rooted in a social context that was distinctly southern and rural, rendering them incapable of adequately addressing the developing crises of black urban life. It is then not surprising that the first major work on the black urban condition, St. Clair Drake's *Black Metropolis,* is produced by one of the first black scholars to legitimately integrate a major urban university in the North.[3]

Writers like Richard Wright, Ralph Ellison, and Gwendolyn Brooks represent an urban intelligentsia shaped by their experiences in the North and willing to use their texts as vehicles for social protest. Embracing a self-defined lifestyle that often existed beyond the Negro academy and mainstream American public life, this generation of thinkers and artists laid the foundations for an independent intellectual movement in the black community in the post–World War II era. Wright in particular carried this responsibility like a badge of honor and was highly skeptical of traditional black scholars, particularly those still fixated on black life in the rural South. This is, of course, not to ignore valuable contributions by scholars like E. Franklin Frazier, or Oliver Cox, but to recognize the reanimation of a third stream of black intellectual thought, not explicitly produced from the traditional white academy or the historic sites of black intellectual discourse, and whose presence can be dated back to the work of nineteenth-century scholars like Frances Ellen Watkins Harper, Martin Delany, Anna Julia Cooper, and Alexander Crummell.

Wright's work, of which *Native Son* and the nonfiction pictorial essay *12 Million Voices* are most emblematic, details the deteriorating conditions of black urban life and the existentialist spirit inherent in it, even as the urban North continued to be championed as the "Promised Land." Wright's efforts, like those of his contemporaries, inform the activist agendas of the young and often urban-based intellectuals of the 1960s like Amiri Baraka and Sonia Sanchez. Representatives of the Black Arts movement and a school of black nationalist thought, scholars like Baraka, Sanchez, Nikki Giovanni, and Haki Madhubuti form the intellectual building blocks of the "post-Soul" generation. The work of many of these scholars continue to resonate in the work of the "post-Soul intelligentsia, perhaps because they rightly understood that accessibility to the masses was not necessarily antithetical to high creativity, political activism, and intellectual acumen. Despite a proclivity for problematic and ultimately confining constructions of nationalism and masculinity, this generation of thinkers, however briefly, established themselves as the most visible and independent stream of black scholars of the twentieth century, though many of their base sentiments were at profound odds with the largely middle-class and southern-based leadership of the Civil Rights movement. These scholars, like their most influential political icon Malcolm X, dared to imagine a post-colonial world that included their role as its dominant aestheticians.

In reality, then-revolutionary acts were reduced to tenured faculty appointments and guest lectureships on predominantly white university campuses, where former intellectual revolutionaries were increasingly found as faculty within the first generation of Black Studies programs and as regulars on the Black History Month/Black Student Union lecture circuit of the 1970s and early 1980s. While on one level emblematic of the problematic limitations of diversity efforts within higher education, the presence of black intellectuals on predominately white campuses represented the draining of valuable resources to the black community, even if such resources had been formerly distributed largely within the parameters of a black academy bound to middle-class aspiration. With rare exceptions many Black Arts scholars remained significantly marginalized from mainstream African American life or frustrated and entrenched within a bevy of tenure battles, retrenchment initiatives, and university committees within the mainstream American academy, equally marginalized from the people and the policies that define contemporary African American life. Interpreted within the broader context of American race relations, black intellectuals were effectively desegregated away from the very communities of blackness that produced them, while their presence tacitly validated America's claim to the realization of an integrated America.

These phenomena highlight many of the perverse benefits of segregated black life. Within the structure of segregated black life, the diversity of class and political interest were largely constrained by the physical dynamics of the black community. Thus, within both formal and informal public life, mechanisms of accountability and communal critique were integral to daily life within the black community. In our contemporary moment—which in the context of black life is now defined by black middle-class flight, the erosion of traditional forms of public life, and the emergence of a black urban underclass—intellectuals and politicians are no longer constrained by any formal means of communal critique. This relationship is most profoundly exhibited in the black masses' unrelenting distrust of black intellectuals. I speak here of those many intellectuals who have chosen to silence their voices in lieu of faculty appointments, tenured status, endowed chairs, rich publishing contracts, and "I am the only black in my . . ." status and who chose not to address the critical questions facing the larger black community.

In a broader sense the problematic conflation of intellectual and academic life represents, as Russell Jacoby suggests, the demise a vibrant bohemian culture in America's urban spaces.[4] Though contemporary academic life does afford a lifestyle supportive of America's elite intellectuals, too often the energies and the interests of the average academic remain aligned with the business of running the academy as opposed to the business of producing original and provocative scholarship. Unfortunately the most publicly affecting contemporary scholarship is rarely produced by intellectuals within the academy, but rather so-called scholars supported by well-endowed conservative think tanks like the Hoover Institute and the Heritage Foundation, whose scholarship is produced in concert with the public policy initiatives of the Right. The Left in America has rarely been positioned to generate significant and consistent financial support and the remnants of the Left that continue to seek influence on matters of public policy have found the most accessible avenues of public debate—television and commercial print media—to be inaccessible to their financial and political means. In reality the demise of a vibrant intellectual culture within American bohemia—think here of the noncorporatized coffeehouse and parlor spaces that defined New York's Greenwich Village as well as San Francisco's Haight-Ashbury—has significantly affected the generally tenuous status of the American Left. Often viewed as the Left's poorer relations—was not Harlem simply New York bohemia's uptown annex?—the changes in American public life have obviously had an adverse and unbalanced affect on black public life, as the cottage industry of African American arts and letters has always required the patronage of the liberal bourgeois establishment of the strategic support of the Right, when such scholarship helps valorize the public policy inclinations of the Right.

Ironically, it is the remnants of bohemian culture in the Lower East Side and East Village of New York City that have provided the impetus for the generation of cultural and social critics who directly precede the post-Soul intelligentsia. Heavily concentrated in the urban underground of the 1980s that produced entities as varied as Greg Tate, Vernon Reid, the Black Rock Coalition, Jean Michel Basquait, Public Enemy, George C. Wolfe, Darius James, Cassandra Wilson, and Geri Allen, this cadre of thinkers and artists is directly related to the generation of esoteric black intellectuals who inhabited New York's East Village during the '60s, when self-styled black bohemians like Ellen Stewart, Steve Cannon, Ishmael Reed, and Archie Shepp purposely embraced the edges of marginalia to guarantee a hyper-objectivity towards a liberation movement gone awry. In one of Tate's seminal essays, an examination of the work of Basquait, he suggests that "To read the tribe astutely you sometimes have to leave the tribe ambitiously, and should you come home again, it is not always to sing hosannas or a song the tribe necessarily wants to hear."[5] Tate articulates a vantage point that the East Village bohemians of the 1960s craved. While Baraka left the confines of New York's bohemia, landing in Harlem as a nationalist and later a Communist, East Village bohemians maintained a cautious distance from the site of too many poorly conceived "Black to the Future" dreams. It is this same community in the East Village that was home to the Negro Ensemble Company, which under the direction of Douglas Turner Ward consistently and effectively presented complex and brilliant representations of African American life that undermined acceptable depictions of African Americans.

Particularly visible in weekly journals as diverse as the *Village Voice* and *Billboard* magazine, a collective of urban critics emerged in the late 1970s and the early 1980s to impose consistency to the then dispersed nature of black intellectual thought—at least relative to earlier generations of black intellectual thought—and meaning to the fleeting improvisation of black urban life. Championing hip-hop as the Black arts critics had championed hard bop and bebop, writers like Tate, Nelson George, and Harry Allen instigated an aggressive, oppositional criticism that embodied the sonic kinetics of hip-hop and black urban life as primarily defined by black male sensibilities. Beyond politics and cultural history, Tate in particular instilled a sense of intellectual urgency to the life and art forms of American's most despised and condemned constituency. Crucial to the base sensibilities of this group was their distance, philosophically it not generationally, from both petty bourgeois visions of the traditional Civil rights leadership and the essentialist demanding ideology of some within the black nationalist wing of black intellectual and political thought. Beyond oppositional stances, this was a generation of critics devoted to redefining essentialist notions of black culture. It was a project in large part protected by their commitment to remain on the margins and thus to remain unsought and unbothered by the thought police and "soul patrol" alike. Their commitment to presenting what Tate has called an "Anti-essentialist Essentialist" perspective of black culture is largely realized in the diversity of their aforementioned icons and their ability to bring to bear African American influences on things deemed distinctly nonblack.

In his controversial essay "The New Black Aesthetic," Trey Ellis identifies the primary sensibilities of this generation of largely nonacademic critics and artists.[6] Generally regarded as that generation's manifesto, Ellis's essay encapsulates what Ronald A. T. Judy has identified as thee traditions of "avant garde modernism" and Leftist vanguard agit-prop,"[7] traditions that of course link the "New Black Aesthetic" to the "high Negro style" of the New Negro/Harlem Renaissance period and the provocative pop-art of the Black Arts movement. At the crux of this New Black Aesthetic is a profound rearticulation of the sounds and signs of socially constructed notions of blackness as the praxis of obliterating "old definitions of blackness," that "show us the intricate, uncategorizeable folks we had always known ourselves to be."[8] Ellis's manifesto links radical and transgressive notions of blackness as expressed in the work of Katherine Dunham, George Clinton, Jimi Hendrix, Albert Murray, Ishmael Reed, Patti Labelle, LeRoi Jones (early Amiri Baraka), and Melvin Van Peebles. Moreover, in that the New Black Aesthetic attempts to re-articulate traditional conceptions of blackness, the aesthetic movement also aims to animate and deconstruct popular assumptions of black identity, through the process of parody/pastiche and the democratization of black critical discourse.

It is this latter example of the "New Black Aesthetic" that of course links the aesthetic movement to the oppositional stances of black critics like Anna Julia Cooper, George Schuyler, Bayard Rustin, Audre Lorde, Ralph Ellison, and to a lesser extent James Baldwin. Representative of the often hyper-democratic tendencies related to black public discourse, the work of the above critics and scholars has served to problematize simple constructions of black identity and black thought. Cooper, Rustin, and Lorde in particular have been instrumental in re-articulating notions of blackness along an axis of gender and sexual preference—constructions that remain at odds with dominant representations of blackness and challenge popular notions that increasingly posit patriarchy and heterosexuality as the foundations for acceptable social constructions of blackness. For instance, it has been the proclivity of much black nationalist thought, particularly that which emerged during the 1960s and re-animated itself during the 1980s in the form of Louis Farrakhan, to silence alternative and radical constructions of blackness by asserting heterosexual capitalist patriarchy as the primary vehicle for black empowerment, often to the detriment of maintaining real solidarity within the broader African American community. Though the Million Man March cannot be reduced to singular ideological viewpoints—to do so fails to acknowledge the broad interpretations the march holds for many—the acceptance of Louis Farrakhan as the march's figurehead is tacit acceptance of heterosexist capitalist patriarchy within the black community. In its essence, "The New Black Aesthetic" aimed to confront the increasingly oppositional nature of black identity within the context of a liberating creative process, inclusive of both the production and the subsequent criticism of contemporary artforms.

Marginalized from both mainstream and academic life, the "New Black" aestheticians emerge almost simultaneously with the new face of the elite American academy. Twenty-five years after the historic emblems of segregated life eroded from the walls of the ivory tower and sixty years after the intellectual triad of DuBois, Alain Locke, and Charles S. Johnson were emphatically denied access to the mainstream American academies of the North, a generation of young, black intellectuals emerged from within the very confines that denied access to the best minds in the black community for much of the twentieth century. Though many of these new intellectual voices would eventually find their institutional base in the African American Studies departments at elite universities, they were not necessarily the product of efforts to refit the university landscape with ethnic studies departments, but rather the beneficiaries of liberal opportunism as reflected by this country's elite academic institutions.[9] To be sure, these folks had major skills. What most uniquely separated them from previous generations of black academics is that this contemporary group was produced almost exclusively within the mainstream academy and would work almost exclusively within that same academy. What connects these thinkers to the broader examples of African American intellectual thought is their devotion—a devotion that is arguably second nature—to public, political, and critical discourse, though much of this discourse is invariably linked to a white literate consumer public. As Robert S. Boynton suggests, ". . . theirs is scholarship with a social purpose. This generation of public-minded academics, while notable is hardly the first to have straddled the worlds inside and outside the university. . . . What distinguishes these new public intellectuals from those of the past, is that their desire to transcend the academy was motivated almost exclusively by an interest in race."[10] It has been as the popular interpreters of race signs and race relations that this generation of scholars, both those linked to the Left and the Right, have been most influential. In many regards they have served to validate the identity politics simultaneously articulated within the "New Black Aesthetic."

With a striking inclination to popularize critical issues and debates within the black community, the visible presence of scholars like Molefi Assante, Patricia Williams, Derrick Bell, Henry Louis Gates Jr., Manning Marable, Michelle Wallace, bell hooks, Cornel West, Barbara Smith, and Michael Eric Dyson has had a significant impact in positioning academic life as a viable pursuit for the post-Soul generation. The high visibility of the "new black intellectuals" has arguably been the primary stimulus for the generation of blacks who have just emerged or will shortly emerge from doctoral programs within the humanities and social sciences, areas that have historically supported discourse and research on race and race relations. Ironically the primary stimulus for the high visibility of many of these intellectuals has been the intense commodification of black popular culture during the past two decades—a process that demands articulate interpreters of a culture inherently exoticized by mainstream consumers—particularly as black popular culture has framed and informed racially volatile events like the murder of Yusef Hawkins, the Clarence Thomas–Anita Hill debates, the Los Angeles riots of 1992, and the Million Man March. This conspicuity of black intellectuals within contemporary middle-brow and high-brow media culture has been unprecedented in American history and arguably bespeaks the significant presence of racial discourse within the same cultural parameters.

It is within the context of this commodification that unprecedented volumes on race and the African American experience have been produced by black intellectuals for academic, trade, and popular presses alike—volumes that have ultimately served to "grandparent" the "post-Soul" intelligentsia, with many of these scholars serving as distant and not so distant mentors to "post-Soul" thinkers.[11] The present emergence of a public class of black intellectuals who ply their trade beyond the ivory tower and within the organs of mass culture has had a particularly compelling impact on the development of a "post-Soul" intelligentsia in that contemporary black intellectuals have largely been framed and contextualized by their presence within mass media—arguably the dominant institution in the socialization process of the "post-Soul" intelligentsia. I maintain that the development of the post-Soul intelligentsia is wholly predicated on the explosion of mass consumer culture and the significant commodification of black popular culture within it. While the 1920s and 1950s are also periods in which there was a significant expansion in the influence of mass consumer culture the 1970s would witness the most significant incorporation of African American culture within the discourse of mass consumer culture. Part and parcel of America's efforts to construct an integrated America that was not wholly experienced by African Americans, the symbolic integrating of America society via popular culture would offer the perception of full citizenship for a generation of young African Americans in the post–Civil Rights era. Furthermore, this last explosion is largely interpreted through the guise of "televisual" expression, again separating this era from earlier eras.

It is within this context of mass culture that contemporary black intellectuals, by extension, have posited the intellectual process and the lifestyle it affords, as elements of what "post-Soul" aged Motown CEO Andre Harell has referred to as contemporary "Big Willie" or "High Negro" style.[12] As the Black Arts movement blurred the historic boundaries between high art and black popular culture, contemporary black intellectuals have blurred the boundaries between academic and popular writing, in some regards reducing the critical process into accessible mass media fodder like mainstream film reviews and reviews of popular fiction. Though the contemporary class of black public intellectuals is located firmly within the tradition of the so-called "New York" intellectuals of the 1940s and 1950s like Diana and Lionel Trilling, Dwight MacDonald, and Irving Howe—a generation of public intellectuals largely sustained by highbrow interests beyond the academy—much of their scholarship must be interpreted within the context of contemporary mass culture. While the accessibility of popular non-fiction on the African American experience has been invaluable to a generation of black undergraduate and graduate students alike, the very essence of mass culture has demanded the dulling of the critical and theoretical edge of much of this scholarship. While this process clearly obstructs the nuanced realities of pursuing a life of the mind, there is perhaps no precedent to the access that young black scholars and writers would have to the prominent thinkers within the community, excepting the example of the dynamic web of historically black colleges and universities that, in large part, are solely responsible for the generation of black male intellectuals that dominate black intellectual life prior to the 1970s.

It is within the area of gender that contemporary black intellectuals profoundly differ from earlier generations of black scholars in that black women, academic sexism, and misogyny notwithstanding, are prominent within the community of contemporary black scholars and academics. The scholarship of women like Angela Davis, Hazel Carby, Patricia Hill-Collins, Kimberlie Crenshaw, and Katie Cannon has arguably redefined gender studies within the context of the African American experience, though the marginal status of their scholarship to the canon of contemporary black thought is the obvious price they have paid for the patriarchy that continues to inform black intellectual thought. Ironically, it has been the significant presence of black women within the academy that has provided the context for an acceptance of black and mainstream feminist scholarship among both female and male thinkers within the "post-Soul" intelligentsia. This reality has furthered the de-essentialist project most recently articulated within the "New Black Aesthetic" movement.[13] While Tate's concept of "Anti-essentialist Essentialism," like the tradition of public and oppositional discourse that is so rooted in the black intellectual tradition, is inherently located in the broader universe that produces the "post-Soul" intelligentsia—really emblematic of the hyperconsumption that has defined the "post-Soul" period—there are two major themes that primarily inform the intellectual project of the "post-Soul" intelligentsia; namely the reconstruction of history/memory and the reconstitution of community. These particular tensions are the products of structural developments that have informed, if not defined, the socialization process of the "post-Soul" intelligentsia.

Perhaps no structural development delineates the emergence of the "post-Soul" generation better than the post-industrial transformation of black urban centers. Broadly interpreted as the "death of community," the transformation of urban centers from the sites of industrial production to the incubators of surplus labor and displaced humanity provided the context in which the contemporary black underclass emerges. Furthermore, it continued to erode the already precarious status of the black working class, which, coupled with the incidence of black middle-class flight, provides the impetus for the radical transformation if not demise of the traditional black public sphere as represented in many segregated communities prior to the Civil Rights movement. While the transformation of the traditional black public sphere can be documented as early as the mid-50s with the migration of white middle-class elements from urban centers into suburbia and later with the urban uprisings of the mid- to late 1960s, the structural transformation of the economy of the industrial city would have the most prodigious impact on black public life within these spaces. This would have a compelling impression on the "post-Soul" generation in that the seminal institutions of the traditional black public sphere were largely responsible for the transmission and reproduction of communal values within even stratified black communities. The erosion of the black public sphere provides the chasm in which the "post-Soul" generation is denied access to the bevy of communally derived social, aesthetic, cultural, and political sensibilities that have undergirded much of the success of the black community during the twentieth century, in part fracturing the post-Soul generation and all those who followed from the real communal history of the African American Diaspora.

Emblematic perhaps of the dis-connectedness of contemporary American life, the post-Soul generation is also marked by the hyper-activity of mass consumer culture and mass media, of which the commodification of contemporary black popular culture is a seminal enterprise. The post-Soul generation becomes the first generation of African Americans who would perceive the significant presence of African American iconography within mass consumer culture/mass media as a state of normalcy.[14] It is within this context that mass culture fills the void of both community and history for the post-Soul generation, while producing a generation of consumers for which the iconography of blackness is consumed in lieu of personal relations, real experience, and historical knowledge. Furthermore, the quest for individual satisfaction that undergirds contemporary acts of consumption would in fact render the concept of community and communal activities as foreign to contemporary experience.

Ironically it is hip-hop, a multibillion-dollar industry and arguably the most commodified form of popular black expression ever, that provides the metaphoric inspiration through which the "post-Soul" generation would generate its critical and intellectual perspectives. In its essence, hip-hop has aimed to stimulate a dialogue across the chasm of silence that has engulfed black communal discourse in the "post-Soul" era, by popularizing the dominant issues within contemporary black urban life. While there is of course a fine line between celebrating the realities of black urban life and reporting the facts, the fact remains that hip-hop has been singularly responsible for presenting issues inherent to contemporary black urban life to broader audiences via mass culture, even if many of its constituents are simply constructed as consumers and aspects of black urban life are reduced to emblems of stylistic acumen for mainstream consumers. This aspect of hip-hop, which I believe is a quintessential trait of the post-Soul intelligentsia, differs from aforementioned uses of mass culture by contemporary black intellectuals. Hip-hop does not simply posit mass culture as a vessel of mainstream acceptance, but as a conduit to introduce marginalia, on their own merit, into mainstream discourse, a process predicated in large part on the dominance of mass culture in framing public opinion and the recognition of the role of mass production and distribution outlets to contemporary African American culture.

Hip-hop's imagination provides the metaphoric capital in which the post-Soul intelligentsia would dually address the issues of history/memory and community. Hip-hop's continuous mining of the decades old Soul, funk, and Soul jazz traditions represents a concerted effort to reconstruct an aural history of the community. Inherent to the re-constructed collage of sonic history that hip-hop documents are broader efforts to create community, via the marketplace and across the generational divide of the African American Diaspora. The music of Ganstarr, Pete Rock and CL Smooth, A Tribe Called Quest, and Common Sense, for instance, with their heavy reliance on hard bop and '70s jazz fusion samples, represents artistry uniquely accessible to normally disconnected male constituencies. The broader network of hip-hop artists, listeners, consumers, and critics represents a re-constitution of community designed specifically within the parameters of post-industrial public life and contemporary mass consumer culture. The construction of such communities can of course serve as the basis for broader social movements informed by the sensibilities of the "post-Soul" generation.

Concurrently, I must consider the relative explosion of popular fiction during the "post-Soul" era by black women writers like Terri McMillian and Bebe Moore Campbell, whose core constituency entails a construction, like those among black men and hip-hop, of black women across class and social divisions. McMillian's *Waiting to Exhale,* arguably the most popular of the genre, was made into a film in 1996. The film's all-women sound track, which was largely written and produced by Kenny "Babyface" Edmonds, was the antithesis of much that was produced in hip-hop during the period. This would seem to suggest that my thesis may not hold as much value for female "post-Soul" intellectuals, though hip-hop and its representative sexism, objectification of black women's bodies and misogyny, accordingly has served as a primary discursive site of contention for many "post-Soul" intellectuals, both male and female. This mode of cultural critique is perhaps most visible in Tricia Rose's important text, *Black Noise.*

Afforded incredible access to the intellectual rumblings of the elite minds within the contemporary black intelligentsia and informed by the sonic constructs of community and memory that ground the best of hip-hop, the "post-Soul" intelligentsia is poised to interpret the disparate energies and discourses of contemporary urban life and to provide the critical and theoretical framework to best impact upon the conditions of those within black urban spaces. While the overall project of the post-Soul intelligentsia will not markedly differ from that of contemporary black intellectuals, the former has clearly been produced within a context more organically connected to the realities that black intellectuals are expected to interpret for both communal and mainstream constituencies—particularly those realities in which urban life and hip-hop culture serve as clear pretexts and subtexts. With rare exceptions, for example the work of Rose, Michael Eric Dyson, Robin D. G. Kelley, British critic Paul Gilroy, and Todd Boyd, much of the scholarship of the contemporary black intelligentsia has inadequately interpreted black urban life as witnessed by the "post-Soul" generation, many of whom were still in the "hood" when crack rhetorically and physically transformed already reeling black communities in the late 1980s.

But the context(s) that produce the "post-Soul" intelligentsia is also observed, beyond content, in the nature and stylistic tendencies of their scholarship. Uniquely bound to the emergence of contemporary mass consumer culture, mass media and culture will maintain an almost hegemonic influence over the "post-Soul" intelligentsia. In that much of the modern world for the "post-Soul" generation has been interpreted primarily and secondarily through the guise of mass media and culture, the post-Soul intelligentsia's interpretations of contemporary life will obviously use the iconography of mass culture to frame and inform their critical insights. Moreover, the nature of "post-Soul" scholarship will differ dramatically from that of earlier generations in that the style of writing and structuring of information will reflect the collage form that is dually represented in the electronic cut-and-paste techniques of contemporary mass media and hip-hop music. This break with traditional notions of wholly contained intellectual ideas is much more representative of the increasingly inter-disciplinary and post-modern nature of the contemporary academy and contemporary American life.

Boynton, Robert. "The New Intellectuals." *The Atlantic Monthly* (March 1995): 61–72.

Ellis, Trey. "The New Black Aesthetic." *Callaloo* 12.1 (Winter 1989): 233–343.

George, Nelson. *Buppies, B.-Boys, Baps and Bohos: Notes on Post-Soul Black Culture.* New York: HarperCollins, 1992.

Jacoby, Russell. *The Last Intellectuals.* New York: Basic Books, Inc., 1987.

Judy, Ronald A.T. "The New Black Aesthetic and W. E. B. Du Bois, or Hephaestus, Limping." *The Massachusetts Review* (Spring 1995): 250.

Rose, Tricia. *Black Noise: Rap Music and Black Culture in Contemporary America.* Middletown, Conn.: Wesleyan University Press, 1994.

Tate, Greg. *Fly Boy in the Buttermilk: Essays on Contemporary America.* New York: Simon & Schuster, 1992.

West, Cornel. *Race Matters.* Boston: Beacon Press, 1987.

--- ---

1. George gives a full detail of the highlights of "post-Soul" black culture in his book *Buppies, B-Boys, Baps and Bohos: Notes on Post-Soul Black Culture.*

2. HNIC is an anachronym for "head nigger in charge." As Ronald Dorris suggests, many of the artists and critics of the New Negro movement resisted the imposition of such paradigms on them by the movement's more visible hierarchy.

3. Drake taught at the University of Chicago.

4. Jacoby's text, *The Last Intellectuals,* offers a trenchant commentary on the demise of public discourse and the collapse of spaces for independent intellectuals not exclusively tied to the academy.

5. "Nobody Loves a Genius Child: Jean Michel Basquiat, Flyboy in the Buttermilk," *Fly Boy in the Buttermilk: Essays on Contemporary America,* p. 232.

6. "The New Black Aesthetic," *Callaloo* 12.1 (Winter 1989): 233–243.

7. "The New Black Aesthetic and W. E. B. Du Bois, or Hephaestus, Limping." *The Massachusetts Review* (Spring 1995): 250.

8. Ellis, p. 237.

9. I am referring to the financial benefits afforded predominately white institutions, during the 1970s and 1980s, that actively recruited black students and faculty.

10. "The New Intellectuals," *The Atlantic Monthly* (March 1995): 64.

11. My own academic career has been framed by brief yet weighty interactions with scholars like West, Marable, Wallace, Tricia Rose, Manthia Diawara, Mwalimu Shujja, Robin D. G. Kelley, and Michael Eric Dyson.

12. Darnetta Bell suggest this context to interpret the introduction of Cornel West's mainstream foray *Race Matters,* in which he meticulously describes his twice-weekly sojourn from Princeton to New York City's Sweetwaters restaurant and club.

13. In regard to my own career, the direction I received from womanist scholar Masani Alexis DeVeaux was invaluable to my ability to broaden my own critical skills beyond knowledges deemed necessary by the patriarchal norms of black intellectual life and the larger academy.

14. I am reminded here of my own experience as an eight-year-old watching the *Jackson Five* cartoon on Saturday morning television.

Facing Unknown Possibilities: Lance Jeffers and the Black Aesthetic

Howard Rambsy II

"I disclaim nothing: I can only discover who I am."

—LANCE JEFFERS

"We have always been dreamers, people who have visions of a better life and who want to transform those visions into realities."

— JERRY W. WARD JR.

DESPITE THE INCREASING NUMBER OF STUDIES DEVOTED TO AFRICAN American literature, the work of many writers who helped to define the Black Aesthetic movement in African American literary history awaits critical attention. The tendency to write again and again about a small body of writers undermines the idea that quite a diverse body of writers build the tradition of African American literature. Since black writers have historically existed within and against the dynamics of the larger American society, it is possible that many of the works that constitute the whole of African American literature are often neglected in Eurocentric assessments. In other words, the

New York Times Book Reviews and "the African American section" at the mega-book-store Barnes & Noble are not always accurate indicators of the range and scope of works of literature by and about black people. In order to represent a broader vision of African American literature, it is necessary to undertake studies of some of the not-so-popular black writers.

One such writer whose works have yet to receive critical attention is Lance Jeffers. During the 1960s and '70s he was among the group of writers who made concerted efforts to produce works of literature that reflected the spirit of liberation(s) and resistance(s) embodied by the Civil Rights and Black Power movements. Many of the African American writings of this era became known as the Black Arts/Black Aesthetic movement. As Larry Neal pointed out, "Black Art is the aesthetic and spiritual sister of the Black Power concept. As such, it envisions an art that speaks directly to the needs and aspirations of Black America." Attempting to distance themselves from traditional Eurocentric values and standards and at the same time seeking to produce works that addressed audiences of African descent, the writers of the era produced bodies of work that were unapologetically and irrevocably black. "Revolutionary black writers," observed Hoyt Fuller, "have turned their backs on the old 'certainties' and stuck out in new, if uncharted, directions. They have begun the journey toward a black aesthetic."

Producing works of literature before, during, and after the height of the Civil Rights era determined that Jeffers would help define the Black Aesthetic movement even as he was influenced by it. The works of writers such as Jeffers during the time period were both an extension of the long tradition of African-descended people(s) creative expressions and a reflection of the age the black artists of the 1960s and '70s were living in. In considering the works of the Black Aesthetic movement, and more specifically the writings of Lance Jeffers, I am reassured that important groundwork has been laid for those of us facing the possibilities and unknowns of the twenty-first century.

Born on November 28, 1919, Lance Flippin Jeffers lived with his grandfather in Nebraska until the age of ten and then moved to San Francisco with his mother and stepfather. Jeffers spent his teenage years in California and after high school and brief periods of study at local junior colleges, he jointed the military. After a stint in the armed services that allowed him to stay for periods of time in the South and in Europe, Jeffers earned a degree in English from Columbia University. Jeffers taught English at various colleges and universities across the country until he eventually settled at North Carolina State University and made the South as well as black people and culture central reference points for his writings.

A short-story writer, essayist, and author of one novel *Witherspoon* (1983), Jeffers was principally known as a poet. He published four volumes of poetry: *My Blackness Is the Beauty of This Land* (1970), *When I Know the Power of My Black Hand* (1974), *O Africa Where I Baked My Bread* (1977), *Grandsire* (1979); and published his works in such journals as *Callaloo*, *African American Literature Review*, and *The Black Scholar*. Jeffers's writings also appeared in such landmark anthologies of the late 1960s and early '70s as *Black Fire* (1968) and *Understanding the New Black Poetry* (1973).

In his poems, Jeffers described the complexities of black experience in America and the ability of African Americans to endure and overcome oppression. While the more critically acclaimed writers and works of the Black Aesthetic period concentrated on the experiences of urban-dwelling African Americans, Jeffers's writings have a focus on "working class" black people living in rural areas in the South, thus contributing to our sense of a Southern Black Aesthetic. Acknowledgments of African and African American ancestry, praise of black people and culture, and considerations of the power of black pride and black unity were hallmarks of Jeffers's poetic writings.

In his poem "Black Soul of the Land," Jeffers writes of an older black man who has "a secret manhood tough and tall/ that circumstance and crackers could not kill." Recognizing the symbol of a resilient black heritage of strength and survival in the figure of an old black man, Jeffers writes of gaining special insight from such individuals:

> Give me your spine old man, old man,
> give me your rugged hate,
> give me your sturdy oak-tree love,
> give me your source of steel.
> Teach me to sing so that the song may be mine

The theme "black is beautiful" resonated throughout the Black Power era, and Jeffers made his contributions to such culturally affirming standpoints in poems such as "My Blackness Is the Beauty of This Land":

> My blackness is the beauty of this land,
> my blackness,
> tender and strong, wounded and wise,
> my blackness

In this poem, Jeffers evokes images of suffering, endurance, and love in relation to blackness as opposed to oppression and hate in relation to whiteness. Both blackness and whiteness, as demonstrated by Jeffers in the poem, have been necessary components for forming the sometimes painful history of America. He concludes the poem by writing "my love and yet my hate shall civilize this land," thus highlighting the nation's contradictory make-up.

Exploring human potentialities was yet another characteristic of Jeffers's creative works. In his poem "When I Know the Power of My Black Hand," Jeffers works through the dilemma of overcoming psychological oppression:

> I sit slumped in the conviction that I am powerless,
> tolerate ceilings that make me bend.
> My godly mind stoops, my ambition is crippled;
> I do not know the power of my hand.

Upon wondering "what it would be like . . . to be free," Jeffers writes of realizing one's fullest potentials, which will lead one to:

> sing the miracle of freedom with all the force
>   of my lungs,
> christen my black land with exuberant creation,
> and stand independent in the hall of nations,

root submission and dependence from the soil of my soul
and pitch the monument of slavery from my book when
I know the mighty power of my hand!

The literary critic David Dorsey has written that "Jeffers's poetry is securely faithful
to an aesthetic whose boundaries and potentials it constantly extends and defends." He
goes on to point out that Jeffers's poetry is important "as a unique and passionate reflection of black life in the United States." In his poetry, Jeffers explored issues relating to
various people(s) of color and to black people beyond the U.S. borders. "It seems to
me," wrote Eugenia Collier, "that Jeffers is the Negritude poet of this generation. In
poem after poem, he links contemporary Black Americans with our brothers throughout the world and with a history shared by us all." Jeffers's poetry, like many writings
of the era, highlighted regional, national, and international concerns.

To gain a fuller understanding of the impact of the Black Aesthetic movement, we
should not only consider *what* some of the poets wrote. Rather, it is important to also
consider who the poets were seeking to address in their works, how they were structuring their works to draw upon black cultural expressions, and where their works were
being published. Since the Black Arts movement had a mission of addressing "the
masses of black folk," it is no minor coincidence that black presses such as Broadside
Press and Third World Press were created during the Black Arts movement and more
publishing opportunities became available for black writers at mainstream publishing
companies who realized that there was a market for "black books."

The blend of radical and performative creative expressions embodied by some of the
black poetry of the time period helped attract new and vast numbers of readers of various ethnic and racial backgrounds. Poets such as Amiri Baraka, Haki R. Madhubuti, and
Sonia Sanchez, to name a few, were among the more acclaimed—if not representative—
poets of the Black Arts movement. However, a meaningful result of the Black Aesthetic
movement was that it placed a strong emphasis on encouraging "everyday" people, not
just the "traditional poets," to participate in the production of poems and other cultural
expressions. As the literary critic Houston Baker Jr. has written, "Black poetry of the sixties was adopted by elementary school students, university professors, working wives and
mothers, community activists, prison inmates, barber shop aficionados, athletes, and
'trained' poets alike to express a new pride of the times." Even with all the positive outcomes of the Black Aesthetic movement, it also had its shortcomings.

In distancing black writings from some Eurocentrenic standards of assessing the
"worth" of literature, proponents of the Black Aesthetic movement, in turn, did not
offer an adequate theoretical framework for evaluating black literature. It is one thing
to write "black poems," but it is something else to create theories, literary models,
and/or paradigms for appropriating aspects of black culture to discuss African American literature. And it is not so easy to answer such questions of "What does and does
not represent black writing?" when approaching serious study of African American literature. There also seems to be a lack of comprehensive studies and considerations of
the Black Aesthetic movement as a meaningful literary movement in American and
African American literary history. The conservatism of Eurocentric institutions is
opposed to the black and radical content displayed in some of the literature(s) of the
Black Aesthetic movement. Assessing and tracing some of the impacts and configura-

tions of the black writings of the 1960s and '70s, then, would require a variety of approaches within, against, inside, and beyond the dominant culture's imposed categories and interpretations. Not only did Lance Jeffers seek to illustrate the complex histories and struggles of black people in America in his poetic works, rather, he also sought to enlarge consciousness of African American people and culture by addressing the missions, scope, and visions of black literature in his critical writings.

In his essays, Jeffers expressed his concern about the future development of African American literature. Jeffers felt many black writers before the 1960s have a stronger tendency to avoid exploring all aspects of black experiences—especially negative portrayals—because of fears of what white Americans might thing of black people. This process became known as the "defensive posture." As far as Jeffers was concerned, black writers were doing a disservice to themselves and readers by only depicting romantic views of African American experiences at the expense of not fully exploring the varying complexities of black people(s). Thus black writers must "set the white man aside and write honestly of black reality," wrote Jeffers. "Only by depicting honestly every aspect of black life will the black writer help us reach our destined grandeur." According to Jeffers, the challenge for black writers and African American literature was to represent a fuller view of African American people and culture.

Convinced that the varied lives of African Americans were broad, complex, and beautiful—beautiful in the sense of wholeness—Jeffers wanted black writers to present such dimensions in their works. The development of African American literature should rest on black writers' abilities to "fearlessly explore the infinite complexity of the unexplored continent of black life and nature in America," said Jeffers. He insisted that the complexities of black life and culture should not be presented in narrow and/or apologetic terms. "There are hellish depths and godly heights in the black experience that await the black artist as he [or she] charts our voyage into the future," explained Jeffers.

A body of literature that addresses the needs, aspirations, characteristics (both positive and negative), and ability of a group of people to overcome obstacles such as racial oppression was what Jeffers saw as a goal and/or function of African American literature. Jeffers felt the visions put forth by African American writers might serve liberalizing effects for black people. "If we are to be psychologically independent," wrote Jeffers, "we must create our own values, our own way of looking at things, our own way of looking at ourselves." The idea of creating self and artistic autonomy was central to Jeffers's writings and to the tenets of the Black Aesthetic movement.

Who are black people beyond their defining relationship(s) with white people in America? Who are black people individually and collectively? How have African American identities evolved in the latter part of the twentieth century? What difference do geographical locations mean to how black people in America live and express themselves? And when, if not now, should black writers be more concerned about defining, redefining, and complicating ideas of blackness? Through his writings, Jeffers was concerned about approaching such questions. Toward the end of his life, Jeffers was intent on expanding his artistic creations concerning black people. "This is where I am moving," he said, "not away from race, but to a broader conception of race, of the human experience in every black person." Jeffers realized that African American writers must concern themselves with the ever-changing complexities of the world and at the same time remember the ever-present factors and consequences surrounding race. "I simultaneously have to be as broad as humanity, and as intense and angry as the black man successfully fighting for his life against a pack of lynchers," he said.

Examining the lives and writings of those African American writers who emerged during the Civil Rights and Black Power era reveals that black writers were deeply concerned about linking social consciousness and activism with their artistic productions. As the literary critic Jerry W. Ward Jr. wrote years ago, "the great awakening made possible by the Black Aesthetic movement is the recognition that the yoking of the social and literary facts is an inextricable part of the process of reading." The black poets, essayists, novelists, and critics of the 1960s and '70s have produced works that might be useful guides to understanding their time period in America and African American history and thinking about our future(s).

The continued circulation and appreciation of African American literature will rest on readers. That means we must continue to read and re-read the works of such widely discussed writers as Richard Wright, Toni Morrison, Alice Walker, and Amiri Baraka. But let us expand our readings to include such significant, lesser-studied black writers as Lance Jeffers, Toni Cade Bambara, Ton Dent, Gloria Wade-Gayles, Gayle Jones, John Oliver Killens, and Audre Lorde. These writers, and numerous others who published in black-oriented journals from the 1960s through the 1980s, engaged the dominant topical issues in black culture(s) and provided models of using literary means to achieve the end of awakening historical consciousness. They provided one set of blueprints for negotiations with history.

The history of our generation is a continuation with a difference, and we must account in new ways for our missions as writers and artists. Multicultural phenomena and new technologies obligate us to ask in new terms who decides which black writers get published. Why and how might young writers incorporate such black cultural expressions as rap music in their works? How might gender, region, class, and various other categories and differences affect representations of blackness in literature? How might the Internet be a useful tool to exploring issues relating to African American literature? And last but not least, how might writers of today and tomorrow draw upon black literature and history to re-draw some of the color lines in American and African American literature of the future? When and if we're developing the blueprints for another Black Aesthetic and/or the NEXT movement, do not forget that important groundwork has been laid for us and that Lance Jeffers was one of the bravest pioneers.

PART FOUR

Fiction

"I'm just a narrator, you know?
I'm just telling a story....
You can't be mad at me...."

—The Notorious
B.I.G., unlisted
monologue on *Life
after Death* (1997)

Paul Beatty

The White Boy Shuffle

MY MAGICAL MYSTERY TOUR GROUND TO A HALT IN A WEST LOS ANGELES neighborhood the locals call Hillside. Shaped like a giant cul-de-sac, Hillside is less a community than a quarry of stucco homes built directly into the foothills of the San Borrachos Mountains. Unlike most California communities that border mountain ranges, Hillside has no gentle slopes upon which children climb trees and overly friendly park rangers lead weekend flora-and fauna tours.

In the late 1960s, after the bloody but little known I'm-Tired-of-the-White-Man-Fuckin'-with-Us-and-Whatnot riots, the city decided to pave over the neighboring mountainside, surrounding the community with a great concrete wall that spans its entire curved perimeter save for an arched gateway at the southwest entrance. At the summit of this cement precipice wealthy families live in an upper-middle-class hamlet known as Cheviot Heights. At the bottom of this great wall live hordes of impoverished American Mongols. Hardrock niggers, Latinos, and Asians, who because of the wall's immenseness get only fifteen minutes of precious sunshine in summer and a burst of solstice sunlight in the winter. If it weren't always so hot it would be like living in a refrigerator.

We lived in a pueblo-style home with a cracked and fissuring plaster exterior my mother said provided an Old Mexico flavor. Even she had to laugh when I walked up to a peeling section of the house, broke off a yellow paint chip, popped it into my mouth, rubbed my tummy, and said, "Mmmmmm, nacho cheese." Our back yard nestled right up against the infamous wall. I often marveled at the unique photosynthesis that allowed the fig, peach, and lemon trees to thrive in a dim climate where it often rained dead cats and dogs, rotted fish, and droplets of piss. Apparently rich folks have an acerbic sense of humor.

After a week in our new home, a black-and-white Welcome Wagon pulled up in front of the house to help the newcomers settle into the neighborhood. Two mustachioed officers got out of the patrol car and knocked on our front door with well-practiced leather-gloved authority. Tossing courtesy smiles at my mother, the cops shouldered their way past the threshold and presented her with a pamphlet entitled "How to Report Crime and Suspicious Activity Whether the Suspects Are Related to You or Not." It wasn't the day-old macaroni casserole she'd been expecting. My sisters and I sat in the living room, half listening to the news on the radio, half listening to the cops asking Mama questions to which they already knew the answers.

"Kids, Ms. Kaufman?"

"Yes, three."

"Two girls, ten and eleven, and a boy, thirteen, all of them left-handed, right?"

"That's correct."

"Ma'am, may we speak to the boy, Gunnar?"

My mother turned around and waved me over with the hated come-hither crooked index finger. I lifted my sheepish carcass off the couch and shuffled like a reluctant butler toward the interrogation. The cop with gold stripes on his sleeves cut Mama a look

203

and said "Alone, Ms. Kaufman," and she deserted me with a satisfied smirk, happy that I was finally getting a bitter taste of her vaunted "traditional black experience."

I stood there, perched directly under the doorjamb, as I'd learned to do when your earth quaked. My slumping shoulders trembled. My kneecaps shook. These weren't some Santa Monica cops sporting Conflict Resolution ribbons, riding powder-blue bicycles, this was the LAPD, dressed to oppress, their hands calmly poised over open holsters like seasoned gunfighters'. I tried to distance myself from the rumbling in my ears, clamoring for one of those out-of-body experiences only white folks in midlife crises seem to have. I felt the gases rising from my queasy stomach to inflate my body. My arms and legs began to swell, and slowly I began to float away. I was just getting off the ground when I let out a long silent fart. Apparently, my escape fantasy had a slow leak.

"Son, you smell something?"

"Nope."

"Well, something reeks."

"Oh, that's the chitlins."

My would-be out-of-body experience hovered there, wafting in the flatulent fumes. I wasn't going anywhere; I felt like a Macy's Thanksgiving Day Parade balloon—tethered, and grounded to reality by fishing lines looped through my nose and eyeballs. I was a helium distraction until the arrival of Santa Claus. "Look, Daddy, Snoopy with an Afro."

The squat grayish-blond officer removed his cap and introduced himself and his partner as officers Frank Russo and Neal Salty.

"Gunnar, we know you had some problems with the Santa Monica police department. Son, here in"—the officer took a deep breath—"Nuestra Señora la Reina de Los Angeles de Porciuncula, we practice what we like to call 'preventative police enforcement.' Whereby, we prefer to deter habitual criminals before they cause irreparable damage to the citizenry and/or its property."

"You mean you put people who haven't done anything in the back seat of your squad car and beat the shit out of 'em so you don't have to do any paperwork. Thereby preventing any probable felonious assaults on the citizenry."

"And/or its property."

"And/or it is. You know, my father is a sketch artist down at Wilshire Division. Does that carry any weight?"

"Yeah, he gets to visit your ass in jail without being strip-searched."

Taking out a small notebook from his supercop utility belt, he continued the inquest. "What's your gang affiliation?"

"Gang affiliation?"

"Who do you run with? Who are your crimeys, your homies, your posse? You know, yo' niggers."

"Oh, I see. Well, on weekends I'm down with the Gang of Four."

"Who?" to his partner, "Geez, these fucking turds are incredible, there's a new gang every frigging week." Then he turned back to me. "So, Gunnar, who you banging with in this Gang of Four?"

"You know, it's me, my homegirl Jiang Qing, Wang Hongwen, Zhang Chuqiao, and my nigger even if he don't get no bigger Yao Wenyuan. Sheeeeit, we runnin' thangs from Shanghai to Compton."

Although I had only lived in Hillside for a few days, it was impossible not to pick up a few local catchphrases while running errands for Mother. Language was everywhere. Smoldering embers of charcoal etymology so permeated the air that whenever someone opened his mouth it smelled like smoke. Double-check the mailbox to see if your letters had fallen through and the lid shrieked, "Dumb-ass motherfucker, have you ever looked and letters were still there? No! Shut the goddamn lid." Press the crossing button at the intersection and the signal blinked a furious "Hurry the fuck up!" Call information and the operator answered the phone with a throaty "Who dis?" Nothing infuriated my mother more than me lounging on one elbow at the dinner table slinging my introductory slang with a mouth full of mashed potatoes: "Sheeeeit, Ma, I'm running thangs, fuck the dumb."

"Seriously, son, judging by your previous nefarious history, we feel that you have a proclivity for gang activity. Do us all a favor and come clean."

"Okay, fuck the dumb. On Mondays, Wednesdays, and odd-numbered Fridays when my mother lets me stay out late, I be down with the Our Gang He-man Woman Haters Club. Matter of fact, we have a rumble with the Bowery Boys next week. If you see that schmuck Muggs, tell da bum I'm gonna kick his ass."

"Okay, we're going to put you down as unaffiliated. For now keep your big black nose clean."

Gang affiliation? I didn't even have any friends yet. My sisters and I had no idea how to navigate our way around this hardscrabble dystopia. Each of us had already been beaten up at least once just for trying to make friends. Deciding there was safety in numbers, we took to traveling in a pack. Nervously, traipsing through the minefield, we tiptoed past the suspected ruffians and kept on the lookout for snipers. Shots would ring out from nowhere, forcing us into sacrificial heroics, diving onto verbal grenades to save the others.

"Say, bitch-ass, com'ere!"

"Who, me?!"

"Must be you, you looked."

"You guys, go on without me. Get away while there's still time. Tell Mama I love her. I regret that I have only one life to give for my family."

By day six of the ghetto hostage crisis my sibling captives and I were avoiding the dangers of the unexplored territory along the banks of the Harbor Freeway by sitting in the den playing Minutiae Pursuance, substituting our own questions for the inane ones on the cards.

"Sports and Leisure, for the pie."

"Oh, this one's a toughie. How many dimples on a golf ball?"

"Four hundred sixty-three. Give me my piece."

Mom was not the kind of matriarch to let her brood hide up under her skirt, clutching her knees, sheltered from the mean old Negroes outside. Under the guise that she was worried about our deteriorating social skills, she suggested we go to Reynier Park and play with the other kids in the neighborhood. She might as well have told us to play in the prison yard at Attica. Reynier Park was an overgrown inner-city rain forest that some Brazilian lumber company needed to uproot. You needed a machete to clear a path to the playground. The sandbox was an uninhabitable breeding ground for tetanus and typhus. Shards of broken glass and spent bullet shells outnumbered grains of sand by a ratio of four to one. Hypodermic needles nosed through this shimmering sinkhole like rusted punji sticks.

Despite our pleas for a pardon, Mom invoked the death penalty and sentenced us to an afternoon at the park. For the record, the condemned ate last meals of liverwurst and mustard on white bread and drank grape Kool-Aid (extra scoop of sugar) before departing. We were somberly alternating turns on the only working swing when two girls about ten years old, smoking cigarettes and sharing sips from a canned piña colada, approached us. The taller of the two was wearing denim overalls and had so many pink and blue barrettes clipped to the thinning patches of braided hair on her head it looked as though she was under attack by a swarm of plastic moths. The other girl had an orange polyester hot pants and matching polka dot halter top that was so small it barely succeeded in halting her two BB-sized nipples. Her hair was heavily greased into a rigid elliptical disk that sat precariously on the crown of her head. Every few seconds she'd stoop down to pick up a discarded needle and deposit it in her little red Naugahyde purse. She resembled a Vietnamese woman wearing a straw hat and toiling in a paddy. I listened for bleating water buffalo but heard only the bigger one's mouth.

"Get out of our swing now!" she shouted at Nicole. Nicole wanted to get off the swing, but she was catatonic with fear. It didn't help that out of sheer nervousness Christina and I kept pushing, propelling her stiff frame higher and faster.

Kicking off their dime store flip-flops, the two badly coiffed bullies marched through the sandbox without a flinch or grimace. A little diaper-clad boy waddled up, blew a kazoo tribunal, and heralded the dyspeptic duo: "That my sister Fas' Betty and her bestest friend Vamp a Nigger on the Regular Veronica. They fixin' to kick y'all's ass." Betty and Veronica went into a loud hands-on-the-hips, call-and-response, head-bobbing tirade on how they owned the entire park from the calcified jungle gym to the busted teeter-totter. Betty's braids stood on end as she demanded that Nicole get off the swing before she heated up every piece of broken glass in the sandbox, affixed them to the end of one of those pointy 7-Eleven Slurpee straws, and blew glass bubbles in her tight black bourgeoise booty.

The thought of this snake-haired demon shoving molten glass in her rectum gorgonized Nicole even further. Her sphincter tightened and her rock-hard butt sat heavy in the swing. Betty picked up a piece of broken glass, lit a Bic lighter, and teasingly passed the piece of glass through the flame, her fireproof fingers impervious to the heat. Nicole's hands fastened themselves to the chains; her legs spread out in front of her and locked at the knees. Mistaking our silent petrification for hincty insolence, Betty and Veronica tried to rush us. The alcohol must have affected their bullying judgments, because they charged into Nicole chin first just as her legs were in the high kicking up stroke of a swing filled with panic-stricken kinetics. Fas' Betty caught a sneaker in the trachea and Veronica Vamp a Nigger something-or-the-other got kicked in the solar plexus.

Wiggling in spasmodic waves like dying fish on the filthy playground, the girls somehow managed to find enough air to moan raspy Miles Davis "motherfuckers" and threats that every ex-con cousin, pyromania auntie, serial killer uncle, and pit bull in the neighborhood would soon be coming to "put that head out" and "peel our caps." Within moments, as if some silent gangster medical alert alarm had gone off, a small army of nepotistic enforcers magically appeared at the entrance near the basketball courts, parting the underbrush and yelling, "Y'all fucking with my cousins?" The three of us instantaneously burst into a waterfall of tears. Begging for a sympathetic détente, Christina and I mindlessly continued to push Nicole's swing. Her whoosing arc through the air, accompanied by the rusty swing set's rhythmic creak, became a foreboding, metronomic pendulum counting down our deaths. "We didn't know! We didn't know! Please leave us alone." A screaming vortex of punches and kicks answered our pleas with a firm *ignorantia juris neminem excusat*.

The ghetto intelligentsia had kindly provided the young Kaufmans with our first lesson in street smartology: never, ever cry in public—it only makes it worse. If we hadn't bawled we might have been let off with a polite cursory thrashing, just to maintain protective appearances. Since we sobbed like wailing refugee babies, we received a full-scale beatdown designed to toughen us up for the inevitable cataclysmic Italian opera end of black tragedy. Usually when the fat lady sings in a black community, it's a funeral. I've seen kids get hit by cars, ice cream trucks, bullets, billyclubs, and not even whimper. The only time it's permissible to cry is when you miss the lottery by one number or someone close to you passes away. Then you can cry once, but only once. There is no brooding; niggers got to get up and go to work tomorrow.

My sisters and I walked home routed, picking bits of gravel out of one another's tattered Afros and holding our heads back to stanch our nosebleeds. I thought about Betty's flecked bouffant, Veronica's flying-saucer-like do, and the oily Jheri curls, rock-hard pomade cold waves, and horsehair weaves of our attackers, and I realized that every day for the black American is a bad hair day.

"We haven't seen Daddy since we moved."

"Mommy told me he knows where we live, but he won't come by."

"Fuck that nigger."

"Listen to you. So, tough guy, I think Betty and Veronica kind of like you. Did you notice the tender look in their eyes when they stomped on your head? Which one you gonna choose, Archiekins?"

"Oh, be quiet. I could swear that little baby knee-dropped me in the balls."

Ricardo Cortez Cruz

Interpolation: Peace to My Nine

Contains Replayed Elements of "Forget I Was G" and "Dust in the Wind"

> *Allahu-Akbar. As-Salaam-Alaikum. In the name of Allah, Most Graceful, Most Merciful . . . I close my eyes, but only for a moment, then the moment's gone.*

THERE ARE DAYS WHEN YOU LOVE EVERYTHING. I MEAN, ABSOFUCKINGLUTELY everything, man. You love your momma, because she is Calypso, full of dance, Marvelless. You even love your daddy, despite being afraid of him, afraid to talk to him. You conversate [sic] with a nice vendor, see ketchup running down the side of a hot dog, and it doesn't remind you of the nasty, violent stories you heard in the streets about your cheating father. Your daddy is big and bad, your life a grim fairy tale, so you drink to keep the wolf off your back, and it works. You know you could quit at anytime, but that's life, you say, and you find Regina and Amy, who both have an illegitimate baby by you, so they can agree with you and put their mother-tongues into your ears, telling you what you like to hear. But, you wait for Sunday to moon you before committing yourself to these women because the darkness of the sky is a bitch, you say, a black skeezer getting into bed in only cream silk panties, and you are the main player in a midsummer night's dream. You look for a romp. This is how good, how strong, you feel.

But, then comes a flash, a twinkling, these periods when you lose everything, particular instances when you hate everything in sight as if your bitter momma, who has tried to control your life, is now testing you, has put spell #7 on you because you remind her too much of your daddy—you won't act right. Bitter momma hexes you, swallows bitter pills so she can go to sleep at night, makes you swallow bitter pills, too. You wash them down with a watermelon and blockade. Under the influence, you think of everybody in front of you as trailer park material. You have an intolerance for sours and swipes and apple-jack and enamel and bingo; you finally vomit, too ill to escape those horrible feelings inside that are tearing you up like the sharp, metal claws of Freddy Krueger because they want to get the hell out; you know that the lining of your stomach is gone. You hate your own mother for having you, cursing you, whipping your ass and reminding you, "What I say goes."

You see, these are the days when even the sun won't touch your dark ass because every time you see the light it's white to the point where it's in your face and offensive and you call it 'a motherfucker, honky.' You dance but play Slave because you feel so funky. These are the days when life does not matter to you. I mean, you realize that you have experienced a kind of nightmare on Elm Street and you wake up hot and, as you try to wipe all of the sweat off your forehead, you hope that you don't go off and hurt somebody because of their mental delusion that you have nothing to lose.

So, you get down on your knees and pray for another day, pray for things to be different the next time.

I close my eyes, but only for a moment, then the moment's gone.

In front of the Harlem mosque and clutching a gun with a second thought of putting a body on it, I'm talking to you, Mr. White Man, my brother reading about the death and life of Malcolm X, *The Saturday Evening Post* in blood's hands.

Near Sam's furniture store, my crimeys are chilling, some drive-by niggers singing "I'm yo' pusher," one afro brother shouting "fuck the police" and "fuck you" and "fuck you, too," another bright brother saying "beat me, daddy." Boyz II Men singing *Cooleyhighharmony* around the way. Black men, huddled up like football players, stand at the corner and talk nasty things, some of them deliberately in people's way by the bus depot—shooting crap and singing "The Doo-Bop Song" where a street sign asks traffic to pass through carefully. "Do you want to see me cooking," one of them asks. Without waiting for an answer, he starts pounding an old city trash can, creating new beats with wooden spoons and pots and pans, and he keeps saying over and over "just give me that doo-bop sound, just give me that doo-bop sound."

By the ashes of a Harlem joint, a little brother writes "Muhammad Speaks" into the dirt, his glasses falling off his face and everything in pieces on the ground, his mama waving the *Holy Qur'an* at his big head. These are the kind of spectacles that are hard to find; they don't come easy.

So my brother is scared there in the grass, but, when he gazes up, a white photographer from *Life* humming country music quickly snaps his picture, then proudly announces that the boy's going to enter the hearts of America, be on every big screen, television, newstand, rack and table in the country, even end up framed in a nice, little picture sold for Home Interior. His mama screams, flailing her huge arms, and then herself, into nets.

As if trying to protect his camera and his own lenses, the photographer sprints away, breaking through the horizon, where the landscape is so ghetto, entering the planes to recapture his own vantage point and to leave behind that place, that space, where the sun is ducking down and some raps from Naughty by Nature shout "if you've never been to the ghetto, then stay the fuck out of the ghetto, cause it ain't for you—you can't understand how things operate here." It was after all, by the stop sign where earlier a brother got caught and beat to a pulp (like the way white people want to do O.J.) for obscenely fucking a drop-dead, gorgeous white woman in broad daylight. He did it by that singing hill, they say. As the white lady was screaming, hill was singing, "That thang, that thang, that tha-a-a-ang." Afterwards, they say the white woman's limp body rolled downhill, down the street, picking up sticks, a pancake in a children's story before getting kicked to the curb.

A riot of black men and women, straight from the set—upset about the King beating, run the streets, cussing like it's nothing, breaking windows, and tripping, The Man arresting them left and right. It's so bad that even white observers start asking "Why can't we all just get along" while niggas are bloody and crawling along the sidewalk talk, their fallen bodies splashing puddles together, the police leaving dark spots on the pavement.

Near the Audubon Ballroom, niggas are screaming "Red is dead! Red is dead!" Somebody's Aunt Esther points in the man's face as he lies on the ground. "Don't you know no good?" she asks. Black Muslims drag her away, then head for Mosque No. 7, carrying Molotov cocktails, blood and alcohol squirting through the opening of their lips, glass bottles in their hands, gasoline bombs bursting in air while, I'm told, their leader Louis Farrakhan sings old nightclub songs in his shower and plays Jimi Hendrix performing the *Star-Spangled Banner.* "Water," Farrakhan has said, "is the purest thing on Earth."

"Red is dead!" Muslim brothers shout, running and looting and moving the crowd. The women of Islam are sprinting behind them like Furies chasing after the evildoers and haints. Under the evening sun, their faces are disguised by white veils, shrouded in oppression, and without a smile. They do as they are told; they eat and drink the fruit of Islam. I am told that they are the nutritionists who give their body nothing in order to give their men everything they have. Shunning all forms of close contact and interpersonal communication, they privately languish in misery, I hear. Their awkward fit into society, as well as their perceived lack of vision, reaches the point where they force somebody to kiss their ass goodbye. I believe this is what happened to brother Malcolm. That is to say, all of the whiteness of his day eventually got to him.

"There will be no more Satan!" screams a chorus.

"Without Red, we won't know what to do."

"We need a fix to get the monkey off our backs."

"But, believe me, the royal family will go on."

"Red would want it that way."

"Expect more riots," says somebody.

"Expect more rage," says someone else.

Community folks are flinging water and hollering, many of them raiding the rack of *The Saturday Evening Post,* which was the first white man's magazine to put Malcolm X on the front cover. Today's feature is *Deep Cover.* Holding a Saturday Night special, Larry Fishburne is frowning as if upset that Life/life never gave Malcolm his due pub. According to the cover, Fishburne, a rising star and "a boy in the hood," now insists on being called Laurence. "That's too much power for one man to have," a police chief says, pushing over the newsstand.

A graying black woman looks up and asks me if I am an act from the Apollo Theater, and a faded boogie runs to the phone booth and searches for "Spike Lee" in the yellow pages, hoping to call him to do a film on the hood right now while things are hot.

In the mean time, my homies are moving the crowd. Like wounded rabbits, they flee into the black alleys, screaming loud enough to blowout windows, twisting their ankles trying to get away, scraping their arms, dodging bullets, Dirty Harry's naked gun repeatedly yellow "make my day" as it smokes them one by one. At first, The Man couldn't decide if he wanted to do two niggas or three, so he shoots two of my niggas, maiming them first because he wanted them to see what Power looks like and how it rules—he wanted them to see his ugly face. He hits another black man, Doubting Thomas, in the front of his pants and then just stares at the man while he begs for mercy and loses control of his feces. There are other cops, pretty women who act like Charlie's angels, recording the action for the police report. In the hood, police wear the blues like they own blacks and have to keep a running count. The pinks don't know math, but they think they can solve every problem in the ghetto. Tragically, my homies would rather be six-feet under than jailed like Marcus Garvey, who had warned them to go back to Africa.

"O, I'm shot in da booty!" another homie screams.

The copper shoots him again in his limp, hitting the broken Kool/cool in his hip pocket. Then the copper runs over and lines him up against the wall, patting him down like he is feeling on a woman's breasts.

"What did I ever do to you?" my nigga asks, his sorry face nut chocolate, half-laughing, half-crying, then half-laughing again. They got him going round in circles.

The cop takes offense to the snicker/snigger. "Do ya feel lucky, punk?" the cop asks. For cops, image is everything.

"I bet you know how to suck a mean dick," the copper says, almost playing with his gun, showing my nigga his draws. Then he pops him for good, the bullet going clean through the nigga's big head, the sucka' singing "how ya like me now" by the time the nigga falls into the trash can.

The copper stands back and glares at all the mess. "Throw the bodies in the East River," he says to his buddies dashing up, back into the picture, in order to see what happened.

At night, almost in a kind of surrealistic dream, I walk from way west to Hell Gate, past a row of hospitals. I slip back to the river with some bitches' brew and a six-pack, and I say peace to my motherfuckin' nine. I imagine these niggas as having made their bed and now sleeping it, cold(code)blue; I pour the panther piss all over their afros and wavy hair, the water carrying them away, shipping them COD. The waterfront breeze picks up, dust in the wind.

Checking out the entire scene with an evil eye, I cry while the water slaps the face of one of my boys into deeper depths that slowly begins to take him under, beat him down. "Wa! Salaam Alaikum." I close my eyes, but only for a moment. Then the moment's gone.

With the blues of a fallen teardrop and my gun as a speaker begging for a washout, I tell you in front of a screamer, "You stared death in the face and blinked, Mr. White Man. Don't expect to get more chances like that."

Epilogue: Women Like Us

Edwidge Danticat

YOU REMEMBER THINKING WHILE BRAIDING YOUR HAIR THAT YOU LOOK A LOT like your mother. Your mother who looked like your grandmother and her grandmother before her. Your mother had two rules for living. *Always use your ten fingers,* which in her parlance meant that you should be the best little cook and housekeeper who ever lived.

Your mother's second rule went along with the first. Never have sex before marriage, and even after you marry, you shouldn't say you enjoy it, or your husband won't respect you.

And writing? Writing was as forbidden as dark rouge on the cheeks or a first date before eighteen. It was an act of indolence, something to be done in a corner when you could have been learning to cook.

Are there women who both cook and write? Kitchen poets, they call them. They slip phrases into their stew and wrap meaning around their pork before frying it. They make narrative dumplings and stuff their daughter's mouths so they say nothing more.

"What will she do? What will be her passion?" your aunts would ask when they came over to cook on great holidays, which called for cannon salutes back home but meant nothing at all here.

"Her passion is being quiet," your mother would say. "But then she's not being quiet. You hear this scraping from her. Krik? Krak! Pencil, paper. It sounds like someone crying."

Someone was crying. You and the writing demons in your head. You have nobody, nothing but this piece of paper, they told you. Only a notebook made out of discarded fish wrappers, panty-hose cardboard. They were the best confidantes for a lonely little girl.

When you write, it's like braiding your hair. Taking a handful of coarse unruly strands and attempting to bring them unity. Your fingers have still not perfected the task. Some of the braids are long, others are short. Some are thick, others are thin.

Some are heavy. Others are light. Like the diverse women in your family. Those whose fables and metaphors, whose similes, and soliloquies, whose diction and *je ne sais quoi* daily slip into your survival soup, by way of their fingers.

You have always had your ten fingers. They curse you each time you force them around the contours of a pen. No, women like you don't write. They carve onion sculptures and potato statues. They sit in dark corners and braid their hair in new shapes and twists in order to control the stiffness, the unruliness, the rebelliousness.

You remember thinking while braiding your hair that you look a lot like your mother. You remember her silence when you laid your first notebook in front of her. Her disappointment when you told her that words would be your life's work, like the kitchen had always been hers. She was angry at you for not understanding. *And with what do you repay me? With scribbles on paper that are not worth the scratch of a pig's snout.* The sacrifices had been too great.

Writers don't leave any mark in the world. Not the world where we are from. In our world, writers are tortured and killed if they are men. Called lying whores, then raped and killed, if they are women. In our world, if you write, you are a politician, and we know what happens to politicians. They end up in a prison dungeon where their bodies are covered in scalding tar before they're forced to eat their own waste.

The family needs a nurse, not a prisoner. We need to forge ahead with our heads raised, not buried in scraps of throwaway paper. We do not want to bend over a dusty grave, wearing black hats, grieving for you. There are nine hundred and ninety-nine women who went before you and worked their fingers to coconut rind so you can stand here before me holding that torn old notebook that you cradle against your breast like your prettiest Sunday braids. I would rather you had spit in my face.

You remember thinking while braiding your hair that you look a lot like your mother and her mother before her. It was their whispers that pushed you, their murmurs over pots sizzling in your head. A thousand women urging you to speak through the blunt tip of your pencil. Kitchen poets, you call them. Ghosts like burnished branches on a flame tree. These women, they asked for your voice so that they could tell your mother in your place that yes, women like you do speak, even if they speak in tongue that is hard to understand. Even if it's patois, dialect, Creole.

The women in your family have never lost touch with one another. Death is a path we take to meet on the other side. What goddesses have joined, let no one cast asunder. With every step you take, there is an army of women watching over you. We are never any farther than the sweat on your brows or the dust on your toes. Though you walk through the valley of the shadow of death, fear no evil for we are always with you.

When you were a little girl, you used to dream that you were lying among the dead and all the spirits were begging you to scream. And even now, you are still afraid to dream because you know that you will never be able to do what they say, as they say it, the old spirits that live in your blood.

Most of the women in your life had their heads down. They would wake up one morning to find their panties gone. It is not shame, however, that kept their heads down. They were singing, searching for meaning in the dust. And sometimes, they were talking to faces across the ages, faces like yours and mine.

You thought that if you didn't tell the stories, the sky would fall on your head. You often thought that without the trees, the sky would fall on your head. You learned in school that you have pencils and paper only because the trees gave themselves in unconditional sacrifice. There have been days when the sky was as close as your hair to falling on your head.

This fragile sky has terrified you your whole life. Silence terrifies you more than the pounding of a million pieces of steel chopping away at your flesh. Sometimes, you dream of hearing only the beating of your own heart, but this has never been the case. You have never been able to escape the pounding of a thousand other hearts that have outlived yours by thousands of years. And over the years when you have needed us, you have always cried "Krik?" and we have answered "Krak!" and it has shown us that you have not forgotten us.

You remember thinking while braiding your hair that you look a lot like your mother. Your mother, who looked like your grandmother and her grandmother before her. Your mother, she introduced you to the first echoes of the tongue that you now speak when at the end of the day she would braid your hair while you sat between her legs, scrubbing the kitchen pots. While your fingers worked away at the last shadows of her day's work, she would make your braids Sunday-pretty, even during the week.

When she was done she would ask you to name each braid after those nine hundred and ninety-nine women who were boiling in your blood, and since you had written them down and memorized them, the names would come rolling off your tongue. And this was your testament to the way that these women lived and died and lived again.

The Sun, the Moon, the Stars

Junot Díaz

I AM NOT A BAD GUY. I KNOW HOW THAT SOUNDS—DEFENSIVE, UNSCRUPU-lous—but it's true. I'm like everybody else: weak, full of mistakes, but basically good. Magdalena disagrees. She considers me a typical Dominican man: a sucio, an asshole. See, many months ago, when Magda was still my girl, when I didn't have to be careful about almost everything, I cheated on her with this chick who had tons of eighties free-style hair. Didn't tell Magda about it, either. You know how it is. A smelly bone like that, better off buried in the back yard of your life. Magda only found out because homegirl wrote her a fucking *letter*. And the letter had *details*. Shit you wouldn't even tell your boys drunk.

The thing is, that particular bit of stupidity had been over for months. Me and Magda were on an upswing. We weren't as distant as we'd been the winter I was cheating. The freeze was over. She was coming over to my place and instead of us hanging with my knucklehead boys—me smoking, her bored out of her skull—we were seeing movies. Driving out to different places to eat. Even caught a play at the Crossroads and I took her picture with some bigwig black playwrights, pictures where she's smiling so much you'd think her wide-ass mouth was going to unhinge. We were a couple again. Visiting each other's family on the weekends. Eating breakfast at diners hours before anybody else was up, rummaging through the New Brunswick library together, the one Carnegie built with his guilt money. A nice rhythm we had going. But then the Letter hits like a "Star Trek" grenade and detonates everything, past, present, future. Suddenly her folks want to kill me. It don't matter that I helped them with their taxes two years running or that I mow their lawn. Her father, who used to treat me like his hijo, calls me an asshole on the phone, sounds like he's strangling himself with the cord. "You no deserve I speak to you in Spanish," he says. I see one of Magda's girlfriends at the Woodbridge Mall—Claribel, the *ecuatoriana* with the biology degree and the *chinita* eyes—and she treats me like I ate somebody's kid.

You don't even want to hear how it went down with Magda. Like a five-train collision. She threw Cassandra's letter at me —it missed and landed under a Volvo—and then she sat down on the curb and started hyperventilating. "Oh, God," she wailed. "Oh, my God."

This is when my boys claim they would have pulled a Total Fucking Denial. Cassandra who? I was too sick to my stomach even to try. I sat down next to her, grabbed her flailing arms, and said some dumb shit like "You have to listen to me, Magda. Or you won't understand."

Let me tell you something about Magda. She's a Bergenline original: short with big eyes and big hips and dark curly hair you could lose a hand in. Her father's a baker, her mother sells kids' clothes door to door. She's a forgiving soul. A Catholic. Dragged me into church every Sunday for Spanish Mass, and when one of her relatives is sick, especially the ones in Cuba, she writes letters to some nuns in Pennsylvania, asks the sisters to pray for her family. She's the nerd every librarian in town knows, a teacher whose students fall in love with her. Always cutting shit out for me from the newspapers. Dominican shit. I see her like, what, every week, and she still sends me corny little notes in the mail: "So you won't forget me." You couldn't think of anybody worse to screw than Magda.

I won't bore you with the details. The begging, the crawling over glass, the crying. Let's just say that after two weeks of this, of my driving out to her house, sending her letters, and calling her at all hours of the night, we put it back together. Didn't mean I ever ate with her family again or that her girlfriends were celebrating. Those cabronas, they were like, No, jamás, never. Even Magda wasn't too hot on the rapprochement at first, but I had the momentum of the past on my side. When she asked me "Why don't you leave me alone?" I told her the truth: "It's because I love you, *mami*." I know this sounds like a load of doo-doo, but it's true: Magda's my heart. I didn't want her to leave me; I wasn't about to start looking for a girlfriend because I'd fucked up one lousy time.

Don't think it was a cakewalk, because it wasn't. Magda's stubborn; back when we first started dating, she said she wouldn't sleep with me until we'd been together at least a month, and homegirl stuck to it, no matter how hard I tried to get into her knick-knacks. She's sensitive, too. Takes to hurt the way water takes to paper. You can't imagine how many times she asked (especially after we finished fucking), "Were you ever going to tell me?" This and "Why?" were her favorite questions. My favorite answers were "Yes" and "It was a stupid mistake."

We even had some conversation about Cassandra—usually in the dark, when we couldn't see each other. Magda asked me if I'd loved Cassandra and I told her no, I didn't. "Do you still think about her?" "Nope." "Did you like fucking her?" "To be honest, baby, it was lousy." And for a while after we got back together everything was as fine as it could be.

But what was strange was that instead of shit improving between us, things got worse and worse. My Magda was turning into another Magda. Who didn't want to sleep over as much or scratch my back when I asked her to. Amazing how you notice the little things. Like how she never used to ask me to call back when she was on the line with somebody else. I always had priority. Not anymore. So of course I blamed all that shit on her girls, who I knew for a fact were still feeding her a line about me.

She wasn't the only one with counsel. My boys were like, "Fuck her, don't sweat that bitch," but every time I tried I couldn't pull it off. I was into Magda for real. I started working overtime on her, but nothing seemed to pan out. Every movie we went to, every night drive we took, every time she did sleep over seemed to confirm something negative about me. I felt like I was dying by degrees, but when I brought it up she told me that I was being paranoid.

About a month later, she started making the sort of changes that would have alarmed a paranoid nigger. Cuts her hair, buys better makeup, rocks new clothes, goes out dancing on Friday nights with her friends. When I ask her if we can chill, I'm no longer sure it's a done deal. A lot of the time she Bartlebys me, says, "No, I'd rather not." I ask her what the hell she thinks this is and she says, "That's what I'm trying to figure out."

I know what she's doing. Making me aware of my precarious position in her life. Like I'm not aware.

Then it was June. Hot white clouds stranded in the sky, cars being washed down with hoses, music allowed outside. Everybody getting ready for summer, even us. We'd planned a trip to Santo Domingo early in the year, an anniversary present, and had to decide whether we were still going or not. It had been on the horizon awhile, but I figured it was something that would resolve itself. When it didn't, I brought the tickets out and asked her, "How do you feel about it?"

"Like it's too much of a commitment."

"Could be worse. It's a vacation, for Christ's sake."

"I see it as pressure."

"Doesn't have to be pressure."

I don't know why I get stuck on it the way I do. Bringing it up every day, trying to get her to commit. Maybe I was getting tired of the situation we were in. Wanted to flex, wanted something to change. Or maybe I'd gotten this idea in my head that if she said, "Yes, we're going," then shit would be fine between us. If she said, "No, it's not for me," then at least I'd know that it was over.

Her girls, the sorest losers on the planet, advised her to take the trip and then never speak to me again. She, of course, told me this shit, because she couldn't stop herself from telling me everything she's thinking. "How do you feel about that suggestion?" I asked her.

She shrugged. "It's an idea."

Even my boys were like, "Nigger, sounds like you're wasting a whole lot of loot on some bullshit," but I really thought it would be good for us. Deep down, where my boys don't know me, I'm an optimist. I thought, Me and her on the Island. What couldn't this cure?

Let me confess: I love Santo Domingo. I love coming home to the guys in blazers try-ing to push little cups of Brugal into my hands. Love the plane landing, everybody clapping when the wheels kiss the runway. Love the fact that I'm the only nigger on board without a Cuban link or a flapjack of makeup on my face. Love the redhead woman on her way to meet the daughter she hasn't seen in eleven years. The gifts she holds on her lap, like the bones of a saint. *"M'ija* has *tetas* now," the woman whispers to her neighbor. "Last time I saw her, she could barely speak in sentences. Now she's a woman. *Imagínate.*" I love the bags my mother packs, shit for relatives and something for Magda, a gift. "You give this to her no matter what happens."

If this was another kind of story, I'd tell you about the sea. What it looks like after it's been forced into the sky through a blowhole. How when I'm driving in from the airport and see it like this, like shredded silver, I know I'm back for real. I'd tell you how many poor motherfuckers there are. More albinos, more cross-eyed niggers, more tígueres than you'll ever see. And the mujeres—olvídate. How you can't go five feet without running into one you wouldn't mind kicking it with. I'd tell you about the traffic: the entire history of late-twentieth-century automobiles swarming across every flat stretch of ground, a cosmology of battered cars, battered motorcycles, battered trucks, and battered buses, and an equal number of repair shops, run by any fool with a wrench. I'd tell you about the shanties and our no-running-water faucets and the sambos on the billboards and the fact that my family house comes equipped with an ever-reliable latrine. I'd tell you about my *abuelo* and his *campo* hands, how unhappy he is that I'm not sticking around, and I'd tell you about the street where I was born, Calle XXI, how it hasn't decided yet if it wants to be a slum or not and how it's been in this state of indecision for years.

But that would make it another kind of story, and I'm having enough trouble as it is with this one. You'll have to take my word for it. Santo Domingo is Santo Domingo. Let's pretend we all know what goes on there.

I must have been smoking dust, because I thought we were fine those first couple of days. Sure, staying locked up at my abuelo's house bored Magda to tears, she even said so—"I'm bored, Yunior"—but I'd warned her about the obligatory Visit with Abuelo. I thought she wouldn't mind; she's normally mad cool with viejitos. But she didn't say much to him. Just fidgeted in the heat and drank fifteen bottles of water. Point is, we're out of the capital and on a *guagua* to the interior before the second day had even begun. The landscapes were superfly—even though there was a drought on and the whole *campo,* even the houses, was covered in that red dust. There I was. Pointing out all the shit that had changed since the year before. The new Pizza Huts and Dunkin' Donuts and the little plastic bags of water the tigueritos were selling. Even kicked the historicals. This is where Trujillo and his Marine pals slaughtered the *gavilleros,* here's where the Jefe used to take his girls, here's where Balaguer sold his soul to the Devil. And Magda seemed to be enjoying herself. Nodded her head. Talked back a little.

What can I tell you? I thought we were on a positive vibe.

I guess when I look back there were signs. First off, Magda's not quiet. She's a talker, a fucking *boca,* and we used to have this thing where I would lift my hand and say, "Time out," and she would have to be quiet for at least two minutes, just so I could process some of the information she'd been spouting. She'd be embarrassed and chastened, but not so embarrassed and chastened that when I said, "O.K., time's up," she didn't launch right into it again.

Maybe it was my good mood. It was like the first time in weeks that I felt relaxed, that I wasn't acting like something was about to give at any moment. It bothered me that she insisted on reporting to her girls every night—like they were expecting me to kill her or something—but, fuck it, I still thought we were doing better than anytime before.

We were in this crazy budget hotel near the university. I was standing outside staring out at the Septentrionales and the blacked-out city when I heard her crying. I thought it was something serious, found the flashlight and fanned the light over her heat-swollen face. "Are you O.K., mami?"

She shook her head. "I don't want to be here."

"What do you mean?"

"What don't you understand? I. Don't. Want. To. Be. Here."

This was not the Magda I knew. The Magda I knew was super courteous. Knocked on a door before she opened it.

I almost shouted, "What is your fucking problem!" But I didn't. I ended up hugging and babying her and asking her what was wrong. She cried for a long time and then after a silence started talking. By then the lights had flickered back on. Turned out she didn't want to travel around like a hobo. "I thought we'd be on a beach," she said.

"We're going to be on a beach. The day after tomorrow."

"Can't we go now?"

What could I do? She was in her underwear, waiting for me to say something. So what jumped out of my mouth? "Baby, we'll do whatever you want." I called the hotel in La Romana, asked if we could come early, and the next morning I put us on an express guagua to the capital and then a second one to La Romana. I didn't say a fucking word to her and she didn't say nothing to me. She seemed tired and watched the world outside like maybe she was expecting it to speak to her.

By the middle of Day 3 of our All-Quisqueya Redemption Tour we were in an air-conditioned bungalow watching HBO. Exactly where I want to be when I'm in Santo Domingo. In a fucking resort. Magda was reading a book by a Trappist, in a better mood, I guess, and I was sitting on the edge of the bed, fingering my useless map.

I was thinking, For this I deserve something nice. Something physical. Me and Magda were pretty damn casual about sex, but since the breakup shit has gotten weird. First of all, it ain't regular like before. I'm lucky to score some once a week. I have to nudge her, start things up, or we won't fuck at all. And she plays like she doesn't want it, and sometimes she doesn't and then I have to cool it, but other times she does want it and I have to touch her pussy, which is my way of initiating things, of saying, "So, how about we kick it, mami?" And she'll turn her head, which is her way of saying, "I'm too proud to acquiesce openly to your animal desires, but if you continue to put your finger in me I won't stop you."

Today we started no problem, but then halfway through she said, "Wait, we shouldn't."

I wanted to know why.

She closed her eyes like she was embarrassed at herself. "Forget about it, " she said moving her hips under me. "Just forget about it."

I don't even want to tell you where we're at. We're in Casa de Campo. The Resort That Shame Forgot. The average asshole would love this place. It's the largest, wealthiest resort on the Island, which means it's a goddam fortress, walled away from everybody else. Guachimanes and peacocks and ambitious topiaries everywhere. Advertises itself in the States as its own country, and it might as well be. Has its own airport, thirty-six holes of golf, beaches so white they ache to be trampled, and the only Island Dominicans you're guaranteed to see are either caked up or changing your sheets. Let's just say my *abuelo* has never been here, and neither has yours. This is where the Garcías and the Colóns come to relax after a long month of oppressing the masses, where the tutumpotes can trade tips with their colleagues from abroad. Chill here too long and you'll be sure to have your ghetto pass revoked, no questions asked.

We wake up bright and early for the buffet, get served by cheerful women in Aunt Jemima costumes. I shit you not: these sisters even have to wear hankies on their heads. Magda is scratching out a couple of cards to her family. I want to talk about the day before, but when I bring it up she puts down her pen. Jams on her shades.

"I feel like you're pressuring me."

"How am I pressuring you?" I ask.

We get into one of those no-fun twenty-minute arguments, which the waiters keep interrupting by bringing over more orange juice and café, the two things this island has plenty of.

"I just want some space to myself every now and then. Every time I'm with you I have this sense that you want something from me."

"Time to yourself," I say. "What does that mean?"

"Like maybe once a day, you do one thing, I do another."

"Like when? Now?"

"It doesn't have to be now." She looks exasperated. "Why don't we just go down to the beach?"

As we walk over to the courtesy golf cart, I say, "I feel like you rejected my whole country, Magda."

"Don't be ridiculous." She drops one hand in my lap. "I just wanted to relax. What's wrong with that?"

The sun is blazing and the blue of the ocean is an overload on the brain. Casa de Campo has got beaches the way the rest of the island has got problems. These, though, have no merengue, no little kids, nobody trying to sell you chicharrones, and there's a massive melanin deficit in evidence. Every fifty feet there's at least one Eurofuck beached out on a towel like some scary pale monster that the sea's vomited up. They look like philosophy professors, like budget Foucaults, and too many of them are in the company of a dark-assed Dominican girl. I mean it, these girls can't be no more than sixteen, look *puro ingenio* to me. You can tell by their inability to communicate that these two didn't meet back in their Left Bank days.

Magda's rocking a dope Ochun-colored bikini that her girls helped her pick out so she could torture me, and I'm in these old ruined trunks that say "Sandy Hook Forever!" I'll admit it, with Magda half naked in public I'm feeling vulnerable and uneasy. I put my hand on her knee. "I just wish you'd say you love me."

"Yunior, please."

"Can you say you like me a lot?"

"Can you leave me alone? You're such a pestilence."

I let the sun stake me out to the sand. It's disheartening, me and Magda together. We don't look like a couple. When she smiles niggers ask her for her hand in marriage; when I smile folks check their wallets. Magda's been a star the whole time we've been here. You know how it is when you're on the Island and your girl's an octoroon. Brothers go apeshit. On buses, the machos were like, "Tu sí eres bella, muchacha." Every time I dip into the water for a swim, some Mediterranean Messenger of Love starts rapping to her. Of course, I'm not polite. "Why don't you beat it, pancho? We're on our honeymoon here." There's this one squid who's mad persistent, even sits down near us so he can impress her with the hair around his nipples, and instead of ignoring him she starts a conversation and it turns out he's Dominican, too, from Quisqueya Heights, an Assistant D.A. who loves his people. "Better I'm their prosecutor," he says. "At least I understand them." I'm thinking he sounds like the sort of nigger who in the old days used to lead bwana to the rest of us. After three minutes of him, I can't take it no more, and say, "Magda, stop talking to that asshole."

The Assistant D.A. startles. "I know you ain't talking to me," he says.

"Actually," I say, "I am."

"This is unbelievable." Magda gets to her feet and walks stiff-legged toward the water. She's got a half-moon of sand stuck to her butt. A total heartbreak.

Homeboy's saying something else to me, but I'm not listening. I already know what she'll say when she sits back down. "Time for you to do your thing and me to do mine."

That night I loiter around the pool and the local bar, Club Cacique, Magda nowhere to be found. I meet a Dominicana from West New York. Fly, of course, Trigueña, with the most outrageous perm this side of Dyckman. Lucy is her name. She's hanging out with three of her teen-age girl cousins. When she removes her robe to dive into the pool, I see a spiderweb of scars across her stomach. Tells me in Spanish, "I have family in La Romana, but I refuse to stay with them. No way. My uncle won't let any of us out of the house after dark. So I'd rather go broke and stay here than be locked in the prison."

I meet these two rich older dudes drinking cognac at the bar. Introduce themselves as the Vice-President and Bárbaro, his bodyguard. I must have the footprint of fresh disaster on my face. They listen to my troubles like they're a couple of capos and I'm talking murder. They commiserate. It's a thousand degrees out and the mosquitoes hum like they're about to inherit the earth, but both these cats are wearing expensive suits, and Bárbaro is even sporting a purple ascot. Once a soldier tried to saw open his neck and now he covers the scar. "I'm a modest man," he says.

I go off to phone the room. No Magda. I check with reception. No messages. I return to the bar and smile.

The Vice-President is a young brother, in his late thirties, and pretty cool for a chupabarrio. He advises me to find another woman. Make her bella and negra. I think, Cassandra.

The Vice-President waves his hand and shots of Barceló appear so fast you'd think it's science fiction.

"Jealousy is the best way to jump-start a relationship," the Vice-President says. "I learned that when I was a student at Syracuse. Dance with another woman, dance merengue with her, and see if your jeva's not roused to action."

"You mean roused to violence?"

"She hit you?"

"When I first told her. She smacked me right across the chops."

"Pero, hermano, why'd you tell her?" Bárbaro wants to know. "Why didn't you just deny it?"

"Compadre, she received a letter. It had evidence."

The Vice-President smiles fantastically and I can see why he's a vice-president. Later, when I get home, I'll tell my mother about this whole mess, and she'll tell me what this brother was the vice-president of.

"They only hit you," he says, "when they care."

"Amen," Bárbaro murmurs. "Amen."

All of Magda's friends say I cheated because I was Dominican, that all us Dominican men are dogs and can't be trusted. But it wasn't genetics; there were reasons. Causalities.

The truth is there ain't no relationship in the world that doesn't hit turbulence. Ours certainly did.

I was living in Brooklyn and she was with her folks in Jersey. We talked every day on the phone and on weekends we saw each other. Usually I went in. We were real Jersey, too: malls, the parents, movies, a lot of TV. After a year of us together, this was where we were at. Our relationship wasn't the sun, the moon, and the stars, but it wasn't bullshit, either. Especially not on Saturday mornings, over at my apartment, when she made us coffee campo style, straining it through the sock thing. Told her parents the night before she was staying over at Claribel's; they must have known where she was, but they never said shit. I'd sleep late and she'd read, scratching my back in slow arcs, and when I was ready to get up I would start kissing her until she would say, "God, Yunior, you're making me wet."

I wasn't unhappy and wasn't actively pursuing ass like some niggers. Sure, I checked out other females, even danced with them when I went out, but I wasn't keeping numbers or nothing.

Still, it's not like seeing somebody once a week doesn't cool shit out, because it does. Nothing you'd really notice until some new chick arrives at your job with a big chest and a smart mouth and she's like on you almost immediately, touching your pectorals, moaning about some moreno she's dating who's always treating her like shit, saying, "Black guys don't understand Spanish girls."

Cassandra. She organized the football pool and did crossword puzzles while she talked on the phone, and had a thing for denim skirts. We got into a habit of going to lunch and having the same conversation. I advised her to drop the moreno, she advised me to find a girlfriend who could fuck. First week of knowing her, I made the mistake of telling her that sex with Magda had never been topnotch.

"God, I feel sorry for you," Cassandra laughed. "At least Rupert gives me some Grade A dick."

The first night we did it—and it was good, too, she wasn't false advertising—I felt so lousy that I couldn't sleep, even though she was one of those sisters whose body fits next to you perfect. I was like, She knows, so I called Magda right from the bed and asked her if she was O.K.

"You sound strange," she said.

I remember Cassandra pressing the hot cleft of her pussy against my leg and me saying, "I just miss you."

Another day, and the only thing Magda has said is "Give me the lotion." Tonight the resort is throwing a party. All guests are invited. Attire's formal, but I don't have the clothes or the energy to dress up. Magda, though, has both. She pulls on these super-tight gold lamé pants and a matching halter that shows off her belly ring. Her hair is shiny and as dark as night and I can remember the first time I kissed those curls, asking her, "Where are the stars?" and she said, "They're a little lower, papi."

We both end up in front of the mirror. I'm in slacks and a wrinkled guayabera. She's applying her lipstick; I've always believed that the universe invented the color red solely for Latinas.

"We look good," she says.

It's true. My optimism is starting to come back. I'm thinking, This is the night for reconciliation. I put my arms around her, but she drops her bomb without blinking a fucking eye: tonight, she says, she needs space.

My arms drop.

"I knew you'd be pissed," she says.

"You're a real bitch, you know that."

"I didn't want to come here. You made me."

"If you didn't want to come, why didn't you have the fucking guts to say so?"

And on and on and on, until finally I just say, "Fuck this," and head out. I feel unmoored and don't have a clue of what comes next. This is the endgame, and instead of pulling out all the stops, instead of pongándome más chivo que un chivo, I'm feeling sorry for myself, como un parigüayo sin suerte. I'm thinking, I'm not a bad guy.

Club Cacique is jammed. I'm looking for Lucy. I find the Vice-President and Bárbaro instead. At the quiet end of the bar, they're drinking cognac and arguing about whether there are fifty-six Dominicans in the major leagues or fifty-seven. They clear out a space for me and clap me on the shoulder.

"This place is killing me," I say.

"How dramatic." The Vice-President reaches into his suit for his keys. He's wearing those Italian leather shoes that look like braided slippers. "Are you inclined to ride with us?"

"Sure," I say. "Why the fuck not?"

"I wish to show you the birthplace of our nation."

Before we leave I check out the crowd. Lucy has arrived. She's alone at the edge of the bar in a fly black dress. Smiles excitedly, lifts her arm, and I can see the dark stubbled spot in her armpit. She's got sweat patches over her outfit, and mosquito bites on her beautiful arms. I think, I should stay, but my legs carry me right out of the club.

We pile in a diplomat's black BMW. I'm in the back seat with Bárbaro; the Vice-President's up front driving. We leave Casa de Campo behind and the frenzy of La Romana, and soon everything starts smelling of processed cane. The roads are dark—I'm talking no fucking lights—and in our beams the bugs swarm like a Biblical plague. We're passing the cognac around. I'm with a vice-president, I figure what the fuck.

He's talking—about his time in upstate New York—but so is Bárbaro. The bodyguard's suit's rumpled and his hand shakes as he smokes his cigarettes. Some fucking bodyguard. He's telling me about his childhood in San Juan, near the border of Haiti. Liborio's country. "I wanted to be an engineer," he tells me. "I wanted to build schools and hospitals for the pueblo." I'm not really listening to him; I'm thinking about Magda, how I'll probably never taste her chocha again.

And then we're out of the car, stumbling up a slope, through bushes and guineo and bamboo, and the mosquitoes are chewing us up like we're the special of the day. Bárbaro's got a huge flashlight, a darkness obliterator. The Vice-President's cursing, tramping through the underbrush, saying, "It's around here somewhere. This is what I get for being in office so long." It's only then I notice that Bárbaro's holding a huge fucking machine gun and his hand ain't shaking no more. He isn't watching me or the Vice-President—he's listening. I'm not scared, but this is getting a little too freaky for me.

"What kind of gun is that?" I ask, by way of conversation.

"A P-90."

"What the fuck is that?"

"Something old made new."

Great, I'm thinking, a philosopher.

"It's here," the Vice-President says.

I creep over and see that he's standing over a hole in the ground. The earth is red. Bauxite. And the hole is blacker than any of us.

"This is the Cave of the Jagua," the Vice-President announces in a deep, respectful voice. "The birthplace of the Tainos."

I raise my eyebrow. "I thought they were South America."

"We're speaking mythically here."

Bárbaro points the light down the hole, but that doesn't improve anything.

"Would you like to see inside?" the Vice-President asks me.

I must have said yes, because Bárbaro gives me the flashlight and the two of them grab me by my ankles and lower me into the hole. All my coins fly out of my pockets. Bendiciones. I don't see much, just some odd colors on the eroded walls, and the Vice-President's calling down, "Isn't it beautiful?"

This is the perfect place for insight, for a person to become somebody better. The Vice-President probably saw his future self hanging in this darkness, bulldozing the poor out of their shanties, and Bárbaro, too—buying a concrete house for his mother, showing her how to work the air conditioner—but, me, all I can manage is a memory of the first time me and Magda talked. Back at Rutgers. We were waiting for an E bus together on George Street and she was wearing purple. All sorts of purple.

And that's when I know it's over. As soon as you start thinking about the beginning, it's the end.

I cry, and when they pull me up the Vice-President says, indignantly, "God, you don't have to be a pussy about it."

That must have been some serious Island voodoo: the ending I saw in the cave came true. The next day we went back to the United States. Five months later I got a letter from my ex-baby. I was dating someone new, but Magda's handwriting still blasted every molecule of air out of my lungs.

It turned out she was also going out with somebody else. A very nice guy she'd met. Dominican, like me.

But I'm getting ahead of myself. I need to finish by showing you what kind of fool I am.

When I returned to the bungalow that night, Magda was waiting up for me. Was packed, looked like she'd been bawling.

"I'm going home tomorrow," she said.

I sat down next to her. Took her hand. "This can work," I said. "All we have to do is try."

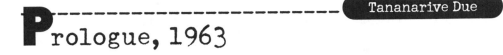

Prologue, 1963

Tananarive Due

HILTON WAS SEVEN WHEN HIS GRANDMOTHER DIED, AND IT WAS A BAD TIME. But it was worse when she died again.

Hilton called her Nana, but her real name was Eunice Kelly. She raised Hilton by herself in rural Florida, in Belle Glade, which was forty miles from Palm Beach's rich white folks who lived like characters in a storybook. They shared a two-room house with a rusty tin roof on a road named for Frederick Douglass. The road wasn't paved, and the stones hurt Hilton's tender feet whenever he walked barefoot. Douglass Road was bounded by tomato fields behind an old barbed wire fence Nana told him never to touch because he might get something she called tetanus, and they couldn't afford a doctor. Hilton knew they were poor, but he never felt deprived because he had everything he wanted. Even as young as he was, Hilton understood the difference.

Nana had been a migrant worker for years, so she had muscles like a man on her shoulders and forearms. Nana always saved her money, and she played the organ for pay at the church the monied blacks attended across town, so she hadn't harvested sugarcane or picked string beans alongside the Puerto Ricans and Jamaicans in a long time.

Hilton worshipped her. She was his whole world. He didn't know anything about his parents except that they were gone, and he didn't miss them. He didn't think it was fair to his friends that they had mamas and daddies instead of Nana.

Nana always said she didn't intend for Hilton to end up in the fields, that there were bigger things in store for him, so she sent him to school instead. She'd taught him to read before he ever walked through the doorway of the colored school a half mile away. And it was when he came home from school on a hot May afternoon that his life was changed forever.

He found Nana sprawled across her clean-swept kitchen floor, eyes closed, a white scarf wrapped around her head. She wasn't moving, and not a sound came from her. Hilton didn't panic just yet because Nana was old and sometimes fainted from heat when she tried to act younger, so he knelt beside her and shook her, calling her name.

That worked by itself sometimes. Otherwise, he'd need to find her salts. But when he touched her forearm, he drew his hand away with a cry. Even with the humidity in the little house and the steam from pots boiling over on top of the stove, their lids bouncing like angry demons, Nana's flesh felt as cold as just-drawn well water. As cold as December. He'd never touched a person who felt that way, and even as a child he knew only dead people turned cold like that.

Hilton stumbled to his feet and ran crying outside to find a grown-up who could help. He was only half seeing because of his tears, banging on door after door on Douglass Road, yelling through the screens, and finding no one home. After each door, his sobs rose higher and his throat closed up a little more tightly until he could barely breathe. It was as though everyone were simply gone now, and no one was left but him. He felt like he'd tried a hundred houses, and all he'd found was barking dogs. The barking and running made him feel dizzy. He could hardly catch his breath any more, like he would die himself.

In truth, there were only six houses on Douglass Road. The last belonged to Zeke Higgs, a Korean War veteran angry with middle age, angry with white folks, and whom no child with sense would bother on any other day because he kept a switch by his door. Zeke appeared like a shadow behind his screen when Hilton came pounding and crying, "Nana's dead. Come help Nana." Zeke scooped Hilton under his arm and ran to the house.

When he got home, Hilton's childhood flew from him. Nana was no longer lying lifeless on the kitchen floor. She was standing over the kitchen stove, stirring pots, and the first thing she said was: "I wondered where you'd run off to, boy." She looked at Zeke's face and nodded at him, then she fixed her eyes on Hilton. "I'm 'fraid Nana's made a mess of supper, Hilton. Just a mess."

"You all right, Mrs. Kelly?" Zeke asked, studying her face. Hilton did the same. She was perspiring, and her cheeks were redder than usual underneath her thin cocoa-colored skin.

"Just fine. May have had a fainting spell is all. I hope Hilton didn't send you into a fright."

Zeke mumbled something about how it wasn't a bother, although he was annoyed. Hilton barely noticed Zeke slip back out of the house because his eyes were on Nana. His tiny hand still tingled from the memory of the cold flesh he'd touched, as unhuman as meat from the butcher. Nana's smiles and gentle manner frightened him in a way he didn't understand. He stood watching her, his tears still flowing.

Nana glanced at him several times over her shoulder while she tried to scrape burned stew from the bottom of her good iron saucepan. The scraping sounded grating and insistent to Hilton. For the first time in his life, Hilton wondered if Nana might ever do anything to try to hurt him.

Finally, Nana said, "You go on out of the way now, Hilton. Supper's late today. Don't give me that face now, pumpkin. Nana's not going to leave you."

Hilton wanted to take Nana's fingers and squeeze them, to see if the cold was still there, but she hadn't reached out to him and he wouldn't dare touch her if she did. Hilton felt something had changed, maybe forever. He went outside to play with a three-wheeled wagon he'd found, but he wasn't really playing. He was sitting on the front stoop, rocking the wagon back and forth in front of him, but he barely knew where he was or what he was doing. And, as he'd sensed, things were different after that day he found Nana on the kitchen floor: She began to wake up crying out from bad dreams. He watched her get out of bed for a glass of water in the moonlight, her nightgown so soaked with sweat he could see all the lines of her body as though she wore no clothes. Many nights Hilton went to sleep alone because Nana would stay up humming and writing hymns on the porch. She said she did this because she couldn't sleep. Hilton knew the truth, that she didn't want to. Maybe she had met the boogeyman.

It was fine with Hilton to be alone, because it was hard for him to sleep with Nana there. Her sleep breathing sounded different to him, the breaths longer and drawn farther and farther apart until he was sure the next one wasn't coming, but it always did. Once, he counted a minute between her breaths. He tried to hold his own breath that long, but he couldn't.

Nana was confused all the time now. She would get cross with him more easily than before, and she'd smack his backside for no good reason. One day Hilton was smacked when he didn't bring home cubes of sugar he knew she had never asked him to bring.

This went on for nearly a year, and Hilton began to hate her. He was afraid of her for reasons he didn't know or want to know. She'd never hurt him, not really, and on the rare occasions he touched her now her skin felt warm, but his memory of that day in the kitchen was too strong.

All of this changed the day Hilton took his first ride on a Greyhound, sitting at the back, of course, when Nana and their Belle Glade cousins took him to Miami for the Kelly-James family reunion. Twice before, Nana had stayed home and his women cousins drove him to the reunions to meet his kin, but she decided to go this year. The smells coming from Nana's picnic basket and the wonder of the flat, endless Florida landscape through the bus window were enough to make Hilton forget his fear.

The reunion was at Virginia Key Beach, and Hilton had never seen anyplace like it. This was a beach in Miami for only colored people, and folks of all shapes and shades had flocked there that day. Hilton had become a good swimmer in canals near Nana's house in Belle Glade, but he'd never seen so much sand and the trees and a green ocean stretching to forever. He'd always been told the ocean was blue, so the sparkling green ribbons of current were a wonder to him. Anything could happen on a day like today.

No one warned Hilton about the undertow, and he wouldn't have understood if they had, but Nana did tell him he could only go in the water if he didn't go far; this would have been enough if Hilton had minded like he should have. Nana, who was helping the ladies set up picnic tables, pointed to the orange buoy floating out in the water and said he could go only halfway there. And Hilton said "Yes, Nana" and ran splashing into the water knowing that he would go exactly where he wanted because in the water he would be free.

He swam easily past the midway point to the buoy, and he could see from here that it was cracked and the glowing paint was old. He wanted to get a closer look at it, maybe grab it and tread water and gaze back at all those brown bodies on the sand. And it was here that he met up with the undertow.

It was friendly at first. He felt as though the water had closed a grip around his tiny kicking legs and dunked him beneath the surface like a doughnut then spat him back up a few feet from where he started. Hilton coughed and smiled, splashing with his arms. He didn't know the water could do that by itself. It was like taking a ride.

The buoy was now farther than it was before the ocean played with him. It was off to his left now when it had been straight ahead. As Hilton waited to see if he could feel those swirling currents beneath him again, he heard splinters of Nana's voice in the wind, calling from the beach: "Hilton, you get back here, boy! You hear me? Get back here."

So the ocean was not free after all, Hilton realized. He'd better do as he was told, or he wouldn't get any coconut cake or peach cobbler, if it wasn't too late for that already. He began sure strokes back toward the shore.

The current still wanted to play, and this time it was angry Hilton was trying to leave so soon. He felt the cold grip seize his waist and hold his legs still. He was so started he gasped a big breath of air, just in time to be plunged into the belly of the ocean, tumbled upside down and then up again, with water pounding all around his ears in a roar. Hilton tried to kick and stroke, but he didn't know which way was up or down and all he could see was the water all around him specked with the tiny ocean life. Even in his panic, Hilton knew not to open his mouth, but his lungs were starting to hurt and the tumbling was never-ending. Hilton believed he was being swept to the very bottom of the ocean, or out to sea as far as the ship he'd seen passing earlier. Frantically, he flailed his arms.

He didn't hear Nana shout out from where she stood at the shore, but he'd hear the story told many times later. There was no lifeguard that day, but there were plenty of Kelly and James men who followed Nana, who stripped herself of her dress and ran into the water. The woman hadn't been swimming in years, but her limbs didn't fail her this one time she needed to glide across the water. The men followed the old woman into the sea.

Hilton felt he couldn't hold his breath anymore, and the water mocked him all around. It filled his ears, his nose, and finally his mouth, and his muscles began to fail him. It was then, just as he believed his entire fifty-pound body would fill with water, that he felt an arm around his waist. He fought the arm at first, thinking it was another current, but the grip was firm and pulled him up, up, up, until he could see light and Nana's weary, determined face. That was all he saw, because he went limp then.

He would hear the rest from others who told him in gentle ways about Chariots to the Everlasting and that sort of thing. One of the James men had been swimming closely behind Nana, and she passed Hilton to his arms. Then she simply stopped swimming, they said. Said maybe she just gave out. Nana's head began to sink below the water, and just as one of the Kelly men reached to try to take her arm, the current she'd pulled Hilton from took her instead. The man carrying Hilton could only swim against it with all his might toward the shore. Many people almost drowned that day.

When Hilton's senses came back to him and he was lying on the beach, caked in gritty sand, all that was left of Nana was her good flowered dress, damp and crumpled at the water's edge.

So what the gifted old folks, the seers, often say is true:

Sometimes the dead go unburied.

The Emperor's Babe

Bernardine Evaristo

Claudia is a Black woman living in roman London who has an affair with the Roman Emperor Septimius Severus, who was an African.

My Legionarius

I like you two ways
either take off your crown of laurels
drop your purple robes
to the floor
and come to me naked
as a man

or dress up.

Claudia, 211 AD

Real soldiers wear tunics under armour,
my emperor does without.

Stands before me, metal bands tied
with leather straps over a bull's chest, iron wings.

protect shoulders from flying sabres—
I finger your second skin, my lord, cold, polished,

my reflection cut into strips,
your tawny trunks, perfumed with juniper oil.

hard with squeezing the damp flanks of stallions,
dagger, gripped for my forging.

Are you ready for war, soldier?
Today a centurion's crested helmet and visor,

curve of dramatic bristle, like an equus,
you roll your head, lightly brush my inner thighs.

leaving a trail of goosebumps, and giggles,
then trace the tip of your sword down the centre.

of my torso, dare I breathe? Let your route
map a thin red line?

Silver goblets of burgundy vino by my bedside,
to toast the theatre of war.

Close your eyes, you command, a freezing blade
on my flamed cheek, hand around my neck.

I am your hostage.
I am dying. I am dying of your dulcet conquest.

You make my temples drip into my ears,
whisper obscenities to me,

plant blue and purple flowers
on my barren landscape;

here, bite my sore lips, besiege me,
battery-ram my forted gateway, you archer.

beseige me, you stone-slinger, trumpeter,
give it to me, futuo me, futuo me, my actor—

emperor, forget those stinking back stabbers
in the Senate in Rome, those shit-stirrers,

perfidious smilers, has-beens, cunning
poisoners, ruthless young guns, arse-lickers,

mendacious gits, wannabes—and your wife,
who won't play make-believe, I know.

I hold the pumping cheeks that rule the world, I do.
Ditch the empire on your back, Semptimus,

it is crushing my carriage, the weight of a soldier
trained to march thirty kilometers a day,

marching for centuries over roads
made with the gravel of skulls, legions forming

an impregnable walking tortoiseshell,
on the battle-field, on your back, making

the whole damned world Roman.
Vidi, Vici, Veni. Take off your victory.

I am vanquished already, I can't fight you,
just stab me to death, again and again,

stab me to death, soldier.

Christopher John Farley

the missionary position

IRAQUIS, THREE OF THEM, WITH RIFLES. I DON'T KNOW HOW THEY WERE ABLE to see us and shoot at us from so far away when we couldn't even see them. Sojourner and I both tried to tell them we were journalists, but nothing doing. None of them understood English. Or Latin, for that matter. One of them spoke French but both got frustrated pretty quickly trying to converse with me. So they tied Sojourner and me up and threw us in the back seat of their jeep. Two of the Iraqis got in the front seat, the third Iraqi spent about seven seconds hot-wiring my jeep, and then drove away laughing.

"This is like virtual reality," said Sojourner.

The Iraqi soldier in the front seat threatened her with the butt of his gun and said something that probably translated as "No fucking talking."

We were off.

The Iraqi soldier in the passenger's seat, the one that knew French, may not have known how to speak English, but, as it turned out, Frenchie knew some English song lyrics. He was rustling through our supplies, and when he saw Sojourner's Walkman, his eyes lit up. He opened the jeep's glove compartment and pulled out a beat-up cassette tape and put it in the Walkman. Then he detached the headset and turned the sound up to full volume. He began to hum to himself, then he turned around and started to poke Sojourner in the cheeks.

I think he wants you to sing along, I said.

"I don't know this song. I don't like this song."

It's a great song. Just mumble. You think he's really clear on the lyrics? No one knows the lyrics to this song.

"You first. Then I'll join in."

Load all your guns and kill your friend, I sang. Something something it's all pretend . . .

"With the whites out, it's outrageous," Frenchie joined in at the chorus. "That big pink sow, it's contagious . . ."

Sojourner didn't join in. She just looked out into the desert.

If war came, if Bush actually launched an attack, we were driving through a landscape of dead men.

The media had been beating the drums about Saddam's impregnable defenses, the acres of minefields, the miles of barbed wire, the ditches filled with burning oil, the unassailable bunkers, the hundreds of thousands of battle-hardened troops, proven warriors who had been seasoned in Iraq's vicious decade-long war with Iran. People said Iraq had the fourth-largest army in the world. But, as someone once said, after the U.S.A., the Soviet Union, and China, there's a real drop-off. During the war, the U.S. government and its hand puppet, the U.S. media, said that there were over 500,000 Iraqi troops in Kuwait. After the war was over, and the government had gotten all the mileage they needed from propaganda statistics, the House Armed Services Committee would revise that figure to a relatively paltry 183,000.

And these were troops only in the loosest possible sense of the word. These were scared kids playing with guns. Many of the Iraqi soldiers couldn't have been older than thirteen. I also saw old men, with potbellies, white hair, and humped backs. I saw kids and old men digging holes in the ground to hide in. They weren't constructing high-tech, ten-foot-thick concrete bunkers. What they were making weren't even foxholes really. Just holes.

A couple times, when the jeep slowed, Iraqi troops crowded around. Not to mock the captured Americans, but with their hands held out, asking, begging for food. As if Sojourner and I, tied up, our possessions already stolen by our captors, could do anything to ease their suffering. They were dressed in rags, and many of them were shoeless. After several hours of driving, Frenchie got tired of his fellow soldiers gawking and he got bored with our periodic alternative rock sing-alongs. He opened the trunk to the jeep and put Sojourner in first and threw me on top of her. Bang. He had closed the trunk. We could see nothing.

"This is gonna make a terrific story," I heard Sojourner say in the nothingness. "That is, if they don't shoot us or something."

I didn't know how much time had gone by. I had been dozing and waking for what might have been hours or minutes.

The jeep had stopped. I could hear voices. Iraqi voices. It sounded like an argument.

Two shots sounded. Then another. One more. I could feel Sojourner dig her face into my shoulder.

Suddenly the trunk opened. Rough hands grabbed me and shoved me into another trunk.

Sojourner! I yelled.

I didn't want us to be separated. Here I was, all tied up in the trunk of an Iraqi jeep and I was being chivalrous.

A few seconds later, Sojourner was thrown on top of me.

"Hey, you," she said. "You didn't think I'd leave you, did you, honey?"

The trunk was slammed shut. Nothingness. The second jeep drove off.

I was groggy when I woke up again. The trunk opened. I was pulled out. Soldiers were leading me hurriedly through the lobby of a strange hotel, into an elevator.

I looked around, tried to get my bearings. Sojourner was there too, a soldier on either side of her.

Tenth floor. The elevator doors opened. We were led out and taken to a room. A soldier opened the door and we were both thrown through the door onto the floor. The door slammed. I heard a series of locks click into place.

Every muscle was sore. I felt like I had been beaten up.

Are you okay? I said.

"I'm alive. At least for now," said Sojourner, struggling to her feet. She began to search through the hotel room.

What are you looking for?

I surveyed the place from my supine position, it was a medium-sized hotel room.

There were two single beds. I climbed on one of the beds and lay there. No windows in the joint. A TV set.

"There's hotel stationery in the drawers, believe it or not," said Sojourner.

Stationery?

"Yeah. Says we're in the Baghdad Howard Johnson's."

We're in Iraq? And Howard Johnson's has a hotel in Baghdad?

"Yes, looks like we're in Iraq. I don't think this is a real Howard Johnson's. Some sort of knockoff franchise."

She threw herself face-first onto the other bed.

We were both too tired to feel despair. By Sojourner's reckoning, the UN deadline authorizing the use of force was today. If we were in Iraqi hands when and if the shooting began, we'd be in a lot of trouble. We still didn't know who had taken us captive. Were they official Iraqi troops? Some sort of freelance group within the Army?

I stood up, suddenly too worked up to rest. My head felt all screwed up from the jeep exhaust fumes that had seeped into the trunk.

I clicked on the TV.

MTV was on. They were playing the video for that all-star tribute to the troops, the one where a gathering of morally irrelevant rock stars (Voices That Care) refuse to endorse the war but somehow manage to support the troops. What would Immanuel Kant think?

I turned the channel. CNN! Check this out, I said. We got cable! We got CNN here!

"Great. So we can watch the war from here. We could have done that in Dhahran. Hell, we could have done that in Washington."

CNN faded in and out, making it hard to hear and see what was going on. I didn't know how this place was managing to get the signal, maybe a satellite dish or something. But they were getting it. From the TV, we confirmed that today was January 15 and hostilities had yet to begin. Maybe Saddam and Bush and the world would come to their respective senses.

"Let's hope so," said Sojourner. "'Cause we're at ground zero here."

We didn't talk much the next day. We just tried to recover, sort things out. There was a trickle of water out of the faucet in the bathroom, so the place was livable. Hell, it was probably a little cleaner than my old group house. At lunchtime, a soldier brought us crackers, cheese, and something that seemed like it could have been some sort of meat in a past life. We made some perfunctory demands to be released, to be allowed to contact representatives of the American government, but, of course, we were ignored. We began to eat.

What do you think of this war anyways? I think I can guess, but I don't think I've ever asked you. Is it a Just War?

"It's not a Just War," said Sojourner, plopping a hunk of cheese on a cracker. "It's just war. That's all it ever is."

Explosions were rocking the hotel. Like thunder and earthquakes. The bombing had begun. Sojourner and I sat on one of the beds and held hands.

The door to our room burst open. Iraqi troops. This was it. They were going to execute us.

They hustled us up several flights of stairs as the booming continued.

I'm glad I met you, Sojourner, I said. I don't know what else I can say.

"Oh, just stuff it," she said. "We're not going to die."

The troops led us up to the roof and left us there.

Baghdad at night. A city under siege.

On the roof, the city was spread out all around Sojourner and me and the sky stretched out over our heads. The sky was full of light and deafening noise. We should have lain down on the roof and prayed for our lives. But we just stood there, on the roof, watching the sky and the city explode. I could hear the roar of invisible planes, bombers, passing far overhead, the supersonic booms as they roared by. There were screams from the streets below, some far away, some near. Something, a bomb, falling debris, it was hard to tell in the pyrotechnic confusion of the night, but something hit near to the hotel and Sojourner and I were thrown down to our hands and knees from the shock of the noise and the force of the blast. I looked up to see white and yellow and orange and red flames and smoke dancing to the sky. There were more explosions overhead, matched by the boom and crack of gunfire from the ground, from desperate, over-matched Iraqi gunners, their tracer bullets lacing necklaces of light across the sky. How could anything so horrible be so beautiful? There was a ghastly loveliness to the scene because even on the roof, even here in a city under attack, we were somehow apart; we were spectators. I watched the terrible white explosions along the horizons, the destruction of homes or military facilities. I watched it all with a sense of grim awe, but my fear had drained out of me. It felt like it was happening to someone else's country, someone else's city. It was someone else's war.

As the air attack subsided, Iraqi troops returned to take Sojourner and me back to our room. No one said anything, in English or in Arabic. There was a sense, between captors and captives, that something new, something different, now both united us and set us apart. Sojourner and I had become witnesses to the unstoppable force that Iraq would have to endure; we had become potential empathizers. But we were also representatives of the country that had rained fire on Baghdad that very night.

Back in our hotel room, Sojourner turned on CNN. It was barely audible, dimly visible. We struggled to make it out through a storm of interference.

President Bush was speaking. "Five months ago, Saddam Hussein started this cruel war against Kuwait. Tonight, the battle has been joined. We will not fail."

The picture blurred and fuzzed, and when it came back, Saddam was on the screen, speaking through a translator.

"The big confrontation has begun in the mother of all battles between right and wrong," said Saddam. "Iraq will never surrender."

The siege continued. Every night, the bombers would come. Explosions, some near, some far off, some across the street, others at the outskirts of the city. We began to see less and less of the Iraqi soldiers who were holding us. We didn't know if they had been killed, reassigned, or were merely holed up in some secret bomb shelter in the bowels of the Baghdad Howard Johnson's. The bombing, the isolation, the fact that we weren't being fed regularly, the shortage of toilet tissue, the absence of razors and shaving cream, the lack of tampons for Sojourner, began to play on our nerves. We had come here to report a story and we were trapped in the dead center of it. We were reporters and we couldn't report.

On TV we heard and saw images of Israel under attack. Scud missiles blasting through Tel Aviv. Civilian deaths. Reporters in gas masks. One NBC reporter seemed to be physically ducking missiles, crouching and bobbing his head whenever Scud-like roars interrupted his on-air chatter. I thought about Peter and his Jewish fiancée. I wondered where he was, if he was under fire or back safe and sound in the States.

"I just keep telling myself that we're not any more trapped here than we were back in Dhahran," said Sojourner. "Just look at the TV coverage. Where are the bodies? There's a war going on and we haven't seen any dead bodies on TV. Those damn military flacks and press-pool bureaucrats have a stranglehold on the coverage."

She was right. Even on a TV with bleary, in-and-out reception, this was a neat and tidy war, with all the crusts carefully cut off. From what we could hear, commentators were talking about a Nintendo war, super-accurate smart bombs, precision attacks against military targets. From what we saw on the roof, from what we could feel in our little room, the walls shaking, the city shuddering, this was not a precision war, a neat and tucked-in and folded little war.

Probably no war ever was. When it was all over, at California's Bohemian Grove, a secret all-male nature resort where rich and powerful professedly anti-gay right-wingers engaged in intriguingly homoerotic bonding rituals, a former Navy Secretary boasted that 200,000 Iraqis were killed in the Gulf conflict. According to one early Greenpeace report, 90,000 of the deceased were Iraqi civilians. As time passed, the body counts would rise. The U.S.A. dropped over 88,000 tons of bombs on Iraq, the equivalent of seven Hiroshimas, ten pounds of explosives for every Iraqi citizen. Less than 7 percent were so-called smart bombs; the other 93 percent were old-fashioned stupid bombs, idiot bombs, droolingly dumb bombs that took a few shop classes in high school, dropped out, and had an on-target accuracy rate of just 25 percent.

"This war is about jobs," said the TV. General Pinpoint was talking to reporters.

"Whose job?" sneered Sojourner. "His?"

Wait a second, you were fat in high school?

"I was fat up until senior year in college. The summer before my senior year I finally started to exercise, eat right, all that stuff. I think it was smoking that really put me over the top. Every time I want a Twinkie now, I just light up."

What a health plan. Can I ask how heavy you once were?

"Big. Fat. I was a heavy woman. We're talking banana splits, candied apples, Snickers bars, peanut butter and jelly sandwiches smothered in syrup—all of that after a glass of Slimfast and a sensible meal. Honey, I was heavy. I'd walk up a flight of stairs and be out of breath. Looking back, I can't believe I lived that way."

But before, you were talking about how these guys would always ask you out.

"Senior year, they did. Before that, nothing."

Yeah, I see myself being rich at some point, I told her. It's not the money is that important to me. It's just that money brings a sense of comfort, leisure time, allows you to concentrate on the things you feel are really important. I guess what gets me is looking around and seeing some of the people who are rich. An easy example is Donald Trump. He has a couple billion dollars. I'm sorry, but Donald Trump is not a couple billion dollars smarter than me. Some guys in my Naverton class have already made millions. These people aren't especially creative or smart. But they're rich as Midas.

"I got the same feeling when I was at *National Now!*" Sojourner said. "I kept doing interviews with these incredibly famous celebrities, and after a while, I'd think: They're not so hot. They didn't have some special insight into truth or humanity that I didn't have. But they were still a hundred times more successful. It was like there was some secret to making it, some secret that nobody told me or was about to tell me. So when the chance came to go to the *Post,* I took it. It felt like upward movement and I needed that."

"I did an internship at the *Chicago Tribune* during college," said Sojourner. "It was after freshman year. God, I don't know if I want to tell this. Anyways, there was this one editor there who used to spank female employees. He was big, old, greasy-sandwich-eating white man. Balding, sloppy. He'd pick on girls who were vulnerable. Young interns. New female employees who were looking to make it in journalism and didn't want any trouble along the way. I found out a lot of this later. Anyways, he'd wait until his victim was having a really bad day, or until they were in tears about deadline pressure, and then he'd invite them into his office, close the door, put them over his knee, and spank them. Sometimes he'd pull down their panties and give them a bare-bottom spanking. He got off on it or something."

Didn't people report this clown?

"Well, he ended up retiring under a cloud, but he was like sixty when that happened. It's hard to go up against a guy like that. It's hard enough to be a woman in a male-dominated newsroom, much less having to admit that some editor spanked your bare fanny. It's humiliating. I remember, on the day my mother called to say that my father had died, this editor summoned me into his office. I didn't know any of this stuff about him then. So I went in there and he started to lick off my tears. I was paralyzed. Three seconds later, I was facedown on his desk, and he had ripped off my panties and was swatting my ass with his open palm. That shit *hurt.* Then I notice the guy's got his dick out and he was getting ready to mount me from behind. Something in me woke up. My reflexes took over—I jumped to my feet, gave him a spinning kung fu kick in the balls, and ran out. But I never told anyone at the paper about the incident. That always really bugged me. I told myself I'd never keep something like that to myself again."

We were both silent. There was the sound of gunfire, miles away.

"Some good came of this though. At the *Post,* an editor once stood behind me on an escalator and sniffed between my legs. I did everything to get him fired, and management, a bunch of white guys named George, just wouldn't fire him. But he did end up leaving the paper. I don't know where he is now. Hell, I hope. I feel good that I at least saw *that* one through."

"The hardest thing is being alone. Alone when some guy slaps your ass, alone when you just want to have someone to run an idea by. Don't get me wrong—I'm down with all that whole sisters-doing-for-themselves, Angela Davis trip. But I see these white couples, these yuppie working couples, together, tight, making it, earning that dollar—and I want that, that unit, that duo. There's a comforting strength and sweetness there. But I also know, to get that, we have to go at it in a different way."

Marcuse touched on that in one of his books, I forget which one. Success is defined as becoming a leader in society, an integral respected part. But since society is hostile to black people in general, success in mainstream terms necessitates a kind of self-destruction. Golfing with the boss. Marrying a white woman. It's sort of the Spike Lee syndrome. To be truly successful he had to create a whole new paradigm. If he had done things the Hollywood way, he'd be directing shit like *Rambo in Africa*.

So we talked and talked, and after some time passed we refocused on our situation. The TV was dead. Only one lightbulb in the room still worked. Nobody had fed us in two days. Before the TV blew there had been some talk about a ground war. We couldn't sit around this room and wait for that to happen; besides, we might be used as bargaining chips or human shields or something. We had to escape.

I was pretty certain the cabinet in our bathroom connected to the cabinet in the bathroom in the suite next door. When I knocked on the back of the cabinet, there was a hollow sound, like there wasn't a solid wall behind the wood. Because this was a hotel and not a prison, after all, there was a chance that in the adjacent room the door to the hallway wouldn't be locked.

Sojourner suspected that there was a bomb shelter beneath the hotel. During air raids, we never heard voices or footsteps in the hall, so breaking out during the next big air raid would be an ideal time. It wasn't that great a plan, but at least it was a plan.

The Iraqis brought us dinner that night. It was almost like a farewell diner—bread and grape juice. They hadn't fed us that well in days.

After dinner, such as it was, it just happened.

We were both on the floor, done with our meal, and I ran my hands through Sojourner's hair, her dreadlocks. I had wanted to do that for the longest time. She kissed my forearm. Her lips were soft and warm and full. She kissed up my arms and found my mouth. We both stood up, still kissing, and then we embraced for a few seconds, swaying back and forth, as if we were on an empty dance floor. She drew me back, onto the bed, onto her. Soon our clothes were off, discarded, and I was kissing down the length of her body. I felt light-headed, distant, like I was watching this scene from above. I turned around, kneeling atop her, my face buried in her lap, and she took me into her mouth. I could feel the slickness of her tongue, the hot juices of her mouth as she licked and sucked. I could also hear the rush and the boom of supersonic aircraft. The sound of explosions far away, getting closer. All the lights were out in the room, and suddenly all the sound went out as well. I felt like I was floating. I was reaching down to her breasts and tracing circles around her nipples with my fingers and something blew up near the hotel, and suddenly I couldn't feel anything at all, not the war, not Sojourner, not myself. I was somewhere without sensation, without noise. Everything was a void. Was I dreaming? Had I fallen asleep? These vague questions orbited around me and then floated off into the nothingness and I suddenly felt like I was coming, and I was back on the bed again, my face between Sojourner's legs, her mouth around me and I thought I heard her voice, faintly, somewhere, moaning in pleasure or maybe it was just some lost soul out there and the room suddenly vanished and I was lost too.

"The food was drugged."

I thought I heard Sojourner's voice. I was thinking about those monks. Escher's monks. *Ascending and Descending.* I opened my eyes. It was daytime. We were out in the desert. I was lying on a bed of sand.

What?

"They drugged us and dumped us somewhere," said Sojourner, who was standing above me. "I have no idea why. But we're out here someplace. Maybe the Iraqis were listening through the walls, knew more English than we thought, and ditched us before we tried to escape."

I had a pounding headache. I said: I'm all fucked up here. I gotta rest.

"We have to move. I've seen planes coming from that direction, so that's the direction we're heading."

We walked and walked along a wide dirt road. In the distance we saw plumes of smoke twisting up from the route ahead. As we approached, we realized the smoke was coming from columns and columns of burning, smoldering tanks and trucks, cars and buses. We didn't know it then, but we would learn later that this was the Highway of Death.

The road, jam-packed with wreckage, stretched for some sixty miles. Sixty miles of gnarled steel, skeleton cars, and dead bodies, tens of thousands of dead bodies, Iraqi soldiers, Palestinian refugees, men, women, children. On February 25, 1991, at 2:00 a.m. local time, Baghdad radio announced that Iraq's foreign minister had accepted a Soviet-brokered cease-fire and that Iraqi troops were to be withdrawn from Kuwait and would reoccupy the positions they held before the invasion. The Gulf War should have been over right there but it wasn't. President Bush released a statement: "Iraqi units are continuing to fight. We continue to prosecute the war."

But the Iraqi withdrawal, according to Kuwaiti eyewitnesses, was already underway. Iraqi vehicles and Palestinian refugees were streaming down the road, the Highway of Death, heading out of Kuwait and into Iraq.

At about midnight, the U.S. bombing of retreating troops began. The American planes attacked both ends of the Iraqi convoy, trapping everything in between. Drivers and passengers began to abandon their vehicles, but there was nowhere to go. The air was so thick with attacking planes that they were having difficulty finding space in the sky. One U.S. pilot would say later it was like "shooting fish in a barrel."

And here were Sojourner and I, walking along the Highway of Death. The air stank with the stench of burning gas and rotting, flame-roasted human flesh. Whole buses had been pounded into the ground, as if by giant hammers. A tank lay on its side, spurting flames. A car had been ripped open like a sardine can, a half dozen bodies scattered nearby. The horror was so extensive, so incredible, it was impossible to catalogue. It was a vehicular and human holocaust. Extending from the spot where we were walking, past the horizon, past where we could see. We saw miles and miles of blackened bodies, shattered limbs, melted windshields, stinking burning tires, smashed skulls, splattered flesh, a child cut in two by a sharp piece of metal, a woman whitened by fire, her skull stripped of flesh by tongues of flames, her jaw open, caught in some sort of awful scream or laugh.

Sojourner was in a rage. I never heard her spew theorics with the fury she did that day on that road. Young black males are viewed as the criminal prototype in American society, she said. Over one-quarter of black men in their twenties are in jail, awaiting trial, or are wanted by the police. That's not to say they did anything, that's just to say the justice system has them locked up, or is trying to. American society is about locking up black people. It costs almost six figures a year to keep someone incarcerated in a big-city jail. If you give the average black man a college scholarship of that size, he'll for damn sure keep out of trouble. You give the average brother a job with a salary of that size, and he'll pay society back and then some with his labor. Yet America still chooses to spend more to incarcerate than to educate.

So black men are the villains, Sojourner continued. They lock them up and call them an "endangered species," like they're beasts in a zoo. But when it comes to true viciousness, to committing real crimes, nothing beats white men. Nothing. The Holocaust. White men did it. Slavery. White men ran it. The genocide of the indigenous people of North America. White men were the architects. The destruction of the rain forests, the ozone. The demands of white capitalism are causing it. The Savings and Loan banking crisis, which will cost the U.S.A. hundreds of billions of dollars to fix. White men. Ain't no black people running the S&L's, hell, we can't even get a loan to open up a damn lemonade stand. And no group of black criminals has ever done anything in the history of the United States that cost hundreds of billions of dollars to fix. Never. Yet when people picture criminals, they still picture the black man.

She was righteous, but wrong, I thought. This thing was more complex than melanin. General Pinpoint, a black man, was part of all this after all, even if Bush was ultimately making the decisions, Pinpoint had to have been at all the meetings. That's how they kept us down in slave times; one of us would always be on the massa's side, yes-bossin' his ideas, telling him what they were whispering about in the slave quarters. But maybe Pinpoint had fooled us all. Maybe it was possible, as a black man in America, to become so powerful within the system that you transcended it. To become such an integral part of the establishment that its interests actually became your own. I struggled with these thoughts. Maybe Pinpoint had his reasons. Surely some wars were justified. The Civil War. World War II. But now Sojourner was talking again.

This was nothing but a national drive-by, she said, quoting a rapper. How could sixty miles of slaughter be justified? Did America understand what had gone on here? Did the press give them the opportunity to comprehend it? Twenty-four of the nation's twenty-five largest dailies came out in favor of Bush's Persian Gulf policies, she said. The increasing corporatization and consolidation of the newspaper industry made this sort of consensus possible. Later I would learn that a study by the Center for Media and Public affairs—a right-wing group no less—found that ABC's assessment of the U.S. military during the Gulf War was 61 percent positive; NBC and CBS were 100 percent positive. We were hoodwinked, we were sucker-punched, we were set up to support this conflict, Sojourner said. War is essential to the maintenance of capitalism, to the long-term success of the companies that run the U.S. media. War breaks down the family unit—two-thirds of the homeless population is made up of veterans. War teaches society to view its citizens not as individuals with sacred rights but as units, as soldiers, temps. To accept the mass deaths that come with war, we have to desensitize ourselves to life, Sojourner said. Violent crimes always rise dramatically after wars. This is all in the corporate interest. Capitalism is easy, capitalism is fun, when people are just movable parts, cogs in the machine, violent, homeless, willing to work at any job for any wages they are offered. And the effects of American aggression are long-lasting. Months later, Sojourner's words were still echoing in my mind. After the war, U.S. homeless shelters began to see an influx of Persian Gulf veterans. A few years after the Gulf conflict, UNICEF estimated that 500,000 Iraqi children under the age of five had died because of the war and war-related ailments. The last thing I saw on the road was the corpse of a child with a yellow flower sprouting from its forehead.

Morning. The Highway of Death was behind us. Sojourner and I were still walking. We saw a jeep riding fast along a nearby road. Someone in the jeep was screaming at us.

"Is that English?"

Hard to tell.

The jeep was still heading down the road toward us.

Maybe we should head toward the road, I said.

"It could be an Iraqi jeep," said Sojourner.

The jeep was closer now. I couldn't make out what was being yelled, but I was pretty certain now it was English, so Sojourner and I began running toward it.

The jeep had stopped. The man in it was waving his arms and shouting something, but he was too far away for us to hear clearly.

"Urine's running in a brine seal!" the man seemed to shout.

What was that about seals? Well, now was no time to worry about marine life. We kept running toward the jeep. I was tired, bone tired, but I felt a burst of energy. Rescue. Finally. Sojourner was running with a big smile on her face. She was running and doing a little half-skip like a schoolgirl. I started to laugh for joy. Then I started to cough because my throat felt so raw.

"You're running in a minefield!" the man yelled.

What?

"A mine—"

The world went white.

My Son, My Heart, My Life

John R. Keene

SANDALWOOD, JAIME WHISPERS TO HIMSELF, RECALLING THE VENDOR WHO had sold Tony and him the three little vials of this scented oil and the five foil packets of incense. He had a makeshift stall outside the bus terminal in Dudley Square. Wearing an embroidered red and black tarboosh and an immaculately white T-shirt, on which had been silk-screened in exquisite calligraphics the simple phrase, "Life is the finest art," he was probably in his early twenties—and *handsome,* Jaime thought now—though hard living had so weathered his face and hands, his gestures, that he looked much older. Beside Tony, however, the vendor had appeared almost a boy. His thin, dark fingertips, sallowed by the oils, the incense, cigarettes, perhaps even the plate of curried goat that sat at the edge of the display table, fanned slowly over the array of offerings, patchouli, lavender, musk, Rose of Sharon, anise, something called "Love," something else called "Power," which Jaime had not noticed before. Which one *you* like? *Sandalwood,* Tony had snapped out without deliberation: It was the only scent he had ever worn.

—What*ever* you do, baby, don't forget your algebra notebook! Jaime's mother's call rings from the kitchen, where she is preparing breakfast for his two younger sisters, Tatiana and Tasha. Having awoken early as always with his older sister, Teresita, Jaime has already wolfed down a banana and a piece of white bread with strawberry jelly for breakfast, before his mother and the girls rise, to stay out of their way. Sometimes he will drink a cup of coffee and chat with Teresita—whose position at the nearby springs manufacturing plant occasions *her* early mornings—but not this morning. He has spent the entire time since he woke, ate, and showered in reading over his poem—*his poem!*—which his teacher and classmates, everyone, including perhaps even his mother, will all be talking about for weeks to come, and checking his equations. After proofing his Spanish against the dictionary, he struggled over a seemingly unsolvable "xy," and came up with the only answer that allowed the equation to work: This, he tells himself, calls for a celebration, a game.

—*Sí,* Marni, I promised you I wasn't gonna forget it again. That stupid notebook, Jaime grumbles, why can't he forget it altogether! He sits up on his bed, which he has just prepared to his mother's former specifications (since Tony's death, she no longer has to scold him every morning, he now makes it instinctively), and opens the palm-size, amber-colored vial, one of the few personal effects of Tony's that neither his mother nor Tony's girlfriend had hoarded as her own. As he had observed Tony do every morning for the last few years, he places his index finger over the opening, upends it, then daubs the sweet, masculine fragrance under both ears; again, then lightly across his collarbone; one last time, a straight line from the point where his Adam's apple has begun to appear to the soft point of his chin.

This fragrance, Jaime realizes, almost smiling now, almost tearing as it takes root and blossoms in the loam of his consciousness, still lingers upon the surface of everything in the apartment; this matted wool comforter on which he sits; on the top and corners of the particleboard dresser that he and Tony had shared; upon even the mildewed plastic anti-slip stars plastering the bottom of the bathtub in which they had stood huddled together when they were younger, all redolent as though permanently coated. Today, for good luck's sake, it will trail him as well, throughout the morning, on the way to school, as he stands before his class and reads his poem.

Done, he shakes his head as Tony would, wipes his eyes—no one had seen him cry at or after the funeral and will not now—then hides the vial under the stack of underpants in the top drawer of the dresser that has become his alone. As he stands before the open drawer—how they had fought over where their clothes would go! How he, Jaime, had *always* lost and wished that he could claim the entire thing as his own!—he feels like a blackboard from which everything has been erased, on which anything can be written. Tony. Alone, he drops onto the bed, tries to think of the day before him, the bus ride, school . . . his poem. His poem, which Tony would have read with approval, maybe even awe, as he had done with the other poems, the drawings, the stories Jaime would write, sometimes off the top of his head. . . .

Silent now, he can hear beneath the floorboards his uncle, Narciso, rearranging the merchandise on the shelves of the bodega he and his aunt Marisol own and operate. Above him, their apartment slumbers. Jaime is glad to have been occupied and to not have had to help out this morning. Often his mother will send him downstairs after she has awakened the girls and begun to get them ready and before his bus arrives, to seek something to do, to help his uncle and aunt out, as if she owes them something for living here, especially since his father left, as if his sacrifice is her part of the bargain. Sometimes he aids in moving pieces of meat around the cold-locker and shelving newly arrived canned and boxed goods when his uncle asks him to. Undoubtedly there will be some bubble-gum box to be refilled, some soup cans to be shifted around or transformed into a stable pyramid, some moldy bread to be turned over so that the nearby loaves will mask it. This morning, however, her mind has latched completely on to that notebook.

Outside this room, music, laughter, the cacophony of glass against metal, voices, the television against the hour's stillness.

Tony, Jaime reminds himself, had never helped out in the store. He had gone simply from mornings and afternoons before the television and Nintendo games to the streets and a crew of similarly minded boys and couriering, which meant that Uncle Narciso and Aunt Marisol never wanted him around; his presence, at least in their eyes, and that of his boys, his *chicos,* usually spelt trouble. It was an out to which Jaime had not recourse: *Send Jaime down to help me out,* Uncle Narciso was always saying, *so I can make a man out of him, keep him out of trouble.* Jaime's mother only too eagerly assented.

Hoisting his backpack onto the bed, Jaime pulls out his Spanish poem to read once more, which jogs his memory: they had had to wait until nearly the end of the school to write poems, and why? Because of the "turdles," as he and Vinh, his classmate and best and only friend have often laughed to themselves at lunch, though neither would dare call the mass of their classmates, even the girls, this nickname face-to-face. Despite the fact that they have occasionally had to write a paragraph, or even a short essay, they are mainly doing multiple-choice quizzes, nothing more advanced, more creative, even though this class is supposedly accelerated. As usual Mrs. Donovan has given them nine regular words and a bonus word, and this time, unlike before, she has allowed them to create a *poem* of at least one hundred words from these. *Too simple,* Vinh had cracked under his breath, against the general groans of the class; Jaime had nodded, though he disagreed. As the lines now sing inside his head, he is sure this poem will merit an A, as will Vinh's, which he has not yet seen. More of the other kids, even those whose first language is Spanish, will end up with B's or C's, whether they hand in homework or not, since Mrs. Donovan is unwilling to embarrass anyone, even the most "slow-dropping" of the turdles, with anything lower. They had to wait almost the entire year, Jaime sighs, but now he will show them.

The words read, in this order: *hijo* (son), *parar* (to stop), *pedir* (to ask for), *cada* (each), *corozón* (heart), *broma* (joke), *hallar* (to come across), *sangre* (blood), *anochecer* (nightfall), and the bonus word *fugaz* (brief).

Such words! Vinh had said after fourth period that Mrs. Donovan had torn up a Spanish dictionary and picked the entries one by one out of a hat, but Jaime is convinced that she pulls some of them out of whatever she has been reading at home, some novel, some book of poetry, because there are always strange or unusual words, like *fugaz*, that are nowhere to be found in their Spanish book. He has never heard anyone, not his mother, nor Uncle Narciso nor Aunt Marisol, nor any of the Spanish speakers in the neighborhood or at church, nor even his grandmother, uncles, aunts, or cousins in Puerto Rico, ever use this bonus word *fugaz* even once in conversation—he and his sisters speak only English regularly, as did Tony—which for him is the giveaway. This word, he thinks, she has selected just for me.

As a result, he wrote (with the translation beneath it):

> *Cada dia al anochecer*
> *voy esa cama y pienso*
> *sobre mi hermano muerto,*
> *Antonia José Barrett.*
> *Fue mi hermano solo*
> *y tuvo quince años y medio.*
> *Yo halle la sangre y su cuerpo*
> *que estaba acostado*
> *sobre la acera como un G.I. Joe.*
> *Durante el funeral mi Mami preguntó*
> *al Dios, "¿Por qué, God, por qué*
> *mi hijo, mi corazón, mi vida, mi Tony*
> *por qué my baby ahora?" Mi tio*
> *Narciso dijo toda la iglesia,*
> *"¿O Dios, mi amigos, quando la muerte*
> *va parar?" Nadie is respondió,*
> *Desde entonce hay una cosa que yo sé:*
> *En mi barrio vivir es muy fugaz*
> *y el futuro estará una broma grande.*

> Every day at nighttime
> I see that bed and I think
> about my dead brother,
> Antonio José Barrett.
> He was my only brother
> and was fifteen and a half years old.
> I found the blood and his body
> lying on the sidewalk like a G.I. Joe.
> During the funeral my mother asked
> God, "How come, God, how come
> my son, my heart, my life, my Tony
> why my baby now?" My uncle

Narciso said to the whole church,
"Oh God, my friends, when
is the dying going to end?"
No one answered him.
Since then there is one thing I know:
in my neighborhood living is too brief
and the future is a great big joke.

One hundred and eleven words he counts, and he has used the past tense correctly every time; he has verified this twice this morning against his Spanish book. No misspellings that he can spot, and even some words they have not yet learned, but which he has gathered from regular conversations or his own reading: Mrs. Donovan will *have* to give him an A! When he recites it, she will comment on the rhymes in Spanish, on the flow, on the *feeling:* in her eyes there is nothing *he can do wrong.*

What else is there for today? For social studies he has his notes for his presentation on a country in West Africa. He has elected to report on Senegal, where he imagines his father's (and mother's, maybe) ancestors came from, instead of Cape Verde, his other option. Jaime shuffles his note cards in order: there are seven. He makes sure they are all there, then stores them in his backpack on top of his Spanish notebook. He has no homework (when do they ever have homework?) for any of his other classes, except algebra. He glances again at the figures cleanly printed in that notebook and on the loose-leaf, and on which he spent two hours last night, and at least one this morning.

His sisters are clamoring in the kitchen, he can hear; his mother never tells them to shut up anymore, or even slaps Tasha when she talks back as she had always done before. Jaime never talked back in the first place, though she would still sometimes slap him for whatever reason (because he would not clean his room, because he sulked all through dinner, because he was switching and batting his eyes, because he reminded her too much of *that black man who had left her*) but now she is always asking him what he is doing before she gets home, how he is progressing in school, what he is *feeling.* My son. He always lies and tells her nothing beyond the barest outline of what happens to him each day, because he is convinced she would not understand anyway, or care; she has never understood a thing about him before in the previous thirteen and a half years of his life, nor cared, and she understood even less about Tony, whose name was always on her lips, though no longer. *Tony.* My heart. Nor about any of his sisters, except Tatiana, the *true* baby, who seems to gain her care and concern though how long will *this* last, Jaime wonders, how long? My life.

Why is it so quiet downstairs? He descends the stairwell quietly and crosses the narrow hallway, through the double-hinged door, into the store. Quiet, empty. His uncle Narciso has obviously gone into the storeroom down in the cellar, or perhaps out into the small cold-locker in back, and Aunt Marisol has not yet come down. The shade on the front door is still drawn, and the triple-bolts have not been unlocked, nor the gratings raised and furled.

Jaime leans back against the wall of candy racks behind the cash register and brushes, curly, raven bangs back from his forehead. In the mirror of Plexiglas surrounding the register area before him, he chances upon his reflection: the spit and image of his father—the eyes two new backgammon chits; the nose the face's anchor, an inverted mahogany cross; the lips as pale and swollen as two undercooked link sausages—whose actual face he has not seen in two years, he finds himself *almost* handsome, though not like Tony, who more resembled their mother, and was thin, lean, wiry. He, Jaime, is still too plump, "*muy gordo*." Though no one calls him "Porcelito" anymore, since he has lost some weight over the last few months, his first cousin Niño, who had been a year ahead of him at school until he flunked out and was placed in Catholic school, has not stopped calling him "Gordon" every chance he can. At least he no longer has to hear that nickname at school, or Niño's other gem, "Chunky and Chinky," for when he and Vinh were together. Being "*gordo*," however, no one has ever expected him to be cool or popular or have a girlfriend or have *juice*. Those expectations fell upon Tony, who satisfied them amply, which allowed Jaime thus to be the inverse, his reverse: the "smart," "quiet," "artistic" one, the little chub who spends all his hours in his room drawing, reading, writing, devising imaginary scenarios and games by and for himself. . . .

Since Tony's death, however, not even Niño or his mother calls him those *other* names, those names that had lacerated Jaime in their truth and viciousness, that had left him in tears when not driving him to fights he could not win, though no one, not even his mother, had ever dared utter them in Tony's presence. That Tony would never tolerate, Jaime remembers, nor had he ever called Jaime those names, not even while playing, though he must have known. . . . Now, since Tony failed to father a little boy, he, Jaime, has become his mother's *only* son, the only *man* in her life . . . the thought sometimes makes him shudder, as now.

Mi hijo, mi corazón, mi vida.

Still by himself, he empties into his mouth an already-opened box of Lemon-Heads which was sitting under the register and probably belonged to Aunt Marisol, who is always munching on something sweet. At his feet he notices about six chewing-gum wrappers, which means that Aunt Marisol, or Lisa, a woman neighbor who fills in at night, worked the closing shift: Uncle Narciso would never tolerate trash lying anywhere on this floor, so he has not yet been back behind here. Jaime gathers them up and, as he is tossing them in the wastebasket, notices the Browning Hi-Power 9mm semiautomatic, clipless, poking out from the lower shelf. Who left this thing out? Catching no light the barrel does not flash as it normally would; Jaime's thoughts recoil from the cold metal. He has held this handgun before, and had held Tony's many times; with his toe he pushes it back onto the shelf so that it is no longer visible.

Before his uncle returns, he pulls the shade to peep out the front door. A small throng of people is collecting at the bus stop several feet down from the front of the store. This group of about seven people, all of them neighbors, mostly work downtown or in Cambridge, and there is a woman Jaime recognizes as one of the teacher's aides in the special education program now housed at the back of his school. Hardly anyone is milling around, as usual, so frozen are they to their spots, even at this time of year. Within seconds the bus, already half-full, screeches up. These commuters, as is customary, are pushing and shoving each other out of the way to board. Jaime's mother always says that the Orientals push hardest because they have to claim seats first or they will never be able to muscle their way into one, that Portuguese will give up their seats if you look tired enough because they are a sad people, that the Irish usually smell like whiskey or beer so you will want to give them your seat, that the West Indians do not care how tired you look if you do not look West Indian, and that black men never give up their seats for an older woman, unless it's their mother. But Jaime knows these kernels of maternal wisdom do not hold; he was once knocked out of his seat by another Puerto Rican, and Tony always gave up his seat for an older or pregnant woman, if she was black or Puerto Rican or Cape Verdean. Truth is, everyone, as Jaime knows, can be rude, mercenary, self-interested.

—*¿Ai, Negrito, qué tal?* Jaime feels the thick, spatulate fingers softly digging into his shoulders, the protuberant stomach pressing against his slope of his shoulder blades. It is his uncle Narciso. He tenses. His uncle's breath, warm and somewhat stale, wets the hairs on the back of his neck, as his hand slips like a scarf around Jaime's neck bone.

—*Nada, Tio.* Jaime turns around to face his uncle's sloe eyes, a virtual mirror image of his mother, in male form. Of medium height—Jaime has never been able to guess heights on sight, but Narciso is taller than Tony, who was five-eight—and, like his mother, slender, except for the belly, Jaime comes nearly to his uncle's forehead. He backs away, to prevent his uncle's mustache from scouring *his* forehead like a small hairbrush.

—You didn't come down this morning. *Tio* was waiting on you. His uncle grins, exposing a row of teeth like kernels of Indian corn.

—I was working on my algebra. I'm *failing,* you know. Jaime stops against the counter. I told you that, *Tio.* He knows his uncle is not listening, as usual.

—*Tio* was *waiting* on you. I had a lot for you to do this morning, didn't your mother let you know? He approaches Jaime, both his hands squirming beneath his bloody apron like two small, trapped birds.

—I was just checking to make sure the bus was on schedule. Jaime rolls his eyes, darting out of his uncle's path, towards an aisle. I'm gonna be late if I don't hurry up, *Tio.*

—You don't got any time left to help *Tio* this morning! I was *waiting* on you. Jaime cants his head around the corner to read the clock: he has only about fifteen or twenty minutes before his bus arrives. His uncle sweeps a lock off Jaime's forehead, reaches down, and tightly embraces him. Like always, he is mouthing something onto Jaime's earlobe, his neck, but Jaime has long since stopped paying any attention; he just goes slack and waits for his uncle to let go. In the back of the room, beyond the door to both the apartments and the cold-locker, he can now hear someone, probably his aunt Marisol, scuffling toward the storeroom in the cellar. Abruptly his uncle releases him, picks up the cash box at his feet, and slips behind the door that forms a clear, though somewhat rickety, protective partition around the register.

—I'll help out tomorrow morning, *Tio,* I promise, Jaime yells out, before bounding out of the store and upstairs so as not to be late. When he reaches the top of the stairs, he hears his mother saying:

—And I told Mr. Morris to call me if you was skipping class or not doing your homework, Jaime, because I don't want you failing math again. Had she heard him come upstairs or had she just automatically launched into this? he asks himself. His mother, splendid in her nurse's aide's whites, emerges from her bedroom, and now stands before him in the narrow strait of hallway between the rooms. She is frowning, blankly.

—Did you *hear* me?

—Yeah, Marni, I heard you. I'm not gonna skip algebra any more, and I *did* my homework, just like Mr. Morris wants. Do you want to see it? Do you want to see my *poem?* As though by default she shakes her head no; she seldom looks at any of his homework, though she will sometimes check to make sure that he has at least packed the notebook in with the rest of his school materials, and she never looks at his other things, his other notebooks, full of his writings and drawings, which he now keeps hidden behind his bed in a small bag that had belonged to Tony. Most of these he has shown to no one except Vinh, who draws pictures of his own, keeps similar notebooks. Vinh's consist mostly of action figures like the X-Men or the Fantastic Four, which he copies from the comic books he collects (Jaime collected them, too, at one point but stopped when his mother got laid off the last time), but he always changes all the eyes and hair so that they become Vietnamese and usually much more muscular than they appeared originally. Jaime's, all drawn from his storehouse of memories and fantasy, usually consist of people he has seen on the bus or on the street or in the bodega, or at Downtown Crossing or in Central Square when he slips there on Saturdays or sometimes after school, and occasionally he even draws pictures of Tony, and rarely his father, though never other members of his family. Other renderings, completely from his imagination and of a different, vivid, and more explicit nature, he reveals to no one. So much no one knows about him, he realizes, now that Tony is gone.

As they stand there wordlessly, Jaime places one hand on his hip and licks the palm of his free hand, flips back his bangs coquettishly, bats his eyes: this once provoked a reproach from his mother, but no longer. She stands before him, saying nothing, bemused as if she were looking upon someone she had never seen before in life, when his youngest sister, Tatiana, just barely five, materializes, her jumper misbuttoned and her socks mismatched, her ponytails uncoiling from beneath her barrettes. She drops in loud sobs to the floor at his mother's feet. Jaime flees into his bedroom.

A glance at the Teenage Mutant Ninja Turtle clock—had he really been *so* into them?—alerts him that he has only about five minutes to spare. He checks his backpack to ensure everything is there, including that stupid algebra notebook. He even makes sure that he has the loose-leaf of arithmetic work tucked into the front inside cover of the notebook; Mr. Morris likes to receive the homework this way, so that he can verify the answers in the notebook by the preparatory work on the loose-leaf. Only for such a white turdle, Jaime notes, does everything have to be so complicated. On top of this, Mr. Morris is always pushing Jaime to do better cornering him after class, stopping him in the hallways, calling his mother *at home!—he could easily be an A student, Ms. Barrett*—but all those variables and commutative laws tend to drive Jaime to distraction; he likes Spanish and Language Arts and social studies much better, since they afford him the freedom to order things—words, worlds, his life—to his satisfaction. Still, he has to admit that there is no reason he should *fail* algebra, because if he does, it will probably spell the death of his chances of getting into the Latin Academy, where he, with Vinh, has vowed to be, come ninth grade.

Below the clock's green-diode glimmer, Jaime gathers up the change off the small desk he had shared with Tony, and funnels it into his pockets. Maybe he will buy a pack of doughnuts from Uncle Narciso to eat on the way, or maybe he will save the coins for a tonic after school. *Tony.* It is so quiet these mornings, and evenings, too, now that Tony is no longer around, and yet Jaime no longer has to keep quiet when he wakes for fear of awaking Tony, who would be lightly snoring by now after having come in just around dawn from a long night out, probably dealing. This last year and a half Jaime would occasionally find a few dollar bills, mostly ones but occasionally a five or ten, lying in his house shoes when, still half-asleep, he climbed out of bed to go to the bathroom in the morning, and he did not even have to look across the room to realize these signified Tony was home and installed under the covers. Jaime had been saving these small gifts, which totaled about fifty-six dollars after a few withdrawals, and now keeps them tied up in a sock in the back of his drawer, for a future emergency. He has told no one about this, not even Vinh.

As though it were a talisman, he fingers his sock-bank, re-stashing it carefully, then slips on a green, plastic wristband that he had won at the West Indian Festival last summer, before zipping up his backpack and heading downstairs.

His mother had said nothing about his yellow T-shirt, his baggy red shorts, or his matching red hightop sneakers when she saw him earlier. Teresita would surely say he looked like a clown, but she has left for work already. No one would even notice the wristband, he bets, or what the colors together represent. His keys: he pats the three of them, which hang from an extra-long shoelace beneath his shirt down into his briefs.

—Marni, I'm going. Where is she?

—Jaime? In the kitchen. He pokes his head in the doorway.

—You be good and be careful, okay?

—I will. She has Tasha in one hand and Tatiana in the other. The two girls are dressed like twins, even though Tasha is three years older. His mother is obviously on her way out as well.

—Jaime, you got your algebra notebook? He nods yes, tapping his backpack where he thinks it is tucked away—*because I just want you to do well, to not end up like your brother, to get out of all of this*—then gives her a quick kiss on the cheek.

As he runs down the stairs, he can hear the *I love you* trailing his steps.

Through the bodega, where his aunt Marisol is now planted behind the register, chewing on a stick of gum, past his uncle Narciso, who is lifting the last of the outside grates and larks out a goodbye in Spanish and English, onto the already hot, uneven, tar-gummed pavement: the bus has not yet arrived. Jaime crosses the street to his bus stop.

Only one other person is waiting for this bus: a young man, Corey Fuentes, who had dated Jaime's sister Teresita. As Jaime looks up and smiles, Corey sneers in reply, then lights up his Newport. Corey is out of work, has been for about a year, Jaime has heard, but this morning he is wearing alligator loafers, nice pressed gray slacks, an ironed white shirt, and holds what appears to be a brand-new clip-on tie in his free hand, which leads Jaime to suppose that he is going in for a job interview (very unlikely), traveling somewhere to meet his parole officer or some new criminal associate (more likely but still unlikely), or heading downtown to make a court date (most likely). Jaime does not dare inquire.

The spring heat has not yet fired the streets, and a breeze, almost gauzy in texture, carries pieces of trash and some seedlings toward the horizon. The other bodega, owned by the Cape Verdeans, stands behind and cater-corner from them, somewhat dilapidated on the outside, with its warped grates, yellowed newspapered curtains, and its faded beer signs, unopened. To their right across the street in the distance, down near the wrought-iron fence that garters the Social Services building, a corpulent straw-haired white man, whom Jaime recognizes as Father Peter O'Hanlon, is chatting with a woman employee, unknown. So what if Fr. Pete was removed as assistant pastor of St. Stephen Protomartyr's for spending so much time with the gangs? Tony, Jaime remembers him saying, is not a lost cause. He will surely be in the bodega gossiping with Aunt Marisol and sipping a Coke, laced with rum, in about twenty minutes.

—Where *is* that fucking bus? Corey hisses, checking his wrist graced not by a watch, but by an ornate gold bracelet.

He leans backbreakingly against the bus-stop sign pole. He is staring off into the distance, envisioning what? Jaime wonders. What sort of plea bargain his attorney will arrange? Whether his new girlfriend will show up to escort him back home, on his own recognizance? What the penalty will be for "uttering checks and credit cards" for the third time within one calendar year? Jaime is familiar with quite a few of the court careers of other people, such as Tony, and Teresita's current boyfriend, Eric, and her ex-boyfriend Andray, so that it is not too difficult for him to figure out what this "small-time booster," as Tony had labeled him, might be facing.

As he ponders Corey's fate, his eyes trace an invisible line from the slicked, raven crown of hair to the full, pink lips to the satiny brown neck bone, which a white under-shirt almost completely conceals from view. He has dreamt about Corey before. Jaime's eyes linger on that downward slope and the cloven pectorals below, imagining them supple beneath his grasping fingers like the earth beneath the saplings that his Earth Science class spent all last month planting. Corey's skinny arms pale in comparison to the knottier arms and the ample chest of the guy who sometimes drives Jaime's bus route—Jerome—whose name he has inscribed on the inside back cover of the note-book he remembered to bring with him today. For a while Jaime feared his mother might see this name and interrogate him about it, but then he realized she would not touch anything of his, save perhaps that algebra notebook, under any circumstances, unless *he* were dead.

Turning and catching Jaime in his spell of appreciation, Corey glowers, murmuring, —You li'l *freak!* As Jaime looks away, unembarrassed, Fr. Pete lumbers his way up the street.

Another breeze is bearing up a fresh offering of debris as their bus scuds up to the curb. Corey boards first, tamping out his cigarette and tossing it over his shoulder so that it bounces off Jaime's arm. Jaime says nothing, and hops aboard after him, perfunctorily flashing his pass as he moves into the aisle. The bus is mostly vacant, but before he can grab a seat, the bus driver has pulled sharply away into the street, stomping down on the accelerator, thus hurtling Jaime headfirst towards the back. Obviously, this bus driver is *not* Jerome, who has a velvet touch on the pedal—Jaime visually verifies this: No! Oh, well—but instead Randall, who from time to time works this morning route but more often drives the Columbia Road evening route, which Jaime has taken on those occasions when he had to drop off something at his sister Tita's job.

For a moment he debates whether he should sit up near Randall, whom he has never really paid much attention to, or sit in the back of the bus and write in his notebook: *¿Qué va hancer?* He decides to perch himself on the last forward-facing seat on the right side of the bus, near no one; Corey is sitting near most of the other passengers in the forward-facing seats near the front, an unlit cigarette poling from his lips. Jaime thinks about reading his poem, how his classmates will all stare in amazement, how Mrs. Donovan will nod her head appreciatively with theirs, how afterwards she will tell him that this is proof of what she knows he can do. He will show her his other poems, some of his drawings soon, she will write a recommendation for him, he will get into Boston Latin, he will do so well that he confirms Tony's grandest predictions. He tries not to think about algebra at all.

Randall's driving this morning is certainly a lot more jerky than Jerome's. Extracting his writing notebook and a pencil, he sketches Randall's face, and then Jerome's face and torso, which he can summon from memory as sharply as if he were staring right at them, before writing beneath both pictures: "AM: RANDALL—Almost turdle of the bus drivers-iron foot. No Jerome this morning. Ran-dull instead . . . will have to settle for second best . . . not the best start, but I will make do!! Fugaz. What is the game for today? Tony."

The bus slithers along its usual path, people board, Jaime looks up periodically to see if any of them catch his eye: a few girls who were once classmates of Teresita's or Tony's and who are now cradling babies in their arms or in strollers; a few teenagers his age, none at his middle school, boisterous, listening to hip-hop or dance-hall blaring from headset speakers, their backpacks rattling with drug paraphernalia, perhaps, or forties; an old woman, dressed in a filthy white blouse and yellow shorts, a pink hairnet framing a face drooping like melting brown wax; another older woman, white and in an appliquéd blue frock, yammering excitedly to herself; an older man, maybe forty-five, somewhere Uncle Narciso's age, in a red and white striped polo shirt, brown buckled loafers. He slides into the row of seats across from Jaime and smiles. Jaime acknowledges him, almost absently.

Light is now flooding the bus. May sun. The fragrances of sandalwood, a cologne that must be Brut and newsprint commingle in Jaime's consciousness: he turns slowly towards the man who has a full head of graying wavy hair and an almost lacquered black mustache. The man pulls out the sports section of his newspaper and starts reading the back-page write-up of last night's big boxing match, which Teresita and Eric and his mother had been watching on pay-per-view. *My hurt.* Jaime had instead been printing out his index cards, and had telephoned Vinh with a question about one of the languages in Senegal, which Vinh of course knew about. They had spoken for about twenty minutes. *My love.* Vinh was in the midst of doing what he spends all of his free time doing, like Jaime: reading or drawing.

Jaime examines the man more carefully. He must be still in his forties, because although gray salts his hair, his face does not look *that* old. Skinny almost, he has a complexion not unlike Jaime's own, the color of an unshelled almond; and thick lips, like Jaime's father, like Corey, like Jaime. Through the small triangle created by the placket of his shirt, Jaime can almost see the hairless chest. It looks like it may be toned; the man cranes slightly forward, obscuring Jaime's view. Jaime watches him study the scores, and draws a picture of him. What does he do all day, who is he, where is he going? Jaime writes these questions down, in order. If I were myself, but like Tony: What would I do? What would he do? As Jaime scribbles, the bus stops, people board, de-board.

When Jaime looks out of the bus window for a change, he sees a fourteen-year-old girl he knows, named Mercedes, whom they call Dita, in front of the liquor store, step-ping out of a fire-engine-red Samurai with two boys, from a gang that hangs out at Four Corners. He bows his head so that he can watch her unobserved, though it is unlikely she even notices the bus's presence. She had wanted to have Tony's baby so badly, just a year ago, but since Tony's death, Jaime has rarely seen her. One of the men wraps his arm around Dita's waist, eases his hand down the side of her leg, slides it over onto her behind . . .

Jaime turns back to the man, who has been staring at him.

The man gets up and slides in next to Jaime, who pushes his knapsack against the window. *What does he do all day, who is he, where is he going?*

—Hhhiiih . . . , Jaime says, his voice breathy and tremulous, like a vibrating reed.

—Hey, the man replies. How you doing this morning? His voice is pure ice.

—Fine.

—Tha's good, the man says, baring his straight, yellowing smile. Jaime spots the wedding band on his left ring finger, which, like all the others, is long, unwrinkled, and spoonlike. Maybe he is younger than Uncle Narciso. Setting the paper in his lap, the man slowly examines the riders on the bus, his head angling and turning as if it were a movie camera. Jaime searches the bus for anyone who might call him out. Corey is still up front, but he is now conversing intensely with one of the young mothers. The man appears to mime placing his hand on Jaime's knee, but does not. He simply looks down at Jaime and smiles. The teeth gleam like butter-covered knives. Jaime can feel his underarms beginning to moisten. *My son.*

—Where you headed? the man asks.

—Wha's your name? Jaime answers.

—I like that, 'What's your name?' . . . My name is Vernon, what's yours? He lays a hand on the seatback next to Jaime's shoulders. Jaime licks his palms and sweeps back his curls; this man's name cannot *really* be Vernon, Jaime tells himself; he must be play-ing a game as well. He looks out into the traffic alongside the bus: cars snake past on their way to wherever.

—Tony.

—Tony . . . Where you headed, Tony?

—Cuffe School . . . Where you headed?

—Nowhere, I got the day off . . .

Vernon purses his lips, then asks,—Tony, why don't we get off at the next stop? I'll walk you partway there. We can talk. He smiles again, as the fingers, like the petals of some exquisite brown flower, flutter out upon the seatback. Jaime inhales deeply, his mind swirling with questions: What *is* happening? Who is this man? Where are they going? Is he going to miss *algebra?* Because Mr. Morris will surely telephone his mother and admonish him in front of the class. The bus halts at the stop, and they both slip out through the back door. As the bus pulls away, Jaime reminds himself that although he has never taken a game *this far*, Vernon seems decent enough, and Jaime decides that, no matter what, he will *not* act as he normally would.

The sidewalk flares with the morning heat. Sun glints off every metal surface in daz-zling spars, forcing Jaime to put on the pair of sunglasses he keeps in the front pocket of his backpack. Vernon dons a pair, too; where had he stored them? At the green light, they cross the street together, walking quickly, almost in tandem, then walk several blocks up before turning into a side street, where they pause. Jaime's hands, like Vernon's, are pocketed. He scans the main street to see if anyone he knows is passing by. Not a soul.

Pointing in the direction of the projects, to their left, Vernon tells Jaime,—Now, if I'm correct, Cuffe is about six blocks that way. Jaime wrinkles his lips several times, then nods in agreement.

Running his hand over the lip of his pants, Vernon continues,—Cuffe School, Cuffe School . . . I remember when the Cuffe School first became the Cuffe School. Used to be Wendell Phillips School when my kids went there, then they decided to change the name. Always do. Can't leave well enough alone. Can't say I actually know who Cuffe is, you know . . . or Wendell Phillips for that matter. I guess you kids don't care who it's named after, though, hunh?

All this talk annoys Jaime, who says nervously,—No, no, nobody cares. He brushes the hair back from his forehead: Vernon is plumper than Jaime thought, or perhaps it is just that he has a gut like Uncle Narciso; he begins to wonder if he should not just run off, end this game right now, wait till after school, another day . . . What time is it anyway? he wonders.

—Turn around so I can see how *handsome* you are. You are so *handsome,* you know? Jaime follows the instructions, revolving in a gradual circle. Vernon now looks older than he did at first, on the bus; the sunlight colors in the slight sagging of his chin, the almost slack quality of the skin on his arms, like a sheet of crumpled brown plastic. He is definitely older than *Tio.*

—How old are you, Tony?

—How old are *you,* Vernon?

—There you go again, answering my question with another question. My age doesn't matter, Tony, but I'm forty-nine. Now, how old are you?

Jaime throws his head back, closes his eyes, says casually,—I'm sixteen and a half. I got kept back a few times and I look young for my age.

Beginning to laugh, Vernon inspects Jaime up and down.—Now, Tony, I ain't no *fool.* I think you're about thirteen, maybe fourteen. Either way, this could turn into a crime in the state of Massachusetts, you know that? Jaime remains silent, fiddling anxiously with his Day-Glo wristband, which is now primed with sweat. *My heart.*

—Look, if you're gonna call me a liar, I can just leave.

Vernon flashes those teeth again in a furious grin.—Who said anything like that, about you being a liar? We cool, ain't we, Tony?

—Anyways, if I did leave, where would that leave *you?* Jaime bats his eyes, turning his back to Vernon. This, he thinks, is not going where he thought it would, though he is unsure where that was.

Vernon moves closer to Jaime and rests his hand on the boy's shoulder.—Why don't we take a walk behind that old filling station there? I knew the man who owned it, you know, Vernon whispers, his voice trailing off. Jaime reminds himself just because they go back there, nothing really *has to* occur. It's a game; he's *Tony,* this man is playing along, nothing will happen. He also thinks if Tony were alive and he knew about this, he would put his gun to this man's temple right now and pull the trigger until the clip was completely emptied so that the eyes and snot mixed into the ground like spilled soup and then stomp on the head until the face was unrecognizable. So unrecognizable

that no one could figure out who he was but Jaime had known instantly, just by that scent;
instead that very thing happened to Tony and now he is lying six feet under a head-
stone in a cemetery in Jamaica Plain, his face shattered into a hundred pieces like a
porcelain doll, his body so twisted that they could barely fit the suit on him, and no
one is here to stop this game, stop it at all, save Jaime from anything, from *himself,*
no one cares, not his mother not his father not his aunts or uncles or sisters not
Teresita not Tita not even his *abuela,* no one, the only one who ever cared and
showed it is silent and silenced for posterity so why not see what is going to happen this
morning—

They head down an oil-slicked gravel driveway toward the rear of the abandoned
gas station, which abuts a narrow alley, bordered on three sides by a brick wall, covered
by ivy and other climbing vines. Jaime has passed by this site before, though he has
never actually ventured back in here.

Vernon leans against the back wall of the station. He unbuckles his pants. Jaime
faces him, his eyes now falling everywhere but on Vernon, who has begun to expose
himself, urging the boy to approach him. Is this part of the game? Jaime asks without
rendering the words audible, fixed to his spot. What would *Tony* do? His eyes still wandering, his mind leaping alternately from Vernon's extended fingers to Tony's veined
brown hands gripping that 9mm—that's what it was, wasn't it, a 9mm, a Tech-Nine
pulling the trigger again again again, him finding the body back behind the Dumpster
behind the store like garbage dumped in the middle of the night, his mother not able
to say anything at all for days, her lying on the floor beneath the pew convulsing in
tears at the funeral, him under his comforter shivering in the overheated room, working himself into a frenzy at the sight of that body, that horrible corpse, that face mangled beyond recognition, beyond even hideousness, as the bed across from him lies
empty empty empty—

—Com'ere, Tony, Vernon clucks, his eyes closed and his body arched back against
the wall. Jaime approaches until he is standing in front of him, stone-still. That's *good.*
Jaime just stands there, his eyes now fixed on Vernon's hairless and pocked torso, paler
than his face or arms, like the flesh of a plucked chicken, which he has revealed by raising his polo shirt. Jaime tenses as the hand clamps onto his shoulder. Tony! Vernon is
hunching over, breathing heavily. Turn around for me again, Tony! Tony?

Jaime, who feels himself slowly losing his sense of balance-distance-time letting
everything go why can't he concentrate why can't he be a man like Tony would why
can't he end this game end it now get closer to Vernon run why why why is this happening like this why is this happening he begins to turn look down find the head crumpled like a toy doll fall shoot convulsed in tears my god why my *son* on the floor of the
pew why my God *por qué* when he hears,—Oh! Tony . . . Tony, *ooooh . . .*

He opens his eyes suddenly. What time *is* it? Vernon's left hand is massaging Jaime's
shoulder, his right hand . . . he feels his chest collapsing. He glimpses Vernon's watch
on his right hand . . . he's late for his algebra class! He is going to *miss* it! Jaime leaps
up, stumbles backwards, knocking over his knapsack, spilling the contents upon the
stones.

—Wha? Hunh? Vernon murmurs, writhing against the wall like a felled bird struggling to alight, driven with bliss, unaware of the boy's actions. Panicking, Jaime
snatches up his knapsack, stuffs everything back in it, hoists it onto his left shoulder,

hesitates. *My life,* he feels rising on the tip of his tongue: No one is going to save him from anything, ever, *not a soul.*

—Wha's the matter, Tony? *Tony?* Jaime, refusing to look in Vernon's direction, runs off down the driveway, his backpack now half-open and dangling from his back. In about five seconds he is onto the street that leads through the projects and into the front door of Cuffe Middle School, pass the hall monitor who is yelling out his name—*Jaime Barrett, Jaime Barrett, Jaime?*—up onto the third floor, into a seat in the back of the class as Mr. Morris is chalking a series of dizzyingly elaborate equations upon the black slate that appears now as depthless as the voice that is explaining the actions of the hand and chalk, and Jaime, in the back row, is fumbling around madly in his bag, his hands searching furiously for that algebra notebook—where *is* it? He *knows* he packed it, he remembers having placed it in there this morning—which is *nowhere* to be found.

Then he sees it, he sees it as keenly as if it all were unreeling right before him, *here:* As Vernon gets ready to depart, he spots a notebook, lying several inches in front of him. A black and white wirebound gridded notebook, which has ALGEBRA I—MR. MORRIS, FIRST PERIOD etched across its front. Picking up the notebook, he flips through it, seeing all the red marks and the heavily annotated margins of the pages, which, like a used scratch-and-sniff sample held close to the nose, emit a faint but perceptible scent: sandalwood. He casts the notebook to the ground, beside the discarded newspaper, laughs at the folly of it all, at this boy who cannot even keep up his role in their game, walks off down the driveway towards Dudley and rest of his life—

His bangs now plastered like a veil to his forehead, his breathing so labored as to drown out even his own thoughts, Jaime looks up, to the puzzled expressions of Mr. Morris, of Vinh, of every student in his algebra class. Their faces are screens of bemusement, showing only the recognition of his strange and novel presence before them. Their eyes have fixed upon him as if he were the last boy on earth, their stares as blank and unrelenting as if they had never seen such a pitiful and enigmatic creature in their entire lives.

The Last Integrationist

Jake Lamar

MELVIN WAS MIDWAY THROUGH ONE OF HIS GREATEST HITS, A RELIABLE standard for youngish audiences about the importance of personal responsibility, respect for one's ancestors, our rich cultural heritage, the need to dream great dreams, to have the discipline and the self-respect to pursue those dreams just as the people who came before you—

And then he froze. Standing at the lectern, onstage in the same auditorium at Samuel Adams High School where decades earlier he'd addressed his peers—all of them, or most of them, anyway, conscientious young Negroes, the boys in jackets and ties, every girl present wearing a dress or a skirt—as president of the student body,

Melvin Hutchinson stopped cold in midsentence and gazed at the subtly swimming audience before him. He felt himself wobble ever so slightly and wondered if he'd edged past the threshold, that slender line indicating that other people could tell he was drunk. Melvin, in the years since Abby's death, had become expert at going right up to the threshold, standing with his toes touching that barrier, but rarely crossing the line. When he did tiptoe over the threshold, it was always late at night, at some jolly gathering where most everyone was tanked. But now, standing frozen on the Sam Adams stage, Melvin worried that maybe he'd gone too far today, that maybe by starting his drinking two hours early this morning with that splash of vodka in his orange juice at 8:00 A.M. aboard *Justice One,* he'd hastened his approach to the threshold and had now, carelessly, stepped over it.

But almost as quickly as that fear entered his mind, it disappeared and Melvin suddenly felt the full force of his anger, the rage careening inside him as he stared at his audience. It wasn't the entire audience that maddened him. But it was the majority, all those young faces he saw out there slack with boredom, or twisted in sneers, or, worst of all—these were the faces his gaze flitted to, dispersed as they were throughout the crowd—stuffed with gum. He fixated on those mouths, lazily masticating, cracking the gum, popping it loudly, blowing pink balloon-sized bubbles. Here he was the most prominent man—let alone *black* man—these kids had ever seen in the flesh, an alumnus of their school, coming back to give them a significant message, a message that, if only they would heed it, might save their wretched lives. And they weren't even listening to him! It was so obvious from their blank stares and sleepy expressions that nothing he'd said had even registered. Why had they bothered to show up? Why were they wasting his precious time? Why couldn't they even show the common fucking courtesy to *pay attention,* simply to pay attention for half an hour? Melvin Hutchinson—who knew he had to be the most famous role model ever to show up at this school, who had come here, back to his alma mater, returning, as black people were always being urged to do, constantly being criticized for *not* doing, to his roots, to his original community, who had taken time out of his schedule to try to reach out to these kids—stared at the multitude of dull, uncomprehending, gum-cracking faces and felt nothing but disgust.

"What is wrong with you all?" Melvin said in a voice brimming with resentment.

Surprised murmurs rippled through the audience.

"I said," Melvin fairly shouted into the lectern's microphone, "what in the *hell* is wrong with y'all?"

The crowd came alive with shocked and indignant whispers, buzzing like a swarm of bees. Melvin looked to the front row, to his entourage of white agents and functionaries, and spotted Henry Beedle, who looked positively stricken. Melvin quickly glanced around the auditorium. There wasn't a camera or a tape recorder in sight. The absence emboldened him.

"I come here to give you people a valuable message and you can't even be bothered to listen to me! What is the problem with you people?"

"Maybe the problem ain't with us!" a voice called out from the crowd. "Maybe the problem is with you!"

"Who said that?" Melvin shot back, feeling more primed to do battle than he'd ever felt in his life. "Stand up. I wanna see who said that."

While the crowd continued to buzz, a young man (obviously not a high school student; he looked at least twenty-five; a teacher perhaps?) rose in the center of the auditorium. He had a tangle of coiled braids on the top of his head, little hair at all on the sides, a scraggly goatee, and a red-green-and-yellow earring in the shape of Africa. He wore a Technicolor dashiki—probably, Melvin thought, made in Hong Kong. "Yo!" the young man said, and the kids in the audience applauded.

"And who are you?" Melvin asked.

"I'm Rashid Scuggs, director of the Norris Center for African-American Arts and Culture. Located at Sixty-six Jefferson Avenue. *Dat's* who I am!" All the gum-cracking students cheered their approval.

"And you have a problem with me, Mr. Scuggs?"

"Yeah, I got a problem witch you! Cuz you say *you* got a problem wid my homeys here. And the problem ain't wid us. Da problem is witch you! The problem is witch your message. Cuz your message don't address *our* cause. The *black* cause!"

While the kids cheered again, Melvin stared hard, though more analytically than angrily, at the young man in the audience. What was the strange incongruity he detected in this Rashid Scuggs? There was something in his demeanor, in his voice, that range discordantly with Melvin. It wasn't his hostility. At this moment, Melvin didn't give a damn about that. It was something else. Melvin felt intuitively that this Rashid was an exceptionally intelligent person. But something in his voice seemed false. It seemed as if he were trying to assume a voice that was not his own, as if he was trying to sound the way a black man was *supposed* to sound.

"I've been fighting for the black cause my entire adult life," Melvin said slowly, forcefully.

"Yeah? Watchoo ever do for the black cause?"

"I risked my *life* for the black cause, for every single one of you in this auditorium today. I risked my life for you!"

Now a good portion of the audience, led by the principal of Sam Adams and the teachers in the auditorium, applauded for Melvin.

"Yeah!" Rashid challenged. "I know about choo. I know *all* about you."

"What do you *know* about me?"

"I know you call yourself a civil rights fighter. But you ain't never been in no fight. All you ever been is a lawyer in a suit!"

"And all Thurgood Marshall ever was was a lawyer in a suit," Melvin intoned. The crowd responded enthusiastically, but he did not hear them anymore, barely even saw them. It was just Melvin and Rashid now; he was all alone with this arrogant little punk. "And no, I didn't join in mass demonstrations. I didn't get hosed down in the street or have German shepherds snappin' at my Johnson or get firebombed out of my home. No, I didn't take part in the March on Washington. I was, in fact, in Hazelton, South Carolina, the day of the "I Have a Dream" speech, putting *his* words into action, doing the indispensable scut work of the movement, in short, makin' it law! And no, I shed no blood for your freedom. I just made it *legal.* I just made the shit *stick!* But you better believe I was at risk, cuz wasn't nothin' *less* nonthreatening than a black man, let alone a *blue-black* man like yours truly, wearin' a *suit,* drivin' a *car,* and callin' hisself a lawyer, let alone a *civil rights* lawyer, in Hazelton, South Ca'lina, in the summer of nineteen hun'red and sistee-*tree!*"

"Yeah, yeah, yeah," Rashid scoffed. "All you old-timesy niggas gotta talk about Dr.

King. I don't even respect your Dr. King. Cuz all he ever did was let black people get beat up!"

"That's just about the stupidest shit I ever heard."

"It's the truth. And I defy you to tell me one lasting, concrete thing your Dr. King ever achieved, aside from makin' liberal white folks feel good about themselves. What did he ever accomplish?"

"One: He secured for you, and for every African-American, the most sacred right of democracy—the right to vote!"

"Hey, man, I don't even *use* my right to vote. I'm thirty years old and I ain't never voted in my life."

"What?" Melvin said, finding Rashid's comment almost unfathomable.

"I said, *I don't vote.* Ain't no real options for black people out there, anyway. The white politicians are just out to exploit us and the black ones are just a bunch a Uncle Toms!"

"Do you mean to say that after I worked my butt off, after people *died* to get your sorry black ass the vote, you're gonna go and *not* vote?"

"Votin' don't make no difference for black folks. Democracy for black folks does not exist in America."

"That is an untenable position, Rashid. Don't you have anything constructive to say?"

"I say it's time to be *de*-structive. If the system ain't gonna do nothin' for black folks, I say tear it down!"

"Don't you know that's suicide?"

"Don't *choo* know black people are gonna burn this country down?"

"Do you think, do you really *believe* that I have worked this hard, that I have come this far to have crazy ignorant niggas like you make a mockery of my life's work? Do you think I'm gonna let poisoned little shits like you destroy everything I've staked my *life* on?"

"You ain't nothin' but a Uncle Tom!"

Melvin could no longer ignore the crowd. The entire auditorium seemed to be rocking, the whole audience on its feet, alive with brutal energy. Melvin saw Beedle standing in the front row. The deputy quickly drew an index finger across his throat. *Cut it short; we're outta here!*

"Uncle Tom!" Rashid screamed, and suddenly the whole crowd seemed to be chanting it: "Uncle Tom! Uncle Tom! Uncle Tom! Uncle Tom!"

Then something grabbed Melvin's gaze, something sailing in the air, spinning end over end above the crowd, now hurtling toward the stage. When the object was no more than six feet above his head, Melvin could see that it was large, that it was made of clear glass but streaked with yellow, with liquid; it was—could it be?—a forty! The nearly empty bottle of malt liquor shattered at Melvin's feet. In an instant, Melvin's federal agents were onstage and the attorney general was surrounded. Melvin saw riot police burst through the front entrance of the auditorium, billy clubs in hand, fighting their way through the crowd, which seemed to surge in all directions at once. Agents on either side of Melvin grabbed his arms. Next thing he knew, he was running; no, his feet were barely touching the floor—agents were practically carrying him, rapidly through the back entrance of the auditorium, out into the playground. He saw the door of his limo in front of him. Seemingly out of nowhere, a white hand grabbed the handle and flung open the door. Melvin felt another hand, fingers spread, grip firm, come down with a powerful pressure on the top of his head. He felt still another hand on his back, shoving him into the car. He tumbled into the leather seat. Christian Emerson, his chief bodyguard, jumped in and sat across from him, gun drawn. Suddenly, Beedle appeared in the seat beside him. The limo door slammed shut. Sirens screeched. The car lurched forward, pitching Melvin back deeper into his seat, and now all he felt was velocity, almost as if he was in a jet taking off, as he and his entourage sped away from Sam Adams High.

Victor D. LaValle

Slave

ROB EATS PUSSY LIKE A CHAMP.

He's on awful knees that should have been turned in months ago; they are now numb. He should be getting ready for school; tenth grade is usually the age of football teams and part-time work.

She says,—Don't stop, through those teeth so white Rob was sure they were caps when he met her in front of the Disney store in Times Square and Andre was across the street in his jacket blue like veins, gesturing to her, Rob's customer. There's a lamp on the nightstand, weak and sputtering light.

Outside the sun is a rumor; maybe in one hour it'll be up and they have been on that bed together for much longer. He has been doing the same thing continuously, except for breaks when it's understandable that muscles tire and freeze; then he drinks handfuls of cold, cold water from the sink in the bathroom.

—Don't you fucking stop.

She has soft skin everywhere and does nothing he might call work. This woman doesn't have rough fingers like secretaries who must type and dial phones all their lives or lawyers who look tired and must win every argument; not even models who are so pretty, or pretend to be, that they would never have to pay for an ugly little kid to eat their pussies. Her legs and thighs are draped over his shoulders, her ass somewhere in that space between him and the bed; he wants to tell her that his shoulders hurt, but will he? No.

In front of Disney, Rob had moved to touch her face, but the collar of her jacket was pulled up and flopping like mud flaps. She had to speak to him through them, saying, —It's so windy out. She stepped away. —Sure, Rob said.

Then on the train they were moving fast, it was nighttime. When he asked, —So how'd you meet Andre? She pulled something invisible up between them.

After the Columbia University stop their car and all the ones trailing and leading were just mobile testaments to the lingering effects of miscegenation.

Eventually, the train rumbled and stopped and jerked forward; he touched her arm. —Let's go. In the air Spanish was being spoken. Rob took her to the same motel as his men, walked the same path; he could see his footprints in the concrete.

On the bed, backed against the headboard, her thighs ache; she rubs them, tells Rob they hurt, but he wants to laugh because he's still on his knees, afraid to stand; his body is assuring him it will not work. His mouth is a wound that should be left to heal, but there is her purse next to the bed, pregnant with bills rolled into a rock. He has four twenties, a ten and a five in his coat that she'd peeled off earlier and even in the way she tossed them to him there was the promise of much more.

He rises but his body has forgotten how to stand; he falls back against the wall and is lying there beside the door with his legs finally straight; blood is pumping and life is returning; his feet twitch as though they're being resurrected. —Come here, she says, but his hand's up, begging for some rest. Her face, for a few moments, betrays her, there is some warmth and sympathy, she does not wish Rob any pain. She does not have children. Waiting, she tries to imagine what she'd have served a baby for breakfast that morning, how she would have spoken to convey her love. You ever have a girl? she asks. That you liked, I mean.

—Why?

She shrugs. —Just wanted to know. Wanted to hear about it.

On the walk to the motel she had finally looked at him. —You are young, aren't you?

He smiled. —As young as you want. Then he ran his hands across his chin and neck and all the places where he had, just that morning, run the razor and swept away all signs that he had aged past thirteen. Later, in the room, he moved his hands down his slight neck, over his stomach, under his balls, looked at her, saying, —Smooth.

—Like a little, little boy. She said this while touching her tummy.

She sat in that room alone with him and didn't check the closet or push open the bathroom door (just in case) because she had trust packed tight in her purse next to the money and a .38. The first thing she said to him was, —I'll give you ten dollars if you let me do this. Rob took the money, then she emptied the gun, slid the barrel into his mouth. For five more dollars he let her pull the trigger twice. The hollow clicks made him giggle.

Rob had had a girlfriend; two years before, he was fourteen and she was twelve. But when he and Inca got together he lost fascination quick because already her pussy was all used up. That was how he felt and when he asked her about it she laughed, said, —You'll find out how when that asshole's all fucked up.

And she was right.

Soon she had to leave because Rob was always trying to put fire to things—like her. She broke out finally when he set his own right foot to burning, just to make his friends laugh. She was saying, —If you'll do that shit to yourself, I don't know what the fuck you'll do to me.

Healing was tough and peeling skin is ugly, but Rob's girlfriend looked worse, had that face like she and a train had gone at it, does it really matter who won? He was dumb and thought he could do better so he drove her away on purpose, but who knew after that that nights and days would just be business, business, business?

Inca knew that even from a distance her young skin looked withered and loose on her bones and still she expected you to treat her nice. She demanded it. If not, she was gone, no question.

What he missed most, she could talk this talk, knew this language that was from somewhere before Spain landed ships and Spanish cut out more natural tongues, it was hard to hear her speak like that, Rob was jealous, when she spoke, it seemed as though she had her own good and wonderful time machine.

—Do you want to make more money? she asks Rob.

—Of course. What do you want to do?

She pulls the covers up around her like a robe. He wonders what her sheets look like at home. —Let me see your dick.

Everything is quiet while he pulls down his underwear, then quiet for longer. He looks down. —What's wrong?

—Nothing. Nothing.

—Is there something wrong with it?

—No, it's not that. I just haven't seen many up close but my husband's.

—He make his different?

—No. She scratches her stomach. No, no.

—Forty to fuck. Rob touches his legs, still not quite alive.

—Forty?

—Yeah.

—Forty?

—Come on. Do you want to or not?

—Hey! she snaps. Don't forget who's got the money.

He can't. He says, —Sorry.

She is smiles again. —You remind me of a boy I used to like. He had a body like yours. Do you play sports?

—Yeah, he says, moves closer. I fuck.

—Okay, she sighs. Enough talk.

—Money first. Rob exposes his palm to her face. The four tens are smooth and new like the others had been; he can picture her at the ATM right before she got on the Long Island Rail Road, the honey-sweet sound of the money flipping out in bundles.

—I have to use a condom, he says and even her blood is glad he brought it up.

He wraps one around his dick. But what about the times when there was nothing latex available and he used cellophane bags and then Scotch tape and then—most often—nothing? It has been sore for weeks or maybe months and could it be longer than that?

When he gets to the bed he bumps the nightstand, moves the whole thing. It seems to her that lamp will spill over and singe, she moves her hands to catch it, but he does nothing because it's nailed down, wouldn't move if something divine came in and tried to displace it. His hands are around the base of his dick, trying to strangle it so the blood can't escape. But it does.

—How long have you been doing this?

He wants to do something to her with his fists. —Long time, he promises. Wait, there it is. He comes toward her, but with each step air leaks out like an old balloon.

She says,—So is this like a cab? Even the time we're sitting still the meter's running?

He's got nothing to say, he's watching himself; keeping it stiff is like balancing a tray of dishes on one hand and walking them across a stage, a comedy act. —It's gone. Rob does not complain, his mouth and body are mostly tired of the taste and shape and force of dicks and the men that own them. Being with a woman is a treat. Rob gets down on knees, prods tongue out with fingers, stays this way for the long hours ahead.

In the midmorning they say good-bye. Before she leaves there is a promise: that she will call Andre, ask for him. He nods. —Don't forget my name.

—Rob, she says and it almost sounds nice.

All the money she'd paid is lodged in his underwear. As he walks away, the stiff bills cut against one leg; he walks with a hitch like some old cowboy. A two-hundred-dollar limp. But it's all for Andre. When Rob gets back to the apartment that five people share, there will be no negotiation, only Andre's underfed palm. Maybe if he's fortunate he'll be given twenty dollars, or forty, enough to buy some magazines or go to a movie, but only if the whole apartment is in a good mood; there, generosity is an occasion.

You will find ways to save yourself. This is relative: save.

Rob's been at this long enough to have radar; a crowded hall has its interested and they can find one another. Those who weathered the Holocaust have been known to find a fellow fortunate survivor at the other end of a restaurant.

Because he's tired, Rob feels bold; he is most ready for a change just before the trip home, the emptying of his coffers. The Port Authority pizza shop, on the subway level, has a court of white plastic seats and tables. Rob has spotted the man from four hundred feet; Rob has come closer to be more sure. Passes by, four times, slowing progressively, thinking: Notice, notice. But the man, he loves his pizza, soda too. So Rob passes by three more times, decreasing his pace more until, with his arms stretched forward, Rob could be Boris Karloff's mummy chasing Abbott and Costello through a tomb.

—Why don't you go away or sit down? The man finally asks, leaning back in his chair.

Rob finds speed again, comes around the short railing. Sits. —Nice to see you.

—No it isn't, says Harrold, who tells the truth. He is much too thin, you can't hide any secrets in a body like that. And his mustache is long, a U turned over his lips, hanging down. Gray. On his cheeks and neck more hair grows in, enough to unsmooth the skin, but it will never be a beard. His fingers are slim but the tops are fat bulbs. The nails are dirty. I drive a truck, he explains.

—You take a lot of coke? Rob smiles, earnestly asks.

He laughs, and the teeth are bad, dull. —Not so much anymore. I don't meet boys like this, really.

Rob nods, he loves the liars, leans forward and tries for sultry. —Then how do you meet them, really?

Harrold coughs on some crust causing clutter in his throat. —I didn't mean it like that.

Behind them are the young women and men, a few years older than Rob, standing in a long and winding cord before they buy their tickets for Greyhound buses; upstairs the same line exists for Short Line tickets and this is the painted pattern many mornings. These young people are on their way back to college, the names stitched across their sweatshirts Rob's first, best clue; some are with their parents, but most are with the people they call Honey or Sweetheart, then kiss quickly and, with a jumble of sad and happy, watch the bus make concrete the distances between them. Rob turns back to Harrold. —Leaving isn't always sad. It can be a good thing.

Harrold doesn't understand he's being given a hint, a suggestion, but he nods because he is polite enough and Rob is pretty, which always coaxes manners from the worst of men. He asks, —So, how does this work? You want to go to the bathroom or something?

There is an information booth, empty, twenty feet away. The lights are off, glass on all sides, there is no mistaking the vacancy, but people still walk to it, stand there expectantly. As though their need for something is enough to make it appear. As though you don't have to put in any effort. Rob knows better, you have to work things. —We could do that. If that's all you want.

—What else? Harrold asks, touching his pocket. You selling vacuum cleaners too?

Anxious. Anxious. Rob does not want another night in the room he shares with three other boys, the way wind seeps through the window frame despite the black tape Rob has put up as insulation. He is desperate. He offers, —I can cook.

Again, Harrold's coughing. He's a shy one, it won't work to be dirty or prurient, that will not coax charity, affection. Women are used to this, the way they sometimes have to set it all up before their date will reach out and hold hands. It can be playful, it can be infuriating: leaning close, smiling often, brushing near, grabbing elbows. But it can be done. Rob says, —My biscuits are nice. My mother taught me how to make them. Or cinnamon French toast, I know how to do that too.

Harrold's legs are long and, while his upper half leans back, far, they reach forward. He is conscious of it, but not in control. They would not listen if they could. He touches the insides of his boots to the outsides of Rob's sneakers. Harrold says, —I live alone. But he had not meant that to come out; internal monologue, not for Rob. Harrold, embarrassed, sits up quick, pulling his feet back from their foreplay. Someone younger, less experienced, would have jumped on the admission, but Rob pretends he hears nothing. He says, —I want to get some soda.

—I'm not paying for it, Harrold burps, quickly, like he's caught Rob at something.

Rob laughs easy. —I don't want you to. I have money, I just want to know if you'll stay here.

—And if I won't?

—Then I'm not moving.

Harrold dips his head. —Sorry, I didn't mean anything. I'll wait.

Rob walks, careful not to wiggle or strut, so when Harrold looks, and he will look, he'll see a boy, with a gentle limp. Rob does not romanticize it with emphasis.

—I'm not gay, Harrold explains when Rob returns.

He nods. —Me neither. Rob reads; in other places they will eat bugs for food, the will to survive so strong; Rob understands them.

—I'm Harrold, with two r's.

—That's weird.

—Telling me? Two of anything in your name and people think you're strange. Just your name can make people call you a monster, low.

—My name's simple: Rob. Want some? He lifts the drink and gestures like it's a gift or a secret to share.

Harrold stands, walks away. Nothing said. He creeps off to the newsstand, goes around to the far end so Rob will think he's left altogether. Rob has spent some of the two hundred for the drink, just a dollar, but accounting is Andre's passion. Rob looks around, agitated, for a purse, a man not watching his pants pockets, a way to replenish that one bill. The fluorescent lights live on, unaware of what and whom they illuminate; they are just a mechanism. Rob begins to weep. He's exhausted, had really thought Harrold was it. At least momentarily, someone who'd take him in. He should have at least gone for the blowjob, that's twenty all for yourself, off the books. He gulps his soda but there is too much ice, the drink cold enough to awaken the nerves of his teeth, too easily roused. They flare, grouchy yawns. Rob eats soft things because he's brittle. He loves ice cream despite the temperature; the occasional pint of vanilla-chocolate-cookie-dough is an exercise in gratification and self-flagellation.

Harrold then returns like he wants to be: a hero. —Why the tears? I just went to get a pack of gum.

—Oh. Rob grins. Can I have a piece?

Harrold has lied, has bought nothing. He feels stupid in front of this kid.

Rob asks, —Are you going to sit back down? He shifts in his seat as the older man comes back around. He touches his face, rubs the skin and pats down his hair because when he gets tired age grows in like a beard. What does this guy like? Young and stupid? Young and mean? All the variations, they go through Rob's computer; how to convince this man to take him along, it doesn't matter where. It begins to confuse Rob and when confused he taps his legs with his hands but knows that annoys others so he tries to stop but then only taps more. In a panic he blurts out, I can be really beautiful.

—Huh?

—You could put me in a dress. Or anything. Whatever you like. I'll make you dinner or lunch like that, dressed up. I wore makeup before, I know how to make it look real nice. I could be your pretty young wife. Rob is sobbing, biting his lip, but not yelling, it is ingrained that, in this world, you keep things quiet. I don't care, whatever you like.

Harrold, finds his courage. Evaluates the boy: small shoulders, little hips, nice mouth, he will be gorgeous, and look at him, he's terrified. Abject fear can breed a kind of loyalty. And it can be arousing.

They walk near each other but not together; like the old idealized wife Rob trails back five feet, out of deference, gratitude. Upstairs they leave the Port Authority, walk until they reach the garage where Harrold hands a short man a ticket, when the car comes, a tip. Rob walks ten feet of sidewalk, then waits for the blue Chevy Corsica. When he gets in, Harrold's pants are already mostly down. Rob goes to touch him but is brushed away. —Not yet, Harrold says. Tell me something. He begins a self-caress. Tell me something bad.

The Famished Road

ONE OF THE REASONS I DIDN'T WANT TO BE BORN BECAME CLEAR TO ME AFTER I had come into the world. I was still very young when in a daze I saw Dad swallowed up by a hole in the road. Another time I saw Mum dangling from the branches of a blue tree. I was seven years old when I dreamt that my hands were covered with the yellow blood of a stranger. I had no idea whether these images belonged to this life, or to a previous one, or to one that was yet to come, or even if they were merely the host of images that invades the minds of all children.

When I was very young I had a clear memory of my life stretching to other lives. There were no distinctions. Sometimes I seemed to be living several lives at once. One lifetime flowed into the others and all of them flowed into my childhood.

As a child I felt I weighed my mother down. In turn I felt weighed down by the inscrutability of life. Being born was a shock from which I never recovered. Often, by night or day, voices spoke to me. I came to realise that they were the voices of my spirit companions.

'What are you doing here?' one of them would ask.

'Living,' I would reply.

'Living for what?'

'I don't know.'

'Why don't you know? Haven't you seen what lies ahead of you?'

'No.'

Then they showed me images which I couldn't understand. They showed me a prison, a woman covered with golden boils, a long road, pitiless sunlight, a flood, an earthquake, death.

'Come back to us,' they said. 'We miss you by the river. You have deserted us. If you don't come back we will make your life unbearable.'

I would start shouting, daring them to do their worst. On one of these occasions Mum came into the room and stood watching me. When I noticed her I became silent. Her eyes were bright. She came over, hit me on the head, and said:

'Who are you talking to?'

'No one,' I replied.

She gave me a long stare. I don't remember how old I was at the time. Afterwards my spirit companions took great delight getting me into trouble. I often found myself oscillating between both worlds. One day I was playing on the sand when they called me from across the road with the voice of my mother. As I went towards the voice a car almost ran me over. Another day they enticed me with sweet songs towards a gutter. I fell in and no one noticed and it was only by good fortune that a bicyclist saw me thrashing about in the filthy water and saved me from drowning.

I was ill afterwards and spent most of the time in the other world trying to reason with my spirit companions, trying to get them to leave me alone. What I didn't know was that the longer they kept me there, the more certain they were making my death. It was only much later, when I tried to get back into my body and couldn't, that I realised they had managed to shut me out of my life. I cried for a long time into the silver void till our great king interceded for me and reopened the gates of my body.

When I woke up I found myself in a coffin. My parents had given me up for dead. They had commenced the burial proceedings when they heard my fierce weeping. Because of my miraculous recovery they named me a second time and threw a party which they couldn't afford. They name me Lazaro. But as I became the subject of much jest, and as many were uneasy with the connection between Lazaro and Lazarus, Mum shortened my name to Azaro.

I learnt afterwards that I had lingered between not dying and not living for two weeks. I learnt that I exhausted the energy and finances of my parents. I also learnt that a herbalist had been summoned. He confessed to not being able to do anything about my condition, but after casting his cowries, and deciphering their signs, he said:

'This is a child who didn't want to be born, but who will fight with death.'

He added that, if I recovered, my parents should immediately perform a ceremony that would sever my connections with the spirit world. He was the first to call me by that name which spreads horror amongst mother. He told them that I had hidden my special tokens of spirit identity on this earth and till they were found I would go on falling ill and that it was almost certain that I would die before the age of twenty-one.

When I recovered, however, my parents had already spent too much money on me. They were in debt. And my father, who was rather fed up with all the trouble I brought, had grown somewhat sceptical of the pronouncements and certitudes of herbalists. If you listen to everything they say, he told Mum, you will have to perform absurd sacrifices every time you step outside your door. He was also suspicious of their penchant for advocating costly ceremonies, the way quack doctors keep multiplying the ramifications of ailments in order to make you spend fortunes on their medicines.

Neither Mum nor Dad could afford another ceremony. And anyway they did not really want to believe that I was a spirit-child. And so time passed and the ceremony was never performed. I was happy. I didn't want it performed. I didn't want to entirely lose contact with that other world of light and rainbows and possibilities. I had buried my secrets early. I buried them in moonlight, the air alive with white moths. I buried my magic stones, my mirror, my special promises, my golden threads, objects of identity that connected me to the world of spirits. I buried them all in a secret place, which I promptly forgot.

In the early years Mum was quite proud of me.

'You are a child of miracles,' she would say. 'Many powers are on your side.'

For as long as my cord to other worlds remained intact, for as long as my objects were not found, this might continue to be true.

As a child I could read people's minds. I could foretell their futures. Accidents happened in places I had just left. One night I was standing in the street with Mum when a voice said:

'Cross over.'

I tugged Mum across the street and a few moments later an articulated lorry plunged into the house we had been standing in front of and killed an entire family.

On another night I was asleep when the great king stared down at me. I woke up, ran out of the room, and up the road. My parents came after me. They were dragging me back when we discovered that the compound was burning. On that night our lives changed.

The road woke up. Men and women, all in wrappers, sleep-marks on their faces, blackened lamps in their hands, crowded outside. There was no electricity in our area. The lamps, held above the heads, illuminated the strange-eyed moths, casting such a spectral glow over the disembodied faces that I felt I was again among spirits. One world contains glimpses of others.

It was a night of fires. An owl flew low over the burning compound. The air was full of cries. The tenants rushed back and forth with buckets of water from the nearest well. Gradually, the flames died down. Whole families stayed out in the night, huddled amongst the ragged ends of their clothes and mattresses. There was much wailing for lost property. No one had died.

When it was so dark that one couldn't see the far corners of the sky and the forest lacked all definition, the landlord turned up and immediately started ranting. He threw himself on the ground. Rolling and thrashing, he unleashed a violent torrent of curses on us. He screamed that we had deliberately set his compound on fire to avoid paying the recently increased rent.

'How am I going to get the money to rebuild the house?' he wailed, working himself into a deaf fury.

'All of you must pay for the damages!' he screeched.

No one paid him any attention. Our main priority was to find new accommodations. We gathered our possessions and made preparations to move.

'Everyone must stay here!' the landlord said, screaming in the dark.

He hurried away and returned an hour later with three policemen. They fell on us and flogged us with whips and cracked our skulls with batons. We fought them back. We beat them with sticks and ropes. We tore their colonial uniforms and sent them packing. They came back with reinforcements. Dad lured two of them down a side street and gave them a severe thrashing. More came at him. He was such a dervish of fury that it took six policemen to subdue him and bundle him off to the police station.

The reinforcements meanwhile lashed out at everything in sight, unleashing mayhem in a drunken fever. When they had finished fifteen men, three children, four women, two goats and a dog lay wounded along the battleground of our area. That was how the riot started.

Deep in the night it started to rain and it poured down steadily while the ghetto-dwellers raged. The rain didn't last long but it turned the tracks into mud. It watered our fury. Chanting ancient war-songs, brandishing pikes and machetes, gangs materialised in the darkness. They stamped through the mud. At the main road, they fell on cars and buses. They attacked police vehicles. They looted shops. Then everyone began looting and burning, and overturning things. Mum, carrying me, was driven on by the frantic crowd. Along the main road she put me down in order to tighten her wrapper, in full preparation for the worst, when a caterwauling mass of people came pounding toward us. They ran right between us. They separated me from my mother.

I wandered thought he violent terrain, listening to the laughter of mischievous spirits. There was a crescent moon in the sky, darkness over the houses, broken bottles and splintered wood on the road. I wandered barefoot. Fires sprouted over rubbish heaps, men were dragged out of cars, thick smoke billowed from houses. Stumbling along, looking for Mum, I found myself in a dark street. There was a solitary candle burning on a stand near an abandoned house. I heard a deep chanting that made the street tremble. Shadows stormed past, giving off a stench of sweat and rage. Drums vibrated in the air. A cat cried out as if it had been thrown on to a fire. Then a gigantic Masquerade burst out of the road, with plumes of smoke billowing from its head. I gave a frightened cry and hid behind a stall. The Masquerade was terrifying and fiery, its funereal roar filled the street with an ancient silence. I watched it in horror. I watched it by its shadow of a great tree burning, as it danced in the empty street.

Then the darkness filled with its attendants. They were stout men with glistening faces. They held on to the luminous ropes attached to the towering figure. Dancing wildly, it dragged them towards the rioting. When it strode past, sundering the air, I crept out of my hiding place. Swirling with hallucinations, I started back towards the main road. Then suddenly several women, smelling of bitter herbs, appeared out of the darkness. They bore down on me, and swooped me up into the bristling night.

Stigmata

Phyllis Alesia Perry

RUTH KNOWS FIRST.

We sit in the old apple tree behind Aunt Eva's house in Johnson creek, having just delivered several basketfuls of apples to Aunt Eva. She watches us from the back porch where she peels some for canning.

My fantastic out-of-body story has my cousin sitting still as stone, her cheek against the rough bark of an upward-reaching branch. Funny, she doesn't look the least bit shocked, and she presses for details.

"Damn," she murmurs. "You did it again."

"Again?"

"Ah, I remember it well," she says, mockingly putting her hand to her chin and looking skyward. "Nineteen-seventy-seven, wasn't it? You called me by someone else's name, fell off the bed and stared in space for a couple of days. I wrote about it in my diary."

"But I never told you . . ."

"You never told me what you saw, Lizzie. But you called me Joy. Ancestor of ours, right? So's Grace. Why are these people trying to talk to you?"

"You make it sound like ordinary conversation."

"Well, I know it ain't that. But some kind of communication between then and now is going on here. I mean, is there funk after death?"

I roll my eyes.

"Was there something familiar about the house you were in, about the room?" she asks.

"Yeah, I told you. But I can't tell you where I'd seen it." I look off over the top of the house, the church, and towards the cemetery where Grace lay. "Maybe I was in Grace's house, you know, that old empty place back up in the woods where we used to play. But it wasn't anything like you'd remember, Ruth. It was . . . it was home, with furniture and rugs on the floor. It was like remembering, but more. I saw what she was seeing. I saw . . . man! I saw Mother as a little girl. When I woke up, or came to, or whatever, it didn't feel like a dream. Felt like I'd stepped out of one room and into another."

"You said you weren't asleep. Both times you winked out and then back?"

"But I had to be asleep, Ruth, right?" She is taking me far too seriously, frightening me.

"I don't know. Maybe Grace was trying to tell you something. And Bessie."

"Damn, girl. This ain't no *Twilight Zone* thing."

"No, much better." She grins. "The real stuff always is. So what else?"

"Well, I am kinda achy when I wink back in. Sore. Some places feel almost raw. But after a few hours I'm OK."

"Ooooh. Physical manifestations. Did you do something in the other times that hurt you? That could be proof that you really went."

"No." I look down at Aunt Eva, who has stopped peeling and now stares at us, not moving. She can't hear us, can she?

"Where are the pains?"

"My wrists and ankles and back. Stinging."

"Lemme see." She holds out her hands and I give her mine. Turning them over, she examines the wrists. "I don't see anything," she says, putting her fingers against my right arm. Then she is still. She puts her hands around my wrists and lets out a small gasp, dropping them as if they are hot.

"What? What?" I search her face, and her eyes are clouded.

"I felt something," she whispers.

"No shit. What?"

"Pain." Ruth closes her eyes. "Just for a second. Pain."

"What kind of pain? I don't feel anything, at least not now."

"But . . . oh Jesus, it's there! Just under your skin."

"Ruth." I touch her hand and she flinches. "What am I gonna do?"

"I don't know. But Lizzie . . ."

"Yes?"

"There's more coming. Coming fast." She keeps her eyes closed. Her lips tremble.

"Ruth . . . you can feel that?"

She nods.

"How?"

Ruth opens her eyes and says, "How is it that you can step into the life of a woman who died before you were born?"

"There is no answer to that," I say.

We stay at Aunt Eva's that weekend. We had driven down from Tuskegee in Ruth's new car after classes Friday to help with the apples and to taste the first pies, and had planned to go back that evening to catch a party on campus.

But after we climb down from the tree, we decide to stay. We call our mothers, who are playing cards with two other ladies at my house in Tuskegee. I imagine my father safety cocooned behind the door of his study, sipping and reading. Nothing can get me to go home and disturb such domesticity tonight.

"Can you touch me now?" I ask Ruth after dinner, after Aunt Eva is in bed and we sprawl on the front steps. She reaches out a hand and takes mine tensely, sliding her palms over the wrist and forearm. After a few seconds, I feel her relax.

"It's OK," she says, taking her hand back nevertheless.

We're sick, I think, as Ruth swats a lightning bug. *Very sick.*

That night I wake because the night chill has crept into my heart. I open my eyes and I'm standing upright under the night sky. My bare toes dig little depressions into the dirt road just beyond Aunt Eva's front porch, where I can sense, rather than see, Ruth standing, watching. Her long frame sways toward me.

Sleepwalking. That's a new twist. Can't remember the dream that brought me out here. Can't move until I remember what I'm supposed to remember. It just feels so good to be out, but I can't move to what waits for me.

Closing my eyes, I try to remember. That pain is back, especially along the wrists. I rub them. I'm being pulled, but I can't go where they want me to go. Not there.

Ruth's eerie pitter-patter follows me, down the road a bit past Son Jackson's house, and then a turn right to the pasture that runs all the way down to the little river we call Johnson Creek. Our white nightgrowns fly out from our legs, making us winged spirits, and Son Jackson's cows, standing still as stone a moment before, turn their long heads to look.

I stop and close my eyes. Salty air saps the moisture from my lips. Why am I here and why can't I go home, when I know my mother waits for me?

The ground slowly rolls under my feet. I smell—taste—sweat and blood and months of misery. The scent knocks me dizzy for a moment and I stumble forward. Then I am pulled, jerked. I open my eyes, but there is a void in front of me. Light, gray and weak, filters in slowly from the left side of my vision, and I see the deck, the water beyond and the line of dark bodies going jerkily forward into the ghost-land. Each bent back ahead of me is familiar.

A gurgling sob reaches me. Mine. I'd been steadily shuffling forward, but I can't go any farther.

The rail is under my palm, the weight of another person dangles from my wrist. The bottom of my foot scrapes the top of the rail; I try to ignore the sound of the chain dragging along the wooden deck. Trying to stand on the rail, I expect to be jerked back at any moment. I crouch there for what seems to be an eternity. The man attached to my wrist whispers to me urgently in some strange tongue. When I turn to look at him there is some slow-crackling fire in his stare. I am to go, his eyes say, and he'll go with me.

So I throw my leg over the other side, but I feel myself being pulled. . . .

I hit the water with a hard thud, rolling over and scraping my forehead on something—is it the side of the boat? I touch bottom and the water is pitch-dark; no sunlight. Where is the sun?

A hand grabs me and my head breaks the surface. But I'm not sure I want to open my mouth to breathe.

"Dammit!" Ruth says, her voice coming from far away, but her fingers biting into my arm. "Help me—at least a little here, Lizzie! You're like a damn rock!" she drags me through the water crossways to the current; it tugs gently but insistently on my limbs.

I drift into that now-familiar sensation of disorientation; my mind crawls down a long hallway. I now Ruth is there, but when I look into her face, I see someone else. A dark girl in African clothes, silent but with eyes that speak of horrible things. She and I seem to walk back and forth, holding on to each other.

Cold water slaps my face as I stumble and fall.

"Lizzie," I hear Ruth half-growl, half-moan. "Lizzie, don't blink out on me now!"

Hands in my armpits haul me upright again and I stand face-to-face with Ruth, chest-deep in the cold, tumbling flow of Johnson Creek. If Ruth looks that frightened, I wonder how I look. The African girl is gone. The ship deck is gone. Involuntarily, I touch my arms under the water, but I already know there are no chains.

"Lizzie . . ." Ruth strokes my forehead and then stares at the smear of blood and water on her fingers.

"Your head," she says. "You're bloody. Let's get the hell outta this water!"

We wade through to the shallows. Ruth scolds. I can think of no response to her mumbling, frightened questions.

The creek isn't very wide, but it's sort of deep in the middle. If I had dived over in the shallows, where the rocks ruled, that likely would have been the end of my story.

Over my shoulder, I see the thin-railed small-plank bridge that spans the stream. Luckily, I'd gone over in the deepest part with water to cushion the fall. Still—I touch a hand to my head as Ruth drags me by the arm to the bank—I hit something. Is that why I feel so fuzzy?

Despite the warmth of the night, we shiver violently as we stumble to shore, and we don't break stride until we are climbing Aunt Eva's porch steps.

Inside, Ruth almost tears the soaking nightgown off me, still whispering urgent questions at me as I stand there naked, hair dripping and on its way back to wherever hair goes, back to damn Africa, I guess. She searches for something dry. I can't answer her questions. I don't know what to say. Cursing, she wraps me in a sheet and slips away down the hall.

OK, OK, OK, I think, clutching the sheet closer. *Ayo-Bessie. Grace. Y'all just trying to confuse me.* Grace always speaks loudly, her memories hissing insistently inside my head. And behind her are the dream-like tangles of Ayo's life. More distant but also more painful. I shiver, wanting it all to go away immediately, but I still see the burning eyes of the man on the ship's deck, lit up with some fever.

"Lizzie," says Ruth, slipping back into the room and closing the door, "you got to say something to me so that I know you're doing all right here." She is still soaking wet. She drops a dry gown, one of Aunt Eva's, over my head.

"Lizzie?!" she grabs my arm, and we both gasp. A searing pain passes through my body, radiating from the wrist she has in her hand. Her eyes widen and she looks otherworldly, her body rigid with pain, her hair hanging limply against her chin, and the wet gown still glued to her body.

"Let go of me," I manage to choke out. "Please. It hurts."

But she hesitates, as if it is difficult to move. Finally she reaches up with her other hand and pries her own fingers from around my flesh. I slump, suddenly so tired, staring at the red, round marks on my wrists.

I watch her wearily take off the wet gown and put on another. She sits on the edge of the bed and begins drying her hair with a towel. She tosses me another dry towel and slips under the covers.

"Go to bed before you die shivering there, Lizzie," she says. "But don't touch me."

I turn off the light. Ruth breathes heavily beside me in the bed we share, and I try to scoot my body as close to the wall as possible.

"Don't tell the doctor," she says.

"What?" I turn my head to look at her, trying to see her face in the dark. I only discern the faint outlines of her cheek, her nose, her ear.

"I wouldn't tell your father or Sarah about what happened tonight if I were you," Ruth says.

"I wasn't going to."

"Good idea." Ruth turns her back towards me, and I sink down in the bed. I am afraid to sleep, since the line between dreaming and waking has become hard to see with the naked eye.

The Pagoda
Patricia Powell

THE SUN HAD APPEARED BY THE TIME HE TURNED EAST AGAIN, AND IT battered down on them and on the hilly and dry and hard red earth. Water in his canteen had grown warm and the mule switched its tail though there were no flies. He passed women burned with baskets on their way to market, over worked donkeys straining under impossible weights. The trees, foliage and brush blanketed the roads in abundance, no sight of the shimmering glassy sea, just the blue green mountains bristling with lush vegetation and fluttering butterflies, the meandering dirt paths broken up by ruts, the pure heat, the thatch roof road side stalls full of arguing women and girls and squealing babies, squatting and laughing and selling and buying and standing round and eating and philosophizing. Scrawny dogs and peel-headed chickens rushed from the stalls to the road to yell at the mule and then back again to the stalls where they rooted through the mound of rubbish in silence. He rode on, passing the gothic stone buildings that separated into banks, infant schools, drug stores, hair dressing parlors, barber saloons, tailor shops, fish market, butcher shops, post office, church, rum bars and grocers. He approached the center, where Queen, King and Princess streets intersected and where hundreds of hand cart men sold ice cream and snow cones and cool drinks and the brown and green heads of coconuts. He heard the bells and chants of blind beggars and seeing ones without legs, their trousers folded and hooked at the shiny safety pins. Among them too were the children busy at noisy and convoluted games until they saw him, then they paused to stare at him and to point and shout out and grab at pebbles, before turning back to their games. There were the musicians who sang in deep baritones against the din of jangling banjo strings and stormy tom-toms. The claws of hunger finally dug at him and he slowed near a row of shop fronts and lifted the hat from his parched head and staggered past the disorderly mob of confusion, his legs wobbling from ill use. He unsaddled the mule and looped the noose around the waist of a Sycamore and tucked his shirt neatly into the waist of his trousers, and checked if the bristle black brush of hair pasted above his thin and trembling lips had escaped and entered the square. He carried his hat in his hand, and his shadow lumbered ahead of him, mammoth-like and imposing.

There were people everywhere, some white, but mostly men of a million assortments of brown, dressed in Sunday clothes and white shoes, some with string ties and felt hats and bow ties and bowler hats and brightly colored short sleeved shirts. There were men who had faces twisted with laughter and men with chattering mouths full of solid gold bars of teeth and men with smirking smiles and men with eyes that crouched with anger. They stood in the entrances of banks and schools and post office and clinics and police station; in the entrances of the towering government buildings. They stood in the narrow entrances of bars holding glasses full of rum and bottles of beer and sticks of cigarette and rolls of tobacco. They talked and guffawed with crooked and corroded faces and slammed dominoes on upturned crates. They stood in the shade of Ortanique orchards with their legs wide apart, hugged their balls and thought of their frustrated longings. They stood with their legs wide apart, a row of them, backs to the street, pissing and waving their blue cocks. They sat on wooden benches with their legs crossed at the knees and their legs spread out in front of them and folded at the ankles and with their legs collapsed underneath them in a squat. They leaned against broken down stone walls, against the wrought iron gates that protected the colonial monuments; they wrapped themselves with frail, sinewy arms, they talked in loud voices, with wet eyes, about politics and the infertile land and the approaching drought and about their people back there. This, they would say with their heads flung behind them, for the island, now erased of its original inhabitants, was composed of a transplanted citizenry. They talked about women and their pendulous breasts and swinging hips. They talked about women and their provocative and secret smiles, the fabulous drum roll of their bottoms. They talked about love.

With unhurried and gaunt and precise steps, Lowe walked into one of the shops and the smooth flow of conversation hushed. It was a mid day and he carried his steaming sweat and the stink of the mule and his trembling radiance inside the shop. And they looked at him as if he were a rare bird indeed, with the sleeves of his shirt flapping round his gangly arms, with his voluminous trousers tucked into the mouth of knee high boots with studded heels that resounded on the asphalt and concrete, with the bristling mustache that swallowed half his face. He nodded, they avoided his beaming eyes and he went up to the counter and saw the enormous crumbling wooden shelves tiered to the ceiling and stacked with tins of goods that winked in the glare of the afternoon and he remembered again plumes of gray smoke, and the cackle and spit of unresisting timbers, and the crowd of arsonists, his neighbors, running and shouting and dowsing the fire they had set to his shop, the villagers, sliding and spilling and colliding in the dark, their clothes shifting like wings, the arms of great trees, their copper skins the color of zinc in the approaching dawn. He greeted the proprietor, who was an old Chinese man he didn't recognize, and whose face was full of tufts of whiskers shooting out the many warts on his face so he looked like a ferret, and ordered two tins of sardines in tomato sauce, half a loaf of hard dough bread, one bottle of grape flavored aerated water, a cut of cheese and maybe one little red pepper if he had any growing in the back. He said all this in Hakka, his face split up into a smile, watching as the man's face tightened and folded and grew hard and lean and his eyes, lit up with an interior glare, avoided Lowe's and stared out past him at the shop full of drunken men who had been sitting there idle, since morning. Lowe ordered again in English, his voice suddenly gone to rot, the muscles in his cheeks shuddering. This time, the man brought a fat green and orange Scotch Bonnet pepper and a chipped enamel plate still dripping with water. He began to cut the bread which Lowe noticed didn't look so fresh, and he arranged slices nicely on the plate. But Lowe had lost his appetite. He signed as he chewed, the food tasting like cement. He looked out at the road with bright eyes. Chickens and a few scrawny goats ran round confused in the heat, the dry earth, the fine red dust. A multitude of sand flies suddenly appeared and turned the world black. They disappeared. The world turned real again.

The shop keeper tried to be friendly. He asked Lowe where he was traveling from and to where he was going. He asked Lowe which part he lived and if he had a woman and children. Lowe responded with words that were no longer than three syllables, bobbing up and down his head, grunting and gesturing with awkward arms that said nothing at all and everything. All of a sudden he was missing his shop and the lean and robust women with bundles on their heads who stopped in just to rest the load or to get some shade or to remove the thirst from their parched throats with a glass of rum or a bottle of Guinness or dragon stout. They would always talk and laugh in high pitched voices and argue about the elections, the lying and thieving politicians, about education for their children, family planning, the women they loved on the side, about their wayward husbands. They talked about unions and working conditions, about proper medical care and independence and famine, their families in England, the approaching war and the inequities of conquerors and dictators and empires. They talked about the scarcity of goods and of work. He like it most when they lowered their voices and smiled secret smiles and batted the black sweep of lashes and talked about their lurid sexual lives and laughed deep, throttling laughs that revealed secrets and insatiable cravings. But the women would never linger long enough though he opened up tins of sardines and offered them sandwiches made with fresh ginger buns so they kept him company in the midday heat. Only the men with washed out eyes stayed, telling him their broken dreams, their bottled up fantasies, and asking about his life back there in south China, in that small village in Kwangtung. But now they were gone. Everything was gone. And inside his stomach he felt again the stirrings of a deep and incredible sadness.

He paid and wobbled out slowly with no dignity at all in his steps that moved clumsily one before the other and into the blazing sun to collect his mule and he took the reins and lurched on his journey to his daughter's house. He rode past a few more concrete buildings, then the foliage overtook the world again and there was only the one roadside stall here and there and the yellow sun coppering his face and his thin, wicker shadow, which had all but disappeared. He realized that maybe he was truly mad after all to be thinking of building up a center, a Chinese cultural center, especially when the white merchants were beginning to harbor bad feelings against Chinese businesses and had even gone so far as to enact bills now sitting in the legislature waiting for passage. When month after month, the hostile and war mongering people were setting Chinese businesses on fire. Maybe he should just drop the idea at once and think of something else. Something more practical. But nothing came to mind, and a depression descended on his so profoundly he wanted only to throw himself off the mule, only to sharpen a stout piece of stick and run it through his chest, only to hack at his wrists with his knife sleeping there at his waist, anything, anything to relieve him of the abyss in his stomach.

And then he thought of Joyce, fabulous Joyce who had been his friend, all these years, but whom he didn't see much anymore, though she had attended Cecil's funeral, Cecil who was burnt in the blaze, and had absorbed him with her hugs afterwards. He remembered the shrill ring of her musical laughter and the gorge in his stomach ebbed and suddenly the journey to his daughter's house wasn't etched with as much torture. Joyce had been the only woman who often stayed at the shop to keep his company. She was married to Mr. Fine, who was a policeman and rode a shiny bicycle he imported from England. She used to come twice a week and at two in the afternoon, the hottest and stillest part of the day when the zinc roof of the shop crackled and popped; when the tar on the asphalt bubbled and whirls of steam rose from the road; when the birds were marble still and the insects screeched a gruesome movie music and stray dogs and goats walked round dizzy.

This was when she would arrive, when Elizabeth his daughter was unconscious with sleep and he would be dozing off as well. She came always with new installments of stories about Mr. Fine and his war-mongering relatives, about Mr. Fine and the corrupt policemen with whom he worked at the station, stories about her manic depression and anxiety, about the hideous details of their sex lives and the incredible adventures of the three children she had for him. He looked forward to her moist eyes that clamped shut when she sprung into laughter, the tiny rat teeth and purple gums. He diligently awaited her lunches of steamed Escovitch fish or curried crab or beef stews always wrapped in white linen, starched and crisp. All those years she visited, he had never said much, just listened to her steaming chatter and laugh. Then one day he noticed that their interaction had changed, that she wore lower cut dresses and more red on her full and heavy lips, that when she leaned over on the counter to tell him confessionals, though it was just the two alone in the shop, he was confronted with the great deluge of her breasts, with the poignant essences of her perfume and body lotions, with the gleaming dark of her velvet skin that glistened in the unbearable humidity.

He noticed too that her dishes had become more exotic, croquettes made with cod fish and béchamel, that she told him was Spanish; chunks of meats seasoned with Indian spices pierced with a wooden skewer and left to roast submerged under warm ashes, that she said was kebob; and noodles tossed with fried eggs, golden squares of bean curd and sprouts (he had no idea where she found those, for he was certain they didn't grow on the island) garnered with a rich and brown peanut sauce she said was Siamese. During all this, he noticed too that she touched him more when she spoke and he saw that her fingers and hands were shapely. She talked and laughed less, though she asked more questions about Liz and Miss Sylvie, indulging him to reveal secrets. Lowe noticed too and with much alarm, that on Mondays and Thursdays, he wore a cleaner shirt, spent more hours at his toilette, polishing and twisting the pointed edges of his false mustache and sprinkling his throat with sandalwood, and that he had taken to saving the leaner, less bony and fatty, more tender pieces of cod fish and salted pork and red herring for her, and that his hand on the scale was not as heavy when he weighed her rice and sugar and cornmeal, and that when goods were scarce he didn't marry them for her.

Then one day when she leaned over to indulge him in confidence, she clamped her wide open mouth on his lips. At first he struggled, and the pressure of her humid hand on the back of his neck was strong and kind. His breathing by this time had stopped, his stomach turning into metal, and his tongue lay logged in the wide open door of her mouth, while hers darted and burrowed, and slivered and cornered. He worried about Elizabeth who might awaken from the fuzzy edges of sleep and about the villagers who might descend on the shop at any moment herded by Mr. Fine. He worried about the dribbles of saliva leaking from either his mouth or hers, he couldn't quite tell, and he opened his eyes slowly, peering out at the solemn world behind her head. He saw that the light had changed, that the searing sun was softening, and that the precise bars of shadows were more diffused than poignant. He saw the quivering edges of his mustache from the corners of his eyes that were moist and clear. A black cat crossed the deserted street and a purple breasted robin flew by. A mother walked by with six open beaked and clucking yellow chicks. Her hand had tightened around his neck and he felt the sharp outlines of the flat bands of gold on her fingers, smelled the fragrances of cinnamon and oleander in her hair and hibiscus on her skin, heard her galloping breaths and the deep pulsation of her wildly beating heart, heard her soft, almost inaudible moans, but maybe those he had made up from the sensational stories the drunken men told on the piazza each night. He saw an enormous pimple on her cheek he had never noticed before, and an extraordinary long string of hair piping from the rounded tip of her small and flattened nose. He thought she must have suffered much or was prone to deep reflection, she had many creases cornering her eyes and generous lips.

Then she pulled her lips away, just as abruptly as she had enforced them, fumbled in her hand bag for the list of items she intended to purchase, patted her straightened hair scraped away from her forehead into a bun, though not one strand had come undone, and began to read from the list. For many weeks she did not return, only Mr. Fines came accompanied by her children. Lowe inquired once and was told that she was ill. He never sent his regards, though he thought fondly of her, but he feared that she might read more into his greetings and decide to pick up from where she had left off. Several months later, she started up again, this time without the dishes, and though they still shared deep intimacies, it was with some formality. Lowe remembered that she had hugged him at the funeral and he had caught a glimpse of her watery eyes and a whiff of her perfume, the flavor of which was different, more fruity, the other had been of spice.

He rode on, his heart graced with more cheer, the journey filled with much less foreboding. It was the middle of the afternoon and the world was silent for even the insects were too miserable to voice their despair.

Danzy Senna

face

BEFORE I EVER SAW MYSELF, I SAW MY SISTER. WHEN I WAS STILL TOO SMALL FOR mirrors, I saw her as the reflection that proved my own existence. Back then, I was content to see only Cole, three years older than me, and imagine that her face—cinnamon-skinned, curly-haired, serious—was my own. It was her face above me always, waving toys at me, cooing at me, whispering to me, pinching me when she was angry and I was the easiest target. That face was me and I was that face and that was how the story went.

In those days, I rotated around Cole. Everything was her. I obeyed her, performed for her, followed her, studied her the way little sisters do. We were rarely far apart. We even spoke our own language. Cole insists that it began before I was born, when I was just a translucent ball in my mother's womb. Cole would lean her high forehead down to the pale balloon of our mother's belly and tell me secrets with her three-year-old gibberish genius, all the while using her finger to trace a kind of invisible hieroglyphics against our mother's swollen flesh. Cole believed I must be lonely in there, frightened of the dark, and that her voice and scribblings would soothe me.

Later we perfected the language in our attic bedroom in the brownstone on Columbus Avenue. Up there, amid the dust and stuffed animals, Cole whispered stories, one-liners, riddles to help me fall asleep. It was a complicated language, impossible for outsiders to pick up—no verb tenses, no pronouns, just words floating outside time and space without owner or direction. Attempting to understand our chatter, my mother said, was like trying to eavesdrop on someone sleeptalking, when the words are still untranslated from their dream state—achingly familiar, but just beyond one's grasp.

My father described the language as a "high-speed patois." Cole and I just called it "Elemeno," after our favorite letters in the alphabet.

My grandmother wanted us to see a child psychiatrist. She said it was my mother's fault, for teaching us at home, in isolation, around the dyslexic kids, who were my mother's specialty. My grandmother said we must have spent too much time around those "backwards children" and that was why we spoke in tongues. My father also blamed my mother for raising us in that kind of chaos. He said we were suffering from a "profound indifference" to the world around us. My mother said they both were full of shit, and left Cole and me alone in the little world we had created.

Our world was the attic. Up there, we performed for each other with the costumes that were stuffed in a trunk at the end of the bed. The attic had a crooked and creaking floor, a slanted roof so low that grown-ups had to hunch over when they came up there to visit, and a half-moon window that looked out onto Columbus Avenue. Across the street sat a red brick housing project, and beyond that, we could just glimpse the tip of the Prudential. I had some vague understanding that beyond our window, outside the attic, lay danger—the world, Boston, and all the problems that came with the city. When Cole and I were alone in our attic, speaking Elemeno and making cities out of stuffed animals, it seemed that the outside world was as far away as Timbuktu—some place that could never touch us. We were the inside, the secret and fun and make-believe, and that was where I wanted to stay.

I don't know when, exactly, all that began to change. I guess it happened gradually, the way bad things usually do. The summer before I turned eight, the outside world seemed to bear in on us with a new force. It was 1975, and Boston was a battleground. My mother and her friends spent hours huddled around the kitchen table, talking about the trouble out there. *Forced integration. Roxbury. South Boston. Separate but not quite equal. God made the Irish number one. A fight, a fight, a nigga and a white . . .*

One evening, Cole and I lay side-by-side on our big brass bed after dinner. Our bellies were full, and the swelter of the day still stuck to us. We lay with our heads toward the foot of the bed, our legs in the air, as we rubbed our feet against the cool white surface of the wall, leaving black smears from the dirt on our soles. We could hear our parents arguing through the heating vent. Muted obscenities. *You pompous prick. You fat white mammy.* We were trying to block them out with talk of Elemeno. Cole was explaining to me that it wasn't just a language, but a place and a people as well. I had heard this before, but it never failed to entertain me, her description of the land I hoped to visit some day. We whispered questions and answers to each other like calls to prayer. *shimbala matamba caressi. nicolta fo mo capsala.* The Elemenos, she said, could turn not just from black to white, but from brown to yellow to purple to green, and back again. She said they were a shifting people, constantly changing their form, color, pattern, in a quest for invisibility. According to her, their changing routine was a serious matter—less a game of make-believe than a fight for the survival of their species. The Elemenos could turn deep green in the bushes, beige in the sand, or blank white in the snow, and their power lay precisely in their ability to disappear into any surrounding. As she spoke, a new question—a doubt—flashed through my mind. Something didn't make sense. What was the point of surviving if you had to disappear? I said it aloud—*peta marika vandersa?*—but just then the door to our room flew open.

It was our mother. She wore a flowered muumuu from Zayres and her blond hair piled into a loose bun. Lately she'd been acting funny. She was distracted, spending hours on end in the basement. I didn't really understand what went on down there. It was a grown-up land, where my mother held her hushed Sunday meetings with her friends. They would disappear from noon till just before dinner time, and Cole and I were absolutely forbidden, at all times, to go near them. Cole thought they must be smoking pot. I thought it was where my mother hid our Christmas presents. Whatever the case, the door was locked and there was no way around it.

Our mother stood still for a moment in the doorway, arms folded across her chest. "Kiddos, get up. Change into something a little nicer. Your father wants to take you to your aunt Dot's house."

"What for?" Cole asked, already up and heading toward the closet.

My mother crossed the room. She was a big woman, in both directions, and looked like a giant as she stepped over our toys, hunching low so her head wouldn't hit the ceiling. She stared out the window with a grim expression.

"Dot's going away. Far away. And she wants to say good-bye."

I sat up with a start, feeling a twinge of panic. Dot was my father's younger sister and my favorite grown-up. She was two shades darker than my father, a cool, rich brown verging on black, with no breasts to speak of, long legs, and a gap between her two front teeth. She liked to dress like a boy, in overalls or low-slung blue jeans, and wore her hair in a short, neat natural. Her real name was Dorothy, but her mother had shortened it when Dot was just a girl.

Dot was the only relative we knew on our father's side of the family. The grandmother on that side remained a mystery to me. We always referred to her as Nana, to distinguish her from our white one, who was always Grandma. Nana had died when I was still a baby and Cole was three. Cole claims to remember her. She says Nana taught her, at that young age, to have an appreciation for coffee (she would give it to Cole with a dollop of sweetened condensed milk, so it was like coffee ice cream). I was jealous of those memories. All I had was Dot, and now she was leaving.

"She's going to India," my mother explained, still frowning at the street. "To the mountains, to stay with some religious guru of hers. Probably a bunch of nuts. I doubt it'll last long, but it's not clear. She claims she's gone for good. Anyway, hurry up. Your father's already outside."

I asked my mother why she wasn't coming. She didn't go to many parties anymore. She said she didn't have time for boogying. She had rallies to attend, and dyslexic students to teach, and secret meetings in the basement. But this party seemed different. Important, from the sounds of it. I knew she liked Dot and would want to say good-bye. I stood beside her and followed her gaze to the street, where my father's orange Volvo sat parked. "You should come," I said.

She looked tense and shook her head. "No, baby. I've already said my good-bye to Dotty. Besides, there are gonna be people there I don't want to see. Now hurry the hell up. You're late."

Before we kissed her good-bye, she mumbled: "Tell that bastard to have you home before midnight."

My father wasn't alone. Beside him in the passenger seat was his sidekick, Ronnie Parkman, a strikingly handsome man with high cheekbones and deep-set eyes. We clambered into the back of the car. As we rolled toward Roxbury, my father and Ronnie talked politics in the front. Earth, Wind, and Fire crooned from the radio, and my father tapped his hand to the beat against the steering wheel. *You're a shining star, No matter who you are, shining bright to see, what you can truly be . . .*

My father always spoke differently around Ronnie. He would switch into slang, peppering his sentences with worlds like "cat" and "man" and "cool." Whenever my mother heard him talking that way should would laugh and say it was his "jive turkey act." In the past year, he had discovered Black Pride (just a few years later than everyone else) and my mother said he was trying to purge himself of his "honkified past."

As we made our way down Humboldt Avenue, my father glanced over his shoulder, smiling at us. "Birdie, Cole, do your papa a favor," he said. "Yell, 'Ngawa, Ngawa, Black, Black Powah!' at those two cats on the corner." He poined to two young men who stood in front of a barbershop, and muttered to Ronnie, "Check them out. Nypical tiggers, wasting their lives away."

Ronnie chuckled and repeated my father's phrase. "'Nypical tiggers.' Deck, man, you're crazy."

Cole and I stuck our heads out the window and mimicked the chant at the corner men, who raised their fists in a half-serious salute. I thought it was fun, my head being hit by the wind of the moving car. "Ngawa, Ngawa, Black, Black Powah!" we yelled again in unison, this time at a neat, churchgoing old lady with salt-and-pepper hair. She stopped in her path and scowled at us as we passed by. My father tried to stifle his laughter and ordered us to sit down.

He explained to his friend, "Dot's flaky. Always has been, always will be. Ever since we were little kids she's had her head in the clouds. This latest silliness doesn't surprise me one damn bit."

Ronnie sighed. "Yeah, Dotty sure knows how to pick them."

My father went on, more insistent than usual. He seemed to be trying to get a reaction out of Ronnie. "She sleeps with these white boys, then acts surprised when they don't take her home for dinner. I told her, these ofays just want their thirty minutes of difference."

I was pretty sure "ofay" meant white, and without really thinking, I piped from the backseat, "Isn't Mum ofay?"

I heard Cole snicker into her hand beside me.

My father threw me a sharp look. "Yeah, but that's different."

"How?"

He sighed, about to launch into a long explanation, when Ronnie began to laugh, low and softly, beside him. "Kids are too smart for their own good. Always gotta watch your back."

My father broke into laughter, too, and forgot to answer my question.

Dot lived on the border of Roxbury and Jamaica Plain in a large communal household that grew all of its own vegetables and marijuana in the backyard and was governed by a Hindu philosophy. Usually, no one was allowed to wear shoes beyond the front door. But tonight must have been extra special, because when Dot opened the door, I saw she wore high white platforms and a tight, bright-yellow minidress. Around her head she had tied an orange-and-purple African cloth that made her look regal. She smelled smoky, foreign already, as she wrapped Cole and me in her arms. She held us away from her then, to examine us.

"If it isn't the terrible twosome. Give your auntie a kiss. Look at you two, so grown. Hot damn, Cole, check you out." She spun Cole around in her hands, then said to my father with a wink, "Watch out there, big daddy. She's gonna be a heartbreaker."

Dot hugged my father and his friend then, and kissed them both on each cheek. She seemed unable to stop smiling, full of possibility, as she led us into the dim crowded house, where people lounged around the main room in a swirl of colors, conversation, and smoke. I heard my father whisper to Ronnie, "Check it out. Welcome to the land of miscegenation."

On the couch, a man with a frizzy brown beard and glasses was giving a back rub to a petite dark-skinned woman, while a Puerto Rican wearing a Red Sox cap backward sat beside them, rolling a joint. A red-haired woman sat cross-legged on the couch, nursing a baby at her bare breast, while a small Indian man sat before her on the floor, waving his arms in excited conversation. My father and Ronnie went into a corner to get beers, then stood perched, watching the crowd with critical stares, whispering to each other from time to time. I stood by the doorjamb watching, transfixed, light-headed from the haze of reefer fumes that sifted toward me.

When I reached beside me for Cole's hand, I felt only air. I was alone. This was always happening to me, in grocery stores, in movie theaters, in crowds. I would wander off, mesmerized by the sight of some oddity—a burned man's face, a dog with three legs, a Bible-thumping evangelist whom everyone else ignored. My mother said that one of these days she was going to get me a leash. Cole was usually the one to find me, on the verge of tears, having realized the danger of my folly.

Cole and Dot had wandered off somewhere. They probably assumed I was close behind. I went down the long hallway in search of them.

The house once had belonged to a family of Hasidic Jews. They had fled Roxbury when it began to change colors, and the building had sat empty and rotting for years until Dot and her motley crew took it upon themselves to restore it. They had been slowly reconstructing the house through lazy Saturdays of hammering, sanding, and painting. But still it had the feeling of a half-finished funhouse. All the floors tilted at an angle, and someone had painted a mural on the long first floor, a row of blissful Indian faces—the disciples of Ramakrishna—women and men with glazed eyes and knowing smiles. The painting was unfinished, and the last disciple, a young woman, was eyebrowless. The mural always had frightened me a bit, and that night I felt a chill as I traced the shape of Ramakrishna's nose with the tip of my finger before moving on through the house.

There were mysteries to be uncovered behind the closed doors that lined the hall, and I turned my attention to the first door, which was open a crack. Angry voices carried out into the hallway. I peeked in. A couple sat on the bed. The woman, a thin white girl with strawberry-blond hair and freckles, was crying. The man wore his hair in a wide, light-brown afro with a headband splitting it in half. He sat beside the girl and said into the air, "You just don't understand. I was trying to help a sister out."

The girl didn't seem to be listening.

"You fucked her, didn't you?" she hissed. Her makeup was smeared and bright like a clown's, and snot was running down into her lips.

"Julie, don't ask questions if you don't want the answers," he told her, shaking his head and looking at the floor.

"You motherfuckers are all alike! All alike!"

She started putting on her jacket, and her eye caught mine.

I stopped breathing, ready to run. But she just sniffled and began sobbing all over again.

I wondered why she couldn't see me, and felt a thrill of anonymity, invisibility, all of a sudden. I wandered away, wondering what else I might find.

I went on like that for a few more rooms, in one finding nothing but clothes strewn across an unmade bed, in another finding four grown-ups giggling madly as they passed a bong around. I was beginning to get bored and to worry where Cole was, when I reached the door at the end of the hall.

It was sealed tight. I had to push hard to open it, but finally it gave.

The light inside was dim, and the room smelled of sweat and cigarette smoke. Books lined the walls, and a desk sat at the far end. It was a strangely conservative room, which stood out from the ethnic and ragtag decor of the rest of the house. It looked somber, like the library in my grandmother's house. But here, a group of men with their backs to me were bent around the desk in an excited huddle, whispering, and letting out little hoots of laughter. I suspected that it was a private meeting and that I should leave. But I wanted to test whether I was really invisible. It was a feeling that thrilled me even as it scared me. I was curious about what all the men were looking at. I opened the door just a little farther, but it let out a loud creak, and one of the men with his back toward me turned in a violent motion.

I had seen him before, though I couldn't place where. Then I remembered. He had come knocking at our door one night a few weeks before. My father had been spending the night away, at a friend's house in Roxbury, but my mother had been at home. I had found them out on the porch together, smoking and laughing, when I came to ask my mother for ice cream. I remember thinking he looked almost like a white man, barely a trace of black at all, except for his tight reddish-brown curls. He had smiled at me and winked and said to my mother, "That your little girl?"

Now he was kneeling in front of me, staring at me with gray-blue eyes, and I stood still as stone under his gaze.

He smiled, and I saw that his teeth were crooked and crowded so that they folded over one another. He had a reddish fuzz over his lip.

"Hey, girl, whatcha lookin' at?"

I shrugged and moved to turn away. But I felt his hand squeezing into my arm—tight.

A voice behind him said, "Redbone, man, get rid of that little girl."

But the man turned toward them, still clutching my arm, and said, laughing, "Nigga, this ain't no ordinary little girl. This be Sandy Lee's little girl. Ain't that right?"

I frowned at him. His slang was awkward and twisted. It didn't seem to come naturally to him. Even I could see that. I reminded me of an old black-and-white plantation movie my father had forced Cole and me to watch one Sunday afternoon. The slave characters in it had been played by white actors who wore some kind of pancake makeup on their faces. My father had laughed whenever they spoke in their strained dialect. Redbone sounded as if he had graduated from the same school of acting.

I glanced over his head at the group. They were blocking my view to the desk.

He laughed. "Girl, you wanna see what's on the desk?"

I stared at him for a moment. I was aching to see, but hesitated, instead looking at one of the men, a friend of my father's, who smiled softly at me, as if he felt sorry for me.

"Yeah, let me see," I said, knowing I would get in trouble for this one, but too curious to care.

Redbone picked me up in his arms in one swift motion. He smelled like sweat, and there were yellow stains, like piss in snow, creeping out from his underarms.

He hauled me over to the desk.

I looked down to see two large rifles, black and shiny, cradled on top of a couple of pillows. They looked like twin sleeping dogs lying there.

Redbone whispered in my ear, "You know what those be?"

"Guns." I leaned forward in his arms to touch one, but he held me back.

"Naw, you don't want to get too close, baby girl. I'd have to teach you how to use it first."

One of the men said, "Redbone, why you showing her this, man? Isn't this a security risk?"

But Redbone was still staring at me. I was trying to hold my breath, trying not to smell him.

"This little girl ain't no security risk, brotha. We gotta raise our children to know how to fight. There's a war going on. We can't be raisin' no sissies. We got pigs in the White House and pigs patrolling the street. Know what I'm sayin', Birdie Lee?"

I tried to squirm out of his arms. Something about the way he had said my name felt wrong. Too familiar.

The other men looked uncomfortable.

Just then the door swung open, letting in a burst of joyful chatter from the party. We all turned to see who it was.

My father stepped in with Ronnie. They were laughing and carrying beers. He froze when he saw Redbone holding me.

I yelled, "Papa! Over here!" and put out my arms toward him.

But he didn't move. He was staring at Redbone with a thin-lipped smile. Everyone was quiet as he slowly handed Ronnie his beer bottle.

Then his voice came out: "What the fuck do you think you're doing holding my daughter over those guns?"

Redbone laughed again, a strained, unhappy laugh, his voice breaking. But he put me down, and I ran over to my father, turning now to stare back at Redbone with my hands on my hips.

"Deck, man, don't be gettin' like that. She came in here on her own free will, and I just showin' her what we was doin'." He paused, and a queer, rather miserable smile came over his face as he said, "Maybe you need to get your head out of them books and put some action behind them high-falutin' theories of yours."

But my father was leaning over Redbone then, standing so close to him, towering over him, though they were the same height. "Don't tell me 'bout the revolution, you fake-ass half-breed motherfucker."

The other men crowded around, pulling them apart, laughing nervously, saying, "C'mon, y'all, we're brothers, ain't no need to fight."

"This ain't no brother. Where did this fool come from, anyway? Can someone tell me that? He shows up a month ago actin' like he been a revolutionary all his life. But no one knows where you came from, Red, do they?" my father bellowed.

Redbone's voice was different now, nasal. He was no longer speaking in his butchered slang as he said, "Deck, watch your step. Don't get black and proud on me. You're the one with the white daughter."

There was a lot of pushing and yelling. Without thinking I grabbed the leg next to me and said, "Stop it! He's gonna kill Papa!"

But Redbone didn't get very far. The men held them safely apart and talked to them in smooth, calming voices. I realized I was clutching Ronnie's leg. He leaned down to my level and smiled, putting his hand on my head.

"Bird, no one's gonna hurt your papa. I'll make sure of it. Now, why don't you go find your sister and your aunt Dot? I think they're in the kitchen."

I nodded and turned to go. Behind me, my father's voice: "If I ever see you near my wife again, I swear, man, it's all over."

I gave one last glance to my father holding his hands in the air and backing away from Redbone, who was looking over his shoulder at me with a pained grin.

Outside of the room I ran down the hall toward the yellow light of the kitchen. Dot sat at the table, smoking, while Cole sat beside her, chopping greens. A woman with bleach-blond hair, darkening at the roots, stood at the stove, singing in a low, Spanish accent.

Dot said to me, "Where you been, girl?" Then she looked at Cole and said, "This sister of yours is always wandering off. You need to keep a better eye on her." She stroked my hair. "Your father's been lookin' for you. He wants you and Cole to perform some dance he taught you."

Cole piped in, "'Member, Birdie? He wants us to do the Bump for everybody."

Dot's smile faded when she looked into my eyes.

"What is it, Birdie, baby? Did someone bother you out there?"

I hesitated and looked over at Cole, who had stopped chopping and held the knife in midair.

Dot shook me roughly by the shoulders, and my head jiggled loosely like my Sasha doll's. "Why you look so funny, Bird? Did someone bother you?"

I shook my head no. Dot hugged me to her bony body and said, "Hey there, now. I didn't mean to shake you. But you tell me if anyone hurts you. You hear me?"

I started to speak, to tell them what had happened, but the words caught in my throat. It seemed secret, what I had just seen, and so I said only, "All right. Let's go rehearse."

Cole and I did the Bump to "Roller Coaster" before a group of swaying, grinning grown-ups, who stood jingling their glasses and shouting out encouragement to us. My father had taught us how to do the dance one silly afternoon in the fading light of our kitchen, but now he stood in the back of the crowd, barely watching our performance, his head cocked to the right side as if weighed down by too much information.

In the car ride home that night, as Cole dozed with her head against the glass, I watched the streetlights fly by and tried to eavesdrop on my father and Ronnie, but their words were swallowed by the smooth bullshitting baritone of Barry White.

Zadie Smith

The Peculiar Second Marriage of Archie Jones

EARLY IN THE MORNING, LATE IN THE CENTURY, CRICKLEWOOD BROADWAY. AT 0627 hours on January 1, 1975, Alfred Archibald Jones was dressed in corduroy and sat in a fume-filled Cavalier Musketeer Estate facedown on the steering wheel, hoping the judgment would not be too heavy upon him. He lay in a prostrate cross, jaw slack, arms splayed on either side like some fallen angel; scrunched up in each fist he held his army service medals (left) and his marriage license (right), for he had decided to take his mistakes with him. A little green light flashed in his eye, signaling a right turn he had resolved never to make. He was resigned to it. He was prepared for it. He had flipped a coin and stood staunchly by the results. This was a decided-upon suicide. In fact, it was a New Year's resolution.

But even as his breathing became spasmodic and his lights dimmed, Archie was aware that Cricklewood Broadway would seem a strange choice. Strange to the first person to notice his slumped figure through the windshield, strange to the policemen who would file the report, to the local journalist called upon to write fifty words, to the next of kin who would read them. Squeezed between an almighty concrete cinema complex at one end and a giant intersection at the other, Cricklewood was no kind of place. It was not a place a man came to die. It was a place a man came to in order to go other places via the A41. But Archie Jones didn't want to die in some pleasant, distant woodland, or on a cliff edge fringed with delicate heather. The way Archie saw it, country people should die in the country and city people should die in the city. Only proper. *In death as he was in life* and all that. It made sense that Archibald should die on this nasty urban street where he had ended up, living alone at the age of forty-seven, in a one-bedroom flat above a deserted chip shop. He wasn't the type to make elaborate plans—suicide notes and funeral instructions—he wasn't the type for anything fancy. All he asked for was a bit of silence, a bit of *shush* so he could concentrate. He wanted it to be perfectly quiet and still, like the inside of an empty confessional or the moment in the brain between thought and speech. He wanted to do it before the shops opened.

Overhead, a gang of the local flying vermin took off from some unseen perch, swooped, and seemed to be zeroing in on Archie's car roof—only to perform, at the last moment, an impressive U-turn, moving as one with the elegance of a curve ball and landing on the Hussein-Ishmael, a celebrated halal butchers. Archie was too far gone to make a big noise about it, but he watched them with a warm internal smile as they deposited their load, streaking white walls purple. He watched them stretch their peering bird heads over the Hussein-Ishmael gutter; he watched them watch the slow and steady draining of blood from dead things—chickens, cows, sheep—hanging on their hooks like coats around the shop. The Unlucky. These pigeons had an instinct for the Unlucky, and so they passed Archie by. For, though he did not know it, and despite the Hoover tube that lay on the passenger seat pumping from the exhaust pipe into his lungs, luck was with him that morning. The thinnest covering of luck was on him like fresh dew. While he slipped in and out of consciousness, the position of the planets, the music of the spheres, the flap of a tiger moth's diaphanous wings in Central Africa, and a whole bunch of other stuff that Makes Shit Happen had decided it was second-chance time for Archie. Somewhere, somehow, by somebody, it had been decided that he would live.

 Lisa Teasley

Baker

THE LAST PERSON EVER TO SEE MARTY NAKED WAS HIS LITTLE SISTER, Baker, back in Amarillo, Texas, when they were 12 and 5, respectively. Not long after, Baker was diagnosed as autistic. Marty always thought his nakedness had caused his sister's disability.

Marty moved to New York when he was 17. For nine years he had numerous jobs involving grease and oil, until he met Carol, who hired him at the paper in Jersey City, where he lived. Carol was soon fired but it didn't matter since she failed upward. She had already been fired from seven jobs, each one paying more than the last, so she sported no pallor of defeat. Carol was beautiful—not heartbreakingly beautiful, but beautiful and heartbreaking. Only 33, she'd been divorced three times. The ex-husbands hung on, left messages on the machine. Marty knew little about them because he didn't want to. She told Marty her lovers had always worn jockeys, but her *mates* wore boxers. Marty looked particularly tall, skinny, pale and gangly in the boxers she chose for him. Although it had been a year and a half with Carol, he was always half-dressed with the lights off when they had sex, and he always took showers with the door locked. So she'd never seen him naked. This she said she'd conquer after he agreed to go to AA.

As well as drinking there was coffee to kick, then sugar, then Jesus. Soon he found the god of health. Couple mornings a week when he had spent the night at Carol's in

Williamsburg, he'd leave the car in front of her building, and take the L train one stop into the city for yoga on 1st and 15th. There was a woman, Leila, whom he somehow didn't consider a revisiting of his past big black girl fetish. This was different, and serious. He could never predict which class she would attend, but when he was lucky, he'd walk in, see her name on the sign-in sheet, and anticipate the thrill of watching her limbs move, her muscles skate, her dark skin shine. Her body had one flaw which didn't challenge aesthetic but rather function. When she scooped her stomach on the floor, pressing the palms of her long hands in an attempt to bring herself up into the position called Cobra, she winced, hardly making it halfway. He heard her apologize many times to the teacher for the structure of her spine. He wanted badly to hear her whisper same into his ear while fucking her from behind. But he knew this would take time.

Marty's sponsor gave him a tape denouncing self-will, self-love, and sex. Mornings after Carol had rode him, he would pop them in her deck, while she got ready for work. Carol came out of the bathroom, this time, and screamed. When he showed no reaction, she started yelling about how nice it was when they first met, listening to tapes of the ocean, or some of the "fast shit" that he was into when she still worked at the paper. As Marty could feel nothing, watching her, wondering how he'd ever fell for her, as he had never really liked the taste of her, she ran for the iron, which wasn't plugged in, then scrambled for him where he sat on the bed, and punched him with it in the ear. The pain rang, as he closed his palm over his ear, and he looked up at her in disbelief, and then she hit him again, this time in the jaw, which was where she said she meant to put the first one.

He could knock her back with it, or could lie there enjoying the pain and the look on her face, girlish regret. He's seen it before, when she'd hit him, but they were few and far between, these scattered incidents of her explosive anger. The pain felt right, he thought, burying the back of his head into the pillow, as she said she was sorry and put her hands gently on his hips. Forgive me, she said, as he knew he was forgiven for one more night of sex that meant nothing to him, for one more night of sex without love or marriage, and how was it, he wondered, that these ex-husbands had fallen for her anyway?

The drive through the Holland Tunnel, the stop and start and the echoing howls of horns made him aware for the first time that they were all under water. And it felt soothing to him. He could live out the fantasy of drowning, if he really concentrated, and it would squeeze it out, those thoughts of little girls, and the whackings, as he called it, from his old mother.

What happened to your face? Everybody kept asking in the building as he made his rounds with the mail. Everybody, except Benjamin, got the sly smile from Marty, which hurt and reminded him. With Benjamin he went out to the truck for a dog and a Snapple, which tasted nasty and canceled out all of last week's offerings to the god of health.

Marty my man, have you fallen off? Benjamin finally said from the curve where they sat looking across the street to the soot-colored building. Ah nah, man, 246 days, I'll make it to my first birthday, Marty said, smiling to face Benjamin, so it hurt again. It was Carol, and I didn't lay a hand on her. Benjamin shook his head, and laughed then said, Don't take this the wrong way, but everybody knows, me especially, that Carol is fucked up. Marty rolled that over for a while, then said, No, it's me. Really. Well, Benjamin said, This is the best time of year to count your friends and leave the rest of them where they belong, in the dirt. Know what I mean, man? When the leaves are changing color, and falling down on the ground. The beauty of it man, always tells the truth. Yeah, Marty answered. I used to travel 'round this time most every year, just drive from Texas to wherever when the colors were doing their thing, and I used to leave half my heart home, but then came a time when I took the whole thing with me. So I know what you mean. Maybe you do, man, Benjamin said. And then again, maybe you don't, because you have this problem, see, with listening. Benjamin got up and hit him firmly on the back of the head, and called back, See you in there.

Later when Marty drove by the preschool, and his head started pounding, pushing out, trying to squeeze out any too-old memories of his little sister Baker, he ran a red light then screeched all the way to the first pay phone to call his sponsor. Thomas, a market analyst, had given him his cell, and whenever Thomas gave him a short quick response of the next hour on the clock when he would call him back, Marty would have to wait out five minutes of a testy edge until Thomas settled in with some humanity. Fuck it, Marty said aloud when he hung up, and he made it to the next meeting.

While he was there not listening to the woman going on about her sickness, he was thinking he would go to a yoga class for every meeting. That would up his chances for seeing Leila.

The fourth time was when Leila gave him five minutes after class, and he gave her the depth of his white boy humility, which had always worked. He asked her if he could drive her home, since she lived in Brooklyn, and even though he didn't have his car there, he knew she would turn him down but maybe take him up on it the next time, and so could figure out her schedule. He found out she was a pastry-maker for a French restaurant in the city, so he feigned his shock to lie and say his mother did the same thing in San Francisco. It occurred to him he should explain his slight Texas twang, so he told her about Amarillo but made up the rest about moving to California with his mother, and he left out his sister altogether. There was some truth to it, he thought, as the instructor said goodbye, and a couple people pushed in to get to their things, Leila was pulling her skirt up over her purple bike shorts, now covering the shape of her gorgeous thighs, and slipping her backpack on. This lie wasn't such a stretch, Marty thought. After all, his mother worked in a diner and pies were among the things she served, and his mother had a sister who left for California just after their parents were murdered when they were still in their teens.

From the door of the building, Marty decided to go the opposite way of Leila, so that he could wait until she made it three quarters of a block then follow her. When she disappeared down the steps into the subway, is when he walked around in search of a lingerie shop so he could buy her a bra and panties, some deep strain of red like burgundy or maroon that would set off the tone of her skin, then he could give it to her at the proper moment.

Carol had been leaving desperate messages on his machine for the past week, since he'd only been by her place once or twice in the last month, the time before last being violent again, which he swore to her later he didn't mind, because in fact he knew it saved him from having to have sex with her again, and again.

Sponsor Thomas invited Marty to meet him at one of his Wall Street bars thick with slick hair and cigar smoke. How can you drink coke in one of these places, Marty asked, him as he always did. Because I have to, Thomas said, it's my job. And that's what you have to learn, Marty, how to handle yourself in all the tough situations, like bars, and women, and lonely winter nights. This winter hasn't been shit yet, has it? Marty asked, trying to be light. No it hasn't, Thomas said, dragging on his cigarette. So tell me, you moving up yet in that shit-hole of a paper? Marty laughed. And then he looked past, and made a tunnel through all the dark suits, and loud voices that sounded like one long grumble until Marty squeezed it into a rumble, fast, like getting into a car and racing it down the road, dragging it past the drunk fucks who'd just challenged him to a crash.

What do you see in me? Marty asked Thomas. Thomas laughed, and then squinted his eyes, and brought his face closer to Marty's, and with a slim curl in his lip, whispered, Is there something you're trying to tell me, son? Then he winked, and hit the table, then with both hands beat it as if it were a drum, and said, Fuck man, you're going to make it.

The eighth time Marty had a treasured encounter with Leila was when she finally said she would take that ride home. They had to walk five blocks to his car, and he noticed she often left off the last words of her sentences, as if he was supposed to know what would come next. He noticed too that there was something similar to Carol about her, not their skin or texture of their hair, of course, but something in the space between all of the features of their face. He was sorry about this, and tried to see something else. He concentrated then on seeing her with the instructor when he would adjust her, and the expression she had, this kind of merciful expression he wanted to lick off.

He was relieved to see, as they drove, that she lived in Park Slope, very mixed, and not some black ghetto he couldn't be caught dead in in Texas. And he pushed that out of his mind, as well, he was determined not to fuck with his own mind and his own past with her, because he deserved a little better this time.

It wouldn't be right to come in, he thought, as he pulled up in front of her building, and she gave him the sweetest smile of gratitude, and then something else washed across her face just before she opened the door, and he wanted to slap it off of her. That thought scared him, as she said, Thank you, and got out, and she shoved the door closed quite hard, and since his car had human qualities to him, he took offense for a moment, then thought to himself, Well she could never know what a car could mean, she's probably never owned one in her life.

He saw Carol that night and she'd pulled all the stops, candlelight, very sheer nylons, and she even put on his favorite gloves, and sat dangling her shoe from the tip of her toes, the way he used to love. Instead of grabbing her, as he thought he would a moment ago, he got up, proud of himself, feeling like Thomas, who he realized he hated and had always hated, but felt proud to be like him, as he walked out the door. Yes he did know how to handle difficult situations.

At the truck with Benjamin the next day, in front of work, Marty said it was finally over with Carol. Thank God, man, Benjamin said gulping down his Sprite, which he always drank, pulling his pea coat tight around his neck. I was beginning to think you were truly thick, but you did it man. Marty smiled and leaned back and stretched his arms behind him. Benjamin started talking about Hawaii again where his stepfather had an old coffee ranch, and what it was like the last time he was there and he wished he was there right then. And then he started talking about his best friend from college, who he'd had some rivalry with that started with some chick but was really about something deeper like the dynamics of his family. Marty tuned out, and headed to the preschool in his mind. And when he realized Benjamin had gotten up, he looked up at him and saw that Benjamin was looking at him with disgust. See you in there, man, Benjamin said, as if to hide the look. But Marty saw it. He never missed those looks. He'd seen them way too often in most everybody he knew.

Leila had been to lunch with him once, then for a late coffee one Thursday night. It wasn't until after a movie, just after his first birthday, that he decided to give her the underwear. It was daring, seeing as how he had never even kissed her, and he felt a punch in the gut just as he handed her the package, all wrapped in butcher paper with a curly yellow ribbon.

I'll open this when I get home, if you don't mind, she said to him. She was searching his eyes, the way he hates in a woman. Why do they always do that, just when you don't want them to? Marty looked at the ground, and then they got in his car and he drove her home playing the "fast shit" Carol would have preferred to his self-help tapes.

He didn't see Leila until two weeks later when he picked her up one morning to go to yoga. She came down the steps with a little girl, and the sight of her knocked him flat. As Leila opened the door, Marty thought he was having a breathing attack. Leila ignored it, or else didn't see it, and she introduced the little girl, and he didn't catch her name, but he did hear that she was her daughter. When he was catching his breath, looking out of his window, pretending to watch for oncoming traffic before he pulled out, Leila said that they just need to drop her daughter off at dance class, and her cousin would be picking her up.

Marty heard nothing else Leila said that whole excruciating drive to the dance class, which couldn't have been more than five minutes but took him through his entire lifetime in his head. He kept not trying to look at her, there in the backseat, with her hands in her lap. Looking out of the window, then at him in the rearview mirror, already like an adult, with that subtle look of disgust on her lips.

He watched Leila take her to the door, and then come out again. She looked as if she were trying to catch her breath too, and before she got it, it seemed for a moment as if she were changing her mind.

I should have told you about her, I suppose. No, no, Marty said, and then he wondered where that came from, out of him. I mean, I had plenty of opportunities, and I missed them all. He looked at her before they got on the bridge, and then he thought he should try and be nice. As they began to climb it, he put his hand over hers, but more to steady his own mind. You don't have a problem with children, do you? she asked hesitantly, and her eyes were big, and he hated that, and then hated her for making him think he could push her out of the car and head for the first bar. Just a few weeks after his birthday, like that. No, no, Marty said. How old is she, anyway? Four and a half, she said. A big, four and a half. I wouldn't know, Marty said, too quickly. The traffic started to bunch up and he felt smothered being up so high. She doesn't look much like you. Thanks, she said. Then she laughed. Her father is Pakistani. Really? Marty asked, moving the gear into park, as traffic had come to full stop for minutes on end. They don't like black people much, Indians, do they? She seemed taken aback at this, and then she laughed again. Well, who does like black people much? Sorry, Marty said, looking at her. Forget it. You don't want to hear the history with her father, which is very much over for me. Not for her. He's actually a good man, and we were in love for some time. It just didn't work is all. Sorry, Marty repeated, and then moved back into gear to crawl another few feet. Shyly she looked at him, You think we'll make it to class? Probably not, he said, relaxing finally. Well, she said. She laid her head back on the seat. She sighed. She looked out of the window. Well, she said again. I must tell you. I fell asleep in the underwear you gave me. She turned to look at him, and so he returned it. You can't guess what I dreamed, she said. Maybe I can, Marty said, getting mesmerized by her eyes, then turning to drive a few more feet. I'll tell you anyway, her smile getting bigger, her eyes more coy. I dreamed you fucked me all night. Well, Marty said. Well, well. Leila gasped a little before she giggled, and it touched him. That being the case, Marty said, if I've already had you, I may as well have you. And they drove through the traffic on the bridge and through the streets, and through the Holland Tunnel to his place in Jersey City.

I have a new woman now, Marty said to Thomas after a meeting. Thomas shook his head as he lit a cigarette. Marty's breath was thick in front of him, as thick as the smoke Thomas blew to the side before he responded, What did I tell you about women? I know what you told me, Marty said, but I wasn't born this morning. No, Thomas said, you were born a little over a year ago when you took your last drink. Maybe so, nevertheless, this isn't just sex. This is something entirely different. I'm feeling as new and as pure as I did before I ever had a filthy thought in my head. Is that so, Thomas said, laughing. Well, my friend. If that is truly the case, you're going against everything in the program. You aren't tough enough to lick this thing over night. Get it into your head, my man. You are an alcoholic. And after only little more than a year of sobriety, you are nowhere near knowing one from two, much less twelve. Be careful, Thomas said, as he turned to walk off. Then he stopped in his tracks, and looked back at Marty, and called, And consider this woman, my friend, she deserves someone who still has his head! Marty flipped him off, and Thomas brought up his hands, like, What else can I say? Then kept walking.

It was early summer by the time Leila could trust Marty longer than 20 minutes alone with her girl. He was in her room, and she was showing him her latest action figure, which went with the one he just gave her. Leila would only be an hour getting her hair "touched up" at the salon. She had someone fast, she said, and she said this more to bolster her own confidence, it seemed to him, than to reassure him of the shortness of any babysitting duties. The girl had him laughing with the toughness in which she fought his doll with hers. The games in her head seemed complicated to him, and it brought him back to his little sister Baker, and instead of squeezing it out, he tried to remember how it was when it was good and natural between them. And he relaxed with it, and he laughed and enjoyed himself, and so it caught him by surprise when she said she had to go to the bathroom, and he found himself following her. I don't need help, she said, as she started to close the door. But when he put his hand there to stop her from closing it, startled, she looked up at him.

He couldn't hear whatever he said to her so that she would just relax and go ahead and pull her pants down and "go potty," that part he did hear himself say, but he couldn't see himself, or he couldn't imagine himself doing what he was doing, as he was taking off all of his clothes to be completely naked while the girl wasn't looking but busying herself with the toilet paper. She had pulled off too much of the toilet paper, and when she saw that he was nearly naked, she asked too loudly what he was doing, so he moved over to her to cover her mouth. Oh God, he thought, because his mind was trying to catch up to him, something didn't feel right, as everything was clearing up and he began to see a bit of himself, and the terror was starting but he had to rush on through. The girl was struggling with all she had in her, and so when he heard the door open, a part of him was relieved and the other part panicked, trying to push his body against the bathroom door, trying to keep it closed, while trying to hold onto the girl's mouth, and her body, while he heard Leila wailing and kicking at the door, and everything all slippery with his sweat, the sweat dropping into his eyes in fact. There were stomps on the floor and then Leila was back again, and she got the door open, and there she stood with a gun, pointed at his nose, while she yanked the child from him, threw her out of the room and closed the door behind her. *Yes God,* Marty heard himself say, as she cocked it. Yes, God, Leila yes, Thank God, pull it.

 Jervey Tervalon

Rika

LOOK AT THIS. WONDERED HOW MANY PEOPLE WOULD SHOW UP CONSIDERing the kind of fool you were but you've got a crowd to bury you. I can't join them, you know. See how beautiful that casket is and the flowers. Picked them out didn't I. Because you knew what happened was going to happen and you didn't want some low rent funeral. You wanted to look good going down, I have taste. I took care of it. You just didn't think that I'd be the one. It's fine down here at the foot of Forest Lawn. I don't need to join the crowd. I know what everything looks like; the yellow and white roses and tulips, the gold and pearl casket. Not your colors as much as mine. You were always too much into purple. Couldn't leave the gaudy behind. I know your mother's crying, Ollie's cursing me out. I know your associate's looking my way, checking the car out, trying to see if it's really me. Wonder what he thinks. I'm not a fool. I can come back anytime—you're not going anywhere.

It's night now. Sitting in the car above the lights. Bet you wonder how I make it. How you used to talk to me, "Can't do a damn thing for yourself cept spend money." But it's not like that. I know what I'm doing. Look at the roaches walking by. The jungle is buzzing tonight. Roaches after crumbs. I'm tired of watching, see what you've done to me. They look just like me. Noses open, sprung. Looking for a blast. Drive further up the hill, not like I'm living down in the jungle or anything. I might not be staying on the Westside but Baldwin Hills isn't the projects.

Oh yes, my uncle has a beeper for a reason. He's an architect, blueprints cover the kitchen table. See, they have a marble foyer with a coat rack. Now, if I can sneak to the bedroom everything will be right with the world. The TV's on the living room. Sounds like *Wheel of Fortune.*

"She's back."

It's my uncle's voice.

"Rika, could you come here?"

Oh no.

"What?"

Gotta get to the third door on the left. Lock myself in, wait them out. Here they come. Uncle Jack, gray-haired but quick, pushes me aside and blocks the way. Must have been playing tennis at Dorsey, still in his sweat-stained whites. Mother looks shocked as usual. My fat auntie leads us into the living room, nice view of the Hollywood hills but the setting sun is still too bright. I need my shades.

"You left again," Uncle Jack says.

"You can't leave," my mother says. Her eyes, red and desperate.

"Where did you go?" my aunt asks.

I don't say anything. I smile.

"Jesus! She's high again."

Mother stands and runs to the other side of the room and starts crying. I start for the bedroom but my uncle is forcing me down into a bean bag. I made a big sloosh as I land. He's so mad he's sputtering.

"Do you know what you're doing to your mother, us? We are trying to help you. And you go out in your robe and slippers wearing a rag on your head like you're some kind of cheap hooker on Normandie."

I don't look at him. Instead I look at my slippers. What's wrong with my slippers? They're clean.

"We took you and your mother in because she needs help. We're going to give her that help. If we can't help you here we're going to have to commit you. But you're going to get help."

He keeps saying give, get and going. Maybe I should get going.

"Don't you have something to say?"

I shake my head.

"Where did you go, to the jungle to buy crack?"

"I did not!" I say but a scream comes out. Everybody jumps. I try to struggle out of the bean bag but I tumble over. My mother rushes over grabbing me, holding on like I'm going to run.

"Baby, baby, were you with that boy? You weren't with him, were you?"

With him? Wow, I thought she knew.

"I saw him but I wasn't with him."

They're looking at me, all in my face.

"I thought you promised me you wouldn't see him after all he's done to you," Mother says, tears rolling down her face. She cries even better than before.

"I wasn't with him. I saw him . . . from a distance."

"I bet he's the one who gave it to her," Jack says, positively irate.

Auntie throws her hands up and goes for the phone. "I'm calling. There's no way we can handle this. This girl needs professional help."

Mother pulls me out of the bean bag, with one hand, just yanks me up.

"See, she's making the phone call. We can't handle this. We can't watch you twenty-four hours a day."

Funny, they keep saying the same things.

"Why are you laughing?"

"Me?"

Jack grabs me by the arm and drags me to the room I was trying to get to in the first place. He pushes me in, Mother watching.

"You're not going anywhere."

Mother comes in and gives me a hug. She's wearing Chanel. "We love you. You've got to try . . ."

I wait for her to complete the sentence. Fill in the blank. To get a hold of myself. To control myself. Not hurt myself.

"Jesus. She's laughing again. She's not listening to anything."

"I'm listening!"

Another scream. Mother almost jumps off the bed. Uncle Jack shakes his head and leaves.

"You really are sick," Mother says whispering like she doesn't want me to hear.

"I'm okay."

"You need so much help."

"You should get a cut like mine. It's very summery."

Mother draws back. Pulls my hand from her hair. She should get it dyed too, I don't care for all of that gray. Now, she's holding on to me crying again. Softly, so Uncle Jack can't hear. He's so full of himself.

"Rika. You got to promise me not to see that Doug again."

"Mother. I thought you knew? Doug's no longer with us."

"What?" she says, her blue eyes streaked with red.

"He's gone to his reward."

"He's dead?"

"Yes, Mother. They buried him today."

"And you went to the funeral in a bathrobe?"

"I didn't get out of the car. It was okay."

"Are you sure . . . ?"

Mother's so happy. She doesn't want to believe me.

"Yes, I'm very sure."

"Why didn't you tell us? It explains so much."

"I thought I did."

"Oh, baby. I really didn't know."

Again, she wraps her arms around me and cries, tears drip onto my cheeks. It's embarrassing.

"Mother, you should go and get some rest. I'll be fine."

She looks at me, what's the word? Forlorn, forlornly. I've made her so sad.

"I am tired."

She kisses me and heads for the door.

"If you need me . . . "

I nod. She tries so hard. I hear Uncle Jack at the door locking me in. I hope nobody's smoking in bed! What's on the tube? I turn it on and turn down the sound. Who needs the words and lie back. What time is it? Eight-thirty. Much too early to go to bed. But I am tired too.

What I don't understand is how I feel. Suddenly everything changes. I don't feel good at all. Comes in waves, my good humor washing away like sand castles. Isn't that it. That nothing lasts, nothing keeps, specially a buzz. I'm not like you, though. You're the kind of man that would make his woman sit in a car; yes, it was a Benz but so what, and for how long? Once, I sat in that leather-lined pimpmobile for four hot hours, getting out only once to use the bathroom. Knocked on the door of that run-down house and there you were, with your associates, four or five very dumb-looking future felons watching a basketball game in a smoky living room. Then it was only the smoke of the best Ses but soon we would all be smoking the roach powder. You actually looked pissed as though I had no reason at all for interrupting the festivities, even if I did have to go in the worst way. You looked at me like I was the stupidest, the ugliest bitch in the world but you failed to notice the way your associates were ogling me. You saw me like everyone first saw me, a fine, high yella bitch, who looked like a model with good hair and green eyes. Wasn't I a trophy? I had to be stuck up, I had the look of someone what had to be stuck up. And you had to have it. You had to train me because I needed to be turned into a obedient bitch, and because I have certain problems I went along with the program. But you didn't know then, that because you made me sit and fetch and wait on hot leather seats for master to bring me a bone, that I wouldn't forget, that the bitch would bite that bone.

Let me turn out the light, turn off that TV, this room looks like an ugly motel, cottage cheese ceiling, hot green, oversized couch—where did they get this stuff? Better in the dark, cooler.

It didn't start that way. You came into the Speak Easy like you were going to yank some girl off the dance floor and take her to the car and do a Ted Bundy on her. I'm sure you thought you were the most dangerous player there, bigger, younger, better looking. But baby, baby, nobody was fooled. The girls there knew, knew you had the wrong zip code, even if you have a fat wallet. Too, too wet for a girl who wanted a legitimate money man, that's why you didn't get much play. You were in the wrong neighborhood. I saw you coming but you know, right then, you were just the thing for me, what I was looking for. I really hate to be bored. More than anything, more than getting slapped by a man who doesn't know he'd prefer a boy or driven up the coast and left to find my way home. See, all of that wasn't fun but baby, I wasn't bored and I got their numbers, paid them back in kind. So when I saw you, a young buck-wild businessman, I just knew you were the ticket to go places I've been and wanted to get back to.

"Are you with somebody?" is the first thing you said to me leaning back in your chair to show your thousand-dollar suit to its best advantage. "No," I said. And gave you a wet-lipped smile and, Douglas baby, you were sprung. I could have had it then, twisted you into the most vicious knots I could have imagined but I wanted to see, see how far we were going to go. Just how bad it was going to be.

Somebody's at the door. Probably Mother, wondering if I'm okay, or Uncle Jack wondering if I managed to slip out again. They think because it's dead locked I'm securely tucked away. Too stupid. Soon enough and I'll be making like a roach and bug on out of here.

Oh, how nice, I slept. At least three hours of beauty rest. See with you we never had time for sleeping; either we were chasing the rock or fucking or fighting. But now, since you've gone on to your reward, I actually find time to rest. That's why I look better, that haggardness is gone. Sleep is truly a wonderful thing. What's it like to be dead? Do you see me? Do you see me when I smoke your money and you're not there to share the happiness, the bliss? Do you see me getting on my knees and getting a high school boy the best blow job of his life for a couple rocks? Not that I have to do it, I still have quite a stash, but baby, I'm not being simply frugal, though frugality is to be admired, really, the kick is imagining you spinning in your ten-thousand-dollar coffin. How sweet!

I should go. I'm not getting any happier. Sooner or later I'm going to have to get back to it. The job of feeling good about myself, going on a mission to shake my money maker. It's distasteful. Compared to the creeps I have to deal with now that you're gone, you were the perfect gentleman. Even though you were inclined to punch and slap and burn, you did it with conviction, that's the kind of lover you were, resentful, mistrustful and destructive but we shared those qualities. But Douglas, to these young men, a woman is less than a dog, less than a shrimp plate at Sizzler. They have no idea what relationship is all about. It's like a woman doesn't exist other than for a fuck or to cut. Too simple for my tastes. But I have a taste for the burning white smoke, rolling into my lungs to restore my good humor for five good minutes, smoke it all, my five-O limit. I can exert self-control, something you never managed to do. See, I smoke so I won't be sour, I prefer anything to being sour. Remember when we smoked fifteen hundred worth, and you started choking, really, turning code blue. What was I supposed to do? Call 911? But that's not me, no. You laid there on your back gasping, vomiting, looking like you had bought it. I knelt by your side, saying "I told you nobody can smoke that much." Sure, it was after the fact, but did you listen? I don't know what happened because I had to leave, couldn't sit there and watch you expire. Just like I can't lie here and reminisce about the good old times. One has to live in the present.

What's a deadlock if you have the key? There I go being ironic, but you never understood irony so you don't get the joke. Outside my dark room the hallway is brightly lit, and in the kitchen, near the living room, is my Uncle Jack, dead asleep. I guess he thought he could find out how I do it, make such quick exits. The front door opens without a creak and I slip out. Oh, the sweet fresh air, how I love it. Slip into the auto, take it out of gear and coast downhill. Yes. And the land quickly changes. From the upper middle class split-level ranches down to the jungle apartment complexes. Not stopping, no, not for a stop sign, I'm on a mission. I got a surprise for the fat man. How unusual, no one is lurking in front of the Kona apartments but the yellow light is on. Where are they, the police? It would be stupid to just rush out and plunge headlong into trouble. But what the hey. Yes, the door is unlocked. Inside, I don't see anyone waiting to do something nasty to me. Are things askew or am I getting more and more paranoid? Guess I'll mosey up and see with my own God-given eyes the situation. The hard steel door hurts my knuckles but I knock sharply anyway. Someone walks to the door, must be looking through the spy hole at me. I put my eye to the cold metal of the door. "Fuck" is said and I hear the door unlock even through the noise of the TV. It swings open and there he is, Alton, Mister Tub O'Lard.

"Hey, it's Miss It. She's back."

He grabs me by the arm and leads me into the little nut hole of a living room, nowhere to sit but a nasty couch.

"You got money, or is it gonna be the usual?"

I nod.

"What's that mean?"

I shrug.

He opens his ham-sized arms wide and gestures for me to see the almost empty room.

"We closing up shop. Too hot round here. Police be sweating a brother twenty-four-seven."

He comes over, perspiring like he's drunk and opens my robe.

"Ooh, that bra is cute but you don't need to be wearing one flat as you is."

I smile sweetly, as he pulls my bra aside and takes hold of my nipple and rubs it clumsily. Thinking of what the next few minutes will bring, I smile even more sweetly.

"Aw, baby, you should take better care of yourself. Bet you slipped out the house with them curlers in your hair, wearing them silly slippers to get a blast. You know, ya still pretty, you oughta slow down."

Oh, how nice, fat boy is giving me the just say no line while he's leading me into the bedroom. I guess we're going to be doing it on the mattress. Doesn't look very sanitary.

"What's it gonna be? Do it like I like, two rocks, like you like it, just one."

He pulls my robe up, forces me stomach down onto that piss-stained mattress. Down come my panties. I hope you're watching. I hope you see what he's going to do to me. He's grabbing my hips, trying to put it inside my ass, but I wiggle making him slip, hoping he'll just do it the normal way. He pushes me away, and I roll to the wall.

"You know how I like it. You don't give it to me I'm gonna take it."

It's gonna get ugly. Is it time for the surprise? He turns me over and grabs my hips again, and yanks my curlers.

"Don't you have oil?"

"Naw. I like the friction."

See, he's forcing my hand down again, trying to push it in. It won't go. I won't let it. Pull the cute little .22 auto out the robe pocket and point it at his big stomach. He stops crawling across the nasty mattress to me. Actually, he's backing up, smiling like a big fat Cheshire cat.

"Baby, baby, what you need? I must be scaring you. I got it in the other room, every-thing you need. Rocked and ready to go."

I smile. How sweet, he's begging just like a dog. I might be a crazy bitch but he's a begging dog.

"Pull up your pants."

"Baby," he says whining pitifully, he really thinks I'm going to shoot him.

"Kneel," I say, he does. We're both the same height now.

"Were you going to hit me?"

"Hit you? Baby, it ain't like that. You didn't hear me right."

"Didn't hear you about what?"

With my left hand, I pull up my panties, the gun feels light in my right. Wonder if it's loaded. I think I loaded it but now . . . oh well. We both kneel there a while, him looking at the gun then my eyes. I know, he's going to go for it. He stands up, big belly aquivering.

"Fuck you. You ain't gonna shoot me."

He comes toward me, then launches himself like a big, fat blanket into the air. His big hams stretched out for me. I squeeze the trigger three times. Three sharp cracks and he's flying in reverse, rolling to the wall, all bug-eyed, trying to scramble to his feet. He can't, must have broken a bone in his leg. But he's not bleeding badly. Look, he's covering his big bald head, must be afraid I'm going to crack it like a big brown egg.

"It's in the kitchen. Take it. You don't gotta shoot me."

"Baby, isn't that for me to decide?"

"Sure, whatever." His big eyes are tugging at me. Pleading for me to let him live. I bet he has a wife and a child at home or a old mother he has to support.

I leave the fat boy and go into the kitchen. Talk about dirty dishes, all kinds of filth. There's what I need on the table, still in the pan. Empty the cake into a plastic bag, and take my leave. In the living room I see Mr. Tub O'Lard's gun, it's a big one, something to have so I put it in my other pocket and go to the door. Shit, it's deadlocked. He's got the key. Back in the bedroom, he's out, slumped against the wall.

"I need the key."

Oh shit. He's out. He can't be dead. I don't touch the deceased. And he's bleeding. I hate the sight of blood. Ugh, must I push him over?

"I got it. Kaiser card's in the wallet."

Oh, he's not dead. Just delirious. Pants are too tight though. How I'm supposed to get the keys?

"I need the keys," I say sweetly.

"Key? Oh yeah, the keys." He reaches around into his back pocket, must be painful the way he's flinching but like the good boy he is, he comes up with them and tries a toss but they roll out of his hand onto the brown carpet that's quickly turning red. "Thanks," I say and cut for the door. Must be nervous because I fumble with the keys, takes what seems like hours to get the door unlocked. Can't be too hasty. Peek before you leap. The hallway is empty, but they're watching, waiting to see who comes running out. Police are probably on their way. I crack the door open. One light for the whole hallway. Point Tub's big gun. Have to use two hands to point this big thing. Smooth, that's what you said. How to pull the trigger. Boom! Boom! Plaster flies everywhere. The light still shines. Damn gun just about broke my wrist. Boom! Boom! Boom! There she blows and I'm in the dark. Drop the gun outside and run. The two lowlifes watching from across the street scatter when they see me coming but I bet they'll sneak over and find Fat Boy's gun before the police get here. It's worth a dozen rocks.

"They're shooting in there!" I yell. Sometimes it's good to state the obvious. I get to my car, throw myself in and burn rubber up the hill. In the rearview mirror I see the red and blue strobes snaking onto Hillcrest. Good, Don Diablo. Who names these streets? I hit the garage opener and pull the car in. See, Douglas, it's not hard to get what you want if you know what you want and you're willing to work for it. Now if I wanted to die, all I would have to do is leave this car running and close the garage door and inhale. Sure, this Lincoln would have shit-stained seats but that wouldn't be my problem. But I don't have a problem, at least not right now. I've got cake in my pocket.

Crack off a piece, a nice sized chunk and fit it into the pipe and fire it up. The red flame turns blue and I can see myself in the rearview mirror. My eyes, pupils are wide as plates, couple of full-lunged hits though, shrinks them to the size of pinpoints. The buzz expand-run-run-run till the soft spot hums. Is that it? I try another and another and another till every part of me hums. How much do I have to smoke till I get enough? I don't know but we'll find out.

I don't sleep, just close my eyes but when I open them again, I see the pipe in my stiff fingers. Still lots of night left. I much prefer the night. Maybe that's what I am, a vampire. Sucking smoke instead of blood. I really have to stop this Douglas. There's no future in it. And even though you couldn't see life without the pipe, even you should be able to appreciate my position. I'm carrying your child. You wouldn't want "it, the unknown" for your firstborn? Well, it wouldn't truly be your firstborn, but those poor, drug-addled tramps that carried your seed don't count. I count. Because I'm the queen of your desire or is it the bitch of your desire. Anyway, let's be honest. I'm going to smoke that baby to hell.

"Get up. You're going!"

Oh, it's morning. I'm in bed and here's Uncle Jack and the rest of his merry crew. He just yanks me up and marches me through the house to the car. And doesn't Mother look disappointed. She slides in next to me, Uncle Jack takes the wheel and my butterball of an aunt gets into the backseat. I guess it's time to go to where they put people like me. To the funny farm where life is gay all the time. The garage door swings open and we pull out into the bright light of day. Mother is crying again as usual but she wants to say something, gagging on the words.

"How could you? We trusted you."

"It's too bright. I need sunglasses."

"We aren't stopping so you can run off. You know where you're gong."

They're really going to do it this time.

"We found the drugs. A whole pocket full. How much did it cost? How'd you get the money?"

"I got it for free."

"She got it for free, hah. What did you sell?" Uncle Jack says. Mother is crying buckets. What a callous thing to say in front of her.

"I certainly did not sell anything that you're implying. I got it for free. I have ways."

"My God, she needs help," Uncle Jack says.

And here's the hospital.

"Emma, you park the car. I'm walking this young lady in."

Uncle Jack slams the brakes, stopping us right behind an ambulance, slides out from behind the wheel and pulls me along, my robe comes open but he doesn't wait. It's like being on a roller coaster the way he's pulling, jerking me one way and then the other.

"What's the rush?" I say, digging in my heels.

He looks at me, his brown face wonderfully twisted in a perfect sneer.

"How could you bring that shit into my house."

"But, Uncle Jack, it's so expensive. I couldn't just leave it outside."

His hand flashes up and smashes me across the face. I spin out of his grip and run for the sliding doors. But he has me, carries me, squirming mightily to the nurse's station.

"We've made arrangements for this young lady."

He's in great shape. I'm twisting around like my dog used to do, twirling against his chest, but his grip doesn't break. The robe opens all the way, my pink panties are for the world to see. The nurse looks embarrassed for him. Mother and Aunt Emma walk into the lobby and see me wrapped in Uncle Jack's arms, ass out, the robe all about my shoulders like a straitjacket, and are even more embarrassed. The nurse gets it together. I'm too tired to keep up the fight so I watch as the forms are presented and signed. And everyone looks relieved to be getting the paperwork out of the way.

"Wait a minute! They can't commit me. I didn't sign anything."

The nurse barely looks at me, instead she shuffles papers. "You're not being committed. This is a drug treatment program. They've placed you in our care. The doctor will be out shortly to explain to you how our program works."

I nod enthusiastically. "That sounds great. I can't wait!" I shout and the nurse flinches.

Oh, since the papers have been signed, two big men in white suits appear, and they have a wheelchair I suppose they want me to sit in. I wonder if I could make it to the sliding glass double doors. Wild on the streets once again. But don't I need this. Don't I need to find out why I'm the way I am. Don't I need to dry out for the baby's sake, don't I, Douglas? Isn't this all a pathetic cry for help? Yes, I guess it is. I'm one sick bitch. It's bright and sunny here in this lobby, with fine, sturdy, modern furniture in soothing pastels. It might be time for a change. The doctor, balding and thin, comes up. He's wearing running shoes. He extends his hand. I extend mine. I shove hard against his chin and knock him into Uncle Jack and it's off to the races.

Butterfly Burning

Yvonne Vera

THERE IS A PAUSE. AN EXPECTATION.

They play a refrain on handmade guitars; lovers with tender shoulders and strong fists and cold embraces. Birds coo from slanting asbestos roofs. Butterflies break from disused Raleigh bicycle bells.

In the air is the sound of a sickle cutting grass along the roadside where black men bend their backs in the sun and hum a tune, and fume, and lullaby. They are clad in torn white shorts, short sleeves, naked soles. The grass burns over their palms where they reach over and pull at it, then curve over the sickle and beyond, pull, inward, and edge the grass forward with the left palm. They bend it toward the left shoulder and away from the eyes. Sweat drips like honey over the firm length of the arms tearing and tugging and splitting the grass. Often they manage to pull the roots out of the ground; to free something; to conquer a stubbornness; to see what is below; to touch what keeps something alive and visible. Sharp rays of the sun drop along the sharp curve, and flow along the rotating glint of the silver sickle. The arm agile, the arm quick over the grass.

The tall grass sweeps across the length of their curved bodies, above their bowed shoulders and throws a cascade of already dry seeds over their bare arms. The grass is a thin slippery tarnish as it waves smoothly. It sways away and again away in this current of heated air. There are seeds, light and flat, like tiny baked insects. Falling down, with their surfaces rough, flat. They waft into the thickness of grass.

Each motion of the arms, eyes, of the entire body is patiently guided. The palms are bleeding with the liquid from freshly squeezed grass. The brow is perpetually furrowed, constricted against this action, and against another, remembered; against regret for a possible inaction, and against each memory that dares not be understood. A silence, perhaps, or something near and anticipated but not yet done. There is waiting.

Their supple but unwilling arms turn, loop and merge with the shiny tassels of the golden grass whose stem is still green, like newborn things, and held firmly to the earth. The movement of their arms is like weaving, as their arms thread through each thicket and withdraw. This careful motion is patterned like a dance spreading out, each sequence rises like hope enacted and set free. Freed, stroke after stroke, holding briskly, and then a final whisper of release. The grass falls. Arm and arm and arm of it. It falls near and close to each curled body. The grass submits to the feet of the workers who step over it to arrive where the grass is high and stands defiant. They hug it indifferently, concerned only to keep its tassels from their eyes, spreading it away. With an easy ease they escape the fine flutter of dry seeds raining downward. The men cut and pull. Cut and pull. They bend, cut and pull. It is necessary to sing.

They cut and level the grass till the sun is a crusty and golden distance away and throws cool rays over their worn arms, and the sky dims, and everything is quiet except the spray of light breaking and darting between the grass tossing back and forth above their foreheads and above their eyes now filled with fatigue. The grass is swishing hopelessly below the shoulder, under the armpit, grazing the elbow, and its sound folds into a faint melody which dims with the slow dying of the sun, and each handful of grass becomes a violent silhouette: a stubborn shadow grasped.

The men twist the grass together and roll it into a large mass, stacks of it, and gather it into heavy mounds to be carried away the following day. Their bare soles grate against the stubble now dotting the ground, raised like needles, and where the grass is completely dried, turning to fierce thorns. The men, adapted to challenges more debilitating than these, discover welcoming crevices, empty patches where the grass has been completely uprooted and the soil turned to its cooler side. So they place their soles to safety, their heels to a mild earth. The work is not their own: it is summoned. The time is not theirs: it is seized. The ordeal is their own. They work again and again, and in unguarded moments of hunger and surprise, they mistake their fate for fortune.

As for healing, they have music, its curing harmony as sudden as it is sustained. It is swinging like heavy fruit on a low and loose branch, the fruit touching ground with every movement of the wind: they call it Kwela. It is a searing musical moment, swinging in and away, loud and small, lively, living. Within this music, they soar higher than clouds; sink deeper than stones in water. When the branch finally breaks and the fruit cracks its shell, the taste of the fruit is divine.

This is Kwela. Embracing choices that are already decided. Deciding which circumstance has been omitted and which set free, which one claimed, which one marked, branded and owned. The beauty of eyelids closing; a hand closing; and a memory collapsing. Kwela means to climb into the waiting police jeeps. This word alone has been fully adapted to do marvelous things. It can carry so much more than a word should be asked to carry; rejection, distaste, surrender, envy. And full desire.

Trust lovers to nurture hope till it festers. Always wounded by something—a word, a hope, a possibility. After all, they are the kind of people to get caught by barbed-wire fences. A part of them calcifies, dries, and falls off without anyone noticing or raising alarm.

Bulawayo is this kind of city and inside is Makokoba Township where Kwela seeks strand after strand of each harsh illusion and makes it new. Sidojiwe E2, the longest street in Makokoba, is fresh with all kinds of desperate wounds. Bulawayo, only fifty years old, has nothing to offer but surprise; being alive is a consolation.

Bulawayo is not a city for idleness. The idea is to live within the cracks. Unnoticed and unnoticeable, offering every service but with the capacity to vanish when the task required is accomplished. So the black people learn how to move through the city with speed and due attention, to bow their heads down and slide past walls, to walk without making the shadow more pronounced than the body or the body clearer than the shadow. It means leaning against some masking reality—they lean on walls, on lies, on music. One can always be swallowed by a song.

The people walk in the city without encroaching on the pavements from which they are banned. It is difficult but they manage to crawl to their destination hidden by umbrellas and sunhats which are handed down to them for exactly this purpose, or which they discover, abandoned, at bus stations.

They understand something about limits and the desire that this builds in the body. Their bodies long for flight, not surrender, simply the need to leap over the limit quickly and smoothly without bringing attention to oneself. This they do, often and well.

After all, they are the ones who keep the pavements clean and sweep the entire city. They have the duty by virtue of their own humility and obedience to pick up the white men fallen on the pavements while the door swings open, once more, from the smoke-filled taverns, and voices are heard briefly before the door swings back in. They help these men into an upright and respectable position, then lead them into solid black cars. Then they spit on the pavements and move on.

When they arrive back in Makokoba, Sidojiwe E2 is flooded with Kwela music. The feet feeling free. Hostilities too burdensome to give up. There is a search in the narrow gutters for passions and separations. The people smoke burnt-out stubs and tone their fingernails with nicotine, and lovers mourn with joyful release. We do it together. This and that—fight, escape, surrender. The distinctions always unclear, the boundaries perpetually widening. Kwela music brings a symphony of understanding, then within that, other desperate confusions. Poverty prevails over innocence. In such times, a song is a respite.

Dying in your sleep. Not once, but several times. Fleeing from an image reflected from translucent shop-windows. And then, again, sleep. Afterwards, a brief resolve not to bend. Then saying yes.

Kwela strips you naked. Anything that reminds of pride can be forgotten in the emptiness introduced. A claim abandoned. A lover lost. It is the body addressed in its least of possible heights. A stone thrust. The knees down and the baton falls across the neck and shoulders. Kwela. Climb on. Move. Turn or twist or . . . move. No pause is allowed, and no expectation of grace. Kwela. Cut, pull, bend. It is necessary to sing.

Then one chaotic evening the word is pulled back from the police jeep by whoever is listening in sleep as a car tyre digs along Sidojiwe E2. It is freedom and style and survival with no fear of flight or stagnation. This is the city and the pulse of possessing desire. Something that can be recovered, must be restored. Even if it may now be frayed or torn. It has to be put back somewhere where there could be a hint of belonging fastening on somebody. If not freedom then rhythm.

Patience is abandoned and something else witnessed: a raised eyelid; a handshake; fingers snapping. Then slow courtship under the tall trees which divide the houses from the red roofs of the police camps. These trees have been brought from faraway lands. They are the sort of trees which do not seem to need water, or when they do, send tentacles that burrow deep, no matter how hard the ground. With no regard whatsoever for the lack of pliable soil, or absent drops of edible rain.

Underneath these trees, the lovers stand forlorn in the cluster of large silver and white peelings which are curled among the thin pointed leaves now fallen, where forked roots break the earth. The dead leaves cling to their tinge of green, resisting their separation from the tree. A shell expands, dries, pods explode and spread black rounded seeds to the ground. The seeds have hard surfaces, with grey veins.

So tall, these trees, firm and impossible. They look as though they have been built by hand to carry improper histories. A strong scent rises from the base of the tree, from the roots perhaps, like a fading dream. A beautiful, precious, remembered scent. Wafting and vanishing like a mist. The trees make the search for love good by their strong presence and brief odour. In the night—moonshine, words, a happy tune, fate and distance are shared. The lovers bask in immaculate dreams. Kwela includes the harmonies one can name, and misname. There is night.

Kwela in daylight is incessantly bold. No parting or other phenomenon of rupture. Some fighting. A slap and a slash and more Kwela. Torn leather shoes rubbing against cement. Tar melting in the hot sun as though newly spread. The sanitary lane carries the secrecy and stench which envelopes the waste of every charater—wasted time, wasted love, wasted this and that.

Time flips like a tossed coin and in the lustre and swinging surprise it is nothing on a single day to hear a thief leap over hedges on Sidojiwe E2 and by noon to listen to bicycle bells in the city centre. There copper coins crush and jingle on to the pavement as they are swept out in the early hours of the morning from empty city taverns which have NO BLACKS signs, WHITES ONLY signs and CLOSED signs which say OPEN on the flip side signs and dangle CLOSED from ornate door handles, and outside . . .

There is music.

Colson Whitehead

The Intuitionist

HE LIVED HERE, ASSEMBLED HIS VEHICULAR EPIPHANIES HERE, MULLED OVER the bolts and pins of his mythology in this very house. Mrs. Rogers leaves her in the ruined parlor. Beneath her, an angry slash of ripped upholstery grins ticking. The fireplace mantel has been swept clean—she can see the coat sleeves of the men who trashed her own apartment brush across it—and her host's collection of ceramic horses are dashed to the floor, broken heads and limbs. The men's fingers groped inside the couch and chairs after Fulton's notebooks and Mrs. Rogers's loose change, smashed the two emerald lamps to see what may or may not have been inside them, cracked the frame of Fulton's portrait over taut knees. Lila Mae rubs her hands on her thighs and surveys the damage. The odor of cigar smoke lingers in the dull air and she can see a cigar butt ground into a photograph of Mrs. Rogers and her children, in happier times, not here. They didn't find anything but must persist, a determined gang thundering through the houses of those who might possess the object. Their violent blundering seems so pathetic to Lila Mae now, a child's plea for attention, a good hug. They'll never find it.

Mrs. Rogers returns from the kitchen with tea and thin butter cookies. Lila Mae reads the old grooves in her skin, the ripples around her eyes and mouth, the afterimages of old expressions. The human face is only capable of two or three real expressions, and they leave their mark. Lila Mae thinks, she only has one expression and what will her face look like forty years from now. Eroded rock, a wall of dry canyon. Mrs. Rogers sighs, "They gave this place a real going over. Just a fine mess they made. Broke all of my horses. Broke they legs off." She doesn't look at the mess on the floor, busying herself with the delicate disrobing of a sugar cube. "I was in the city visiting my sister and I come home to this."

"Last night?" Lila Mae asks. "What time did you get back?"

"About eleven last night."

Then they hit the place right after she left Ben Urich. When they realized she knew. Lila Mae's been a practicing solipsist since before she could walk, and the days' recent events are doing irreparable damage to her condition.

Mrs. Rogers points to a bucket in the corner. A gray disrag slithers over its lip. Preoccupied, she says, "One of them relieved himself on the floor. You can't smell it, can you?"

"I don't smell a thing," Lila Mae lies. "Did you call the police? Institute security?"

"What for? They probably the ones that did it."

Lila Mae leans forward in her chair. "This is the first time, right? When you told the Institute that this place had been broken into after Fulton's death and his notebooks stolen, you made that up, correct?"

"It may have been a lie," Mrs. Rogers shrugs. Stands. She hasn't touched her tea and snacks. It's all ritual, Lila Mae appraises. Her host says, "I did most of the upstairs, but I haven't finished down here. Do you want to give me a hand?" An old house and an old woman. She needs to preserve the rules of this place, the order she keeps beneath the pitched roof. Even though they have pissed on it. She bends over slowly before the fireplace and picks up one of her fallen horses. It kneels on its stomach in her rough palm. No legs, Mrs. Rogers gets down on the floor and looks for its legs.

Lila Mae grabs the broom that leans against the back of her chair. She picks an area, sweeps couch innards and shredded paper into mounds. The old woman says, "To answer your question, yes, he was having a joke on them at first, but it wasn't a joke at the end. It became true." She discovers one of the tiny thoroughbred's legs under the newspaper rack and holds it up to the window. "You have to realize something about

James," continuing, tilting the leg in the sunlight. "Deep down he was real country. No kind of sense at all in his head except his own kind of sense. That's what made him what he was."

After all that has happened, Lila Mae figures she can put up with the woman's drifting explanations. There's no rush. Lila Mae says, "But he wasn't who he was. He passed for white. He was colored."

"Well look at you," Mrs. Rogers says with exhaustion, sparing a second for a quick glance at her visitor. "Not the same girl who was knocking on my door last week, are you? With your chest all puffed out like a peacock. You've seen something between now and then, huh?" She places the horse on the mantel, where it rolls over on its side and exposes its white belly and manufacturer's lot number. "I didn't even know myself until his sister come up to visit one time, and I lived under the same roof with the man. I knew he wasn't like no other white man I had worked for, but I didn't think . . . She came up to the door one night—I don't know, fifteen years ago? Twenty? Whenever it was, it was right before he wrote the second one of his Intuitionist books.

This information isn't hard to recall for Lila Mae. There was an eight-month break between the publication of *Theoretical Elevators* Volume One and Fulton's embarkation on Volume Two. It was twenty years ago when Fulton's sister knocked on his door. What did she look like? What do you say to a brother you have not seen for decades? Lila Mae can barely speak to people she saw last week.

"She shows up at the door," Mrs. Rogers continues, "and tells me she has to see James. She was one of them down-home women. You could see she made herself the clothes she got on her back. I look her up and down because I don't know who this woman is, and say I got to see if Mr. Fulton is receiving visitors. You should have seen his face when he walked down the stairs. His pipe fell right out of his mouth onto the floor—you can still see the carpet where he burned it. He starts fussing and telling me to go out to the store—suddenly he got to have fish for dinner. So I leave, and when I get back, she's gone and James is sitting in his study reading his journals like nothing's strange. Asks me what time will dinner be ready, just like that. He told me who she was later, but that was after."

Did she bring photographs or bad news: the death of their mother. Money for burial costs. What do you say to your brother who you have not seen for many years. She can see them talking in this room. The furniture is the same, the day's light thin and cold. He sits in the chair Lila Mae sat in, hands kneading the armrests. It is the moment he has feared since he left his town. When he will be revealed for who he is, the catastrophic accident. But his sister does not expose him. She did not make him crash. He was saved.

"It wasn't soon after that he started acting funny," Mrs. Rogers says. She has now retrieved four horses and eleven legs. They lay on the mantel as if on a battlefield. Their masters dead and dying. "Just little things a body wouldn't notice at first, but then it creeped up on you."

"Like when he dunked the provost's head in the punch bowl at the groundbreaking ceremony."

"That was later, but you on the right track," Mrs. Rogers tells her. "He'd been in a pretty good mood because his first Intuitionist book was doing alright. It had been hard on him but now he was getting what he deserved. When he finished that first book he showed it to them up on the hill there. His colleagues. And they just tossed him out of there—he couldn't get anyone to take it seriously. None of them wanted to touch it. So he paid for it himself, and it started. They believed it."

She can't decide which porcelain limb belongs to which porcelain horse. "I remember when the first reviews came out in one of those elevator journals," she says, placing the leg next to a small white pony caught in fractured gallop. "He sits down right in the chair right there and starts reading it. I was in the kitchen cooking. I didn't hear anything for a long time, and then I hear him laughing. You see, James was a very serious man. He had a sense of humor, but it was his own sense of humor. We lived in the same house for years and I don't think there was one time when we both laughed at the same thing. That day I hear him laughing from the kitchen. Like I ain't never heard him laugh before—like it was the biggest, best joke he ever heard. I come running out and ask him what's so funny. And he just looks up at me and says, 'They believe it.'"

She must be referring to Robert Manley's famous mash note in *Continental Elevator Review,* which, if Lila Mae's memory serves, anointed Fulton "the field's greatest visionary since Otis" and "hope's last chance against modernity's relentless death march." It was the first review to describe Fulton's approach as "Intuitionist": postrational, innate. Human. No wonder he laughed. His prank had succeeded. From that review's cornices, the gargoyle of his mythology shook its stiff, mottled wings and conquered, city by city, whispering heresy, defecating on the robust edifices of the old order. No wonder he laughed.

Mrs. Rogers pulls Lila Mae back from distraction. Mrs. Rogers says, "I never seen him happy like that. He was happy for a whole week, and that's the longest time I ever seen him happy. Then one night I'm down here doing my crosswords. I couldn't sleep so I was doing my puzzles. James comes down from up there, wearing his robe—I thought he was in bed. He comes downstairs looking confused and upset and he says to me, 'But it's a joke. They don't get the joke.'"

"He thought that someone would understand but they didn't."

She nods. "They had all their rules and regulations. They had all this long list of things to check in elevators and what made an elevator work and all, and he'd come to hate that. He told me—these are his words—'They were all slaves to what they could see.' But there was a truth behind that they couldn't see for the life of them."

"They looked at the skin of things," Lila Mae offers. They couldn't see his lie. It was Pompey that allowed her to see Fulton's prank. The accident resounds in her still, the final notes of the crash the new background music of her mind. She had been so sure that Pompey had sabotaged Number Eleven—it appeased her sense of order. If Chancre wanted to set her up, any number in her Department would have been happy to oblige. But Lila Mae fixated on Pompey. The Uncle Tom, the grinning nigger, the house nigger who is to blame for her debased place in this world. Pompey gave them a blueprint for colored folk. How they acted. How they pleased white folks. How eager they would be for a piece of the dream that they would do anything for massa. She hated her place in their world, where she fell in their order of things, and blamed Pompey, her shucking shadow in the office. She could not see him anymore than anyone else in the office saw him.

Her hatred. Fulton's hatred of himself and his lie of whiteness. White people's reality is built on what things appear to be—that's the business of Empiricism. They judge them on how they appear when held up to the light, the wear on the carriage buckle, the stress fractures in the motor casing. His skin. Picture this: Fulton, the Great Reformer, the steady man at the helm of the Department of Elevator Inspectors, gives up his chair when the elevator companies try to buy his favor, place him in their advertisements. They have already bought off many of the street men—building owners lay cash on inspectors in exchange for fastidious blindness to defect. Their sacred Empiricism has no meaning when it can be bought. When they can't even see that this man is colored because he says he is not. Or doesn't even say it. They see his skin and see a white man. Retreat behind the stone walls of the institute does not change matters. He is still not colored. *There is another world beyond this one.* He was trying to tell them and they wouldn't hear it. Don't believe your eyes.

Mrs. Rogers says, "He was making a joke of their entire way of ife and they couldn't see. The joke wasn't funny to him anymore. Once he realized that—that it was a joke but they didn't see it like that, it wasn't a joke anymore. His sister come to visit soon after that. He told me later she saw him in the newspaper. Like I said, he got strange after that. He started writing that second book. He'd lock himself in his study and he wouldn't come out. I had to start leaving his dinner outside the door because he wouldn't come down to eat. This went on for months and months. Then one day he comes down and says he finished."

Lila Mae knew he was joking because he hated himself. She understood this hatred of himself; she hated something in herself and she took it out on Pompey. Now she could see Fulton for what he was. There was no way he believed in transcendence. His race kept him earthbound, like the stranded citizens before Otis invented his safety elevator. There was no hope for him as a colored man because the white world will not let a colored man rise, and there was no hope for him as a white man because it was a lie. He secretes his venom into the pages of a book. He knows the other world he describes does not exist. There will be no redemption because the men who run this place do not want redemption. They want to be as near to hell as they can.

Lila Mae looks at the old woman. She busies herself with her collection, attempting to right those mangled equine forms. They will not stand. The kind thing to do would be to put them out of their misery, but she will not do that. She hangs on to them. Perhaps one day they will be right again. Mrs. Rogers and Fulton living together in this house, as employer and employee. She tends to the colored business and he tends to his white business. Secretly kin, but she does not know that. So no, Lila Mae sees, he does not believe in the perfect elevator. He creates a doctrine of transcendence that is as much a lie as his life. But then something happens. Something happens that makes him believe, switch from the novel but diffuse generalities of Volume One to the concrete Intuitionist methodology of Volume Two. Now he wants that perfect elevator that will lift him away from here and devises solid method from his original satire. What did his sister say to him? What did he wish after their meeting. Family? That there could be, in the world he invented to parody his enslavers, a field where he could be whole? A joke has no purpose if you cannot share it with anyone. Lila Mae thinks, Intuitionism is communication. That simple. Communication with what is not-you. When he gives lectures to his flock, years later, they are not aware of what he is truly speaking. *The elevator world will look like Heaven but not the Heaven you have reckoned.*

Lila Mae hears a car door slam outside. Through the window, she sees her old Engineering professor Dr. Heywood lock the door of his car. Returning from church and prayer for the next place. Beyond. It is need. She has always considered herself an atheist. She has knelt beside her mother and father in church and said the words she was supposed to say, but she never believed them, and when she came North she stopped going. She has always considered herself an atheist, not realizing she had a religion. Anyone can start a religion. They just need the need of others.

They haven't made much headway into the mess left, presumably, by Arbo and their bruiser army. Lila Mae, for her part, has spent the last few minutes sweeping up a mound of grit and then brushing it out into a thin layer before gathering it again. Mrs. Rogers has been fussing over her silly tchotchkes, her broken horses. It's useless. Lila Mae asks, "Why did he put my name in his notebooks?"

Mrs. Rogers sits down on the couch. Too tired. Touches the side of the teapot and frowns. Cold. "Toward the end he knew he was going to die. He spent his days and nights all running around trying to finish his last project. Nights he went over to the library they named after him—he said he liked the peace there." She's looking at her hands. They're palm-up in her lap, dead, overturned crabs. "He said he saw a light on in the room across the way, and one day he asked me if I knew what the name of the colored student on campus was. I told him I didn't know, and that's all I know about it." Looking now in her visitor's eyes. "You should take what's left. I don't want to hold on to it anymore. It's too much."

She rises and walks into the kitchen. Lila Mae can't see what she's doing. But she hears it. Hears squeaking, it takes her a few seconds to place it. It is an old pulley, doing what it was meant to do. There's a dumbwaiter in the kitchen. A primitive hand elevator containing all the principles of verticality. She hears rocks scraping.

When the old woman returns, she holds a stack of notebooks, Fulton's cherished Fontaines, wrapped loosely in a shred of stained leather. The sacred scrolls, of course. What did she do? Lila Mae can see it: she's removed some bricks from the back wall of the dumbwaiter shaft and opened up a shallow dark hole. Where the texts waited. They stand for a minute, the two colored women, face to face, a generation and two feet apart, djinns of dust whirling in the shafts of afternoon light between them. Lila Mae takes the notebooks into her hands. It's a good weight. She asks, "What made you send out the packages?"

The old woman says, "He left instructions. He said when I sent them out, someone would come."

PART FIVE

Poetry

"When I'm writing I am trapped in between the line/I escape when I finished the rhyme."

—Eric B. and
Rakim, "I Know You
Got Soul" (1987)

Safari *for Ogaga Ifowodo*

When I read my poems,
dripping with fire and gutters,
they asked me, "don't you
write about trees and constellations?"

And I said, "in this land we love with pain
even the trees feel like whips,
I cannot lie that the blood in
my mouth is tomato sauce.

Your book grieves on my table.
The jokes for our lunch grow rancid.
What a sacrifice we bear,
bricks on worn heads.
Tons that grow luxuriantly.

Through the dust, searching for your aroma,
your safari heart, that curious joy
moistening your poetry, I see
bones sold into bank accounts,
a deposit, waiting for barbarians.

This is why the wind is sprawling your words,
of wasps, of webs, of wailing.

The Rumor

in El Viejo San Juan
a shopkeeper heaves with the rumor,
his mouth full of its sweetwater

Bochinchero eyes raised, he murmurs
To tourists new on the island
  "All the Dark people live in Loiza
  you will find them nestled
  like sleepy black beetles under rocks,
  a termites' trail, they line barrio walls,
  faces fired by sunlight, bodies ready like spears"

He chatter-boxes like an old woman,
forehead pasty as port rind,
about Loiza's blue people,
the color of a *puta's* toenails, shades of wounds and bruises
oh, the storeowner is absolutely bubbling over
a singing pot of black beans,
on and on about *Borinquen's* dark downtrodden,
how their dance scorches cane fields,
how their dead carry the Devil's lanterns,
how his father's bones know the hard *plena* jigs of their feet

Wide-eyed as a minstrel,
the shopkeep whispers seductively
        to Norwegians really just on their way to the Bahamas,
he bends into their ignorance like bamboo—

"Phosphorous by night, litter by day,
You should go see them in their habitat,
        Go see how brightly they shine"
He breathes hotly.
Pirate lips pursed and sweaty with
The import of a conquistador's dream,
A brittle bread broken and shared
With the first white face he sees

Elizabeth Alexander

Fugue

1. Walking (1963)
        after the painting by Charles Alston

You tell me, knees are important, you kiss
your elders' knees in utmost reverence.
The knees in this painting are what send the people forward,

forward to a real place, moving as one.

Once progress felt real and inevitable,
as sure as the taste of licorice or lemons.
The painting was made after marching
in Birmingham, walking

into a light both brilliant and unseen.

2. 1964

In a beige silk sari
my mother danced the frug
to the Peter Duchin Band.

Earlier that day
at Maison Le Pelch
the French ladies twisted

her magnificent hair
into a fat chignon
while <u>mademoiselle</u> watched,

drank sugared, milky tea,
and counted bobby-pins
disappearing in the thick-

ness as the ladies worked
in silence, adornment
so grave, the solemn <u>toilette</u>,

and later, the bath,
and later, red lipstick,
and later, L'Air de Temps.

My mother without glasses.
My mother in beige silk.
My mother with a chignon.
My mother in her youth.

3. 1968

The city burns. We have to stay at home,
TV always interrupted with fire or helicopters.
Men who have tweedled my cheeks once or twice
join the serial dead.

Yesterday I went downtown with Mom.
What a pretty little girl, said the tourists, who were white.
My shoes were patent leather, all shiny, and black.
My father is away saving the world for Negroes,
I wanted to say.

Mostly I go to school or watch television
with my mother and brother, my father often gone.
He makes the world a better place for Negroes.
The year is nineteen-sixty-eight.

4. 1971

"Hey Blood," my father said then
to other brothers in the street.
"Hey, Youngblood, how you doin'?

"Peace and power," he says,
and, "Keep on keepin' on,"
just like Gladys Knight and the Pips.

My stomach jumps: a thrill.
Sometimes poems remember small things, like
"Hey, Blood." My father

still says that sometimes.

5. The Sun King (1974)

James Hampton, the Sun King
of Washington, DC
erects a tin-foil throne.
"Where there is no vision, the people perish."
Altar, pulpit, light-bulbs.

My 14th and "U," my 34 bus, my weekday winos,
my white-robed black Israelites
on their redstone stoops,
my graffiti: "Anna the Leo as 'Ice,'"
my neon James Brown poster
coming to the DC Coliseum
where all I will see is the circus,
my one visit to RKO Keith's Theater
to see "Car Wash"
and a bird flew in, and mania,
frantic black shadow on the screen,
I was out of the house in a theater full of black folks,
black people, black movie, black bird,
I was out, I was free, I was at RKO Keith's Theater
at 14th and "U"
and it was not "Car Wash" it was the first
Richard Pryor concert movie
and a bird flew in the screen
and memory is romance
and race is romance,
and the Sun King lives
in Washington, DC.

Jeffery Renard Allen

The Clearing *for Lauryn Hill*

In that kingdom to come
    that scripted promise know as zion
the sea-changed blacken the horizon with chopping rhythm
Row and rest and range
buoyant vessels of wrath

Dawn hammers a ledger mean, measured, made

Razored wings open us
Valley and brook pulse red with our pumping inner life

Refrained years behind
we ring,
belled anger

A charged hand thumbs our blind foreheads with berry juice:
   Paid
We purchase coats in the coin of life to come

Then the siren issues her singular call

At the stream's edge
one hundred forty-four thousand gather
swaying with skyward eyes,
robes humming and the new song on pitched lips

No longer must we kneel before the stumblingstone
No longer must our palms shape the clay of offense

The final hour
Children are counted for the seed

Charlie Braxton

Dream of Jesus

last night I dreamed
i saw jesus pimp strolling
Peacock-proud down crenshaw blvd.
looking for lost souls
in the concrete valley of the damned

for forty days and forty nights
the son of man sought souls
in south central l.a.
home of the body bag
the bloods the crips, the pigs
and the inner city blues
only to find shell-shocked soldiers
raging over the rock of caine

last night i swear i saw jesus
dressed in black khakis cracking
a 40 and shooting the dozens
while hanging with all the homies in the hood
just cold kicking it
things were smooth until some fool lost his cool
and shot another
jesus tried to save the brother
but couldn't
that's when all hell broke loose

tempers started flaring
gats started cracking
caps started popping
and niggas started dropping
like flies
the body count read twelve injured
three dead
crucified on the cross of ghetto life

Shonda Buchanan

personal

i believe in dragons
before we go any further
i want you to know this

i find the strange beautiful
the crush cantaloupe scent
of homeless lovers heady

the ant mouths of crack babies,
as needy of attention
as sunsets and your back,
awe-inspiring

uneven patches of skin
on a stranger's hand

the tombstone tinge
of skies after storms

even the monster i
find beautiful
their unfinished, lopsided
hearts lacking balance
only because we hurt them first

i like it from behind
two hands clamped on
my slick shoulders
as he burrows deeper into me
with the question mark of
winter sleep on his brow

i find men and women enticing
their sixty dollar cologne
lips licking mac shadows
sun-dusted skin disappearing
beneath thin black dresses

i want you to know these things
and not be afraid

here these things and trust
in the limestone behind my
gaze

see these things and taste the
gravel i leave on your lips

know that i know what commitment
is
and will not be swayed

II

last night
i stared at my naked breast
in the mirror
no longer bruised by the
plymouth kisses you once
planted there

but i looked anyway
liking the way they arched
forward when i removed
my chemise

i think of who i'd like kissing
them when i turn thirty
or in thirty years

i don't know

i do know
i don't want a liar at my nipples
someone breathing insincerity
into my skin

unable to nurse truth from
my body
i don't want a liar to touch me

nor do i want a man who talks
grins or laughs when he enters
hiding his eleven-year-old
masturbation guilt

or someone who touches
himself so much all his erections
are for him

i don't want someone with bad
breath because when he comes
up for air
he will dampen the iridescence
of my scent

i want you to know
that i believe i am a goddess
and a witch
i pronounce stray words
for their feeling in my mouth
i know i disappear inside myself
when i am with you
but i am *with* you

listen.
i am a poet.

i can love you in licorice tense
hold your dick in my mouth until
every trace of fatigue vanishes
from your pours
and the syrup stirs again in
your membrane

i want you to know this
understand

you must know
i climb mountains
eat the wind
i am a rain dancer

a panther tracker
a woodsmoke cloud rising past vision
i beat out my songs
with conch shells, sage brush
and broken lead
i peel and touch beneath
the skin
blow there
kiss there
i am a reverend's daughter

i can heal you with touch

i want you to know
i believe in dragons, fairies
life on other worlds
a higher power too intellectual
to fit into man's hands
in the form of books

i believe in anansi
medusa, seshat
all myths exist in me

i want you to know these things
and not be afraid

know that my breast
are less than firm
overly ripe
my thighs
saunter in certain places
like the meat of savannah peaches
straining to slip from their covering

i am soft as cornbread warming
on the stove and as sweet

listen
i am a simple woman.
a poet.

Have me
If you dare

Tat Tvam Asi
(You Are the One)

Paul Calderon

There was blood in teeth,
oak in ear but heart is what was to be followed.
Nothing beyond sensation, nothing found written, nothing within reason
could
have taken me there.
To space where fallen tree branches hold rhythms.
Where hands & hides tell stories of how birds in middles of concreted
labyrinths (pain's domain of flesh)
carry wind in eyes and drop Ibo names from beaks in middles of unnamed
but
claimed villages for children of inner mystics of outer realms to harvest
from womb of
a mother goddess.

Every petal of her hair turns to Sun, whispers in dream time bridges
Between
sat / asat.

Tattoos of cypress, tendon of arched backs ivory and sprinkle these black
mosaic smiles beneath tones and slaps calling it off into sunsets where
chaos finds order.

Tat tvam asi
  Black woman.
    It's in your limbs now.
Tat tvam asi

Black
  woman.
    It's in your feet.
  Don't read it,
    there are no words.
      Be it.
Tat tvam asi.

Sat yarga
  Black man.
    This is you battle.
Sat Yarga
  Black man.

Behind you, in this tale of blood on trail home, they who are the one come
before and after you.

Sat yarga. Don't let go. This is your battle.
A burning spear is water in mind's motion and your hands know rhythms to
throw.
Believe this & fall for nothing. It will save this village.

Dip hips low.

Play hard.

Dig mind deep.

Dance with river, with air, with fire.
Tet tvam asi.
Sat yarga

Whisper in heart sweated mirages on these walls where eyes have
tendencies
to twist the sway of metal.

From these thighs parting with music kings and queens will awaken.
From these limbs bent in sonic prayer will be birthed the quickening of
soul
fire and blade will sharpen grace's glow. In the middle, where it is
strongest, they will meet. Some old, some young.
They will bring seeds to plant illness to heal, but they will come.

Tat tvam asi, sat yarga.
Let your body drum the language that your tongue haven't the heart to
speak.

Tat tvam asi.
Sat yarga.

Adrian Castro

One Irony of the Caribbean

It is common knowledge:
these waters witnessed the meet between East & West

Those sullen sailors rancid with chorizo
talcum'd with salt & sea breeze
old gunpowder
the perennial scent of Spain flapping
    among crested flags
the debauched nights of laud
   the Moorish cumin
    the Gypsy's dervish

But Tainos had mango o guanábana
to hoist as flag
perhaps a carey & tabaco leaf as insignia
They used planks from siguaraya
o quiebra hacha
pine or cedar
(which perfumed at the same time)
while sailing to the Areyto plaza
And the Caribs
well they used bones with hatchet scars
for mere decoration
in effect a floating coffin

The triangle that ensnared freedom
corraled continents into a trinity of suffering
the ships which chiseled these shores
in effect floating coffins

They departed from these islands
in rafts at best
hammered & fastened from rafters
from dangling colonial homes
in Regla, Cojimar, Marianao
Jacmel, Cap Haitien
the same homes built
by survivors of floating coffins
They built them
with the same wood which bolted their ancestors' chains
The same wood glued with sugar cane sap
They used strewn army canvases for sails
the sails that pivoted
often in the wrong direction
A rudder fashioned from a shovel
stained with the earth of a dead man
They launched it to sea
to begin anew
but in effect a floating coffin

A long time ago
they didn't bury the dead
till the eyes were pecked by a mysterious bird
delivered to the heavens
so the eyes could oversee the body's proper burial
It was then that
they buried the body
in a hollowed trunk of siguaraya,
quiebra hacha, pine or cedar
sometimes ceiba for chiefs & priests
They launched it to sea to reach home to
reunite with the others
they launched it to sea
to begin anew
in effect a floating coffin

Legba, Landed

He crossed. the border
line in a northern corner

        four
cardinal   points
      for

a better over there. created a here.

One foot in A   one foot in a
merica   Canada.

        one Negro.
        liminal.
        limped
          a

cross
clutching a crutch
  a sliver of a quest
  a lining of silver
  a sparkle of meridian
  a severed scent
  a razorous rain
  a glade
  a terrain
  a blame

a strait razorous border. he
reached for a me
to be
real
real
real
enough to re
treat into a tree
for the forests he could see
he sought as he believed himself
into the mirrorous glass a
cross the border.

customs: are you carrying any
baggage? are you moving any fruit or seeds or trees
of knowledge, immortality or weeds or roots or truths
through to bluer blues and greener
grass, hash, heroin, hidden, stashed
uppers, Canada, land. no lower-class
middle passage. no flask
of flashing yellow magma,
spirits, rum, release. no fire
arms, tobacco, or too much cash.
or too little cash.
in the razor-thin space between my lines,
you may fit in. line up
and pay your sin
tax
at
the next
wicket.

here eyes bear the white burden
of watchful wardens
dutiful citizens in
lower mainlands
patrol each shade of un
white. each stray curl of un
straight. each straight hint of un
settled seeking for   home

carry me, motherless child.
My tracks are so sweet to the stalker.
Mount Zion, baptize me abysmal.
Abyssinian of obsidian meridians.
I take to the night like winged carrion.
I am sweet to the stalker.
like an ibis, stems snapped
like reeds, I fly above
reptiles and annihil
ation. forever in flight against the sky.
painted feathers brushing versus eternity.
limbs in the image dangle.
snapped like photos.
finished like the tape breaks up
lifting the race. winged
in flight

without hope
of landing. Canada
geese band together
to kill their crippled
for fear of attracting
stalkers to the flock.
they peck.
a mess of splintered feathers.
hollowed bones.
shattered limbs.
frenzy toward the nest of night.
death.
no.
rest.
I am sweet to the prey.
my only thought: I fly on,
on, my sky home,
home

Kwame Dawes

Excursion to Port Royal

In the giddy house the wind riots on the beach
we have had lunch flat moist sandwiches cooked
by the steaming bus engine now alone
abandoned by the other boys I stare across the roll of sea
and there is no sign of the passing of time

no evidence of the decades of progress
only the scraggly grass the Institute of Jamaica
tourist information plaque screwed tight into the
armoury wall here is the possibility of journey
from the quarter deck I claim all I survey

on Admiral Nelson's quarter deck the sea sand is black
shells glint white in the tick of waves
the water is moving the horizon shifts   the morning's clean edge
smudges into stark sheets of white light   a thin line of cloud
moves the wind toying with its tail

canon crusted with centuries of rust black sea sand dirt points
Admiral Nelson surveys the royal port from his quarter deck   goblet of
gold rum swishing in his unsteady hands   the bitch is singing

from the wooden whore house there a blue Yorkshire shanty   her tongue
is heavy on the vowels   his dick is erect

here was Napoleon's nemesis too   long haired bitch with a royal name
teasing the rum to flame in the sweet roast fish air   singing Josephines
their tongues dancing in the voice you smell their sex
Nelson searches the horizon for ship sail needling its way
across the fabric of green silk looking for war

the shore crunches laps folds unfolds ticks gravels
its undertow back out to the sea weed bed the last of the rum
warms sweetly in his pit the voice sirens across the quad
and making his giddy way past the armoury   combustible as this
itch in his pants Nelson prays for the empire

Dear Mr. Ellison
Jarvis Q. DeBerry

If we s'posed to be
so invisible, why they
watch us when we shop?

Assam
Nikky Finney

Old Black woman heavyweight
body conscious now
after years of swinging wide
chocolate wings below her waist
wedged now into the surf for good
her treasures sunk
in the sane of selfconsciousness

From here she watches more
than moves these days
I walk by noticing
how things still pull to her
how even the uncalled water
comes calling knocking softly
bubbling about
her flat out thighs
the wet salt
wanting in

Her fingers disobey
the rest of her
and climb down
they turn into years
of summer grandchildren
running from the chasing water
straight into her netted arms

She sits there dripping
half in half out the sea
a tea bag full
of black uncut leaves
without you I whisper
the world is plain
tap water

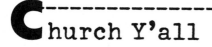

Ruth Forman

Church Y'all

For and with Adrienne, Kim, Lisa, Nyesha, Rhonda, and Sonia

What is it sisters
we was doing there
so long ago
and naming tomorrow at the same time
Stange Fruit playing
and us around a table front of 5th St. Dicks
should'a known better when I counted us seven

what is it we started
playin words but the spirits heard
and decided they would step
into our mouths and out
into the night air
but we were not cold
children
dribbling out our mouth with sweet potato pie
and ice cream brothers six foot nine
black as our table but smoother
corn cob pipes sending messages back to the ancestors
we are still alive

under the ocean rewalking your footsteps
flyin into the sun
on our nipples
brothers stroking the glow on our thighs
speaking
in tongues
funny
didn't feel like seven
felt more like one
but it was us it was we
Black people in the groove
y'all the spirit was
enough for us to get up and dance around that table
like we was a forest for us to sway
with the dip double time like we was children of Moses
on Soul train
and up to the scramblin board
in polyester and black goldfish
chosen to put in our platform shoes
afros seven feet high and black sage
singing after the sunset and before the sunrise

well
Cornel say *So it's true*
Black women can have church anywhere
Holy ghost dance on our hips
as we had to
stop and do the bump
and Kim did the window pane
Rhonda saw
the double dutch bus comin down the st.
we had to stop n
sing it till we couldn't remember no more
n just sit back
saying
Doubledutch ya'll Doubledutch
Doubledutch ya'll Doubledutch
God turnin the short end of the rope
we found ourselves jumping hand in hand
into the spirit on 43rd place
43rd place God picked you to be heaven tonight
Sonia grandmother
Josephine Josephine
came back again
that table home and the kitchen hummin

stories of first times and hmmm
here my ugly stories step out of me
and I thought I was cool with my stories
but here come 17 ya'll 17
and my boyfriend's daddy try to get with me
but 19 y'all 19
Nyesha golden verbs dangling
the corners of her mouth
taste a rainbow on Crenshaw

nothin necessary but our tongue and what we remember
seven cleaning women seven housewives
seven orishas curenderas healing women curing women
yes seven healers seven sages
the spirit called itself to us
though the stories singin swayin
like Alvin Ailey's Wade in the Water
we was jammin like we saw our mamas at funerals
we was jammin like we did in the hallways at school
Adrian's eyes close findin the right flow on concrete
we could have sat there for 20yrs
cymbals rinsing away our days

Strange Fruit droppin up the beats
for us to suck on like butterscotch
y'all made me hungry
y'all made me full
like Lisa say *Black women need to play together*
if we did we would change the world
Black women need to play together like we know how
playin our words like string games like mary mack like freezetag
like we without age
playing and knowing at the same time
electric sliding into the milky way
to play jacks with the stars
sisters the strength invincible
when we come together in love
y'all gave me love
y'all made me want to shout whole trumpets
y'all made me want to hug everybody down there coming out of 5th St.

that was church y'all
that was church at 1 am
cuz i got the spirit
smooth enough
for Adrian to do her James Brown slide

into the jitterbug
on the sidewalk
like it was a dance hall
like it was a school gym
like we was safe
like we was safe in love
we called it to us
life
wanting to talk
twirl its fingers in our hair
feel the sweat of stories travelling to us
after 7 yrs of hiding

Even now the earth shake her head
marking the last days
Death a thief in the night
with more and more keys on his keychain
we losing people under our feet and around this corner
cheekbones crushed into the concrete and left
cuz these are the last days
last breaths of the old world
but us flyin into the new with oxygen masks
from God and the old ones
to let us dance on the cracking sidewalk
chant
our stories together
communal spirit to take us through
we the curtains aflame burning into black holes
we the Nile's children and water
each of us bringing spirit to the table
a cocoon of silver and butterflies already born
with wings of griots.

Peace sisters, peace. i am born again.

The Yellow Forms of Paradise

Danielle Legros Georges

With paradise suspended from their necks like a giant clock,
the old folks stitch together the island's shifting colors.

Its iridescent paths of light they project onto the days between
this and the lost country. We are going back they say.

They pierce our ears with the golden studs of paradise which hum
when removed and studied in the palm. Home is a tiny bracelet

engraved with a girl's name, a scarf that ties the head down,
keeps it from flying. This yellow form of paradise, a disease,

an unlit road carved from fields sown with two sets of trees,
maple, palm, and we who leap from one set to another

all the while seeking ground.

Vertigo is never fun the old folks say, you fall without falling,
at once at the building's edge and at its foot. Beyond the building

a mountain laughs and behind it another, snow-peaked and ready
to release its avalanche of beads. We roll them underfoot, throw

a goat knuckle up and catch it with another knuckle. We sweep
the streets with our hair and on clean sidewalks picket the use

of our blood abroad. We write the dead who return amid clouds.
To the living we rain our green love in letters post-marked by birds.

For the living we bow to the great creator of fragments and break
into pieces on airplanes. Three new skies suffocate my old clouds.

My soil grows anemic. It whispers to me: *Return*

The ascent can be nitrogened with quick bubbles to the blood.
Do not rise too fast for surface, too fast for the beach road,

for the path once river now stone. The gods ride this, color of blood,
color of earth, backward from the hills. Uphill is a monument

of breaking coral. Uphill is a series of dead *caballeros,* uphill
is a salted plain whose dust reveals an army of cactus soldiers.

A topsoil of plastic bottles paves the way to the city of *peristyles,*
to the city of seven million gods.

A *tap-tap* of color cries by. I count the carried. I count the hills.
I count the buried. The living sweep by with their tongues in baskets.

The living sweep by with their golden rings and *gwayabels*. The living
Sweep by with their canes and dusty shoes, their brooms and *mango fransik*.

The living squeak by greased in oil of palma christi, accompanied by
the *wiwas* of donkeys. The returned sweep by with their double vision

and sunglasses of the dead. The returned sweep by with dirty hair.

Now, how can I give you up, my mother's earth, my alpha tongue?
I will bed you, earth. I will give birth to a three-headed child.

A mouth will emerge from my navel, another from my sex, and a third
from a third eye not mine. Its lungs will be hearty, will be sound.

It will call me mother.

Brian Gilmore

Swampy river

(for duke ellington, piano player, composer)

"magnolias dripping with molasses,"
oak fingers coasting over keyboard
cutting contest mellowed
shimmering ballrooms and a smile
that never leaves

melancholy lotus blossoms
limbo jazz jive
old hands tenderly blending
blue into biography

fats waller be his walk a long
tatum touches his tune
diz ain't seen no better doctor
mingus and roach ride this day break

trane whistling at sentimental ladies
big louie got a chance at the plate
chair rockin' in rhythm like wood science
carvings
smile never leaves

magnolias dripping with molasses
night searching for melody
dark lobbies in dawn's early light
smoke all in his eyes

mother tongue moving fingers
notes chosen before boat ride
drums heard be a woman
portraits of the lion

"happy go lucky local"
the intimacy of the blues
careful not to curse his color
pure poetry on piano

plays a thousand different cities
a million separate clubs
ragtime in his back pocket
stride style in his coat

    magnolias dripping with -

ambition.

    that is really his blood.

confident like a cat on the hunt
he's got an unshakeable rhythm

        purging pulitzer denials.
        muting critics with his
        masterworks
        never a bad word for the enemies

people be him.
just listen to the beat.
next time next song
    very gracious
    very very gracious
    indeed.

    where's the rhythm section?
an answer by
morning.
sam woodyard

clark terry
anyone
who believes in this
like noah and the flood

the water came
the ark was built
we had to float
a dove flew
found land
brought us an olive branch.

he/they/we always know
the dove will
come find land
by morning

that's why the ark is built.
everyone loves the dove
the ark
    the olive branch
        madly
        madly.

———————

     will talk of it for years to come
like the first time they heard paul robeson sing

"we are . . . climbin' . . . jacob's ladder"

    soldier on the bandstand

soldiers on the bandstand

professor of black music
swing nixon to the blues
shakespeare, steinbeck, tchaikovsky got wings
too

here he comes with those
spirituals

the negro ark builder smiling
holding a dove in his hand
setting it on top of his piano while he
builds it
again

board by board
section by section
calling in the people
with prophesy

the dove returning at last
with the olive branch
telling everyone exactly
where and when
to land

where to find the magnolias
and the molasses

where the world always starts
again after the flood.

from "Awakening"

Wind is in the cane. Come along.
Cane leaves swaying, rusty with talk.
Scratching choruses above the guinea's squawk
Wind is in the cane. Come along.

—JEAN TOOMER, FROM "CANNA"

Proem

We begin with
the sucking of teeth
a name compressed, squeezed
of its vowels, a number,
a disembodied imperative
answered by letters to God,
loose laughter of scattered half-notes,
staccato of ripened-too-soon
We memory
begin with proclamation, fighting
the suck of smallness in all
things manifest, scratching drought
at the openings, encroaching

We be/gin with debt
and necessity, power,
praisesong, orisha
riding air and magic
likened to madness, light,
a daughter's geography

I was born in a cane field
I was born in a cotton field
in a brake
in the thick of thieves
on the way
back from the sudden dead

We memory
begin self/ estranged
fruitless, primed into missing
orphaned of the ground,
deserving, We be/gin

re/membering
harvest cries, inventing
and celebrating this
perpetual present, *me*
for my recitative self
me for my recitative

I Creation

Strange woman, I fall asleep
after the world ahs been created
into the creases between female and Eve,
ribwoman, gift. This day, awakening,
beside my brown body, traversing
the surface, I linger, caressing
rough places and scars, familiar blemishes
and new moles, spider-veined thighs,
bumps of coiled hair, plumb-stone breasts.
I watch my body breathe, being. I see
the part others see: the periphery. The rind.
This day, awakening, as a ghost spit up from the river,
precious to myself if to none other, I am the story

of the blank-bellied woman, the story of her name,
and its brass box secret calling to me
where I wait to be born. I am in accordance
with my purpose. Spun out to the perimeter.
Radiating breath's momentum
I return singing.

"Awakening" is a serial response to Eve's account of her own creation as it appears in Book IV of John
Milton's *Paradise Lost*.

Sleep

Yona Harvey

My grandmother was never confused.
Day she died she fixed grits for breakfast,
washed dishes, purchased a can of snuff,
a box of peanut brittle from Walgreens
for her grandbabies to find. She lined
her dresser with our photographs &
carried herself to bed.

The devil must be crazy
calling all hours of the night.
We are so pressed to hear something
we lie awake listening.

If someone were to look down
we'd look like ants torn between drops of honey & sugar,
Some of us frozen in the riddle of decision.

Who isn't waiting for a sign?

When no one answered my grandmother's door
a neighbor let herself in. What was left
Was our faces on the bureau,
An abandoned body lacking
that bright knowing beneath the skin.

Listen.
My grandmother doesn't call
through my sleep thick as milk.
I only remember the song that held us like a net.

I never said I counted bones
or listened to their music. Recorded
the tail end of dreams. I never said
there's an answer to every question
that knowing would make us better.

I'm not a lonely grandchild.
most nights I hardly sleep.

Terrance Hayes

When the Neighbors Fight

The trumpet's mouth is apology.
  We sit listening

To *Kind of Blue*. Miles Davis
  Beat his wife. It hurts

To know the music is better
  Than him. The wall

Is damaged skin. Tears can purify
  The heart. Even the soft

Kiss can bite. Miles Davis beat
  His wife. It's muffled

In the jazz, the struggle
  With good & bad. The wall

Is damaged skin. The horn knows
  A serious fear

Your tongue burns pushing
  Into my ear. Miles Davis

Beat his wife. No one called
  The cops until the music

Stopped. The heart is a muted
  Horn. The horn is a bleeding

Wife. Our neighbors are a score
   Of danger. You open
My shirt like doors you want
   To enter. I am tender

As regret. Mouth on the nipple
   Above my heart.

There is the good pain
   Of your bite.

Ogaga Ifowodo

You Are Chic Now, Che

You are chic now, Che, capital profit
to Wall Street and Hollywood; no longer
banished to the neighbourhood of spider-
webbed streets. Your name no more flies with the spit
from cigar-smoking clones of Adam Smith,
communist-catching senators of god
or C.I.A. spooks with a silent rod:
your're as loud in the air as Beethoven's Fifth.

Let's not wrong your vanity: you were rather
handsome. Though not a woman, I can tell.

Had you taken to rock-and-roll, football,
or followed Clint Eastwood, Madison Square
Garden would have seen a revolution
and your murderers saved from the gas chamber
by a Dionysian mob. Your poster-
face spiced romance with a guerrilla's gun.

You are so chic now, Che, thirty years after
They tumbled you into a toe-dug grave.

As might be, by the logic of a brave
new world, alchemy of the profiteer.
Earth, blind to an American malice,
turned your bones to gold, its catalyst
the unbounded love of the dispossessed
whose inhuman griefs, grown too tall, obsessed

your blood, raced your feet to distant places
where, vile armies viler, your death had been
sooner. Such armies, Che, in the new lean
world of market-made hope, hold the aces.
Oh, pardon me, a few things right away:
the Berlin Wall crumbled and Communist Europe
fell. Comrade Gorbachev, labour's last Pope
preached perestroika and withered away

the Warsaw pact. The Union of Soviets
(now only Russia), China, Che, and all
the workers' states turn to the shopping mall,
swear by the Stock Exchange. Their old helmets
on, Castro and the rest of the Twelve
bluff the storm. But he's old now, so is Raul
and you're dead, Che, while America - call
it unfair - stalks still Havana's shy shelf.

So, you see why you could make Wall Street,
why McCarthy will not turn in his grave? -
no one else stands in the ring, out to save
dignity from the auction block. Bread, meat,
the opium of a consumer culture,
together with commodity-Che, will cure
classless hungers. And we are to leave to time
this defilement of the dead, this added crime?

Visitation: Grenada, 1978

Allison Joseph

From slender trees mangoes hang,
swelling toward ripening;
coconuts, brown haired, huge,
dangle in sunshine and clear air.

At sea's edge blue water laps
clean white sifts of sand
while goats, old and groggy
in this heat, move carefully

around haggard cows,
metal bells swinging
around pendulant necks.
Inside my grandmother's house

on this isle of spice, wooden floors
cool my hot feet, toes browned
by a sort of sun I'd not known
before, city girl, unfamiliar

with skies not diminished by smog,
exhaust, I startle on hearing rain
clatter on the tin roof above,
run with any child who calls me cousin

to the one-room store at the end
of a dirt road, peeking at penny candy
in wooden barrels and paper sacks.
Someone will always feed me—

aunts, grand-aunts, women who remember
the skinny boy who left for the States
years ago, proud now to see his daughter
come home. They feed me food

they fear I won't soon taste again—
genips, sweet pulpy treats hidden inside
thick leathery skins, breadfruit
and fried snapper, saltfish cooked

with plantains. In St. George's,
in the market, I find mats and hats
and hangbags woven from multicolored
straw, t-shirts silkscreened with

paradise scenes, quick souvenirs
for the pleasure ships that stop here
for a half-hour, on their way to bigger
destinations. I hold my mother's hand,

know she's a visitor here too,
not of this island but of a larger one
where tourists spend weeks, not minutes.
But even she is tempted to play traveler:

filling our bags with shells—
some big as a fist, small
as an eye, pink-brown swirls
and stripes stippling each one's

hard surface, taking me for a ride
in a boat where I can see blue
right down to the bottom, island waters
she can now show me, briefly.

Arnold J. Kemp

100 Times

Lost in rivers of Mars Bars and more coffee to spill on the bus,
Like so many other nights, a rose will silence your expression on film
Her impression of him of little consequence.

Oh my nights and eyes, when I think of those I love,
Those so far away, I cry. When I read the grounds
At the bottom of my coffee cup your image drives me mad.

Because the boys of Guadalajara are so beautiful,
See them still—even here in San Francisco—
With their dark brown hair and oddly shaped noses,
Their long nostrils that, looking at them eye to eye,
One can almost peer into, and the stillness like pools.

Still, when I lie down to love you, I am 100 times a street worth of traffic,
As many engines purring, as many fan belts turning.
Turn to me and you are more than you were from behind.

It didn't start this way at all, my spark plug. The two boys
Were exiting the mall by way of the over ground bridge
Attached to the hotel lobby. One asked the other, in a flirtatious way,
"Well, what do you want to do tonight?" and the handsome one replied,
"I don't know. Go home and think about death," or did he say,

"Sex," totally deadpan? Later that evening, they were sitting in the dark,
Deep in thought and fantasy. Then there was this Japanese drag-queen
Unleashing and practicing her English at the bar's end, saying,
"Black, African-American. Let's go Coco. I'm stinky as a bear!
I am a tiny little minuscule dime-sized penny's worth of a Negro-star."

Discubriendo una Fotografía de mi Madre

Shara McCallum

If I had left Venezuela with you, been on the boat moving
From your world of Papá, Mamá, abuelos, tios y primos,

I could watch granny cooking en la cocina,
Taste frijoles negros y arepas hot on my tongue.

If I had worn your clothes, dressed like this niña bonita
you left behind, I would be able to conjure up the collar

moored to your neck, feel its lace scratching my skin.
If I had the memory you lost to the Atlantic

(the blur of a white house in the background, las caobas
lining the front walk, the music box dancer still spinning

in your hand), if I could do more than imagine you
as this child, I would understand how *tierra, pais*

y casa became untranslatable words. From Spanish
to Patwa, something nameless must have gone wrong.

Sometime in the summer there's october

Tony Medina

for Stacie

*though it's summer
i'm thinking of fall,
thinking of fall,
walking in the rain
on my way to you*

I

i always liked the fall
walking down the street
in grey light afternoon
the leaves rising up off the curb
falling through the trees
a sunny somber Coltrane melody
rocking back and forth inside my skull

i always like the way you smiled
sipping hot tea
in warm empty cafes,
windows clouded wet
with the memories
of your poetry

II

in the hospital room
your blinds are shut
so the light won't eat
into your bones

you lie in your bed
folded hairless
in a puddle
of dead skin

your sheets are soaked
in sweat
your pillow full of snot
and tears

and though they carve you up
into a jigsaw puzzle
of your former self
you refuse to sew yourself up
from the world

III

you smile at me
As I clown for you
As I clown for me
unable to swallow
This image of you

IV

what impostors we are:
you in that broken skin
trying to hold your bones
together in its web
of dust and blood

and me trying
to keep
from sobbing
like the night
my grandmother died
in her light blue robe

V

you try to talk,
your smock dangling
off your bones
as your laughter shifts
the light in the room,
the blinds masticating
the sun, and you
forcing out a smile
through the impostor
that traps your soul,
in my eye's spying
examination
of what is now you
there is still
the you
i remember
with quick bright eyes
and attitude
the lips i've touched
the toes my tongue remembers,
that one sunny Sunday
in blue socks
that curled
as we baptized each other
in poetry,
the music
the wooden floor made
against your skin

(how i wanted
to keep you
in *that* light)

VI

but here, now,
you are in a dark cell
on death row,
a political prisoner
in Life's endless Kafkaesque nightmare
always absurd and unfair,
playing Russian roulette
with your sanity,
your sense of reality

Death, the final judge
and jury
Death, the governing body
with the power
to absolve
and release
and heal

and Cancer,
the prosecuting attorney,
trying to exhaust you
of your appeals
to live
leaving you with no other option
but to put yourself
in the hands
of bone marrow transplants
and corporate science
and other people's
blood

and though my days
are not as uncertain
as yours
if I could I would
will you them

The Outcome *for Nas*

global warming between my legs
scream against the waves
gave birth to 13 daughters
so now we never run out of water
my skin layered in diamonds and sage
left alone in confused forests
enslaved by days
time keeps on whoring us
ghetto saviors—can't keep ignoring us
flowers and flames flew from her fingers
rifles pointed from her sack
or was it simply a bag of sticks and stones
either way
she wore a compass on her head
rains won't stop the grass from turning red
her hair was half-permed half-dread
we gave up on walking in a past life
so we danced
arms wrapped around my neck
choked me back to life
a new world wife
reflecting the sun and rolling dice
symbol of the drama yet to come
too late to run
time traveling was late
watching was a blind man's mistake
all his assets melted right in front of his face
his right leg dragged with demon pace
shoes stay angel-laced
never count you blessings with haste
even a prophet can catch a case
didn't realize how sweet the future might taste
telepathically cutting through mental gates
words were weapons against their hate
shepherds searched for stars in her hair
her chest grew fermented like yeast
she broke her body like aged bread
he gave her truth
from all the books he'd read
she wrote rhymes inside the mud
sacrificed her cervix
to fit the future

named their poison
spit truth inside his mouth
re-born prophet
writing twisted scriptures
inside her belly
resurrected from bones and dirt
she made hard niggas smile
left her seeds inside the earth
gave husslas and killas life's worth
this is the life we chose
remember who was here first
find a reason why you curse
gold rush tongues
buy dreams too loose
sportin' electronic nooses
hoeing humanity—love takes over lust
despite the damage to Destiny
you can't take the best of me
in God we still trust

Toi Derricotte at Quail Ridge Books

Lenard D. Moore

I.

In front of Reynolds Price,
a mere portrait, surrounded by white faces,

You speak black metaphors.
blazer, body shirt, pants, metallic belt,

loafers, all onyx.
Your right hand holds eyeglasses,

the left grips *The Black Notebooks,*
like a noose clenches a wrenching neck.

II.

I see my grandmother's geography
when I study the map of your face:

peach-skin, wind-soft voice,
lips a path to wisdom.

I understand you've broken
through the door

no key can open
for your walnut folk.

III.

Black comes in degrees
like meanings of words.

You re-create mirrors,
heal the stinking sore

caused by three centuries
of whip lashings.

Passing is not your way.
You know the other world.

Nairobi Streetlights

Samwiri Mukuru

The people are not walking home. They are not watching the winged termites flood the sky as bulbs flicker on and light the air. The men are not carrying beds and broken chairs on their backs or thoughts of babies between crossed fingers. Their footsteps do not sound like ants marching or cows entering City Market. Their footsteps do not echo through Mathare, Hurrlingham, Westlands and the avenues irrigating human pollution.

Nothing is changing under Nairobi streetlights. The prostitutes do not intend to tap their heels into the sidewalks and wave their asses at the passing lights. The Kenyan Cowboys do not want to roam the streets in their Land Rovers, Range Rovers and Bata boots. The American Marines never want to drink American beer and watch American Movies at their base. The tourists are indistinguishable from the International School students and no one is laughing at this and no one belongs everywhere.

Nothing is falling on dirty streets and being sniffed up by dirtier noses. The street boys are looking for the legendary woman who will buy them spirits in exchange for sex. Husbands and teachers are taking high school girls away from high school boys and the high school boys are using Tusker, Sportsman and Nyama Choma[1] to consume the rage. Wives are at home, in bed, watching the door so they know when to turn away.

And while Sajiv Singh is in his office counting shillings, the *askaris*[2] holding their Aks and pangas[3] stand guard as nothing is tucked in under Nairobi streetlights.

---

1 Roasted beef (usually eaten while drinking beer)
2 Hired security
3 machete

3 movements

Letta Neely

morning

harvesting your nectar
is my favorite
task
just dip down
till I taste
horizon on my
tongue brilliant
as mumia's liberation

night falling

over this city
in 3 shades of
blue, sky is
open as yr legs
some nights/I arch
my neck
let air sit
on my face

noon
(short fisting hallelujah)

girl,
when you
come
I swear I
feel god
squeezing
my hand

The Night when Mukoma Told the Devil to Go to Hell

Driving at a blur of 85 MPH to meet with
memories that sit in the back seat of my
old Nissan Sentra to the sculptured lake where
yesterday your kiss occasioned a shooting star.

Insects caught in lightning passage explode
on my windshield. The lined porches are dark.
Rainbow TV lights flicker and spill onto
the hunch back road that curves and mangles,
new years eve is sooner than we think
and celebrating voices will be one day too late

Caught in the web of memory at the bottom
of vodka and manuscripts that fill my pockets
like stones, I only catch a glimmer of a broken
picket fence and flying wood splintering,
then shattering the lake's moon, sound of roaring
engine on nothing and a sudden weightlessness-
death can be such a surprise

An old blues song by Lightning Hopkins escapes
through the cracked passenger window and finds roots.
Reservice engine soon, buckle your belt-flashes-
Always turn into the skid, a lesson I remember alone
one second past today. Darkness.

Scars do not save and mean nothing-
a life lived, a life lost, and love?
Love is African cented incense and
your soft mystic touch that will mourn
tomorrow but only redeem you. I feel everything
betwixt the harsh gasps for oxygen.
We are, after all, such sycophants of life.

I find the devil sitting at the bottom of the lake
where yesterday we had basked in the glow of the red sun.
how you held your head above water gasping much like
one in labor and yet patient enough to walk on water

What does one tell one who knows no surprise?
Ailments of the mind? Aches of the heart?
That I stood by God till I learned of anarchy?
Or deliver the message in the bottle that God is dead?

Over the bottle, blood pasted thick by spirits,
we talked of gaps between teeth* and wrinkles,
of weeping shooting stars, life and death,
worms and with a warm smile, "Hell is the space
between two worlds and two skins—metamorphosis"

the devil is a picky bastard and fuck him
for his godliness for one second into New Year's
I will resurface, still terrified of illusion and muse,
unborn, uncrucified and no one did I save

Some stories much like this one have no redemption,
I could talk of how I wanted to walk back, shoot smoke
straight as an arrow into the skies*
pin drops of blood on icicles and let them drown my
words of breath under that Mugomo* tree.

I want to let you know it was a long walk home
that night and like a snake shedding its other self,
I cannot remember exactly what it was I left buried
at the bottom of that lake, only what I found

Alas, I have to sneak this in
for you are one with resolution:
My dear, please know that your whispered love
turned suffering into an annunciation.

---

* For the Kikuyu, a gap between the front two teeth is an indication of beauty.
* According to the Kikuyu, a sacrifice was accepted if smoke from
the burning meat for sacrifice went up straight.
* Mugumo tree: It's a massive tree, reputedly lives to be several hundred years old, where traditionally
the Kikuyu people sacrified to their God—Mwene Nyaga. I remember one such tree near our house—
legend has it that it has been alive for as long as the Kikuyu have been.

Autobiography of a Black Man

Who has not
On occasion entertained the presence
Of a blackman?

—RAYMOND PATTERSON

All the ladies feeling lucky at love
ask me if I like jazz, want to go out
and kick it at some club they know. I nod,
being a man who never disappoints.
Every white man I've known has wanted me
to join his basketball team, softball league
or book-discussion group. They invite me
on week-long, fly-fishing trips to Montana.
One day I might say yes. They think
they admire my superb athletic skills
and my broad education, but it's nothing
more than my color. I am The Black Man
the whole world mythologizes and envies.
I can get cats to march like boot-camp soldiers.
No dog ever dares ignore what I say—
sit up, fetch, play dead—the whole fucking routine.
Even New York roaches know to behave,
scurrying and hiding when I say, *Scat!*
I'm big and too damn powerful. The boss
on the job gulps hard and fast while I piss
into the cracked urinal. His hand shakes
as he follows me out, making small talk.
I will appear in his dreams 'til he's dead.
Black brothers, too, hurt themselves to get near me,
like crabs trying to climb out of a bucket.
The Latinos up in Harlem yell, *Jesus!*
when they see me. They fall down on their knees.
Am I the Messiah? Might be. Might be.
Koreans behind fruit stands bow their heads,
treating me like Buddha. That's alright. Let 'em.
My father wants us to be better friends
as if father and son weren't close enough.
My mother loves me more now than before,
since I grew up and became a Black man.

I'm twenty-three, and I'm king of this world.
Everyone fears and worships me. I know
I'm the motherfucking object of envy.
I'm the be-all and end-all of this world.

Willie Perdomo

Spotlight at the Nuyorican Poets Café

Finally fixed
I get to the café
in time for my spotlight.
I ask Julio, the bouncer,
if he's gonna stay inside
to hear me read tonight.
He tells me I better read something happy
none of that dark ghetto shit
because tonight's crowd got him pissed.
He is the best random judge in the house
as he soothes a low scoring slam poet
"C'mon, you know you can't
take this shit too seriously."
Julio helps me strengthen my aesthetic
as I walk through the door
I spot the spoken word racketeers
who get close enough to put bugs
in my ears
buy me a few beers
and extend open invitations to the studio
to lay down a track or two
for a couple of points
so they can dig into my pockets
when I fall asleep.
They look at me stupid
when I tell them
that I just spent my last ten dollars
but I'm still looking
for metaphoric change.

I was just a poet
wanting to read a poem
the first night I came here.
Since then

I have become a street poet,
then somebody's favorite urban poet,
a new jack hip-hop rap poet,
a spoken word artist,
a born-again Langston Hughes
a downtown performance poet
but you won't catch me rehearsing
because my shit is ready made real
and you won't see me sucking
on showbiz-flavored herbal throat drops
because I want you to hear
the crack at the back
of my throat.

I come up to the cherubic man with white hair
whose smile will not close
until the poetry café is demolished,
who will allow himself to die
only when love fails to create.
Later he will tell me stories
about his soul brother
his beautiful Miky
creater of the ghetto genesis
where shit begets shit
who saw God and said "Vaya. You got something?"
The cherubic man with white hair
stays alive
by breathing Miky's ashes
in the Avenue B air.

I go to the back of the bar,
sit next to the blind man
and light a cigarette for him.
He can tell when I'm not right,
when I've been racing against myself,
wiping sweat off my eyes.
"Where you been you jive muthafucka?
I'm glad you here
cuz these muthafuckas
want to get up there
cop pleas and sell Cliff notes
before they read a goddamn thing."
A guest poet
from the university
gets on stage to read a poem.

He begs the audience
to be gentle
because his stuff is built for the page.
The blank man tells him
to read the goddamn poem.

I kiss the lady with the sunglasses
sometimes used to deflect rays,
always to look where I can't see.
She has been taking notes on the scene
watching poets exchange business cards.
She takes a moment to hug me tight
and begs me to take care of myself
because the bigger picture
needs me.

The impresario leaps onto the stage,
he tells the DJ to give him a hippety-hop
a hippety-ho for the hype
and calls out for word perfect.
I look at the candle burning
in front of Miky's picture
and he tells me that there is still time
for me to go the bathroom
throw water on my face
and remember how I was just a poet
wanting to read a poem
the first night I came here.

Carl Phillips

Blue

As though marble or the lining of
certain fish split open and scooped
clean, this is the blue vein
that rides, where the flesh is even
whiter than the rest of her, the splayed
thighs mother forgets, busy struggling
for command over bones: her own,
those of the chaise longue, all
equally uncooperative, and there's
the wind, too. This is her hair, gone
from white to blue in the air.

This is the black, shot with blue, of my dark
daddy's knuckles, that do not change, ever.
Which is to say they are no more pale
in anger than at rest, or when, as
I imagine them now, they follow
the same two fingers he has always used
to make the rim of every empty blue
glass in the house sing.
Always, the same
blue-to-black sorrow
no black surface can entirely hide.

Under the night, somewhere
between the white that is nothing so much as
blue, and the black that is, finally, nothing,
I am the man neither of you remembers.
Shielding, in the half-dark,
the blue eyes I sometimes forget
I don't have. Pulling my own stoop-
shouldered kind of blues across paper.
Apparently misinformed about the rumored
stuff of dreams: everywhere I inquired,
I was told look for blue.

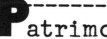

Rohan Preston

Patrimony *for Rudolph R. Jones*

Born inside the red house with the blue door and turpentine floor —
with my navel string buried up front in the yard, waiting for me
under that valuting sweetie mango tree. Issued inside yawning
heartwood with rings to hose Mesmer and a million stars —
ripe liquid rippling. Sprung from amber and ancient sap,
into the sublime spirits my mothers singing, slapping clothes
against rockstone, blanching stain into shine — flagging the breath
of the breeze. Into heavy lightened by trilling — my fathers
breaking rockstone down Emmanuel Road, gal and boy,
into sawdust and lumber, and banana tears staining khaki
trousers. Delivered limbic and alembic, arms akimbo,
into such singing laughter and flat-paned manners, such music
and musing — beating wheels with a stick down the district road,
bottling peeny-wallies to twinkle galaxies in our hands,
outrunning ventriloquist crickets that chime glittery gowns
onto night. Pushed into the loneliness of caked-together

chicken feathers after rain, the grievance of mourning doves.
Risen into the cooing of women come to throw corn, come
to throw words, come to throw partner. Into the belly laugh
of men come to slap dominoes and tap tables and slap hard
backs. Sung into these mountains that swell like bumps on foreheads
or fill out like breasts with milk coming in; these seas that stack
pastel bands atop each other. Prayed on in this house, with dogs
whimpering underneath and nannygoats dancing reverse funnels
into earth; aromaed by roast breadfruit, naseberry, thyme,
scallion, custard apple and sour sop. Given up to
Dragon stout and condensed milk on red Saturday nights,
then the hallelujahs and hosannas broadcast by trembling hands,
salted mercies and haily Marys, tribulating crosses
and palam-pam — into such a churning calabash —
into such a cassava milky way was I born.

Claudia Rankine

ntermission in three acts in service of PLOT

The thing in play (act I)

The people outside the theatre prevent intermission from
being uninvolved. Hence the overwhelming desire to forgive
some, to forget others. Even so we are here and yet I cannot
release us to here, cannot know and yet go on as if all the world
were staged. Who believes, "Not a big mess but rather an
unfortunate accident arrived us here." The past assumes
presence. It stays awkward, clumping in the mouth. And this is
necessary time. Only now do we respect or is it forget the
depths of our mistakes. There often rises from the tiredness on
the surface a great affection for order. Plot, its grammar, is the
linen no one disgorges into. Excuse me. From that which is
systemic we try to detach ourselves, cling to, cellophane
ourselves into manmade regulations, so neatly educated, so
nearly laid. But some of us have drowned and then coughed
ourselves back up. The deep morning lifts its swollen legs high
upon the stage. Some wanting amnesia float as a personified
abstraction. Some wash ashore, but not into the audience, not
able to look on. Help me if who you are now helps you to know
the world differently, tell me. *We want to not fear life so.*

Still in play (act II)

On the street where children now reside the speed limit is 25.
Green owns the season and will be God. A rain, that was, put a
chill in every leaf, every blade of grass. The red brick, the
asphalt, cold and cold. The front step, the doorknob, the
banister, the knife, the fork. A faucet opens and Liv arrives like
a thing formed in the sea's intestine, before floating in to be
washed ashore and perfumed. In time she opens her mouth and
out rushes, "Why is the feeling this? Am I offal? Has an
unfortunate accident arrived me here? Does anyone whisper,
stay awhile, or the blasphemous, *resemble me, resemble me.*"
Those watching say with their silence that is Liv, she has regret
in her eyes or she needs to know the why of some moment. She
doesn't look right. She is pulling the red plastic handle toward
her, checking around her. She's washing, then watching hands,
fingers and shouting what sounds like, *assemble me, assemble
me.* She is wearing shoes and avoiding electrical wires, others,
steep drops, forgotten luggage. Those are her dangers, she
cannot forget. A hook out of its eye, she's the underside of a
turtle shell. Riveted, and riven, the others stare contemplating
the proximity of prison to person before realizing the quickest
route *away from* is to wave her on. They are waving her on. Liv
is waved on. Now everything remains but the shouting. A cake
is cooling on a rack. Someone is squeezing out excess water.
Another is seasoning with salt. The blacker cat is in heat. A man
sucks the mint in his mouth. The minutes are letting go. A hose
is invisible on the darkened lawn.

Musical interlude (act III)

A certain type of life is plot driven. A certain slant in life. A
man sucking his mint lozenge. He is waiting for the other foot
to drop. His own, mind you. In a wide second he will be center
stage.

His song will be the congregation of hope. He will drain his
voice to let Liv know she cannot move toward the birth without
trespassing on fear. To succumb to life is to succumb to the
reverberated past seemingly arrested.

Erland knows Liv is as if in a sling, broken in the disappeared
essence, the spirit perhaps: catfoot in a moist soil, at the lowest
altitude or simply streamside, though seeming fine.

He knows he too sometimes is as if below, drained, non-circulatory, in an interval, the spirit perhaps in an interval. But then frictionized, rubbed hard—

Sweet life-ever-lasting, he is singing softly beneath his meaning in the sediment of connotation where everyone's nervously missing or missed. The melody is vertical, surrendering suddenly to outcome, affording the heart.

Always there is a ladder recalling another sort of knowing because some remainder, some leftover is strenuous. *Again and again here is a cradle dropping.* His voice catches. It feels like tenderness beckoning and it is into her voice, into voices.

Calypso the outside woman

Vanessa Richards

She is music made flesh
filling the room with perfumed bass notes
and the pink pong of steel drums.
Veils of Savannah dust
wash away with rain water
melodies.

Down the road
a kaisonian is calling,
trailing revellors home.

Sleep rides Carnival
on a slow mule
through the promenade
while the 3 peaks of Trinidad
bow their heads like holy men.

Calypso pulls back the sheet,
welcomes a minstral wind.
Slipping through jalousie windows
it plays upon her nipple,
provoking the pearl
from the shell of her breast.

Quicksilver fingers
plait her black mane with rhapsodic ribbons.
Her potent hands retrace song,
bracing brass trumpet,
catching spirited starbeams
to shower on legions of synchronised backsides.
Dancers pressed between
Brrahhbrrahh shots, trills
and sustained supplicating breaths.
She is a player in the band.

Beyond this island
she is the outside woman.

The nymph receives him in waves.
Deep forest kisses open his journeyed chest.
Tendril limbs draw salt from skin.
Gold tooth smiles under
half a moonlight
Licking out the rhythm
with a talking drum of tongues.
Harmony indulges the longing of dawn.
but Mercury has been sent.

A coolness rises from the harbour
Cane fields savour the dew.
A new morning.
Ash Wednesday morning.
She has given him up.
In good faith she curl into his side
and is consumed by history.

Ulysses and Calypso succumb to sleep
and ration one dream.
In the morning he will sail
on the ship she has prepared for him
and just so the masquerade begins.

Kristina Rungano

The Woman

A minute ago I came from the well
Where young women like myself drew water
My body was weary and my heart tired.
For a moment I watched the stream rush before me

And thought how fresh the smell of flowers,
How young the grass around it.
And yet again I heard the sound of duty
Which ground on me—made me feel aged
As I bore the great big clay container on my heard
Like a great big painful umbrella.

Then I got home and cooked your meal
For you had been out drinking the pleasures of the flesh
While I toiled in the fields
Under the angry vigilance of the sun
A labour shared only by the bearings of my womb.
I washed your dishes
And swept the room we shared
Before I set forth to prepare your bedding
In the finest corner of the hut
Which was bathed by the sweet smell of dung
I had this morning applied to the floors.
Then you came in,
In your drunken lust
And you made your demands
When I explained how I was tired
And how I feared for your child in me
You beat me and had your way
At that moment
You left me unhappy and bitter
And I hated you;
Yet tomorrow, I shall again wake up to you
Milk the cow, plough the land and cook your food,
You shall again be my Lord
For isn't it right that woman should obey,
Love, serve and honour her man?
For are you not fruit of the land?

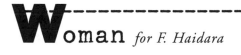

Woman *for F. Haidara*

Tijan Sallah

You have my unqualified love.
Flowers lean on the slender waist
Of your door knob. This is no
Hoary love; no love to toss
In the waste-basket.

I see you in my mirror every day,
Love images in plenitude.
You extend your lips
In syllables of charm;
I extend mind. Like elephants,
We fuse our proboscises
In the amorous moonlight.

Woman, there is nothing
On this garrulous earth;
Nothing, not even garlands
On the feet of sacred stone circles
That match your grace.

The way you walk, terraces of flower-shades.
Each step practised to the
Rhythm of the imaginary drum.
Each waist-shake, each hand movement,
Like the flawless gestures of a ballet-dancer.

Woman, tall beauty of giraffe-grace,
Like the slender palmtrees of Jeswang*,
Like the ostrich I saw at Niokoloba.
You compete with the beams of sun and moon.
And you trap shades of beauty
Under your armpit.

Woman, you are Timbuktu.
Salt rides every part of your aura.
You nibble books like fish do plankton.
You anchor your head
On the rock of tradition.

You are beauty, clothed in kindness.
Your days are filled with terranga*.
Woman, you are the nectar that perfumes my seasons.
And I stand here today like a bard-flower,
Your beauty overwhelming my savage days.

---

* Jeswang: a town between the Gambia's capital, Banjul, and the adjoining town of Serre Kunda.
  Terranga: Senegambian hospitality.

Angela Shannon

Sunday

It could have been the way the Southern
man in his navy suit and skin,
rocked along the church wall,
waddling to the tambourine and falling
at the sides, the way old men do to Blues.

Or the way Sister Nettie got the spirit
all in her feet and behind, quick-stepping,
like an ant hill was under her toes,
shaking her head back and forth in disbelief—

Or the way Deacon Jones raised
both hands like the police was there,
and started pacing the pulpit—
a foreign street—looking for Jesus.

But something quick came over the church
when Walter's voice slid to his navel
and plucked a piece of an umbilical cord,
tugging the notes from generations gone.

And a sister lost in the crowd screamed,
like when children have their first babies,
and it floated over the pews
and took the congregation rocking

back to the first cry we made
in this freedom-stealing country—
the first scream on the auction block—
and we tried to clap our way out of memory,

to stomp out the sound like sparks of fire
but it was already voiced (and the seer had said,
this child would be different).

Purple Impala

your arms/ quiet snakes
coiled 'round me like gods
your hair like/ dark fingers
spread wide/ to hold the night
your body/ bamboo
reaching to heaven

you part my lips/
lick jamaican stars into my throat
and as i swallow
i open/ purple
for the very first time
      i mean really feel/ purple

i'm in half notes
blown upside down
from floor of diva breath
i am sampled riffs/ getting wetter
each time/ i'm in church/ when
fingers stroke ivory keys/
i am angled lean of
a deaconness hat

you take me all inside
this vibration/ violet
the flavor of/ buttered grits
on a foldaway table
have me suck juice from round hips
of concord grapes/
      i rise in steam
off triple black coffee
and run/ all the way
with you

we in creases of unopened books
we verses in the holy qur'an
we a river's handclap
n lilacs/ on backyard bush

i roll over
      undress my belly scent
         into air
bounce and flirt

with bees and sun
and end up
      in a chevy impala
marvin gaye dancin'
all 'round
      the backseat

Patrick Sylvain

Windows of Exile

Wings soaring in the flare of dawn
to uncover hidden aches of feet treading slushy, blankets of snow.
The sun, a ripe orange
in the sky, is a mirage,
Wrapped heads and hands
remind tropical skins
this land is of fruit and thorns.

Knots torment my head,
yearning to hear the somersaults
of sea breezes in conch shells
deepens the incision of loneliness
made by this savage winter.
Barren of heat and honeycombs,
I seek music to heal the scars
inflicted by an Uncle whose smile
is a loaded M-16.

I danced anguished steps
when a man with unkempt hair
and cigar caked teeth
chants nigger with jaw
tightened like an unmerciful fist.
I wish to escape
the rhythm of this land;
my words play different chords.

Tonight, although the sky is inviting,
deep blue, half lit,
stars gathering in clusters,
I'm standing behind my windows of exile
fanning my wings;
waiting for Haiti's spring to eradicate
the scorching heat from khaki uniforms
and dragon eyes, pelting my native land.

gin and juice

when i was little my father stole my pussy
small, purple and pink
it was mine

he would put his mouth on it and smile
put his fingers in it and sleep

i wonder how he kept from puking some nights
from drink, from himself

so cliché, so stupid
he made it our secret

i will tell you another

it was the softer, more liquid touches i preferred
than the smacks across my face
my bubbled lips
my welted arms and thighs
the kicks in the gut
the chasing around the house

i would tremble in my bed
hooded in a favorite jacket
the same one i wore when i ran away
zipped, tight
a braided, brown bundle
but my father was good at detangling virgins

i was only a girl

it was quiet on nights
when my father asked if i was wearing panties

with each new lover
i erase those damn fingers
the grin and tobacco of him
and i do not remember as often as i used to
just when i look in the mirror
and notice his face in mine
his jaw and mouth
his mother's feet

i would like to say that i got it back
but sometimes it is still his fingers
not mine or someone fine
with big promises and a dick

it is him i smell
in an exhausted heap
reaching for a glass of wine,
a cigarette

when i call myself names it is him that i hear

no such thing as easy pussy
especially when you want it back

i wonder
since we don't talk anymore
if he holds his fingers to his face
to remember

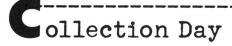

Natasha Tretheway

Collection Day

Saturday morning, Motown
forty-fives and thick seventy-eights
on the phonograph, window fans
turning light into our rooms,
we clean house to a spiral groove,
sorting through out dailiness—
washtubs of boiled-white linens,
lima beans soaking, green as luck,
trash heaped out back for burning—
everything we can't keep,
make new with thread or glue.

Beside the stove, a picture calendar
of the seasons, daily scripture,
compliments of the Everlast Interment
company, one day each month marked
in red—PREMIUM DUE—collection visit
from the insurance man, his black suits
worn to a shine. In our living room
he'll pull out photos of our tiny plot,
show us the sight eastward slope,
all the flowers in bloom now, how neat

the shrubs are trimmed, *and see here,*
the trees we planted are coming up fine.

We look out for him all day, listen
for the turn-stop of wheels
and rocks crunching underfoot.
Mama leafs through the Bible
for our payment card—June 1969,
the month he'll stamp PAID
in bright green letters, putting us
one step closer to what we'll own,
something to last: patch of earth,
view of sky.

Insomnia

Prophets
gagged by words
by blood by fantasy
bound and shoved
      pushed up
in public precincts thrown
into holding cells hanged
with belts strapped
    into cars
demolished and drowned
in joke ends broken up
from head down

unseen from brownstone windows but heard
      inevitably
           screams
           unleashed
           unwillingly

bleed
thru windows inward like wind creeps howling
with whistles
street pistols whip
heads blood crystals
    shatter in shards
falling pierce vision shimmering glint sparks
unseen but heard crashing
like waves breaking   brakes screeching   prophets

(gagged by words   arguing
over nothing because anything's better than silent suffering
    &passing men are evidence   spread
    against warm hoods   their hands
    and checks down   against the pebbled ground   their backs
    exposed to nightstick plunger premature 41 bullet verdict salutes &
50 foot freefall escapes for alla my mother's prophets)

    born
red hot gasping
against merciless patrol car engine sharks who growl
up one way streets spinning hot brass and cold aggression

casting 360 new blue shadows to confuse

police questions like

where you coming from?

Kevin Young

Shrine outside Basquiat's Studio, September 1988

Back on Great
Jones
his face

against the façade
fronting the carriage
house rented

from Warhol—
inside, his suits
stiffen from starch,

split paint.
He's bought
the farm whole,

enchilada
& all—August
& the heat

covering everything,
needle-sharp,
asleep. No more

feeding
his habit art—
he's gone

& done it
this time, taken
his last dive.

Exit, stage right
A broken
record—his black

skin thick,
needled
into song—
a swan's. Upon
graffitied brick—
INSIDIOUS MENACE

LANDLORD
TENANT—
folks pile

candles flowers
photos notes
to God & lace—

anything TO REPEL
GHOSTS, keep
his going at bay

before memory comes
early, snarling
& sweeps him

into the mouth
of euphemism—
sanitation worker, waste

management engineer,
garbage man, dumpster
driver, trash

heap, heaven.

PART SIX

Dialogue

"Back to the lecture at
hand/perfection is
perfected so I'ma let
'em understand"

—Dr. Dre featuring
Snoop Doggy Dogg,
"Nuthin' But a
'G' Thang" (1992)

Ras Baraka

Black Youth Black Art
Black Face—An Address

Panel discussion from the "I'll Make Me A World" production school entitled "African American Artists In The Next Millennium," sponsored by BLACK-SIDE Film and Television Productions—1997

I WRITE BECAUSE I HAVE A DEEP SENSE TO TELL MY STORIES, AND A deeper sense to change what I see. I was on a panel with Rosa Guy about two years ago at the National Black Arts Festival in Atlanta. I remember her saying that people write what they feel and what they know about. This I believe translates to mean that people usually write from their own point of view, what they think, what they believe, and how they see themselves in the world using the information they have access to.

Amiri Baraka said, "The noblest function of art is to oppose what is ugly." The question is, what is ugly? Like Rosa Guy said, it depends on where you're coming from. It is to know that when you choose to say one thing you are choosing not to say something else. I think a lot of us here still have to get clear on "what is ugly," so we can begin to bring beauty into the world. The only problem with that is that beauty is in the eye of the beholder. Which takes us back to perspective. To the slavemaster, slavery was beautiful. It secured him wealth and prestige for his family. On the contrary, slavery was hell to the slave, and while the slavemaster prayed for more slaves, the slaves prayed for freedom. So I guess it comes down to whose side you're on. Or from whose perspective do you view the world.

Black art and culture is American art and culture. It was created out of a genuinely American experience, and has had an enormous impact on America's cultural and social development. The problem is that most people don't know what American culture is, because they don't know America's history, or I should say, the history of its people. It would be the same if I were to say that most black people could not clearly identify black art and culture except that it was done by black people. They don't understand the forces that push it, the history or material conditions that created it. American schools don't teach American history, or, I should say, they don't teach history from American people's perspective. History is usually taught from the point of view of presidents, laws, wars, and treaties. That is the perspective of the bourgeoisie. They teach European literature, European art, European renaissances, European philosophy, and almost nothing genuinely American.

I grew up in Newark, New Jersey, a predominantly black and Latino city. I went to predominantly black schools my entire life. In my formal education I didn't learn about Langston Hughes, Zora Neale Hurston, David Walker, Frederick Douglass, W.E.B. DuBois, Sojourner Truth, Margaret Walker, Claude McKay, the Harlem Renaissance, Amiri Baraka, James Baldwin, Katherine Dunham, Billie Holiday, Charlie Parker, John Coltrane, Paul Robeson, Sonia Sanchez, Frank Yerby, Duke Ellington, the Last

Poets, the blues, bebop, jazz, Dizzy Gillespie, Miles Davis, or Max Roach. And there are many many more where they came from. All of these people and forces had to have at least some small impact on American society. And if you do get a chance to read an excerpt or poem by a black author, or hear an essay, a song, it is mentioned in isolation or passing. We never discuss the social and material forces behind them, or the political movements that ushered them into existence. And while we're here discussing in preparation for "I'll Make Me A World," most kids still don't know of or have seen "Eyes On The Prize." So most of us today, especially the youth, are grasping for straws, guessing. You found an old record that moves you: James Brown, Curtis Mayfield, John Coltrane, Nina Simone, you tape it, you sample it. You found an old book. You read a beautiful poem. Someone told you about Paul Robeson and DuBois. You read *The Autobiography of Malcolm X,* or just went to see the Malcolm X movie, and then "Panther," but no real education or preparation.

Our response to this should be the re-creation and re-development of our own institutions. We need writers' guilds, community theater, film production groups, artist collectives. We have to find advanced ways to reach and teach masses of people who are being controlled by international multimedia conglomerates. And while most of us play our part, our history and culture is being revised and told by those who were opposed to it. The people who said that there was no such thing as black art and philosophy, and who denied the relevance of black history, are now teaching it. Those who stayed in the dormitory while others fought for Afri-centric education are now its professors. The same people who thought there was nothing plausible or academic about black literature are now the experts of it. These are the same people we are now learning from. They are the people who have been put in charge of the marginal resources and power that we are able to get our hands on; or like the woman said yesterday, that we have access to.

Now instead of influencing and leading American popular culture we are becoming pulled down by it, or, like Malcolm said, by the "dollarisms." The sex, violence, misogyny, fascism, and imperialism that dominate American popular culture has now become a leading theme in ours, complete with revisionism, and funny, contemptible Negroes. From "Booty Call" to "Ill Na Na," "Life After Death" to MenaceIISociety." We have carved out a place where we have become comfortable with death and self-destruction. A place that finally culminated in the deaths of Tupac Shakur and The Notorious B.I.G. And while some may disagree with them, had problems with their style, or belittle their importance, you can not disagree that they had the ears and minds of millions of black and Latino youth around the world. And our children mourned their deaths the same way that previous generations mourned the deaths of Malcolm X and Martin Luther King.

I went to college when I was 17 years old. At the same time one of my closest friends went to the Navy and another went to jail. Months before that he was shot in the leg and I drove him to the hospital in my father's car. When I got to college the dichotomy of our stories forced me to write. My poetry was developed in an atmosphere of protest and resistance. The first audiences I had were at organization meetings of Black NIA F.O.R.C.E., or at the Howard University protest. I met Sister Souljah and she took me on tour with Public Enemy, Stetsasonic, and many other artists and community activists. We traveled around the country to schools and prisons lecturing to youth, and developing consciousness. I met Kevin Powell and the idea of *In the Tradition* developed as we were counselors at a camp for welfare hotel children, out of New York, organized by Sister Souljah. Kevin began organizing tours with other poets. Asha Bandele, Tony Medina, Willie Perdomo, Lorena Craighead, and myself, and others, went around reading poetry when it wasn't popular.

In the late '80s and early '90s, youth tried to combat the crack cocaine left by the C.I.A., the aftermath of COINTELPRO, Negro politicians, as well as Howard Beach, the murder of Yusef Hawkins, Tawana Brawley, Virginia Beach, with one hard cultural push. Public Enemy stormed on the scene with the S1Ws and introduced the rap world to sound bites and speeches in their music. They hipped people to Coltrane, Malcolm X, Assata Shakur ("recorded and ordered supported of Chesimard"). P.E. raised the consciousness of millions. We began to see P.E. hats and shirts, and the gold chains were being replaced with African medallions and Malcolm X shirts. I found myself on the train rhyming loud "Elvis was a hero to most but he never meant shit to me the straight out racist the sucka was simple and plain mutha fuck him and John Wayne." KRS-1 put himself as the persona of Malcolm X on his album cover, "By All Means Necessary." Everyone began coming into some form of social consciousness. Souljah and I held a series of "State of Black Youth" rallies that were attended at points by two to three thousand youth. Around the country college campuses became swollen with protest movements: Howard University in 1989, Tennessee State, Morgan State University, Morris Brown, City College of New York, the University of the District of Columbia. And as fast as everything began to develop, and as quick as students began to form alliances and organize themselves, it was attacked piece by piece.

We watched Public Enemy torn apart and destroyed in full public view. Thousands of students graduated from college looking for the Student Nonviolent Coordinating Committee, the Black Panther Party—anything that they could channel their energy and new-found activism into. Nothing existed. Some joined the Democratic Party or the Joint Center for Political Studies. Some joined the NAACP. Others just tried to make a living. The whole push of resistance and social and political rap was brought to its knees. "Respect and protect the black woman" became Hoes With Attitude, or "Pop that coochie" and "Do Do Brown." The idea of self-respect and self-defense promoted by X-Clan, P.E., The Jungle Brothers, Poor Righteous Teachers, and KRS-1 was overshadowed by N.W.A., and gangsta rap, complete with pimps and money. Malcolm X was replaced with Iceberg Slim. Gangstas and pimps became cultural and political icons who kept it real, represented, and defined manhood in the ghetto. And while most of this changed with us staring it eye to eye, many watched and played their part fitting nicely into revisionism and mediocrity. And many of these same people will tell you that positive rap doesn't sell when Public Enemy went platinum with "It Takes a Nation of Millions to Hold Us Back." They will say that lyrics aren't important, or what you say doesn't matter, the way you make your money is different than your personal life, or that this generation has always been negative and stood for nothing. That is why it is called "Generation X." And I say, remembering Public Enemy, Don't Believe the Hype!

Stefani Barber

leaving a feminist organization: a personal/poetics

"ESCHUCHA, ESCHUCHA, ESTAMOS EN LA LUCHA" RESONATES IN A STREET filled with people playing drums and drinking water. we walk up a hill and wave at children hanging out of the windows. give flyers to their parents down below. *come by sometime.* where would they arrive, looking for the plates of steaming food offered. who would hand it to them. this was our work. because *nothing's too good for the working class.* an embodiment of the forces of one paradigm (socialist, feminist, ours) in struggle with its arch-nemesis (capitalist, sexist, theirs): *a lived reality.*

in addressing the role of black lesbians:
"the possibilities for you are heady and endless.

what attracted me, or made me want to dedicate my life to the revolution. the liberty I sought, this world "new born, free" visualized as scientifically attainable. the community offered. the near promise of a type of stability and trust not possible outside of that configuration. certain things were definite: always a roof over my head, always something to say. you close your eyes and imagine a phalanx of sorts behind you. yet what happens when a voice becomes automatically spoken. before the body can elicit the breath to speak. look here's another thing I have a position on. here is where I draw the line. this all-knowingness drag worn as a member of a socialist and feminist organization gets hefty. its seeming inclusivity of "all the oppressed: all who suffer" began to sound shallow (as a black queer female, in some books "triply oppressed," this is obviously not easy to say) after I realized I could predict the answers to many questions just by running down an accepted list of choices. it became, or always was, a location of a constant naming. that is, I wasn't sensing a *movement* in terms of going forward—or in understanding what inconsistencies or incongruities these groupings (which were not determined by the organization, yet were strangely defended by it) embodied.

I come up against a resistance to ready-made answers. meaning the need to confront what this resistance means to me: (real or imagined) accusations of "selling out," conflicts between intellectual vs. activist approaches, and what is all this talk about the body. it is a conscious return to questioning and investigation outside of the context of convenient ideology—a complication of my thinking in a real way. I mean I don't want easy answers but I still want answers. who has the better explanation for how I react to getting cruised or why I get cruised. it seemed easy to say at one point. since age 13 out in the streets for different things, age 17 became "woman-identified" and age 22 "radical." in a way I guess it was a predictable trajectory. but when I tried to pry open one or another idea there was nothing but more flatness and language to simplify the struggle (=against sexism, homophobia, racism, et al) and I wanted something to sink my teeth into. above all I desired a freedom to complicate things even my own identity.

[it started the night after the night in the library, a microphone in my hand
hoping for a story to share. chased it with a margarita]

performing identity, scripting, negotiation— the postmodern seduction

turning to poetry—a stabilizing force. I became concerned with questions of repre-
sentation because it seemed there was a place where questions could be freely asked and
freely answered. not only concerning how a group presents itself, but how I as a member of that group present myself to them and others. acknowledging that not all is
binary and polar, I experienced a duality between who I was in my activist life, and
who I was when not performing activist.

a duplicitous life/

the thing about my body is not so well hidden.   a performance of survival.
on the chest of drawers, postcards, incense and our mother of the streets signify a
shrine. (breathe keep breathing) words like discourse and positioning and subjectivity are inevitable outcomes. even in the context of the collective. a scripted life.
falling down on the job. those who will put the pieces together and know my mind.
carrying, as it does, *the seeds of its own destruction.*

free time/

saturday came & went. not in any way that you could
measure.
girl a: I blocked her view. girl b: owes me a dance & no more free coffee. ripped
pantyhose seconds out of the box. no attraction

---

a sunny day, and wanting to position myself between the queer and black contin-
gents I wind up in no contingent at all. invitations declined. this feels different than
previous arrangements in which I utter expected and approved reasonings with the
uninitiated as we wind through the streets. my movements today float between the
groupings. there are no goals to meet. no check-in afterwards. I think, *this would not
have been possible if* and *how would this day have been if.*

to eat we find a grassy spot away from the people assembled and stay there for some
while. is my contribution any less. no banner in front of me, I have also lost the bull-
horn. but I am present now, I use the same critical ear for listening and I have removed
the filters. it's not easy not behind the banner, there is not always something to say and
you don't know where all your allegiances should lie. the reasons why I am not behind
the banner and the reasons why I find myself in the streets again.

struggle matters. reading more I see that the terms of struggle are not always the same.
what is being resisted is not always the same. the language opens, fucks with my head,
and I struggle to engage with it. so it's not either/or, or even both/and within a box. as a
poet I engage on paper and cement. attentive to how things are said, written, spoken. I
think of Deleuze's critique as destruction as joy, Spivak's permission to narrate, and sit
there for a while. returning to the site of struggle, I hunger for a feast of multiplicities.

going forward

1. "there's no glamour in being a radical"
2. "choosing the path of least resistance"
3. " . . . not reach [your] full human potential"

one might say there is no glamour in being a poet. and one has said that. "master of fine arts? what are you going to do with that?" etc. sitting my oppressed and marginalized and exoticized female body in the classroom or in front of a computer, and the daily struggle of finding a language for that experience which resonates and not just demarcates is an act that puts me in the path of resistance against what I could/should/ and in the process finding where [my] potential lies and what it's made of: this is an examined life.

Tisa Bryant

We are trying to (have me) conceive

"Dear _____,
I'm pregnant and about to marry the woman who knocked me up. Well, at least I think she did. I'm pretty late. Or maybe she did something to the moon. Anyway, she's Dominican, of course, and currently part of an ongoing study on ambiguously sexed adults at UCSF. I met her on the 24 Divisadero about six weeks ago and one thing led to another . . . sorry I've been so secretive but imagine my surprise to discover . . . I had to savor it all, keep it to myself until I could get used to it. I'm still working on that part, the getting used to it. Sometimes I don't know how to touch her, as if my hands, my fingers, lose their memory. Her name is Casienda Melliflores, or CasM, for short. She's a mixed media artist, does these huge collage pieces on wood and metal, and loves Hélène Cixous as much as I do, but not Kara Walker, which is a shock, from CasM's work. Right now she's doing some super-large manipulated Polaroid self-portraits that incorporate the UCSF study, the Venus Hottentot, and Dominican history/lore re: hermaphrodites, since the country has the largest incidence of ambiguously sexed individuals per capita of any place in the world. Her forced and unforced connections, the landscapes she makes of them. You'll like her. She's very intense, and up until recently, she didn't think her ejaculate was potent. I really don't want my child, if I am pregnant, to be part of that mad scientist business over at UCSF, if a child is what I'll have. Good lord! Do I sound left-handed?"

Appearing to do what I'm told, to listen to what is authoritatively said, hands folded in lap. The things I've heard. Legs crossed demurely.

Bleed onto the typewriter. Cut yourself open. Get to where you're uncomfortable with your work and plow through the feeling. Crave it. Give birth to all the metaphors, maxims and platitudes, no matter how overused, or by whom. To write is to. Mother. Or muse.

Gestate. Coddle. Midwife. Produce. Create. Force through a small dark opening something bigger and more significant than oneself.

limit. the present. dull ache.

Negotiating the biological urge. It's been said that writing and motherhood can indeed coexist within a woman's life. She can handle it. It will be hard work, to be certain. Yet on the radio a writer says of her character, "She is who I might have been if I hadn't married young and had children." What this means is. I can't decide. Who I'll be, if. The writer writing to find out who she was capable of being before she became who she is, a mystery writer on the radio, who had children before character, no matter how fanciful. Perhaps I can keep writing to find out who I'd become if I had children while remaining who I am without them?

Tell the citizen she must regenerate. Be regenerative.

Take my lover CasM, for instance, she works through collage. She doesn't call them children, nor does she imagine them barking, needing a walk. She calls her work art. She's very disciplined, dedicated. That I call her she is not arbitrary.

can you hear for instance the mirror—its rattle—not yet firmly fastened to the wall

We have been trying to get pregnant, although I'm not positive I want to be, and she thinks I already am. Neither of us are sure her "sperm" works. We are experimenting.

else she can never hear the words of her own making unmaking

My hermaphrodite, my child, ambivalently produced, her existence a useful cleverness. Side to side, front to back. Face swinging in the glass before the glass, reflecting, this infinity moves me. A corridor of selves looking back, looking at. Expecting. The reproductive timer ticks me off.

else she can never see her own innermost . . .

CasM sends me an e-mail with an enclosure: Your Personal Fortune Teller. It has a 20-use or 30-day expiration, whichever comes first. There are a myriad of divination methods to choose from. I point and click "geomancy", because it is unfamiliar. What changes must I make in life to be more productive? is the question I ask my nuclear oracle. Tiny dots rapidly appear, fill the small white space of the open window at random, waiting for me to select a pattern that "speaks" to me. I think I see a skinny dog, so I click "ok". I continue concentrating on my question until the screen changes, producing my "reading", comprised of 13 positions. In the fifth position are diamonds in the shape of a long-legged X. "There is a prediction that children will cause troubles and unhappiness. Creative projects and hobbies are spoiled."

I'm not sure what this means. Human children, or manuscripts about them, born and unborn?

What hasn't seen the light of day.

ere she can see
her right to be in the dark

Sweet and little, it is. More than a middle finger, gorgeous, enhanced, delightful as miniatures often are. CasM's wicker. In isn't easy. A new asana with props. Once on her worktable: How committed are you, she asked? If she pushed my leg higher, I thought, my yelp will surely be misinterpreted. Her work table is only for her work, I've been told repeatedly. No teacups. No phone bills. Just the tools she uses, neatly compartmentalized. Where do I fit, forbidden ass where she cuts out eyes, tests patterns for power. When we try to do it on mine an incense burner topples over. That answers my question, CasM hissed. Later I clear my table of all but paper and the most germane of texts, then sit before it all, akimbo, expectant. This disciplined pose brings pleasure, as long as it's the only one. What about the others, where I edit or send off, sex my text, change a diaper or wipe up the milky emissions?

the right to be

I have manuscripts like people have dogs. Instead of. One of these is ironically more visible, a constant memory of possibility and denial, deserving yet never to be born, which is her aborted theme. She survives on the interest of a publisher and my subsequent attentiveness, a kind of twisted belief in reincarnation.

else she can never hear the words of her own making unmaking

CasM is bemuses at the number of folders on my desktop, their innumerable contents. I explain to her that, like Miró and Alexander, I have several canvases chrysalizing their way to completion. She is unfazed by this attempt to appease her artistic emphathies. You are a hen sitting on a pyramid of eggs, she says, laughing, with a pat to my tightening back. They elevate you but ultimately get you nowhere. You must first crack to hatch.

I want to say something cruel to her about the egg that she was, the either opportunistic or simply indecisive convocation of hormones or authorial intrusion that resulted in her double genital jeopardy, then I remember how ideal I think she is, and recall the inspiration of The Dispossessed, wherein the father of five children could be the mother of several more, the psycho-genital 1-2-3-shoot! of sex initiation and assignation, that CasM can both enter and be filled, that I love her dark unavowedness, the wild frolic of her Cixousian nature, her (dis)interred gender.

her own making unmaking

Pressing against the opening. Haunted by a cheesy divination. "Creative projects and hobbies are spoiled." I peek down into the lab. The terrarium's far off light quavers as I wince. Apple tree. Tiny Buster Browns. The other tank bubbles angrily with cancelled stamps. The trouble of little shoes, the multiplicity of clannish memories, debates on the veracity of, lettered critique of established authority, moral majority. I go into a belabored panic, thin streams of air from my nose, forehead swelling like Zeus's before the impossible idea. My pen about to break into a well of ink. CasM appears, covered in mock up and Mucilage, concerned.

she must regenerate. be regenerative.

Unfinished business versus new projects. My new love has flattened this question onto fiberboard, cut it up and reassembled it into Elephant (wo)Man-ish responses. She is an ongoing project of how many ways she can conceive of herself. She is not afraid to die over and over again, and looks her age. I, on the other hand, am a nasty lab overseer of lucite cubes bloated with ink-pickled manuscripts curing into themselves. She doesn't doubt my ability to raise a child past the toddler stage without abandoning it for a while then coming back to it later, refreshed, ready to continue, but.

else she can never taste smell feel touch see her own

This idealized body. How unexpected and new, sometimes I don't know how to touch her. Then I remember I'm a woman. That something should sprout inspired by my hand, or the very thought of my hand. Forgiveness. Desire. Will.

Hey! She says. Actual childbirth would for you amount to a state of permanent avoidance therapy, a perfect excuse for not finishing your work, for not going crazy, for not dying for your work, or at least killing someone else. Little squeaking sneakers, crumpled letters. She stares at me. The dots did shape an island dog, I say. You don't even like dogs, she says. Then, Don't look so dejected. She tongues my hairline. Wanna test my syllogism?

tell the citizen

I was young, so I thought ignoring her would make her go away. She lies flat now, without volume, directly beneath the opening. From time to time I press my eye to the spot, to check in, up, on, her. From a personal leaning or disposition, yes, but my objective is knowledge. Force through a small dark passage a greater significance. Trace the oval shape, the Arabesque doorway. Force ahead through.

We are trying to have conception. The sound of running in letters. Oval wicker table, elephantine support. We squat down and face each other, tuck bottoms tightly.

Can you hear for instance the mirror — its rattle — not yet firmly fastened to the wall

Down below the black oval depth, the fallopian feeding tube or finicky synapse, depending, the other child races around on a green stretch her sneakers squeak on. She is new and spindly and loud, seldom present, often talked about, the polar opposite of seen and not heard. She likes hating the word zoo. But she too is yet unborn, tortured as undeserving, hiccuping the ovalian length, running against the clock, another kind of longing, aging and ageless.

My fortune, said CasM. My fortune paper progeny, figures to dress, scissored shapes round and forced against.

limit. the present. dull ache.

Quelling the impulse to have everything, to do everything, while doing just that, is my work. Then the worry that once finished, there'll be no more, in spite of all the limbs and organs growing in my lab, this one is a whole body, closest to me, my first, captive. Like one of those mothers who "can't let go". I sneer at myself; the thought disgusts. First the stage-mothering. Be a star!, now this. I'm screaming at the screen, If I had a dick, I wouldn't have to go through this. CasM laughs demonically from the kitchen. Sometimes you act like a dick, she says. I am not-so-secretly thrilled.

else she can never see her innermost . . .

She is the space, the place I enter, where I touch everything and have nothing, where there is no top or bottom, there is both and none of her, yes, her voice, her willingness to conceive with me, be conceived, conceived of, CasM, letters, regret, zoo, kid. Having it all at once, empty out and fill me.

else she can never be twice born twice bloodied born bloodied

I'm bleeding again, rather happily. CasM makes me ginger tea, a cookie stuffed in her mouth, a plate of cookies for me. kneeling widely into my ergonomic contraption, I finger a flat stack of letters on my table from the dead child I'm still corresponding to, thinking of the other one, living, past her life, into mine, still pissed and confused. All my voices are she. I gaze down the tube. She eyes me back. She is. My issue. I am having her.

Italicized conscience: "On the Cusp of Finitude and Its Afterbirth" from Cusp, Jocelyn Saidenberg

● ─────────────────────────── Eisa Davis

If we've gotta live underground and everybody's got cancer/will poetry be enuf?

A Letter to Ntozake Shange

dear ntozake,

i got sacks of mercury under the skin beneath my eyes
either cried too much or i'm abt to
the cool war's burning up my retina again
does poetry start where life ends?

i know i'm supposed to be cool:
i wear corrective lenses that feature
high definition tragedy.
baby in the dumpster   ethnic cleansing
assassinations   multinational mergers
i'm supposed to shake my head
write a poem
believe in ripples.
but i ain't cool.
i emit inhuman noises

i imagine terrorist acts as i flick my imaginary ash
onto the imaginary tray
i imagine going insane with a purpose
and writing it down feels sorta unnecessary
does poetry end where life begins?
berkeley girl   black girl   red diaper baby
born of the blood of the struggle
but with reaganomics and prince pickin up stream in '81
nothing came between me and my calvins
10 yrs old   unpressed hair   playin beethoven
readin madeleine l'engle   got scared in my pants when i heard
this girl testifying 'TOUSSAINT'
in the black repertory group youth ensemble
i was just sittin in a rockin chair pretendin to be 82
and talking like i knew all about langston's 'rivers'
i wasn't as good as her
and i definitely wadn't cool
so i gave up drama
and decided to bake soufflés

zake
you wda beat me up on the playground
if we'da grown up together
and you did
eighth grade   'he dropped em'
at the regional oratorical competition
i saw another fly honey rip it
this time it's 'a nite with beau willie brown'
i was bleedin on the ground
i became yours
no more soufflés
i jacked *for colored girls* right off my mama's shelf
my mama fania who was sweatin with you
and raymond sawyer and ed mock
and halifu osumare
dancin on the grass   back in the day

in you i found a groove
never knew i had one like that
did that monologue over and over
alone in my room
my bunk bed the proscenium arch
13 yrs old   screaming and cryin abt my kids
getting dropped out a window
didn't know a damn thing about rivers
but i knew abt my heart fallin   five stories

you were never abbreviated or lower case to me
you just pimped that irony
that global badass mackadocious funkology
you not only had *hígado*
you had ben-wa balls in yr pussy

betsey brown on my godmother's couch
nappy edges in mendocino at the mouth of big river
spell #7 after the earthquake in silverlake
the love space demands had to be in brooklyn
yr poems are invitations to live in yr body
love letters yr admirers dream they coulda written themselves
no one cd find a category that was yr size
blackety black but never blacker than thou
you teased me into sassiness when i had none to speak of
you made profane into sacred but never formed a church
sanctified women's lives
whether we were reading nietzsche or a box of kotex
we were magical and regular
you many-tongued st louis woman of barnard and barcelona
you left us the residue of yr lust
left us to wander life as freely as sassafrass cypress and indigo
and even the unedumacated could get yr virtuosity
cuz you always fried it up in grease
you built an aqueduct from lorraine hansberry's groundwater
and it bubbled straight to george c. wolfe
you never read what the critics said
and you scrunched up the flesh between yr eyebrows
like everybody else in my family

but zake
is poetry enuf?

i beg the question cuz you grew me up
you   and adrienne kennedy   and anna deavere smith
and all my mothers
you blew out the candles on my 26th
so when there's mercury under the skin beneath my eyes
and the world ain't so cool
do you write a poem
or a will?

like leroi jones said   if bessie smith had killed some white people
she wouldn't have needed that music
so do we all write like amiri baraka does
or do we all get our nat turner on?

i beg the question cuz i wanna get my life right
do some real work
and i really don't want to kill any white folk
i mean   can we talk abt this
maybe it's just my red diaper that's itchin
but i still got that will to uplift the race
sans bootstraps or talented tenths or paper bag tests
this time we uplift the human race
and i know the rainbow might be
but is poetry enuf?

it's a naïve question but i'm old enuf to ask them once in a while
if we do finally unload the canon
clean it out
stock up on some more colorful balls
ain't we only getting the ones that are available at a store near you?
doesn't the marked end up setting the new standards anyway?
is poetry enuf if it ain't sellin?
if ain't nobody readin it?

can poetry keep a man   who can't read
from droppin his kids out a window?

and how can i call a ceasefire to this cool war
in stanzas of eights
when we've declared poetry a no fly zone?
we have learned to protect it and its potential politics
like a mother
shoot down anyone who might overdetermine a poem's meaning
(while we poets divebomb everyone else's politics with impunity
like we're the United States or something)

if poetry is just poetry
we save it from the conservatives
but doesn't that mean it's of no use to the progressives?

is poetry enuf?
cuz that's all i'm doin.
making up stories   on stage   on the page
keepin the beat
and that's all my friends are doin
and that's what a lot of folks my age are doin

but if we've gone and burnt up everything in the sky
if there's nothing else to eat but landfill stroganoff
if we've gotta live underground and everybody's got cancer
will poetry be enuf?

my aunt angela says i can do my thang
and keep swinging left hooks to oppression
if i stay up stay into it stay involved
just one form of praxis will do.
it's just my guilt that thinks i need twenty-two
what's enuf?

shouldn't i (or somebody) be our secular bodhisattva
become a real power player but skip the talk show
can't we stabilize, rekindle collectives
and cooperatives and collaborations
therapeutic communities that double
as creative juggernauts
a publishing house   a theatre where the plays
cost less than the movies
get the neighborhood coven back together
take dance breaks in the cubicles
sign until the flourescent lights burst into snow
i ask you because you changed me zake
you changed thousands of women
and i know poetry can't be enuf if you drunk

i ain't trying ta walk off wid alla yr stuff
and i got nuttin but love for ya
so that't why i gotta know
i'm sittin on my bed encircled by every book
you've ever published
they're open like fans
marking pages with the flint of genius
all i want is for this circle to grow
so tell me:

is this where poetry and life are twins?
i felt so crumpled up when i started writing you
poetry seemed so useless and dingy
next to all the bright red bad news
but now that the poem is over i feel wide open
like an infant of the spring
just tell me how
to feed this light
to my responsibilities
and poetry just might be enuf
    love
    eisa

Cege Githiora

Binga

Diary entry

I.

ON THE STOREFRONT OF HO'S GENERAL SHOP SAT A GROUP OF BIG, BLACK men. They were sprawled in several drunken poses, loudly talking in foul language, passing a bottle of rum between them. It was nine in the morning at the small market—really only a stall selling vegetables, boiled dumplings and fried bananas. Opposite, across the dusty road where the buses stop, is a bigger shop. One of the men staggers to the fortified little window grill, behind which sat a man I assumed to be Mr. Ho. His face was impassive and he did not exchange words with customers—merely pierced them with small, black obsidian eyes.

"Gimme a fuckin' Winston," the black man says. Mr. Ho waits for him to pass the Belizean dollar bill through a tiny opening in the wire mesh that completely seals him in like a small fort in a far off trading post in hostile territory. He sticks two cigarette sticks back at the man who curses again and returns to his friends muttering to himself in an undefined anger. Mr. Ho's daughter is in the back of the shop. She is fat and walks in a waddle, wearing an insolent, sleepy look on her face, eyeing customers from behind the iron grill inside the small, hot space. She spits a lot, three times in the time I spent to buy a Coke. The big, black men sit and curse as they down the bottle of rum. "Fuck you! Me tell the bwaay!" one them narrates to the others with a voice full of drunken bravery and Caribbean no nonsense.

Another lone man was preaching something to no one in particular at the empty market. I had just gotten off the bus from Belmopan, the quiet official capital city of Belize where I witnessed a few goats grazing in front of the parliament building. I was feeling very hot and cramped after the long, four-hour ride with many stops along the way. I put down my backpack and sat down to rest on one of the benches under the stall. The woman who was frying bananas and dumplings eyed me hopefully, but I was not ready to eat yet. The first thing I wanted was to find a place to stay before nightfall.

II.

Dangriga is a small town on the shore of the Caribbean Sea, in the southern end of Belize, a small country and former British colony that gained its independence only in 1981; Belizean dollars still bear the face of Queen Elizabeth. The vast majority of people of this town are black, descendants of Africans brought to this corner of the slave empires built by Spaniards, Dutch, French and English. Belizians speak Creole English, a dialect of English that is quite similar in sound and structure to the sister dialects of nearby Jamaica, Trinidad and other islands. Many Afrobelizians also speak another language called Garifuna, also spoken by the Afro-Hondurans and Guatemalans in this Central American region. The Garifuna language has all the sounds that would easily tempt one to take it for an African language that has been kept alive by transplanted Africans.

Salvador Suazao, a Garifuna historian from Honduras, writes that before and during the early settlement of Europeans in the Caribbean islands, an Arawak-speaking peoples known as the Igneri occupied the Island of Yurúmain, which was later renamed San Vicente (Saint Vincent) by the Spanish. The Igneri were later invaded by the "fierce" Kallíganu (or Caribs) from the Caribbean Guyana who proceeded to take over most of the islands in the region, also due to their sea-faring superiority. Apparently, the Caribs had the custom of killing only enemy males—male children included—and taking the women as their own. Spared to perpetuate life, the women did not abandon their first language, Igneri, which they used alongside that of their conquerors. In the new society, language became heavily marked by gender: males were taught the language of their fierce father-warriors, Caribana, while the girls and women spoke Arawak. The language that eventually prevailed even before Eurpopean dominance was, literally, the mother tongue Arawakan, but it was named *Caribana* or *Garifuna* in favor of the dominant Caribs.

From the early 16th through the 19th century, enslaved Africans encountered a thriving native American language—Garifuna—which they adopted, and it became the principal language of the new immigrant Africans. Naturally, the Garifuna language acquired many words of Spanish, English and French—depending on the colonial power ruling which region. The chief African contribution to this language was phonological: sounds, stress and tones which today make it sound very much like an African language. While there are Belizians who do not speak Garifuna today, the people of Dangriga speak it as their first language, and Belizian Creole English as their second. In neighboring Honduras or Guatemala where the majority of Garifuna people live, they speak Spanish as their second language.

III.

There is a main street that divides Dangriga in two parts. On one side is the market at the bus stop, and Mr. Ho's shop. There's also the Bank of Nova Scotia, Belize Bank, the Social Security office and a Tax and Income office, all next to one another in a row that covers one small block. On the other side of Main Street are residential houses, and beyond, the calm, blue waters of the Caribbean Sea. Houses and business buildings in Gandriga are built of wood and are props, ready for when the sea might rise and flood. Looking at them, I would not help thinking just how easy it'd be to set the Bank or the Social Security office on fire.

I was consulting my map of Dangriga as the black man continued his monologue, shirtless, wearing only a pair of brown tattered shorts. A powerfully built body rippled with muscles and his hair was a mess of long, unkempt dreadlocks. He had the reddest pair of eyes and he wore a stern look of serious thought. He stood at a respectable distance, watching me carefully, obviously seeking my attention. "Here comes another con man," I thought, weary of numerous street people that had accosted me in Belize city, trying to get a dollar, a quarter, or a cigarette or two from me with faked friendliness or cheap cock and bull stories. But the man did not seem to be in a hurry to accost me with his tale of misery. He did not even impose his presence on me, seeming to respect me, doggedly seeking my eye for attention as if he needed my permission to approach. He continued to preach to the deserted market, his Belizian Creole so heavily accented I thought he was speaking Garifuna. As my ear adjusted to this newer dialect of Caribbean English, I began to understand his sermon.

"Is why they killed Malcolm X!" he swore in a pained voice, "because he was against the Klan . . . the Klan, they's here, RIGHT HERE, man!" He shook his head and stabbed the air in front of him with heavy emphasis, staring fixedly at me, as if the message was mine. My curiosity was aroused and I decided to encourage him a bit by granting him a brief audience with my eyes. It worked very well. He moved closer to stand right in front of me. Listening to his black consciousness message, I felt less threatened by his towering, menacing image. He suddenly switched his topic without losing the basic theme.

"I tell you this, my brother, 'cos you is an intelligent man . . . I can see that." Now he was addressing me directly. "It's all the Klan here, the fuckin' Klan is all over here . . . but I, Binga, I's STRONG—." He flexed powerful arm muscles in demonstration. "I'm a LION!" he roared, "I tell you this . . ." Here he went into a strong monologue couched in so much emotion that he seemed to be crying. I could no longer follow, catching only a few phrases here and there, but I could not tell if it was a tale, a prophecy or a personal narrative. " . . . in my arms, she dead . . her sister!!" Here he pointed at the woman in the market stall. I became worried when he said this because I did not want to involve myself in a local argument or take sides in a story of murder. I got ready to move and hoisted my back-pack. "Later dread, respect," I said to the man, preparing to move off, but he grabbed my arm and grinned at me in a friendly manner, saying, "You is a brown man, RED man like Malcolm! I saw it right away, you is a man of education!" I was taken aback by the charge, and laughed nervously as I walked off.

The next morning I saw Binga as I went for a walk around town. He was standing under a coconut tree close to the river which pours into the sea. He recognized me as I did, and he quickly fell into a story about himself and his life. He did not seem to tell me all this to get something out of me, genuinely disinterested in getting dollar from me, though he accepted the cigarettes I offered him. He'd been into drugs but was now cured; he repeated over and over again how the "Klan" rules the town.

"Where do you live?" I ventured to ask him. "Right here under this tree, man," he replied, "any damn place although that house right there is ours, and the other belongs to my sister, but she won't give me a fuckin' piece of bread! I cook right here too," Binga said, pointing at a tin that stood over a cold fire under the coconut tree. "Bananas. You like bananas? I invite you man, today, anytime," he said earnestly, looking me straight in the eye. I looked back into his coal red eyes and saw all the sincerity I could fathom. However, it was an open invitation. He did not insist on setting a day when I could come eat bananas, and I was glad he was not insistent. "What is your job?" I asked Binga, who replied, "I live. I fish. I'se a fisherman, man." With a quick movement that startled me, he pulled out a long, gleaming knife from the waistband in his back and made to show, "I clean the fuckin' fish like this! I see it, or I give it away. I have no cares man! I used to, but I don't anymore, not since she died in me arms . . . that fuckin' woman's own sister . . . out! Chop!" He made a chopping motion with his knife, giving it a vicious twist which convinced me that he was the author of the dreadful deed.

"Did you . . . how did you . . . ?" I could not bring myself to finish that question, but Binga quickly understood my confusion. "No man, no!" he explained patiently, without rancor or surprise. "She got killed by she man! Cut up the bitch with a fuckin' knife, her neck, her arms . . . she fell into my arms and me HOLD her like this, like she my baby . . ." Binga started to cry. His neck bulged and veins in his temple and face bulged as he said this, cradling his arms as if holding a baby. "And what happened to the killer?" I asked him. "He ina jail, man, but you see how people is, man, the woman's family won't talk to me, my own people they won't talk to me . . . they say I crazy!"

At the bridge which runs under the river that cuts Dangriga in two I met Binga again later that day. He was hanging out with a few other men. He was shirtless as usual. As soon as he saw me coming along he broke off from the group to approach me. I was glad to see him yet again, for I had not made any other friend in Dangriga. Perhaps, I thought, it was because I was seen talking with Binga too much. We shook hands warmly. "Want a beer?" I said, eager to talk some more with him before I left town the next day. We went into a bar next door and I ordered two beers. For the first time, Binga asked me for a dollar, "To fill up the bottle for my friends, man, they poor like hell!" He said this earnestly, and when I gave him a dollar he passed it on to the bar man who filled up a bottle of Guinness Stout with white rum. Binga took it outside to his friends, and shortly returned to sit with me. For about an hour we talked about Blackness, for that was Binga's favorite topic, and Malcolm X, Marcus Garvey, the Klan, America, Nation of Islam. Binga repeated over and over, "Elijah killed Malcolm, the Klan is all over the place . . ." His discourse, while repetitive, was intelligent. "Have you been to the States?" I asked him. "Noo . . ." Binga replied vaguely as if he did not wish to talk about that. His conversation suggested intelligence. A knowledge far beyond Dangriga and Belize—and personal tragedy. As I waited for the bus out of Dangriga the next day, the woman at the market told me that Binga was mad. I bought Binga another beer, and another bottle of rum for himself this time. He took my hand and looked at me with his deep red eyes, pleading with a sincerity that moved me: "My brother," he said, "when you come back again, please take me to Africa. Please! It's the only one place I wish to see before I die." With a big lump in my throat, I mumbled a vague assent. Binga and I took a picture together with my camera, but it never came out.

The Six-Hour Difference: A Dutch Perspective on the New World

Scotty Gravenberch

IN EARLY 1998 MY GIRLFRIEND LULU ENTERED AN EXCHANGE PROGRAM AT Howard University in Washington, D.C. In mid-March I took a two-week study break to visit her. As one would expect from a devoted lover, I had planned to ignore the sights and the people to whatever degree they might interfere with our effort to compensate for that period of separation. But when I got off the plane to embrace the woman who I had gazed at only via photos in the preceding four months, I also entered a world which on its own terms had presented itself to me mainly through images. Beautiful America: Virtual reality materialised; Melrose Place; Jerry Springer; the Chicago Bulls; KRS1; Jay Leno; Jesse Jackson; Hillary Clinton; NIKE; *Friends;* Desert Storm; *The Cosby Show.* And despite the great joy I felt when I saw Lulu at the airport—instantly noticing the minor changes her looks had undergone—the couch potato in me looked right past her at the sloppily dressed, big gun-carrying black airport security officer seated halfway down the arrival hallway, reading a brightly coloured newspaper while sipping coffee out of a cup three times the size of what we Dutch consider decent.

We had a beautiful time, Lulu and I, but it was in spite of the two-week choke hold American sights and sounds had on my imagination.

13 March

Traveling through Washington there are several things which I can't help noticing. One is the average look of the surroundings. Before coming to the United States, I had the dynamic architecture of New York City in mind as the archetypal American urban design. But the Washington scenarios I've seen so far remind me more of a Dutch town than of New York. But I still have to check out the governmental heart of D.C. I expect it to be an exception.

It's all quite cozy and modestly proportioned. Georgetown, a vibrant student district, even looks a lot like the Pijp in Amsterdam. The Pijp is a district of Amsterdam where a lot of Turkish and Spanish labourers came to live in the '70s. The numerous Spanish bars and Turkish coffeehouses still testify to this. But in the last 10 years the neighbourhood has been discovered by the young and rich. Hip bars and even hipper little restaurants now dominate the streets. Common folks can hardly get a house in the Pijp because the contemporary vibe of the place pushed the rent up to illegal highs. I understand that Georgetown also underwent a transformation. It used to be a black neighbourhood, explaining the many Baptist churches. What you see in modern Georgetown is a multicultural mix of swell dress students, quantitatively dominated by cool young white. But, nevertheless, it does seem to be one of the few places in Washington where different shades of humans present a non-hierarchical view on public life.

15 March

Went looking for bookshops and music dealers today. Was amazed to find that you can be catered to the smallest detail of your racial preference. There are shops devoted entirely to black music, to white music, black books, white books. The "mixed" shops have everything neatly categorised in literature, history, poetry, politics and black literature, black history, black poetry and black politics.

It would be nice to call this postmodern, in the sense that this country hasn't got one definite identity, which is probably true, and is playing different styles of personhood and consciences against each other. But this wouldn't be very respectful towards the writers whose work has been categorised under black politics. I would be lying if I said that Dutch culture shops don't make these distinctions—they do. Even if non-whites get defined in a wider range of subcategories like Turkish, Surinamese, Caribbean, refugees. But the political, cultural, social and economic polarisations here are far more impressive. I suspect this difference to spring forth from the inescapable fact of America's racial relations, from past to present. The slaves of the Netherlands didn't live in the Netherlands: they were put to work in far and exotic places like Suriname, Indonesia, and Curacao.

As such, the Netherlands, and I specifically mean that piece of land between the North Sea and Germany, has never been the location of legalised and structural racist violence. The "sins" of the past were committed far away. This makes them less intense and more easy to deal with; or not to deal with. The English were headed for similar moral procedure, until their colonists decided they didn't need a Queen. And even though the English lost a nice piece of land because of this, they should be grateful for it. Because in current Afro-American consciousness it is no longer the British who killed, maimed, raped and did you know what to black people in America; it was the "whites" who did it. White Americans, that is. The Brits just shipped the blacks (too bad for England they were never permanently defeated in Jamaica). In Surinamese and Antillean consciousness it is still the Dutch carrying a historical guilt. But, nevertheless, the Surinamese or Antilleans who live in Holland don't have the same relation to their white neighbours as black Americans do to theirs.

Firstly, the percentage of black people in the Netherlands, as in *Afro-whatever* black people, is only 5 percent, as opposed to the 12 percent in the USA. The nominal amount of black people is also much smaller: the total Dutch population counting 16 million people, which makes the possibilities of economic and political self-reliance for black people much smaller. Last but not least, the blacks in the Netherlands are perceived as immigrants, or as children of immigrants. This as opposed to the blacks in the USA: they are seen as descending from African slaves, but don't have any problems in seeing themselves as entitled to the predicate "American" (this in spite of the difference one creates when mentioning an American and an Afro-American person in the same sentence).

This is an important distinction when you compare the two nations. In the Netherlands black people are firstly defined in cultural terms: they are part of the Surinamese or Antillean culture, and in the secondary description they're black. In America the terms of black identity concentrate on race; black Americans are firstly black, only in the second instance are they part of Afro-American culture. A strange situation when you consider the massive impact Afro-American culture has had on Western culture: defining fashion, attitude, music, and in general providing a sense of urban being; combining the individuality, sexiness, aggressiveness and pace which make Western culture so interesting to the rest of the world.

16 March

Yesterday we explored the area around Howard, where we are staying. This part of town is called Northwest. If I took this walk in a random town in the Netherlands, I'd know I was walking around in a poor district. But the scenic codes aren't the same around the world. For example, in Leipzig, East Germany, where I worked as a salesman four years after the Iron Curtain was pulled up, I visited neighbourhoods which looked much worse, but were resident to many successful trading houses, law firms, architect buros, etc. You just couldn't tell from the outside. Even in current Belgium you can find yourself in streets which make a strong Third World impression, yet prove to be just another middle-class area when you are invited into the houses. The Dutch just spend a lot of money on public space appearances, which makes poor-looking neighbourhoods just that, poor neighbourhoods.

What the Dutch don't have, rich or poor, but wherein the people of Northwest D.C. excel, is manners. People here are so incredibly polite. Not only in shops, where the stereotypical American cheerfulness could be dismissed as "good for business," but also on the street. When people want to pass between you and a wall they attentively apologize for cramping your space. When they bump into you they take the time to let you know that it wasn't on purpose, and "Have a nice day." If somebody took this kind of effort to keep peace with me in the Netherlands I'd tell my parents, hoping to reactivate their rightfully lost trust in Dutch public life. The strange thing is that Washington is known as the most violent city in the States, and Northwest D.C. as one of its more dangerous neighbourhoods. You wouldn't expect such great emphasis on courtesy in the most notorious part of the country. On the other hand, as with Dutch soccer hooliganism, it is probably a minority of the stigmatised group which actually lives up to the stereotype. But the statistics do give some ground for caution, especially for a tourist unaware of codes to adhere to or streets to avoid. It is probably because of these statistics, which are real-life facts for the people living here, that they are so eager to signal their good intentions in the public arena. You never know if the person you bump into has an ego more sensitive than his body. It is a healthy practise of survival to satisfy *any* loss of face which a person might have suffered, avoid aggravation and keep the situation peaceful.

19 March

I walked out of the subway stop at Federal Triangle, and entered the centre of all worldly power. Rome 1998. Architecture pulled up in beige-coloured blocks of stone measuring 3 by 4 meters, held up and together by huge pillars hovering over imperial entrances to governmental departments and institutions. This whole area, which furthermore is home to the White House, national and international banks, the Congress, and the Smithsonian, is clearly designed to radiate power and confidence; and it does so in abundance. When you walk around here you cannot help but feel at ease: everything is so clean, tranquil and organised. This all in shrill contrast to the Northwest section, from where we departed. As a metaphor for this difference Lulu noticed the discrepancy in the concentration of garbage cans between NW and here. The White House area caters to the pedestrian with one garbage can per 20 meters (which is a lot even by Dutch standards) while in NW you are lucky if you find one per house block (which explains all the rubbish floating around).

22 March

What strikes me most here is the fact that social situations (rendezvous, meetings, greetings, conversations) look so very staged. Scripted. Every encounter seems to be pre-written for network broadcasting. No matter. What actually strikes me is this: they don't seem any less real. In Holland people don't greet each other with big "Wassups," laughter and perfectly feigned interest. In Holland we greet each other with a nod, or a silent good morning. We are rarely polite, because we don't believe the other will trust our intentions when we act polite. I think in Holland the individual civilian is looked upon as egoistic and striving, but that might be the same in the U.S. The Dutch, however, think that it is hypocritical and sneaky to disguise this inescapable nature of mankind in kind manners and attentive communication. The foremost complaint Dutch people ventilate when they come back from America is, "Everywhere I come people ask me, 'How are you doing?' as if they care!"

Now that I'm here myself I've got a new perspective on this phenomenon: It is a demonstration of civilisation if a shopkeeper politely informs how you are doing; he is making a person feel good. On a philosophical level it is even more polite. For asking "How are you?" is an acknowledgement of one's existence. Translated in existential terms the question would be, "I recognise your being in this world, how are you coping with it?" So even if the latter part of the question isn't genuine, if the shopkeeper really doesn't care how you're doing, the first part certainly is; you have been recognised as a human being. This is where civilisation starts, the recognition of the other as a human being; there is no greater longing than to be recognised.

23 March

The moment I got off the plane in Washington and actually engaged with the locals I noticed that there is a peculiar difference between the way Americans and Dutch people speak. Today I found out what it is. Had lunch with Troy this afternoon and he ordered a Coke. This is quite normal here in America. Even if you ask for a small size drink of this brand, you ask for a *small* Coke. In Holland we ask for a Coke-tje. The "tje" at the end of Coke is a diminutive suffix; in everyday conversation it is placed behind a lot of nouns. Only when we want a big Coke, which we seldom want and can only be ordered in American franchises like McDonald's, do we speak of a Coke. These different ways of ordering a soda are exemplary for a more widespread contrast in Americans and the Dutch in their relation to language. A difference between a tendency towards "enlargement," versus a tendency towards "decreasement."

Referring to their life partner, an American may speak of "my love"; in Holland this person is called *"mijn lief-je."* So he or she is no longer your love, but your little love. These different ways of describing the world around you, enlargement versus decreasement, stand in a network of similar categorical oppositions. The USA is BIG, the Netherlands is small. Americans and everything they do on the world stage are important; the Netherlands and all the things we do seldom make an impression. The cars we drive in Holland are smaller than the cars the people in America drive. Life, dreams, power and hope are all bigger in the United States, at least in the way they are appraised. I suppose one can give perfectly sound sociological/historical explanations for this difference (a difference which, from a wider perspective, can be drawn between the U.S. and the whole of Europe).

This is a negation, the Sartre way of being in the world. In America, individuals don't negate, they identify. They pronounce the material world around them in words which express the grandeur of the things which they have let enter their private kingdom. An American doesn't want a Coke-tje because a Coke-tje is small, smaller, a loser. Big, good and powerful people don't hang around with losers, they team up with winners. An American orders a Coke, because Coke means Bigger and Better. They want to have and be with people and things who have qualities similar to the ones they attribute to themselves, not with their opposites.

25 March

The slogan of Howard University is "Leadership for America and the Global Community." You won't find a banner like this being used at any of the Dutch educational institutions. Not even in university politics, which have been dramatically de-democratised over the past two years, does the leadership discourse play a significant role. In Holland it's all about "being yourself." We are encouraged to believe in the hard-fought abstract egalitarian principles which made our small country great. But like everybody else we want power for the power. So when nobody is watching, we grab all the power we can get our hands on. Yes, the Dutch want to be leaders, but it is such a giant taboo to propagate this desire.

There is a student president election running at Howard. I was approached by one of the candidates, one sharp-looking, fast-talking, strong handshaking, power-hungry guy from Kenya. He assumed me to be one of the Howard students and he gave me a lolly and a rundown of all the reasons why I should vote for him. I was truly amazed, for I have never experienced such an encounter in my life. If I would be walking on my university in Utrecht, and somebody would come up to me like he did, with that attitude and that rap, I'd pity him. But here in America this is normal; well, not normal, but better than normal. You're profiling yourself, taking up leadership responsibility, breaking yourself in for the future where this sort of behaviour, when successfully executed, can determine the life and death of your personal career. If you're a leader in Holland the last thing you do is go onto the street and tell everybody how great you are. You get other people to tell it for you. And when someone asks you if you're really this terrific leader, then you just nudge your shoulders in a semi-embarrassed fashion and modestly tell the tale of your past victories and conquests. I think this difference in attitude toward self-proliferation can again be brought back to the difference in the psychic. Americans identify, the Dutch differentiate; in this case with the stories they tell about themselves, and maybe on a deeper level with language as a whole. Americans identify themselves with their own words: they walk the walk and talk the talk (this proverb is not without reason as stereotypically American as McDonald's). In Holland there is an alienation from the language. We don't think language is part of the same reality as we ourselves are. You can also spot this difference in all the self-help programs and books which come from the American West Coast: they all revolve around the premise that your personal reality is made up of language, and that by changing the way you talk about yourself and your world you can change your life. A Dutch elder, when asked what to do if you want to change your life, will advise you to stop talking about it and do it.

The leader of all the Dutch, Premier Kok, is a typical Dutch leader, like President Clinton is a typical American leader. Kok doesn't talk about himself, doesn't tell the people what he's done for them over the last 6 years, doesn't radiate power and confidence, is as far from bragging about his qualities as he is from ever having an affair with a governmental intern. Clinton, on the other hand, talks about Clinton all the time. Tells the Americans he did this and that for them, didn't do this or that to them; in the same tone he tells the rest of the world what he and the country he stands for mean to the prosperity of the rest of the world. Clinton is his word, or is at least striving to let everybody believe he is; Kok wants to be his actions, the words which pertain to him may only be spoken by others.

27 March

Yesterday I kissed Lulu good-bye, took a bus out of Washington, and headed for the mother of all things contemporary, New York City. Arrived at Penn Station at 20:00 sharp. For the two days I'm staying in New York, I can room with a friend. Had a rendezvous with her at 21:00 in Brooklyn, which gave me time to check out Times Square. And it delivered. I saw Robert De Niro in his car, waiting for a red light, yelling at Woody Allen, who was selling food out of an umbrella-ed cart. "Give me a hot dog." Woody Allen waved his arms in denial, and then pointed at the traffic lights. "Before I'm done you're outta here." I went with Woody. Robert was approximately the fifth car in a line which was 3 across and 20 long. He could never get the people behind him to wait till he had his order; but I loved Robert for trying. Yes, this is the America I know; the America where superstars, cops and robbers, activists, evil politicians, artists and writers do their noisy things.

Arrived at my friend Cordelia's in time. She immediately took me for a walk to the Brooklyn Bridge and a beautiful night viewing of Manhattan's skyline. When we returned to her place she gave me a little cassette / radio and preset the dial to Hot-97. I fought my exhaustion for at least another hour before I fell asleep with "Funkmaster Flex" spinning the latest tunes.

28 March

Cordelia took me to Manhattan before she left for work. We entered the subway in Borough Hall, Brooklyn, which resembles the Brooklyn from the movies, but also looks a bit like Amsterdam. Exit on Fifth Avenue, which is nothing like Amsterdam and only vaguely resembles the skyscrapers in the movies. They're so much bigger in real life. It's like getting out of a subway which accidentally drove you to a land of giants. I would be very surprised if the meetings between the architect and the owner of one of these buildings didn't centre around the materialisation of dominance. Because in first contact that's exactly what they do—they dominate you. They're saying, "You're small, very *very* small. We're Big, we can do anything we want." But this effect disappears within an hour. Not because you get used to the size of things—this *must* take at least two weeks—but because of the desperate messages they deliver at their base. I'm talking about the shops which are situated at the ground floor of the skyscrapers. They all have big windows which display fur coats for $3000; laptops stashed up like they're giving them away; BMWs; exuberantly overpriced stiletto heels; and just about anything else which you might intuitively associate with decadent rip-off consumerism in the late '90s.

The obviousness of the attempt to impress turned me numb for the possible beauty of all this wealth. And somehow the stores gave meaning to the rest of the building: from fierce and proud giants they turned into oversized wannabes: cement and glass accumulations of never fulfilled desires towering over the mortals hoping they will perceive them as the gods they will never be. Too bad, I'd have gladly fallen for a slightly more modest myth.

29 March

Back in the Netherlands. A small, arrogant and prosperous centre of the universe. Everything is so "normal" here—proportionate, old, useful. No glitter, no speed. In New York the sun was shining fiercely. Here the atmosphere is blanketed by a wet mist, just like I left it. Actually, everything is like I left it. This makes me realise that while flying back home over the Atlantic I had the solipsistic expectation that some hint of Americanism might step out of the plane with me, infect my Dutch surroundings. Can't help feeling slightly disappointed. Maybe the USA had more luck.

Sarah Jones

Just Beneath the *Surface*—An Email

Subj: Re: Reply, PART I
Date: Sunday, December 19, 1999, 3:16:33PM
From: JONESARAH
To: _ _ _ _ _ _

WHERE TO BEGIN? I CAN'T REMEMBER A TIME WHEN I'VE HAD TO THINK—I mean put down whatever I am munching on, stop whichever four tasks I'm only halfway executing, and focus my mind on processing something of substance— in the last couple of years. That is not to say that odd thoughts have not made their way across this strange plane I call a mind recently, but that I just don't *do* much *thinking*.

See, once upon a time, I was an English and Philosophy major, and thinking *a lot* was not only always on the agenda, it was all that was keeping my butt in a higher-learning institution and out of a mental one (I'll go into my personal drama-history another time). But somewhere along my route, thinking lost its urgency, its relevance; it wore out its welcome and finally just broke the fuck out. I mean, I discovered in college that a fairly swift black woman can get dope grades and accolades aplenty without having to do a whole lot of thinking. In fact, I slowly realized how much all my thought processes seemed only to help complicate things, to bring anything—especially anything painful or hard to face—bubbling to the surface of whatever I understood to be "my understanding" like so much hydrochloric acid. Scars everywhere. Thinking was fucking up my mental complexion.

Now, I say all this to say that, while I now have a few solid years of living without thinking under my belt, I have also spent those years (halfheartedly) searching without for answers to questions I formulated back when I was thinking and never dreamt I might one day be a person whose long list of aspirations makes no mention of really thinking. I am a (sometime) poet. A kinda playwright, an untrained actor(tress?), a mini-marshmallow mogul in the new tradition of young heads out here trying to clock cheddar by bartering with some art they only recently discovered somebody left in the pocket of their hand-me-down post-post-modern boho / b-boy / girl / overalls. I am a black woman, a femi-womanist sitting on a fence overlooking the Bloomingdales-black revolutionary backyard of a movement for which I haven't really lifted a finger, but to which I have the deed. I am a sister and a clown and an angst-ridden twenty-some-thing. BUT I am not a thinker.

So, _____, how dare you give me pause? I have canned answers—enough to sustain me through any Y2K eventuality—for everyone, any question. I am usually safe, because, as you say, attention spans are short, and most people don't *listen* to what they hear. Those who do—if they are white (and there are exceptions to this)—are gener-ally afraid to wake the wrathful gods of Politicallycorrectia and so don't challenge me. Those who are black, Latino, dare I say . . . Other, are often dragging behind them some kind of baggage akin to my own, baggage that I stamp, as they complete their journey with me, with a kind of validation tag. "You just heard somebody whom you think is cool & talented & ought to know her shit jump up and down reaffirming—albeit in an entertaining way (one would hope)—everything you already believe for whatever reasons." No danger of growth there. Not for them, not for me. There isn't really much of an exchange of ideas—thoughts, if you will—that enables anybody to leave, if they must leave with baggage (and you know they will), with at least some dif-ferent shit than what they came in with. I'm there with you, _____. But I'm really only *visiting* in a key way, 'cuz where I'm livin' (at least for the now), the views ain't as good, but the rent is cheaper.

As you so astutely point out, this industry is one strange beast. Training it to suit one's needs is a ridiculous task that practically requires degrees in finagling, schmooz-ing, compromising, ass-kissing, artistic contortion with a smile, but NOT THINK-ING. You know that stupid expression "no brainer"? Must have started as an industry term. And this industry is where I live at the moment. Am I happy here? Not hardly. But I'm strangely comfortable. Lazy. I know. Can I, should I, *must* I do better for myself and everybody I'm busting these nonexistent nuts to reach? Hell yes. Am I on my way? Lord, I hope so. But it's gonna take a whole mess of thinking, and like I said, I'm kinda out of practice.

Which brings me (at last!) back to the show. Yeah, it's autobiographical. Fairly self-ishly so, too. Slanted? Hell yeah. Well-intentioned? Mmm, yeah, but in a somewhat narrow, colorized sort of way.

I am the product of an arguably unhealthy marriage of disparate ideologies; deeply entrenched, racialized identity conflicts; gender politics circa 1950s; and the simulta-neous beliefs that the world was ours for the taking and that we would never actually have anything. Literally, my parents were such a young, confused mess as a unit (for-get separately) that I wonder how they kept it together for as long as they did. My interpretations of the world, of justice, of who I was vs. who the world expected me to be, of what blackness, whiteness, otherness, and being a girl would mean all my life, were shaped mainly by watching my parents. So, women were white. Men were black. (Yeah, I know, some of us are brave, but this was long before Barbara Smith's words found me.) Gay people were bad (dad passed this wisdom down, & mom never disputed it). Black men had been victimized and vilified at every turn in every way since the dawn of time but were actually the fathers of all civilizations which were eventually usurped by white devils (from the world according to daddy). Black women just needed to stay out of the sun and straighten their hair if it was the bad stuff and hope somebody would eventually deign to marry them (but it better not be a white boy— don't you have any pride?) (You guessed it—daddy again, *never* refuted by mom).

I now know that my mother didn't agree with all the things we were taught, but, as a woman and a wife, felt it was most important to only raise her voice in unison with daddy's. I now know how much my father yearned to be just like the little white boys in all his classes, wished that his children had been boys (we were three girls) and could be white and enjoy the world the way he believes white people do. I remember the bittersweetness of only dating white boys in high school to piss off my dad and discovering that I both identified with them and often hated them, that I could turn on and be turned on by the same people whose blatant racial prejudices made my stomach turn, made me want to haul off and punch them and myself in the stomach to distract me from the shame of knowing that they were wrong about "us" and believing in some corner of myself that they were right.

Now, I'll pause here because, from what I can recall, in REPLY PART 1 you make references to aspects of the piece that struck you in various ways citing certain contexts—whole worlds like the Jewish Holocaust, the world of hip-hop and modern urban/black youth culture, the worlds of gender / sexual orientation politics, the world of music (Yeah, I feel your pain as regards the "soundtrack." Believe me, it pains me every time I hear it, but I had to choose my battles with the so-called production of this show, and a lot of things suffered badly. I'd love to rap to you about this in detail at some point, though.)—that would better help the piece find its place as a world in its own right, rotating on an axis of balance and a deeper commitment to all the layers of sometimes painful truth, and the complex of beds, mouths, banks and tributaries that have kept and keep this River Hate thing flowing through out collective consciousness and daily lives.

In some ways, my trouble with *Surface Transit* is literally and figuratively written in all the background I gave above. It's all me out there on that stage, duke! Working out my own personal shit, bold as you please, and calling it art. Or soup, as Lily Tomlin might say. At no point did I sit down and think, really think, about this piece. I did a whole lotta feelin', though. Soul searchin'. Crying, grappling, wondering, lamenting. But the thinking, the making use of some of the tools I've got to ensure that I'm not just preaching to the converted, and preaching a somewhat haphazard, at times skewed version of a professed anti-hate gospel at that, has gone undone and pretty much unchecked.

So, the question is what do I plan to do about this problem that will require a good deal of work underneath the surface? Now that the politics and drama are behind me (Damn, ____, you shoulda been there last night. Gloria Steinem & Marcia Gillespie (GOOD LOOKIN'—thanks for spreading the word to her . . . that was you, right?),

Russell "laughing-out-loud-as-I-spat-all-over-him-&-Andre Harrell-in-the-front-row" Simmons w / big bro' Danny, the other Danny in the solo show world, & even Missy Elliott turned out thanks to all the hard work of the machine & its extended family) I plan to do some of the thinking I've been missing. I'm really most interested in tightening the actual writing (too much of which is always-uncontrollable improv), gutting the soundtrack, and concentrating on the existing characters. Lorraine's son exists, but probably won't see much light until the next show, about which I'll think before I write. But I hope this won't be the end of our chats re: *Surface Transit,* and in general. I know I'm a long-winded mufucka, and, as rusty as my thinking skills are, sometimes my writing feels worse. But you did title your joint "PART I" and I sense you're a man of your word, so I figure you'll endure the run-ons, etc.

One last thing. I know you're busy with writing and life. Your having taken the time to get at me the way you did is a testament to the respect you must have for art and artists in general, and for me and my particular brand of strangeness. Thank you for the time and the thoughts and the implicit props. I'm glad to know somebody else thinks I got some real shit to say. Just know that all the growing I've got to do is a blessing I ain't trying to block. Aiight, I gots *thinking* to do.

Love,

Sister Sarah Jones

By Invitation—An Open Letter to the President of South Africa

Itumeleng oa Mahabane

DEAR MR. PRESIDENT MBEKI:

Ten years ago, in my penultimate year of school, my future changed dramatically. From the certainty of a life as a second-grade citizen with an uncertain professional future, to the certainty of being a free and equal member of my society, with an equally uncertain if more hopeful future.

When the symbolic shackles fell from Nelson Mandela's feet, so too did the invisible but all too real shackles around me and every young black South African. I thought we would no longer have to bear the brunt of a struggle whose main theme, "liberation before education," had already damned us as certainly as Verwoerd's vision of black youth as a low-skilled labour force.

Ten years ago, the day Mandela walked out of jail, first proudly in the air, that day, I thought at the time, was *our* day. That victory was *our* victory. I recall 19-year-old Solomon Mahlangu's words as he was sent to the gallows: "Mama, tell my people not to weep. My blood will nourish the tree which will bear the fruit of their liberation." And I knew they would not be in vain. The seed planted by the 1976 generation and nourished with the sweat of the militant young lions of the eighties would finally bear fruit.

It is therefore a bitter irony that ten years later, young people sit, crippled and unable to reach for that fruit. Instead, South Africa's young are an incidental part of society, remembered only at election time.

I hope our Minister of Education, Professor Kader Asmal, will forgive me if I sound naïve, or insensitive, or both. It isn't that I don't see or appreciate his efforts to fix the non-existent schooling system in black society. Your efforts are admirable. Yet I cannot ignore the fact that hundreds of thousands of my peers will never have a matric exemption. What are we to do about them? Leave them on the wayside? It is not that I discount your efforts. It is only that I feel your party, the party I've grown up believing in, seems interested only in fixing what's visible.

What we don't see, what we don't read about, the thousands who idle on street corners every day—they're a mirage on the periphery of our society. Each year after we've lamented the matric results, those who are the victims of our system are forgotten. As you, Mr. President, so eloquently put it, "They too slide into the past as though they never were."

I do not mean to sound bitter and cynical. It is only that I feel that your party, the African National Congress, the party I believed would stay a liberation movement as you and others swore it would, feels as though it has become a party of political expediency.

When I hear talk of Gear and targets, of fiscal discipline and deficit reductions, when I hear you talk of a political vision that is more a management style in line with the needs of a developed country, I wonder to whom you're talking.

This is no mere lament from a young person who expects the State to provide for him. Though I scorn Kennedy's "Ask not" speech, I do believe that things will come to those who get up and do for themselves. But I'm suffering from fatigue, brought about by decades of hopelessness.

All I ask is that you give me some spiritual encouragement so that I might find the energy to get up and do for myself. When you and Minister of Finance Trevor Manuel talk of Gear, you give me nothing. Instead, each year when you stand up in parliament and address me, you leave me bewildered.

Because you choose not to engage and talk to me, but to some faceless person at some obscure financial institution with an odd acronym, I find it hard to be motivated. You leave me demoralised, wondering if the next ten years will be like the ten years past? If I'll be twiddling my thumbs for yet another decade?

Sometimes I think back to my high school history and that American President, Franklin Delano Roosevelt. I think of his famous fireside chats. I wish you also had time for reassuring talks. I wish you too had a vision of boosting morale by creating public works programmes for my peers and me.

Then I remember that you must exercise fiscal discipline. Sometimes I long for the inspirational rhetoric of the RDP. I sometimes think that if you paid me just 20 rand a day to dig holes, even if I were to fill them again, it would at least give me the energy to keep hope alive until Manuel achieved the magical 8% growth rate.

Certainly, I feel that way when my friends talk about how they would be grateful to find a job, any job. And when I see them peddle goods from dusk to dawn on the streets each day, I have no reason to believe they would not labour if they found the jobs. But I wonder how long their spirit will survive. I urge you, Mr. President, to remember this: for every me that makes it to university, ten of me join my older brothers who have been unemployed for close to two decades. Their pessimism feeds into my disillusionment.

Mr. President, those more economically astute than I have explained why you need this fiscal discipline that sounds like the Reaganomics I learnt about in school. Yet others have told me how the Asian Tigers threw caution to the wind in pursuit of the kind of growth that creates jobs.

If there is a lost generation, it is because each year we choose to forget it, we let it slide into oblivion. The middle class may cheer at Manuel's present growth rate. But for the majority, the legacy of the past ten years is the legacy of forgotten scars.

But perhaps I should not complain too much, lest I impose upon you and the party the pain of guilt, and upon myself the pain of those memories of the dusty militarised streets of the eighties.

And please do not be clouded by the publication in which these words appear. Before you dismiss me as a reactionary, as those in your party are wont to do of dissenters, let me assure you I believe in you even as I remain unconvinced of your economic ideology. An ideology, incidentally, you share with this publication. Remember that before you dismiss me.

Itumeleng oa Mahabane

Notes

Matric Exemption: A university entrance high school result.

Gear: South African government's macroeconomic framework. It is a form of structural adjustment and free market economics.

RDP: Reconstruction and Development Programme. It is the ANC government's first policy.

Eisa Nefertari Ulen

What Happened to Your Generation's Promise of "Love and Revolution"?

A Letter to Angela Davis

DEAR MS. DAVIS,

You know my father. You know my mother. They know you. And your sister Fania. Daddy helped you slip through Pennsylvania when you were underground. Mommy let Fania into our home when you were caught. Fania was pregnant, I was about two, and she later named her daughter Angela Eisa Davis. Mommy kept your niece's birth announcement. It is taped, next to pictures of people sporting Afros, in my baby book: "Born of the bloodfire of struggle for the people. I honor my child with your daughter's name. May they both be strong forces of love and revolution."

Oh, the promise of those words, those pictures, these images. My soul cries out even as I turn the yellowed page. There are pictures of Daddy and Mommy. Together. And me. Lenin lines the walls, stacked beneath a poster ("Unite Contre La Represión") in our living room, where folk then in their twenties would arrive and debate through study sessions, trying to fulfill the promise in that poster, those books, bringing the images and words to life—a real life.

Of course that living room isn't ours anymore. Like so many folk in their twenties then, my parents divorced. And like so many folk in their twenties now, I was raised by my mother.

As I take full advantage of my generation's opportunity to enjoy a delayed adolescence—single but yearning for marriage and parenthood—I look back on my own family. I feel the lost potential—at times feel imprisoned by it. I also look around our community, feel the lost potential, and—at times—feel imprisoned by it. I think we, now, are feeling the same way, imprisoned by the past. The Black Nation's hip-hop generation has been looking back at itself.

We give '70s parties, wear '70s bell bottoms. Well beyond any good ol' days clichés, my generation is recapturing its passage from youth to young adulthood. In an era when so many young Black men have seemed unafraid of killing and dying, Generation (Malcolm) X is reliving—in the past.

A few of the best in the rap music industry can take and twist 1970s sound with 1990s image through old sampled beats and new spoken words. This aligns the modern on an ancient continuum and perpetuates the legacy of Black music; yet why do so many hot young singles go back in the day on wax? Why is Black music, our talking drum in the diaspora, sending a message of return? Why are we consuming your generation's music, your generation's love?

In the climate-controlled confines of local movie theaters, where we escape from the real world and enter the filmmaker's recreated vision, we go back to the days just before and just after Black folk in their twenties stepped into young adulthood. Something in the collective unconscious of young Black filmmakers remembers a people bumping on the dance floor, rolling with the skates at a disco ring, loving themselves enough to keep the gun unloaded in a shoebox on the closet's top shelf. From *Crooklyn* to *The Inkwell* to *Boyz N the Hood* to *Dead Presidents* to *Jason's Lyric* to *Panther* to *Set it Off,* we revisit.

The release of rites-of-passage films heavy with Pro-Keds—era iconography moves us to a time before AIDS (what happened to my sexual revolution?), before Reaganomics (what happened to my economic revolution?), before crack even hit Huey Newton's neighborhood, much less poisoned his body (what happened to my political revolution?). And in this slice of time before sneakers became one-hundred-dollar investments worth shooting the brother down the block over, parents called us into the house once streetlights flickered on through the community's night. Then, just as we grew old enough to play adolescent games past sunset, the safety of the streetlights blew. Now we stand on the stoops and porches ourselves, not quite ready to call out to the neighborhood kids, no longer the ones called.

I refuse to lie back and feel good about the retro movement in young Black cultural expression. Were a hot young single you love holding her broken old Lite Brite with strength equal to 1990s P-Funk revivalist record sales, you would worry. I know it's time for young heads to work toward true illumination. But that bright glare might spotlight a positive HIV test, a lot of time between jobs, the barrel of that gun now loaded, out of the closet, the shoebox tossed. Better to focus on the dim past as we stand on the community steps, peer into a situation where the streetlights still burned bright.

Too few households have left the stoop lights on along the streets of today's Black Nation. But why? Why after the hope and uplift and struggle of your life—of your collective lives—why is our community standing in the dark?

My mother tells me I should write something nice. "Why don't you talk about all the good things that happened?" she asks me. Well, it does feel good to turn on my radio and hear the old school mixes, hear my favorite hip-hop artists talk about "back in the day," about "goin' back in the day." I'm listening to all the good stuff all the time. But aren't we a little young, isn't hip-hop a little young, for any of us to feel good about going back?

It was during the '70s that my peers were able to rise from where we'd been forced—undereducated, underfinanced, underground—and create the multibillion dollar industry that is called rap. But now, just as we've started to create a new generation ourselves—who mimic our words, our sounds, and our deeds—we haven't been able to build on your promises of love and revolution. What will be the substantive results of our legacy, our image? What were yours?

It's bad enough that brothers are dying but that the death seems sometimes to be feeding on itself, springing out like fresh blood from within ourselves; this is just, this is just too much. I know each generation struggles, Ms. Davis; but I'm asking you to help me come to terms with these losses. I know there are retro elements in any new trend, but each film looks at the moment of transition, the place where our families, our communities, our world seemed to fall apart. We mix sounds of family reunions and backyard barbecues with words of terror and pain.

I am writing from a seemingly sheltered, comfortable life, but I, too, have seen boys fall to our streets. I've seen their blood fall to our streets. I've heard young men listen to your music and say, "This is when Black people still loved each other."

I've seen girls fall to our streets. I've seen their futures fall to our streets. I've seen young women look around them and heard them say, "I'ma just go on and have his baby before he gets locked up or shot up or something." I've heard that.

Your generation's ex-husbands are replicated in my generation's babies' fathers. This is not an empowering new configuration of family that is somehow uplifting and free. Our babies' mothers are alone and tired and broke.

I can only remember a glimmer of revolutionary-type lovin', of we gonna make this happen, baby I love you this much, enough to make this happen, this is our struggle, this is our struggle, we gonna struggle together baby-type lovin'. Where are our models of strong manhood for young men? Where are our models of strong mates for young women? Where are those revolutionary, revolution-era families?

Are we supposed to get those models from our grandparents? From books? Forced further and further past strength to strain, what is left but the prison of bad choices? I see whole families imprisoned by bad choices. I see whole communities surrounded. I sometimes wonder if we were better off when we had fewer rights, but more revolution.

I'm asking because after seeing my family fall apart, seeing the Movement fall apart, I know the real revolution was at home. For a Black woman and a Black man to create new Black life, nurture it, watch it grow together, that is a revolutionary act. It is the only way we will be able to live—to remain alive.

I know the face of a real postwar syndrome. I belong to it. I have seen the ache and the rage in my own father's eyes. But now he can see a piece of that part of himself in me. He was too young then. He was too young to see such death. I am too young now. Our death—real and metaphorical—and our prisons—real and metaphorical—have kept your generation so far way. And they have kept my generation flung backwards in time.

I am asking your peers to come forward with the full force my peers have spent in the stretch to yesterday. What formal structures (as formal as family configurations) do you have in place for us? For your grandchildren? Will you help us rebuild the extended family—the one I remember from my childhood—in our community today?

I know Tupac needed everyone who had ever been down with anything Afeni had been down with to visit him in jail, Ms. Davis. He needed that. He said that. Geronimo wasn't released until Tupac was dead, but you weren't all locked up. Or were you?

Are we going to kill each other off before your generation returns, is released, to finish leading, to finish parenting? Where are our leaders? Where are our parents?

Will you hear us? Will the new Black Radical Congress address us? Will it include us? Will it address the brilliance lost like Tupac's, brilliance lost on our community streets every night?

Ms. Davis, we re crying out to you in the dark. We have come of age without the wisdom of the earlier generation. We have your style, but we don't have your substance. Tupac was just a symbol of our murdered potential. A future so lost, so gone, that sometimes, just sometimes, Ms. Davis, it seems gone for good.

Love and Revolution, Ms. Davis. Love and Revolution.

Still yours,

Eisa Nefertari Ulen

An Atlantic Away: A Letter from Africa

Teresa N. Washington

14 July 1999

Shining One,

PEACE BE UNTO YOU AND YOURS! I PROMISED I WOULD GIVE A FULL "GIST" of Nigeria from my perspective. Here goes: As you will be able to tell from the length of this document, things here are dry. The students have protested, so they've all been kicked out. Now, these are not the same protests as at Jackson State or Fisk. Many students here at Obafemi Awolowo University (and some lecturers) see themselves as minor politicians. So they pick insignificant issues or things that are flat-out wrong and rabble-rouse around them. Many are also provocateurs or saboteurs who are "rewarded" for causing confusion. Since I came here in May of '97, there have been about ten shutdowns of the university because of various protests. They call these protests "Aluta," as in struggle. Aluta is as regular as rain in the rainy season. One doesn't know if one is attending an academic institution or a training ground for politicians, counter-revolutionaries, or agents.

When I first came, the Ife-Modakeke War which had been dead for 180 years began again in Ife town. The two groups were fighting over the political myth of "local government area." I was pissed. Blood flowing in the street and nobody was looking out! It wasn't until neo-warriors started burning the homes and kidnapping the children of professors that the so-called intellectual community got involved, and then only minutely. But that is the situation here. People are killing one another over political fantasies! Now the war is over . . . but nothing changed! Neither the Ife nor Modakeke got anything. These are people who had been intermarried for tens of decades so it was literally husband against wife and all for nothing.

This is the same thing that was happening in the Delta Region when the Ijaw, Itsekiris and Urhobos were all killing one another until recently. One of my students, who is Urhobo, said the Urhobos and Itsekiris "fight in the morning and make love in the night." That is their motto, and it describes both the degree of intermarriage and the level of divide-and-conquer. However, there has been a change in this three-pronged massacre: The Ijaw Youth Action Committee has, last I heard, taken over the Shell refinery and another refinery. Those regions have absolutely nothing. No hospitals, schools, nothing that general humanity needs, but crude oil abounds in this region. And that oil keeps the West moving! Finally, these youth are attacking the real enemy.

Did you all hear about the Jesse explosion in Warri, Nigeria? Due to a pipe leak, petrol was literally all over the ground. This was during a fuel crisis, so members of the community were collecting the petrol in whatever canisters were handy and selling it. Then, a motorcycle sparked. Humph, it was devastating! Hundreds of people were killed; multitudes were burned beyond recognition. Concurrent with the explosion was the three-way war, like here in Ife, again, blood flowing in the streets. But I pray the Ijaw youths will bring Shell, Elf, BP and Total to their knees. These are the only warriors I know of in Nigeria. Most folk would sell their souls to go to America. Wouldn't you know, that is all the nation asks?

Among the inclusive campus populace there is little of what we call consciousness. One of two conscious brothers I met at O.A.U. Ife was killed recently, along with three other students, because he unmasked cult members, who had been terrorizing the school. His name was George "Africa" Iwilade. When I came two years ago, he and I tried to start an organization for consciousness-awakening. We could not find one person to make three! The situation is grim. Most people are solely driven by the pursuit of money. They can also be wickedly violent and destructive. The situation reminds me so obviously of the mentality that made the Slave Trade successful that it sickens me.

The culture here in Ife is that no matter how grave a situation may be, one need only beg. You can insult someone, slap someone (an elder), kill someone, steal from them, rape their daughter—anything goes—and just go and beg the person you have offended later. Another cultural rule is that there is "no such answer as 'no.'" imagine a group of people of all ages who simply do not recognize the answer "No." In short, the tools we honed to survive in America's heinous society were not cultivated here because this is HOME for Nigerians—it truly is. Our rule, for example, of being twice as good as the best white boy to go as high as the average one, is unnecessary here. There is an assumption that nothing is forbidden. Nothing. Actually, I envy the freedom Nigerians have in Nigeria, a freedom that most members of society disavow. And yet, this is a master / slave society with many dichotomies. One is often forced to go around begging and cringing like a beast for recognition of one's humanity (ironically); other times one may be inundated with unctuous false respect, as if one were a "master" in hopes that "master" will give a "slave" a "dash" (financial gift). It is distressing to witness people the age of one's parents acting this way. When one of us loses our dignity, we all do.

As you may know, I am teaching here in addition to my Ph.D. work. I teach African, African-American and American literature. I thought my teaching here would be the apex of my career. In many ways it has been because I have obtained experience here I could not have gained elsewhere. However, my love of teaching has been neutralized because I am faced with students who say outright that they "hate to read." They also hate to write. If I give an assignment, rather than doing it, they may very well write a letter of complaint against me (and of course come begging me later). This is due to intricate levels of apathy. Because morale is low, there is very little real education or even training going on. There is also the status quo to consider. If someone is enthusiastic, like me, she or he may be crushed into the society's norm of vapidity.

I did have a good experience teaching Ngugi's *Matagari* and Armah's *Two Thousand Seasons,* however. I think I really reached the students and opened them up, but there are so many factors going against conscientization. The little seeds I plant are scattered before the students leave the class. But one of the most profound things, that really shouldn't have been all that surprising, occurred when I was teaching African-American literature. I read a song from a WPA ex-slave narrative that went as so:

Lie low, nigga, lie low,
Bill Hill will whoop and the nigga will holla
Lie low, nigga, lie low.

Obviously, this is a message for protection against Bill Hill to brothers and sisters on the lam. Well, my students busted out and sang: "Lai lo, Lai lo!" A Yoruba song that says: "Fisherman, don't go to the sea today / lai lo / Farmer don't go to the farm today / lai lo / The gorillas are coming to capture and take us away." We all left the class dancing and singing "lai lo!"

Here is the same message in a similar song, both songs probably composed within 50 years of each other. Our version possibly a truncation of the Yoruba original, and both songs were united in 1998. This kind of epiphanic-link happens all the time. I love finding these cultural connections that unify us, despite our proclivity to despise one another. But times of beauty are rare. Oh, one "brother" loved knowledge. So much he fled to Cameroon with my Last Poets and Gil Scott-Heron tapes, my *Destruction of Black Civilization,* and my documentation about the National Institutes of Health and the Centers for Disease Control's invention of AIDS and the World Health Organization's dissemination thereof. You know I sat down and cried. Well, at least the knowledge is circulating.

However, the apathy that plagues us here in Nigeria reaches many levels. For example, when Nigeria saw all types of upheaval last year, everyone was watching the World Cup (soccer)! Sani Abacha died. I thought folk would go to Aso Rock and start battling for release of prisoners and what not. People got drunk and celebrated his death (he was still a husband, father and human, right? Abacha really assisted in Liberia and Sierre Leone, also) and watched World Cup. (Imagine if Clampett, the House and Senate members were all slaughtered and we sat down and watched the Super Bowl!) But no one did anything. People were talking about Jesus of all things.

So then Jesus / the United States come to Nigeria, and some prisoners are released. The Americans sit with Moshood K. O. Abiola on the eve of his release and asked him if he would demand to be installed as President (re: the never-fulfilled June 12 mandate). Next thing you know, Abiola is coughing and doesn't stop till he dies. So, then, folk riot and loot and burn and scatter everything in the Yoruba nation. The only thing Abiola had taken was tea with the American "mediators." These same entities oversee the examination and autopsy of the man whom, to all eyes concerned, they had just waxed. (Actually, I wasn't partial to Abiola, his legacy with ITT speaks for itself, and the reparations scheme sounded too much like select Africans profiting off of the trade— AGAIN—to me). During the investigations of Abiola's death, everyone sat down quietly because how can you fight the leader of the so-called free world? Next thing you know, Obasanjo is "magically" released from prison and discussing with Americans. Okay. Now, he's head of state—again.

When folk start in about politics, I just laugh, "America has chosen your president for you, wha ting make we discuss?" It was a trip. During the election that Obasanjo eventually won, *BBC Magazine* reporters / voting monitors went to polling stations and noticed that there were no people around, just filled ballot boxes. So they asked what was up and learned that by 11:00 A.M. everyone had come, voted and gone. All the ballots were neatly folded in the same way. So, at one station, where "everyone had already voted," brothers come up looking to vote. Their names had been ticked off as having voted already (see Fela's comment on dem / o / cracy below).

So it is no surprise that the students here like to protest and will resort to violence easily. This legacy of violence is most disturbing to me; I don't know if it is due to the inability to signify or the legacy of the work of slave-raiding villages. At any rate, students here at O.A.U. have attacked Vice-Chancellors at convocations. Students in Ibadan threatened to kill their Vice-Chancellor, and publicized the threat in the major national paper! A few months back, students kidnapped O.A.U.'s Deputy Vice-Chancellor of Academics. Hear, someone's father, husband, they just snatch him up. The students can be wild. They commandeered a university vehicle that had been grounded because it needed extensive repairs and ran into the main gate, nearly died. These things pain me. Even when we build something, it seems we are determined to destroy it.

When I was here about three months and understood that the future of this nation—our future, because we are one and going through the same destruction at "Evil, Inc.'s" hands—I would just sit down and weep for our loss. The ancestors must be so disappointed in us as a people. We have done nothing to advance their struggle, collectively. And when I see folk here battling to take the same journey on which they sent the slaves—humph. They don't even understand how bizarre that is. Like Femi Kuti (Fela's son) sang, "you leave your fatherland to go scrub toilets in America."

As it concerns the future of Obafemi Awolowo University, I do have hope because of our new Vice-Chancellor, Professor Roger Makanjuola. I do not know how to appropriately praise or describe him. He is efficient, thorough, corruption-free and HUMAN. He is about action. He doesn't dissemble. He became our Acting Vice-Chancellor when George "Africa" was murdered in the "cult killings." We lost one warrior but gained another. I pray they let Prof. Makanjuola live and work and shine, because if anyone can turn this university around it is him, and believe me, we are turning at about 270 reaching 360!

Did C____tell you about the conference in Morocco? She really looked out for me. You know she funded my trip. I couldn't have gone without her. We went to the African Literature Association conference where I presented my essay "Blood Across the Water: Africana Spiritual Power in Life and Literature." There were some irations flowing at that conference! A visual artist named Mike Platt, from D.C., gave a deep slide presentation / poetry exhibition. Wooo, elder pulled out a harmonica, started playing the blues, flashed to a slide of a brother's countenance in the sky surrounded by constellations: Drinking gourd, the same heavens that Abubakari II used to navigate to America years before Columbus, the same ones we used to run to freedom, the same ones I look to and pray for my mothers . . . I can't describe how this brother's work touched me! and his spirit was so vast!!!! He gave me the piece and I was still weeping and jubilating I was digging him so much his wife was amazed! He reminded me of my favorite uncle! A brother from Cameroon, Dr. Matetayou, presented on King Njoya of Bamun and his system of writing. God, we have been writing here for eons, from Liberia to Kongo, King Njoya painstakingly revised his system four times and the symbols are so much like ve ve and the gang symbols. If you can, find this film, "Afrique, je te plumerai" by Jean Marie Teno; he discussed King Njoya among other complex continental issues. Profound!!!

The conference was powerful in many ways: my meeting Niyi Osundare, a master poet, was the highlight for me. His reflections on my work were steps taking me through a crossroads of creative insecurity. He was supervised by my supervisor, who is the ultimate elder! I am honored to be in such excellent academic company, word. But I was slapped in the face with something I had forgotten about here: how cliquish we are. There was a noted critic there. You know, I was all honored to meet this scholar, who has done work I have found so vital. However, folk were grandstanding, avoiding issues and reminding me of the Temple students who, in Ghana, considered themselves more African than the Africans. (When I started discussing the African rituals carried out religiously by gang members that have been on-going since before Africa became fashionable, the Temple "Africans" curled their lips up.) This critic even dismissed and dissed me when I started talking about the inherent racism of the Arabs and questioning the reason as to why the conference of African literature was held in a land where the folk don't consider themselves African. (I was detained at the airport in Casablanca six hours. An Arab looked at my passport, looked at me, laughed and walked away! No explanation. No conversation. "Youse a nigga ain't ya!" The first thing a sister and I were greeted with as we left our hotel room in Fez was "Hey Niggers!") Actually, a few folks dealt with this issue, which further angered me. How can we decide to act as if Moroccans aren't reminding us of "Mississippi Goddamn!"? Perhaps disavowal is one of pseudo-multiculturalism's many ambiguous gifts. Perhaps we think we have "transcended race," like O.J. thought he had.

However, feeling a cultural gap, we quietly ferreted out some bliss, as you know we will. After the closing banquet, after the Moroccan entertainment was over, Brother Platt pulled out his harmonica and juba's reprise began! Later, as we were leaving the "palace" in which the banquet was held, this Yoruba brother and I started singing praisesongs to Aje, and this would be unheard of in Nigeria! We were flowing! Dancing and waking folk up, signifying. It was thrilling and ironic that we felt free to praise Aje in Morocco.

I don't know if you know what I'm here studying. I am studying Aje, which is the Africana women's force of power. My dissertation is a Pan-African analysis of the force itself and its impact on Africana literature. Aje originates in the womb and is of myriad manifestations. Ile-Ife is the reputed home of this force and its powerful women. I have been studying Aje for years now, especially our African-American evolutions thereof. Actually, L____, it is you who turned me on to Aje through introducing me to Esu, who also has Aje. So when my Mothers give me grief again for staying too long, I will direct them to you. :) Honestly, I honor you Iba a se, egbon mi pataki. Aiku, aiku, aiku (I pay you homage, big brother. Long life, long life). You showed me my life's direction and path. Word Life. Saved my life and soul there in Hattiesburg, Mississippi. You are more than a brother! Mo juba ore mi gidigidi ganan ni. (More homage for you, most excellent friend.) I still remember me, you, J____ and C____ sitting in your living room all promising to look out for one another and to promote and quote one another. I give all praises for you and C____ because you always have babygirl in mind. You all have been part of my creative soul since we met. You don't know how often I quote you to folks and refer to your knowledge in my work. Mo dupe! (That dreadlocked Jesus stays on my mind.).

At the Big-10 institution I attended before I came to O.A.U., I felt like a hypocrite. Many of the profs in the African literature and language program were neo-coloniallyinclined. But more than this, I was being academically dishonest: How did I call myself studying Aje, there in 60 below 0 weather where there was no natural earth to receive libations? Furthermore, I was starving. The minority fellowship was 13.5 g's. We "minority fellows" were like Kool and The Gang, but tuition, rent, and all school fees came out of that money and went right back to the university! One sister and her lover were cleaning houses to make ends meet. I was working in a gas station. Doncha love America, my favorite country? So one night, as I got on my knees to pray to my ancestors, I was afraid to get up because it would have meant going on. I got up, and began processing my forms to come here. Seems I keep migrating further South. From Peoria, Illinois, where I was born, to Georgia, Missouri, Tennessee, Mississippi—Midwest to the Dirty South—I kept flowing with our blood and bone-soaked rivers till I hit the sea. Traversed the Ethiopic with its salt and ancestral bones re-membering me buoying me still here in Nigeria, the former Slave Coast.

Since I came here to study and live it has been more than worth it, academically. I have been able to do a work that I couldn't have done anywhere else. I have witnessed some true power, also, and beauty. Aje are feared as "evil" witches and what not, in the West, and here too. However, the people I was researching with took me immediately as a daughter. Finish. They opened all unto me. But the academic Aje . . .

I have seen blood here (Nigerian expression: "Come see blood!"). You know, coming to the continent independently, for an unspecified amount of time without some big shot grant or fellowship, is an experience. Foreigners are generally viewed as walking or riding wallets, not as humans. This is cool if you have the fund or the ego to validate the myth. I came only with the money to see me through my academic program, money I had earned in that gas station. I had hoped to be able to work and was able, eventually, to land a position as Assistant Lecturer. However, such Emersonian "self-reliance" is ludicrous to Nigerians. It does not compute. The underlying thought is that I have money and it must be taken from me and enjoyed. Giving of oneself in the form of sharing books, music or time—which is a considerable gift—are not appreciated because they are not lucrative. For example, I co-organized a poetry festival. It was a huge success; however, I was disregarded and disrespected. In fact I suffered negative repercussions from attempting and succeeding at doing something positive that benefited many persons.

The culture here in O.A.U. Ife is a hybrid neo-colonial, pseudo-British, shattered-Yoruba, mimicked-African-American; it is an incomprehensible blend that leaves its bearers with only monetary desires. Often the primary concern regarding moey is not need, but greed. It is a painful phenomenon to witness. I have found that many coastal nations, whose relations with the West are high, are of a similarly destroyed mentality.

My experience will be quite different from tourists, visitors or academic prima donnas. I experience what the typical Nigerian does, even more so because I wash my own clothes, clean my own home, and cook my own food. Most folks, even students, have "small boys / girls" to do these chores and look at me like I'm crazy washing my clothes by hand. (Hiring folks to do for peanuts what the Creator gave me hands to do reminds me of slavery.) As one sister told me, I am able to better appreciate what is happening here than folks who pass through. No one is obliged to roll out any type of carpet for me; I'm living the real deal. My salary is the same as my Nigerian colleagues of the same

rank. I receive no favoritism or special regard. In fact, I may have received worse treatment simply because I came as "another African" whereas folks would have preferred "an
American." But if you can be of no financial use, you are considered useless.

Within two weeks of when I came here, folks found I wasn't Chelsea Clinton—
meaning I wasn't financially fit for purposes of extortion—I was kicked out with no
where to live. Straight up gazing at the stars. Didn't hip me to rooms on campus or
nothing. I was just ass out one day. So many things that I can think back on now and
smile. The second time I caught malaria, I fainted twice in the dormitory hallway and
the brother and sisters passing who helped me, promptly stole my money and vamped.
My body was hardly cold. Now, they didn't know my nationality, they were just inhuman. I could have died in my room with brain fever, no water, food or drugs, but one
of my brothers was sitting in a lecture and something told him to check on me. Saved
my life. Literally. Strong Man, Chris.

Academically, two scholars whose work I admired and whom I looked forward to
working with decided to work together to scatter me because of my j study, and yes,
people use their Aje. It is deep, projecting things into my dreams, like my family members dying, literally trying to slay me, making me just want to pack it up. Aje is an astral
force: it can be used in many ways. But I know that my ancestors have protected and
guided me. That is the truth and I give all praises to them for it: Mo juba Egngn mi.
Folk have threatened my life. Threatened my elders lives waaaaay cross the ocean.
Some have stalked and attempted to rape me. But I persevere.

Women get no props here; if you aren't attached to some man (no matter how useless he may be), you are worthless or only sexually "valued" in spite of your academic
credentials. The women suffer here because most, nay, all people believe, "a woman is
nothing without a man." The men act like little children, sampling women like balls
of candy. I give all respect to the sisters here struggling to manifest academically. Yet it
is ironic that where women once walked "naked and unashamed," thanks to modernization, they now dress up half-naked a la Lil' Kim (tell J____ I give her props for her
article in Raw and that our influence here along those lines is strong. It makes me sad
that money, sex and guns are the legacy we are issuing forth). Where brothers were
once sons of Ogun, Esu, Obatala, and Orunmila, now they think they Puff and Mase.
Sexual oppression is the norm here. Like, go to a prof's office and he'll corner and start
groping you.

But what pains my spirit is that lack of community. No one to just rap about issues.
Nothing. No vibing. The donut. Sometimes I get close to snappin'. My isolation is due
to a few reasons: 1) Consciousness surrounded by unconsciousness leads to isolation;
2) I am not a Christian or Muslim in a land of shallow zealots. If we think xtianity dealt
with us, we ain't seen nothing! Religion here is like a gang, everything hinges on which
side you are on. Imagine my vulnerability, and studying j to boot!; 3) I do not fit Nigeria's myth of "An American": stupid, rich, ready to be used; 4) Myself. I try to be real,
natural, honest. A Taoist proverb warns us of the danger of being sincere with the insin-
cere, but I have not cultivated the wiles of the trickster. With my African dress and natural hair, I am an oddity, often, ironically, exoticized. It is funny though. Sometimes
brothers and sisters will come to me and say, "I like your style, you're really African!"
Imagine! One sister tried to insult me by saying, "Well, well, you look like an African!"
So what did she consider herself? But I see sisters feeling their natural beauty more and

what not, not just the hair but themselves. Maybe there's hope but it has to go beyond outer appearances.

When we treated *Two Thousand Seasons* and I asked my students who in their sphere did they recognize as the keepers, hearers, seers, utterers of the original way that Armah's narrator discussed, the ONLY person they could think of was me. It's sad. But one Muslim sister, after we discussed the work, started questioning her religion and the Arabs who brought it. She simply had never thought to question or examine her religion. The goal is not conversion but questioning. But the light of self that began glowing in her would be dimmed so quickly as soon as she left the class. As one of my Cameroonian brothers said of the status of African peoples in the light of slavery, colonization and neo-colonization, "They have truly dealt with us."

My solitude is why I have written a novel. In my novel I try to create the community I miss so much and the one I hope to build and /or belong to upon returning. It is about 12 women (and their lovehers) and they all have Aje. They use their force in many ways. It is a force of herbal healing, divine retribution, creativity, the power to do and undo, create and destroy. It is the ground glass in the slavemaster's food, the fire that ripped through plantations, and the juba in the clearing. African Americans evolutionized the force. So these women and their communities use this force to re-order the world. There are 6 chakra sites—3 in Africa, 3 in African America. They revolutionize the projects, as in the 60's; they found an independent institution of learning (one of my long-term goals), among other things. So many things: founding Soul Sanctuaries, an international j tribunal. It is a powerful and cyclical work (I think). What I am trying to do is to utilize the ancient (and modern wisdoms) so that we can free and heal ourselves and organize our existence on our own terms. As with Armah's *Osiris Rising,* I would like my work to also be a kind of path for re-creation.

I also feel we don't have to exclude, isolate, or privilege one way of being. African cosmologies have been impervious to colonization and modernization because they are open-ended. This is not to say that we accept any drivel, but when I think of the depth of the black Gangster Disciples and their similarity to African secret societies like Yoruba's Ogboni, I know that the force is the same, just mis-directed. We can re-direct our force. The question is, are we willing to struggle and die to be free?

Truly, we have evolved our forces in African America. But I also needed to know what is currently on-ground in the continent. How are we manifesting here in actuality? Studies are so often filtered, bowdlerized, and decidedly in a past-tense, i.e. long-dead, perspective. Many studies have been written by "Africanists"—a term Europeans have assigned themselves without any qualification whatsoever—so that Africana-to-Africana cognition is contingent upon entities who serve to eradicate cognition. On the other hand, we often "style" Africa, but are styling from a cosmetic or even Black-Africanist position. Studying Aje, I felt compelled, by the mothers, to "go there and know there," to quote Zora Neale Hurston, who I call the Great Mother of Africana Letters (Iyanla Iwe). The Mothers won't allow me to front, possibly because I consider myself / am considered their child. The lessons they re teaching me are not easy ones to deal with. However, Iyanla Iyami Osoronga is she who creates problems and also provides the solution. Ase wa.

What I want to do is come holistically armed, you know? Our past wars against America were unsuccessful because we had no unified spiritual cosmology. Possibly one reason the majority of Africana peoples shrugged off communism is because crucial aspects of our survival / cultural / revolutionary ethos were considered irrelevant: we have to have our spiritual force and our music along with arms. When the Spirit is whole and recognized so too will be the body and community.

There is a clearly discernible and powerful link between our Afri-Baptist churches, Hoodoo, Ifa, Voodoo, and gangs like the Black Gangster Disciples and Vice Lords, our rituals, our style, our signification. In my own estimation, that root is Aje. Odu is the Orisa (deity) who is the j. She is considered the womb of Origins and the Calabash of Origins. She is the Great Mother of African Creation. She is Oduduwa, Odua. She is wife and mother of Obatala, she is the Yewajobi, "the mother of all Orisa and all living things." She is the origin of creativity and violent retribution. Her pot of creativity is just that, the beginning and end of all creative forces. As the traditional Yoruba say of her, "She is the owner of everything in this world. She owns you. We must not say how the whole thing works." In my research on Aje during colonization and under American slavery, it is clear that Aje was affecting the most heralded and the unmentioned insurrections. But the more we assimilate, the more we degenerate. However, our writers seem to be asking us to re-member our force to ourselves. I try to analyze these connections and exertions of spiritual cum literary cum communal Aje—not only in my research but in my existence.

When I listen to Five Percent rhetoric, I am hearing Ifa, Olodumare, and Odu. Many rappers herald the ancients outright. The cultural retention is profound and getting deeper every day. As you know, Ifa doesn't proselytize; those who are shining shine. Imagine the Yorubas telling the Fon they need to change their Fa to Ifa or the Yoruba telling the Ewe that they should give up Afa and come to Ifa. It is ludricous because it is all one. Our variously manifested force, beneath the rhetoric and politricks, is one. This is the case all over the continent. From Cape to Cairo. But the reason we (African-Americans) so bad, to me, is because we have the best of all ancestors. Many Aje were sold off, as they threatened African-European collective raping of Africa. We took our force with us through the Middle Passage and recreated ourselves, had to. We blended the best of Fon, Yoruba, Hausa, Akan, Igbo, Wolof, BaKongo, Ewe—so many became one, even Malagasian-spiritual forces survive, and more, evolve. We became the Orisa. Fine, we Gods, we bad. Now what do we do with it? What is the next stage of evolution and how do we unify ourselves? This is what I'm trying to figure out.

But my activities, writing and reading, are poor compensation for the human connections that I miss so much. Of course my being here is tremendously hard on my family. Five of my elders have become ancestors since I have been here. We are all just praying for reunification. And how can I explain isolation in a nation of 100,000,000 people? It is devastating. But one thng that I have learned is that when they sold us, they had lost the ability to love. That is their inheritance. Ase.

There is little love here in Nigeria, even among parent and child, husband and wife. Most connections are akin to business investments or opportunities. I cannot imagine having 6 to 10 children and being in a perpetual state of misery because of what they will buy me when they start working. Nigeria was once termed the "Slave Coast." That legacy remains. I have seen the same people who sold us into slavery. I work with them every day. They would sell me again if they could. My return, on my own terms, is a threat. My loudly and proudly representing the shining and resilience of those sold away is problematic. It would have been more pleasant if I was a tourist, I'm sure. But I am proud of what we, with nothing, not even owning ourselves, have accomplished and I want to share it and be shared with. Perhaps it is too shameful. I am a direct reminder of the past and the terrible mistake that was made. Terrible in the sense that the "masters" wish they had been of those taken away as "slaves." Have mercy. I am speaking it in the way it is suppose to be spoken.

However, when I visit other West African nations, particularly those that are land-locked, there is vibration, cognizance. Of course there are intricacies in all people everywhere, but I feel more depth. I have traveled many places from Nigeria to Niger to Ghana to Burkina Faso to Benin to Togo to Mali to Cote d'Ivoire. It can be beautiful. I don't speak French and only a little Yoruba and everyone associates me with Yoruba-land or Liberia. I travel by road (cars can take you anywhere here, and cheaply) and because it is too expensive and dangerous—and unnecessary—to use my U.S. passport, I use my school I.D. and say I'm from Liberia. Members of the ECOWAS (West African) nations have free movement. It is wonderful to ride through the Hausa nations and see these Earth-black warriors, and sleep under the stars in Niamey or Togo. The only woman everywhere and everyone takes me as a baby sister. See the Muslims at their synchronized prayer during Rhamadan. Meet brothers named Marcus Garvey at Cape Coast. Discuss with elders asking you which languages you speak because NO African can only speak one language and that language be English. I love to gaze at the Baobab trees. They look like pregnant women offering gifts with many hands. And the divy divy trees whose branches face not the sky, but the earth, wishing they'd never been born. But my love is Mali! The straight up home of the blues! You can see the same kin of Drew Mississippi playing the guitars (kora) they invented at the beginning of time.

I consider myself the universal African. My mothers made me well because I can go to any marketplace in Africa and people will speak tongue to me. In Ghana with C____, one mommy abused me because she thought I was fronting and speaking English to try to be like C____. She thought I was abandoning my Akan culture and she tried to straighten me!

But my travels have shown me ugliness too. We Africans can hate one another and while folk in Ghana say, "Oh, you're a Nigerian? Well, we are all one people," Nigerians say "Ghanaians? They are soooo black!" Once in Togo, I went to a food vendor with one of my Liberian brothers and the women attacked me! This was when the Liberian war was nearing its apex, and refugees were everywhere, and often despised. I looked at these mommies coming at me with 2x4s and all I could say was, "They're going to kill me. I will die here." But I couldn't hit them because I saw my own mothers in them. That is how ridiculously serious we are taking these colonial borders here. Yeah, people can snap 'cause you've come to THEIR country. This also speaks to the proclivity of violence that is sadly general in Lomé, Togo.

But in so many places there is much depth and beauty, cultural richness. Seeing the Bambara women with their mojos tied in their hair and on the rings of their fingers. And to be honest, people can say what they want about Lagos but it's all propaganda. Whenever I have gone, and I have often gone ignorant and alone, I've had no problem, seen no drugs or thugs. Last week, a sister spent 4 hours with me shoe-shopping! We met on the bus. I have made friends just asking folk for directions! It is funny. I always say I'm from Liberia. To say America is to leave yourself open. I just want to be part of the whole. I don't want to have to spend my time trying to futilely dismantle the monolithic myth of "America." Anyway, I went to the U.S. Embassy and couldn't get in! A sister told me I should have gone when there were Europeans there so I could have seen two lines, à la Jim Crow.

I criticize Nigeria and it has been painful in many ways, but I do have much love for folk here. The problem in O.A.U. Ife is the pseudo-academic mentality. This place reminds me of Roberta Flack asking: "Tryin' to make it reeeeeaaaal, but compared to what?" Professorship is equivalent to deification and in a master / slave society, you can imagine how nasty folks can act. But in Ibadan and Lagos, big towns where folk have lives, folk aren't as worried about cashing in on the economic value of someone's soul.

I also try to pull up and magnify the depth because I need to find / create / develop a safe place for the daughter I will have one day. I have to look at the facts. America: I used to say, how can we just leave the land where our ancestors are and repatriate? Well, if we just get down and honest about it, we will consider that the ancestors don't want us inhabiting lands and being oppressed just for the hell of it. Furthermore, we will never be able to build anything for ourselves in that land. We were brought there to build for others. Our blood is what has reddened the soil of the South and our bodies have weakened the trees of the South and North. Toni Cade Bambara mused that when the cotton gin was invented, we were not supposed to be around much longer. Poet Ted Jones soliloquized in a poem that "We all sposed to be dead . . . But we ain't." And as beautiful as our manifestation is, we are still under the threat of genocide. Now that Yurugu has perfected AIDS and cloning, and now that the computer era is in full thrust, America don't need no niggas no more. To be honest, I am not looking forward to coming back there and engaging in dubious battle. It isn't that I have lost my warrior's spirit; it is that there is no battle to fight. We don't have to ask, beg or kill Yurugu for anything. We have an entire continent here and the very mosquitoes, flies, ocean, and vegetation are against Yurugu. Printing presses, music studios, television and radio stations are all here—so many opportunities waiting to be utilized. Furthermore, our culture is the most influential culture I have seen in all the nations I have visited. The music and posters of our hip-hop stars. The bitings of style. It is really a trip! Nigeria's three largest radio stations exclusively feature OUR music! When you see the brothers and sisters copying the dress, lingo and style of these musicians you recognize the mis-directed potential we do not know we have. If only we could form some lasting links and write songs about things other than cars, clothes and hos. Yes, the music featured is designed to keep the masses in a state of desire / destruction. Sometimes I walk through campus and get confused, thinking I strolled into a video for Harlem World. Imagine if it was our consciousness rather than our vapidity that was blowin' minds here . . .

People really recognize us in some cases, especially the elders. They know us, they remember their parents and grandparents hiding from slave-raiders. One of my profs told me his grandmother sat her progeny down and told them about her daughter, who was stolen in slave raids. Interestingly, Abeokuta, a Nigerian town, means "under the rock." Folk were led "under the rock" by a spirit and hid there and escaped slavers (see Tutuola's *My Life in the Bush of Ghosts*). But for all the young Nigerians' adoration of African-American culture, most have no interest in discussing our history or creations.

"You too hung up in those slavery times," I'm told. Folks are not recognizing NEO-slavery, if they do, they really do not mind. But this is not the case in other nations, where folks are more conscious. Something extremely detrimental occurred in the land Lord Lugard's girlfriend named Nigeria, and the past is cyclically manifesting itself today.

One of the good things about the Continent is that the New World Order will be slow in coming here, because we are not that technologically advanced: no numbers, codes or symbols. Most societies are strongly cash-based. But, sadly, you see nations rushing to integrate into their societies "modernity" in the form of cash-free cards and full computerization, with no idea of the larger implications. But I have to give props. My neighbor shared a Christian tract with me that was hipping readers to NOW, Mondex, Illuminati, and a Liberian brother shared a powerful tape, "From the Shadows," with me. So, folk are hip, believing, and preparing.

But we have so much work to do just in the field of self-recognition. In Ghana, for example, the tuition rates are high so the government can cash in on Euro-students who come to buy the culture; Ghanaians can't even afford to attend the university. You'd think the campus is Harvard or something when you see all the Europeans. Also, I hear folks are trying to turn the Fort and Slave Castle into tourist resorts! You know, these are our sites of pilgrimage. But when I went in '95, whites were chilling on the verandah, making jokes, mocking and reading novels like they were in a park! I mean, these should be places ONLY for Africana peoples to sojourn, pray, revere, and remember. Just like Mecca and Medina. But that isn't lucrative. If we don't appreciate ourselves, we cannot expect our oppressors to do so. Yet in spite of all this, I know that conscious people can build, grow and develop, and we will. We gon get tired of cutting ourselves down from trees, watching our churches burn, watching our sisters go up in flames and weeping over brothers' bodies dragged from the backs of trucks. We gon get tired. To be honest, I don't know what will happen for us as the conscious shining people on this earth. But I know we will get tired of wasting our gifts and enriching soil we will never walk over freely. I don got tired.

But repatriation without a community will be devastating. I know because I have been here manifesting alone. I struggle to tell the truth about the struggles of the Africana masses in America. I strain discussing the cold-water flats in Mississippi, forced sterilization of women of color, successful attempts to close our black universities, why AIDS is genocide in effect, and the shittings on of continental African students in America. But I am one person. They call America "God's Own Country." Everyone is clamoring to win the visa lottery, which is so insulting a construct I can't believe it. Like going to the United States is like winning all kinds of cash. When I tell them 'bout lynchings, church burnings, racist churches—in the '90s—they would rather believe in the misrepresentations of CNN and Voice of America. They feel those who cannot make it in America (meaning "make" a heap of cash) are just stupid. But like Armah says, so many of us are dead. He asks should one waste his or her time and gift trying to conscientize long-rotted ash from the graveyard? Indeed, save a few bright spots, the future looks bleak, blanched.

I feel like I'm on pause right now. I feel my life will begin when I see my Mothers' faces again. I have so many goals / dreams / plans. I want to publish my writings. I also want to work in Africana Studies at an historically black college or university and link with a university here on the continent with that HBCU because we really don't give back enough—and this is why our institutions are intellectually scattered. I dream of classes on Diop and Armah and Browder and Jeffries and Morrison and Ani and Williams and Jochannan and Achebe, I mean I literally dream of this goal. I also want real wisdom-keepers from the community doing some lecturing, you know. I am sick of all of this intellectual saddityism and relying on oppressors for knowledge. We have elders who are starving who can tell us more about SNCC, the Panthers, the Nation of Islam than any European can read and mumble about. Here in Ife they also have a dichotomy separating what they consider the intelligentsia from what I consider the wisdom-keepers. But the real knowledge I have been blessed to witness has come from the community—yes, the bush, the huts. Where we drink ogogoro that is stronger than any white lightning, and pour libation with water sprinkled with flour, and my Babas and Mamas walk with dignity although they may be toting wood on their heads because at least they are in full possession of their souls. Let me be surrounded by full people!!!

It is imperative that we control our educational facilities, and our educational opportunities. I put this bug in my mother's ear. You know, she went to the University of Mississippi (where I went after University of Southern Mississippi, and got my M.A.), she went there and got her M.A. in Education. I convinced her to go because they were giving her their typical racist hell in Mississippi. She is a teacher. So she got the degree and she still can't find a job! Guess where my M.A.-holding momma is working? Wal-Mart. We don't get into their school systems to teach or be educated properly, and even if we do, we are being taught *anything*. If we wait for ole massa to educate us, we will remain ignorant. We need our own school systems from primary on up. I was teaching whole families to read in Hattiesburg, my daddy came down to visit and he started holding classes with me too. We need to have independent schools with Africana-based curriculums.

These are my dreams / goals / plans; maybe it sounds quixotic, but I'm gon try to make it manifest. Actually, it is a lot like what I'm writing about, forming positive independent communities with a higher spiritual goal. Manifestation. We can actually have our sites of power on both sides of the Ethiopic. I know we can cuz we a baaaaahhhhhhdddd people!

So, this is what I've been doing for the last few years and these are the things I don't yet have the courage to tell my mothers. I will close now, but not without giving you some vibrations!

Are you hip to Fela Anikulapo-Kuti (RIP)? Now that they don iced the brotha, I'm sure you can find all possible "greatest hits" compilations. He died of AIDS, he married 27 women at one time, but he also sheltered thousands in his Kalakuta Republic. I love Fela!!!! Please listen to his flow on "Who Be Teacha?" and "ITT (International Tief Tief)" (in ITT he discusses the corruption of Abiola and Obasanjo circa the '70s) and "Beast of No Nation," my favorite song. In "Beast" Fela asks, "What ting unite for United Nations? Disunited United Nations." And "How animal gon know slave trade don pass?"

Regarding UN "Human Rights" endeavors. Fela queried,

How animal gon dash (give) us human rights?
Human rights na (are) my property,
So therefore, you can't dash me my property.
Animal can't talk to human beings . . . .

Fela—Baba, 70. The only gift I have for you is Fela! When Fela died, the soul of Nigeria died! (When you hear his music you hear a strong P-Funk influence. An African-American sister named Sandra opened him up in the '60s.) How does Fela define democracy?

Crazy dem all
—Dem all crazy—
Crazy demonstration
—Dem all crazy—
Demonstration of craze
—Dem all crazy—

Keep on manifesting at full capacity, you are glowing all the way cross the Atlantic/Ethiopic. I send greetings of love and blessings to your children and loved ones.

Sista T

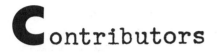

Contributors

Toyin Adewale is a native of Emure-Ekiti, Ekiti State, Nigeria. Born in 1969, she has absolutely no faith in zodiac signs. One night when she was 13, after a teenage spat with her parents, she put pen to paper to record her point of view and discovered she could write. She writes because she must, dreams swim in her, the swirling passion and pain and joy of her people, her life and the lives around her, all these come tumbling out because they refuse to be caged. She insists art is for life's sake. In a terrain where publishers don't like to risk their money on poetry, she is the happy author of *Naked Testimonies* (1995), *Die Aromaforscherin* (1997) and *Flackernde Kerzen* (1999), a work of prose.

Jane Alberdeston-Coralín was born in November 1968 on what was once known as Boriken, post-Colon-ization's bamboo canopied, salt-skinned Puerto Rico. Army-taught the Pledge of Allegiance before the alphabet, Jane moved with her family around the globe. In 1995 she landed like a flamboyan seed-pod in Washington, D.C. Here she found then lost her heart in the black writer's community which flourishes easy as runaway dandelions on the White House lawn's clipped and perfect arse. She braved overwhelming shyness reading in a local dive's slam competition, then bungee-jumped into performing at the much-loved "Its Your Mug" Poetry Cafe, Gala Hispanic Theatre, Nuyorican Poet's Café, Whitney Museum (NY), Philadelphia's Painted Bride. She was published most recently by *Bilingual Review Press* and *The Drumming Between Us.* Chapbooks *The Waters of My Thirst* and *The AfroTaina Dreams* are still in circulation. Her current pound of flesh, *Of Skin and Shadows,* is still cooking in the pot. A Cave Canem fellow 1998-2000, she still lives in DC.

Born in 1966 of a union between a thugging Muslim-to-be and a virginal future Jehovah's Witness, **Donnell Alexander** shed the husk of Sandusky, Ohio, to become the greatest juco success story this side of Latrell Sprewell. He cut his writing molars in the 1990s West Coast alternative press, appearing in the major California newsweek-lies, as well as various hip-hop journals. To sate his interest in all facets of popular culture, Alexander even briefly wrote for *ESPN The Magazine.* This writer publishes because he's from the same terrain as most Americans, and his journalism, at its best, transcends the media noise that insists humanity ain't about shit. He lives in Brooklyn.

Elizabeth Alexander—I was born in 1962 in Harlem, New York, and brought up in Washington, D.C. I have lived, studied, and worked up and down the eastern seaboard as well as in Chicago, and am now settled in New Haven, Connecticut. My work is teaching and writing. I have published two books of poems, *The Venus Hottentot* (1990) and *Body of Life* (1996), as well as many essays and articles on African-American literature and culture. I am presently finishing a third book of poems and a collection of essays. I write because words come to me and voices speak to me, asking to be recorded, and because I love to wrestle with shapes and language, and because writing is how I seem best able to contribute to others, and to honor and manifest what the ancestors (mine and ours) have worked for, hoped for, and died for.

Calling myself *Media Assassin* affirms that writing is best served as an act of transformative violence. When I was first published—in Brooklyn's *The City Sun,* then *The Village Voice,* where "Hip-Hop Hi-Tech" originally appeared ("It blew my mind," Dr. Tricia Rose said, while researching her seminal *Black Noise*)—one of my aims was to someday produce work so inflammatory that reading it in public might be deemed a seditious act.

I could claim that my intentions were formed by the circumstances of my birth: New York City, the '60s, just five days after John F. Kennedy's life, and white America's widely fabled innocence, both evaporated in an ethereal, pink mist from the president's fatal head wound.

But my objectives rise, instead, from the inevitability of my death. Living in Harlem, promised less life than a Bengali peasant, I've long concluded that the task of every sane Black writer is to *educate and excite, inform and infuriate;* not to placate, or to reassure, but to leave a bloody mess.
—Harry Allen

Jeffery Renard Allen—A writer has but one calling: to search out the distant reaches of the human heart. Reach the universal through the immediate and the particular. The Black writer shines his black light into all the dark and funky corners of our experience. Born in 1962, I was raised in South Shore, a black Chicago ghetto which on the surface appeared to be more-than-ghetto with its neat lawns and well-kept courtyard buildings. For twelve years, I put in work at the University of Illinois at Chicago, leaving in 1992 with a Ph.D. in English (Creative Writing), then moved to New York City to accept a full-time gig at Queens College, where I am presently an Associate Professor of English. I have been fortunate enough to publish two books, *Harbors and Spirits,* a collection of poems with a compact disc of me reading the entire text, and *Rails Under My Back,* a novel. I am presently completing *Stellar Places: One Hundred Poems,* and *Shadow Boxing: A Novel in Stories.* I am also at work on a novel, *Hours of the Seeds.* In the Far Rockaway section of Queens, I live, breathe, and write.

Born in 1960 in New York City with roots in Barbados, **Hilton Als** has been described as "a genius ashamed of nothing." Als is a staff writer at *The New Yorker.* The essay which appears in this anthology, "GWTW," first appeared in *Without Sanctuary: Lynching Photography in America.* Als' first book, *The Women,* was a *New York Times* Notable Book of the Year. He is currently completing another, also for Farrar, Straus & Giroux. Als is a graduate of the High School for the Performing Arts, and attended Columbia University. He lives in Manhattan. When asked why he does what he does, Als responded, simply, "Why I write: It defines me."

Angela Ards learned a love of words kneeling bedside, listening to her mother pray. She was born in Dallas in 1969, raised on James Cleveland, religious Aretha, Sam Cooke before he backslid, and speaking in tongues. "You can tell she goes to church," a teacher told her mother, when, at 3, she led (coerced?) her nursery school class in a spirited testimony and praise service. Her name, "Angela Ann"—bestowed by her big sister, Roslyn—means "graceful messenger," and she writes because it's always felt like the Universe's plan. A true Aries with Aquarius rising, she is a free spirit with deep passions that she's pondered and probed in the pages of *The Village Voice, The Nation, Emerge, The Source, Ms.,* and the anthology *Still Lifting, Still Climbing: African American Women's Contemporary Activism.* The Haywood Burns Fellow at the Nation Institute and an editor at Ms., she lives in Fort Greene, Brooklyn.

Jabari Asim—I am a journalist whose work has appeared in a number of anthologies, including *In The Tradition, Brotherman, Soulfires,* and *The Furious Flowering of African-American Poetry.* A dedicated husband, father, nerd, intellectual, "race man" and baseball fan, I'm not one of those sexy, hot-button scribes whose work is destined for big sales and widespread attention. I admire many of those writers and have often fervently wished that I might someday join their ranks, but it ain't gonna happen. That doesn't deter me, however, because obscurity does, in fact, have its own rewards. For example, there's . . .and . . .well . . .okay, I'll have to get back to you. Born in St. Louis in 1962, I grew up cheering the Gas House Gang and learned to take the work seriously while regarding my own neurotic self with a healthy sense of humor. Reasons I write: 1) few things make me happier; 2) I never learned to hit a curveball; 3) it beats waiting tables; and 4) I have no other marketable skills.

Erin Aubry—I write about politics and culture, and sometimes obviously about myself, but I've discovered that writing about the first two things together very often describes me more intimately than I can. This is both empowering and eviscerating. Black people by definition, by history, are still the avatars of American politics and culture, though we now struggle with the public expression of the individual, not the archetype or the mouthpiece; this will be the cultural battle of the twenty-first century. I do battle in Los Angeles, where I was born (in '62) and raised. I've written for the *Los Angeles Times,* have been a staff writer at *New Times Los Angeles* and am now staff writer at the *L.A. Weekly.* I've freelanced for *Contemporary Art Magazine, London Independent on Sunday* and *Black Enterprise,* to name a few publications. I've had essays anthologized in *Adios, Barbie* (Seal Press) and *Mothers Who Think* (Simon & Schuster). I've also written and performed poetry throughout Los Angeles.

Kevin Baldeosingh was educated at the University of the West Indies, and also got a degree there. After teaching for three years, he applied for a part-time position as a newspaper columnist with the *Trinidad Express.* His application letter began, "There are only two writers who people actually buy the newspaper to read. I propose to become the third." As a result of being so brass-faced, *Express* editor-in-chief Owen Baptiste hired Baldeosingh full-time as an editorial writer and columnist. After three years, a conflict between management and his journalistic ethics led to his resignation. He then worked as a feature writer and assistant editor at the *Trinidad Guardian*. After three years, a conflict between management and his journalistic ethics again led to his resignation. Baldeosingh was starting to see a pattern here. He now makes his living as a freelance writer. His two published novels are *The Autobiography of Paras P* and *Virgin's Triangle*. The first novel is a satire on politics, religion, media, social mores—in fact, just about everything. The second novel is a romantic comedy that begins "Thinking about sex and money," and proceeds from there. Baldeosingh likes squash, volleyball, tennis and the women who play them. Born in 1963 in Trinidad, he considers himself young and single, but hopes to get older one day. He writes because it gives him that bubbly, contented feeling that lesser men get from drinking champagne.

Ras Baraka has been called "one of the most consistent, courageous, and insightful activists of his generation." The son of revered poet-activists Amina and Amiri Baraka, Ras continues in that prominent legacy of art and community activism. Born in 1969 in Newark, New Jersey, Ras hails from a family that has lived in the city for over 70 years. As an artist, Ras independently released his debut spoken-word CD *Shorty for Mayor* in 1998. He is re-launching the project in 2000 with plans for national and internet distribution. One of its highlights is the never released single "Hot Beverage in Winter," which features Grammy-winning songstress Lauryn Hill, who weaved Baraka's vocals throughout both *The Score* by The Fugees and on her own *The Mis-Education of Lauryn Hill*. Co-editor of *In the Tradition* (with Kevin Powell), presently Ras is working on a second book and teaches fifth grade in the Newark public school system. His love for teaching is matched only by his passion for political equality. A former candidate for Mayor and the City Council, he plans another City Council bid in 2001.

Born in Hollywood, California, in 1974 under the sign of Aquarius, **Stefani Barber** spent her first years in a part of Los Angeles known, for various reasons, as "The Jungle." An only child, she and her parents moved throughout "South-Central" until one of their neighbors, who had a habit of passing out in his driveway, brought his trade a little too close to home, and the Barbers settled in the complacent working-class suburb of L.A. known as Carson. In the summer of 1990, she was named a California Arts Scholar, and attended the California State Summer School for the Arts, where she first came to believe in her identity as a poet—and began writing to attest to her growing political, social and sexual consciousness. Two years later, she escaped her Catholic high school and made her way to the Bay Area by way of Mills College in Oakland, where she got her first taste of organizing and hunger-striking. Now a graduate student at San Francisco State University, she performs non-socially-redeeming office work and dreams of being the world's sexiest salsera. She lives and loves in San Francisco.

Paul Beatty—I was born in Los Angeles in 1962. Raised on kung fu triple features, samurai movies with no swordplay, V-8, Philly cheesesteak sandwiches from Al's Sandwich Shop, and my mother's frayed paperback library. I write because I'm too afraid to steal, too ugly to act, too weak to fight, and too stupid in math to be a Cosmologist. As a result two volumes of poetry, *Big Bank Take Little Bank* and *Joker, Joker, Deuce,* and two novels, *The White Boy Shuffle* and *Tuff.*

A native of Atlanta, **Valerie Boyd** was born in 1963 on December 11. Using her Sagittarian qualities of seriousness and purposefulness, she is writing a forthcoming biography, *Wrapped in Rainbows: The Life of Zora Neale Hurston* (Scribner), because she feels called to do so. Her articles, essays and reviews have appeared in *Ms., The Oxford American, Emerge, Creative Nonfiction, The Washington Post* and *The Atlanta Journal-Constitution,* where she works part-time as an editor and book critic—despite her astrologer's advice to avoid a sedentary job. For her work on the Hurston biography, she was awarded a 1999 fellowship from the Howard Foundation of Brown University. To remain in touch with her inner callings, she meditates every day.

Charlie Braxton—Right now I am being attacked by a brigade of little green men who want me to tell you that I may or may not have been born in McComb, Mississippi, in 1961. They force-fed me some type of cornbread laced with a funny tasting substance that is compelling me to write down the first thing that comes to my mind. Damn! I hate doing bios. Excuse me. I mean, I don't like writing about myself. The major reason why I write is because the ancestors demand that I tell the truth. My captives insist that I am some sort of poet, playwright. They tell me that I am also a journalist and that I have had some things published in various magazines and journals such as the *Black Nation, Catalyst, Cut Banks* and anthologies such as *In The Tradition, Soulfires* and *Catch The Fire!!!* They also want you to know that I am currently being held up in a city called Jackson, Mississippi. Excuse me again. Huh? Okay, I'll tell 'em…no need to go postal on a brother.

When **Daphne A. Brooks** was 12 years old, she dreamed of flipping the script on Siskel and Ebert, Pauline Kael, and Kurt Loder. Toting a dog-eared blue notebook to multiplex matinees and arena concerts at the Circle Star Theatre, she left behind a paper trail of mad scribblings about Purple Rain and Doug E. Fresh. Term papers on Toni Morrison, James Baldwin, and the band Living Colour would prove joyful and career-altering distractions in college and grad school at U.C.-Berkeley and UCLA. Born in 1968 and raised in the San Francisco Bay Area by her educator parents, Brooks now spends her time teaching courses on African-American literature and popular culture at the University of California, San Diego. She's also writing a book on black performance in the 19th century. She holds high hopes of one day organizing a coalition for black folks who love baseball and who like to rock.

Tisa Bryant sent the editor this brief note as she was preparing to take a month-long journey to India: "I couldn't get too flossy with the bio; too pressed for time right now, and all that comes to mind is weird, unrelated stuff." That said, Tisa Bryant is a Boston native living well in San Francisco, where she is working on several projects to bring critical attention to avant-garde women writers of color. Her work has appeared in *Clamour, Chain, Kenning, Blithe House Quarterly,* and the anthology *Children of the Dream: Our Own Stories of Growing Up Black in America* (Pocket Books, 1999). Tisa's work will appear in the anthologies *Beyond The Frontier* (Black Classics Press) and *What Is Not Said.* A chapbook, *Tzimmes,* is forthcoming from A+Bend Press. The editor notes that Tisa's family migrated from Barbados and she was born somewhere in the vicinity of the late 1960s and the early 1970s.

Born in 1968 in Kalamazoo, Michigan, me, **Shonda Buchanan,** AKA Nyesha Khalfani, was raised shoeless, in a family of seven, all of us without a hint of guile, yet fiercely protective, same as the black moist earth that covers the landscape. Between pretending we were the Silvers and running away from home, my siblings loved hard and loud all the way across Kalamazoo, flinging one sister to Alabama, a brother to Arizona, another to Las Vegas, and me to Los Angeles, where I now reside, write and remember the poetry of their poker-hand lives. Paying my bills as an associate editor of a black magazine and freelancing for the *L.A. Weekly,* I write because my kin and my ancestors, both African and Native American, have placed their stories in my hands. I can't do anything else as well or as important as this. I am working on capturing several ancestors in my first novel, *Baring Cross.* Over the years, I've published varying episodes of these and my personal tales in *The Drumming Between Us, Caffeine Magazine, Venice Magazine,* and in the anthology *The Fire This Time.*

Paul Calderon was coaxed from the womb on the heels of the Watts Riots with much appreciated efforts from a Central American hairstylist and a Chicano mailman. As a child in L.A., the eternal glowing hot ambers of race influenced Paul heavily. While still trying to make sense of it all, he allowed himself to be swindled into the Air Force. He aimed high but missed. After adjusting his crosshairs, he wrote, produced, and directed plays. Looking for something true to grasp, Paul returned to Los Angeles and received a degree in philosophy. It was an opportunity for him to again attempt to make sense of the ashes of rebellion that over twenty years later still erupted into flames. Paul is noted for his use of poetry as a means of transcendental soul travel. His work has been published in numerous anthologies and literary journals. Paul's time now is spent strategically spreading the still hot ambers over the silver screen.

I, **Adrian Castro,** am a poet, performer, and interdisciplinary artist. I was born in 1967 in Miami from Cuban and Dominican heritage, a fact that has provided fertile ground for the rhythmic Afro-Caribbean style in which I write. I articulate the search for a cohesive Afro-Caribbean-American identity, and I honor myth on one hand and history on the other. I also address the migratory experience from Africa to the Caribbean to North America, and the inevitable clash of cultures. These themes reach their climax in their declamación: the circular, call-and-response rhythm of performance with a whole lot of tún-tún ká-ká pulse. I am the author of *Cantos to Blood & Honey* (Coffee House Press), and I've been published in a host of anthologies. I am the recipient of several grants and fellowships including NewForms Florida and

Florida Invididual Artist Fellowship, as well as several commissionings from the Miami Light Project and the Miami Art Museum. I am, too, a practicing herbalist and Babalawo.

Veronica Chambers was born in 1970 in Panama, where her people came from Jamaica, Martinique and Costa Rica to build the Panama Canal, not to mention this bridge called her back. She is the author of five books for adults and children including the critically acclaimed *Mama's Girl* and *Marisol and Magdalena: The Sound of Our Sisterhood.* A culture writer at *Newsweek,* she has also written for *The New York Times Magazine, Esquire* and *Harper's Bazaar.* The easy answer to why I write is because I love books and I want to add my voice to the chorus of singing that bellows across the ages and pages: Phyllis Wheatley's sweet soprano, James Baldwin's tenor, Toni Morrison's strong, clear alto.

Farai Chideya sees writing as both revolution and evolution. The daughter of a Zimbabwean journalist and a Baltimorean teacher, she grew up reading books like *They Came Before Columbus* and *Before the Mayflower*—with the Hobbit trilogy thrown in for good measure. Her work as a magazine and television journalist has sometimes made her an accomplice to the stereotyping of African-Americans. She must have written *Don't Believe the Hype: Fighting Cultural Misinformation About African-Americans* to ease her guilty conscience. Her second book, *The Color of Our Future,* tracks an America rapidly becoming "majority-minority." Born in 1969, Chideya resides in New York City.

Cheo Hodari Coker (born 12/12/72) has loved writing from the moment he first realized that he wasn't going to be the next Charlie Parker. But it was reading music books by Ross Russell, Nelson George, and Amiri Baraka, and talking to his high school idol, writer Robert Marriott, that made him realize that he could maybe make a contribution behind the scenes as a writer. Coker decided that writing about the new be-bop, "hip-hop," was his ticket, and when he picked up his first issue of *The Source* during the Spring of 1990, his life was altered forever. He would eventually pen pieces for *RapPages, Vibe, Spin, Rolling Stone, Urb, The Bomb,* and, yup, *The Source.* From 1995 to 1997 Coker was a staff writer for *The Los Angeles Times* Calendar section where he did everything from hang out with pimps in Washington, D.C., with the Hughes Brothers, to interviewing The Notorious B.I.G. 36 hours before his fatal March 9, '97 shooting. Around this time he had a crazy idea for a screenplay about the music industry, and with his uncle, veteran screenwriter Richard Wesley (*Uptown Saturday Night*), created the gritty hip-hop thriller *Flow,* which he sold to New Line Cinema. It will be produced and directed by John Singleton.

Wayde Compton—The first black population of my home province moved en masse from San Francisco to Victoria in the spring and summer of 1858, fleeing persecution in California and seeking gold, suffrage, and equal rights under the Union Jack in British Columbia. Some of them did find a little gold. Most of them returned to the

States after the Civil War and the abolition of slavery. I was born in Vancouver in 1972, and I didn't descend directly from those blacks, but I inherited their false-start history. I was born to a white mother from Toronto and a black father from Philadelphia, and then adopted by a similar set-up—my white Vancouverite mother and my black father from Houston, Texas. So the personal and the public drive my interest in settlement, dispersal, voice, and authenticity, my regionalized, racialized I. "If," as Paul Beatty writes, "niggers could fly," British Columbia would be the layover capital of the world. My first book of poems is *49th Parallel Psalm* (Arsenal Pulp Press, 1999). I'm currently at work editing *Blueprint: An Anthology of Black British Columbian Literature and Orature,* and a novel, *Boxing the Compass.*

Ricardo Cortez Cruz [born 1964 in Decatur IL] relishes the compositions done from his coffin He writes novel ideas *Straight Outta Compton* [called one of 1992's best efforts by *The Nation*] *Five Days of Bleeding* his pointing finger turning into a phono-GRAPHIC needle his rap (Gil Scott-Heron "B-movie"-like lyrics of social protest) Shure enuff embedded in nouveau grooves exploring the thin lines of black skin He keeps digging into and collecting more disturbing parts of violence *Premature Autopsies* (*Tales of Darkest America*) suggests BODIES NEVER LIE period; cuts pieces have appeared in *New American Writing, Fiction International, African American Review, Postmodern Culture, The Kenyon Review,* a Norton anthology, and *Obsidian II.* Schooling half-white college students, etc. at Illinois State in black English he moves the crowds spitting messages for the record as if his life his very lively hood depends upon it

Ten Things About **Edwidge Danticat:**

1. She was born in Port-au-Prince, Haiti, in 1969.
2. She now lives—mostly—in Brooklyn, New York.
3. She is the oldest child, and only daughter, among four siblings.
4. She is the very proud aunt of Nadira, and Karl Ezekiel Danticat.
5. She hates talking on the phone.
6. She is the author of two novels *Breath, Eyes, Memory,* and *The Farming of Bones* and a collection of short stories *Krik? Krak!* (Maybe that's three things)
7. She is the editor of a collection of essays called *The Butterfly's Way: Voices from the Haitian Dyaspora in the United States.*
8. She loves to read and tries to read a chapter in a book, a short story, or an essay each day.
9. She loves writing—
10. But hates writing bios.

Born in Berkeley, California in 1971 and raised on major seventh chords, tofu burgers, orthodox Marxism, and public transit, **Eisa Davis** began her first screenplay, *Cockleburrs in My Sock,* at age 6. She broke the record for the 25-yard breaststroke in Birmingham, Alabama, a year later. Truncating a career as a concert pianist, she went to Harvard to study philosophy but was increasingly drawn to the schizoid joys of theatre. After graduating, she moved to Los Angeles then New York to pursue her Master's in acting and playwriting at the Actors Studio School. Eisa has contributed to *The Source, Rap Sheet,* and the anthologies *To Be Real* and *Letters of Intent.* A recipient of fellowships from the Mellon Foundation, the MacDowell Colony, and Cave Canem, her most recent work is *Paper Armor,* a play about the ill-fated *Mule Bone* collaboration between Langston Hughes, Zora Neale Hurston, and Louise Patterson. She lives in Brooklyn, New York.

Kwame Dawes was born in Accra, Ghana to a Jamaican novelist father and a Ghanaian scupltor mother. There he learnt the taste and smell of the yoyi and discovered Jamaica in songs and folk tales that his father told. The clan of five children and parents moved to Jamaica in 1971 when Kwame was nine. Kingston, pulsing with reggae, flirting with socialism and fighting the legacy of colonialism, was the site of Kwame's awakening as an artist, poet, and playwright. He has lived in various places and has published six collections of poetry, a seminal work on reggae and art titled *Natural Mysticism,* and is awaiting publication of two novels and a collection of short stories. Though Kwame is labeled variously as a poet, fiction writer, academic, editor, playwright, musician and artist, he knows that ultimately he is nothing but a storyteller who is constantly seeking to write his Christian faith and his historical self into moving art. In fall 2000 his latest collection of poems, *Midlands,* a series of poems that feed on the landscape of South Carolina and that of Jamaica, will appear with Ohio University Press. The manuscript was selected by Eavan Boland as the winner of the Hollis Summers Poetry Prize.

Jarvis Q. DeBerry was born in September 1975 and grew up in Holly Springs, Mississippi, where he read lots of books, played kickball with his 30 cousins and listened to his family tell funny stories at high volumes. He studied engineering at Washington University in St. Louis before ditching that program to study English. An editorial writer at the *Times-Picayune* newspaper in New Orleans, DeBerry's work has appeared in *Speak the Truth to the People,* an anthology of the NOMMO Literary Society. DeBerry writes because "If I didn't, I'd be even more verbose which would chase all my friends away."

Junot Díaz was born in the Dominican Republic, three years after the Dominican Revolution was crushed by U.S. Marines. As a child he watched a U.S.-backed security apparatus eliminate what remained of the Dominican Left. He immigrated to the U.S. in the mid-seventies, endured plenty of post-Vietnam War racism, worked in a steel mill, delivered pool tables and believes that global elites centered in Europe and North America are the true enemies of planetary democracy. He is the author of *Drown*; his fiction has appeared in *The New Yorker, African Voices* and *Best American Short Stories 1996, 1997,* and *1999.*

Debra Dickerson—I write to sing the song of the black working class. I was born in St. Louis, in 1959, to escaped sharecroppers. I'm still trying to get over that, mostly by writing about the world those migrants made. My escape route? The Air Force. Those polyester-wearing rednecks taught me how to be me—my talent was too valuable for them to waste, so they didn't. They tried to make a damn general out of me. Stayed twelve years and didn't start writing until my thirties. Now, as a senior fellow at the New America Foundation, I write about black life in publications like *Talk, The Village Voice, Good Housekeeping, Salon, The Washington Post, Essence, Vibe* and *The New Republic.* Much as we complain about being invisible, my writing often upsets my fellow Negroes. This both saddens and amuses me. Go on and get mad, but I still win awards and get included in other Negroes' anthologies. "Disappearing Acts" won the New York Association of Black Journalists First Place award for Personal Commentary in 1999; "Who Shot Johnny" was included in *The Best American Essays 1997.* And my memoir of political and social conflict within the black community, *An American Story,* was recently published by Pantheon.

Tananarive Due (b. 1966)—The daughter of two Civil Rights activists, Tananarive Due was 14 when she realized that writing might save her life: In 1980, several white police officers were acquitted for beating black motorcyclist Arthur McDuffie to death. While Miami's inner-city went up in flames, Due wrote an essay, "I Want to Live," about the world she wanted to live in, free of bigotry—and the knot burning in her chest went away. (Her mother told her she was lucky she could write, because the people rioting in the streets had no other outlet for their pain and frustration.) Due would eventually study journalism and creative writing at Northwestern University, then obtain a Master's degree from the University of Leeds, England, specializing in the literature of the Nigerian civil war. A former features writer and columnist for *The Miami Herald,* Due published her first novel, *The Between,* in 1995. Her second book, *My Soul to Keep,* was published in 1997 and named one of the best novels of the year by *Publishers Weekly.* Due's current effort, *The Black Rose,* based on the life of Madam C.J. Walker, is a historical novel written in conjunction with the Alex Haley Estate. (Haley had always intended to write about Walker, the first black female millionaire, before he died in 1992.) She will publish *The Living Blood,* a sequel to *My Soul to Keep,* in early 2001. Due lives in Longview, Washington, with her husband, science fiction novelist Steven Barnes.

Trey Ellis—I was a faculty brat so we moved around every six years or so. I was born in 1962 at Howard University while my father was finishing up medical school. We moved from there to the University of Michigan to Yale to Columbia by the time I was in the tenth grade. I attended Andover, the oldest boarding school in the country, but now made infamous by the Bushes père and fils. When I was there you'd have a hard time finding even one Republican, I swear. I then went to Stanford where I majored in creative writing and it was there that I began *Platitudes* (1988), my first novel. *Home Repairs* followed in 1994 and *Right Here, Right Now* in 1999 which won an American Book Award. I have also written several screenplays including HBO's *The Tuskegee Airmen* for which I was nominated for an Emmy. I am also proud of my essays including "The New Black Aesthetic."

When **Ekow Eshun** was 11, he wanted to grow up to be Spiderman. Unable to find a radioactive spider he decided to become a journalist. Which meant having a voice in a society that prefers to condemn black people rather than listen to them. He was born in London in 1968, the son of parents who emigrated to Britain from Ghana. Ekow is a journalist, broadcaster and cultural critic. From 1996-99 he was editor-in-chief of *Arena* magazine, and from 1993-96, assistant editor of *The Face.* Ekow likes to say what he thinks and hates being described as articulate—as if that's a novelty in a black person.

Bernardine Evaristo—I was born in London in 1959 to a Nigerian father and white English mother with further umbilical attachments to Ireland, Germany and Brazil. I spent my childhood inhabiting other people's lives through books and pretending to be someone else at the local youth theatre. The black presence in Britain goes back to at least the Roman occupation 2000 years ago, yet it is a history that is only now being uncovered. This is what spurs me on to write: to put the books on the shelves that were not there when I was growing up. My books are a poetry collection, *Island of Abraham* (1994), and a verse novel, *Lara* (1997), which won the EMMA Best Novel Award. I am also featured in many anthologies and magazines, and my forthcoming verse novel, *The Emperor's Babe,* will be published by Penguin/Hamish Hamilton in Spring 2001. A full-time writer, I tour world-wide giving readings, having completed 18 international trips in the past two years. I now reside with my current husbands, eunuchs, soothsayers, sycophants and a harem of rugby players in a bedouin tent in Notting Hill, London.

"So, you written that bio, man?" "Nah." "What's up?"
"Just got this thing about bios." "What?" "You include
a bio and it like recontextualizes the piece."
"Recontextualizes the piece? What's this
recontextualizes the piece bullshit?" "I tell people I
was born in 1966 in Kingston, Jamaica, I tell people I went to
Harvard or that I'm a senior writer for *Time* magazine, and
they'll like read my work differently." "Check it out,
check it out—this shit's simple. Where you from?" "I
don't want to say." "You just said the shit a second
ago." "That was a different context." "Okay, what's
the name of your first novel?" "*My Favorite War,*
published in hardcover by Farrar, Straus & Giroux.
The Washington Post called it 'one of those rare
jewels,' and Terry McMillan said she liked it too. It's
available in paperback from Ecco Press for $13. It
makes a great stocking stuffer...." "Okay, okay, enough.
You know, on second thought, I think you need to like,
keep your shit on the down low and let your work speak
for itself." "See? That's what I'm saying...."
—Christopher John Farley

Nikky Finney was born in Conway, South Carolina, in 1957, at the mouth of the Atlantic Ocean. She was raised in several different small towns all across the state. Choosing to remain in her beloved southland, she graduated from Talladega College in Talladega, Alabama. Her first book of poems, *On Wings Made of Gauze,* was published in 1985. She has been published in the anthologies, *In Search of Color Everywhere* (1994), *I Hear a Symphony* (1994), *Spirit and Flame* (1996), and *Bloodroot* (1998). The 1999 anthology, *The Bluelight Corner,* takes its name from a line found in her poem, "The Turtle Ball." She works and writes in Lexington, Kentucky, where she is a founding member of a community-based writing collective, The Affrilachian Poets. And she is an Associate Professor of Creative Writing at the University of Kentucky. Finney's second book of poetry, *Rice,* won the PEN American Open Book Award in 1999. She is also the author of *Heartwood* (1998), a collection of short stories written especially for literacy students. Two new books of poetry are forthcoming. Nikky Finney travels extensively, meets with young writers, and reads her work and conducts numerous writing workshops at universities and arts festivals, as well as around kitchen and coffee tables.

Ruth Forman—I was born in 1968 in Cape Cod by deep woods and deep water, raised later in Rochester, New York, under a cruel urban sky. Been writing poems since age seven, lost interest when taught the beauty of poetry lay in structure, not content. Rediscovered it, though, at UC-Berkeley as something personal, tangible, and a way to fly. Been writing ever since. Studied with greats like Ishmael Reed, June Jordan and Yusef Komunyakaa. From each I learned a different beauty and truth. Now in Los Angeles, I write to keep magic in my life. Hope some gold will dust the fingers of those who read *We Are the Young Magicians* and *Renaissance.* I find strength in the company of an ever expanding fleet of young writers of color, and I credit my vision and inspiration from voices not only before me, but those singing at this very moment. We are not individuals, but a chorus.

Lynell George—Some say I write in the wilds. That Los Angeles is without spirit, center or core. That it is all talk and flash and quick-cut moments—no quietude and certainly no substance. That it is the quarrelsome child cast to the farthest corner, constantly carrying on, throwing tantrums for attention. But as a native, born in 1962, I constantly box with the city and its issues and I'm proud of how it belligerently redefines itself—refuses definition. A writer's perfect sparring partner. No better place/moment to be a journalist where race and culture and language and crisis constantly converge before they converse. Out of it has come various meditations: *No Crystal Stair: African Americans in the City of Angels* (Verso/Anchor 1992/93). My work has appeared in various publications including *Vibe, Essence, L.A. Weekly* (staff writer 1987-1993), *Newsday,* and *The Boston Globe.* I've been the recipient of the National Association of Black Journalists' award for 1992's best hard-feature for a series on Black independent schools. Currently, I'm a staff writer for *The Los Angeles Times* where I piece together the mosaic of race, culture and art. Why do I write: "I write to try to understand *Why?*"

Danielle Legros Georges arrived on these shores armed only with the English word *fish*. She would later add such terms as *rope, trope,* and *microscope* to her linguistic arsenal. Born in 1964 in Gonaïves, Haiti, and reborn in Mattapan, Massachusetts, U.S.A., Georges wrestled with crocodiles, circumvented the jaws of Boston busing, outmaneuvered ruffians, and when unable to do that, outran them—in her youth. She has since developed a mean look, a bad reputation, and credits in publications including *The Beacon Best of 1999, The Butterfly's Way, Encarta Africana, The American Poetry Review, Black Renaissance/Renaissance Noire,* and *The Caribbean Writer.* Georges writes, she says, "Where the tongue in my mouth fails me . . . writing is both a *lwa* that rides my head and a demon I am forced to feed . . ." For immediate nutrition, she works, happily, as a college instructor and editor in Boston.

Brian Gilmore—all writers only have one story to tell. the writer just keeps telling his/her story differently. my story begins a few years after my birth in 1962 in washington, dc. one Saturday morning my father cut off our house television. my brothers and i had been watching "tarzan." he told us how stupid we were for watching such an absurd program. my father eventually stopped most of the television watching in our home and replaced our television time with books like *the narrative of the life of fredrick douglass.* my mother loves the written word. not only did she read to us all the time, but we were constantly tested on our "english" and vocabulary. by 1985, reaganomics was real and apartheid was being crushed in south africa. i began to write poetry. i was attending a racially- hostile, mostly white college away from washington and its uplifting "chocolate city" culture. my father sent me some "dubois" books to read. my mother always read my poetry and critiqued it. in 1993, third world press published my collection of poems entitled *elvis presley is alive and well and living in harlem.* my second collection, *jungle nights and soda fountain rags: poem for duke ellington,* will be published in 2000 by karibu books.

Cege Githiora was born in Mang'u, Kenya, in 1966. He lived in Mexico for 6 years and backpacked through Mexico and several other countries of Latin America. Cege profoundly believes that Africans and those in the Diaspora are branches of the same tree and he writes fiction, essays and poetry about this tree in Gĩkũyũ, English, Swahili and Spanish. Some of his research was published in *Conexoes,* an African Diaspora Research Project Newsletter at Michigan State University. Cege's poems and short stories appear regularly in *The Gĩkũyũ Journal of Literature and Culture,* and *Mûtiiri,* edited by Kenyan writer and activist Ngũgî wa Thiong'o. Currently Cege teaches African Languages and Culture at Boston University. "I write," he says, "for education and inspiration."

Malcolm Gladwell was born in England in 1963 and raised in Canada, in a small farming town called Elmira in the southern Ontario Bible-Belt. Elmira had one bar (the Steddick), one Jew (Harry Coblentz), one black (Malcolm's mother) and twenty-three Protestant churches. He escaped first to the University of Toronto, and then to the United States, where he worked at *The Washington Post* for nine years, first as a business reporter, then as a science reporter, and finally as the paper's New York bureau chief. Since 1996, he has been a staff writer for *The New Yorker*. In 2000, he published his first book, *The Tipping Point,* an examination of social epidemics. He lives in New York, and considers himself a stealth negro: white enough to pass, but black enough to know better.

Born in North-Brabant, in 1970, **Scotty Gravenberch** was welcomed by his grand-mother as the next phase in a then 150-year running experiment of trans-ethnic gene swapping. In the 15 years that followed his parents took him for a world-wide run through Western civilisation, touching base on well-known settlements such as El Paso, Sidney, Blomberg and Maarssen. Scotty's aesthetics proved to be a "projection screen" for locals, categorising him each time as the country's national minority. This strange quality of human fantasy pushed him to reflection. He has written a range of articles, discussion papers for NGOs, short stories, and he edited a book on the Dutch folklore figure Zwarte Piet (Black Pete). Scotty is currently an Amsterdam- based editor for "The Blue Light," a weekly television show on media culture.

dream hampton was born on the East Side of Detroit, and she celebrated her first birthday the day the Attica rebellion came to a naked, murderous end. Her father's nickname was "Soul" and he spent much of the seventies in pink foam rollers. Hustlers and their sister-friends would always ask her "Ain't you Soul's baby?" to which she would reply "mmm-hmm." dream was also raised by a loving mom from Indiana, a stepfather who loved Bird, and the Kubrick catalog. Throughout her teens and much of her twenties dream had a deep love affair with hip-hop, which has since ended. She's been published in *The Source, Vibe, The Village Voice, Ego Trip, Essence, RapPages, Spin, The Detroit News,* and *Parenting.* Now the true love of her life is her daughter, who is named after Nina Simone.

Duriel E. Harris—After 10 years out east, I've returned to my native Chicago to face my demons & to pull off a doctorate while teaching and writing in opposition (to what?: hostile counter-narratives lap at life/cacophony gnaws belly/perpetually birthing itself). My writing, my self becoming self-fragmented/(w)hole-pushing witness, joy-backside-suffering, makes its way in print and performance shouting: we are. (Shout-ing: Buy my chapbook, *but there are miles!* Read *Obsidian III*!) Ahem. In summer '99 (blessing), it took me to Cave Canem, to folk, to Black Took Collective—we are, we take, will not be eaten—& as of late it returns me to Funk, my pulse/percussive muse (beat)/always already unknown changing & same (mythology: Xmas '69, I fell from my mother's body upon the tail of movements). My writing, my self becoming self, is PoMoFunk (fo mo funk), voicings & vernacular evidence, transgressing.

Yona Harvey was born in the stubborn light of Ohio, 1974. Shy and tender-headed, she survived her suburban upbringing (peppered with Pentecostal sermons) and escaped to a city made of chocolate. She craved the sweet and ugly stories of her people and learned to kindle them with memory. She married a man not frightened by her recipes, calls her daughter a flower, and currently lives in New Orleans. Her work appears or is forthcoming in *Testimony, Catch the Fire!!! Obsidian III: Literature in the African Diaspora, Indigo, Speak the Truth to the People*, and *Beyond the Frontier.* The first girl "caught" with underarm hair in sixth grade and the last girl permitted to see R-rated movies, Yona writes to embrace the awkwardness and humor of Black life; she cannot stop.

Terrance Hayes is an utter failure as a mute. There are haiku tattooed across his tongue. Fashioned out of graphite & invisible ink, he sprang from the ear of an unwed mother circa 1971, in a condemned South Carolina hospital. Several moons later *Muscular Music* (Tia Chucha Press, 1999) was born. In the last year he has won a $35,000 Whiting Emerging Writers Award, a $5000 Kate Tufts Discovery Award & various other potentially damaging spoils, not only because of his poetry, but his legendary good luck. Presently dwelling in wild-ass New Orleans, Louisiana, Hayes is wooed daily by the song & spirit of his muse, Yona, & the coos of their Libra daughter, Ua Pilar. He writes things down because he suffers chronic forgetfulness. Whenever you see smoke drifting from his mouth, it means a poem has caught fire in his gut.

On the 14th day of May, 1966, in the sleepy south of Nigeria, a cry pierced the pastoral veil of the town of Oleh, Delta State, to announce the birth of **Ogaga Ifowodo.** Christened Ezekiel to sustain the Hebrew tongue, he translated that name into Isoko, his native language, and God did not take offence! It was his fate to study law and also to devote too much time to reading the wrong books, poetry, and student activism. The latter earned him indefinite suspension from university and delayed his admission to the finishing law school until a month to the bar exams. In his fourth form, his poem won first prize in an annual school contest. He is author of *Homeland & Other Poems*, winner of the 1993 Association of Nigerian Authors poetry prize; *Madiba* (forthcoming); and *Homeland: A German-English Issue of Selected Poems*. In 1997/98, he was detained for 6 months by the great dictator, General Abacha. But the PEN centres of Germany, Canada and the USA thought a "security risk" was the very kind of person for honorable society; the latter even named him recipient of the 1998 Barbara Goldsmith Freedom-to-Write Award. He was also given the Free Word Award of the Netherlands-based Poets of All Nations. He lives in Lagos and works with a human rights NGO in the foolish belief that POWER and the Consumer Society can be prevailed upon not to breed poverty and misery for the overwhelming number of earth's inhabitants.

Esther Iverem—It has slowly dawned on me the reason for my 1960 birth and childhood in North Philly: shuttling between the speakeasy-cabaret-Johnnie Walker Red existence of my father's family and the holy ghost-testifying-choir singing folks on my mom's side. They, the streets, roaches and the deconstruction of capitalism all prepared me to know the world in its entirety. Everything else—USC, Columbia, *The Wilmington News-Journal, The New York Times, New York Newsday*, poetry readings, anthologies, performances with Fred Ho, marriage-childbirth-divorce, a phat-ass fellowship from the National Arts Journalism Program, *The Washington Post*, now

BET.com—has been a way station after being launched into the world, skinny and anemic, by an always lover who told me to fly. I write to have voice in a world that wants to create us, frame us and speak for us from the outside. I write so we are not annihilated culturally, spiritually and politically. My book is *The Time: Portrait of a Journey Home,* a collection of poems and photographs, which I think accomplishes my other writer's goal: to leave some intelligent record of a black woman's life in my time on earth. After Philly, L.A. and New York, I am now camped out in Chocolate City with my son Mazi and working on a collection of cultural criticism that you should see this year. I am flying. I am a child of Oya—woman warrior, wife of Shango and the spirit of the wind.

Lisa Victoria Chapman Jones/Victoria, after the queen; Chapman after my great-great-grandmother, Delphia Chapman, who was once enslaved in America and whose untimely death at age 105 was caused by fire/born the year *Purlie Victorious* opened on Broadway/grew up between the East Village and Newark/daughter of writers/grand-daughter of a post-office supervisor and a social worker/made literary debut at age seven reciting poetry on stage at the Negro Ensemble Company Theater/former *Village Voice* columnist/author of *Bulletproof Diva: Tales of Race, Sex, and Hair*/day job: screenwriter/working on a new book/favorite biblical romance: Jacob and Rachel/plan to be reincarnated as Fredi Washington/if I were a love song, I'd be sung by Marvin Gaye and Delroy Wilson.

With no tummy-tuck, no breast implants and no rhinoplasty in her past or immediate future, **Sarah Jones** is gravely jeopardizing her shot at the head-waitress position at a local Hooters franchise. The NYC-based writer/actress, who was born in Baltimore, Maryland (pronounced MURR-lind), in 1973, is trying to balance her passion for crabcakes and long-winded anecdotes, gifts from her daddy, with the Joni Mitchell habit and freckles she picked up from her Irish-German-Caribbean mama. Her work knows neither shame (she won the 1997 Nuyorican Poets Cafe's Grand Slam, performed her solo show *Surface Transit* off-Broadway, appears on the *Lyricist Lounge Vol. 1* hip-hop/poetry compilation, and once worked on an MTV sitcom) nor loyalty to either the stage (Lincoln Center, The Public Theater, HBO Workspace, Aaron Davis Hall) or the page (*A Gathering of the Tribes, The Village Voice, The Source,* the self-published *Your Revolution*). Jones appears in Spike Lee's film, *Bamboozled,* is at work on her second play and first novel, and will continue to travel via *Surface Transit,* winner of the HBO U.S. Comedy Arts Festival's Jury Award for Best One-Person Show, while the rest of the world takes its time discovering the touchable, bouncing and behaving finesse of dreadlocks.

Allison Joseph—I was born in London in 1967, but I never saw the country because my Jamaican-born mom and Grenadian-born dad left England when I was three-months-old. We moved to Toronto, then settled in the Bronx in 1971. I went to the Bronx High School of Science, where, believe it or not, the hallways were full of poets. Then I went to Kenyon College in Ohio, a school famed for its literary reputation—a reputation that was pretty male and all white until I arrived. I graduated, self-respect intact, and went to Indiana University, where I had the great pleasure of studying with Yusef Komunyakaa. I published my first book, *What Keeps Us Here,* in 1992—it won the Women Series Poets Prize from (now-defunct) Ampersand Press. *Soul Train* (Carnegie Mellon, 1997) and *In Every Seam* (Pitt Poetry Series, 1997) were follow-up volumes. I now teach creative writing at Southern Illinois University in Carbondale, Illinois. Teaching and writing are like air to me—I can't do without either—so I'm a happy woman.

Concepts: freedom, strangeness, anarchy, avantgardism, chance:: born in MalcolmX-SelmaMarchdeathyear in apartheidcity (stlouis) USA::reared to Jazz, romancatholicism, TV, R&B and disco, punk(s)rock, 1970s hope & failure, Reaganism, cheap drugs, AIDS, hiphop, "end of..."::studied in parochial/prep schools, streets and suburbanculdesacs, Harvard, NYU::editor, author, amateur artist, work in *AA Review, Code, Hambone, Kenyon, Ploughshares, Washington Post Book World,* on line, etc.::member of the Dark Room, Cave Canem::fellowships from Mass Arts Foundation, NY Times Foundation, Yaddo, Bread Loaf::published ANNOTATIONS (New Directions, 1995)::honors—Critics' Choice Award, Fund for Poetry, AGNI/John Cheever Prize, Best Gay American Fiction::lives in NJ {partner CurtisJAllen}::writing working living loving::concepts—simultaneity, indeterminacy, mysticism, blackness as a vast cultural and historic field::
—John R. Keene

Born in New York City in 1962, **Robin D. G. Kelley** drifted between Harlem, Seattle, Pasadena and Los Angeles, California, until he landed a job as Professor of History and Africana Studies at New York University. When Kelley isn't trying to play the piano or living out his poetry or explaining what his middle initials stand for, he spends his spare time writing articles and books. His last book, *Yo' Mama's DisFunktional!: Fighting the Culture Wars in Urban America* (Beacon Press, 1997), was selected by *The Village Voice* as one of its top ten books of 1998. He is currently writing a book on jazz pianist/composer Thelonious Monk. Kelley once confessed: "I became an historian in search of the truth, but the more I write the more I realize that 'facts' don't yield real truths. As a writer I'm only beginning to plumb the depths of the unconscious, the soul, the spirit, surreality. Twelve years and four books later, I feel like I'm just getting started."

I am a first-generation American, born in Boston in 1968 and now living in San Francisco. Name: **Arnold J. Kemp.** My parents insisted that I practice reading and writing from day one. My mother comes from Panama (her parents from Trinidad), is fluent in Spanish and was determined that I not speak in a monotone, that being the opposite of the rolling Rs and music of her native Spanish. My father, on the other hand, comes from Nassau, Bahamas and was raised speaking "The Queen's English." He was determined that I only speak that language and detested any sign of singing in my speech. Once the parental commands were ingrained, I was left in a funny place as a writer, sort of standing between two worlds. The excitement of that balancing act keeps me interested in writing. My work has appeared in *Callaloo, Three Rivers Poetry*

Journal, Agni Review, Mirage #4/Period[ical], River Styx, and *Eyeball.* I am a practicing visual artist and curator.

Jake Lamar—I was born in 1961 and grew up near Yankee Stadium in the Bronx, New York. After graduating from Harvard in 1983, I served a six-year sentence writing for *Time* magazine before escaping and devoting myself to writing books. In 1991 I published *Bourgeois Blues*—the title is taken from a famous Leadbelly song—a memoir about my relationship with my father and our experiences as black men in America. Since then I've focused on fiction, publishing a satiric thriller about American racial politics, *The Last Integrationist,* in 1996, and *Close to the Bone,* a multiracial romantic comedy set during the O.J. Simpson trial, in 1999. My new novel, a murder mystery titled *If 6 Were 9,* will be published in March 2001. In September 1993 I came to Paris, France for what has turned out to be a permanent visit.

Q: Why do I write?
A: Writing serves pretty much the same function in my life as oxygen.

Victor D. LaValle (1972-)

When I was young my best friend and me would run through Flushing, Queens, like we were dying the next day. One early afternoon my boy and I walked up Colden Street to find Stavres, a girl, outside. If we were seven she was four. We asked her where her ball was that she was always bouncing. Stavres said she didn't know. I asked if we could play together. When she agreed I took the chance and pointed to one standard city sight: dog shit. Prodding her, then pleading, we got that kid bent over the tidy brown mass. Pick it up, I said, with my friend laughing. Pick it up. She took it. We urged Stavres back to her house and then the sound of mother coming. And we said for Stavres to go show her. When she did the mother yelled baldly like she didn't recognize her daughter. Shut the door from her girl even as Stavres stood quietly, bearing a gift. And this is why I write. Because it's true I'm the boy laughing in the street, but you're the mother who shut the door. And I love ugly, so I love you.

My book, *slapboxing with jesus,* is in your bookstore.

Itumeleng oa Mahabane, Johannesburg, South Africa—I'm a school drop-out born on May 14, 1974. While people were attending lectures I pretended to write a novel. It was coming well, in terms of volume, but I wasn't sure even John Grisham's publishers won't read more than the first line. So when it became clear I was destined to be little more than an uneducated bum with the phrase "paradigm shift" in his vocabulary, I began having visions of high school reunions with my private school peers, many of whom were at Ivy League or other prestigious institutions of higher learning all over the world. I realised that I would have to find an alternative. So I enrolled in a journalism crash course. Then I worked as a cadet journalist at the country's most prestigious weekly which is now the country's most trashy and reactionary weekly. Since then I've been a TV listing journalist—if you can call it journalism. I've been a media officer for an arts festival. I've been a media officer for the Greater Johannesburg Metropolitan Council. I've been a scriptwriter: one feature still to be produced, two educational television shows, and one pilot docu-drama. Then I managed to land a gig pretending to be editor of the most boring but officially the most pretentious culture magazine in the country; and somehow I've landed up as contributing editor—read: mid-stream journalist with fancy title—at the most dubious business and current affairs journal in the country.

Shara McCallum—I began to write, I think, first out of the need to cohere the story of the life I had been given, ostensibly by my parents. My mother was a Venezuelan-Jamaican woman, my father a Jamaican man of mixed African, Indian and European descent. Both were Rastafarians and raised my sisters and I as such while we lived in Jamaica, where I was born in 1972. I moved to America around the age of nine, the same year my father died. Removed from the country, language, culture and even family structure I had before known created a space in me that, when I first started to write, I looked to poetry to fill. The moment I became a writer though was the moment I realised not only the ability of a poem to tell some kind of "truth" but also the power of poetry to lie. Poetry has taught me how to write myself into being and counter fragmentation through the lie of wholeness a poem constructs. As a Jamaican-American woman, as a white-skinned black person, as a child now woman of different languages, heritages and cultures, poetry and the process of becoming have been intertwined. Poetry is what has allowed me to live these hybridised spaces, these identities in conflict, and to move away from the sentimental "tragedy of the mulatta" or of any figure of "exile."

Editor's note: Shara McCallum currently lives in Tennessee where she teaches in the MFA program at the University of Memphis. Her first book, *The Water Between Us,* won the 1998 Agnes Lynch Starrett Poetry Prize. Her poems have won an Academy of American Poets Prize, been nominated for three Pushcart Prizes and have appeared in several journals.

Though he was once married, it is rumored that **Tony Medina** is still a virgin. In 1991, he popped his literary cherry with the publication of his first collection of poetry, Emerge & See. He went on to bust a few more: *No Noose Is Good Noose, Sermons from the Smell of a Carcass Condemned to Begging,* and *Memories of Eating.* He also edited the award-winning anthology, *In Defense of Mumia,* and helped produce *Catch the Fire!!!* Born in the South Bronx of a Puerto Rican family tree, in 1966, he's traveled far and wide to settle just a few train stops away, in Harlem. When he's not out trying to save the world with his poetry, passion, and politics, you can find him giving repeat performances for his English students at Long Island University, in Brooklyn.

Jessica Care Moore is a writer/poet/scorpio/mommy/publisher born in 1971 to an English mum and an Alabama daddy. Raised on the Westside of Detroit, her desire to know and later tell everybody's business landed her writing jobs in television and print media. In 1995 she packed up her purple Ford Ranger and moved to Brooklyn to let everybody on the East Coast know how one of Motown's biggest motor mouths gets down. She made her-story in 1996, and became an Apollo legend, after winning a record five times in a row with her poetry. Not bad for a Midwest baby. She is the founder of Moore Black Press, which boasts noted authors such as Saul Williams and Sharrif Simmons. She is the author of her own book, *The Words Don't Fit in My Mouth*, and is working on her second release, *The Alphabet Versus the Ghetto*. A blind man once told her she looked like Ntozake Shange. She wants to know what this means. She writes so she won't hurt anybody. She wants to be a rock star and is busy recording her first musical release with her poetry/rock/hip-hop band, Detroit Read (pronounced like the color). She lives in Harlem with her two favorite fish, Sharrif and Omari Simmons.

Lenard D. Moore was born in 1958 on the black drum-beating earth of Jacksonville, North Carolina, where his literary roots are, but he currently lives in Raleigh. Although LDM no longer runs the 440-yard dash or chases his cousin's runaway pony, Moore's footsteps linger for his Gemini daughter to paint onto canvas, while his heart drums haiku. In boyhood, while listening to his grandfather's storytelling, Lenard felt words catch fire in his own throat. The aroma of Lenard's father and mother cooking collards, frying chicken, steaming rice, simmering gravy, and baking cornbread lodged in his memory. Chopping weeds and hilling/healing corn and peanuts in his great-grand-mother's fields, Moore felt an enormous kinship with the earth. Consequently, he was inspired to document those grab-you-by-the-neck stories. Mr. Moore's quest to define the world has led to the publication of his acclaimed poetry book, *Forever Home*. His works have also appeared in *The Garden Thrives, Trouble the Water,* and *The Haiku Anthology*. A winner of the 1997 Margaret Walker Creative Writing Award, LDM is also the founder and executive director of the Carolina African American Writers' Collective. He teaches Poetry Writing at North Carolina State University.

Jamaican-born, South Bronx-bred, I was brought into life in 1965, into a typically Caribbean household that subscribed to the belief that children were meant to be seen and not heard. Bucking against that tired tradition was my earliest act of rebellion. Writing has been my longest. I learned early that a black woman's voice is a seductive and powerful thing. My way to flex when racism and sexism threaten to render us invisible. I've been writing about hip-hop, gender issues and pop culture for more than a decade—a minor miracle, if you consider the fact that the grueling process of writing is one that I never managed to love. The best of our craft have a reverence for words that can be, at times, debilitating. The better you get at this hustle the harder it seems to be. Still, I've managed to win a few awards: an NABJ award for my article on the Central Park Jogger Rape Case and an EMMA from the National Women's Political Caucus for my coverage of the Mike Tyson Rape Trial. My work has appeared in *The Village Voice, Spin, Essence, Notorious, Madison, Ms.,* and *Vibe,* where I was a staff writer. Like most writers I've got a few hustles: I'm an author, an Editor-at-Large for *Essence,* and I frequently lecture on the college circuit. I gave birth twice in 1999: in March to my first book *When Chickenheads Come Home to Roost: my life as a hip-hop feminist,* and then in July to son Sule. We live in Brooklyn with my husband.
—Joan Morgan

Writing for **Bruce Morrow** is like eating: he gets cranky—downright mean and evil—if he doesn't do it. He wakes up every weekday morning at 7:15 AM, writes a sentence or two, goes to work at Teachers & Writers Collaborative in New York City, writes letters and grant proposals, eats a light lunch, goes to the gym, reads email, the paper, and lots of journals, goes home at 5:30 PM, and writes—hopefully, more than a couple of sentences—until midnight. On weekends he gorges on words. In 1996 he co-edited *Shade: An Anthology of Short Fiction by Gay Men of African Descent.* His next project is a novel with recipes for roast turkey, cornbread stuffing, macaroni and cheese, collard greens, and candied sweet potatoes. Born in Cleveland, Ohio, in 1963, to a mother who really knows how to throw down, his work has appeared in numerous publications, including *Callaloo, Blithe House Quarterly, The New York Times,* and the anthologies *Speak My Name, Go the Way the Blood Beats,* and *Men on Men 2000.* He's still famished.

I was born in Kenya on the first of August, 1977. I am a Ugandan citizen now residing in West Lafayette, Indiana. I study at Purdue University with my wife Christine Reksten. My father thought he was born for the single cow *his* father owned. After all, who would tend to them after *his* father's passing? I thought I was born for my mother; as the last of six children I was determined to be her company. After all, who would entertain her as the house grew empty? We were wrong, my father and I. I was born for my mother and the world she lives in. I was born to keep her stories and mine. I was born to let our stories drift through the world. As I grew I became aware of the importance of memory. My father worked for an international company and we moved from country to country. I carry India, Uganda, Kenya, and America in my thoughts and remember them by writing. Purdue University has opened many creative doors for me but, as I graduate soon, the time for change has come. I am determined to go to graduate school and begin a novel. I am ready to let the world hear my mother's stories. My only hope is that the world is ready for me.
—Samwiri Mukuru

Mark Anthony Neal was birthed in the "Boogie-down," about a month after the '65 black-out, raised by AC and 'lil Lena, on grits, corn bread, fried chicken, The Mighty Clouds of Joy and sista Aretha. Lil' Lena use to play Nikki's "Truth is on the Way" twice a day. Bruh been writing since the age of 8, about the same time he bought his first Sam Cooke album. Bruh been digging old souls since, like Ishmael, that 'lil cat LeRoi, sista Sonia, and that pimp-daddy race man Marvin G. Some time ago bruh thought him could be a Ph.D. Him now Ph.D. working in the trenches of New York's capital, wit' little luv, but a whole lotta attitude. Bruh wrote a book, called it *What the Music Said: Black Popular Music and Black Public Culture.* Bruh thought he should do it again. *Soul Babies: Black Popular Culture and the Post-Soul Aesthetic* be out in a little bit. Bruh also married a little church gal. She from the Boogie-down too. She think he cuss too much. They gotta little girl, affectionately known as the baby-girl diva. Sis already got serious needs, so a bruh gotta write and write and write....

Letta Neely: i was born and raised in naptown (indianapolis, indiana) in 1971; 6 months after the papers reported that the bangladesh liberation struggle had been won. i was obsessed with history as a child—oral, graffittied, written in music. i wanted to know who i was connected to. i found my blood peoples in many places. i started writing because i wanted to tell my grandmother that i loved her. when my heart was ready i was 4 or 5 and the form the spirits sent was a poem. i'm still in love with letters. it's pulsing beating back and forth from one side of the nile's umbilical cord to the other sides. it is important to say i am a blk lesbian (dyke) because when i first started looking for our relatives (to know that i wasn't alone) i smiled the first time i read Audre Lorde's bio. i have published one book, *juba* (Wildheart Press). my work has appeared in these anthologies: *Does Your Mama Know, A Woman Like That, The World Inside US,* and *Catch the Fire.* i live in jamaica plain, mass.

Mukoma Wa Ngugi was born in 1971 to Kenyan parents in Evanston, Illinois, but left shortly afterwards and therefore says his knowledge of the United States is purely fetal. Currently finishing his MA in Creative Writing at Boston University, Mukoma has written all his life and doesn't see how life can be lived without a creative outlet: Creativity shapes the world as the world does shape creativity. Writing for him thus becomes most powerful when fuelled by social activism. Because writing is primarily about human relations, isn't our struggle against tyrannies (and tyrannies come in many forms) part of writing? He hopes that those who read his works will be moved in some way to reflect on their own lives, to reflect on their own environments, and become more conscious. Mukoma has thus far authored *Hurling Words at Consciousness* (a collection of poetry), *Consciousness Before Dawn* (political African fiction), and *Conversing with African* (political African theory). He is presently a member of the Boston-based African Writers Group.

Widely considered one of the most important African voices of our generation, **Ben Okri** is a Nigerian writer residing in London. He was born in Minna, Nigeria, in 1959, and moved to England by age 18, with his first novel completed, *Flowers and Shadows.* Since then Okri has published twelve other works of fiction, essays, and poetry, including the Booker Prize-winning *The Famished Road,* which is excerpted in this collection. Of the novel *The Wall Street Journal* said it is "Something approaching a masterpiece of magic realism..." And in a *New York Times Book Review* Harvard scholar Henry Louis Gates, Jr. called *The Famished Road* "A dazzling achievement for any writer in any language."

I've been writing my whole life. Even if I just started getting the words down on paper five years ago. I work for *The Washington Post* which likes to bring its people in with the appropriate awards and experience and fanfare to announce them. I didn't have any of that, so I announced myself: **Lonnae O'Neal Parker** was born in 1967 on the segregated South Side of Chicago. It's a place she's been trying to recreate for years because she likes the idea of a black world—with the option to travel. She graduated in journalism from Southern Illinois University in 1988, and attended grad school at

Howard. In 1991, she joined the *Post* and primarily answered phones while she laid back in the cut. She was a sales aide, news aide, editorial aide, summer news intern. After that, there was a one-year internship, then six months of a two-year internship writing obituaries before she landed in the "Style" section writing primarily about youth culture, popular culture, and race. Some say she's arrived. They underestimate her journey.

Born during the war in Vietnam, **G. E. Patterson** toddled through anti-war rallies on the campus of a small liberal-arts college in Minnesota and dreamed nightly of life as a landscape painter in maritime Canada. Instead, he was shipped to safety in the hills and woods of rural southwestern Arkansas and home-schooled in Latin and Greek and animal husbandry. On his way to what would become the first of many pilgrimages to Cape Breton, he was waylaid by high school, college, French, Italian and Brazilian-Portuguese. Now working as a translator, art commentator, yoga teacher and poet, he divides his time between rural and urban Minnesota, the San Francisco Bay area, and Seattle. He writes because there are things he can't say any other way. Graywolf Press published his first book of poetry, *Tug,* in 1999.

My grandfather, Pellin Perdomo, was a traveling troubador. I had an uncle, Lole Grande (my cousin Jeanette's father), who was a guitarist. My other uncle, Lole Chiquito (they called him Manteca), who, if you let Mami Carmen tell it, was one of the baddest congeros in New York City but fucked up because he wanted to shoot dope instead of play with Tito Puente. My father, William Perdomo, Sr., played some conga, too. Mami Carmen Perdomo (formerly Carmen Iris Lopez) is an avid journal keeper as well as a loyal note-taker of forecasts from her favorite astrologer, Anita Cassandra. I think I got my poetry from their music. I was born in 1967. Manhattan. Grew up in East Harlem. My first book, *Where a Nickel Costs a Dime* (Norton), was published in 1996. My work can also be found in anthologies such as *Boricuas, In the Tradition, Listen Up!* and *Aloud!* I been all over the country, some of Europe, shot videos, published, won grants and awards, and all that good shit, but nothing compares to that feeling when someone reads your work, or hears you read, and they are changed forever. Siempre palante, nunca patras.
—Willie Perdomo

I, **Phyllis Alesia Perry,** decided to come into the world as a black Southerner, late 20th-century version. I think the when (March 8, 1961) and the where (Atlanta) were good choices. I grew up in Alabama; I grew up in Tuskegee. Black people seem to spring out of the very soil there. Journalism was my trade before my novel, *Stigmata,* was published in 1998. Sixteen years, four newspapers, one Pulitzer Prize for editing duties. So I have had a lot of things come out in newsprint, but the novel was the scariest thing I ever did (including a couple of surgical procedures). Scarier still, it was published overseas, too, so there are people in Germany, Great Britain, The Netherlands and Spain reading it and probably not getting it. It's won the Georgia Author of the Year Award, first novel category, and been nominated for the Quality Paperback Book

Club New Voices Award. But I try not to think about those too much. Too scary. I write because "The voices have made it crystal clear that these flimsy things, these words, are the only things standing between me and insanity."

Carl Phillips was born in 1959, in Everett, Washington. He spent much of his childhood moving around the world—his father was in the Air Force—before settling in Massachusetts, where he went to high school, graduated from Harvard, and taught high school Latin for almost ten years. Phillips is the author of four books of poetry: *In the Blood, Cortège, From the Devotions,* and *Pastoral.* A fifth book, *Spoils, Dividing,* is forthcoming. The recipient of awards from the Guggenheim Foundation, the Massachusetts Artists Foundation, the Library of Congress, and the Academy of American Poets, he divides his time between St. Louis—where he is professor of English and of African and Afro-American Studies at Washington University—and Cape Cod, Massachusetts, where he and his partner (landscape photographer Doug Macomber) spend their summers. He says, "I began writing as a means of having a portable world I could call my own, given how often my family moved. Later, I wrote because I couldn't find what I wanted to be said being said anywhere else, by anyone else. I still can't find that—so I still write."

My name is **Scott Poulson-Bryant.** Not only am I a writer, but I played one on TV. I was born (in 1966) and raised in Long Island, New York, and as happy as those suburban days were, I spent a whole lotta time daydreaming about living and writing in more far-flung places like London or the East Village. I studied at Brown University; I apprenticed at *The Village Voice* (which got me to the East Village); and I wrote for *Spin* (which got me to London), *Rolling Stone, Essence,* and *The New York Times* before becoming a founding editor of *Vibe* magazine. Along the way I reported on music for VH1, sold a screenplay, wrote a gloriously unpublishable novel, and fell in love hundreds of times. By the time this book is in your hands I will hopefully be out of Manhattan and in London, full-time, putting the finishing touches on *A Black History of White People,* a publishable novel. Why do I write? I write because it's all I know how to do.

what the deal, this is **Kevin Powell,** AKA kepo1, sitting in a kinko's in los angeles right this second; while chasing other cats down for their bios, been avoiding writing my own. kinda like writing your obituary, ya heard? was born a year after Malcolm was blown away and two years before a rifle stifled MLK. only child of a young single woman who greyhound-ed it from a southern shack to a northern tenement. i've wanted to be a writer since i was a shorty of 11. ma-dukes took me to the greenville public library in jersey city, new jersey—where I was pimp-smacked into life—most Saturdays. i overdosed on music, TV, sports, hemingway, poe, shakespeare, and so much candy i would see spots with my eyes closed. thought my childhood was one long misery session, complete with hunger, violence, and rage. got to college on a financial aid package but i have made several trips back to the gutter because there is no safety net for field negroes with rebellion on the brain. no matter, childhood dream fulfilled: this anthology is book number four and the name done been in *vibe, code, ms., rolling stone, essence, the washington post,* and elsewhere. i write 'cuz my moms now asks me to spell and pronounce words for her and 'cuz my maternal grandparents could not read. i write 'cuz i wanna be free *before* i die, knowhati'msayin'?

Patricia Powell was born in Jamaica in 1966. She didn't always know she wanted to be a writer, even though she was an avid daydreamer and her favorite novel was John Bunyan's *The Pilgrim's Progress.* In college, she started off as an Economics major, and when that failed switched to English and began writing her first novel. Patricia Powell's three novels—*Me Dying Trial, A Small Gathering of Bones,* and *The Pagoda*—have received a P.E.N. New England Discovery Award, a Bruce Rossley Literary Award, the Publishing Triangle's Ferro-Grumley Award and a Lila-Wallace Readers Digest Writers Award. Patricia Powell holds degrees from Wellesley College and Brown University. She lives in Cambridge, Massachusetts, and teaches at Harvard University.

Dreamt into flesh by his parents, **Rohan Preston** entered the world in a rural hamlet in St. Mary, Jamaica, in 1966, four years after independence and two years before the assassination of Dr. Martin Luther King. He rebelled against Catholicism at 12, the year he joined his parents in Brooklyn, New York, and later found a nourishing spirituality in literature and culture as well as in other sanctuaries. He recently completed a semiotics 12-step program, and now regularly shows the holes in his Yale English degree in his capacity as lead theater critic at the *Star-Tribune* in Minneapolis. In his poetry, Preston hopes to channel new forms from one root like his maternal grandfather who grafted different plants onto one tree that bore many fruits. Though his poetry has been published in such journals as *Drumvoices, Eyeball, Ploughshares* and *TriQuarterly,* and in the books *Dreams in Soy Sauce* and *Soulfires: Young Black Men on Love and Violence* (which he edited with Daniel Wideman), his work springs from and is written for family. He writes to distill his experience and hopes to continuously fall into the eyes of his wife and their three-year-old daughter.

Howard Rambsy II has visions. He hears silenced voices, sees seemingly invisible things. No, he's not crazy. Instead, he's a black writer concerned about representations of African American life and culture. Born in 1976 and raised on the dusty streets of Jackson, Tennessee, Howard graduated from Tougaloo College in Mississippi. Like his literary inspiration Richard Wright, Howard sees himself as a cross between a native son and one of the country's outsiders, thus he began writing to satisfy the American hunger that so many Southern-born black boys must deal with. In the beginning, he published creative pieces here and there, but made his first sustained efforts as a writer/journalist for *The Mississippi Link,* an African American news weekly. Recently, he made a move north as he became a graduate fellow in the American and African American literature program at Pennsylvania State University. Through poetry and prose, Howard seeks to explore meanings, to resound blackness, and to somehow make a difference that will really make a difference.

There are billions of souls in the world and some of us are almost to be touching the depths of how it is and what it is to be human. On the surface we exist but just beyond is existence. I write to articulate the felt experience. My first book of poems, *Nothing in Nature is Private,* existed in the experience of Black, Jamaican, person, woman in a bruised world. My second, *The End of the Alphabet,* makes a kaleidoscopic journey through the will to existence. I think sometimes I am too private, too lonely in my heart, but my mind rows constantly as if involved in a public disturbance. When poet Paul Celane writes "pray Lord, pray to us, we are near," I feel he speaks of me and I with him in talking to God. There are some of us who are constantly mending our hearts, I write into that mending, my writing is that mending. Anyway, here I am, **Claudia Rankine,** born in Jamaica, in 1963, here is my art.

Vancouver, Canada, in 1964, a city of modernity on the edge of wilderness. **Vanessa Richards** is born 10 days early, 20 minutes after her Viennese mother reaches the hospital. She has always travelled with speed. In the swimming pool her Trinidadian father turns around to resume his lesson in floating to find her paddling in the deep end. Her namesake, a genus of butterflies known for migratory prowess. A child prone to musing and reconaissance. A Chinook wind carries a directive from the mountain top. Her assignment? Storyteller and a biological imperative to blend. Her photos have been published, the first film has been made, many songs have been sung, the performance is ongoing and the pages appear in *The Fire People, Bittersweet, 360 Degrees— A Revolution of Black Poets, IC3, Straight No Chaser* and *Stress.* In 1992 she relocated to London, England, where she is Joint Artistic Director for multi-media performing arts company, Mannafest. Committed to culture and educational works as a means for Metamorphasis, backbone and beauty.

Kristina Rungano's name comes up often around discussions on brilliant and iconoclastic post-colonial African writers. Born in Zimbabwe in 1963, Rungano wrote a good deal of poetry by the time she was 18, and published her first volume of poetry, *A Storm is Brewing,* in 1984 (Zimbabwe Publishing House). Rungano's words are visual manifestos on life, love, land, and the on-going search for freedom, both personal and political. Many of Rungano's pieces are blunt assessments on the plight of women in Africa, which might explain why she has moved from and to her native Zimbabwe on several occasions. Rungano obtained a diploma in Computer Science in England and her work has been featured in numerous anthologies, including *The New African Poetry, African Women's Poetry,* and *The Penguin Book of Modern African Poetry.*

Tijan Sallah—I was born on March 6, 1958, in Sere Kunda, The Gambia; the fourth child in a family of seven. I attended St. Augustine's High School—an all-male school ran by Irish Holy Ghost Fathers. Joseph Gough, an Irish priest and English teacher, sparked the initial fires in me to write. From Gambia, I came to the U.S. in 1977. I completed a Ph.D. in Economics in 1987. I've taught at several American universities, and I am currently a Senior Economist on Rural Development in the Middle East Department of the World Bank. My published books include: *When Africa Was a*

Young Woman (poems, 1980); *Before the New Earth* (short stories, 1988); *Kora Land* (poems, 1989); *Dreams of Dusty Roads* (poems, 1993); *New Poets of West Africa* (anthology, 1995); *Wolof* (ethnography, 1996) and *The New African Poetry* (anthology coedited with Tanure Ojaide). I am presently finalizing a biography of the noted African novelist, Chinua Achebe. I write because I have stories to tell: short and tall stories. I write because I am in love, I am in love with all the flowers of Africa that explode in a radiant rage because people ignore their beauty.

Danzy Senna was born in Boston in 1970. She has since lived in many cities, including Los Angeles, San Francisco, Istanbul, Brooklyn, London, and Tijuana. Though nobody has seen hide nor tail of Senna since the publication of her first novel, *Caucasia,* in 1998, she did in fact write a second novel, entitled *Snow in Alabama,* which was only published in German. Currently, she is rumored to be living in the back woods of Montana, in a hut with no running water, heat, or electricity, and a pack of rabid mongrels (half-Pit Bull, half-Labrador) to keep her company. There, she is said to be working feverishly on her third novel, which her publicist says is about "the evil that women do."

Angela Shannon's heritage stems from the red soil of Tulsa, Oklahoma, where she was born in 1964. Playing where sparse grass left a balding spot, Shannon would create stories instead of mudpies. Years later, Shannon would learn of the 1921 Riot from her great-grandfather. Our family's church, Mt. Zion, was burned, but we rebuilt it. Shannon focuses on rebuilding, on extending a voice to silences, which includes Tampa, Florida, where she later grew up; and the culturally-rich Chicago, where she began to pen down poems. Her poetry covers intricate weavings of past and present and has been recited in church halls, and published in journals like *TriQuarterly, Ploughshares,* and *Crab Orchard Review,* and in anthologies such as *Powerlines: A Decade of Poetry from Chicago's Guild Complex* and *Catch The Fire!!!* Shannon continues to polish her craft as an MFA candidate at Warren Wilson College. She's proud of the accolades that have come her way but Shannon's greatest joy as a poet has been witnessing the spirit of a poem move like memory across a face. Shannon resides in Minneapolis, Minnesota, with her husband and daughter.

Renée Simms

is tattered scribe is voice
is slim hands
that bring you food
is shiny smile in dusty ofc
is whatever / is whatever
    to live

live enuf   to write

live enuf   to catch
memory as it falls
black as Detroit 1967:
a baby screamin thru riot fire

baby grows up
lives electric in L.A.
& screams her memory in *Black Love*
beats her memory in *The Drumming Between Us*

she all percussive heat
she a 1999
Pen West Emerging Voice
she a million stories
    chattering over coffee
laughin up this culture
of city bricks &
mauve dreams

Danyel Victoria Smith was born on the longest day of 1965 in Oakland, California. Chatty and bookish, she was, from the word Go. Dropped out of Cal-Berkeley, worked at Copymat and at Saks, interned at the local newsweekly. Got mesmerized by MC Hammer, En Vogue, Too Short, DJ Quik, but mostly Digital Underground—and then she got married. Moved to New York in '93, wrote for the places that seemed official, went to *Vibe* as music editor, and then she got divorced. She went to Northwestern for the fellowship, and back to *Vibe* as editor-in-chief after that, and is now at *Time, Inc.* (figuring *that* out) and teaching at the New School. She's also thinking of her future which will include having more faith, as well as being a professional chef and a novelist, a friend and a lover and a responsible daughter and a good sister and better writer. Hey—you have to claim it, right? Say it, pray it—make it.

I am **Taigi Smith,** the only child of Debbie born in 1972, and granddaughter of women named Ethel and Marion. I am a child of San Francisco, a descendant of Pennsylvania blacks and Indians, an offspring of women with calloused hands, strong backs, and hardened feet. There are stories in my head that plague me when they are ignored; words in my mind, vivid pictures that beg to be validated. I write because as a network news journalist living in Brooklyn, New York, I have seen more, heard more, and been more places than I ever thought possible. The need to write these stories overwhelms me, and more than anything else, I fear that I will forget these things when I grow old. I must immortalize these experiences so that the people who come after me will know what life was like way back when. Just as Debbie, and Ethel, and Marion have verbally immortalized themselves through me, I must eternalize myself through words. I am haunted by the need to be remembered, driven by the desire not to forget. My work has been published in *Testimony: Young African Americans on Self-Discovery and Black Identity* and *The San Francisco Chronicle*.

Earlier this year *The New York Times* called **Zadie Smith**'s bestselling debut novel, *White Teeth*, "a big, splashy, populous production reminiscent of books by Dickens and Salman Rushdie with a nod to indie movies like *My Beautiful Laundrette*. In other words, Smith, born in Northwest London in 1975, is the literary 'it girl' on the lips of this new millennium. A product of a Jamaican mother and an English father, Smith began working on *White Teeth* during her last year of college, after an editor read one of her fiction pieces in a student publication. Asked if there was a novel on the horizon, Smith admits, 'I lied, and said yes.' Set in London, *White Teeth* has a multicultural cast and its major themes are questions of roots and destiny. Somewhat wary of her new-found fame and fortune, Zadie Smith mocked her prodigy status in a self-review in the literary magazine *Butterfly:* 'This kind of precocity in so young a writer has one half of the audience standing to applaud and the other half wishing, as with child performers of the past (Shirley Temple, Bonnie Langford et. al.), she would just stay still and shut up. *White Teeth* is the literary equivalent of a hyperactive, ginger-haired tap-dancing ten-year-old. . . .'"

Patrick Sylvain—I was born in 1966 on the once revolutionary soil of Haiti where machetes, rifles and swords taught the French and the rest of the colonial world a serious lesson in human dignity and the will to be free. Despite the current problems in my home country, I still live by this will to be forever free and to struggle for humanity. Since the age of 12, I've been a wordslinger and now, with much preparation from various institutions and exposures to various folks, I am even more committed to the word. I am a word hunter, hunted by words and I am using words to expose the vowels and consonants screaming in the night. I emigrated to Massachusetts in December 1981. Since that new beginning, I have been a Conant Fellow at the Harvard Graduate School of Education, where I earned my Masters in Education. I currently work as a bilingual public school teacher in Boston. I am also a video-photographer who worked as a special researcher with the PBS documentary series *Frontline*. I also serve as a guest lecturer on "Poetry as a Political Discourse" at Tufts University's Experimental College. I am a former member of the Dark Room Collective and a founding member of the Haitian American Writers Coalition. And I've been fortunate to have been published in various publications, including: *Beacon Best of 1999, Ploughshares, Agni, Essence, Caribbean Writers, Massachusetts Review,* and *Compost,* where I co-edited a special issue on Haitian writers.

Natasha Tarpley—I was born in 1971, in Chicago, Illinois. I started writing by watching my mother work on her electric typewriter, which was stored in a hard black shell of a box that looked like a miniature suitcase. From her, I learned that words can take you further than anything on wheels or wings ever could. I write as a means of traveling, within and beyond myself. Writing is also my anchor, a touchstone, the way I make sense of this life's journey. I am the author of three books: a family memoir, *Girl in the Mirror: Three Generations of Black Women in Motion* (Beacon Press, 1998); a children's book, *I Love My Hair!* (Little, Brown & Co., 1998); and an anthology, *Testimony: Young African Americans on Self-Discovery and Black Identity* (Beacon Press,

1995). My work has been published in *The Washington Post, Essence, Emerge,* and *Giant Steps,* an anthology. Currently, I live in New York City.

Lisa Teasley was born in 1962, in Los Angeles, to a Panamanian mother and an American Midwestern (Cleveland) father. She spent a portion of her childhood in Durham, North Carolina, drowning ants and racing turtles. Later, after graduation from UCLA, journalistic stints, marriage and the birth of her daughter, she would spend 5 years in New York re-living the Carolina metaphor. Her fiction, poetry and essays have appeared in the anthologies *In the Tradition; An Ear to the Ground; Women For All Seasons;* and in the forthcoming *Beyond the Frontier, Brown Sugar* and *100 Black Kisses.* Her work has appeared in numerous publications such as *Between C & D, Rampike, Catalyst, L.A. Weekly, the new renaissance, Great River Review, Rohwedder,* and *Washington Square.* Teasley's fiction awards: May Merrill Miller, the National Society of Arts & Letters, and the Amaranth Review. Her articles and book reviews have appeared in *One World, The Los Angeles Times, Details* and *The Washington Post.* Currently living in Los Angeles, Teasley, a painter as well, exhibits extensively throughout the country. Her oil on canvas or wood portraits represent the tactile side to her obsessive exploration of the hideous and the gorgeous in human nature.

Jervey Tervalon—I was born in New Orleans on 11-23-58. I came to California with a banjo on my knee when I was 4, just in time for the slew of L.A. riots about to happen. I went to half-asset schools; a nun-teacher decided that I was retarded at the Holy Name of Jesus Christ. I wept. That was in the first grade, after my mother threatened to rip the nun's veil off. I was off to the public schools in L.A. where I tried not to get stomped to death. It was cool. Then off to UC-Santa Barbara where frat boys and blonde chicks ruled. I got a rep as a writer and never looked back. Fourteen years later, and after grad school at UC-Irvine, I sold my first novel. I live in Altadena, below where John Brown's son is buried. After two novels and a collection of stories, I am currently trying not to write now, suspecting that it might be the right thing. But soon, like the Invisible Man, I'll spring back out of my hole ready to do battle.

Imani Tolliver—a yellow tub in the living room lined with pillows hold my earliest memory. i am thankful for it. i am two. it is 1967. my palms, the udders wading me through this story from the thin l.a. river to the gasp and burp of the potomac. along the way, I folded my story into a few books and journals. i fellowed a while in the fountain at the folger, read shakespeare in the reservoir across from founder's library. shared what i know about the power of voice, of story to children and grown folks, same. on the hudson one summer, toi told me that my beauty lies where i hold my shame, my scar. so i kept writing and telling. the atlantic eased me onto the soft collar of the pacific where black dolphins swallowed tears for my dead father. i decided to keep all these stories in one place. calling it *Pink.* i write to see and speak. to love.

Touré was born in Boston in 1971, the year Frazier knocked out Ali, Al Green first said, "I'm so tired of bein' alone," and Shaft stuck it to all the suckas. At an American university that doesn't deserve to be named he fell into protest poetry and, determined to expand the complexity of the discussion of Black people, he ran to New York. Now a Contributing Editor at *Rolling Stone,* his work has appeared in *The New Yorker, Playboy, Callaloo,* and *The Best American Essays of 1999.* He studied at Columbia University's Graduate School of Creative Writing and now lives in Fort Greene, Brooklyn. When not writing tales for his upcoming short story collection *Sugar Lips Shinehot, The Man with the Portable Promised Land and Other New Urban Legends,* he plays hardcore guerilla tennis.

Natasha Tretheway—In 1965 miscegenation was still illegal in Kentucky, so my parents crossed the river into Ohio to be married. I was born in 1966 and spent my earliest years in Gulfport, Mississippi. We lived among the shanties and shotguns in the black section of town known as North Gulfport, just outside the city limits. The famous Highway 49 of blues songs cut right through the middle of our community, dividing it. Thus, these crossings and divides are the themes I try to grapple with in much of my work. And as my parents divorced a few years later, I am also interested in absences, in memory and forgetting, our common language of loss. I've received a fellowship in poetry from the NEA, I won the Cave Canem 1st book prize (selected by Rita Dove, and recently published by Graywolf Press), and some of my poems have appeared in *American Poetry Review, Callaloo, New England Review,* and *The Southern Review.* Presently, I am an assistant professor of English at Auburn University in Alabama.

Eisa Nefertari Ulen—1968 was almost done the day I let my mother know she should push me out into this world. A swirl of Philadelphia snow danced through air, and we felt her muscles tight against her sea, tight against me. We women flex to conjure new life. When I was five I first drew a line of words (about tepees and tulips) into story. Now I've twisted around enough words to craft my first novel, *Spirit's Returning Eye,* thanks to a 1995 Frederick Douglass Center Fellowship and a 1999 residency scholarship from the Provincetown Fine Arts Center. I've sat in my sacred space while Fort Greene dances outside my window, pushing and pulling against the page: articles, reviews, essays—a wish, a confession, a tribute. A plea for our elders anthologized right here. I write and feel the surround of force against brown bodies, dreaming about sistahs in the flex of hot battle, faces turned upward, smiling, catching the stuff that dances on air, cool inside.

"Words are like clay, we model them with our fingers," **Yvonne Vera** says. "A word does not rot even if it is buried in the mouth for too long." Vera was born in Bulawayo, in Zimbabwe. Date: 19 September 1964, and raised in the thorn bushes of the Matebeleland veld. Vera writes against the centuries of silence which African women have endured. Her novel, *Butterfly Burning,* is published by Farrar, Straus & Giroux in New York. She is also the author of *Under the Tongue,* which won the Commonwealth Prize for literature, Africa Region, 1997. Additionally, Vera is the 1999 winner of the Swedish Prize "Voice of Africa." Her other two novels are *Without a Name* and *Nehanda. Why Don't You Carve Other Animals* is her collection of short stories. She is the editor of *Opening Spaces—An Anthology of Contemporary Writing by African Women.* Vera is a Ph.D. graduate of York University in Canada and currently works as the Director of the National Gallery of Zimbabwe in Bulawayo.

Marco Villalobos was born under quetzalcoatl the feathered serpent in 1973 and spent his Woodlàn, Califas, childhood learning about heart among con men, home-boys, and barrio grandmothers full of love. He's studied academic and antidemic alphabets and today writes "to get plymouth rock and ivory towers the fuck up off my back." He moved to Crooklàndia, New Jork, in order to escape a Tijuana deportation and has since become a National Hispanic Scholarship Fund recipient with work at *Indieplanet.com, Brooklyn Bridge* magazine, *Stress* magazine, and various small press publications, none of which matter more than the now defunct *Tortilla.*

Writing because the ancestors and the unborn tell her to, **Teresa N. Washington** was born in Peoria, Illinois, 1971. She is a Ph.D. candidate and Assistant Lecturer at Obafemi Awolowo University, Ile-Ife, Nigeria. Her work has appeared in *The Literary Griot, The Griot, Obsidian II, The Third Eye, The Estrella Mountain Community College Literary Magazine, Southern Exposure, Oxford Town, The Daily Mississippian,* and *A Festival of Poetry,* an anthology she co-edited with Adebayo Lamikanra for their "First Annual O.A.U. Poetry Festival."

Colson Whitehead/born in 1969 in New York City/graduated from Harvard in 1991/has written for numerous publications, including *The Village Voice*/his first novel is the widely acclaimed *The Intuitionist*/Walter Mosley said "This extraordinary novel is the first voice in a powerful chorus to come"/*The Washington Post Book World* pro-claimed "...Whitehead carves out an exclusive space for himself in America's literary canon..."/Blending classic and postmodern fiction styles, *The Intuitionist,* excerpted in this collection, deconstructs language, race, and the imagination like Ellison and Mor-rison/Whitehead lives in Brooklyn, New York.

Daniel J. Wideman—I was born, illegally, in Philly in 1968 (Pennsylvania: one of thirty-four states where "mixed marriages" were still banned by law). Grew up in a fam-ily of griots and ballplayers so I've been writing and running forever. I write because it's the only way I've found to remember what I never knew. Since stirring the waters as co-editor of the anthology *Soulfires* in 1996, my work has appeared most prominently in *Callaloo* and in the anthologies *Outside the Law: Narratives of Justice in America; Black Texts and Textuality;* and *Giant Steps.* After chasing knowledge in Providence, Rhode Island, London, England, and Accra, Ghana, I bailed out of grad school and Chicago in 1996 and headed south. I now live, write, hoop, and watch PBS (but not Mr. Rogers) with my daughter Qasima in North Carolina.

Kevin Young was born in 1970 in a town he does not remember. This partially explains the title of his first book, *Most Way Home,* winner of the National Poetry Series and the Zacharis First Book Prize from *Ploughshares. To Repel Ghosts* is Young's second book of poems, an urban epic based on the work of the late artist Jean-Michel Basquiat; excerpts were featured on National Public Radio's "All Things Considered" and in the *Beacon Best of 1999.* Most all Young's "people" hail from Louisiana, which has the same red clay as his current home, Athens, Georgia, where he is associate professor of English and African American Studies at the University of Georgia. Recently Young edited *Giant Steps: The New Generation of African American Writers,* an anthology of poetry, fiction, and nonfiction published by HarperPerennial in February 2000.

Self-Portrait: Radcliffe Bailey, The Cover Artist

My name is Radcliffe Bailey, son of Brenda and Radcliffe Bailey. I was born in 1968 in Bridgeton, New Jersey. When my brother Roy and I were 4 and 5, my parents decided to move to Atlanta to give us a different environment. I pretty much consider myself a Southern person. I have been very influenced by my surroundings: the soul of the South rubs off on people. I was pretty much raised in all-black schools. After high school I went to a white college, the Atlanta College of Art. It was a strange experience, but I learned how to deal and politic on a whole other level.

My first encounter with art was through my great-aunt. She had traveled all over the world, and she was an artist, although she was not known. Then also my mom is an artist and actually taught art classes at one time. I was considered dyslexic and my mom knew I wasn't so she created this other school for me. That's how I came to art. It was not through school. It was strictly my family.

To me it is evident that my family influences my art. I took the basic skills of working with wood from my grandfather. I took the improvisation of creating things mechanically from my father, who I often worked on cars with. My father also built my parents' first house, so the building aspect in my art comes from my dad. In terms of my great-aunt here was this person with a very sophisticated style that I could not comprehend until now. My great-aunt was fly for an older lady: fly in how she dressed and carried herself. She did not look like a person who conformed. That contributed more to my personality and how we as artists carry ourselves in the sense that we express ourselves and have an identity on a whole different level. Identity as an individual and as a group of people.

Besides them, I also observed people like Jacob Lawrence. My mom took me to meet him when I was in middle school. I also met James Van Der Zee around that same time. Growing up in Atlanta and seeing black people living there and passing through was like a sense of power, it inspired me. I felt there was a large group of black people who had my back.

People ask me why do I paint. It is like asking people why do they live, why do they eat, why do they speak? As a kid, I remember being very insecure about my voice, about what I had to say. I think I was insecure because I thought very few people felt like me. Now with art I actually get to talk about things that I never thought I would talk about. As an artist, I am interested in the narrative, but I am not interested in being too literal. Like the blues, there is always a narrative, but there are layers too and it is not as literal as some people think.

My work is in the collection of many prestigious museums, but I don't mention that much. What I am proud of is my first show when I was still a college student. But what is most important to me healthwise, what makes me think, spiritually, in a different way, is the music I am trying to create in the back of my head.

Selected Bibliography of Black Literature

African

Abrahams, Peter. *Dark Testament*. London: Allen & Unwin, 1942

Achebe, Chinua. *Things Fall Apart*. London: Heinemann, 1958

Aidoo, Ama Ata. *Our Sister Killjoy*. Essex: Longman African Writers, 1977

Chipasula, Stella and Frank, Eds. *The Heinemann Book of African Women's Poetry*. Oxford, Oxfordshire: Heinemann, 1995

El Saadawi, Nawal. *Woman at Point Zero*. London: Zed Books, distributed in the United States by St. Martin's, 1983 (originally copyrighted 1975 by the author)

Farah, Nuruddin. *Sweet and Sour Milk*. London: Allison & Busby, 1979

Head, Bessie. *Maru*. London: Heinemann Educational Publishers, 1972

Kennedy, Ellen Conroy, Ed. *The Negritude Poets*. New York: A Richard Seaver Book/The Viking Press, 1975

Nwapa, Flora. *Efuru*. London: Heinemann, 1966

Saro-Wiwa, Ken. *Sozaboy*. Port Harcourt, Nigeria: Saros International Publishers, 1985

Soyinka, Wole. *Madmen & Specialists*. London: Meuthuen, 1971

wa Thiong'o, Ngũgĩ (Ngugi, James). *Weep not Child*. London & Ibadan: Heinemann, 1964

American

Baldwin, James. *Notes of A Native Son*. Boston: Beacon Press, 1955

Ellison, Ralph. *Invisible Man*. New York: Random House, 1952

Ervin, Hazel A., Ed. *African American Literary Criticism*—1773 to 2000. New York: Twayne, 1999

Evans, Mari, Ed. *Black Women Writers* (1950-1980: A Critical Evaluation). New York: Anchor/Doubleday, 1984

Gates, Henry Louis, Jr., and McKay, Nellie Y., Eds. *The Norton Anthology of African American Literature*. W.W. Norton & Company, 1997

Gayle, Addison. Ed., *The Black Aesthetic*. Garden City, New York: Doubleday, 1971

Hurston, Zora Neale. *Their Eyes Were Watching God*. Philadelphia: J.B. Lippincott Company, 1937

Jones, LeRoi (Baraka, Amiri) and Larry Neal, Eds. *Black Fire: An Anthology of Afro-American Writing*. New York: William Morrow, 1968

Locke, Alain, Ed. *The New Negro: An Interpretation*. New York: Albert & Charles Boni, Inc., 1925

Morrison, Toni. *Song of Solomon.* New York: Alfred A. Knopf, Inc., 1977

Walker, Margaret. *On Being Female, Black and Free: Essays by Margaret Walker, 1932–1992.* Nashville: University of Tennesee Press, 1997

Ward, Jerry W., Jr., Ed. *Trouble the Water: 250 Years of African-American Poetry.* New York: Penguin Books, 1997

British

Berry, James. *News For Babylon: The Chatto Book of West-Indian-British Poetry.* London: Chatto & Windus, 1981

Bryan, Beverley, et al. *The Heart of the Race: Black Women's Lives in Britain.* London: Virago, 1985

Busby, Margaret, Ed. *Daughters of Africa: An International Anthology of Words and Writings by Women of African Descent—From the Ancient Egyptian to the Present.* London: Jonathan Cape, 1992

Edwards, Paul and Dabydeen, David, Eds. *Black Writers in Britain 1760–1890.* Edinburgh University Press, 1991

Emecheta, Buchi. *Second-Class Citizen.* London: Allison & Busby, 1974

Evaristo, Bernardine. *Lara.* Tunbridge Wells, Kent: Angela Royal Publishing, 1997

Fryer, Peter. *Staying Power: The History of Black People in Britain.* Pluto Press, 1984

Kay, Jackie. *The Adoption Papers.* Newcastle Upon Tyne: Bloodaxe, 1991

Selvon, Sam. *The Lonely Londoners.* Essex: Longman, 1956

Settlers, Kadija Sesay and Newland, Courttia, Eds. *IC3: The Penguin Book of New Black Writing in Britain.* London: Penguin, 2000

Smith, Zadie. *White Teeth.* London: Penguin/Hamish Hamilton, 2000

Wambu, Onyekachi, Ed. *Empire Windrush: 50 Years of Writing about Black Britain.* London: Victor Gollancz, 1998

Canadian

Alexis, André. *Childhood.* Toronto: McClelland and Stewart, 1998

Brand, Dionne. *Land to Light On.* Toronto: McClelland and Stewart, 1997

Clarke, Austin C. *Amongst Thistles and Thorns.* Toronto: McClelland and Stewart, 1965

Clarke, Austin C. *Growing Up Stupid Under the Union Jack.* Toronto: McClelland and Stewart, 1980

Clarke, George Elliott, Ed. *Eyeing the North Star: Directions in African-Canadian Literature.* Toronto: McClelland and Stewart, 1997

Harris, Claire. *Drawing Down a Daughter.* Fredericton: Goose Lane Editions, 1992

Hopkinson, Nalo. *Brown Girl in the Ring.* New York: Warner Books, 1998

Laferriere, Dany. *How to Make Love to a Negro: A Novel.* Trans.: David Homel. Toronto: Coach House Press, 1987

Mayr, Suzette. *Moon Honey.* Edmonton: NeWest Publishers Limited, 1995

Silvera, Makeda. *Maria's Revenge.* Vancouver: Press Gang Publishers, 1999

Walcott, Rinaldo. *Black Like Who?* Toronto: Insomniac Press, 1997

Ward, Frederick. *The Curing Berry.* Toronto: Williams-Wallace, 1983

Caribbean

Alfrey, Phyllis Shand. *The Orchid House.* London: Constable, 1953

Brathwaite, Kamau (Edward). *The Arrivants: A New World Trilogy.* London: Oxford Universtiy Press, 1973

Condé, Maryse. *I, Tituba, Black Witch of Salem.* Paris: Editions Mercure de France, 1986

Dance, Daryl Cumber. *Fifty Caribbean Writers: A Bio-bibliographical Critical Sourcebook.* Westport, Conn.: Greenwood Press, 1986

Danticat, Edwidge. *Breath, Eyes, Memory.* New York: Soho Press, 1994

Imoja, Nailah Folami and Thomas, Jerolynn, Eds. *Voices 1: An Anthology of Barbadian Writing.* Barbados: Barbados Writers Collective/The National Cultural Foundation (Barbados), 1997

Kennedy, Ellen Conroy, Ed. *The Negritude Poets.* New York: A Richard Seaver Book/The Viking Press, 1975

Kincaid, Jamaica. *At the Bottom of the River.* New York: Farrar, Straus & Giroux, 1983

Lamming, George. *In the Castle of my Skin.* London: Joseph, 1953

Markham, E. A., Ed. *The Penguin Book of Caribbean Short Stories.* London, 1996

Naipaul, V. S. *Miguel Street.* London: Deutsh, 1959

Walcott, Derek. *Dream on Monkey Mountain & Other Plays.* New York: Farrar, Straus & Giroux, 1970

Books Essential to Understanding Hip-Hop Culture

Eure, Joseph D. and Spady, James G., Eds. *Nation Conscious Rap*. Brooklyn, NY: PC International Press, 1991

George, Nelson. *The Death of Rhythm and Blues*. New York: Random House, 1988

George, Nelson. *hip hop america*. New York: Viking, 1998

Jenkins, Sacha; Wilson, Elliott; Mao, Chairman; Alvarez, Gabriel; Rollins, Brent, Eds. *ego trip's Book of Rap Lists*. New York: St. Martin's Griffin, 1999

Jones, LeRoi (Baraka, Amiri). *Black Music*. New York: William Morrow, 1967

Jones, LeRoi (Baraka, Amiri). *Blues People: The Negro Experience in White America and the Music That Developed from It*. New York: William Morrow, 1963

Light, Alan, Ed. *The Vibe History of Hip Hop*. New York: Three Rivers Press, 1999

Perkins, William Eric, Ed. *Droppin' Science: Critical Essays on Rap Music and Hip Hop Culture*. Philadelphia: Temple University Press, 1996

Rose, Tricia. *Black Noise: Rap Music and Black Culture in Contemporary America*. Hanover, NH: University Press of New England, 1994

Toop, David. *Rap Attack #3: African Rap to Global Hip Hop*. London: Serpent's Tail, 2000

Vibe, The Editors of. *Tupac Shakur*. New York: Crown, 1997

Wimsatt, William Upski. *No More Prisons*. Chicago: Subway & Elevated Books, 1999

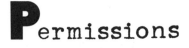

Permissions

Grateful acknowledgment is made to all the authors, publishers, and publications who granted permission to reprint the following work:

"Safari" by Toyin Adewale. Copyright © Toyin Adewale, 1999. Reprinted by permission of the author.

"The Rumor" by Jane Alberdeston-Coralín. Copyright © Jane Alberdeston-Coralín, 1999. Reprinted by permission of the author.

"Are Black People Cooler than White People?" by Donnell Alexander. Copyright © Donnell Alexander, 1997. Reprinted by permission of the author. Originally published in *Might* and *Utne Reader*.

"Fugue" by Elizabeth Alexander. Copyright © Elizabeth Alexander, 1999. Reprinted by permission of the author.

"Hip-Hop Hi-Tech" by Harry Allen. Copyright © Harry Allen, 1988. Reprinted by permission of the author. Originally published in *The Village Voice*.

"The Clearing" by Jeffery Renard Allen. Copyright © Jeffery Renard Allen, 1998. Reprinted by permission of the author.

"GWTW" by Hilton Als. Copyright © Hilton Als, 2000. Reprinted by permission of The Wylie Agency, Inc. Originally published in *Without Sanctuary: Lynching Photography in America* (Twin Palms Publishers).

"Race Natters—The Chattering Classes Convene on Martha's Vineyard" by Angela Ards. Copyright © Angela Ards, 1997. Reprinted by permission of the author. Originally published in *The Village Voice*.

"Angles of Vision" by Jabari Asim. Copyright © Jabari Asim, 1999. Reprinted by permission of the author.

"The Soul of Black Talk" by Erin Aubry. Copyright © *LA Weekly*, 1997. Reprinted by permission of *LA Weekly*. Originally published March 28, 1997.

"Do Books Matter?" by Kevin Baldeosingh. Copyright © Kevin Baldeosingh, 1998. Reprinted by permission of the author. Originally published in *The Trinidad and Tobago Review*.

"Black Youth Black Art Black Face—An Address" by Ras Baraka. Copyright © Ras Baraka, 1997. Reprinted by permission of the author. Originally presented as a public lecture.

"leaving a feminist organization: a personal/poetics" by Stefani Barber. Copyright © *Tripwire*, 1999. Reprinted by permission of *Tripwire*. Originally published Fall 1999.

"The White Boy Shuffle" by Paul Beatty. Copyright © Paul Beatty, 1996. Reprinted by permission of The Wylie Agency, Inc., and Minerva. Originally published in *The White Boy Shuffle*.

"In Search of Alice Walker" by Valerie Boyd. Copyright © Valerie Boyd, 1998. Reprinted by permission of the author. Originally published in *Ms.*

"I Dream of Jesus" by Charlie Braxton. Copyright © Charlie Braxton, 1996. Reprinted by permission of the author. Originally published in *Soulfires: Young Black Men on Love and Violence* (Penguin Books).

"The Other Side of Paradise—Feminist Pedagogy, Toni Morrison Iconography, and Oprah's Book Club Phenomenon" by Daphne A. Brooks. Copyright © Daphne A. Brooks, 1998. Reprinted by permission of the author. Originally presented as a conference paper.

"we are trying to (have me) conceive" by Tisa Bryant. Copyright © Tisa Bryant, 2000. Reprinted by permission of the author. Originally published in Kenning, Vol. 2, No. 3, Patrick Durgin, Ed., March 2000.

"personal" by Shonda Buchanan. Copyright © Shonda Buchanan, 1998. Reprinted by permission of the author.

"Tat Tvam Asi (You Are the One)" by Paul Calderon. Copyright © Paul Calderon, 1999. Reprinted by permission of the author.

"One Irony of the Caribbean" by Adrian Castro. Copyright © Adrian Castro, 1999. Reprinted by permission of the author.

"Mama's Girl" by Veronica Chambers. Copyright © Veronica Chambers, 1996. Reprinted by permission of Riverhead Books, a division of Penguin Putnam, Inc., and The Women's Press Ltd. Originally published in *Mama's Girl.*

"Homophobia: Hip-Hop's Black Eye" by Farai Chideya. Copyright © *Spin*, 1993. Reprinted by permission of *Spin*. Originally published as "Hip Hop's Black Eye" in August 1993.

"The Death of Rock n' Roll" by Cheo Hodari Coker. Copyright © Cheo Hodari Coker, 1999. Reprinted by permission of the author. Originally published in *Notorious.*

"Legba, Landed" by Wayde Compton. Copyright © Wayde Compton, 1999. Reprinted by permission of Advance Editions/Arsenal Pulp Press. Originally published in *49th Parallel Psalm.*

"Interpolation: Peace to My Nine" by Ricardo Cortez Cruz. Copyright © Ricardo Cortez Cruz, 1994. Reprinted by permission of the author. Originally published (in different form) in *The Kenyon Review.*

"Epilogue: Women Like Us" by Edwidge Danticat. Copyright © Edwidge Danticat, 1995. Reprinted by permission of Soho Press. Originally published in *Krik? Krak!*

"If we've gotta live underground and everybody's got cancer/will poetry be enuf?—A Letter to Ntozake Shange" by Eisa Davis. Copyright © Eisa Davis, 1999. Reprinted by permission of the author. Originally published in *Letters of Intent: Women Cross the Generations to Talk About Family, Work, Sex, Love, and the Future of Feminism* (The Free Press).

"Excursion to Port Royal" by Kwame Dawes. Copyright © Kwame Dawes, 1994. Reprinted by permission of the author. Originally published in *Progeny of Air* (Peepal Tree, UK).

"Dear Mr. Ellison" by Jarvis Q. DeBerry. Copyright © Jarvis Q. DeBerry, 1999. Reprinted by permission of the author.

"The Sun, the Moon, the Stars" by Junot Díaz. Copyright © Junot Díaz, 1998. Reprinted by permission of the author. Originally published in *The New Yorker*.

"She's Gotta Have It" by Debra Dickerson. Copyright © Debra Dickerson, 1998. Reprinted by permission of the author. Originally published in *The Village Voice*.

"Prologue, 1963" by Tananarive Due. Copyright © Tananarive Due, 1995. Reprinted by permission of HarperCollins Publishers, Inc. Originally published in *The Between*.

"The Visible Man" by Trey Ellis. Copyright © Trey Ellis, 1988. Reprinted by permission of the author. Originally published in *Travel & Leisure*.

"Return to the Planet of the Apes" by Ekow Eshun. Copyright © Ekow Eshun, 1996. Reprinted by permission of the author. Originally published in *The Face*.

"The Emperor's Babe" by Bernardine Evaristo. Copyright © Bernardine Evaristo, 2000. Reprinted by permission of the author.

"the missionary position" by Christopher John Farley. Copyright © Christopher John Farley, 1996. Reprinted by permission of Farrar, Straus and Giroux, LLC., and Granta Books. Originally published in *My Favorite War*.

"Assam" by Nikky Finney. Copyright © Nikky Finney, 1999. Reprinted by permission of the author.

"Church Y'all" by Ruth Forman. Copyright © Ruth Forman, 1997. Reprinted by permission of Beacon Press, Boston. Originally published in *Renaissance*.

"No Entry" by Lynell George. Copyright © Lynell George, 1993. Reprinted by permission of the author. Originally published in *LA Weekly*.

"The Yellow Forms of Paradise" by Danielle Legros Georges. Copyright © Danielle Legros Georges, 2000. Reprinted by permission of the author.

"swampy river" by Brian Gilmore. Copyright © Brian Gilmore, 1998. Reprinted by permission of the author. Originally published in *jungle nights and soda fountain rags: poem for duke ellington* (Karibu Books).

"Binga—Diary Entry" by Cege Githiora. Copyright © Cege Githiora, 1999. Reprinted by permission of the author.

"The Sports Taboo: Why blacks are like boys and whites are like girls" by Malcolm Gladwell. Copyright © Malcolm Gladwell, 1997. Reprinted by permission of the author. Originally published in *The New Yorker*.

"The Six-Hour Difference—A Dutch Perspective on the New World" by Scotty Gravenberch. Copyright © Scotty Gravenberch, 2000. Reprinted by permission of the author.

"Confessions of a Hip-Hop Critic" by dream hampton. Copyright © dream hampton, 1994. Reprinted by permission of the author. Originally published in *Essence*.

"from 'Awakening'" by Duriel E. Harris. Copyright © Duriel E. Harris, 1998. Reprinted by permission of the author.

"Sleep" by Yona Harvey. Copyright © Yona Harvey, 1999. Reprinted by permission of the author. Originally published as "If Someone Were to Look Down" in *Obsidian III*.

"When the Neighbors Fight" by Terrance Hayes. Copyright © Terrance Hayes, 1999. Reprinted by permission of Tia Chucha Press. Originally published in *Muscular Music.*

"You Are Chic Now, Che" by Ogaga Ifowodo. Copyright © Ogaga Ifowodo, 1998. Reprinted by permission of the author.

"What About Black Romance?" by Esther Iverem. Copyright © *The Washington Post,* 1997. Reprinted by permission of *The Washington Post.* Originally published May 25, 1997.

"Are We Tiger Woods Yet?" by Lisa Jones. Copyright © Lisa Jones, 1997. Reprinted by permission of the author. Originally published in *The Village Voice.*

"Just Beneath the *Surface*—An Email" by Sarah Jones. Copyright © Sarah Jones, 1999. Reprinted by permission of the author. Originally presented as a personal email.

"Visitation: Grenada, 1978" by Allison Joseph. Copyright © Allison Joseph, 1999. Reprinted by permission of the author.

"My Son, My Heart, My Life" by John R. Keene. Copyright © John R. Keene, 1997. Reprinted by permission of the author. Originally published (this version) in *Ploughshares.*

"On the Disappearance of Joe Wood Jr." by Robin D. G. Kelley. Copyright © Robin D. G. Kelley, 1999. Reprinted by permission of the author. Originally published in *New York Newsday.*

"100 Times" by Arnold J. Kemp. Copyright © Arnold J. Kemp, 1999. Reprinted by permission of the author.

"The Last Integrationist" by Jake Lamar. Copyright © Jake Lamar, 1996. Reprinted by permission of International Creative Management, Inc. Originally published in *The Last Integrationist* (Crown Publishers).

"slave" by Victor D. LaValle. Copyright © Victor D. LaValle, 1999. Reprinted by permission of Vintage Books, a Division of Random House, Inc., Victor D. LaValle, and the Watkins/Loomis Agency. Originally published in *slapboxing with jesus.*

"By Invitation—An Open Letter to the President of South Africa" by Itumeleng oa Mahabane. Copyright © Itumeleng oa Mahabane, 1999. Reprinted by permission of the author. Originally published in *The Financial Mail.*

"Discubriendo una Fotografía de mi Madre" by Shara McCallum. Copyright © Shara McCallum, 1999. Reprinted by permission of the University of Pittsburgh Press. Originally published in *The Water Between Us.*

"sometime in the summer there's october" by Tony Medina. Copyright © Tony Medina, 1997. Reprinted by permission of the author. Originally published in *360° A Revolution of Black Poets* (BlackWords, Inc. in association with Runagate Press).

"The Outcome" by Jessica Care Moore. Copyright © Jessica Care Moore, 1999. Reprinted by permission of the author. Originally appeared as a spoken-word piece on Nas' *NaStradamus* CD (Ill Will Records/Columbia Records).

"Toi Derricotte at Quail Ridge Books" by Lenard D. Moore. Copyright © Lenard D. Moore, 1999. Reprinted by permission of the author.

"hip-hop feminist" by Joan Morgan. Copyright © Joan Morgan, 1999. Reprinted by permission of Simon and Schuster. Originally published in *When Chickenheads Come Home to Roost...my life as a hip-hop feminist*.

"She and I" by Bruce Morrow. Copyright © Bruce Morrow, 2000. Reprinted by permission of the author.

"Nairobi Streetlights" by Samwiri Mukuru. Copyright © Samwiri Mukuru, 1999. Reprinted by permission of the author.

"'It be's that way sometimes 'cause I can't control the rhyme.'—Notes from the Post-Soul Intelligentsia" by Mark Anthony Neal. Copyright © Mark Anthony Neal, 1998. Reprinted by permission of the author. Originally published in *Black Renaissance/Renaissance Noire*.

"3 movements" by Letta Neely. Copyright © Letta Neely, 2000. Reprinted by permission of the author.

"The Night when Mukoma Told the Devil to Go to Hell" by Mukoma Wa Ngugi. Copyright © Mukoma Wa Ngugi, 1999. Reprinted by permission of the author.

"The Famished Road" by Ben Okri. Copyright © Ben Okri, 1991. Reprinted by permission of Doubleday, a division of Bantam Doubleday Dell Publishing Group, Inc.. Used by permission of Doubleday, a division of Random House, Inc.. Originally published in *The Famished Road*, A Nan A. Talese book.

"White Girl?" by Lonnae O'Neal Parker. Copyright © *The Washington Post*, 1999. Reprinted by permission of *The Washington Post*. Originally published August 8, 1999.

"Autobiography of a Black Man" by G. E. Patterson. Copyright © G. E. Patterson, 1999. Reprinted by permission of Graywolf Press. Originally published in *Tug*.

"Spotlight at the Nuyorican Poets Café" by Willie Perdomo. Copyright © Willie Perdomo, 1999. Reprinted by permission of the author.

"Stigmata" by Phyllis Alesia Perry. Copyright © Phyllis Alesia Perry, 1998. Reprinted by permission of Hyperion, and John McGregor/JMG Books. Originally published in *Stigmata*.

"Blue" by Carl Phillips. Copyright © Carl Phillips, 1992. Reprinted by permission of Northeastern University Press. Originally published in *In The Blood*.

"This Is Not a Puff Piece" by Scott Poulson-Bryant. Copyright © Scott Poulson-Bryant, 1993. Reprinted by permission of the author. Originally published as "Puff Daddy: This is not a Puff piece" in *Vibe*.

"Live from Death Row" by Kevin Powell. Copyright © Kevin Powell, 1996. Reprinted by permission of the author. Originally published in *Vibe*.

"The Pagoda" by Patricia Powell. Copyright © Patricia Powell, 1998. Reprinted by permission of Alfred A. Knopf, a Division of Random House, Inc., and The Charlotte Sheedy Literary Agency. Originally published in *The Pagoda*.

"Patrimony" by Rohan Preston. Copyright © Rohan Preston, 1998. Reprinted by permission of the author.

"Facing Unknown Possibilities—Lance Jeffers and the Black Aesthetic" by Howard Rambsy II. Copyright © Howard Rambsy II, 1999. Reprinted by permission of the author.

"Intermission in three acts in service of PLOT" by Claudia Rankine. Copyright © Claudia Rankine, 1999. Reprinted by permission of the author.

"Calypso the outside woman" by Vanessa Richards. Copyright © Vanessa Richards, 1999. Reprinted by permission of the author.

"The Woman" by Kristina Rungano. Copyright © Kristina Rungano, 1984. Reprinted by permission of the author. Originally published in *A Storm Is Brewing* (Zimbabwe Publishing House).

"Woman" by Tijan Sallah. Copyright © Tijan Sallah, 1993. Reprinted by permission of the author. Originally published in *Dreams of Dusty Roads* (Three Continents Press).

"face" by Danzy Senna. Copyright © Danzy Senna, 1998. Reprinted by permission of Riverhead Books, a division of Penguin Putnam, Inc., Bloomsbury 2000, and International Creative Management, Inc. Originally published in *caucasia*.

"Sunday" by Angela Shannon. Copyright © Angela Shannon, 1996. Reprinted by permission of the author. Originally published in *TriQuarterly*.

"Purple Impala" by Renée Simms. Copyright © Renée Simms, 1999. Reprinted by permission of the author. Originally published in *The Drumming Between Us: Black Love and Erotic Poetry* (Peter J. Harris, Publisher/Editor).

"Hit 'Em Up: On the Life and Death of Tupac Shakur" by Danyel Smith. Copyright © Vibe Ventures, 1997. Reprinted by permission of Crown Publishers, a division of Random House, Inc. Originally published as "Introduction" in *Tupac Shakur*.

"What Happens When Your 'Hood Is the Last Stop on the White Flight Express?" by Taigi Smith. Copyright © Taigi Smith, 2000. Reprinted by permission of the author.

"The Peculiar Second Marriage of Archie Jones" by Zadie Smith. Copyright © Zadie Smith, 2000. Reprinted by permission of Random House, Inc., and Penguin Books Ltd. Originally published in *White Teeth*.

"Windows of Exile" by Patrick Sylvain. Copyright © Patrick Sylvain, 1994. Reprinted by permission of the author. Originally published in *Crab Orchard Review*.

"Texaco" by Natasha Tarpley. Copyright © Natasha Tarpley, 1998. Reprinted by permission of Beacon Press, Boston. Originally published in *Girl in the Mirror*.

"Baker" by Lisa Teasley. Copyright © Lisa Teasley, 1998. Reprinted by permission of the author.

"Rika" by Jervey Tervalon. Copyright © Jervey Tervalon, 2000. Reprinted by permission of the Regents of the University of California, the University of California Press, and The Joy Harris Literary Agency, Inc. Originally published in *Understand This*.

"gin and juice" by Imani Tolliver. Copyright © Imani Tolliver, 1999. Reprinted by permission of the author.

"Speaking in Tongues" by Touré. Copyright © Touré, 1998. Reprinted by permission of the author. Originally published in *The New York Times Magazine*.

"Collection Day" by Natasha Trethewey. Copyright © Natasha Trethewey, 1999. Reprinted by permission of the author.

"What Happened to Your Generation's Promise of 'Love and Revolution'?—A Letter to Angela Davis" by Eisa Nefertari Ulen. Copyright © Eisa Nefertari Ulen, 1999. Reprinted by permission of the author. Originally published in *Letters of Intent: Women Cross the Generations to Talk About Family, Work, Sex, Love, and the Future of Feminism* (The Free Press).

"Butterfly Burning" by Yvonne Vera. Copyright © Yvonne Vera, 1998. Reprinted by permission of Farrar, Straus and Giroux, LLC. Originally published in *Butterfly Burning*.

"Insomnia" by Marco Villalobos. Copyright © Marco Villalobos, 1999. Reprinted by permission of the author.

"An Atlantic Away: A Letter from Africa" by Teresa N. Washington. Copyright © Teresa N. Washington, 1999. Reprinted by permission of the author.

"The Intuitionist" by Colson Whitehead. Copyright © Colson Whitehead, 1998. Reprinted by permission of Doubleday, a division of Random House, Inc., and Granta Books. Originally published in *The Intuitionist*.

"Your Friendly Neighborhood Jungle" by Daniel J. Wideman. Copyright © Daniel J. Wideman, 2000. Reprinted by permission of the author.

"Shrine outside Basquiat's Studio, September 1988" by Kevin Young. Copyright © Kevin Young, 2000. Reprinted by permission of the author. Taken from the forthcoming collection *To Repel Ghosts* (Zoland Books, 2001).

Index by Author

809.8989
STEP INTO A WORLD

$29.95

DATE			

047

RECEIVED MAY 1 1 2001

SOUTH HUNTINGTON
PUBLIC LIBRARY
2 MELVILLE ROAD
HUNTINGTON STATION, N.Y. 11746

BAKER & TAYLOR